AMERICAN IDEAS
AND
EDUCATION

AMERICAN IDEAS
AND
EDUCATION

Frederick Mayer

CHARLES E. MERRILL BOOKS, INC.
COLUMBUS, OHIO

872

To Erica —
whose greatness
inspired this book

Preface

This work places education at the core of American culture. The founders of our nation, men like Jefferson and Franklin, regarded this civilization not only as a unique political experiment but also as the expression of a new educational ideal that would produce genuine enlightenment and emancipate mankind from the superstitions of the past. To see education as the center of the American experiment is to see the perpetual vitality of American ideals, ideals that must be redefined in every generation.

This book encourages a greater appreciation of the American heritage. This appreciation does not mean idolization of the past, rather the ability to see the past in perspective and thus regard it as a prelude to a more constructive future. The Jeffersonian view was that no generation has an infallible view of history; each age must make its own contributions and develop its own educational philosophy.

Because so much of American education, from the Puritans to the present, has depended on religious participation and leadership, the religious and philosophical background of American ideas has been stressed in this work. The great colleges were founded under religious auspices. Elementary education in early America meant study of the Bible and the catechism; frequently the school teacher acted as an assistant to the minister. Theology has always been at the center of Catholic education in the United States. This emphasis on religion implies not a championing of a particular religious viewpoint but awareness of, and respect for, the religious enterprise that has illuminated so many of our philosophical and educational strivings.

To make the story of *American Ideas and Education* more meaningful, I have related theory and practice, thinkers and social currents. Ideas do not develop in a vacuum: they depend on the prevailing social environment, and, in turn, they have an impact on thought, actions, and institutions.

In every way, I have related education to a larger framework, based on theoretical concepts. The advantage of theory, especially in philosophy, is that it gives us perspective, broadening our vistas and freeing us from the pillars of immediacy.

The most important contribution of this book is its encouragement of an affirmative philosophy of education on the part of the reader. More is needed than mere description of ideas, classification of systems, and marshaling of facts. We must have dedication and enthusiasm for our own times if we are to leave our stamp of individuality upon history and if new foundations and ideals are to be created for the education of the future.

I want to acknowledge the debt this work owes to the inspiration of Dean Tracey Strevey, Dean Irving Melbo, Dr. Leonard Calvert, Dr. Lester Sands, Dr. Emery Stoops, Dr. Roy Harris, Richard Neutra, Dr. William Melnitz, Michael Birnkrant, Eugene Vale, Minna Coe, and Kimmis Hendrick. My profound thanks also go to Susan Goldstone and Julia Estadt of Charles E. Merrill Books, Inc., for their editorial guidance and interest in the book.

FREDERICK MAYER

Redlands, California

Permission Acknowledgments

Grateful acknowledgment is made to the following publishers and individuals for permission to reprint material for which they hold the copyright or for which they are the authorized publishers.

To The Beacon Press: for citations from John Dewey, *Reconstruction in Philosophy.* Copyright 1948.

To Columbia University Press: for citations from Joseph Blau, editor, *American Philosophic Addresses,* 1700–1900.

To Harcourt, Brace & World, Inc.: for quotations from Antoine de Saint-Exupéry, *Flight to Arras.*

To Robert M. Hutchins: for quotations from his Bedell Lectures.

To The Macmillan Company: for quotations from W. H. Kilpatrick, *Philosophy of Education.* Copyright 1951.

To Paul R. Reynolds & Son: for citations from William James, *Pragmatism.*

To Charles E. Merrill Books, Inc.: for quotations from Robert S. Fleming, *Curriculum for Today's Boys and Girls.*

To Robert N. Montgomery, Chancellor, Muskingum College: for citations from the William Rainey Harper Memorial Conference.

To *Phi Delta Kappan:* for quotations from Daniel Schreiber, *The Dropout and the Delinquent;* and from Frank Brown, *The Non-Graded High School.*

To Yale University Press: for citations from John Dewey, *A Common Faith.*

Part of the historical material of this work is based upon the author's study in American thought published by W. C. Brown Co., Dubuque, Iowa, Copyright 1951 by Frederick Mayer.

Photo Credits

Part One, "Foundations of Creativity"—The University of Washington Student Union Building, Courtesy of Ted Splesel from Rapho Guillumette Pictures

Chapter 1, "Education and the American Scene"—Guided tour of United Nations Headquarters, Courtesy of the United Nations

Chapter 2, "The Creative Ideal"—Courtesy of Joseph Nettis from Free Lance Photographers Guild, Inc.

Chapter 3, "The Spirit of American Philosophy and Education"— Courtesy of H. Armstrong Roberts

Part Two, "The Search for Enlightenment"—"Drafting the Declaration of Independence," after Chappel, Courtesy of Charles Phelps Cushing

Chapter 4, "The Religious Background and Education"—John Calvin, Courtesy of Mercury Archives

Chapter 5, "The Impact of Puritan Education"—Schoolhouse, Tappan, New York, in Colonial days, engraving by James Smillie from picture by Robert W. Weir, Courtesy of Charles Phelps Cushing

Chapter 6, "The Age of Edwards"—Statehouse and churches on New Haven Green, Yale buildings in background, as Edwards saw them, *ca.* 1756. Painting by William G. Munson, Courtesy New Haven Colony Historical Society

Chapter 7, "The Liberal Tradition"—Benjamin Franklin flying a kite in a thunderstorm, from a lithograph by Currier & Ives, Courtesy of Charles Phelps Cushing

Chapter 8, "Materialistic Currents and Education"—Courtesy of Mercury Archives

Chapter 9, "The Impact of the Revolution"—"The Boston Boys and General Gage," engraving and picture by C. W. Sharpe, Courtesy of Charles Phelps Cushing

Chapter 10, "Jefferson as Thinker and Educator"—Statue of Thomas Jefferson in the Jefferson Memorial, Washington, D.C., Courtesy of Philip Gendreau

Part Three, "Pioneers of Progress and Education"—Abraham Lincoln as a boy, picture by Eastman Johnson, now shown at Berea College, Berea, Kentucky, Courtesy of Charles Phelps Cushing

Chapter 11, "Impact of European Educators"—John Pounds, founder of the Ragged Schools, England, Courtesy of Mercury Archives

Chapter 12, "Emerson and the Educational Renaissance"—Ralph Waldo Emerson, Courtesy of Free Lance Photographers Guild, Inc.

Chapter 13, "Horace Mann"—First graduating class (1857), Antioch College, Courtesy of Antiochiana, Antioch College, Yellow Springs, Ohio

Chapter 14, "Henry Barnard"—Henry Barnard, Courtesy of Mercury Archives

Chapter 15, "Thoreau and Educational Ideals"—Walden Pond, Concord, Massachusetts, Courtesy of Charles Phelps Cushing

Chapter 16, "New Vistas"—Statue of Booker T. Washington on Tuskegee Institute campus, Tuskegee, Alabama, Courtesy of A. R. Simons from Monkmeyer Press Photo Service

Chapter 17, "Whitman and Education for Democracy"—Crowd in street, Burlington, Vermont, Courtesy of Philip Gendreau

Chapter 18, "The Ideals of Harris"—"The School of Athens," engraving by A. H. Payne from Vatican mural by Raphael, Courtesy of Charles Phelps Cushing

Part Four, "Dawn of Reform"—Child labor, Courtesy of Philip Gendreau

Chapter 19, "Man Against Nature"—French scientist Jean Rostand (son of Edmund Rostand) examining toads, Courtesy of Delmos from Rapho Guillumette Pictures

Chapter 20, "G. Stanley Hall"—Courtesy of Waly Nichols from Free Lance Photographers Guild, Inc.

Chapter 21, "The Progressives and Critics"—"Blindman's-Bluff: How long will this Game last?" (a Boss Tweed Cartoon), by Thomas Nast, Courtesy of Charles Phelps Cushing

Chapter 22, "The Ideals of Parker"—Courtesy of Roy Pinney from Monkmeyer Press Photo Service

Chapter 23, "Progress of Idealism"—"The Charioteer of Delphi," Courtesy of Philip Gendreau

Chapter 24, "William James"—Courtesy of Philip Gendreau

Part Five, "Idealism and Pragmatism"—The Acropolis from Constitution Square, Courtesy of Bernard G. Silberstein from Rapho Guillumette Pictures

Chapter 25, "John Dewey"—Dr. John Dewey, Courtesy of Ewing Galloway

Chapter 26, "The Culture of Normalcy"—Courtesy of the *Columbus Dispatch,* Columbus, Ohio

Chapter 27, "Ideas of the New Deal"—Run on bank at Millburg, Massachusetts, July, 1930; F.D.R. broadcasting, 1936 (photo by Harris & Ewing); WPA workers cleaning up flood debris, Louisville, Kentucky, February, 1937—all photos courtesy of Franklin D. Roosevelt Library, Hyde Park, New York

Chapter 28, "Santayana"—Statue of Carducci the poet, erected on outskirts of Bologna, Italy, in 1928, Courtesy of Philip Gendreau

Chapter 29, "William Heard Kilpatrick"—Courtesy of Dennis Hallinan from Free Lance Photographers Guild, Inc.

Chapter 30, "Contemporary Trends in Philosophy and Education"—Courtesy of Leif Skoogfors from Free Lance Photographers Guild, Inc.

Chapter 31, "Robert Hutchins Revisited"—Robert Maynard Hutchins, Courtesy of *Columbus Dispatch,* Columbus, Ohio

Part Six, "Levels of Education"—Courtesy of Sybil Shelton from Monkmeyer Press Photo Service

Chapter 32, "The Bases for Elementary Education"—Courtesy of Philip Gendreau

Chapter 33, "The High School"—Photo by William R. Simmons, Courtesy of the Ford Foundation

Chapter 34, "Leadership in Higher Education"—Courtesy of Hays from Monkmeyer Press Photo Service

Chapter 35, "Arts of Communication"—Courtesy of Nevan from Monkmeyer Press Photo Service

Chapter 36, "Delinquency and Education"—Photo by Arthur Leipzig, Courtesy of the Ford Foundation

Chapter 37, "New Horizons"—Courtesy of A. Devaney, Inc.

Chapter 38, "The Education of Women"—Class experimenting in quarry around 1890, Courtesy of Antiochiana, Antioch College, Yellow Springs, Ohio

Chapter 39, "Education and Parents"—Father and son at Metropolitan Museum of Art, New York City, Courtesy of Ruth Block from Charles Phelps Cushing

Part Seven, "Conclusion"—Courtesy of Joseph Nettis from Free Lance Photographers Guild, Inc.

Chapter 40, "Art and Creativity"—"The Fish" (1924), by Constantin Brancusi, 1876–1957, Courtesy of Museum of Fine Arts, Boston

Chapter 41, "The Philosophy of Creative Teaching"—Courtesy of Max Tharpe from Monkmeyer Press Photo Service

Chapter 42, "Existentialist Ideals and Education"—Photo by Homer Page, Courtesy of the Ford Foundation

Chapter 43, "The Coming American Renaissance"—"The Spartan," symbol of Michigan State University, Courtesy of A. Devaney, Inc.

Table of Contents

PART THREE

PIONEERS OF PROGRESS AND EDUCATION

PART FOUR

DAWN OF REFORM

PART FIVE

IDEALISM AND PRAGMATISM

PART SIX

LEVELS OF EDUCATION

PART SEVEN

CONCLUSION

AMERICAN IDEAS
AND
EDUCATION

PART ONE

Foundations of Creativity

CHAPTER ONE

Education and the American Scene

THE STRUGGLE FOR EDUCATION

In a complex period of transition many Americans do not have a full appreciation of the public school system. The teacher is not respected sufficiently, and financial support for schools is lacking. Many students take their education for granted. When school bond drives fail, imaginative programs have to be cut and needed enrichment has to be curtailed. Regressive critics regard adult education as being unnecessary; they want to educate only the young.

We forget that American education is the result of vision and sacrifice. Benjamin Franklin was attacked bitterly because he wanted to broaden the base of education and make learning more functional. Thomas Jefferson was called an atheist because he insisted on the separation of state and church in our school system.

Horace Mann was called a perverter of morality because he wanted an enlightened system of discipline. He gave up a flourishing legal practice, for he wanted to defend the rights of humanity. Booker T. Washington started as a slave and against incredible odds

5

educated himself while working as a janitor at Hampton Institute. At Tuskegee Institute he helped to expand the basis of industrial education and he gave a new sense of self-respect and identity to the American Negro.

In 1834 Bronson Alcott established the Temple School in Boston featuring new pedagogical methods and the use of the Socratic dialogue. His school was open to all races and religions. He taught modern subjects and stressed the controversial issues of his time. For all this he was attacked bitterly and eventually his school failed. Still, he did not give up his idealism and later became superintendent of schools at Concord. Wherever he went he spread the gospel of education. He talked to teachers, businessmen and church groups. Sometimes he would ride for miles on horseback in the middle of the winter to spread educational enlightenment. His fundamental philosophy, which symbolizes the spirit of American education, is contained in his incisive question: "Are not our pursuits our prayers: our ideals our Gods?"

The significance of education is illustrated dramatically in the life of Helen Keller. Before she met her teacher her world was narrow; there was no hope and no future for her. The darkness which surrounded her was complete. After she met her teacher, Anne Sullivan, a new horizon opened up. She entered a world of books and ideas — a realm which transcended her own frailties and which gave significance to all her strivings. Once Helen Keller was asked whether blindness had discouraged her. Her reply was that it had made her more conscious of the needs of humanity, that the worst blindness was callousness, a hardness of the spirit. To see meant understanding, building a bridge between human beings, and this could be accomplished by those who were blind as well as by those who had normal sight.

Great thinkers contributed to the spread of American education. Emerson felt that if adults were not educated there could be no creative democracy. He lectured to vast audiences on the need for expanding the intellectual horizon and developing a genuine American philosophy of education. When he gave the Phi Beta Kappa speech at Harvard, in which he called for an intellectual declaration of independence, his remarks were received with scorn by most academicians, who thought that he was carried away by shallow enthusiasm.

Thoreau called for an aristocracy of the intellect. He wanted to transform New England villages so that they would overcome their cultural stagnation and become genuine intellectual centers where the great books of the past and present would be explored.

William James developed a pragmatic philosophy to make ideas concrete and to universalize education. He called for a close association between philosophers, educators and psychologists, who through common efforts could bring about a true American Renaissance. Many thinkers, especially Royce, attacked him because he spoke in terms which could be understood by a vast audience. Did this not popularize philosophy too much? Did this not betray a superficial education? Some of his critics felt that the real mark of profundity in education was philisophical incomprehensibility. Strongly academic thinkers objected to James' emphasis on action. To them, theory was the core of life; abstraction was the only worthwhile realm. To apply theory concretely to man's institutional system, especially to education, was a denial of the fact that education could only appeal to the élite and that the masses could only master a rudimentary vocational training.

In our time, Robert Hutchins has been the object of severe attacks. Critics objected when he tried to create a genuine intellectual community at the University of Chicago. His defense of academic freedom was not received with approval by regressive circles. When he insisted that the college president be a thinker instead of a fund raiser and public relations expert, his view was received with cold disdain in some administrative circles.

Why do we so often attack our most enlightened prophets? Why do we usually recognize their greatness only after they are dead? Why do we idolize mediocre ideas instead of first-rate ones? Why are we guided by the persuaders of public relations who are interested in favorable images rather than in objective appraisals? The reason is that education as yet has been a half-hearted concern. We have not developed sufficient enthusiasm for it and we have only given lip-service to its ideals. We have separated theory and reality, ends and means, the classroom and the community. We have used our knowledge to rationalize our prejudices. Our real values have not been determined by education, but by the agencies of communication, like the press and television. We have been prisoners of assumptions which originate with the idols of the tribe and which create a narrow perspective and a limited view of life. We tend to live on the surface and evade the deeper issues. Our moral sense is not stirred and we resent the prophets of enlightenment who demand awakening and alertness. Many of us have slumbered so long that we are like the prisoners of the cave in Plato's famous allegory. Intellectual darkness becomes habitual; the light of wisdom is too strong and too overwhelming for many of us.

Most important, we do not act according to our convictions
Scholarship is removed from life. As Emerson stated:

> There goes in the world a notion that the scholar should be a recluse,
> a valetudinarian — as unfit for any handiwork or public labor as a
> penknife for an axe. The so-called practical men sneer at speculative
> men, as if, because they speculate or *see*, they could do nothing.
> I have heard it said that the clergy — who are always, more universally
> than any other class, the scholars of their day — are addressed as
> women; that the rough, spontaneous conversation of men they do
> not hear, but only a mincing and diluted speech. They are often
> virtually disfranchised; and indeed there are advocates for their celi-
> bacy. As far as this is true of the studious classes, it is not just and
> wise. Action is with the scholar subordinate, but it is essential.
> Without it he is not yet man. Without it thought can never ripen
> into truth. Whilst the world hangs before the eye as a cloud of beauty,
> we cannot even see its beauty. Inaction is cowardice, but there can
> be no scholar without the heroic mind. The preamble of thought, the
> transition through which it passes from the unconscious to the
> conscious is action. Only so much do I know, as I have lived.
> Instantly we know whose words are loaded with life, and whose not.
> The world — this shadow of the soul, or *other me* — lies wide
> around. Its attractions are the keys which unlock my thoughts and
> make me acquainted with myself. I run eagerly into this resounding
> tumult. I grasp the hands of those next me, and take my place in
> the ring to suffer and to work, taught by an instinct that so shall the
> dumb abyss be vocal with speech. I pierce its order; I dissipate its
> fear; I dispose of it within the circuit of my expanding life. So much
> only of life as I know by experience, so much of the wilderness have
> I vanquished and planted, or so far have I extended my being, my
> dominion. I do not see how any man can afford, for the sake of his
> nerves and his nap, to spare any action in which he can partake.
> It is pearls and rubies to his discourse. Drudgery, calamity, exaspera-
> tion, want, are instructors in eloquence and wisdom. The true scholar
> grudges every opportunity of action past by, as a loss of power.
> It is the raw material out of which the intellect molds her
> splendid products.[1]

Education is not merely an intellectual process. It involves our
view of man and society and demands a sense of appreciation and
relatedness. Education fails when it is removed from common concerns, when the teacher becomes a coward and removes himself
from the crucial issues of his time. His voice, his ideas, his idealism
are needed in the perplexity and turmoil of experience, in improving

---

[1] *The American Scholar.*

the tone and outlook of society and in fighting against the evils which threaten the survival of man.

Our progress in education is measured by our capacity for genuine appreciation. This demands a reverence for ideas; man is not just a biological creature, a slave to the mores of his environment. He is not merely a replica of economic institutions. He does not live merely by immediacy.

Education begins when we become conscious of our own powers and of the debt we owe to others. Thus we develop understanding and genuine self-trust, and we affirm our ties to humanity. We acknowledge our vast debt to the past, to all the pioneers who suffered and sacrificed so that we could be educated. At the same time we realize, as Jefferson did, that the world belongs to the living and we learn how to develop our own views and our own patterns of appreciation without being overwhelmed by the insights of the past.

THE AMERICAN CONTRIBUTIONS

As we consider America's contributions to world civilization, we may ask what has been our most distinctive contribution. What will be remembered most vividly in world history? Some might say that our concept of individual freedom is most significant. This ideal, which has deep implications for politics, religion, and education, has made for an open society. It has given our society a dynamic tone while protecting the individual against the encroachment of the state. It encourages diversity of thought and a degree of tolerance of unpopular opinions.

Freedom is difficult to appreciate fully without having experienced the ravages of totalitarianism with its concentration camps, secret police, brain washing techniques, and the fear of informers. Freedom has a social meaning and cannot merely be taken for granted. Some people in our society want to curb freedom because they will not learn to tolerate unpopular opinions. They feel that only their ideas matter and that their opponents are criminals whose voices should be silenced. Others look for an infallible leader who will do the thinking for the multitude and supply magic remedies for all our dilemmas. *Escape From Freedom* by Erich Fromm describes the feeling of a large number of individuals in our society who long for the security of authoritarianism. Erich Hoffer, in *The True Believer*, describes the fanatic who hates reason and analysis, is an extremist and a crusader, and who wants to crush his enemies violently and totally. Riesman, in *The Lonely Crowd*, portrays individuals who want to lose their sense of identity and who yearn for social adjustment and an other-directed life. Whyte, in *The Organization Man*, portrays the modern business enterprise as a security institution which provides a shelter for the cautious individual who is afraid to venture for himself and express his own identity. The organization in such a system becomes a goal in itself which gives status and recognition and develops a sense of smugness and complacency among its employees.

Freedom in a democracy is weakened in times of crisis. During much of the 20th century the U.S. has been in a state of emergency. In times of crisis, the demagogue attracts a wide following by promising easy solutions and total victories. He simplifies every issue. He has a black and white perspective and believes that his supporters will be saved, while his enemies will be damned. He is afraid of diversity which would undermine his power. By his distrust of freedom he opens the door to a totalitarianism of the spirit. He is just as dangerous as the forces who advocate economic determinism.

Some might point to our system of technology as our most significant contribution. Undoubtedly, the American inventive genius is unexcelled. Our skyscrapers are the largest; our freeways are the most extensive; our progress in electronics and automation equals or surpasses that of other nations. But technology does not increase our happiness. The freeways during the rush hours are symbols of confusion and neurosis. Our large cities create a sense of alienation. Our technical sciences have surpassed the humanities. Moreover, we are conscious of the destructive possibilities of science. The same satellite that goes around the globe can spread awesome devastation. The same airplane that reaches New York in a few hours can bring about total destruction from the sky. The tools of scientific research obey both democratic and totalitarian masters. Medical research can be applied to prolong the life, or it can be used for awesome bacteriological warfare which would strike at the very roots of human existence. Science, without a creative system of education and without the humanities and an adequate value system, opens the door to the brave new world so ably described by Aldous Huxley.

Others may regard our way of life as America's most unique achievement. In this nation the opportunity for the individual cannot be over-estimated. The average man has comforts and luxuries that only the aristocrat possesses in other countries. We can travel more than people of other nations. We have more extensive means of amusement; we have a wider range of experience regardless of social class or age.

Still, there is another side to this optimistic picture. Great American writers like O'Neill, Steinbeck, Lewis and Fitzgerald picture a vast emptiness, a sense of loneliness that can be felt in the city as well as in the rural districts; among the rich as well as among the poor. The sense of quiet desperation, described by Thoreau, gives a bleak outlook to many people's lives. Tension has become a major national problem. Our newspaper headlines feature crime and delinquency — symbols of social disorganization. We tend to overeat while much of the world lacks an adequate diet. More than ever we are conscious of psychosomatic ills. Psychiatrists are working overtime to clarify the innumerable anxieties which plague so many of us.

The negative aspects of certain patterns of individual and social behavior should not be exaggerated. They are symbols of discontent which can be changed, or at least modified, through constructive education and an affirmative view of life.

This implies a view of education which is close to that of Epicurus and in our time to that of William James. Education thus must leave its isolationist environment and deal with the anxieties of man so that we can achieve more serenity. Education fails if it does not give us an adequate value foundation, if it does not give us a sense of social obligation, and if it does not imbue us with a sense of direction. To leave value analysis to professional philosophers and professional psychiatrists is to abdicate one of the most important functions of education—the development of objectives for individual and social enlightenment.

EDUCATION — OUR GREATEST GOOD

The more we think of America's contribution to world history, the more we are apt to think of our system of universal education. To be sure, we are just starting in that direction, and are conscious of vast problems; the drop-out problem, for example, condemns many to idleness and unemployment. Our illiteracy rate is still too high; many have developed an illiteracy of the spirit. Education can produce greatness and fulfillment; it can also create seeds of decadence and disintegration.

Education is the main hope of our country. Without it, freedom becomes merely a slogan and representative government becomes tyranny. Without education, the public taste disintegrates, technology cannot advance, and human relations return to the state of the jungle: material advancement becomes a journey in organized superficiality.

The real challenge of our time is in human relations. To remove the ghettos of the spirit is the responsibility of the teacher. To live with compassion and with wisdom in a spirit of charity is the task of education. Not merely to drift, not merely to repeat the biases of our environment, not to adjust to a mediocre environment — these are the imperatives for all in a democracy.

To attain this objective, we need more than a stress on fundamentals or a return to traditional education. Our biases can be strong and unchallenged even if we have excellent facilities for communication. In education, as in technology, the past cannot be recovered. The more we see the past realistically, the less idyllic it appears and the less we will tend to imitate it in times of unprecedented and increasing complexity.

Education must appeal to a pluralistic audience and must become more flexible and creative than ever before. Leaders with a sense of public responsibility will have to be trained. Gifted students with social awareness will have to be encouraged. The average student must never be neglected and the handicapped child must be treated with compassion and imagination. A real audience for culture has to be created — and we must encourage the solitary genius who expands the frontiers of knowledge. Research and teaching have to be valued with equal fervor. The authentic individualist who does not want to submerge himself in the masses and who delights in his own ideas and conclusions should be treasured. The education of the community is just as important as the education of individuals, for man cannot exist in isolation: if the community does not support cultural goals, a wasteland of stagnation is the result.

The need is to make education universal, to achieve and actualize its ideals and expand its insights. All classes, all groups, all religions, all races have to be educated with fervor and enthusiasm. This means cultivation of the senses as well as of reason, of discipline as well as interest, emphasis on the heart as well as on the mind, on the arts as well as on the sciences, on man as a social being as well as on man in search of solitude, on parents as well as on children, on teachers as well as on students. What matters is the quality of our allegiance to education. To be a Pharisee, to stand still, to rest upon our achievements, is to open the door to regression.

This implies a more dynamic and enterprising view of education. Let us remember that entire civilizations have declined because of self-satisfaction and because the creative minority did not live up to its responsibilities. Rome in the second century A.D. looked back to its past glory and felt a false sense of security. It neglected the foundations of the future and did not develop adequate leadership. All these factors contributed, at least partially, to the decline of Rome, which succumbed to the gospel of materialism and expediency.

Just as decline involves excessive traditionalism, so greatness involves the forward look. As Emerson reminds us:

> Trust thyself: every heart vibrates to that iron string. Accept the place the divine providence has found for you, the society of your contemporaries, the connection of events. Great men have always done so, and confided themselves childlike to the genius of their age, betraying their perception that the absolutely trustworthy was seated at their heart, working through their hands, predominating in all their being. And we are now men, and must accept in the highest mind the same transcendent destiny; and not minors and invalids in a protected corner, not cowards fleeing before a revolution, but guides, redeemers and benefactors, obeying the Almighty effort and advancing on Chaos and the Dark.[2]

Our destiny depends on our view of life and, to a great extent, on our educational system — its content and its methodology, its quantity and its quality, and most important, its impact on society. Education is measured not by slogans, not by theoretical goals, but by its concrete influence on the lives of individuals and nations. Like religion, education demands an inclusive loyalty and, as in religion, the outward form is not as significant as the inward spirit. The heart of man and his relationships have to grow; otherwise he faces a dim future.

The real teacher expresses his ties to the past and acknowledges the debt which he owes to his predecessors. He sees education as a persistent struggle and a perennial quest. The problems that Jefferson and Mann faced are still with us today. They relate to the struggle between superstition and enlightenment, between democracy and aristocratic values, between creativity and stagnation, between faith in man and distrust in his abilities.

American education represents the aspiration of human beings to live in a free society, to develop their rational capacities, and to settle their disputes in a peaceful manner. This is not a static dream. It has to be redefined by every generation. We must never feel that the dream cannot be realized. To be sure, the concrete obstacles are immense and the forces of regression and darkness are well organized. But this is only an incentive to greater effort and more profound determination.

---

[2] *Self-Reliance.*

CHAPTER TWO

The Creative Ideal

SIGNIFICANCE OF CREATIVITY

The importance of creativity cannot be stated too strongly. For the individual it may decide his destiny: it may awaken him from intellectual slumber; it may give him new goals and new satisfactions; it may turn despair into hope and defeat into victory. For this nation a creative attitude may spell the difference between a respectable second-rate status and first-rate achievement.

Certainly, in quantitative achievement it will be difficult for the U.S. to keep up with totalitarian countries like Russia and China. We know that today the Russians are producing more scientists than we are and are graduating more engineers — some of them tend to be proficient and well trained. But the U.S. can excel in boldness and new ideas and in a flexible program which encourages the creative individual. Creativity in education is not a luxury; it is our primary need and our greatest hope for a promising future.

Creativity involves four phases, according to Wallas in *The Art of Thought*. The first is preparation, when new ideas are being tried

15

872

out and new hypotheses are being tested. The creative individual is subject to a multitude of stimuli. His mind represents a theater of emotions and feelings. In the second period, incubation, the unconscious mind takes over. Feelings and hypotheses are arranged in a degree of order. This phase is the prelude to an illumination, which is an almost mystical process. The distance between creator and idea, between ego and non-ego is temporarily bridged. It is a process of union which is felt on both the rational and the intuitive level. The last phase, verification, is when the new ideas are subjected to rigorous tests. Again a problematic situation arises, for the true creator is never in a state of rest and self-satisfaction.

Richard Neutra, when he finished designing a house, which may have curbed his rest for weeks, was already planning other projects. By the time he finished his masterpiece, *Survival Through Design,* he had ideas for several more books. At night he could seldom sleep because he conceived so many new ideas. Roy Harris, who worked so brilliantly in musical composition, at the same time was planning for a center for creative artists and found time to lead seminars for gifted students at U.C.L.A.

The creative individual is open to life. He does not reject new ideas. He is a transcendentalist in the sense that he always goes beyond immediacy. At the same time, he finds significance in things which ordinary people take for granted. He has unusual vitality, which is not merely physical but spiritual and emotional. He is both self-centered and compassionate in his generosity and acceptance of others. He is not afraid to dream and to theorize and to live in a world of fantasy. He usually dislikes formulas and all types of rigid thinking. While others regard their work in a superficial way, he is deeply involved in his productions. His work becomes a key to his strivings and ideals. He has unusual persistence not only in the application of his ideas, but in his ability to meet obstacles. His thinking involves relatedness and analogy; he is basically a Gestaltist in his psychology. This view implies not vague generalizations but an attempt to see the wholeness of life.

Creativity, it should be pointed out, is not confined to one area. It is as significant in science as in art, in human relations as in philosophical theory. It can be found in all social classes.

As compared with the average individual, the creative person usually experiences more emotional storms, has more capacity for feeling, is more intuitive, has more feminine traits without being effeminate, has a greater degree of perception, has greater powers of concentration and responds more negatively to coercion and rigid standards.

OBSTACLES

Creativity is hindered by dullness. As Thoreau stated:

How long shall we sit in our porticoes practising idle and musty virtues, which any work would make impertinent? As if one were to begin the day with long-suffering, and hire a man to hoe his potatoes; and in the afternoon go forth to practise Christian meekness and charity with goodness afore-thought! Consider the China pride and stagnant self-complacency of mankind. This generation inclines a little to congratulate itself on being the last of an illustrious line; and in Boston and London and Paris and Rome, thinking of its long descent, it speaks of its progress in art and science and literature with satisfaction. There are Records of the Philosophical Societies and the public Eulogies of *Great Men!* It is the good Adam contemplating his own virtue. Yes, we have done great deeds, and sung divine songs, which shall never die — that is, as long as *we* can remember them. The learned societies and great men of Assyria,— where are they? What youthful philosophers and experimentalists we are! There is not one of my readers who has yet lived a whole human life. These may be but the spring months in the life of the race. If we have had the seven-years' itch, we have not seen the seventeen-year locust yet in Concord. We are acquainted with a mere pellicle of the globe on which we live. Most have not delved six feet beneath the surface, nor leaped as many above it. We know not where we are. Beside, we are sound asleep nearly half our time. Yet we esteem ourselves wise, and have an established order on the surface. Truly, we are deep thinkers, we are ambitious spirits! As I stand over the insect crawling amid the pine needles on the forest floor, and endeavoring to conceal itself from my sight, and ask myself why it will cherish those humble thoughts, and hide its head from me who might, perhaps, be its benefactor, and impart to its race some cheering information, I am reminded of the greater Benefactor and Intelligence that stands over the human insect.

There is an incessant influx of novelty into the world, and yet we tolerate incredible dullness.[1]

Creativity means a search for reality. As Thoreau said:

. . . Let us spend one day as deliberately as Nature, and not be thrown off the track by every nutshell and mosquito's wing that falls on the rails. Let us rise early and fast, or breakfast, early and without perturbation; let company come and let company go, let the bells

---

[1] *Walden.*

ring and the children cry—determined to make a day of it. Why should we knock under and go with the stream? Let us not be upset and overwhelmed in that terrible rapid and whirlpool called a dinner, situated in the meridian shallows. Weather this danger and you are safe, for the rest of the way is down hill. With unrelaxed nerves, with morning vigor, sail by it, looking another way, tied to the mast like Ulysses. If the engine whistles, let it whistle till it is hoarse for its pains. If the bell rings, why should we run? We will consider what kind of music they are like. Let us settle ourselves, and work and wedge our feet downward through the mud and slush of opinion, and prejudice, and tradition, and delusion, and appearance, that alluvium which covers the globe, through Paris and London, through New York and Boston and Concord, through Church and State, through poetry and philosophy and religion, till we come to a hard bottom and rocks in place, which we can call *reality*, and say, This is and no mistake. . . . If you stand right fronting and face to face to a fact, you will see the sun glimmer on both its surfaces, as if it were a cimeter, and feel its sweet edge dividing you through heart and marrow, and so you will happily conclude your mortal career. Be it life or death, we crave only reality. If we are really dying, let us hear the rattle in our throats and feel cold in the extremities; if we are alive, let us go about our business.[2]

Dullness and conformity both conspire against creativity. Conformity substitutes the group for personal insight. The cult of conformity has subtle symptoms which extend to all aspects of our institutional system. Conformity is based on imitation and adjustment. There can be just as much conformity in a non-conforming group, such as beatniks, as in a more conventional group. Mothers and fathers who protest against conformity often will see to it that their children adhere strictly to parental standards. Public speakers will decry the cult of conformity and yet by their actions will support it.

Creativity is held back by rigid standards and definitions. In a small college in Southern California two of the most creative individuals, both drama majors, were expelled because they would not conform. They did not turn in term papers, their class attendance was spotty, and they refused to work in courses which they found irrelevant and boring. They objected especially to the requirements which tended to interfere with their own creative pursuits.

In earlier education the assumption was that no student could be educated who did not know Latin or Greek. Today we regard these requirements as obsolete. Some of our own requirements may appear just as inadequate and superficial to future generations.

---

[2] *Ibid.*

Creativity is also blocked by lack of understanding. In large classes the instructor tends to look upon the individual as an object, with no real personal involvement. This impersonal atmosphere defeats genuine education and genuine growth.

Another hindrance to creativity is lack of drama. This implies not just spectacular actions by the teacher but a type of intensity which is communicated to the student. The student senses how the instructor really feels about his subject, how he really thinks and whether he is actually interested in his students.

Stated another way, creativity is inhibited by an uncreative peer group, uncreative teachers and administrators, uncreative adults, uncreative values, uncreative agencies of communication, and an uncreative way of life. A mother said to me recently that she could not understand why her child would not read more; after all, they had a magnificent collection of books. She neglected to say that she was so busy with her clubs that she had little time for intellectual activities and that her husband was so busy making money that he seldom opened a book, but read mainly financial reports.

The peer group defeats creativity when the exceptional individual is not accepted and when the introspective individual is made to feel insecure because he pursues his own interests rather than the standards of the group. Teachers inhibit creativity when they follow a narrow schedule and when they become defensive about their work. Administrators limit creativity when they slight human relations and when they are pre-occupied with the mechanics of their work. Adults conspire against creativity when they become impatient with the questions of children. Our values tend to be uncreative when they are overly concerned with the material conditions of existence. Our agencies of communication, as is well known, overemphasize violence and sensationalism, and appeal to the limitations and sensate desires of man, instead of stimulating his curiosity. In fact much of modern man's way of life is deliberate superficiality, deliberate waste and deliberate escapism. Thoreau was right when he remarked that we are determined to die before we start to live.

Creativity involves an acceptance of life and at the same time a transvaluation of existence. We see the limitations of man, yet we attempt to transcend them. In the classroom we realize that we can provide only a clue to experience and wisdom, that we are fighting many follies. Yet at the same time we are not discouraged or disheartened. We begin to realize that external standards are less important than personal and social fulfillment. We learn to appreciate all students — the intelligent and the backward, the gifted and the slow learners. We are able to realize the fallibility of our insights and are ready to learn from life.

Too many teachers have stopped developing their intellectual and creative drives. They have become interested in the ritual of education. They worry about tests and subjects and requirements, and they succumb to quantitative evaluations. They do not ask those soul-searching questions without which education becomes a stereotyped process.

NEW ATTITUDES

Creativity in education involves a profound change of attitudes. The community needs to value success less strongly and be more interested in its teachers. School boards should worry less about mechanical facilities and be more concerned with human resources. They should be less restrictive and be more supportive of genuine creativity. The agencies that educate, such as the library, the lecture forum, television, radio, the newspaper, and the school, have to overcome their isolation and work together in common programs. Parents and other adults must be enlisted in the learning process. The community should value its creative leaders and encourage them in their endeavors. It should reward the creative individual in financial and spiritual terms while he is alive and not wait until he has passed away to praise him.

Administrators, who should be concerned about qualitative educational growth, should be bold and unafraid of new ideas. Some of them today are status-seekers and defend the past against the present. In public education they worry too much about their relationship with the school board; on the college level they are preoccupied with the Board of Trustees or the Board of Regents. Some tend to be so defensive that they develop inadequate patterns of communication; others are so involved in paper work and committee meetings that they become technicians.

One of the most impressive and creative college presidents of our time is Ralph Prator, president of San Fernando Valley State College. His success is based on his humanity. His board, faculty, students and community leaders all feel his warmth and concern. He is never defensive. He welcomes new concepts in the curriculum. His door is always open, even to freshmen. He will take professors and deans on camping trips. He has a deep concern which he communicates to a vast audience. His is a large institution, yet he sees to it that all individuals are valued and that real communication and interaction exist between faculty and students.

Creativity in teaching implies less emphasis on grades and examinations, less memorization of formulas, and more stress upon independent work. It means a problem-centered type of instruction. It implies a constant dialogue between student and teacher and encouragement of "bull sessions" in depth. Often in the classroom the digression may be more valuable than the formal lecture. This does not imply the encouragement of chaos: the wise teacher knows how to balance structure and spontaneity, content and methodology; he knows how to be directive and non-directive at the same time. The class, to be successful, has to be a vital experience on both the intellectual and the emotional plane. Ideas which are not felt deeply have little lasting impact.

The student, however, cannot abdicate his own responsibility. His task is not merely to prepare for a profession or a trade. He should not become merely proficient in his learning. He should not strive for mere success or group acceptance. Rather he should learn to explore the esthetic and intellectual realms. He should not be afraid to face the turmoil of questions. He should seek not the easy answer, but the more soul-stirring dilemmas. Above all, he should not specialize in a narrow field. His challenge is not to become an expert, but to develop a pattern of general understanding.

The student's primary task is one of clarification. He has to clarify his own self-concept, his relationship to others and his attitude toward society. He has to understand his goals and attempt to actualize them. Merely to be an intellectual bystander is not enough; merely to develop tools of communication is an inadequate process. He has to look upon education as a state of being which becomes the center of his life and which gives meaning to all his consequent experiences.

CHAPTER THREE

The Spirit of American Philosophy and Education

SEARCH FOR PHILOSOPHICAL PERSPECTIVE

The great issues in American education depend on philosophical perspective. Thus in colonial times the assumption was that education had primarily a religious meaning. Its task was to prepare dedicated ministers and to develop an audience which would appreciate spiritual truths and follow the ideals of the ecclesiastical leaders. In the 20th century, on the other hand, the religious concern has been supplanted by science which has become the center of the curriculum. The scientific method with its tentativeness and rigorous verification governs almost all parts of the American educational system. Still, the conflict between reason and faith, theology and science, has not been settled even in our own time. Many thinkers, such as Reinhold Niebuhr, feel that unless education is unified by theological concerns it will be dominated by fragmentary issues.

We are still discussing problems which emerged in colonial times. For example, should education be controlled locally or by the federal government? Should there be a strict separation of

state and church? Should education be mainly for the élite or for
the masses? Should the humanities or the sciences be the center
of education? Should the teacher be the follower or the leader of
society? Should the freedom of the teacher be curbed in times of
crisis? Should education be completely objective or should it allow
for indoctrination? Should it be book-centered or experience-centered?
Should it stress primarily the past or the insights of the present?
Should it dwell upon interest or effort on the part of the
students? None of these problems can be understood without
philosophical clarification.

THE FUNCTION OF CRITICAL THOUGHT

In many ways philosophy has been a stepchild in American
culture. The reason for this neglect is quite obvious. Americans,
since the founding of this nation, have been concerned above all
with practical functions, and they have had little inclination for the
life of the spirit and the enjoyment of reason. It has been pointed
out many times that the American civilization resembles ancient
Rome, and that, like the Romans, we are seldom original when it
comes to philosophical concepts.

In colonial times the progress of philosophy was hindered by
the ecclesiastical tradition. Like the medieval scholastics, the colonial
teachers started their philosophy with a profession of faith. There
were two ways of thinking: one severely orthodox, usually Calvinistic;
the other scientific and Newtonian and usually exposed to the antagonism of the clergy. For a time it appeared that the scientific tradition
would prevail. It won able champions in Paine, Rush, Franklin, and
Jefferson; however, the forces of reaction were too strong and the
forces of tradition became basic in the making of the American mind.

What impresses the reader especially in colonial philosophy is
its emphasis on God. Whereas the modern American very seldom
thinks about God — he is too occupied with secular ideals and the
pursuit of happiness and money — the citizen of colonial times had
an intense awareness of the divine governance of the universe. He
looked upon God as an awesome judge who would punish the sins
of mankind in a merciless way. All this has changed, and in the
twentieth century God is viewed as a kind father, perhaps like a
chairman of a corporation who is constantly trying to improve the
universe and who will reward us for our cooperation. Thus today
there is a spirit of democracy in our religious and philosophical

beliefs; man and God are engaged in a partnership and they are working together to improve the world and to fight the forces of evil.

Throughout colonial times the spirit of idealism was strong. Technically, it was largely derived from Berkeley and the Cambridge Platonists, and it held that the external world depends upon man's mind and that the material substance has no metaphysical reality. This idealistic philosophy was concerned largely with man's inner life and had a disdain for scientific experimentation. Naturally, it accepted the immortality of the soul, the reality of God, and the need for the intervention of religion if man was to be saved. Religion meant the Protestant tradition, not Catholicism, which was regarded with great distrust in colonial times.

Such idealism did not make for a mystical spirit. To be sure, we find strains of mysticism in Jonathan Edwards and John Woolman, but it was a restrained type of mysticism which emphasized the *distance* between man and God. The colonial thinkers would have had little understanding of Meister Eckhart, who identified man and God. The general tendency of colonial thinking was *theistic,* rather than pantheistic.

Idealism was also manifested in the field of education. American textbook writers like Samuel Johnson were enthusiastic about abstract moral principles, which were duly summarized and which were to be guides to virtuous behavior. This tendency can be observed not merely in education but also in politics, economics, and international relations. The outstanding charters of the American nation like the Declaration of Independence and Wilson's Fourteen Points all have this combination of idealism and metaphysical vagueness. It is not surprising that Americans such as Ely Culbertson and Cord Meyer have been in the vanguard of the World Federalists, who believed in a world government which would ultimately obliterate all national distinctions and in this way make wars impossible.

The idealistic attitude has several advantages: It makes for a broader perspective on the part of the philosopher; it lends dignity to the educational enterprise; it inspires us with faith in the future. The weaknesses of this attitude are that it leads frequently to a disdain for science and a disregard of actuality. It is much easier to draw up a series of resolutions about the universe than to deal with it in a concrete and experimental manner.

While the idealistic strains are strong, we cannot neglect the forces of materialism in American education. We find them already in colonial times, and they were represented by such thinkers as Joseph Buchanan, Thomas Cooper, and Benjamin Rush. The materialists were more concerned with science than with theology; unlike their European comrades they still accepted the truths of Christianity, except that they substituted the material substance for the soul substance. Thus they were still tender-minded, although they had absorbed at least a few whiffs of the scientific spirit.

However, materialism became the "evil" movement of American thought. Idealists like Josiah Royce in the nineteenth century regarded materialism as a subversive cause, and in the twentieth century dialectical materialism is regarded with deep antagonism both by the professional philosopher and by the general public.

Still, the forces of materialism are well organized in American life. The worship of the machine, the desire for economic success, the emphasis on application, the drive for bigness — all indicate that the average American appreciates, above all, a quantitative evaluation of life.

ACADEMIC THOUGHT

The academic philosopher is not immune from this materialist trend. He wants to have as many students as possible; if he teaches at a university, his thinking is evaluated according to the number of books he produces. Frequently it does not matter what type of book he writes so long as it gains favorable reviews and attracts a wide reading audience. In fact, philosophy is not a leisurely occupation in the United States. The philosophy teacher usually has five or six classes a week; if he is in charge of introductory classes, he may have to lecture to hundreds of students.

Furthermore, the philosopher must attend committee meetings and faculty meetings. If he is successful, he may join the administrative staff, in which case his period of creativity usually ceases. To keep up professionally, he writes articles and works on a textbook and yearns for the time when he will be as famous as Dewey and Santayana.

The academic atmosphere is responsible for much of the stagnation of American philosophy. It makes for a spirit of aloofness and isolation. American thinkers look at the universe from the perspective of their own offices, which are usually located in Gothic buildings — a gentle reminder of the Middle Ages. How different was the method of Whitman, who experienced all aspects of life and who was at home in the slums as well as in the educational institutions! How different was Jefferson's way of life, which led him to an active participation in political and economic affairs. Reading his works, we find both detachment and a penetrating understanding of political actuality. He was writing not merely to fellow philosophers, but to all educated citizens. In contrast, much of academic philosophy is an empty monologue with no relevance to the pressing political and economic problems of our time.[1]

Spengler noted that contemporary philosophy lacks the spirit of originality. The terms may be new, the phrases may be stated in a different manner, but vitality of thought is lacking.[2] Does this superficiality indicate the disintegration of our culture? Does this mean that we have reached a point of spiritual and intellectual exhaustion? No definite answer is forthcoming.

Most regrettable is the increasing warfare between the different schools of American philosophy. It is strange that this warfare can be taken so seriously. Being exposed to an abundance of frustration and being old-maidish in their outlook upon life, many philosophers fight their intellectual battles with religious fervor. Actually most of these conflicts are as important as the medieval controversy over the existence of universals. What an abuse of intellectual capacity! What a waste of time!

Many American thinkers are imbued with the belief in eternal truths. Thus they are constantly speaking of justice, beauty, moral values, and so on. In this way they echo the thoughts of Emerson, Theodore Parker and other transcendentalists, who believed in absolute moral ideals. But the transcendentalists were rebelling against the harsh philosophy of the Calvinists. To them moral ideals had a *vital significance* and they applied them to the institutions of their time. Thus both Emerson and Thoreau were in the vanguard of the forces which were trying to abolish slavery. However, in the twentieth century this stress on absolute principles stands most of the time for an escape from concrete actuality.

An eternal truth is a contradiction in terms; for truth, whatever it means, is uncertain and changing and dependent on the cultural environment in which we live. It is like a capricious woman, moody and unpredictable. Truth must be rediscovered in every generation. New experiences modify previous standpoints, and constant read-justment is required.

Why do so many American philosophers defend so sedulously the concept of eternal truths? From Jonathan Edwards to William E. Hocking they have talked about a changeless ideal realm. For

---

[1] Cf. Runes, ed., *Twentieth Century Philosophy*, p. 227.
[2] Spengler, *Decline of the West*, vol. 1, p. 367.

one thing, they exaggerate the power of reason, thus writing the biography of the universe according to their own experiences. Moreover, personal frustration impels the philosopher to find escape in eternal truth; a "lost horizon" quite different from the chaos of his environment. It must not be forgotten that American philosophy arose under the dominance of a mathematics which stressed invariable axioms. Now, long after new systems of mathematics have come into existence, our thinkers are still talking about eternal laws.

Another stumbling block in academic thought is the commentator spirit. This tradition is derived from the medieval period when the monks, as the guardians of knowledge in Europe, collected books assiduously. They had a vast respect for authority, ecclesiastical and secular, and Plato and Aristotle became infallible guides to truth. The same spirit can be observed in American philosophy — only the frame of reference is different — reliance upon James, Royce, and Dewey instead of Aristotle and Plato. This worship of authority prevents original thinking and develops the "rationalizing spirit." Truths are accepted *a priori* and philosophical debates reflect dogmatic standpoints which are defended in a rigid, uncompromising manner.

Philosophers frequently quarrel over minor points of interpretation. Commentators comment upon other commentators, and sometimes a third and fourth commentator will try to show that all were wrong in their interpretation. This civil war among the footnotes has never been won, and is just as fierce today as in 1200 A. D.

Still, to be objective, we must not omit the advantages of the academic method. It made for greater precision in philosophical controversies; it encouraged scholarly research and broadened the horizon of the thinker. In the nineteenth century American knowledge of Greek philosophy was most inadequate, but in the twentieth century some of the outstanding classical scholars can be found in this country.

Most academic thinkers are unable to understand the exuberance of Socrates, the wit of the Sophists, and the poetry of Plato. Socrates talked with the common people; his laboratory was the market place, his book was Athens and his students were of all types and ages. Philosophical scholarship has made Greek thought dull and overly technical and has missed the vital qualities of the eminent Greek minds. In short, it has pictured the past according to its own axioms and viewpoints, and this has made the past into a genteel museum rather than into a living monument.

INFLUENCE OF SCIENCE

In the twentieth century science has exerted an unceasing influence upon American education. Today science replaces theology as the core of the curriculum, and some philosophers maintain that their primary task is to criticize the concepts and categories of science. They build their systems upon the postulates of science, which are constantly changing with the discovery of new facts about the physical world. The renowned scientific theories of present-day philosophers will be as antiquated in the next century as Herbert Spencer's are today. New theories of matter and non-Euclidean geometry have profoundly modified our views of the universe. There is no reason to doubt that these are just beginnings in a series of far-reaching intellectual changes.

Most American philosophers do not have an adequate scientific background to interpret the present developments in higher mathematics and natural science. Their generalizations are sometimes amusing from the standpoint of the professional scientist. The scientists, on the other hand, when trying to relate their fields to other areas of inquiry, are often like Alice in Wonderland, and get caught in the maze of their own specialization.

The scientific spirit was especially strong in James, Dewey, and to a lesser extent in Santayana. In James it led to an open-minded attitude regarding the universe and to a rejection of traditional philosophies. James viewed philosophy and education through the perspective of psychology, rather than theology. The spirit of the pioneer was in his soul; he thought that the universe was constantly growing and that man's freedom could not be denied. However, the scientific spirit was not completely dominant in James. He had a fondness for psychic research, and he was extremely tender-minded when it came to religion.

Dewey perhaps was the most enthusiastic champion of the scientific method, which he wanted to apply to all fields — including education. His approach was hypothetical and tentative and, like James, he demanded a reconstruction of traditional concepts. But Dewey lacked poetic insight and, like Heraclitus, was fascinated so much by the concept of change that he was unable to picture the goals towards which mankind is marching.

Santayana formed a striking contrast to Dewey. Santayana approached philosophy through poetry and was extremely sophisticated in science. He called himself a materialist, but in every way he was different from the eighteenth century American materialists like Benjamin Rush, Joseph Buchanan, and Thomas Cooper. Santayana did not idolize the realm of matter; and his sympathy was for the realm of the spirit. Nor did his materialism disturb his basic religious views, which he held in a symbolic and allegorical manner. The great mistake, according to Santayana, is man's confusion between the realms of fact and poetry. Much of science, like religion, is merely poetry, a symbolic picture of the universe, and should be so held by a sophisticated spirit.

Certainly science does not offer magic solutions to the American thinker, who more than ever realizes the destructive power of the new technological weapons. It is doubtful, however, if he can go back to the theological certainty of the colonial period. Such an escape would only widen the cultural lag in American life between technology and intellectual concepts. *Neither science nor theology offers a panacea for the crisis of our culture.*

EDUCATIONAL IDEALS

The deficiencies of American education are connected with the general deficiencies of American culture. Like ancient Rome, American civilization is eclectic and borrows from other nations. Santayana once described the United States as a young nation with an old mentality. Technologically we are impatient with obsolete machines, but in the field of culture we often worship the past and adhere to outworn traditions.

The general tone of American civilization is utilitarian. This implies an emphasis upon application rather than interest in pure knowledge. The inventive genius of America is unexcelled, but our interest in the humanities lags behind that of some European countries.

In colonial times men such as Jefferson, Adams, and Washington were like philosopher-kings, but after Jackson the common touch prevailed in politics and it was thought that too much interest in speculation upon theoretical matters would spoil the politician for practical life. Many of the later statesmen like Jackson were practical, down-to-earth and rather contemptuous of the intellectual; of course there were notable exceptions such as Lincoln and Wilson.

Since success in the United States has usually been measured in financial terms, educators were often looked upon with contempt, for they ranked low in economic terms. A myth developed that almost anyone who was a failure in economic life could be a teacher. While in Europe, the teacher, especially the college professor, was regarded with respect, in the United States the teacher often became a glorified technician; his opinion was regarded with scorn by practical men who felt that what mattered was actuality, not ideal standards.

The rapid physical growth of the United States precluded too much occupation with spiritual and intellectual matters. The influx of a variety of racial and national groups made training in citizenship and Americanization almost the first duty of educators. The task of the schools was to develop a new civilization, to establish a common basis for understanding and citizenship.

Still we must not underestimate the great advantages of American education. American education indeed is an audacious experiment in democracy; it gives a chance to poor and rich, to men and women, to members of all classes of society, to all races and all creeds. The state university offers an extremely cheap form of higher education, while private colleges have numerous scholarships to offer the meritorious student, and it is not too difficult for a student to work his way through college. In many nations the secondary schools are reserved for the few, but in the United States high school is for all and graduation from high school is becoming the rule rather than the exception.

Co-education has been of immense value to American education. It has created greater equality of the sexes; it has made contact between boys and girls more informal; also it has explored at least some of the esthetic and intellectual resources of American women.

The separation of state and church has aided the progress of American education. This separation has prevented ecclesiastical control and has given impetus to freedom of thought and freedom of expression. Separation of state and church has protected the rights of various minorities who otherwise might have experienced oppression.

It does not imply the exclusion of moral and spiritual ideals from the public school system; rather it implies that philosophies and religions should be discussed in an objective manner, without government-imposed bias or prejudice. The ideal of the American school system is spiritual freedom for all and coercion of none.

The possibilities of adult education are especially great in American education. Adult classes often specialize in vocational training and Americanization programs; a great need exists to expand liberal education for adults. Promising signs are the Great Books program and the various activities of the adult section of the Ford Foundation.

American education owes a great debt to the charitable efforts of various foundations. Among them we should mention the Carnegie Foundation for the Advancement of Teaching, the Commonwealth Fund, the John F. Slater Fund, the Julius Rosenwald Fund, the Milbank Memorial Fund, the Payne Fund, the Phelps-Stokes Fund, the Rockefeller Foundation, the Russell Sage Foundation, the Danforth Foundation and the Ford Foundation. The administrators of these foundations have given valuable guidance to American education. Intercultural education has been furthered through such organizations as the National Conference of Christians and Jews, the Council against Intolerance in America, and the Bureau for Intercultural Education. Religious groups have made a determined effort to eliminate religious and racial prejudice. Enlightened governors have used education as a method of bridging the gaps between various nationalities. Many important cities have a local mayor's committee on unity.

Scientific training has been promoted vigorously in American education. The Massachusetts Institute of Technology and the California Institute of Technology are among the foremost scientific institutions in the world and attract internationally famous scholars. The Princeton Institute of Advanced Studies offers a haven for those interested primarily in research. It has attracted men of the calibre of Einstein and Oppenheimer.

It is encouraging to notice that the scientific institutes are promoting knowledge of the humanities. The basic idea is that the scientist is not merely a specialist, but that he should be informed about other areas of knowledge, and that he must fulfill his duties not only as a research worker, but also as a citizen.

The United States has been an educational haven for refugees from abroad. Many of them would have been killed by the Nazis and Russians if it had not been for the generosity of various American schools and colleges.

All in all, the American contribution to education is truly remarkable. *Education is America's best hope for the continuation of democracy, for the containment of totalitarianism, and for the achievement of equality and freedom not only on this continent but throughout the world.*

PART TWO

The Search for
Enlightenment

CHAPTER FOUR

The Religious Background and Education

THE MEDIEVAL IDEAL

American education was directly influenced at its inception by the religious ideals of Europe. In early colonial times, supernaturalism reigned supreme, and it dominated the minds of the American thinkers to such an extent that they were never really emancipated from it.

To appreciate the development of American philosophy, we must look to the Middle Ages, the period of faith in which the Catholic Church directed the destiny of Europe. The best expression of this age can be found in Aquinas (1225-1274), who brilliantly synthesized in the *Summa Theologica* the dogmas of the Church and the philosophy of Aristotle.[1]

Aquinas believed that education should serve the Church. He believed that the teacher represented the authority of spiritual truth. He could not tolerate error which might lead to eternal damnation.

[1] Cf. Gilson, *The Spirit of Medieval Philosophy;* Poole, *Illustrations in the History of Medieval Thought;* McGiffert, *A History of Christian Thought,* 2 vols.; Mayer, *A History of Ancient and Medieval Philosophy.*

The postulates of his philosophy are symbolic of the medieval quest for certainty. Aquinas maintained that the existence of God could be proved philosophically, but that certain mysteries of the Church, especially the Incarnation of Christ and the Last Judgment, could not be dealt with by reason but must remain a subject of faith. To Aquinas the realms of faith and reason were complementary. The wonders of God could be studied as much by the scholar as by the average man who believed in miracles.

To Aquinas the universe appeared as a hierarchy in which the lower forms of life were determined by the higher realms. All forms of life had their preconceived function; like Aristotle, Aquinas was a firm believer in final purposes.

He taught that human institutions are to fulfill a moral function. Thus he stressed that the state is to prepare the individual for the future life and that rulers are to be guided by the dictates of morality. However, the realities of political life of his time did not allow for the development of a real ethical system. In the Middle Ages there were bloody wars between feudal principalities; later the world was ravaged by turbulent wars which cost millions of lives.

During the Middle Ages the spirit of supernaturalism developed to such an extent that a common faith existed both for the educated scholar and for the common citizen. Aquinas supported the belief in miracles, for miracles strengthened the faith of the masses and aided in the advancement of the Church. Objects relating to Christianity —relics, the bodies of martyrs, sacred places—were regarded with awe by the populace.[2]

The difficulty for the common people was that relics were expensive and that pilgrimages likewise required financial resources. The Church thought that by Masses and the use of candles the sojourn of the sinner in purgatory might be shortened. However, Masses and candles cost money.

The Church was inextricably involved in the feudal system and had vast holdings in all parts of Europe. There were taxes which exacted much sacrifice from the common people, who often were required to pay for the expensive tastes of ecclesiastical leaders. The death tax was especially burdensome, while the monasteries took advantage of the plight of many of the poor serfs. The investiture tax was resented by all classes of society, for it affected both the peasants

---

[2] We must not underestimate the splendid contributions which the Church made to medieval culture. Cf. H. O. Taylor, *The Medieval Mind*, 2 vols.; Henry Adams, *Mont-Saint-Michel and Chartres*.

and the aristocracy. All were required to pay a special tax on the accession to office of an archbishop or abbot.

Heretics arose who taught that the Church should go back to the apostolic ways of poverty and that the popes should live like Christ. The serfs naturally listened to these teachings, for they resented the numerous exactions of the Church; and the nobles and the kings assented, for they were eager to obtain the rich Church lands.

The moral condition of Christian religion had disintegrated, in spite of numerous attempts at reform. Many of the parish priests lived in a state of complete ignorance and immorality. The papacy itself, as St. Bernard pointed out, had not set a high example. What was worse, the great schism split western Christianity apart and Europe witnessed the unedifying spectacle whereby two or three popes excommunicated each other.

The conciliar movement attempted to establish a broad democratic foundation for the Church government. It was influenced by a faith in the importance of the individual and the belief that his decision should be supreme, not the pope's. Christian religion was to be accessible to all.

The doctrine of indulgences was especially important in the development of the religious revolt. In itself it was a rather poetic doctrine which said that the work of the saints had produced a surplus of merit from which all believers could draw by the performance of good works, but it was used by some Church leaders to produce money. Great rallies were held in western Europe, and often the speakers would go beyond good sense and sound theology and would say that all types of sins could be forgiven if a specified amount of money were paid. Even more amusing, sins could be forgiven before they had been committed. These gatherings were somewhat like the bond rallies in the United States during the second World War and provided entertainment as well as religious edification. To the pious, however, the indulgences almost became as sinful as banking operations, and the reformers challenged the doctrine that the Church could shorten the stay of the sinner in purgatory.

There were, likewise, abuses connected with the confessional. During the thirteenth century the formula of absolution was "I absolve thee." In earlier times it had been "May the Lord absolve thee." Therefore the most corrupt priest had the power which could open the gates of heaven and make possible men's salvation or damnation. More and more, theologians like Wycliffe and Huss protested against this shallow interpretation of the confessional.

It must not be overlooked that the Church had failed in its crusades and that the forces of feudalism were disintegrating. The peasants and the merchants joined forces in assaulting the fundamental tenets of feudalism which were being upheld by the Church. The supernatural system of morality as taught by Catholicism was totally inadequate for the new morality of the middle classes, which believed in profit, labor, and in an infinite accumulation of worldly goods.

Moreover, the Church had failed in combating the Black Death. Religious fanatics, called the flagellants, would beat themselves until their blood ran freely, for they thought that by their sacrifice they could turn the pest away. Yet, they did not stop the pest, and in spite of their efforts and persecution of the Jews, who were thought to have poisoned the wells, the pest took millions of lives. Thus even the common man realized that faith was not sufficient to combat the ravages of disease.

Intellectually, scholasticism, the system of medieval philosophy, was disintegrating. It must be remembered that this theology was so complex that it could be understood only by the few. The theological debates of the scholars relating to the problem of particulars vs. universals had little interest for the common people, who wanted definite and comprehensive answers to their religious questions.

With Duns Scotus, scholasticism became extremely abstruse. For the questions he discussed were merely refinements of scholastic casuistry. As a member of the Franciscan order he stressed faith, and he made a sharp distinction between philosophy and theology. Duns Scotus was opposed vigorously by the followers of Aquinas. The jealousy between the two orders further undermined the unity of the Church.

Scientific inventions and geographical discoveries brought into glaring daylight the provincialism of the scholastics. The new educators belonged to the middle class. They were frequently men of the world, while most of the theologians were monks whose theories were as aloof and as sterile as the cells in which they originated.

It had been the ambition of Aquinas to destroy the influence of Averrhoës, the Mohammedan thinker, but in this he was unsuccessful. Averrhoës had stressed the doctrine that something may be true in philosophy but false in religion. The theory of a double truth was utilized by the skeptics, who said their conclusions in philosophy did not challenge the fundamentals of theology, which rested on faith, not on reason.

A more careful reading of Aristotle indicated to the scholars of the Renaissance that the Greek thinker did not believe in personal immortality and that he did not accept the theory of creation out of nothing. The material world was now regarded, not as an allegory of an unseen reality, but as the main object of man's scientific knowledge.[3]

Likewise the theistic emphasis diminished. The distance between man and God had been emphasized by Augustine, Anselm, and Aquinas, who all thought that it could be bridged only with the aid of the Catholic Church. Mystics of the fourteenth and fifteenth century like Eckhart, Tauler, and Suso stressed the fact that God is within man, and, instead of dwelling upon human inadequacy, they were conscious of the divinity of man. Eckhart especially was opposed to the formal rites of religion. Instead of a vocal and formalistic religion he favored the spirit of quietude and contemplation. He sought a religion based upon the personal awareness of Christ, a religion which excluded the search for material rewards. In the mystics the spirit of original Christianity emerged in a new form.

It may be asked now in what ways medieval thought influenced the American mind. In the first place, a dualism entered the American scene. Life was regarded as a struggle between good and evil. The Puritans had, like Augustine and Aquinas, a personal awareness of the devil, and they were certain that there could be no compromise between the forces of goodness and of wickedness. This dualism never disappeared completely; today we find a political version of it, for example, in the struggle between democracy and totalitarianism.

In the second place, medieval philosophy imbued the United States with a theocentric perspective. Even the Reformation did not change this essential emphasis of the Middle Ages; it merely made it less orthodox and less institutionalized. The stress on God and the beyond characterized early American education. Notice how different this ideal is from Greek thinking, which believed in man, reason, and nature. Philosophy was regarded in the American colonies as a secondary enterprise which had the function of substantiating religious truths. Although later, in the age of transcendentalism, the theocentric perspective lessened to some extent it never disappeared. For the American thinker, most of the time, regarded the universe in a moral light, and he felt that it was his task to indicate and to describe the progress from evil to goodness and from bar-

---

[3] *Cf.* J. F. Randall, Jr., *The Making of the Modern Mind* for a comprehensive survey of the change in philosophical attitude which took place at the end of the Middle Ages.

barism to civilization. He might pretend like William James to be tough-minded in his description of science; still he would have room for faith and God in his philosophical system.

In the third place, medieval philosophy made for an anti-scientific spirit in American thinking. Did not the medieval philosophers regard the universe as an allegory? Did they not accept the reality of miracles? The same spirit can be found in the Puritan thinkers of Colonial America, especially in John Cotton, Winthrop and the Mathers. With the coming of the age of enlightenment, science was accepted more readily by the American philosophers. In fact, Franklin, Jefferson, Paine, and Rush regarded science as the tool for man's emancipation. But the opposition to science never ceased; it only became more genteel and more refined. Hence Emerson and Royce regarded a mechanistic concept of life with contempt and instead urged a consideration of *spiritual truths*.

In short, the medieval ideal of life gave to the United States a double perspective, almost a dual personality. On the one hand, it created a vigorous and deterministic technological system, guided by practical considerations; on the other hand, it inspired a faith which made for an awareness of religious ideals and which imbued some of its adherents with fanaticism. Thus it is a mistake to believe, as many European observers have, that the foundation of American culture is purely functional and utilitarian; on the contrary, it is basically supernatural: the pragmatic concept is secondary in American life.

Even today, much of Catholic education depends on medieval ideals. Institutions, such as Loyola and Notre Dame, combine medieval philosophy and modern science.

Jesuit education cultivated the classics. The study of Greek and Latin was encouraged and the student was taught that no education was complete without the mastery of ancient tongues. In 20th century Jesuit institutions modern languages are stressed with equal fervor.

Jesuit teachers are extremely well trained. Memorization and drill are encouraged so that a solid mastery of subject matter is achieved. Students are treated with individual attention; different methods are used for slow learners and for brilliant students.

Theology is the center of the Jesuit curriculum. It makes the knowledge of God man's highest achievement. The sciences and arts are to be mere preludes to religious understanding. The aim of such an educational system is to produce a many-sided individual who cultivates his physical, intellectual and spiritual powers in the service of God.

THE REFORMATION

Denying the infallibility of the pope, Reformation thinkers like Martin Luther stressed that religious truths depended on the faith of the believers and that they could be interpreted by the common people. The Bible thus became the authoritative organ for the reformers, and faith replaced scholastic reason. The Reformation dwelt on man's personal faith and his experience of God; religious philosophy became more subjective and individualistic. Yet the ideals of the Reformation did not lead to a sudden emancipation of the human mind; the basic emphasis was still authoritarian and otherworldly.

This spirit is especially revealed in Calvin (1509-1564), who magnified the majesty of God. To Calvin, *man's depravity and God's infinite perfection were the keystones of reality.* Much of early American thinking was merely a restatement of Calvin's *Institutes of the Christian Religion,* and Calvin became such an influence on the American mind that we can almost say that early American philosophy contained only two factions: those who were in favor of a Calvinistic concept of life and those who were opposed to it.

Specifically, what did Calvin contribute to the American mind? First, a theocratic view of life.[4] Thus, as in Calvin's Geneva, in Boston the church and the state were identified. Crimes against religion were frequently punished by secular authorities. This meant that, in spiritual matters, freedom could not prevail. For there could be only *one* way of evaluating God and the church.

Secondly, Calvinism made for puritanism in morals. Undoubtedly the severity and austerity of colonial times have been exaggerated; still we must not forget the horror with which early Americans regarded all forms of luxury, ornamentation, and dissipation. Prohibitions included not only card-playing, dancing, and drinking, but even the shortening of women's dresses.

Thirdly, Calvinism made for an activist spirit. Theologically, it was taught that God elected the sinners and that this was done in an inscrutable manner; no one could be certain who was saved

---

[4] *Cf.* Parrington, *Main Currents in American Thought,* vol. 1, p. 12.

and who was damned. Men thus *labored* to become eligible for heaven. As in their economic endeavors, they could not sit still and contemplate life; instead they wanted to conquer, by force if necessary, the kingdom of heaven.

Besides Calvinism we should mention the ideals of the Separatists. They felt mankind's corruption more strongly than other religious groups. Certain that reform from within was inadequate, they became isolationist, urging their followers to avoid all contact with official ecclesiastical institutions. They were motivated by the belief that Christ would soon return and establish a new government and a new world.

The following are some of the positive educational contributions of the Reformation:

(1) The ideal of universal education. Luther believed in education of the rich and the poor, and of girls as well as boys.

(2) The Reformation gave impetus to State control of education. Luther felt that the Church should not be allowed to control education. Some of his more radical followers favored a complete separation of state and Church.

(3) Reformation leaders developed outstanding textbooks for education.

(4) The Bible was translated into German by Luther and it often became the center of education.

(5) Recommendations were made by the Reformation leaders for periodic inspections and surveys of the school system.

(6) Moral ideals and concepts were made central in education, especially in Calvin's Geneva.

(7) The Protestant leaders stressed the importance of great teachers. Requirements for teaching were made more exacting.

(8) Education, mainly through Luther's influence, stressed physical training as well as the training of the mind.

(9) The responsibility of the family in the process of education was emphasized. Luther thus affirmed that education starts in the home and that parental example is all-important.

THE RADICAL SECTS AND EDUCATION

It must not be forgotten that the Reformation unleashed a multitude of radical forces. We find them especially in the ranks of the Anabaptists, who were far more opposed than Luther to the Catholic Church. To them religion was an intensely emotional matter. Among their preachers we find men who had little intellectual training, but believing they were guided by the spirit of God, willingly endured persecutions to propagate their gospel.

In their social ideals, they made much of the virtue of simplicity. Opposed to elaborate church buildings and to luxurious living, they spoke of man's inner life which contained the spirit of God. They protested against warfare and became conscientious objectors. The ruling authorities of the sixteenth century suppressed them mercilessly.

In the Anabaptists we find the seeds of revivalism. They were so emotional in their religious attitude that they regarded a rational faith as utterly inadequate. The same spirit can be found in the *Great Awakening* in the colonies and in Mormonism and Millerism. That religion is based on the dictates of the heart, rather than on the demands of the intellect, was emphasized most clearly by William James in his *Will to Believe*.

What repels sophisticated observers of the American scene is this attitude of credulity. Reading Santayana's *Persons and Places* and *Middle Span*, we find that Santayana could never reconcile himself to the naïve spirit of the American thinker. Santayana could not appreciate the compulsive power of faith and the compulsory optimism which he found in William James, whom he regarded as a spiritual descendant of the Protestant tradition.

Among the radicals of the Reformation we find the Quakers, who rebelled against all types of ecclesiastical authority. Guided by the spirit of love and brotherhood, they regarded all forms of authoritarianism as invalid. They believed in quiet contemplation. In this way they were quite different from the Anabaptists, who were so vocal and enthusiastic in their expression of religious ideals.

To the Quakers warfare was an absolute evil. Thus they refused to bear arms and to support military authority. This brought persecution and immense suffering; still they adhered to their ideals, and they did not compromise with militarism.

From an educational standpoint, their doctrine of human nature is especially interesting. The Quakers, unlike the Calvinists, insisted that man is good and that he possesses an inner light through which he can find truth. We find the same emphasis on the goodness of man in Transcendentalism, which owed much to the Quaker concept of life.

Outstanding Quaker leaders such as William Penn believed that it was their task to live up to the teachings of Christ. In this spirit William Penn concluded a treaty of friendship with the Indians, and he suggested that a universal league be established which would prevent war among the nations. However, the ideals of Penn were too advanced for his time and even today they have not been realized.

To be objective, we must be conscious also of the weaknesses of the Quaker ideal. To some extent, its lack of organization proved to be harmful. This encouraged internal schism and made almost for anarchy. Also the Quakers in the United States were frequently extremely puritanical. Thus they could not appeal to the youth, who wanted pleasure and the good things of life. Furthermore, the Quakers did not believe in formal education. Hence, their leaders lacked the theological and philosophical background which we find in Calvinistic thinkers, especially in Jonathan Edwards.

In educational methodology, the Quakers were far advanced compared with their contemporaries. Thus William Penn in his *Reflections and Maxims* urged a compassionate system of discipline and he believed that nature is to be the guide for educators. Opposed to memorization, Penn believed in meaningful instruction which was to emphasize actual experience. He anticipated John Dewey in his stress upon active learning and in his opposition to classical book knowledge.

CHAPTER FIVE

The Impact of Puritan Education

THE PURITAN SPIRIT

The philosophy of Puritanism was based on theological foundations. Accepting the reality of Divine Providence and human depravity, it held the Bible to be an infallible source of revelation, and it spoke with assurance of the divine status of Christ. It had a most picturesque doctrine of man; although man was a creature of lust and wickedness and was eligible for damnation, he could be saved provided he followed religious ideals and persevered in his righteousness. If God had elected him for heaven, the devil could not tempt him and lure him into his evil abode. Puritan eschatology taught that resurrection involved not merely man's spirit but also his body. For sinners this meant that their bodies would actually burn in hell and that their damnation would be eternal. In many ways it was a harsh concept of life, for it appeared certain that the majority of human beings would be damned, while only the minority would be saved.[1]

---

[1] Cf. Perry, *Puritanism and Democracy;* Miller, *The New England Mind;* Schneider, *The Puritan Mind.*

PURITAN SCHOLARS

Among the Puritan scholars we find Increase Mather, who wrote *An Essay for the Recording of Illustrious Providences.* As the title indicates, this book is full of miracles and contains a detailed description of witchcraft. To Mather, history revealed the guidance of God, who, in His righteousness, punished all sinners, especially free thinkers and Quakers, whom Mather linked together. There was little effort on his part to investigate scientifically the supernatural events which he described in his book.

Cotton Mather followed in the footsteps of his father. Reading his diary, we find an almost psychopathic spirit. With an intense consciousness of evil, he thought it was his task to defend New England against the devil. He was merciless in his opposition to those who differed from him, and did much to cause the witchcraft craze, which remains one of the dark spots in American history. He frequently used the executions of his victims as occasions for public sermons in which he praised the providence of God.

In 1699, Cotton Mather published a work entitled *A Family Well-Ordered*, which summarized his educational and philosophical creed. The book is divided into two parts: one is addressed to parents, the other dwells upon the obligations of children. Mather made much of the authority of parents. Their commands were to be obeyed without hesitation. Parents were to be models of piety and deportment. The home was to develop the fundamentals of reading and writing as well as encouraging an interest in arithmetic. But most important was religious instruction, which meant prayers, daily Bible readings, and faithful church attendance.

In the last half of the book, Mather emphasized the duties of children toward their parents, teachers, ministers, and public officials. The virtues which he recommended for children were obedience and labor. Obedience would develop religious ideals and prevent the tortures of hell-fire. Labor implied a constant application of religious truths to daily life.

Mather pictured in eloquent terms the fate of the wayward child. An outcast of society, his soul would burn in hell — not just for a limited time, but for eternity. No mercy could be shown him because in his defiance he had violated the commands of God and of society.

SYSTEMS OF EDUCATION

Elementary education in early America meant study of the Bible and the catechism; frequently the school teacher acted as an assistant to the minister. Teachers were scrupulously supervised by the community and had to be models of piety and temperance. Massachusetts in 1642 enacted a law which provided for some elementary instruction in "the principles of religion and the capital laws of this country."

In New York, as a contract of 1682 reveals, the teacher often had janitorial duties:

SCHOOL SERVICE. . . . When the school begins, one of the children shall read the morning prayer, as it stands in the catechism, and close with the prayer before dinner; in the afternoon it shall begin with the prayer after dinner, and end with the evening prayer. The evening school shall begin with the Lord's prayer, and close by singing a psalm . . .

CHURCH SERVICE. I. He shall keep the church clean, and ring the bell three times before the people assemble to attend the preaching and catechism. Also before the sermon is commenced, he shall read a chapter out of the Holy Scriptures, and that, between the second and third ringing of the bell. After the third ringing he shall read the ten commandments, and the twelve articles of our faith, and then take the lead in singing. In the afternoon after the third ringing of the bell, he shall read a short chapter, or one of the Psalms of David, as the congregation are assembling; and before divine service commences, shall introduce it, by the singing of a Psalm or Hymn.[2]

Important in elementary education was the horn-book, the first textbook used in elementary schools. It consisted of a sheet of paper covered with transparent horn, and contained religious instructions, the Lord's prayer and the elements of the alphabet. Later came the *New England Primer* which was taught to thousands of children. The *Primer* made much of the doctrine of original sin and encouraged children to lead a moral life if they did not want to face the tortures of hell-fire. The sentiment was Calvinistic:

---

[2] *Annals of Public Education in the State of New York, 1626-1746*, pp. 65-67.

In Adam's Fall
We Sinned all.

. . .

Thy Life to Mend
This Book Attend.

. . .

A Dog will bite
A Thief at night.

. . .

The Idle Fool
Is whipt at school.[3]

Now the Child being entered in his Letters and Spelling, let him learn these and such like Sentences by Heart, whereby he will be both instructed in his Duty, and encouraged in his Learning.[4]

THE DUTIFUL CHILD'S PROMISES:

I will fear GOD, and honour the KING.

I will honour my Father and Mother.

I will obey my Superiors.

I will Submit to my Elders.

I will Love my Friends.

I will hate no Man.

I will forgive my enemies, and pray to God for them.

I will as much as in me lies keep all God's Holy Commandments.[5]

Various types of schools emerged. In New England there were town schools supported by tuition and public funds. These schools provided scholarships for students who had financial needs. Dame schools were designed for the education of women. It was thought that women were less rational than men and hence their schools dwelled upon feminine graces and the three R's were taught with

---

[3] *New England Primer*, 1690.
[4] *Ibid.*
[5] *Ibid.*

less intensity than in the schools designed for boys. Coeducation was not allowed, for it would lead to immorality and low standards, according to most colonial thinkers.

Tutors were frequently employed by wealthy families. Some tutors had only a superficial education, but others had profound learning and they fostered the love of learning which distinguished so many early American statesmen such as Adams and Jefferson.

There were schools designed for training in business and occasionally apprentices received instruction after they had finished their occupational tasks.

Secondary education was stimulated by the law of 1647 which has been called the "Old Deluder Act":

> . . . It being one chief project of the old deluder, Satan, to keep men from the knowledge of the Scriptures, as in former times by keeping them in an unknown tongue, so in these latter times by persuading from the use of tongues, that so at least the true sense and meaning of the original might be clouded by false glosses of saint seeming deceivers, that learning may not be buried in the grave of our fathers in the church and commonwealth, the Lord assisting our endeavors,—
>
> It is therefore ordered that every township in this jurisdiction, after the Lord hath increased them to the number of fifty householders, shall then forthwith appoint one within their town to teach all such children as shall resort to him to write and read, whose wages shall be paid either by the parents or masters of such children, or by the inhabitants in general, by way of supply, as the major part of those that order the prudentials of the town shall appoint; provided, those that send their children be not oppressed by paying much more than they can have them taught for in other towns; and it is further ordered, that where any town shall increase to the number of one hundred families or householders, they shall set up a grammar school, the master thereof being able to instruct youth so far as they shall be fitted for the university. . .[6]

The Act provided for a fine if its provisions were not carried out, but for decades many communities found it difficult to establish satisfactory schools. The Boston Latin School, founded in 1635, was imitated by such communities as Salem, Dorchester, Newbury and Roxbury.

In Virginia, philanthropists like Symms and Thomas Eaton provided money for grammar schools, but most families with sufficient income employed private tutors. The Jesuits established a secondary

---

[6] Massachusetts (Colony), *Records of the Governor and Company of the Massachusetts Bay in New England*, vol. II, p. 203.

school in Maryland and another one in New York. In 1696 Maryland opened the King William's School which gained wide fame in the colonies. The Quakers established the William Penn Charter School, which had a more compassionate view of discipline than usually prevailed in the older schools.

The Latin schools emphasized the classical languages; occasionally even Hebrew was studied. Ancient history rather than modern events was stressed. The teacher was the absolute authority; his word was law and disobedience was punished severely.

The education of the poor was not completely neglected. This was due mainly to the efforts of the Society for the Propagation of the Gospel in Foreign Parts, which helped to establish its first school in New York in 1704. The teachers of this school were trained both in the classics and in religion. Under strict control of the society, they could be dismissed at once if they expressed heretical thoughts.

The Academy movement, stimulated by Franklin, developed a more secular and utilitarian view of education. The first Academy opened in Philadelphia in 1751; others like Dummer's (1761), Phillips Andover (1778) and Phillips Exeter (1783) also emphasized a more practical view of education and were interested in training lawyers and physicians as well as ministers.

Intolerance held back early colonial education: until 1691 no person could vote in Massachusetts who was not a participant in a Puritan congregation. Catholics, Jews and atheists could not vote in Pennsylvania. Even Rhode Island, which was one of the most tolerant states, denied the franchise to atheists and Catholics. Maryland under Catholic control was less intolerant than other states. When the Church of England took over in Maryland, restrictive legislation was passed against dissenters and the schools became pillars of religious orthodoxy.

HARVARD

Many of the famous American universities were founded between 1636 and 1736. Harvard was given a charter in 1636, William and Mary in 1693, Yale in 1701, Princeton in 1746 and Columbia University, first called King's College, in 1754.

The Puritan spirit was well represented by Harvard, which was to train ministers and which was founded so that the ecclesiastical spirit could be perpetuated. The following are some of the regulations which prevailed in 1642:

1. When any scholar is able to read Tully, or such like classical Latin author *extempore*, and make and speak true Latin in verse and prose *suo (ut aiunt) Marte*, and decline perfectly the paradigms of nouns and verbs in the Greek tongue, then may he be admitted into the College, nor shall any claim admission before such qualifications.

2. Every one shall consider the main end of his life and studies, to know God and Jesus Christ, which is eternal life; John xvii, 3.

* * *

8. They shall be slow to speak, and eschew not only oaths, lies, and uncertain rumors, but likewise all idle, foolish, bitter, scoffing, frothy, wanton words, and offensive gestures.[7]

The rules at Harvard were reinforced in 1650:

No scholar whatever, without the foreacquaintance and leave of the President and his Tutor, or in the absence of either of them, two of the Fellows, shall be present at or in any of the public civil meetings, or concourse of people, as courts of justice, elections, fairs, or at military exercise, in the time or hours of the College exercise, public or private. Neither shall any scholar exercise himself in any military band, unless of known gravity, and of approved sober and virtuous conversation, and that with the leave of the President and his Tutor.

No scholar shall take tobacco, unless permitted by the President, with the consent of their parents or guardians, and on good reason first given by a physician, and then in a sober and private manner.

To the intent that no scholar may misspend his time to the dishonor of God and the society, or the grief and disappointment of his friends, but that the yearly progress and sufficiency of scholars may be manifest, it is therefore ordered, that henceforth there shall be three weeks of visitation yearly, foresignified publicly by the President of the College, between the 10th of June and the Commencement, wherein from nine o'clock to eleven in the forenoon, and from one to three in the afternoon, of the second and third day of the week, all scholars of two years' standing and upwards, shall sit in the Hall to be examined by all comers, in the Latin, Greek, and Hebrew tongues, and in Rhetoric, Logic, and Physics; and they that expect to proceed Bachelors that year, to be examined of their sufficiency according to the laws of the College; and such that expect to proceed Masters of Arts, to exhibit their synopsis of acts required by the laws of the College.[8]

---

[7] Joseph Quincy, *The History of Harvard University*, 1840, I, pp. 515-519.
[8] *Ibid.*, pp. 517-519.

SAMUEL JOHNSON AND EDUCATION

Samuel Johnson did much to invigorate and liberate education in the United States. He studied at Yale and later became a tutor there. Although he started out in the Congregational Church, he became dissatisfied with its doctrines and turned to the Church of England. In 1722 he took orders and became a missionary in Stratford, Connecticut. He carried on a wide correspondence, and he was in contact with the noted thinkers of his age, including Colden and Berkeley. He was named president of King's College (Columbia), an office which he held for nine years; afterwards he returned to Stratford, where he died in 1772.

Among his works the most significant are *An Introduction to the Study of Philosophy* and *Elementa Philosophica*. Both are written in a systematic spirit, and they were outstanding texts of the colonial period. What distinguished Johnson, above all, was his acquaintance with European ideas, and thus he was far more cosmopolitan than most of his contemporaries.

Johnson divided philosophy into three parts: rational, natural and moral. Rational philosophy deals with the structure of the mind, natural philosophy with physical events and scientific phenomena, while moral philosophy deals with ethics and religious ideals.

Philosophy, according to Johnson, has many advantages. It teaches us the correct ways and methods of thinking, it enlightens us regarding natural objects, and it prescribes rules of action. In all its fields philosophy aims at *happiness*. This does not mean, however, hedonism, for we soon realize that the pleasures of the senses are inferior to those of the spirit. Furthermore, reflection tells us that we are not autonomous in our moral life, but that we depend on others. Egoism thus is subordinated to altruism.

In his metaphysical concepts he adhered to a dualistic concept. Matter he regarded as inert and passive, while the Mind he regarded as active. The laws of the physical world, he said, are guided by the Mind. This idealistic emphasis is intensified in his later teachings.

The educational influence of Locke is evident throughout Johnson's writings. Both men spoke of the *tabula rasa*, the blank tablet which the human mind contains at first. Still, this indicates to Johnson mainly man's dependence on spiritual truths. Furthermore, in his philosophy, as compared with that of Locke, reason plays a more important part than sense experience.

It would be a mistake to regard Johnson as a mechanist. In his cosmology he made much of *teleology*. Purposes govern the universe; both the material and immaterial realm are guided by God's providence.

In his religious views, Johnson reacted strongly against the determinism of the Calvinists. He felt that the doctrine of God's sovereignty violated moral ideals. Did it not make God into a despot? Did it not picture God as a merciless judge? This was not all. From a philosophical standpoint, it was also inadequate, for it was based on an anthropomorphic concept of time. It stated that God has foreknowledge; in reality, however, this is merely a human trait, for God comprehends all of time simultaneously.

Elementa Philosophica

According to Johnson there are three sources of knowledge: (1) sensation; (2) imagination and memory; and (3) intellectual light or intuition. The third source is the most important, for through it we perceive universal laws and the relation of ideas. Intuition indicated to Johnson that the universe is sustained by God and that matter is merely a passive principle.

In his *Elementa Philosophica* a Deistic spirit appears; it is still rather tenuous and obscured by theological foundations; yet it appears that Johnson regarded ethical laws as the laws of nature. He thus felt that the laws of reason and conscience were the same.

Johnson believed in an innate moral sense. This is the source of man's education, and it distinguishes between right and wrong. He went back to Socrates in his maxim that we must know ourselves, but to Johnson this imparts also a knowledge of our relations with society and with God.

He stressed the reality of man's *freedom*. God has endowed every man with liberty of choice. However, this also involves the possibility of sin, which stands for man's opposition to the laws of God. When we are wicked it is our own fault, not the fault of God.

Johnson was interested in the problem of evil. Using Stoic arguments, he indicated that evil frequently has an educational value. Through it we learn about real values and real ideals and we develop moral integrity.

Johnson As Educational Leader

As a college president, Johnson was far more liberal than many of his contemporaries. He was opposed to denominationalism and he did not believe that higher education should be governed by narrow religious ideals. King's College, which he headed, was far more liberal than Harvard which, in his time, was largely a pillar of orthodoxy.

His liberal spirit was evident from the beginning. He wrote the advertisement for the opening of the college, which included these comments:

> . . . as to Religion, there is no Intention to impose on the Scholars the peculiar Tenets of any particular Sect of Christians, but to inculcate upon their tender Minds, the great Principles of Christianity and Morality, in which, true Christians of each Denomination are generally agreed. — And as to the daily Worship in the College, Morning and Evening, it is proposed that it would ordinarily consist of such a collection of Lessons, Prayers and Praises of the Liturgy of the Church, as are for the most Part taken out of the Holy Scriptures, and such as are agreed on by the Trustees, to be in the best Manner expressive of our common Christianity. — And, as to any peculiar Tenets, every one is left to judge freely for himself, and to be required only to attend constantly at such Places of Worship on the Lord's Day, as their Parents or Guardians shall think fit to order or permit.[9]

---

[9] *The New York Mercury*, May 31, 1754.

CHAPTER SIX

The Age of Edwards

LIFE AND WORKS

Jonathan Edwards (1703–1758) was one of the eminent American clergymen and educators. It has been the custom to regard him as the outstanding representative of philosophical Calvinism, but this classification is too limited. He transcended Calvinism in his leaning on Plato and Berkeley, and his philosophical speculations revealed a wide acquaintance with the sciences, especially with Newtonian mathematics. There was also a mystical strain in his character which indicated an emotional awareness of God.

Born in Connecticut in 1703, Edwards in his youth displayed unusual intellectual gifts. Like Johnson, he attended Yale, becoming a tutor there in 1724. He left the academic profession to join the ministry, first as assistant to his grandfather, then as a regular minister in 1729. After many years of preaching, he was dismissed from his position in 1750. Before, he had contributed to the revival of religious feeling by his powerful sermons in which he showed how God's wrath is turned against sinners.

After his dismissal, he became a missionary to the Indians and devoted himself to philosophical inquiry. Later he became president of the College of New Jersey (Princeton); he died in 1758.

Among his works we find two sermons especially noteworthy: *God Glorified in Man's Dependence* and *A Divine and Supernatural Light.* In 1746 he wrote his *Treatise Concerning Religious Affections,* which was highly regarded by William James. In 1754 he wrote his essay on the *Freedom of Will,* and in 1755 he composed *Two Dissertations: The Nature of True Virtue* and *The End for Which God Created the World.* Finally, in 1758, he wrote *The Great Christian Doctrine of Original Sin Defended.*[1]

What is noteworthy in the works of Edwards is the combination of rationalism and mysticism. Edwards wrote not merely as a philosopher but also as a man of faith. His cardinal concept was the majesty of God and His constant providence. He tried to synthesize all aspects of life: reason and faith, science and religion. The Aquinas of Calvinism, Edwards produced works that are veritable summaries of the religious faith of the colonial period.

IDEALISM

The starting point of Jonathan Edwards' religious philosophy is idealistic. This spirit is revealed in his early treatise, *Notes on the Mind.* All existence, he affirmed, has a mental correlation. We observe events and phenomena, but they only exemplify the laws of the mind. Causation thus depends on God, whose presence unifies nature and whose activity preserves the order of the universe.

The phenomena of nature exist according to divine ideas. Here the Platonic influence is evident. Phenomena refer to a higher law – God's providence.

Early in life, Edwards reflected upon the problem of Being. What is real? What is appearance? What is the source of illusion? He possessed a mind which was not satisfied with superficial explanations, but which inevitably insisted upon a cosmic perspective.

Unlike Newton, Edwards did not regard space as absolute. Space, according to him, is finite and contained *within the universe.* In this way he tried to combat scientific absolutism, which frequently

---

[1] Cf. McGiffert, *Jonathan Edwards;* Smyth, "Jonathan Edwards' Idealism," *American Journal of Theology* I (1897), 950-964; Allen, *Jonathan Edwards;* Winslow, *Jonathan Edwards;* Schneider, *The Puritan Mind,* chs. III, IV, and V; Faust and Johnson, *Jonathan Edwards;* Müller, *Amerikanische Philosophie,* pp. 17-39.

looked upon space and time as two absolute principles of reality.

Both space and time are finite, but God transcends temporal limitations. In God there is no present, past, or future. Man, however, according to Edwards, is determined by time and is forever conscious of its dictates. Being finite, man can grasp only a partial aspect of truth; yearning for God, the principle of perfection, man finds permanent meaning.

In his theory of education, Edwards made much of intuition. Through this capacity he showed that the mind has an immediate awareness of spiritual truths and comprehends esthetic perfection. We start with sense experience, but this is not the end of knowledge; we ascend to reason and then to revelation as revealed by the divine light of God.

How can we distinguish between error and truth? How do we know that our senses do not deceive us? The answer of Edwards followed Calvinistic lines; we must rely on revelation and the Bible.

Which is more important, reason or revelation? The reply of Edwards is quite categorical: *revelation*. However, he made it clear that there is no essential conflict between these two capacities. For revelation is guided by definite laws and reveals God's majesty and perfection to man.

Important also is Edwards' concept of freedom. He argued vigorously against the Arminians, who believed in free choice. He felt that if their doctrines prevailed, they would undermine all religious striving.

The Arminians based their concept on three foundations. First, they maintained that the will is self-determined. Against this viewpoint Edwards spoke about the conditioning factors of volition. Frequently, Edwards held, man's will is determined by outside forces. Moreover, if man were autonomous he would be like God; this viewpoint appeared impious to Edwards.

Second, the Arminians believed in indifference. This means that our mind can deliberate with perfect freedom in choosing a certain action. It implies the possibility of an equilibrium. Edwards, however, asserted that our motives are never perfectly balanced and we must choose necessarily. He cited the example of a man touching some square on a chessboard and he indicated how this action was determined by previous associations.

The Arminians' third principle was contingency: they held that there is no necessary relationship between cause and effect. Edwards, argued that the mind is strictly determined in its choices and that man's behavior is not chaotic but law-abiding.

Edwards' conclusion is that man's will is determined by God. This is the key to both his theoretical and his educational philosophy.

GOD AND MAN

We are dependent on God not only for salvation but for all truth and understanding. Through God we learn to love Christ and through him we have wisdom and faith. This dependence on God is absolute.

The nature and contrivance of our redemption is such, that the redeemed are in everything directly, immediately, and entirely dependent on God: they are dependent on him for all, and are dependent on him in every way.

The several ways wherein the dependence of one being may be upon another for its good, and wherein the redeemed of Jesus Christ depend on God for all their good, are these, viz., that they have all their good of him, and that they have all through him, and that they have all in him: that he is the cause and original whence all which it is obtained and conveyed, therein they have it *through* him; and that he is that good itself that is given and conveyed, therein it is *in* him.

Now those that are redeemed by Jesus Christ do, in all these respects, very directly and entirely depend on God for their all.[2]

God is the cause of all good.

It is of God that we have our Redeemer: it is God that has provided a Savior for us. Jesus Christ is not only of God in his person, as he is the only begotten Son of God, but he is from God, as we are concerned in him, and in his office of Mediator: he is the gift of God to us: God chose and anointed him, appointed him his work, and sent him into the world.

And as it is God that gives, so it is God that accepts the Savior. It is God that provides and gives the Redeemer to buy salvation for us.[3]

Thus we must exalt God alone.

Let us endeavor to obtain, and increase in a sensibleness of our great dependence on God, to have our eye to him alone, to mortify a self-dependent, and self-righteous disposition. Man is naturally exceeding prone to be exalting himself and depending on his own power or goodness, as though he were he from whom he must expect

---

[2] *Works,* IV, p. 170.
[3] *Ibid.*

happiness, and to have respect to enjoyments alien from God and his Spirit, as those in which happiness is to be found.

And this doctrine should teach us to exalt God alone, as by trust and reliance, so by praise. *Let him that glorieth, glory in the lord.* Hath any man hope that he is converted, and sanctified, and that his mind is endowed with true excellency and spiritual beauty, and his sins forgiven, and he received into God's favor, and exalted to the honor and blessedness of being his child, and an heir of eternal life; let him give God all the glory; who alone makes him to differ from the worst of men in this world, or the miserablest of the damned in hell. Hath any man much comfort and strong hope of eternal life, let not his hope lift him up, but dispose him the more to abase himself, and reflect on his own exceeding unworthiness of such a favor, and to exalt God alone. Is any man eminent in holiness, and abundant in good works, let him take nothing of the glory of it to himself, but ascribe it to him whose "workmanship we are, created in Christ Jesus unto good works." [4]

It may be asked why God created the universe. Was it for the happiness of man? Or was it determined by God's own nature? Edwards answered emphatically that it was caused only by God's desire for self-expression. When God created the universe he expressed only his own perfection.

Some may object that this concept makes God extremely selfish. But Edwards felt that only God has real Being, whereas man has a secondary reality. When we love ourselves, we are addicted to illusion, but when we love God, we find certainty and absolute understanding.

Thus we find almost a Platonic ladder in Edwards. We start with the love of the self, then the love of nature as revealed in scientific truths, afterwards we turn to the Bible and to religious ideals, but the climax is the love of God, not because we expect any reward but because through it we understand reality. The good man, in loving God, is not motivated by practical ideals, and he does not expect any material results. He loves God because in this way he transcends all finite illusions and limitations.

ETHICAL IDEALS AND EDUCATION

Edwards' view of God reminds us of Spinoza, but we cannot be blind to his harsh doctrine of man. To those who believed that man is good and not naturally depraved he replied that such a

---

[4] *Ibid.*, p. 178.

doctrine is absolutely false. No, man is a creature of lust and wickedness. Although man was made in the image of God, he sinned and thus became eligible for eternal damnation. This may appear harsh to sentimentalists, but not to Edwards, who justified this viewpoint by saying that *a sin against infinite perfection demands infinite punishment.*

Some may still be in doubt and ask why every man shares the sin of Adam. Again, the answer of Edwards is categorical: the human race is the same in spite of the centuries which have elapsed since Adam. Consequently, we are naturally depraved, and we all share his sin.

One of the sermons of Edwards is entitled, *The Justice of God in the Damnation of Sinners.* In it he showed how thoroughly man is wicked.

How much of a spirit of pride has appeared in you, which is in a peculiar manner the spirit and condemnation of the devil! How have some of you vaunted yourselves in your apparel! Others in their riches! Others in their knowledge and abilities! How has it galled you to see others above you! How much has it gone against the grain for you to give others their due honor! And how have you shown your pride by setting up your wills, and in opposing others, and stirring up and promoting division, and a party spirit in public affairs!

How sensual have you been! Are there not some here that have debased themselves below the dignity of human nature, by wallowing in sensual filthiness, as swine in the mire, or as filthy vermin feeding with delight on rotten carrion? What intemperance have some of you been guilty of! How much of your precious time have you spent at the tavern, and in drinking companies, when you ought to have been at home seeking God and your salvation in your families and closets?

And what abominable lasciviousness have some of you been guilty of! How have you indulged yourself from day to day, and from night to night, in all manner of unclean imaginations! Has not your soul been filled with them, till it has become a hold of foul spirits, and a cage of every unclean and hateful bird? What foul-mouthed persons have some of you been, often in lewd and lascivious talk and unclean songs, wherein were things not fit to be spoken! And such company, where such conversation has been carried on, has been your delight. And what unclean acts and practices have you defiled yourself with![5]

What stupidity and sottishness has attended your course of wickedness; which has appeared in your obstinacy under awakening dispen-

---

[5] *Ibid.*, p. 234.

sations of God's word and providence! And how have some of you backslidden after you have set out in religion, and quenched God's Spirit after he had been striving with you! And what unsteadiness, and slothfulness, and great misimprovement of God's strivings with you, have you been chargeable with, that have long been subjects of them! Now, can you think when you have thus behaved yourself, that God is obliged to show you mercy? Are you not, after all this, ashamed to talk of it being hard with God to cast you off? Does it become one that has lived such a life, to open his mouth to excuse himself, or object against God's justice in his condemnation, or to complain of it as hard in God not to give him converting and pardoning grace, and make him his child, and bestow on him eternal life! Or to talk of his duties and great pains in religion, and such like things, as if such performances were worthy to be accepted, and to draw God's heart to such a creature! If this has been your manner, does it not show how little you have considered yourself, and how little a sense you have had of your own sinfulness?[6]

Edwards showed how man has slighted God.

And why then may not God justly slight you? When sinners are sensible in some measure of their misery, they are ready to think it hard that God will not take more notice of them; that he will see them in such a lamentable distressed condition, beholding their burdens and tears, and seem to slight it, and manifest no pity to them. Their souls they think are precious: it would be a dreadful thing if they should perish, and burn in hell forever. They do not see through it, that God should make so light of their salvation. But then, ought they not to consider, that as their souls are precious, so is God's honor precious? The honor of the infinite God, the great King of heaven and earth, is a thing of as great importance (and surely may justly be so esteemed by God), as the happiness of you, a poor little worm. But yet you have slighted that honor of God, and valued it no more than the dirt under your feet. You have been told that such and such things were contrary to the will of a holy God, and against his honor; but you cared not for that. God called upon you, and exhorted you to be more tender of his honor; but you went on without regarding him. Thus have you slighted God! And yet, is it hard that God should slight you? Are you more honorable than God, that he must be obliged to make much of you, how light soever you make of him and his glory?[7]

---

[6] *Ibid.*, p. 235.
[7] *Ibid.*, p. 236.

Man has been ungrateful; why should God have mercy?

God has tried you with a great deal of kindness, and he never has sincerely been thanked by you for any of it. God has watched over you and preserved you, and provided for you, and followed you with mercy all your days; and yet you have continued sinning against him. He has given you food and raiment, but you have improved both in the service of sin. He has preserved you while you slept; but when you arose, it was to return to the old trade of sinning. God, notwithstanding this ingratitude, has still continued his mercy; but his kindness has never won your heart, or brought you to a more grateful behavior towards him. . . [8]

In his *Thoughts Concerning the Present Revival of Religion in New England,* Jonathan Edwards defended himself against the charge of emotionalism. Religion, he held, had to appeal to man's feelings; otherwise he would not be conscious of the wages of sin. He attacked those who wanted to protect children from his sermons, for the nature of the child was as corrupt as that of the adult. Like St. Augustine, Edwards believed in the evils of children and he enumerated such evils as inattention in school, laziness, truancy, gambling, and avoiding church services.

His ideal child was Phebe Bartlet who, before she was five, had heard one of the sermons of Jonathan Edwards and who was a model child at home. She would pray several times a day and she would talk with her parents about the dangers of hell-fire. When she stole some fruit, she confessed her sins without reservation. The highlight of her existence was the Sunday sermon which Edwards preached and which she followed with complete attention.

We should note the difference between Edwards and modern educators like James and Dewey. To Edwards, education is a process of purging man's desires; to the pragmatic thinkers, education is the "reconstruction of experience." To Edwards, children are naturally wayward; to James and Dewey, children have creative interests which determine the educative process. To Edwards, the teacher is the servant of the church; to the pragmatic educators religion can be found as much in the classroom as in an ecclesiastical institution. To Edwards, physical punishment is the core of education; to James and Dewey, physical punishment represents an obsolete device which indicates inadequacy in the adult.

---

[8] *Ibid.*, p. 237.

THE IDEALS OF WOOLMAN

Quite different from Edwards was John Woolman (1720–1772), who represents the Quaker spirit in philosophy. Born in 1720 in New Jersey, he worked on his father's farm and prepared himself for the Quaker ministry. His education was limited, but he had a variety of occupations; he taught school, he drew up wills and he surveyed land. But whatever he did, he remained faithful to his Quaker ideals. Travelling widely, he visited the South and New England and the middle colonies. He died in 1772 in England from smallpox, while engaged in relief work among the poor.

He believed in living up to the precepts of the New Testament; he opposed slavery, war and the profit system, and he remained humble through his life. Like William Penn, he favored friendship with the Indians and a better deal for the landless masses.

Like Laotze, Woolman believed in *simplicity*. He abhorred great wealth, for it only leads to a struggle for power, and alienates its owner from religious truths. Man is tortured by a multitude of desires which lead only to oblivion. We are guided too much by social approval, which turns out to be only an illusory good.

The task of education is to teach us a correct way of life. This is best represented by Christ; like Him we should be willing to suffer and be persecuted for the ideals we hold. We must not be afraid of the obstacles, for man's spirit, according to Woolman, cannot be broken.

In his doctrine of man, Woolman was far more optimistic than Edwards. Woolman believed that man is good and that he is the vehicle for God's spirit. Man thus has infinite potentialities. Evil is merely an illusion and ultimately will be overcome by the creative powers of God.

To Edwards, God appeared as a merciless judge while Woolman spoke of God's mercy and regarded Him as a loving father who would always protect mankind, down to the worst sinner.

The religious experience, according to Woolman, cannot be represented by cathedrals and churches. It can be grasped only in silent worship when we feel God's presence within us. Away then with the sacraments and elaborate theology! Away with dogmatism! God's truth includes all — Christians and unbelievers, Jews and Gentiles.

How can the reform of mankind be accomplished? Through education. He definitely believed in the method of the Yogi, rather than that of the Commissar. Love, according to Woolman, has immense potentialities. By turning the other cheek, by replying with kindness to evil, we will create a new social order in which all men will be brothers and children of God.

Where Edwards saw an evil and corrupt nature in children, Woolman saw their innocence. He opposed physical punishment; harshness would only stifle children and produce submissive adults. He believed that their natural capacities should be stimulated so that they would want to learn and to lead a simple life.

Woolman made much of the power of example on the part of the teacher. What the teacher said, what he professed to believe, were less important than his conduct. The teacher's example of kindness and morality would bring out the goodness in children and society. He should study individual differences among his students so that he could use the best methods of instruction. His task was to lead the young and the old in the paths of love which could unite all races and all social groups.

CHAPTER SEVEN

The Liberal Tradition

BACKGROUND

Historically, the liberal spirit in American education dates back to the Renaissance, which brought about a revolution in the thinking of man. The localistic and provincial outlook of the Middle Ages, which had pictured the earth as the center of the universe now gave way to a heliocentric perspective. The work of Copernicus, Galileo, Brahe, Kepler and Newton brought about this expanded world view.

At first, the new scientific ideas were exposed to persecution; well known are the sufferings of Galileo at the hands of the Inquisition. But, in the age of Newton, the heliocentric viewpoint was taken for granted by the educated world. Not just the universe had changed but also man; for he had lost his status as lord of creation. More and more scholars were conscious of man's infinitesimal position in the vast astronomical world.

The thinkers reacted differently: to Bruno it meant a ready acceptance of pantheism; to Gassendi, Epicureanism was the only alternative; to Bayle, skepticism seemed to be the best answer, while to Pascal only faith seemed valid. But Pascal's belief in revelation was different from the medieval acceptance of the dogmas of the Church. To Pascal faith was an alternative to complete despair.

The new universe was dominated by laws, not by miracles. It was far more sober than the picturesque world of Aquinas. Faith in miracles continued, but now they were based upon the foundations of science. Were not the alchemists seeking for the philosopher's stone and for perpetual health and prosperity? Did they not combine in their work magic with chemistry?

Theology had been displaced as the queen of the sciences. The Humanists laughed at the old-fashioned utterances of the theologians. The students at the universities were enraptured instead by the study of languages and by the excitement of the physical sciences.

Aristotle was debunked. In the Middle Ages he had been an authority not only in religion but also in science, and regarded as the master of knowledge. His reputation was not ended, but at least it was challenged. The revolt was violent on the part of Sir Francis Bacon, and when his inductive logic challenged the Aristotelian foundations of knowledge, the theory of the Church was likewise imperiled.

The new method in science respected the facts of nature. Particulars instead of generalities were emphasized; in addition, patience became a prime virtue for the scientists. In the *Discourse on Method*, Descartes tells how he constantly checked and reviewed his conclusions. Here we find a precursor of the hypothetical method of modern science.

These advances created an unbounded spirit of confidence in man's ability, and the Renaissance became an age of optimism. A feeling prevailed that no discovery and no scientific advance lay beyond human achievement.

It is interesting that modern civilization started with such naive faith in man's possibilities; today there is a spirit of skepticism regarding man's ability to control nature. It is easy to explain this Renaissance spirit of self-confidence, for in this period man was just beginning to be emancipated and was overwhelmed by the novelty of his inventions. He was almost as eager as a freshman in college. In the twentieth century, he has been exposed to so many inventions and has seen so many scientific miracles that he has become almost as sophisticated and skeptical as a college senior.

HUMANISM AND EDUCATION

It was the Humanists who made the Renaissance victory of the scientific spirit possible. Most of them, like Reuchlin, Colet, and

Erasmus, were pious Christians who still accepted faith in God as the primary condition in life. They had great respect for authorities, especially for Greek and Roman scholars. Erasmus almost made Socrates a saint, and Reuchlin enjoyed nothing better than the study of the Hebrew language. Reuchlin had a persistent enemy in Pfefferkorn, a Jewish convert to Christianity who wanted to destroy all of Jewish literature, but Pfefferkorn was defeated in the end, and the study of Hebrew prospered at the European universities.

The Humanists popularized scholarship. Now the universities became social and political storm centers as well as agencies of active religious reform. Unfortunately, the Humanists were too much concerned with exactness and with scholarship. They venerated the works of the Greek thinkers.

At the same time, scholarship became cosmopolitan. Erasmus was a traveller in many lands, and he confessed that he was a citizen of Europe, not of any one nation. He taught at Cambridge, and he lived at Paris, Venice, and at Basel. Everywhere scholars followed him, and his letters and books reached a wide audience.

The primary aim of the Humanists was to invigorate the spirit of religion by basing it upon reason rather than upon superstition; most of them had a hostility for natural science. Still their work, ultimately, contributed to the spread of the scientific spirit, since it strengthened the cooperation of the European scientists. Moreover, the Humanists stressed an attitude of detachment instead of fanaticism.

BACON'S UTOPIA OF KNOWLEDGE

Francis Bacon's (1561–1626) achievements were even more influential in the development of the scientific perspective than the work of the Humanists. To be sure, his outlook upon life was Machiavellian; he did not hesitate to betray his best friend, he was open to bribery. Still, at the same time, he had a penetrating view of human nature as was shown by his *Essays*.

Bacon had no worship of Aristotle; instead, he turned to the pre-Socratic philosophers. A mechanistic explanation of the universe, as given by Democritus, appealed to him more than Aristotle's search for final causes. His own method was based upon induction, arriving at generalization on the basis of exhaustive enumeration of specific facts. This method was to revolutionize both the scientific and the religious outlook of mankind, for it stressed experience, exact measurement, and rigorous verification. Indeed, the system of empirical science, as used by the American pragmatists, represented a triumph of Bacon's inductive method.

The obstacles to scientific progress are called idols by Bacon. The first are the idols of the tribe. Bacon charges that all knowledge is limited by the anthropomorphic element, and is a reflection of man rather than of the objects which he investigates. The human mind seems to be so constituted that it submits more readily to affirmation than to negation. Bacon in his *Novum Organum* points to the persistence of superstitions. He counsels the students of science to look more to the negative instances and to adopt a doubtful attitude rather than one of ready affirmation.

How often our scientific statements are determined by our religious beliefs! Bacon was opposed to any theology in science and to the psychological foundation of theology which regards science as a secondary device. Is there not a universal tendency of mankind to believe before investigating the objects of faith?

The idols of the cave deal with individual human errors. Some minds stress analysis, others are more inclined to synthesize facts; some are impressed by tradition, others crave only novelty. In religion this means that every theology is an autobiography of its creator, that there can be no one universal system of belief. Moreover, every age will have its own theories of religion and will change the conclusions of the past generation.

The idols of the market place deal with the confusion in words. Here Bacon strikes a heavy blow at the vague phrases of the scholastics. The confusion of words has continued in modern times, in spite of the progress of the science of semantics, which is attempting to create a universal scientific language.

The idols of the theater stand for the persistent reign of tradition. The past enslaves both philosophical and religious systems. Bacon advocates a constant re-examination of ideas. Vigorously he points out that scientific philosophy cannot be based upon ancient authorities.

The tone of his philosophy is secular; no wonder that he was often accused of atheism. But he repeatedly makes it clear that he is a patriotic Christian. His famous statement that "a little philosophy inclineth a man's mind to atheism; but depth in philosophy bringeth men's minds about to religion" indicates his own outlook. There is, however, no pious feeling in Bacon; religion is simply another institution which must be accepted by all law-abiding subjects. Here his spirit approaches the sophisticated philosophy of Hobbes.

The result of his work is faith in an educational utopia, rather than in a religious heaven. In the *New Atlantis*, he outlined an advanced system of scientific training, and spoke of miraculous inventions which were to transform the universe. Like many modern Americans, he had an unbounded faith in technology and was awed by the possibilities of the new science.

THE PROPHET OF SOLITUDE

Scientific faith reached a climax in the teachings of Benedict Spinoza (1632–1677). His life was filled with tragedy. He was expelled from the Jewish faith for denying that the Old Testament taught the doctrine of immortality, for saying that angels may be only delusions in the human mind and for claiming that God may have a body. It was a solemn moment in his life when the edict of excommunication was read. It ordered that no one should communicate with him and that he was to be cut off from all the members of his family.

Spinoza is one of the few philosophers who did not defend a preconceived idea and who was not an apologist for an established faith. Most philosophers claim that they are completely objective, but, like Descartes and Leibnitz, they are usually guided by very human biases. Spinoza reached this attitude of detachment only after an intense period of suffering. He was economically independent as a lens grinder, and he owed allegiance to no religious or political party.

Various strains combine in the philosophy of Spinoza. Foremost is the influence of Descartes with his doctrine of God as the absolute substance, his separation of mind and body, and his rejection of final purposes as a valid explanation of science. There is the influence of Maimonides, who tried to give an allegorical explanation of the Old Testament. Spinoza's system also has remarkable similarities to the philosophy of Bruno, but it was even more influenced by the new developments in mathematics.

Spinoza tried to transform philosophy and religion into a geometric system. It was an audacious attempt and it failed; human experience cannot be enclosed into narrow mathematical categories. His proofs are not substantiated by the theories of modern science, for his system rested upon a static, almost Pythagorean universe. Still, the spirit of his teachings has a lasting meaning for philosophy and education.

The God of Spinoza has no passions, no feelings, no intellect, no human attributes whatsoever. He is all inclusive. Such a God is difficult to love but can have real meaning for the intellectual. In Spinoza determinism reigns supreme, and man must adjust himself to the established scientific order. The universe is not concerned with good and evil, for in life both suffer alike.

To some, this determinism invokes melancholy reflections; but to others, who think deeply, it is a cause for rejoicing, for this determinism is also the source of man's freedom and gives to the universe a basic and unceasing regularity. We find the same spirit in two modern American thinkers: Santayana and Morris Cohen.

Spinoza emphasized that real knowledge leads to freedom and advocated that man should see life under the aspect of eternity. This may be an exaggeration. At most, man can see existence under the aspect of history, yet such detachment leads away from egotism and can create a love of God without any expectations of rewards. Is this not the free man's faith of all ages?

The climax of his ideals is represented by the following well-known passage of his *Ethics:*

> . . . whence it appears, how potent is the wise man, and how much he surpasses the ignorant man, who is driven only by his lusts. For the ignorant man is not only distracted in various ways by external causes without ever gaining the true acquiescence of his spirit, but moreover, lives, as it were, unwitting of himself, and of God, and of things, and as soon as he ceases to suffer, ceases also to be.
>
> Whereas, the wise man, in so far as he is regarded as such, is scarcely at all disturbed in spirit, but being conscious of himself, and of God, and of things, by a certain eternal necessity, never ceases to be, but always possesses true acquiescence of spirit.[1]

Naturally, Spinoza rejected the doctrine of physical resurrection. The only immortality is that of the intellect, which is rather inadequate for the average person. Essentially the religion of Spinoza is for the intellectual aristocrat. The virtues he preaches, like objectivity, detachment, the constant search for knowledge, the intellectual love of God, are for the few, not for the many.

DEISM

The spirit of the age of enlightenment produced a new type of philosophy: Deism. Deists believed in a rational universe. Their religious ideals were extremely systematic. The universe was regarded as a clockwork guided by absolute laws.

The religion of the Deists was immortalized by Pope in his *Essay on Man:*

---

[1] *Ethics.*

All are but parts of one stupendous whole,
Whose body Nature is, and God the soul;
That, changed through all, and yet in all the same;
Great in the earth as in the ethereal frame.

. . . .

As full, as perfect, in vile man that mourns,
As the rapt seraph that adores and burns:
To him no high, no low, no great, no small;
He fills, he bounds, connects and equals all.

. . . .

And spite of pride, in erring reason's spite,
One truth is clear, Whatever is, is right.

The first generation of Deists was still quite conservative. John Locke believed in God, revelation, and the immortality of the soul. Later Deists like Voltaire were more radical and they frequently became atheists and challenged the validity of revelation. The same tendency can be observed in American culture, which started with a rather conservative reaction against Calvinism and ended in the defiant tones of materialism.

THE BEGINNING OF THE REVOLT

The American ideal of freedom was upheld dramatically by Roger Williams, whose protest against religious oppression has become a landmark in American democracy.[2] He was born in England, studied at Cambridge and in early youth was influenced by Puritanism. In 1631 he came to New England where he tried his hand as a minister; first at Plymouth, then at Salem, but he was regarded as a dangerous radical and was expelled from Massachusetts. In 1636 he fled to Rhode Island and established a haven for dissenters and others who were suffering from an overdose of orthodoxy. In his work he was aided by Anne Hutchinson, who constantly shocked the genteel and who was a most capable theologian.

Williams believed above all in the separation of state and church. He made it clear that the state cannot determine the religious beliefs of its citizens and that freedom of conscience cannot be violated.

In this way he paved the way for full freedom of religion, which later became a prominent feature of American constitutional theory.

---

[2] Cf. Straus, Roger Williams, the Pioneer of Religious Liberty; Carpenter, Roger Williams: A Study of the Life, Times, and Character of a Political Pioneer.

Although Williams was a radical in his own time, we must not forget that his religious philosophy was generally quite orthodox. He believed in God and in the atonement of Christ, and he accepted the infallibility of the Bible.

In his social views he fought against English imperial power, and he urged cooperation and friendship with the Indians.

Among those who, like Williams, fought for liberalism in religion, John Wise (1652–1725) is especially important. His father was an indentured servant, and thus John Wise had to struggle hard to obtain an education. He graduated in theology at Harvard and then became a minister. Most of his life he spent in a parish at Ipswich. Among his significant works we find *The Churches' Quarrel Espoused* and *Vindication of the Government of New England Churches*.

Wise believed in the goodness of man. Religion to him was a matter between man and God. He regarded coercion in spiritual matters as entirely illegitimate. Enlightened theologically, he fought against the witchcraft craze and thus incurred the enmity of the New England oligarchy.[3]

Wise derived man's powers from the state of nature. In this state complete equality prevails. Man's freedom is absolute both internally and externally. Describing three forms of government, democracy, aristocracy and monarchy, Wise regarded democracy as the best form of government, for in it men can best find themselves, and it exemplifies the light of nature.

Mayhew, like Wise, was a minister and a student at Harvard. He anticipated Unitarian ideals in his insistence on man's free will and man's innate goodness. A radical in politics, Mayhew fought against the Stamp Act and he urged the colonists to unite against English aggression. His democratic ideals, which influenced American liberalism, are well represented by his sermon: *A Discourse Concerning Unlimited Submission and Non-Resistance to Higher Powers.*[4]

In this sermon he protested against both civil and ecclesiastical tyranny. He explained how tyranny is usually small in the beginning and grows until it becomes a cruel burden on mankind. The best defense against tyranny is an educated democracy. This means no absolute rulers either in the ecclesiastical or civil realm.

In vivid words, Mayhew described the results of tyranny. He pictured the ignorance and brutality of the tyrants, the suppression

---

[3] For an excellent discussion of Wise see Parrington, *Main Currents in American Thought*, vol. I, pp. 118-125.

[4] For the role of religion in the revolution see Baldwin, *The New England Clergy in the American Revolution;* Humphrey, *Nationalism and Religion in America, 1774-1789.*

of education, the destruction of natural resources, and the enslavement of noble minds.

Christian submission, Mayhew pointed out, does not imply passivity and resignation. Civil rulers are to be resisted when they violate the rules of God and when they disregard the common good of society. The people are sovereign, not the princes. Governments are instituted for the welfare of the masses, not for the sake of their rulers.

In Mayhew liberalism rests upon a common-sense foundation. He was not a technical philosopher; thus he showed little knowledge of the classical systems of philosophy. Primarily, he was a man of action who had more regard for the desires and demands of his heart than for the dictates of reason.

PALMER

The career of Palmer was as stormy as that of Mayhew. He was born in 1764 in Connecticut and attended Dartmouth, where he studied theology. He became a Baptist but was expelled from that denomination because of his radical opinions. Then he became a follower of the "Universal Society," which was regarded with great disapproval by the orthodox religious leaders. Finally he turned to law and went to New York, where he became a leader in Deistic circles. In New York he was one of the founders of the Deistical Society, which was based on eleven fundamental principles.

1. The universe is the product of one supreme God who should be worshiped by man.

2. Man is a moral and intelligent being and possesses the natural capacity for happiness.

3. The religion of nature, arising out of man's moral capacity and being a symbol of civilization, is the "only universal religion."

4. Basic religion involves the love of truth and the practice of virtue.

5. Vice always brings about the ruin of mankind.

6. Benevolence and beneficence are fundamental in man's conduct.

7. A religion based on malice and persecution cannot be the product of divine forces.

8. Mankind can progress only through education and science.

9. There must be civil and religious liberty.

10. Religious opinions are not subject to human authority.

11. Human activity should be directed to the acquisition of science, truth, virtue and happiness and should be opposed to all forms "of superstition and fanaticism."

ETHAN ALLEN

Ethan Allen (1737-1789) was not as well educated as Palmer, but like the latter he was an opponent of religious fanaticism. He fought in many military campaigns, and his exploits during the Revolutionary War have almost become legendary. Most of his life he lived in Vermont, where he took a leading part in political affairs. So outspoken was he in his philosophical opinions that he was hated by the orthodox clergy. University presidents attacked him with fervor, especially Timothy Dwight of Yale and Sparks of Harvard, to whom Allen was the symbol of atheism and vulgarity.

As an individualist, Allen regarded religion from a subjective viewpoint. Certain that God exists, he felt that God reveals himself in the rational structure of the universe. With vigor he supported the doctrine of personal immortality.

His major work was entitled *Reason, the Only Oracle of Man.* In the first chapter he points out that while science has prospered, religion still has been held back by superstitious notions. He felt that it was his duty to enlighten mankind regarding the attributes and works of God so that the light of reason and education could shine more brightly.

He was certain that God could not be understood completely. Still, a rational concept of His being could be achieved, and in this manner man could acquire a more exalted view of his destiny both on earth and in the beyond.

The fundamental mistake in religious philosophy, according to Allen, is the identification of God with His works. This has led barbarous nations to worship the sun, which they considered to be divine. Throughout the universe Allen found a dominant purpose which made for order and harmony.

It is interesting to note that Allen believed in the *eternity* of creation. The reason he gave is quite simple. Since God is eternal and infinite, creation likewise must be eternal. He believed in a plurality of worlds and is thus related to the pre-Socratic philosophers.

God, according to Allen, can have only one essence. In this way he attempted to refute the doctrine of the trinity, which he regarded as absolutely invalid and as the source of idolatry and superstition.

As for miracles, they are rejected categorically as contrary to the rational structure of the universe. The only way man can master life is by rational means. Actual effort thus counts for more than prayer. Morality is best achieved through education. We should thank God for giving us moral ideals and rational concepts by which we can improve our destiny.

Rejecting the orthodox view of humility, Allen reminds us that we should act like free men, not like slaves facing an arbitrary monarch. As free men we should not ask any special favors for ourselves, but we should be conscious of the welfare of the universe.

PAINE'S PHILOSOPHICAL AND EDUCATIONAL IDEALS

The clearest expression of Deism was achieved by Thomas Paine (1737–1809), whose *Age of Reason* became the gospel of the Deists.[5] His viewpoint was determined by a variety of influences. His Quaker background made for tolerance and cosmopolitanism; his acquaintance with Newtonian theories gave him a scientific background for Deism; his studies of the classics, especially of Socrates, Plato, Aristotle, and Cicero encouraged his love of reason and harmony. He thought that the classical view of culture was far superior to that of Christianity.

He was also interested in comparative religions, and studied the faiths of the ancient Egyptians and the Druids. While he lacked scholarly penetration, he had an intense enthusiasm for knowledge. He wrote on a variety of topics, ranging from Freemasonry to the cosmological proof for the existence of God.

The *Age of Reason* is dedicated to the American citizen. He pointed out that every man has a right to his opinion and that reason is the best weapon of civilization. At the outset he summarized his creed:

I believe in one God, and no more; and I hope for happiness beyond this life.

I believe in the equality of man, and I believe that religious duties consist in doing justice, loving mercy, and endeavoring to make our fellow-creatures happy.

... My own mind is my own church.

---

[5] Cf. Woodward, *Thomas Paine, America's Godfather;* Conway, *Life of Thomas Paine.*

All national institutions of churches — whether Jewish, Christian, or Turkish — appear to me no other than human inventions set up to terrify and enslave mankind and monopolize power and profit.[6]

He stressed the fact that no church has a monopoly on revelation.

Every national church or religion has established itself by pretending some special mission from God, communicated to certain individuals. The Jews have their Moses; the Christians their Jesus Christ, their apostles and saints; and the Turks their Mahomet — as if the way to God was not open to every man alike.

Each of those churches show certain books which they call *revelation*, or the word of God. The Jews say that their word of God was given by God to Moses face to face; the Christians say that their word of God came by divine inspiration; and the Turks say that their word of God (the Koran) was brought by an angel from heaven. Each of those churches accuses the other of unbelief; and, for my own part, I disbelieve them all.[7]

As for Jesus, his teaching principles were admired by Paine.

Nothing that is here said can apply, even with the most distant disrespect, to the real character of Jesus Christ. He was a virtuous and amiable man. The morality that he preached and practiced was of the most benevolent kind; and though similar systems of morality had been preached by Confucius, and by some of the Greek philosophers, many years before, by the Quakers since, and by many good men in all ages, it has not been exceeded by any.[8]

The significance of Paine's philosophy can scarcely be exaggerated. He popularized   technical thinking and brought it down to the level of the masses.

He gave voice to the dominant ideals of the enlightenment as represented by faith in reason, the goodness of man, the need for science, a mechanical universe, and God as the great architect.

His eclecticism is the mark of much of American thinking. He borrowed from a variety of sources, including the classical philosophers and the French and English Deists. His originality consists in his synthesis of the various authors on whom he leaned and in applying their concepts to his own period.

Paine represented an extremely optimistic current in philosophy. He felt certain that the future would witness the emancipation of mankind and the destruction of tyranny both in the civil and religious

---

[6] Paine, *The Age of Reason.* (Credo.)
[7] *Ibid.*, ch. II.
[8] *Ibid.*, ch. III.

realm. Although he was exposed to violent personal attacks, he never lost his faith in the rationality of man.

Most important, Paine looked to education as the main tool for man's advancement. Education was to provide for real enlightenment: the state and the church were to be separated; free inquiry was to prevail in the classroom. Reason was to govern all aspects of our institutional system.

FRANKLIN'S THEORIES

The Deistic currents are especially strong in Benjamin Franklin (1706–1790). In his youth he leaned in the direction of determinism, which is revealed in his *A Dissertation on Liberty and Necessity, Pleasure and Pain,* but this treatise probably was an extreme reaction against his pietistic background at home. Later he felt that this early work did not present his real opinions, and he became more conservative in his religious and philosophical theories.

His learning was astounding. Among the philosophical authors with whom he was acquainted we find Pythagoras, Plato, Epictetus, Aristotle, Seneca, Cicero, Bacon, Tillotson, Fénelon, Voltaire, Mandeville, Locke, Shaftesbury, Collins, Bolingbroke, Paley, Lord Kames, Adam Smith, Hume, Du Pont de Nemours, Priestley, Paine, and Condorcet.

At the age of twenty-two, he composed his articles of faith, which are an excellent introduction to his philosophical opinions. He stated:

I believe there is one supreme, most perfect Being, Author and Father of the Gods themselves. For I believe that Man is not the most perfect Being but one, rather that as there are many Degrees of Beings his Inferiors, so there are many Degrees of Beings superior to him.

Also when I stretch my Imagination thro' and beyond our system of Planets, beyond the visible fix'd Stars themselves, into that Space that is every Way infinite, and conceive it fill'd with Suns like ours, each with a Chorus of worlds forever moving around him, then this little Ball on which we move, seems, even in my narrow Imagination, to be almost Nothing, and myself less than nothing, and of no sort of Consequence.

When I think thus, I imagine it great Vanity in me to suppose, that the *Supremely Perfect* does in the least regard such an inconsiderable Nothing as Man. More specifically, since it is impossible for me to have any positive clear idea of that which is infinite and incomprehensible, I cannot otherwise than that he the *Infinite Father* expects or requires no Worship or Praise from us, but that he is infinitely above it.[9]

Thus he stressed the transcendence of God; but man has a natural capacity for devotion and he needs an outlet for this drive.

And since Men are endued with Reason superior to all other Animals, that we are in our World acquainted with;

Therefore I think it seems required of me, and my Duty as a Man, to pay Divine Regards to SOMETHING.

I conceive then, that the Infinite has created many beings or Gods, vastly superior to Man, who can better conceive his Perfections than we, and return him a more rational and glorious Praise.

As, among Men, the Praise of the Ignorant or of Children is not regarded by the ingenious Painter or Architect, who is rather honor'd and pleased with the approbation of Wise Men & Artists.

It may be that these created Gods are immortal; or it may be that after many Ages, they are changed, and others Supply their Places.

Howbeit, I conceive that each of these is exceeding wise and good, and very powerful; and that Each has made for himself one glorious Sun, attended with a beautiful and admirable System of Planets.[10]

Franklin conceived of God as a wise architect. He thought that He had some of the traits we possess, especially reason and wisdom. Thus there is a natural kinship between man and the Deity. Also, inferior gods intervene between the highest Deity and man. Thus we can detect a note of polytheism in Franklin's system.

Above all, the goodness of God was emphasized by Franklin, who had no use for Calvinistic concepts.

I conceive for many Reasons, that he is a good Being; and as I should be happy to have so wise, good, and powerful a Being my Friend, let me consider in what manner I shall make myself most acceptable to him.

Next to the Praise resulting from and due to his Wisdom, I believe he is pleas'd and delights in the Happiness of those he has created; and since without Virtue Man can have no Happiness in this World, I firmly believe he is not offended, when he sees his Children solace themselves in any manner of pleasant exercises and Innocent Delights; and I think no Pleasure innocent, that is to Man hurtful.

I love him therefore for his Goodness, and I adore him for his Wisdom.

---

[9] Franklin, *Articles of Belief and Acts of Religion.*
[10] *Ibid.*

Let me then not fail to praise my God continually, for it is his Due, and it is all I can return for his many Favours and great Goodness to me; and let me resolve to be virtuous, that I may be happy, that I may please Him, who is delighted to see me happy. Amen![11]

Generally, a strain of conservatism prevailed in Franklin; he tried to persuade Thomas Paine not to publish his radical opinions in religion. To support his views, Franklin pointed to the majority of men, who are too weak to stand by themselves and who need the comfort of religion.

THE EDUCATION OF SOCIETY

When Franklin came to Paris in 1777, he became a favorite of the sophisticated Parisian society. They liked his simplicity, his sense of humor, and his scientific talents. They all knew how he had risen from poverty to wealth; how he had struggled against reverses, being a child of a family of seventeen. Franklin had done much reading in his youth, including the famous French thinkers. He was, indeed, a man who represented the best possibilities of democracy. His career showed how much could be done in a society which was free from the restraints of a social caste system.

To Franklin, agriculture was the noblest activity of man. He had studied history sufficiently to know that countries acquired wealth in three ways: through war, which meant plunder; through trade, which represented, frequently, corruption; and through agriculture, which, to Franklin, meant complete integrity.

In his political theories, Franklin was in favor of universal manhood suffrage, a unicameral legislature directly responsible to the voters, and annual elections as the best guarantees for a strong democracy.

He had faith in the future of the United States, as can be seen in his letter to Charles de Weissenstein.

Our expectations of the future grandeur of America are not so magnificent, and therefore not so vain or visionary, as you represent them to be. The body of our people are not merchants, but humble husbandmen, who delight in the cultivation of their lands, which, from their fertility and the variety of our climates, are capable of furnishing all the necessaries and conveniences of life without external commerce; and we have too much land to have the least

[11] *Ibid.*

temptation to extend our territory by conquest from peaceable neighbours, as well as too much justice to think of it. Our militia, you find by experience, are sufficient to defend our lands from invasion; and the commerce with us will be defended by all the nations who find an advantage in it. We, therefore, have not the occasion you imagine, of fleets or standing armies, but may leave those expensive machines to be maintained for the pomp of princes, and the wealth of ancient states. We propose, if possible, to live in peace with all mankind; and after you have been convinced, to your cost, that there is nothing to be got by attacking us, we have reason to hope, that no other power will judge it prudent to quarrel with us, lest they divert us from our own quiet industry, and turn us into corsairs preying upon theirs. . .[12]

EDUCATIONAL BELIEFS

To Franklin, the purpose of education was to destroy aristocratic ideals. He noted that many wealthy students who went to Harvard hired poor scholars to do their work for them. Their degrees were thus obtained fraudulently. Education, he held, should prepare the middle classes for public duty.

Franklin had little respect for the classics. In this way he anticipated the pragmatism of Dewey and Kilpatrick. The classics, only too often, he stated, were obsolete. They had no real relevance to his own time which had to make its own discoveries and learn to stand on its own feet. Like Emerson, Franklin was an apostle of self-reliance, which meant trust in one's own energies rather than dependence upon the insights of the past.

The virtues which he prized in education were typical of middle class standards. They included the formation of sound habits: Was not extravagance to be avoided? Would not laziness lead to moral disaster? Was not drunkenness a constant danger? Like Aristotle, Franklin preferred the life of moderation and thought this concept should be emphasized in the schoolroom.

Mere knowledge, he asserted, was not the main goal of education. Too often the scholar was a recluse who was arrogant about his learning. Too often he gave absolute answers when he should have asked more penetrating questions. Scholarship tended to be detailed and analytical, when a broad view of life would help the advancement of society.

---

[12] *To Charles de Weissenstein,* July 7, 1778.

Education, to Franklin, implied the ideal of service. Self-interest rightly interpreted meant the same as service to one's neighbor. Education was to include a knowledge of man's social being. To serve one's fellow man was both a privilege and a responsibility — a privilege because it widened one's horizons and a responsibility because society depended on the creativity and originality of its leaders.

While he did not overlook the classical languages, Franklin mainly stressed correct knowledge of English. This meant more than competence in grammar and verbal eloquence. It meant more than skill in writing. English was to be mastered as a tool of communication; American literature and history were to be the keys to enlightenment. He vigorously promoted English as the language for German immigrants in Pennsylvania. Without a common language, he said, anarchy would result and the nation would not prosper in industry, politics, and science.

Like Jefferson, Franklin favored the training of both body and mind. If only the mind were cultivated it would lead to narrowness of perception and would create individuals unfit for public service. On the other hand, mere physical training would provide a brutish existence and would create individuals who would lack depth and awareness and who would miss the greatest excitement, the life of the mind. Education should create good habits both intellectually and physically.

Pragmatic in his philosophy of education, he cherished the sciences, especially mathematics and physics. He had no use for Aristotelian logic which he regarded as being part of an obsolete age. The method which he favored was one of discovery and depended on application. He felt that the worship of authority, especially in science, constituted a roadblock and made progress more difficult.

How could education be tested? How could its effect be verified? Franklin answered that our way of life was the best test of education. If we develop intolerance and dogmatism, if we worship the past, if we only imitate the ancients, then obviously education has failed. The task of education was to create enlightened human beings who explored their own capabilities and who were able to live with their neighbors and tolerate the frailties of others. Tolerance was to be the core of education, and was to be extended to the lower classes, even to the colored minority.

He was influenced by the Quakers in his regard for the unfortunate members of society. He aided the education of orphans; he was interested in the training of Negroes. In every way he was concerned with the education of the common laborer, whose worth, he thought, provided the real foundation of society.

Franklin looked to the Academy movement for a new educational pattern. The academies, he hoped, would fight against denomination-alism; they would explore new teaching methods and broaden the realms of knowledge by introducing practical subjects.

Franklin stressed the knowledge of history:

> If history be made a constant part of their reading, such as the trans-lations of the Greek and Roman historians and the modern histories of ancient Greece and Rome, etc., may not almost all kinds of useful knowledge be that way introduced to advantage, and with pleasure to the student?
>
> Geography, by reading with maps and being required to point out the places where the greatest actions were done, to give their old and new names, with the bounds, situation, extent of the countries concerned, etc.
>
> Chronology, by the help of Helvicus or some other writer of the kind who will enable them to tell when those events happened, what princes were contemporaries, what states of famous men flour-ished about that time, etc. The several principal epochs to be first well fixed in their memories.
>
> Ancient customs, religious and civil, being frequently mentioned in history, will give occasion for explaining them, in which the prints of medals, basso-relievos and ancient monuments will greatly assist.[13]

History leads to . . .

> Morality, by discanting and making continual observations on the causes of the rise or fall of any man's character, fortune, power, etc., mentioned in history; the advantages of temperance, order, frugality, industry, perseverance, etc. etc. Indeed the general natural tendency of reading good history must be to fix in the minds of youth deep impressions of the beauty and usefulness of virtue of all kinds, public spirit, fortitude, etc.
>
> History will show the wonderful effects of oratory in governing, turning and leading great bodies of mankind, armies, cities, nations. When the minds of youth are struck with admiration at this, then is the time to give them the principles of that art, which they will study with taste and application. Then they may be made acquainted with the best models among the ancients, their beauties being particularly pointed out to them. Modern political oratory being chiefly per-formed by the pen and press, its advantages over the ancient in some

---

[13] *Proposals Relating to the Education of Youth in Pennsylvania, 1749.*

respects are to be shown, as that its effects are more extensive, more lasting, etc.

History will also afford frequent opportunities of showing the necessity of a public religion, from its usefulness to the public; the advantage of a religious character among private persons; the mischiefs of superstition, etc. and the excellency of the Christian religion above all others ancient or modern. . .

On historical occasions questions of right and wrong, justice and injustice, will naturally arise, and may be put to youth, which they may debate in conversation and in writing. When they ardently desire victory for the sake of the praise attending it they will begin to feel the want and be sensible of the use of logic, or the art of reasoning to discover truth, and of arguing to defend it, and convince adversaries. This would be the time to acquaint them with the principles of that art. Grotius, Puffendorff, and some other writers of the same kind, may be used on these occasions to decide their disputes. Public disputes warm the imagination, whet the industry, and strengthen the natural abilities.[14]

History inspires:

When youth are told that the great men whose lives and actions they read in history spoke two of the best languages that ever were, the most expressive, copious, beautiful; and that the finest writings, the most correct compositions, the most perfect productions of human wit and wisdom, are in those languages, which have endured ages and will endure while there are men; that no translation can do them justice or give the pleasure found in reading the originals; that those languages contain all science; that one of them is become almost universal, being the language of learned men in all countries; that to understand them is a distinguishing ornament, etc. they may be thereby made desirous of learning those languages, and their industry sharpened in the acquisition of them. All intended for divinity should be taught the Latin and Greek; for physic, the Latin, Greek, and French; for law, the Latin and French; merchants, the French, German, and Spanish; and though all should not be compelled to learn Latin, Greek, or the modern foreign languages, yet none that have an ardent desire to learn them should be refused; their English, arithmetic, and other studies absolutely necessary being at the same time not neglected.

If the new *Universal History* were also read it would give a connected idea of human affairs, so far as it goes, which should be followed by the best modern histories, particularly of our mother country; then of these colonies; which should be accompanied with

---

[14] *Ibid.*

observations on their rise, increase, use to Great Britain, encourage-
ments, discouragements, etc. the means to make them flourish, secure
their liberties, etc.[15]

Franklin thought that it was the responsibility of the school to
train both leaders and followers. The leaders were to be stimulated
to live up to high standards of proficiency, while the followers were
to develop patterns of appreciation. Culture was to be universalized.
It was not to be the privilege of an aristocratic minority, rather it
was to be the possession of the middle class.

A proponent of adult education, Franklin stressed the value of
discussion. This was a method whereby new ideas could be discovered, whereby liberals and conservatives could meet together
and exchange viewpoints. In his time there was far more contact
and understanding between liberals and conservatives than in our
own period, which has encouraged bitter controversy rather than
rational discussion.

The best type of education, Franklin asserted, was self-education.
It meant that the formal schooling was only a prelude, that book
knowledge was only an overture to the mastery of the book of life.
His ideal teacher was Socrates. Did not Socrates appeal to the young
and the old? Did not Socrates teach in the market-place? Did not
Socrates use discussion as the main tool of education? The difference
between Socrates and Franklin was that Socrates had no real scientific interests, while Franklin was concerned with the pragmatic
application of ideas.

Franklin believed that education had no frontier. It did not start
at a certain time nor could a man ever stop learning. Often the
greatest lessons, he asserted, would be learned from those who had
no formal education. The more a man would understand life, the
more he would see how fallible his thoughts were.

Franklin represents the best traits of the educated mind. He was
urbane and tolerant, he promoted the arts and sciences, he had a
vast sense of public responsibility. He never stopped discovering new
ideas. He had faith in democracy not merely as a political movement
and as a social ideal but as an intellectual concept. His aim was to
fight ignorance and superstition and to promote free inquiry.

---

[15] *Ibid.*

CHAPTER EIGHT

Materialistic Currents and Education

FOUNDATIONS

The materialistic philosophy in the United States was a natural reaction to the immaterialism that we find in Berkeley and Johnson. It was part of the enlightenment which emphasized the enjoyment of physical pleasures and which believed that science was the best tool for the achievement of genuine education.

As scientific principles were applied concretely, inventions multiplied. Every school boy knows about the amazing achievements of Benjamin Franklin and Joseph Priestley. The science of physiology was stimulated especially by Benjamin Rush, who gave a mechanistic account of man's emotions.

Translations of French authors aided in the development of materialism. Mention should be made of Buffon's *View of Nature* and Condorcet's *Progress of the Human Mind*. Cabanis became popular in the colonies and the works of Holbach were read eagerly. As American statesmen were in constant contact with France, especially through Jefferson, French ideas penetrated colonial thinking.

95

Most of the up-to-date French thinkers of the eighteenth century had materialistic leanings. Among the champions of materialism were Condillac, Helvétius, Cabanis, and Holbach. Voltaire, as a Deist, seemed almost conservative, for he still believed in God and thought that the cosmological argument for His existence was valid in philosophy.

Many of the materialists were engaged in revolutionary efforts. They wanted to liberate the human mind and to remove the obsolete institutions which stood in the way of progress. Many of the radicals in the American revolutionary movement combined free-thinking with a belief in absolute democracy.

TRAITS OF AMERICAN MATERIALISM

Generally speaking, the American materialists were rather tame when compared with their European counterparts. They accepted the existence of God, and most of them believed in personal immortality.

Morally, they avoided a hedonistic emphasis. In fact, they thought that materialism would produce a more sublime ethical system. Instead of following the impulses of man's physical nature, they appealed to reason as the highest organ of authority.

Most of the time the American materialists lacked originality. They repeated in the main the theories of Condillac, Helvétius, and Cabanis. They were constantly attacked by the orthodox ministers and the philosophy professors for being subversive. However, these charges were generally exaggerated. In fact, from the perspective of the twentieth century they appear to be rather conservative in their viewpoint.

COLDEN

A moderate spirit is manifested in Cadwallader Colden (1688-1776), who was only a lukewarm materialist. He was born in Ireland, took his medical studies in London, and in 1710 came to the United States. He achieved high political distinction, becoming a member of the Governor's Council of New York, and in 1761 he was named Lieutenant-Governor of New York.

Among his works, two are especially significant, *First Causes of Action in Matter and the Cause of Gravitation* and *The Principles of Action in Matter*. Both deal with his views of the Newtonian system and stamp him as one of the most brilliant scientific minds of colonial America.

His view of knowledge being *dynamic*, he rejected the theory of Locke that our minds are purely passive. There is a reciprocity between objects and the mind; both are active and involved in a process of change.

He sought to refute the viewpoint of Johnson that material substances are passive and purely secondary; rather he regarded them as creative. Causality thus is real and does not depend on the intervention of God, as the idealists asserted.

One of Colden's most interesting essays is his *Introduction to the Study of Philosophy*, which he wrote for the sake of the young man entering college. In it he inveighed against the ecclesiastics, who he thought had obstructed the progress of education. He mentioned especially the sad fate of Galileo. With scorn he treated the old school logic, which only obscured real truth. The syllogism, he asserted, perpetuates tradition and is the enemy of experimental science.

BUCHANAN

Joseph Buchanan (1785-1829) is best known for his *Philosophy of Human Nature*, which appeared in Kentucky in 1812. He was educated at Transylvania University, and he studied in Philadelphia, but he never finished his course. A physician, he gave a thoroughly scientific interpretation of man and the universe.

Among those who influenced him, especially important was John Locke, who gave him his empirical bent. Hartley supplied him with the concept of the association of ideas and the conviction that our mental processes can be understood without rationalistic *a priori* postulates. Hume introduced a skeptical element in his philosophy, and the influence of Erasmus Darwin made for a naturalistic view of evolution.

Buchanan was certain that a metaphysical dualism which separated mind and matter was unjustified. For mind and matter are united and express a common principle of activity. Mind does not express a separate principle, but only a refined state of material activity.

Buchanan stressed the fact that the intellect is not autonomous. As a physician, he knew that physiological changes in man produce mental changes. Now if man's intellect were independent, as the idealists asserted, physical changes would have no influence on it and would not modify its behavior.

Like Holbach, Buchanan regarded man as a machine. Man's behavior must be studied experimentally without making any spiritualistic assumptions. Thus especially important are man's reflex actions.

Man's knowledge, according to Buchanan, can achieve only *probability*. Our ideas do not correctly mirror the external world; causality generally is based on custom, not on absolute logical laws. The only type of education which gives us certainty is based on mathematics. In this field the axioms we use correspond exactly to external objects.

Following Hume, Buchanan stressed the doctrine of necessity. Man's behavior is determined by his environment, and uniformity prevails in his character. Using the doctrine of the association of ideas, Buchanan held that it explains adequately man's choices. Ideas naturally group together; we favor those which give us pleasure and which prove to be functional, while we reject those which give us pain and which science proves to be obsolete.

In his psychology he emphasized the importance of *habit*. Without habitual intellectual training our mind becomes sluggish and loses its vitality. He applied this concept to education, and he urged that teachers should be concerned to inculcate right habits into their students, so that they would find intellectual pursuits more stimulating and pleasant.

PRIESTLEY AND COOPER

Joseph Priestley, fleeing from persecution in England, came to the United States in 1794. In England he was regarded as a subversive thinker, and the same suspicion followed him to his adopted country.

He made it clear that the mind and body are closely related and that matter has been misunderstood by the idealists, who neglected its dynamic properties. With care he examined the concept of an immaterial substance, and he came to the conclusion that it had no validity in philosophy. For everything we perceive and know has material manifestations.

His critics charged that his doctrines showed that the soul is not immortal. Naturally a storm arose in orthodox circles. Furthermore, he was vague regarding the attributes of God, and he leaned in the direction of pantheism.

Priestley's teachings were perpetuated by his son-in-law, Thomas Cooper, whose career was almost as eventful as Priestley's. A follower of Jefferson, Cooper strenuously opposed the Federalist principles;

he agitated for the rights of the states, and he supported nullification ideas in South Carolina.

Among Cooper's works the most significant is his *View of the Metaphysical and Physiological Arguments in Favor of Materialism.* It indicated an excellent knowledge of the history of physiology and demonstrated his logical powers. He first described the idealistic philosophy and then proceeded systematically to tear it down.

The idealists stressed that the soul has nothing in common with matter. Cooper asked: How can the two substances react? Actually the idealistic argument proved to be a boomerang, for it left the immaterial substance in a hopeless condition in which it proved to be without causal efficacy.

What is most striking in the system of Cooper is his stress upon external factors. He believed that the behavior of man is determined by environmental factors. Thus an American citizen will have different ideals and habits from a Chinese. He urged the educators to be more hypothetical in their assertions and less dogmatic and to study the influence of environment on man's intellectual and social life.

BENJAMIN RUSH

Rush in many ways was the most notable of the materialistic thinkers, and he contributed much to the development of American culture, especially in his work with the insane.

He was born in 1745 in Byberry, Pennsylvania. He attended the College of New Jersey (Princeton), from which he received his A.B. in 1760. Then he studied medicine in Scotland and in London. After he returned to the United States he took up medical practice and then was appointed professor of chemistry at the College of Philadelphia.

His rise from that time was meteoric. In 1776 he was elected a member of the Continental Congress; three years later he became Surgeon-General. In 1786 he was responsible for the establishment of the first free dispensary in the colonies; he became a professor of medicine at the University of Pennsylvania. From 1797 to 1813, when he died, he was treasurer of the United States mint.

He was a prolific author. His works included: *A Syllabus of a Course of Lectures on Chemistry; Sermons to Gentlemen upon Temperance and Exercise; Essays, Literary, Moral and Philosophical; Medical Inquiries and Observations upon the Diseases of the Mind;* and *Three Lectures upon Animal Life.*

His concept of life was optimistic; he thought that education and science would eventually eradicate human misery. He pointed out that no man is depraved; if he acts in an anti-social manner, this is merely due to physical and environmental factors. Anticipating modern methods of psychiatry, Rush believed that criminals should be treated as humanely as if they were physically ill.

In his ethical theory he stressed the action of the will, which represents man's moral faculty. The moral faculty, according to Rush, can be investigated scientifically, for it is influenced by external factors.

Deeply religious, Rush did not deny God's providence, which is revealed as much in the material as in the spiritual world. Even if the soul is material, this does not imply its destruction after the death of the body. In fact, Rush contended that the material soul may be immortal.

An excellent summary of his educational system occurs in a speech which he made entitled *An Inquiry into the Influence of Physical Causes on the Moral Faculty*. He made it clear that man's conscience remains mysterious and beyond scientific investigation.

> It has long been a question among metaphysicians, whether the conscience be seated in the will or in the understanding. The controversy can only be settled by admitting the will to be the seat of the moral faculty, and the understanding to be the seat of the conscience. The mysterious nature of the union of those two moral principles with the will and understanding is a subject foreign to the business of the present inquiry.
>
> As I consider virtue and vice to consist in *action*, and not in opinion and as this action has its seat in the *will*, and not in the conscience, I shall confine my inquiries chiefly to the influence of physical causes upon that moral power of the mind, which is connected with volition, although many of these causes act likewise upon the conscience, as I shall show hereafter. The state of the moral faculty is visible in actions, which affect the well-being of society. The state of the conscience is invisible, and therefore removed beyond our investigation.[1]

He was certain that physiological factors influence man's moral faculty. For example, he told of a woman who had excellent habits but who could not refrain from stealing. What made her case especially strange was the fact that she was well off.

He described the effect of climate upon man's moral capacity.

> Not only individuals, but nations, derive a considerable part of their moral, as well as intellectual character, from the different portions

---

[1] Quoted in Blau, *American Philosophic Addresses*, p. 317.

they enjoy of the rays of the sun. Irascibility, levity, timidity, and indolence, tempered with occasional emotions of benevolence, are the moral qualities of the inhabitants of warm climates, while selfishness, tempered with sincerity, and integrity, form the moral character of the inhabitants of cold countries. The state of the weather, and the seasons of the year also, have a visible effect upon moral sensibility. The month of November, in Great Britain, rendered gloomy by constant fogs and rains, has been thought to favour the perpetration of the worst species of murder, while the vernal sun, in middle latitudes, has been as generally remarked for producing gentleness and benevolence.[2]

He turned also to the effect of certain drinks upon man's behavior.

Fermented liquors, of a good quality, and taken in a moderate quantity, are favourable to the virtues of candour, benevolence, and generosity; but when they are taken in excess, or when they are of a bad quality, and taken even in a moderate quantity, they seldom fail of rousing every latent spark of vice into action.[3]

He made it clear that his scientific views did not detract from Christianity.

It is true, Christianity was propagated without the aid of human learning; but this was one of those miracles, which was necessary to establish it, and which by repetition, would cease to be a miracle. They misrepresent the Christian religion, who suppose it to be wholly an internal revelation, and addressed only to the moral faculties of the mind. The truths of Christianity afford the greatest scope for the human understanding, and they will become intelligible to us, only in proportion as the human genius is stretched, by means of philosophy, to its utmost dimensions. Errors may be opposed to errors; but truths, upon all subjects, mutually support each other. And perhaps one reason why some parts of the Christian revelation are still involved in obscurity, may be occasioned by our imperfect knowledge of the phenomena and laws of nature. The truths of philosophy and Christianity dwell alike in the mind of the Deity, and reason and religion are equally the offspring of his goodness. They must, therefore, stand and fall together. By reason, in the present instance, I mean the power of judging of truth, as well as the power of comprehending it. Happy era! when the divine and the philosopher shall embrace each other, and unite their labours for the reformation and happiness of mankind.[4]

---

[2] *Ibid.*, p. 326.
[3] *Ibid.*, p. 327.
[4] *Ibid.*, p. 342.

Rush applied his moral ideals to politics. Unlike Machiavelli he did not believe in a dualism of moral standards. Rather, he emphasized that virtue must be the goal of all men. Only in this manner can civilization, progress and peace be maintained.

Advanced for his time, Rush pleaded for an educational system which would advance all classes. Women were to be educated to their full capacity. No social distinctions were to be tolerated. No bias was to be allowed in the classroom.

CHAPTER NINE

The Impact of the Revolution

SIGNIFICANCE OF THE REVOLUTION

The American revolution was a rebellion on the part of the middle class, which demanded full recognition and demonstrated by its success that it was ready to assume complete governmental power. It was not as bloody and violent a struggle as the French revolution nor did it involve the common people as did the Russian revolution of 1917. Actually, it was a revolution by the minority; only one-third of the male population were in favor of it; the rest were either indifferent or pro-English or lukewarm in their sympathy for the revolutionary cause.[1]

This indifference can be best explained by the geographic distances of the United States; inadequate transportation made both physical and mental communications extremely difficult. The population was composed of many nationalities, with a variety of interests,

---

[1] For a discussion of the significance of the American Revolution see Parrington, *Main Currents in American Thought,* vol. I; Adams, *Political Ideas of the American Revolution;* Merriam, *A History of American Political Theories.*

and a common revolutionary ideal was almost impossible to achieve. In more recent times, revolutions have become explosive because they have affected a larger number of people and because the new weapons have made violence more scientific and more extensive.

The cause of England was pursued very zealously by the Tories, who usually were determined enemies of the Americans, but the Whigs found in the colonial ideals a justification of their own rebellion against arbitrary government in England. Many of the generals, like Howe, were openly in favor of the colonial cause; others, like Gay, had little heart for the fighting; and some, like Cornwallis, were poor strategists. The English soldiers were of poor quality and they deserted in large numbers.

Nevertheless to succeed, the American revolution needed trained leaders and discipline. Both factors were often non-existent. The second Continental Congress was a glorified debating society. The Army often acted like a mob; it was badly fed and sometimes indifferent to fighting. The states did not tolerate any real Federal control and were unwilling to resort to conscription. Hence, the struggle was won mainly because the opponent was so split and because the English leaders had no real desire to continue the struggle.

The revolution developed a radical philosophy of government, but, after it succeeded, a counter-revolution took place which reached a climax in the reign of the Federalists. It is not surprising to note that the Federalists were fervently pro-English and rigidly opposed to French ideals. If they had won a permanent political victory, the United States would have never achieved complete independence from England.

This counteraction against liberalism takes place invariably in the course of a revolutionary movement. France thus endured the dictatorship of Napoleon and later the conservatism of Louis Philippe, and Russia had to make concessions to the old system during the period of the New Economic Policy.

BASIC CAUSES

England, during the reign of James I and Charles II, was determined to maintain strict control of the colonies. In the years of the Civil War, she was too occupied at home to pay much attention to colonial development. Moreover, she needed the aid of the American colonies in fighting France. Beginning with Charles II, navigation and trade acts were passed which curtailed colonial trade and which made it obligatory that all ships and three-fourths of the crew must be English. These measures signaled the triumph of an oppressive English policy.

This policy implied that the mother country had the right to control the colonies, that the mother country should derive great economic benefits in colonial trade, and that she would defend the colonies by maintaining a large army and a large navy. Ultimately, it meant that the colonies had to pay for the defending forces.

The colonial merchants, especially, resented the English control, since it limited their manufacturing activity, decreased their profits, brought about unjust taxation, and prevented the full development of American industry. Together with these economic abuses, the English policy led to serious infringement of colonial liberties. The Townsend Acts, for example, allowed customs officials to search any colonial home for smuggled goods.

From 1770 until 1773, there was a period of relative tranquility. Lord North repealed the Townsend Acts except for a small duty on tea. It seemed that the colonies would not rebel against the mother country. But it was only a short calm before the violent outbreak.

The revolution was aided immensely by the Intolerable Acts of 1774, which extended the Quebec boundary to the Ohio River and gave legal sanction to the Catholic religion in Quebec. This legislation alienated the staunch Protestants and was opposed by all those who believed in the westward expansion. Moreover, these acts kindled the flame of revolution by forbidding town meetings except through express permission of the governor, and permitting trial in England of Americans who had advocated treason against the king.

The Intolerable Acts had been the outgrowth of the Boston Tea Party. The damage had not been great — only ninety thousand dollars worth of tea had been destroyed, but the punishment was harsh, and the harbor in Boston was closed until all the tea had been paid for. The extreme measures of the English government gave excellent ammunition to the arguments of the American radicals.

A revolution, if it wants to capture the imagination of the common people, must have an adequate slogan. The Americans found it in "No taxation without representation." Patrick Henry made an historic speech which was climaxed by the phrase, "Give me liberty or give me death." These slogans were psychological aids in the revolutionary struggle.

A variety of causes and ideals motivated the revolution. The merchants were struggling for an expanded capitalistic system in the United States and were intent upon promoting free enterprise for themselves. The farmers on the western frontier were struggling to get rid of the hated central authority which was symbolized by English control and English taxes. Their ideal government was one which governs least. The Scotch-Irish and the Germans had personal prejudices against England, while the rich plantation owners of the South resented England because they were perpetually in debt to the London merchants. A revolution thus would relieve them from this economic burden, and they thought that it would also increase their own wealth.

Many of the political leaders of the United States resented the pretensions of the Royal governors. The legislatures frequently controlled the purse strings and thus were able to coerce the governors. Here they had a precedent which promised success in their struggle against English absolutism, for to them the king was only a magnified governor.

The Puritans likewise contributed to the agitation against England. To them, the English system of the eighteenth century was like a veritable Babylon. They looked upon it somewhat in the same light as the inhabitants of a straight-laced Middle-Western town might look at the sinful ways of New York. They were certain that in America a new morality was being established which could not be guided by the wicked English influence. Some were afraid that England might set up a Bishop of North America; they remembered only too well the arbitrary actions of the various archbishops of Canterbury, especially of Laud.

Most opposed to England were the frontiersmen, who knew of no class distinction and regarded English aristocracy with contempt. The struggle was made real by the dislike of the frontiersmen for the tax collector. Again and again taxes were important issues in American history; this antagonism to taxation did not cease after the revolution was won.

EUROPEAN BACKGROUND

Most of the revolutionary leaders had a wide acquaintance with European ideas. They read not only eminent writers of the seventeenth century like Locke, Filmer, and Sidney, but they were acquainted with the outstanding Greek thinkers and the French Encyclopedists as well as with Rousseau, who played a prominent role in the political discussions of the colonies.

John Locke was especially important in his influence upon the rebellion. He was a protagonist of the Glorious Revolution of 1688, and to many the revolution of 1776 was only a continuation of the English assertion of middle-class rights against the pretensions of an arbitrary aristocracy.

The right which Locke defended most vigorously was that of *private property*. Whoever tried to violate it was usurping the legitimate limits of power. To Locke the government was not an absolute institution; rather its justification was found in utility. Here he differed sharply from Hobbes, who thought that the people had no right to rebel against established authority.

The colonial thinkers appreciated Locke for his common sense attitude. He was not a man who, like Descartes, spoke of innate ideas, nor did he discuss abstruse questions of morality. The colonial minds approved his plea for tolerance; they noted that he did not go too far and include atheists and Catholics. They noted, too, that in his theory of education he rebelled against classical training and dwelt upon the importance of practical subjects.

To the more radical, Rousseau offered even more convincing arguments against absolutism. Although Rousseau's treatment of the history of society was unscientific, it appealed to the colonists, for he talked about an utopian state of nature, when men were truly pure and happy and free from the corruption of the arts and science. Then the devil appeared when private property was introduced, with a division of labor and the resulting system of serfdom. Rousseau knew that the function of the government was the protection of property, that its laws were not based upon justice but were designed to legalize class oppression. Thus, governments were founded upon the use of force and, if they were to be overthrown, violent means must be used.

Rousseau's equality implied a destruction of economic privileges. In the nineteenth century, educational reformers again and again would appeal to him and they would find in him an ideal description of the state of nature, which contrasted sharply with the rapid rate of industrialization which America was experiencing in that period.

PAINE AND ADAMS AS AGITATORS

Samuel Adams and Thomas Paine were the foremost agitators for American independence. Both were greatly skilled in coining phrases and in framing slogans that appealed to the man in the street. In later days, their work would be continued by journalists and news commentators. The same simplicity of style that is found in Paine's *Common Sense* can be seen again in Ernie Pyle's description of the G.I. of World War II.

Adams was a master strategist in committee meetings. This was important because in the United States changes are brought about mainly through small specialized groups.

Adams, like Paine, attacked the personal character of the king. Many of his middle-class followers regarded this as an act of treason, for the king was regarded almost as a divine person. But the frontiersmen approved, for they saw in the king a symbol of oppression and a relic of feudalism.

Paine completed the work of Adams. In his *Common Sense,* he used two powerful arguments. First, he showed that a liberal system is the best form of government. England posed as a democratic state, but, in reality, it was just as arbitrary as Spain or France. Theoretically, the Parliament of England was independent of the Royal power; practically, it was a tool of the king, whom he called a "crowned ruffian."

Paine ended with a passionate appeal:

> O ye that love mankind! Ye that dare oppose not only the tyranny but the tyrant, stand forth! Every spot of the old world is overrun with oppression. Freedom hath been hunted round the Globe. Asia and Africa have long expelled her. Europe regards her like a stranger, and England hath given her warning to depart. O! receive the fugitive, and prepare in time an asylum for mankind.[2]

DECLARATION OF INDEPENDENCE

The thoughts of Paine were echoed by the American Declaration of Independence. It is an impressive document; the language is clear and succinct; it abounds with noble ideals.

John Adams said that Congress had debated over the new ideas for two years, and Richard Henry Lee saw the distinctive influence of John Locke. The real value of the document lies in its succinct organization and its idealistic philosophy. It answers the question regarding the general function of executive power, to the effect that governments are instituted for the advancement of the individual and that political systems must be justified by their utility.

The preamble is typically American. The phrase, "decent respect to the opinions of mankind," has been used again and again in American history. It is not enough that certain political and economic actions are taken. They must be able to stand publicity; they must convince other nations as well as the citizens at home. Psychological

---

[2] *Common Sense.*

warfare is not a new invention in American history, for it started with the Declaration of Independence, which impressed European liberals as much as it enlightened citizens at home.

In the first body of the Declaration of Independence, there is a statement that all men are created equal; that they are endowed by the Creator with certain inalienable rights; that among these are life, liberty, and the pursuit of happiness. These truths were not self-evident in colonial times. To John Adams, to Gouverneur Morris, and Alexander Hamilton these were distasteful ideas; it seemed clear to them that men were born unequal and that their rights were dependent upon governmental authority.

The Declaration speaks of the pursuit of happiness. The sophisticated European will smile, and he will ask how happiness can be established by law. Having experienced the oppressions and the abuses of government authority, he does not believe that this pursuit can be guaranteed by anyone. Here, indeed, was an optimistic philosophy. It revealed the faith of the American colonist in a glorious future.

How far the American mind had traveled from the austere pessimism of Puritanism! To the latter, life on earth was only a temporary sojourn, a valley of sorrow; the aim of existence, according to the Puritans, was virtue, not happiness. To the later Americans, the pursuit of happiness implied the pursuit of self-expression.

RESULTS OF THE REVOLUTION

What were the social results of the American revolution? Above all, it led to an intensification of nationalism. This is part of the life history of the revolutionary ideal. The French experienced the same feeling after their successful struggle against absolutism, when they regarded themselves as a chosen people whose task would be to spread the ideals of liberty, equality, and fraternity. Similarly the Russians, after their revolution was established, became extremely nationalistic and almost deified their country and their leaders.

A religious ideal developed in the United States. George Washington became a semi-divine figure and his Farewell Address became the Bible for American foreign policy. The dark days of the American revolution were glorified by later thinkers. The struggle of MacArthur in 1942 thus is compared with Valley Forge.

At the same time, the revolution changed the social structure of America. Many loyalists fled to Canada or returned to England. When they came back after the peace treaties, they found that their estates had been broken up and their political influence undermined. Democracy expanded, with the suffrage being extended to many members of the lower classes, and determined efforts were made against slavery. Virginia, Maryland, South Carolina and Delaware forbade the importation of slaves, although Delaware did not strictly adhere to this policy.

The method of landholding was liberalized; primogeniture and entail were abolished. The tenant system was abolished in the North after the large estates had been divided. It must be remembered that some estates like those of Fairfax were almost provinces in themselves. If they had not been divided, their owners might have set up an aristocratic government for the United States.

The revolution had a constructive effect on religious freedom, for it gradually led to the disestablishment of the churches. Education was not now reserved for the sons of patricians but was opened to the lower classes. Intelligence replaced social status in the colleges. The new republic was interested in sponsoring science because in this manner it would increase the welfare of the nation as well as add to its prestige in international affairs.

Was the English influence permanently uprooted in the United States? On the contrary, in many ways the revolution strengthened the English position. For now, there were no direct political ties but only a common interest in world affairs. With the passing of years, the Tory influence in England was undermined and a similar philosophy of government existed in both nations. More and more the United States relied upon the protection of the English Navy; when European governments threatened to make inroads in the new world in the period of Metternich, English and American statesmen fought side by side and promulgated the Monroe Doctrine. This policy of dependence upon England was fully demonstrated when America entered World War I; it reached a climax in the December days of 1941.

From the standpoint of education, the English ties have produced too much intellectual dependence on the part of America. No wonder that the American mind is occasionally provincial. Language training, especially in the Asiatic tongues, is frequently neglected, because many think that the English language is completely sufficient for communication abroad.

LEADERSHIP AND THE EDUCATED MAN

Leadership in the United States has usually lagged behind technological progress. With a few exceptions like Lincoln and Wilson, the quality of political leaders has deteriorated since Colonial times. Reading the books and journals of Jefferson, Hamilton, Paine, Franklin, and John Adams, to name only a few of the outstanding minds of that generation, one receives an impression of a true culture, a grasp of the political realities and the economic factors that guide civilization.

It is true, of course, that knowledge at this time was less complicated, and that it was easier to keep up with current ideas than in the atomic age, when learning is departmentalized. It cannot be denied, however, that the leaders of colonial times had greater respect for education because they saw the intimate connection between knowledge and a stable democracy.

In colonial times there was greater contact between liberals and conservatives than exists today. We tend to have too many artificial barriers. We are frequently too specialized to be able to communicate in an adequate way. We substitute slogans for deliberation. We seem to lack the splendid faith in man which leaders like Franklin had.

Political affairs, at this period, were conducted for the few, not for the man on the street. As the basis of representative government has expanded, it has adjusted itself to the thinking of the most ignorant and the most uneducated. Again and again, in recent times, political ideas and economic issues have been simplified to such an extent that decisions were made, not on the basis of cool, detached and objective thought, but through appeal to emotional slogans. The political mind in America has deteriorated in a very real sense; yellow journalism has won a partial victory, the superficial headline governs the thinking of the average man, to whom the sound of a voice seems to be more important than the political thinking behind it.

Real leadership in a democracy requires careful deliberation, an exchange of viewpoints, a weighing of all the alternatives. This does not imply that there should be endless discussions, interminable controversy with no decision being achieved, but it does mean that there should be less oratory, less appeal to sectional interests, and more consideration of the common cause.

Another reason for the deterioration of political leadership is the personal note in modern politics. Since the President and Congressional leaders today are in constant contact with countless reporters, news columnists, television commentators and society editors, all their personal traits are emphasized. To be appealing to the man on the street, a news story must have definite human interest. Scandal is welcome; many of the reporters do not care about objective evidence and accept rumor as readily as fact.

To the dispassionate observer, it appears that political prejudices have become more intense since the Civil War. Again and again, the voices of disunity can be heard. They are so imbued with the cause they defend that they become fanatic. They lack detachment when it comes to their cause. On the other hand, the colonial leaders like Washington and Jefferson had a great sense of objectivity.

Ever since the Civil War, the corruption of political life has been a danger. Low-water marks were reached in the Grant and Harding administrations. Thus the idea has developed that political enterprise is necessarily associated with undesirable moral traits. Here, a definite paradox develops. The American system depends upon the participation of the most enlightened political leaders; it can prosper only when there is a general interest in the issues of the day. Yet, at the same time, the most intelligent very frequently regard politics as a dirty business and leave the conduct of governmental affairs to professional machine politicians.

The frontier, to some extent, has delayed the development of real leadership. Its heritage was best represented in the revival meetings, which were filled with impassioned appeals and mass repentance. A preacher, if he wanted to succeed, had to be a prize fighter for God. Cartwright is a notable example of this type. When the frontier invaded politics, it demanded the same traits in national life; hence, a leader who was aloof, broad-minded and cosmopolitan in his approach could not succeed.

Political leadership has suffered grievously by the campaign psychology. Usually the opposition leader makes so many promises that his antagonist responds by doing the same. Thus begins a race between rival programs of Utopia. Unfortunately, when the campaign is over, these promises are forgotten and very little deep thinking has been done about the specific issues underlying the campaign.

As yet in the United States, the opposition party has not developed a sense of responsibility as it has in England. It is not the function of the opposition simply to obstruct the will of the majority. A negative attitude is never sufficient in political and economic affairs. Rather, it is necessary for the party that is out of office to create a responsible program which can be put into action when its opportunity comes.

THE ARTICLES OF CONFEDERATION

Lack of leadership was the fundamental factor which doomed the government under the Articles of Confederation. At this time, the position of the colonies was somewhat like that of the United Nations today. All the states were zealously guarding their own rights and privileges and were unwilling to give up their sovereignty. They had created a political machine which was extremely cumbersome; amendments to the Articles could be made only by unanimous vote; any state thus had the right of veto. In important matters, nine states had to consent before action could be taken. The representatives, moreover, had no definite term and they could be recalled at any time.

Here again, the United Nations Organization offers a parallel. There is no real continuity of representation. In many nations, the foreign minister is subject to the ever-changing winds of political life at home. If he displeases powerful forces at home, he may be recalled at any time. Usually when a new foreign minister is appointed he has different policies from his predecessor; matters which were settled before have to be threshed out again, and it takes some time before he is thoroughly informed about the basic international problems.

The Articles of Confederation were defective, because, as in the United Nations, no real executive power existed. The United Nations is more fortunate in having developed the rudiments of a court system, but how important are laws if they cannot be enforced, and how effective is the power of the court if it is prevented from passing on the most important matters?

The Articles of Confederation were deficient in still another matter. No provision was made for the control of commerce by Congress. Here again, the United Nations charter exhibits a similar lack. In the atomic age, control of trade is one of the paramount necessities. There can be no real supervision of international commerce until definite laws and commissions are established which govern trade practices, not just in one area, but everywhere.

In colonial times, the liberals and the more radical leaders were in favor of maintaining strict state sovereignty, while the conservatives were intent upon providing for a stronger federal union. Today the roles have been reversed. The conservatives are the enemies of an international government, while the liberals are in favor of such a step.

THE CONSTITUTION

The Constitution was devised to establish a government of laws rather than of men. Today, most scholars in the United States have lost faith in rigid laws and judge them according to pragmatic test. They ask, how do they promote common welfare, how do they affect social progress, how do they meet the needs of everyday life? It was different in the eighteenth century, which believed in eternal laws of society. To the founders of the Constitution, the universe was as rational and orderly as a machine, and they thought that there was a correspondence between the exact laws of science and the laws which would be framed for mankind.

The system of checks and balances has prevented dictatorship in the United States. The most important check upon the executive branch of the government is the Senate. In the *Federalist,* it is explained how the Senate should act as a watchdog upon the lower house and how it should give stability to the legislative program. Senators, being elected for a longer time, would be better acquainted with the laws of the United States, and, being older and more experienced, they would contribute mature judgment.

It was the task of the liberals to change the rigid spirit of the Constitution as it was adopted at Philadelphia. Richard Henry Lee, the spokesman of the opposition, tried to show that the instrument was undemocratic and that it placed the majority at the mercy of the minority. Others, like Clinton, attacked it as a tool of the rich merchants and of the aristocratic party in the United States. The liberals asked why the supporters were in such a hurry to have their document ratified. Above all, they wanted guarantees that the basic freedom for which they struggled would be protected. Most of the liberals were desperately afraid of the strong central authority, which reminded them of the despotism of the old world.

Educational Implications

The Constitution was not directly concerned with education. The first and tenth amendments left educational control to the individual states. The Northwest Ordinance (1787) made provisions for the support of education in each township.

Indirectly, the Constitution influenced education by its protection of free inquiry and its separation of state and church. This gave an elastic spirit to American education and it prevented the type of ecclesiastical domination which has plagued so many countries in the Western world.

The various state constitutions made provisions for the support and encouragement of education. The following citations indicate the states' concern for culture and education.

Pennsylvania made the following provisions for education:

Laws for the encouragement of virtue, and prevention of vice and immorality, shall be made and constantly kept in force, and provision shall be made for their due execution; and all religious societies or bodies of men heretofore united or incorporated for the advancement of religion or learning, or for other pious and charitable purposes, shall be encouraged and protected in the enjoyment of the privileges, immunities, and estates which they were accustomed to enjoy, or could of right have enjoyed, under the laws and former constitution of this State.[3]

In 1776, North Carolina declared,

That a school or schools shall be established by the legislature, for the convenient instruction of youth, with such salaries to the masters, paid by the public, as may enable them to instruct at low prices; and all useful learning shall be duly encouraged, and promoted, in one or more universities.[4]

Vermont stated that,

A school or schools shall be established in every town, by the legislature, for the convenient instruction of youth, with such salaries to the masters, paid by each town; making proper use of school lands in each town, thereby to enable them to instruct youth at low prices. One grammar school in each county, and one university in this State, ought to be established by direction of the General Assembly.

Laws for the encouragement of virtue and prevention of vice and immorality, shall be made and constantly kept in force; and provision shall be made for their due execution; and all religious societies or bodies of men, that have or may be hereafter united and incorporated, for the advancement of religion and learning, or for other pious and charitable purposes, shall be encouraged and protected in the enjoyment of the privileges, immunities and estates which they, in justice ought to enjoy, under such regulations, as the General Assembly of this State shall direct.[5]

Georgia decreed:

The arts and sciences shall be promoted, in one or more seminaries of learning; and the legislature shall, as soon as conveniently may be, give such further donations and privileges to those already established as may be necessary to secure the objects of their institution;

---

[3] *Pennsylvania Constitution, 1776.*
[4] *North Carolina Constitution, 1776.*
[5] *Vermont Constitution, 1777.*

and it shall be the duty of the general assembly, at their next session, to provide effectual measures for the improvement and permanent security of the funds and endowments of such institutions.[6]

Massachusetts, in 1780, stated:

Whereas our wise and pious ancestors, so early as the year 1636, laid the foundation of Harvard College, in which university many persons of great eminence have, by the blessing of God, been initiated in those arts and sciences which qualified them for public employments, both in church and state; and whereas the encouragement of arts and sciences and all good literature, tends to the honor of God, the advantage of the Christian religion, and the great benefit of this and the other United States of America, it is declared, that the president and fellows of Harvard College, in their corporate capacity, and their successors in their capacity, their officers and servants, shall have, hold, use, exercise, and enjoy all the powers, authorities, rights, liberties, privileges, immunities, and franchises which they now have, or are entitled to have, hold, use, exercise, and enjoy; and the same are hereby ratified and confirmed unto them, the said president and fellows of Harvard College, and to their successors, and to their officers and servants respectively, forever.

And whereas there have been, at sundry times, by diverse persons, gifts, grants, devises of houses, lands, tenements, goods, chattels, legacies, and conveyances heretofore made, either to Harvard College, in Cambridge, in New England, or to the president and fellows of Harvard College, or to the said college by some other description, under several charters successively, it is declared that all the said gifts, grants, devises, legacies, and conveyances are hereby forever confirmed unto the president and fellows of Harvard College, and to their successors, in the capacity aforesaid, according to the true intent and meaning of the donor or donors, grantor or grantors, devisor or devisors.

And whereas by an act of the general court of the colony of Massachusetts Bay, passed in the year of 1642, the governor and deputy governor, for the time being, and all the magistrates of that jurisdiction, were, with the president, and a number of the clergy, in the said act described, constituted the overseers of Harvard College, and it being necessary, in this new constitution of government, to ascertain who shall be deemed successors to the said governor, deputy governor, and magistrates, it is declared that the governor, lieutenant-governor, council, and senate of this commonwealth, are, and shall be deemed, their successors; who, with the president of Harvard College, for the time being, together with the ministers of the Congregational churches in the towns of Cambridge, Watertown, Charles-

---

[6] *Georgia Constitution, 1798.*

town, Boston, Roxbury, and Dorchester, mentioned in the said act, shall be, and hereby are, vested with all the powers and authority belonging or in anyway appertaining to the overseers of Harvard College; *Provided,* That nothing herein shall be construed to prevent the legislature of this Commonwealth from making such alterations in the government of the said university as shall be conducive to its advantage and the interest of the republic of letters, in as full a manner as might have been done by the legislature of the late province of the Massachusetts Bay.[7]

Regarding literature, it provided:

Wisdom and knowledge, as well as virtue, diffused generally among the body of the people, being necessary for the preservation of their rights and liberties; and as these depend on spreading the opportunities and advantages of education in the various parts of the country, and among the different orders of the people, it shall be the duty of the legislatures and magistrates, in all future periods of this Commonwealth, to cherish the interests of literature and the sciences, and all seminaries of them; especially the university at Cambridge, public schools, and grammar-schools in the towns; to encourage private societies and public institutions, by rewards and trades, manufactures, and a natural history of the country; to countenance and inculcate the principles of humanity and general benevolence, public and private charity, industry and frugality, honesty and punctuality in their dealings; sincerity, good humor, and all social affectations and generous sentiments among the people.[8]

Pennsylvania also provided that

The legislature shall, as soon as conveniently may be, provide by law, for the establishment of schools throughout the State, in such manner that the poor may be taught *gratis.*

The arts and sciences shall be promoted in one or more seminaries of learning.[9]

Ohio made the following provisions:

That the general, great, and essential principles of liberty and free government may be recognized, and forever unalterably established, we declare —

That all men have a natural and indefeasible right to worship Almighty God according to the dictates of their conscience; that no

---

[7] *Massachusetts Constitution, 1780.*

[8] *Ibid.*

[9] *Pennsylvania Constitution, 1790.*

human authority can, in any case whatever, control or interfere with the rights of conscience; that no man shall be compelled to attend, erect, or support any place of worship, or to maintain any ministry, against his consent; and that no preference shall ever be given by law to any religious society or mode of worship; and no religious test shall be required as a qualification to any office of trust or profit. But religion, morality, and knowledge being essentially necessary to the good government and the happiness of mankind, schools and the means of instruction shall forever be encouraged by legislative provision, not inconsistent with the rights of conscience.

That no law shall be passed to prevent the poor in the several counties and townships within this State, from an equal participation in the schools, academies, colleges, and universities within this State, which are endowed, in whole or in part, from the revenues arising from the donations made by the United States for the support of schools and colleges; and the doors of the said schools, academies, and universities shall be open for the reception of scholars, students, and teachers of every grade, without any distinction of preference whatever, contrary to the intent for which the said donations were made.[10]

Indiana stated:

Knowledge and learning generally diffused through a community being essential to the preservation of a free government, and spreading the opportunities and advantages of education through the various parts of the country being highly conducive to this end, it shall be the duty of the general assembly to provide by law for the improvement of such lands as are, or hereafter may be, granted by the United States to this State for the use of schools, and to apply any funds which may be raised from such lands, or from any other quarter, to the accomplishment of the grand object for which they are or may be intended. But no lands granted for the use of schools or seminaries of learning shall be sold, by authority of this State, prior to the year eighteen hundred and twenty; and the moneys which may be raised out of the sale of any such lands, or otherwise obtained for the purposes aforesaid, shall be and remain a fund for the exclusive purpose of promoting the interest of literature and the sciences, and for the support of seminaries and the public schools. The general assembly shall, from time to time, pass such laws as shall be calculated to encourage intellectual, scientific, and agricultural improvement by allowing rewards and immunities for the promotion and improvement of arts, sciences, commerce, manufactures, and natural history; and to countenance and encourage the principles of humanity, industry, and morality.

---

[10] *Ohio Constitution, 1803.*

It shall be the duty of the general assembly, as soon as circumstances will permit, to provide by law for a general system of education ascending in a regular graduation from township schools to a State university, wherein tuition shall be gratis, and equally open to all.

And for the promotion of such salutary end, the money which shall be paid as an equivalent by persons exempt from military duty, except in times of war, shall be exclusively, and in equal proportions, applied to the support of county seminaries; also, all fines assessed for any breach of the penal laws shall be applied to said seminaries, in the counties wherein they shall be assessed.

It shall be the duty of the general assembly, as soon as circumstances will permit, to form a penal code, founded on the principles of reformation, and not of vindictive justice; and also to provide one or more farms to be an asylum for such persons who, by reason of age, infirmity, or other misfortunes, may have a claim upon the aid and beneficence of society, on such principles that such persons may therein find employment and every reasonable comfort, and lose by their usefulness the degrading sense of dependence.

The general assembly, at the time they lay off a new county, shall cause at least 10 per cent to be reserved out of the proceeds of the sale of town-lots in the seat of justice of such county for the use of a public library for such county. . .[11]

The Ordinance of 1787 was especially important.

Religion, morality, and knowledge being necessary to good government and the happiness of mankind, schools and the means of education shall forever be encouraged.[12]

WASHINGTON

The ideals of education are eloquently stated in Washington's Farewell Address. Never tempted by his vast power, he was not speaking as a militarist, but as a man who was anxious to promote the future well-being of the nation.

It is undeniable that geography has made some of his ideas about American policy obsolete. Washington was conscious of the distance that separates the United States from Europe. Under these conditions there was no need for entangling alliances. He was a realist; he knew that the army was weak; there was no real naval power, United States commerce was almost negligible, and England was strongly en-

---

[11] *Indiana Constitution, 1816.*
[12] *Ordinance of 1787*, Article III.

trenched in the Northwest. By staying out of European affairs, the peaceful development of American industry could be assured.

But this speech was not really a call for isolation, for the dominant ideal of the speech was a stress upon liberal intercourse with all nations. This meant, to Washington, that the extremes of partisanship must be avoided in foreign affairs.

> In the execution of such a plan nothing is more essential than that permanent, inveterate antipathies against particular nations, and passionate attachments for others, should be excluded; and that in place of them, just and amicable feelings towards all should be cultivated. The nation which indulges towards another an habitual hatred or an habitual fondness is in some degree a slave. It is a slave to its animosity or to its affection, either of which is sufficient to lead it astray from its duty and its interest. Antipathy in one nation against another disposes each more readily to offer insult and injury, to lay hold of slight causes of umbrage, and to be haughty and intractable when accidental or trifling occasions of dispute occur. *Hence frequent collisions, obstinate, envenomed and bloody contests.*[13]

Washington went on to say that if extreme passion exists against one nation, reason is frequently overruled; foreign affairs thus are conducted on the basis of irrational considerations.

By warning against large military establishments, Washington served well the cause of education. He realized, however, that in a world governed by power politics, military preparedness could not be neglected. At the same time, he knew that whenever military leaders have been given too much power, liberty has been endangered. Like Jefferson, he desired to subordinate military authority to civilian control.

Educational Views

George Washington was interested in a national university. In 1795 he wrote:

> A plan for the establishment of a university in the Federal city has frequently been the subject of conversation; but in what manner it is proposed to commence this important institution, on how extensive a scale, the means by which it is to be supported, or what progress is made in it, are matters altogether unknown to me. It has always been a source of serious reflection and sincere regret with me that

---

[13] Washington, *Farewell Address.*

the youth of the United States should be sent to foreign countries for the purpose of education. Although there are doubtless many, under the circumstances, who escape the danger of contracting principles unfavorable to republican government, yet we ought to deprecate the hazard attending ardent and susceptible minds, from being too strongly and too early prepossessed in favor of other political systems before they are capable of appreciating their own.

For this reason I have greatly wished to see a plan adopted by which the arts, sciences, and belles-lettres could be taught in their fullest extent, thereby embracing all the advantages of European tuition, with the means of acquiring the liberal knowledge which is necessary to qualify our citizens for the exigencies of public as well as private life; and (which with me is a consideration of great magnitude) by assembling the youth from the different parts of this rising Republic, contributing from their intercourse and interchange of information to the removal of prejudices which might perhaps sometimes arise from local circumstances.

The Federal city, from its centrality and the advantages which in other respects it must have over any other place in the United States, ought to be preferred as a proper site for such a university. And if a plan can be adopted upon a scale as extensive as I have described, and the execution of it should commence under favorable auspices in a reasonable time, with a fair prospect of success, I will grant in perpetuity 50 shares in the navigation of the Potomac River towards the endowment of it.[14]

INFLUENCE OF THE REVOLUTION ON PHILOSOPHY AND EDUCATION

(1) In summary, it must be remembered that many of the outstanding American thinkers took an active part in the development of American ideals. Thus, Washington, Franklin, Paine, Jefferson, Allen and Witherspoon were not ivory-tower scholars but had a lively concern with political and social problems. Ever since the revolution American thinking has been less closely associated with political ideals and instead has become more interested in technical epistemological problems.

(2) The revolution expanded the outlook of the American thinker. Now there was more interest than before in continental philosophical concepts and, later in the nineteenth century, in Indian and Chinese wisdom. Before the revolution, American thinkers were

---

[14] *To the Commissioners of the Federal District on the National University;* 1795.

rather provincial and almost entirely dependent on the Anglo-Saxon heritage; afterwards they absorbed a greater variety of ideas and grew to have a more cosmopolitan perspective.

(3) The revolution encouraged the new scientific spirit. It was the hope of outstanding American leaders such as Franklin and Jefferson that science would provide the basis for a new culture. Consequently, scientific studies now became as important as theology had been in Puritan Boston. This does not imply, however, that the religious influence was uprooted; on the contrary, it became stronger especially in the West because of the revival movement and the growth of the Methodists and the Baptists. Still, the march of science could not be stopped, and its advancement continued unchecked throughout the nineteenth and twentieth centuries.

(4) The revolution made for an optimistic spirit in American education. We have already found the same tendency in the Declaration of Independence. The philosophers saw how much had been accomplished by the colonists and how far they had traveled in search for freedom and justice. Naturally the old doctrine of the depravity of man lost its attraction, and it was replaced by a vigorous *faith in man.*

(5) The revolution encouraged the spirit of individualism in thought. Did not the Declaration of Independence stress the fact that governments exist for the benefit of the individual? Was not the Revolutionary War mainly dependent on the efforts of the individual states? Traditionally, American thinkers have been suspicious of centralization and too much governmental control. We find this emphasis on decentralization in such diverse men as Jefferson, Royce and Brandeis.

Thus the revolution did not lead to collectivism; rather the immediate result was a zealous attempt to maintain the rights of the states.

The individualistic heritage in the United States made for a dislike of all types of totalitarianism and for a laissez-faire type of economic system. Self-reliance became the keynote of much of American ethical thinking, which had little use for the collectivistic spirit which developed in Europe in the nineteenth and twentieth century.

Self-reliance stamped the educational system in the United States. It meant an emphasis on American ideals and traditions and the rejection of many old European patterns.

CHAPTER TEN

Jefferson as Thinker and Educator

CAREER

Thomas Jefferson was one of the most brilliant figures in the history of American education. He studied at William and Mary, where he majored in law. In 1769 he was elected to the House of Burgesses. There he was closely associated with Patrick Henry, the inveterate enemy of English imperialism. We have noted his work in the Continental Congress, where he helped to draw up the Declaration of Independence. He was responsible for religious freedom in Virginia and also aided in destroying the remains of feudalism there. He became governor of Virginia, then ambassador to France; then Secretary of State, Vice-President, and finally President of the United States.

He promoted the cause of education as first rector of the University of Virginia. Not only was he a great statesman, but he was also a thinker of unusual stature.

INFLUENCES

Philosophically, he drew upon a variety of sources. At William and Mary he was introduced to philosophy by Mr. Small, who, however, had little knowledge of metaphysics. Small's lectures dealt mostly with scientific and moral problems. Philosophy at William and Mary occupied a rather minor place in the curriculum.

Among the thinkers who conditioned Jefferson's thinking, special attention should be given to Cicero, from whose writings he absorbed a faith in natural moral capacities and in the possibilities of education. Like Cicero, Jefferson was skeptical of supernatural truths.

Lord Kames' *Principles of Natural Religion* also had an impact on his thinking, as did Locke, Ferguson, Stewart, Ellis and, above all, Bolingbroke. While he stayed in France he was on friendly terms with Demeunier, Morellet, Mably, Condorcet, and Cabanis. He was well acquainted with Destutt de Tracy, whose system he admired greatly. In fact he regarded Tracy as one of the most astute and able thinkers of all time.

While he respected the materialistic thinkers, he did not agree with their theories. He felt that they gave only a mechanistic account of man and he was opposed to their stress on self-interest. No valid moral system, according to Jefferson, could be based primarily on egoism.

PHILOSOPHICAL AND RELIGIOUS IDEALS

Jefferson felt that moral ideals could not be reduced to a scientific basis:

I think it lost time to attend lectures in this branch. He who made us would have been a pitiful bungler if he had made the rules of our moral conduct a matter of science. For one man of science, there are thousands who are not. What would have become of them? Man was destined for society. His morality therefore was to be formed to this object. He was endowed with a sense of right and wrong merely relative to this . . . The moral sense, or conscience, is as much a part of man as his leg or arm. It is given to all human beings in a stronger or weaker degree, as force of members is given them in a greater or less degree. It may be strengthened by exercise, as may any particular limb of the body. This sense is submitted indeed in some degree to the guidance of reason; but it is a small stock which is required for this: even a less one than what we call common sense. State a moral case to a ploughman and a professor. The former will decide it as well, and often better than the latter, because he has not been led astray by artificial rules. In this branch therefore read good books because they will encourage as well as direct your feelings.[1]

It is most important for us to be just and humane and to engage in activities which promote kindness and the brotherhood of man. He emphasized that the religion of Jesus is simple and can be applied to all men:

1. That there is one only God, and he all perfect.
2. That there is a future state of rewards and punishments.
3. That to love God with all thy heart and thy neighbor as thyself, is the sum of religion. These are the great points on which he endeavored to reform the religion of the Jews.
But compare with these the demoralizing dogmas of Calvin:
1. That there are three Gods.
2. That good works, or the love of our neighbors, are nothing.
3. That faith is every thing, and the more incomprehensible the proposition, the more merit in its faith.
4. That reason in religion is of unlawful use.
5. That God, from the beginning, elected certain individuals to be saved, and certain others to be damned; and that no crimes of the former can damn them; no virtues of the latter save.[2]

He held that Calvin had perverted the Christian faith:

Had the doctrines of Jesus been preached always as pure as they came from his lips, the whole civilized world now would have been Christian. I rejoice that in this blessed country of free inquiry and belief, which has surrendered its creed and conscience to neither kings nor priests, the genuine doctrine of one only God is reviving, and I trust that there is not a young man now living in the United States who will not die an Unitarian.

But much I fear, that when this great truth shall be re-established, its votaries will fall into the fatal error of fabricating formulas of creed and confessions of faith, the engines which so soon destroyed the religion of Jesus, and made of Christendom a mere Aceldama.[3]

In a critical analysis of comparative systems of ethics, he noted that the ancient philosophers were especially great in their precepts

---

[1] *Letter to Peter Carr*, August 10, 1787.
[2] *Letter to Dr. Benjamin Waterhouse*, June 26, 1822.
[3] *Ibid.*

which relate to the individual, but when they discussed social ethics they were defective. Their range was limited, and frequently they omitted a consideration of the welfare of humanity.

As for the ancient Hebrews, their concept of God was frequently arbitrary. They violated the sound dictates of morality and were anti-social when it came to other nations. Furthermore, Jefferson did not think that God should be described in such merciless terms as the Hebrews used in the Old Testament.

He made also a critical examination of Jesus and noted that, like Socrates and Epictetus, he left no writings behind and that his teachings were perverted by his followers. Since he died at an early age, his moral system could not be completely developed.

In spite of all these defects, Jefferson emphasized that the moral system of Jesus is the most sublime of mankind.

> 1.   He corrected the Deism of the Jews, confirming them in their belief of one only God, and giving them juster notions of his attributes and government.
> 2.   His moral doctrines, relating to kindred and friends, were more pure and perfect than those of the most correct of the philosophers, and greatly more so than those of the Jews; and they went far beyond both in inculcating universal philanthropy, not only to kindred and friends to neighbors and countrymen, but to all mankind, gathering all into one family, under the bonds of love, charity, peace, common wants and common aids. . .
> 3.   The precepts of philosophy, and of the Hebrew code, laid hold of actions only. He pushed his scrutinies into the heart of man; erected his tribunal in the region of his thoughts — and purified the waters at the fountain head.
> 4.   He taught, emphatically, the doctrines of a future state, which was either doubted, or disbelieved by the Jews; and wielded it with efficacy, as an important incentive, supplementary to the other motives to moral conduct.[4]

In picturesque terms he described his own religion, which would avoid all the errors of the Platonists:

> I am a *real Christian*, that is to say, a disciple of the doctrines of Jesus, very different from the Platonists, who call *me* infidel and *themselves* Christians and preachers of the gospel, while they draw all their characteristic dogmas from what its author never said or saw. They have compounded from the heathen mysteries a system beyond

---

[4] *Syllabus of an Estimate of the Merit of the Doctrines of Jesus, Compared with Those of Others.*

the comprehension of man, of which the great reformer of the various ethics and deism of the Jews, were he to return on earth, would not recognize one feature.[5]

As to myself, my religious reading has long been confined to the moral branch of religion, which is the same in all religions; while in that branch which consists of dogmas, all differ, all have a different set. The former instructs us how to live well and worthily in society; the latter are made to interest our minds in the support of teachers who inculcate them. Hence, for one sermon on a moral subject, you hear ten on the dogmas of the sect.[6]

Religion is primarily a private matter:

What we all agree in, is probably right. What no two agree in, probably wrong. One of our fan-coloring biographers, who paints small men as very great, inquired of me lately, with real affection too, whether he might consider as authentic, the change of my religion much spoken of in some circles. Now this supposed that they knew what had been my religion before, taking for it the word of their priests whom I certainly never made the confidants of my creed. My answer was, "say nothing of my religion. It is known to my God and myself alone. Its evidence before the world is to be sought in my life; If that has been *honest and dutiful* to society, the religion which has regulated it cannot be a bad one."[7]

Writing to Peter Carr in 1787, he pointed out that faith can best be gained by avoiding all prejudices:

Fix reason firmly in her seat, and call to her tribunal every opinion. Question with boldness even the existence of a god; because, if there be one, he must more approve of the homage of reason, than that of blindfold fear. You will naturally examine first the religion of your own country. Read the bible then, as you would read Livy or Tacitus. The facts which are within the ordinary course of nature you will believe on the authority of the writer, as you do those of the same kind in Livy and Tacitus. The testimony of the writer weighs in their favor in one scale, and their not being against the laws of nature does not weigh against them. But those facts in the bible which contradict the laws of nature, must be examined with more care, and under a variety of faces. Here you must recur to the pretensions of the writer to inspiration from god. Examine upon what evidence his pretensions are founded, and whether that evidence is so strong as that

---

[5] *Letter to Charles Thomson,* January 9, 1816.
[6] *Letter to Thomas Leiper,* January 21, 1809.
[7] *Letter to John Adams,* January 11, 1817.

its falsehood would be more improbable than a change in the laws of nature in the case he relates.[8]

He urged him not to be timid in his quest for truth:

> Do not be frightened from this inquiry by any fear of its conse-
> quences. If it ends in a belief that there is no god, you will find incite-
> ments to virtue in the comfort and pleasantness you feel in its exercise,
> and the love of others which it will procure you. If you find reason to
> believe there is a god, a consciousness that you are acting under his
> eye, and that he approves you, will be a vast additional incitement;
> if that there be a future state, the hope of a happy existence in that
> increases the appetite to deserve it; if that Jesus was also a god, you
> will be comforted by a belief in his aid and love. In fine, I repeat
> that you must lay aside all prejudice on both sides, and neither be-
> lieve nor reject anything because any other persons, or description of
> persons have rejected or believed it. Your own reason is the only
> oracle given you by heaven, and you are answerable not only for
> rightness but uprightness of the decision.[9]

Religion, according to Jefferson, should never be determined by the magistrates:

> The care of every man's soul belongs to himself. But what if he
> neglect the care of it? Well what if he neglect the care of his health
> or estate, which more nearly relate to the state. Will the magistrate
> make a law that he shall not be poor or sick? Laws provide against
> injury from others; but not from themselves. God himself will not
> save men against their will. . .
> I cannot give up my guidance to the magistrate, because he knows
> no more of the way to heaven than I do, and is less concerned to
> direct me than I am to go right. . .
> No man has power to let another prescribe his faith. Faith is not
> faith without believing. No man can conform his faith to the dictates
> of another. The life and essence of religion consists in the internal
> persuasion or belief of the mind. External forms of worship, when
> against our belief are hypocrisy and impiety. Rom. 14.23. "He that
> doubteth is damned, if he eat, because he eateth not of faith: for
> whatsoever is not faith, is sin. . ."[10]

It is clear that Jefferson, in spite of his attacks on the ecclesiastical authorities, retained his faith in God. He noted that atheism flourishes

---

[8] *Letter to Peter Carr,* August 10, 1787.
[9] *Ibid.*
[10] *Scraps Early in the Revolution.*

most of the time in Catholic countries, while Deism prospers in Protestant nations. He accepted the theory that the earth was created, but he did not follow the Biblical accounts of creation.

Among ancient philosophical systems, he appreciated above all that of Epicurus. He contrasted the simplicity of the Epicureans with the fogginess of the Platonists. Mysticism had no place in Jefferson's philosophy. He charged Plato with borrowing indiscriminately from other philosophers and with establishing a system based on confusion. He maintained that the followers of Plato had made matters worse when they added to the obscurity of the Platonic system and synthesized it with Oriental concepts of life.

EDUCATION AND KNOWLEDGE

Jefferson was convinced that democracy without education was an impossibility. Among the objects of primary education he noted:

1. To give to every citizen the information he needs to transact his own business.
2. To enable him to calculate for himself and to express and preserve his ideas, contracts and accounts in writing.
3. To improve, by reading, his faculties and morals.
4. To understand his duties to his neighbors and his country, and to discharge with competence the functions confided to him by either.
5. To know his rights; to exercise with order and justice those he retains; to choose with discretion the fiduciary of those he delegates . . .
6. And, in general, to observe with intelligence and faithfulness all the social relations under which he shall be placed.[11]

Jefferson was opposed to European education.

But why send an American youth to Europe for education? What are the objects of an useful American education? Classical knowledge, modern languages and chiefly French, Spanish, and Italian; Mathematics; Natural philosophy; Natural History; Civil History; Ethics. In Natural philosophy I mean to include Chemistry and Agriculture, and in Natural history to include Botany as well as the other branches of those departments. It is true that the habit of speaking the modern languages cannot be so well acquired in America, but every other article can be as well acquired at William and Mary College as at any place in Europe. When College education is done with and a young man is to prepare himself for public life, he must cast

---

[11] *On the Objects of Primary Education.*

his eyes (for America) either on Law or Physic. For the former where can he apply so advantageously as to Mr. Wythe? For the latter he must come to Europe; the medical class of students therefore is the only one which need come to Europe. Let us view the disadvantages of sending a youth to Europe. To enumerate them all would require a volume. I will select a few. If he goes to England he learns drinking, horse-racing and boxing. These are the peculiarities of English education. The following circumstances are common to education in that and the other countries of Europe. He acquires a fondness for European luxury and dissipation and a contempt for the simplicity of his own country; . . .[12]

He was proud of his educational labors and agitated for new ideas:

I am now entirely absorbed in endeavours to effect the establishment of a general system of education in my native state, on the triple basis, (1). of elementary schools which shall give to the children of every citizen gratis, competent instruction in reading, writing, common arithmetic, and general geography. (2). Collegiate institutions for ancient & modern languages, for higher instruction in arithmetic, geography & history, placing for these purposes a college within a day's ride of every inhabitant of the state, and adding a provision for the full education at the public expence of select subjects from among the children of the poor, who shall have exhibited at the elementary schools the most prominent indications of aptness of judgment & correct disposition. (3). An University in which all the branches of science deemed useful at this day, shall be taught in their highest degree. This would probably require ten or twelve professors, for most of whom we shall be obliged to apply to Europe, and most likely to Edinburg, because of the greater advantage the students will receive from communications made in their native language. This last establishment will probably be within a mile of Charlottesville, and four from Monticello, if the system should be adopted at all by our legislature who meet within a week from this time. My hopes however are kept in check by the ordinary character of our state legislatures, the members of which do not generally possess information enough to perceive the important truths. . . .[13]

He proposed the following organization of the university after his plan was approved:

Encouraged, therefore, by the sentiments of the Legislature, manifested in this statute, we present the following tabular statements of the branches of learning which we think should be taught in the

[12] *To John Bannister, Jr.,* 1785.
[13] *To George Ticknor,* 1817.

University, forming them into groups, each of which are within the powers of a single professor:

I.   Languages, ancient:
      Latin,
      Greek,
      Hebrew.

II. Languages, modern:
      French,
      Spanish,
      Italian,
      German,
      Anglo-Saxon.

III. Mathematics, pure:
      Algebra,
      Fluxions,
      Geometry, Elemental,
                    Transcendental.
      Architecture, Military,
                    Naval.

IV. Physico-Mathematics:
      Mechanics,
      Statistics,
      Dynamics,
      Pneumatics,
      Acoustics,
      Optics,
      Astronomy,
      Geography.

V.   Physics, or Natural Philosophy:
      Chemistry,
      Mineralogy.

VI. Botany.
      Zoölogy.

VII. Anatomy,
      Medicine.

VIII. Government,
      Political Economy,
      Law of Nature and Nations,
      History, being interwoven with Politics and Law.

IX. Law, municipal.

X.   Ideology,
      General Grammar,
      Ethics,
      Rhetoric,
      Belles Lettres and the fine arts.[14]

---

[14] *Report to the Commissioners Appointed to Fix the Site of the University of Virginia.*

He emphasized the modern languages:

The considerations which have governed the specification of
languages to be taught by the professor of modern languages were,
that the French is the language of general intercourse among nations,
and as a depository of human science, is unsurpassed by any other
language, living or dead; that the Spanish is highly interesting to us,
as the language spoken by so great a portion of the inhabitants of
our continents, with whom we shall probably have great intercourse
ere long, and is that also in which is written the greater part of the
earlier history of America. The Italian abounds with works of very
superior order, valuable for their matter, and still more distinguished
as models of the finest taste in style and composition. And the
German now stands in a line with that of the most learned nations
in richness of erudition and advance in the sciences. It is too of
common descent with the language of our own country, a branch
of the same original Gothic stock, and furnishes valuable illustrations
for us. But in this point of view, the Anglo-Saxon is of peculiar value.
We have placed it among the modern languages, because it is in fact
that which we speak, in the earliest form in which we have knowledge
of it. It has been undergoing, with time, those gradual changes which
all languages, ancient and modern, have experienced; and even now
needs only to be printed in the modern character and orthography to
be intelligible, in a considerable degree, to an English reader. It has
this value, too, above the Greek and Latin, that while it gives the
radix of the mass of our language, they explain its innovations only.[15]

He stressed religious freedom — a radical idea for his time:

In conformity with the principles of our Constitution, which places
all sects of religion on an equal footing, with the jealousies of the
different sects in guarding that equality from encroachment and
surprise, and with the sentiments of the Legislature in favor of freedom
of religion, manifested on former occasions, we have proposed no
professor of divinity; and the rather as the proofs of the being of a
God, the creator, preserver, and supreme ruler of the universe, the
author of all the relations of morality, and of the laws and obligations
these infer, will be within the province of the professor of ethics; to
which adding the developments of these moral obligations, of those
in which all sects agree, with a knowledge of the languages, Hebrew,
Greek, and Latin, a basis will be formed common to all sects. Pro-
ceeding thus far without offence to the Constitution, we have thought

---

[15] *Ibid.*

it proper at this point to leave every sect to provide, as they think fittest, the means of further instruction in their own peculiar tenets.[16]

Jefferson was concerned with the expansion of knowledge. A bill he introduced stated:

Another object of the revisal is, to diffuse knowledge more generally through the mass of the people. This bill proposes to lay off every county into small districts of five or six miles square, called hundreds and in each of them to establish a school for teaching reading, writing, and arithmetic. The tutor to be supported by the hundred, and every person in it entitled to send their children three years gratis, and as much longer as they please, paying for it. These schools to be under a visitor who is annually to chuse the boy of best genius in the school, of those whose parents are too poor to give them further education, and to send him forward to one of the grammar schools, of which twenty are proposed to be erected in different parts of the country, for teaching Greek, Latin, geography, and the higher branches of numerical arithmetic. Of the boys thus sent in any one year, trial is to be made at the grammar schools one or two years, and the best genius of the whole selected, and continued six years, and the residue dismissed. By this means twenty of the best geniuses will be raked from the rubbish annually, and be instructed, at the public expense, so far as the grammar schools go. At the end of six years instruction, one half are to be discontinued (from among whom the grammar schools will probably be supplied with future masters); and the other half, who are to be chosen for the superiority of their parts and disposition, are to be sent and continued three years in the study of such sciences as they shall chuse, at William and Mary.[17]

The people, Jefferson stated, are the guardians of knowledge.

By that part of our plan which prescribes the selection of the youths of genius from among the classes of the poor, we hope to avail the state of those talents which nature has sown as liberally among the poor as the rich, but which perish without use, if not sought for and cultivated. But of all the views of this law none is more important, none more legitimate, than that of rendering the people the safe, as they are the ultimate guardians of their own liberty. For this purpose the reading in the first stage, where *they* will receive their whole education, is proposed, as has been said, to be chiefly

---

[16] *Ibid.*
[17] *Notes on Virginia,* 1782.

historical. History, by apprising them of the past, will enable them to judge of the future; it will avail them of the experience of other times and other nations; it will enable them to know ambition under every disguise it may assume; and knowing it, to defeat its views. In every government on earth is some trace of human weakness, some germ of corruption and degeneracy, which cunning will discover, and wickedness insensibly open, cultivate, and improve. Every government degenerates when trusted to the rulers of the people alone. The people themselves therefore are its only safe depositories. And to render even them safe, their minds must be improved to a certain degree. This indeed is not all that is necessary, though it be essentially necessary. An amendment of our constitution must here come in aid of the public education. The influence over government must be shared among all the people. If every individual which composes their mass participates of the ultimate authority, the government will be safe; because the corrupting of the whole mass will exceed any private resources of wealth and public ones cannot be provided but by levies on the people. In this case every man would have to pay his own price. The government of Great Britain has been corrupted, because but one man in ten has a right to vote for members of parliament. The sellers of the government, therefore, get nine-tenths of their price clear. It has been thought that corruption is restrained by confining the right of suffrage to a few of the wealthier of the people; but it would be more effectually restrained by an extension of that right to such numbers as would bid defiance to the means of corruption.[18]

Education does not apply merely to the mind.

If the body be feeble, the mind will not be strong — the sovereign invigorator of the body is exercise, and . . . no one knows, till he tries, how easily a habit of walking is acquired . . . Not less than two hours a day should be devoted to exercise, and the weather should be little regarded. A person not sick will not be injured by getting wet . . . Brute animals are most healthy, and they are exposed to all weather, and, of men, those are healthiest who are the most exposed. The recipe of those two descriptions of beings is simple diet, exercise and the open air.[19]

Learning, above all, must promote science. A knowledge of the classics alone is not adequate.

When sobered by experience, I hope our successors will turn their attention to the advantages of education. I mean of education on the

---

[18] *Ibid.*
[19] *Letter to Thomas Mann Randolph, Jr.*, August 27, 1786.

broad scale, and not that of the petty *academies,* as they call themselves, which are starting up in every neighborhood, and where one
or two men, possessing Latin and sometimes Greek, a knowledge of
the globes, and the first six books of Euclid, imagine and communicate
this as the sum of science. They commit their pupils to the theatre
of the world, with just taste enough of learning to be alienated
from industrious pursuits, and not enough to do service in the
ranks of science.[20]

Jefferson felt that education of the masses provided the best safe-
guards for liberty. It must be remembered that in his age mass education was regarded as a revolutionary idea.

Generally, his concept of culture was functional and utilitarian.
Like John Dewey, he disliked the snobbishness of traditional liberal
education. Education, according to Jefferson, is to liberate the mind
and to apply the fruits of science to our daily life.

MORALITY AND EDUCATION

In his moral system, Jefferson protested against all types of
coercion. Only in an atmosphere of freedom can man develop his
capacities. Liberty and reason go together; one demands the other.
Throughout his life he fought against tyranny.

He abhorred vague metaphysical inquiries. Thus he had little
use for speculations regarding the union of mind and body. He urged
the scientists and philosophers to study man empirically.

Against the spiritual hypothesis, he urged the reality of matter
and motion. Our mind does not contain innate ideas, rather it can be
modified by experience. Here the influence of John Locke is especially evident. Nature itself cannot be reduced to a uniform law;
rather it contains so much diversification that pluralism is the best
method of science. What is real, the universal or the individual substance? Jefferson answered categorically: the individual. This is in
line with his democratic ideals. Nature, Jefferson asserted, presents
us only with individual things. We arrive at universals by grouping
individuals together.

The rational life is best achieved through tranquility and serenity.
The greatest pleasure is the pleasure of the mind. Whatever fate has
in store for us, it cannot deprive us of intellectual curiosity.

Like the ancient philosophers, Jefferson believed in freedom
from external values. Fame, riches and power are fleeting. We must

---

[20] *Letter to John Adams,* July 5, 1814.

seek certainty within ourselves. Whatever happens in life, we must cultivate an attitude of fortitude. In this manner no external reverse can touch us.

Man, according to Jefferson, is naturally good. If guided by wise teachers and a benevolent government, he will develop into an excellent citizen. We are made for mutual cooperation; we are all social animals. Our sense of right and wrong is native; it is as much part of us as our physical senses.

How can we measure our moral actions? How can we be certain that we are right? The pragmatism of Jefferson emerges, for he believed that utility, above all, is the standard for our actions. This does not imply, however, a Machiavellian concept of morality, for Jefferson believed that cruelty, injustice and tyranny could never be justified morally.

In all our actions we are to look forward rather than backward.

> The Gothic idea that we are to look backwards instead of forwards for the improvement of the human mind, and to recur to the annals of our ancestors for what is most perfect in government, in religion and in learning, is worthy of those bigots in religion and government, by whom it has been recommended, and whose purpose it would answer. But it is not an idea which this country will endure; and the moment of their showing it is fast ripening.[21]

We are to avoid extravagance.

> Among many good qualities which my countrymen possess, some of a different character, unhappily mix themselves. The most remarkable are indolence, extravagance, and infidelity to their engagements. Cure the two first, and the last would disappear, because it is a consequence of them, and not proceeding from want of morals. I know of no remedy against indolence and extravagance but a free course of justice. Everything else is merely palliative; but unhappily the evil has gained too generally the mass of the nation to leave the course of justice unobstructed. The maxim of buying nothing without the money in our pocket to pay for it, would make of our country one of the happiest on earth.[22]

Good humor is one of the best aids to civilization.

> It is among the most effectual, and its effect is so well imitated and aided, artificially, by politeness, that this also becomes an acquisi-

---

[21] *Letter to Joseph Priestley,* January 27, 1800.
[22] *Letter to A. Donald,* July 28, 1787.

tion of first rate value. In truth, politeness is artificial good humor, it covers the natural want of it, and ends by rendering habitual a substitute nearly equivalent to the real virtue. It is the practice of sacrificing to those whom we meet in society, all the little conveniences and preferences which will gratify them, and deprive us of nothing worth a moment's consideration; it is the giving a pleasing and flattering turn to our expressions, which will conciliate others, and make them pleased with us as well as themselves. How cheap a price for the good will of another! When this is in return for a rude thing said by another, it brings him to his senses, it mortifies and corrects him in the most salutary way, and places him at the feet of your good nature, in the eyes of the company. But in stating prudential rules for our government in society, I must not omit the important one of never entering into dispute or argument with another. I never saw the instance of two disputants convincing the other by argument.[23]

He summarized his ideals of the educated man in ten rules:

1. Never put off till tomorrow what you can do today.
2. Never trouble another for what you can do for yourself.
3. Never spend your money before you have it.
4. Never buy what you do not want because it is cheap; it will be dear to you.
5. Pride costs us more than hunger, thirst and cold.
6. We never repent of having eaten too little.
7. Nothing is troublesome that we do willingly.
8. How much pain have cost us the evils which have never happened.
9. Take things always by their smooth handle.
10. When angry, count ten, before you speak; if very angry, an hundred.[24]

THE EDUCATION OF POLITICS

The political theories of Jefferson have become part of the American dream. While Hamilton believed in a strong central government and despised the people, Jefferson had faith in the masses and favored decentralization. Hamilton, like Hobbes, believed that man was essentially evil, whereas Jefferson stressed the potentialities of every individual. While Hamilton favored full industrialization of the United States, Jefferson relied upon an agrarian democracy.

---

[23] *Letter to Thomas Jefferson Randolph,* November 24, 1808.
[24] *Letter to Thomas Jefferson Smith,* February 21, 1825.

(1)   Basic in his political philosophy was his faith in the equality of man. He regarded every man as his brother. Writing to Adams in 1814, he stated:

> I agree with you that there is a natural aristocracy among men. The grounds of this are virtue and talents. Formerly, bodily powers gave place among the *aristoi*. But since the invention of gunpowder has armed the weak as well as the strong with missile death, bodily strength, like beauty, good humor, politeness and other accomplishments, has become but an auxiliary ground for distinction. There is also an artificial aristocracy, founded on wealth and birth, without either virtue or talents; for with these it would belong to the first class. The natural aristocracy I consider as the most precious gift of nature, for the instruction, the trusts, and government of society. And indeed, it would have been inconsistent in creation to have formed man for the social state, and not to have provided virtue and wisdom enough to manage the concerns of the society. May we not even say, that that form of government is the best which provides the most effectually for a pure selection of these natural *aristoi* into the offices of government?[25]

(2)   He believed that all government power rests on majority rule.

> It is my principle that the will of the majority should always prevail. If they approved the proposed Convention in all its parts, I shall concur in it cheerfully, in hopes that they will amend it whenever they shall find it works wrong. I think our governments will remain virtuous for many centuries; as long as they are chiefly agricultural; and this will be as long as there shall be vacant lands in any part of America. When they get piled upon one another in large cities, as in Europe, they will become corrupt as in Europe. Above all things I hope the education of the common people will be attended to; convinced that on their good sense we may rely with the most security for the preservation of a due degree of liberty.[26]

(3)   Laws are to be progressive and are to be changed when new conditions arise.

> Some men look at constitutions with sanctimonious reverence, and deem them like the ark of the convenant, too sacred to be touched. They ascribe to the men of the preceding age a wisdom more than human, and suppose what they did to be beyond amendment. I knew that age well; I belonged to it, and labored with it. It deserved well

---

[25] *Letter to John Adams,* October 28, 1814.
[26] *Letter to James Madison,* December 20, 1787.

of its country. It was very like the present; and forty years of experience in government is worth a century of book-reading; and this they would say themselves, were they to rise from the dead. I am certainly not an advocate for frequent and untried changes in laws and constitutions. But I know also, that laws and institutions must go hand in hand with the progress of the human mind.[27]

(4)   The states are the best watchdogs of liberty.

Our country is too large to have all its affairs directed by a single government. Public servants at such a distance, and from under the eye of their constituents, must, from the circumstances of distance, be unable to administer and overlook all the details necessary for the good government of the citizens, and the same circumstance, by rendering detection impossible to their constituents, will invite the public agents to corruption, plunder and waste. And I do verily believe, that if the principle were to prevail, of a common law being in force in the U.S. (which principle possesses the general government at once of all the powers of the state governments, and reduces us to a single consolidated government) it would become the most corrupt government on the earth.[28]

(5)   Rebellion is justified in the defense of freedom. Thus he was not worried about Shay's rebellion.

Yet where does this anarchy exist? Where did it ever exist, except in the single instance of Massachusetts? And can history produce an instance of rebellion so honourably conducted? I say nothing of its motives. They were founded in ignorance, not wickedness. God forbid we should ever be 20 years without such a rebellion. The people cannot be all, and always, well informed. The part which is wrong will be discontented in proportion to the importance of the facts they misconceive. If they remain quiet under such misconceptions it is a lethargy, the forerunner of death to the public liberty. We have had 13 states independent 11 years. There has been one rebellion. That comes to one rebellion in a century and a half for each state. What country before ever existed a century and a half without a rebellion? and what country can preserve its liberties if their rulers are not warned from time to time that their people preserve the spirit of resistance? Let them take arms. The remedy is to set them right as to facts, pardon and pacify them. What signify a few lives lost in a century or two? The tree of liberty must be refreshed from time to time with the blood of patriots and tyrants. It is its natural manure.[29]

[27] *Letter to Samuel Kercheval,* July 12, 1816.
[28] *Letter to Gideon Granger,* August 13, 1800.
[29] *Letter to William S. Smith,* November 13, 1787.

His political principles are summarized in his inaugural message of 1801.

It is proper you should understand what I deem the essential principles of this government and consequently those which ought to shape its administration.

I will compress them in the narrowest compass they will bear, stating the general principle, but not all its limitations.

Equal and exact justice to all men, of whatever state or persuasion, religious or political:

Peace, commerce, and honest friendship with all nations, entangling alliances with none.

The support of the State governments in all their rights, as the most competent administrations for our domestic concerns, and the surest bulwarks against anti-republican tendencies.

The preservation of the General government, in its whole constitutional vigor, as the sheet anchor of our peace at home, and safety abroad.

A jealous care of the right of election by the people, a mild and sage corrective of abuses, which are lopped by the sword of revolution, where peaceable remedies are unprovided.

Absolute acquiescence in the decisions of the Majority the vital principle of republics, from which is no appeal but to force, the vital principle and immediate part of despotism.

A well disciplined militia, our best reliance in peace, and for the first moments of war, till regulars may relieve them: The Supremacy of the Civil over the Military authority.

Economy in public expense, that labor may be lightly burthened.

The honest payment of our debts and sacred preservation of the public faith.

Encouragement of Agriculture, and of Commerce as its handmaid.

The diffusion of information, and arraignment of all abuses at the bar of the public reason.

Freedom of Religion, freedom of the press, and freedom of Person under the protection of the Habeas Corpus: And trial by juries, impartially selected.[30]

SIGNIFICANCE

In all his labors Jefferson was a true son of the enlightenment. With his complete faith in science, reason, and progress, he represented the Deistic ideal of life. As a supporter of peace, he was

---

[30] *First Inaugural Address,* 1801.

grateful that in the United States the bickerings and petty quarrels of Europe had no place. With all his power, he tried to keep the colonies out of European entanglements.

To him democracy was almost a religious gospel. He felt that most of the evils of Europe could be traced to the crowned heads of the various countries. This dislike of kings has become part of the American tradition.

The keynote of the system of Jefferson was his insistent faith in freedom. He believed that the flame of freedom which had been kindled in the colonies would spread throughout the globe. Tolerant in his political and religious opinions, he zealously defended the right of others to differ and even to assail him personally.

In education he followed the rule of Epicurus together with the precepts of Christ. Impatient with metaphysical disputes, he was interested above all in practical matters. He made it clear that Christianity must go back to its early purity and be purged of its Platonic content. He defended absolute freedom in religion and thus had no use for a state church.

To him all moral rules were summarized in the following statement: "Fear God and love thy neighbor." The test of morality was utility, the way in which it promoted common happiness. He was certain that no nation could violate moral rules and still prosper, for a disintegration of morality inevitably led to tyranny.

To promote the welfare of mankind Jefferson urged above all the cultivation of education. Writing to Colonel Yancey in 1816 he stated that, "If a nation expects to be ignorant and free, in a state of civilization, it expects what never was and never will be."

JEFFERSON AND THE 20TH CENTURY

Jefferson is especially important in our era, which has seen a wholesale assault upon democracy. Two major world wars, depressions, and the rise of dictatorships in many countries have undermined the faith of many people in the possibilities of a free society. Fanatics of the left and right claim that in times of crisis democracy is an impossibility and that its machinery is too slow and too inefficient to meet the challenges of our time.

The 20th century has been in a constant state of emergency. The violent military conflicts have cost the lives of millions of human beings. Jefferson, who was a careful student of history, pointed out that wars never aid democracies; they only strengthen the power of the élite and create an attitude of belligerency incompatible with peaceful living. Jefferson was opposed to entangling alliances because they curtailed freedom of action and because they inevitably created counter alliances and in this way spread the seeds of conflict.

Jefferson pointed out that the great problems of life could not be solved by violence. Force would create a world of illusion; it would imply a compulsory return to the past. He believed that in the long run reason would prevail over force, for man's mind could not be permanently curtailed. An opponent of militarism, Jefferson believed that civilian authority must be supreme, otherwise a state of permanent emergency develops with the result that the prospects for mutuality are decreased.

The 20th century has seen a vast concentration of military power, especially in totalitarian societies. The influence of the military extends not only to the government, but to economic institutions and education. The military promise protection against external aggression, but the security which they uphold is never completely realized. In the armament race of the 20th century all nations feel insecure because they are all threatened by annihilation.

Ours has been an age of extremism. The extremists of the left and the right are united by a common dislike of reason and by a common prejudice against an objective discussion of public affairs. They are so imbued with their cause, that they want to eliminate the freedom of their opponents. Jefferson reminds us that once freedom is curtailed, it can seldom be regained and that truth has nothing to fear in the market-place of public debate. To Jefferson, no opinion was absolute and no cause was sacred. This implied an emphasis on fallibilism — an important concept for 20th century man.

In a time when public opinion can be easily manufactured, when stereotypes can be created, when base emotions can be aroused, when propaganda can triumph over information, Jefferson reminds us that critical knowledge is a foundation of decision making in a democratic society. Jefferson felt that it is not enough to be a specialist or to be a scholar; what matters is participation in public life. Every man, he asserted, owes an obligation to himself and to society to improve his mind and to study the issues which determine the fate of mankind.

He set an example to posterity by his own habits. He would arise at dawn and write letters and answer correspondence. In fact, he wrote over 50,000 letters in his lifetime. His library was one of the best of his time. Books, to him, were pathways to emancipation. Before he went to bed at night he would read great authors in their original language. Even in advanced age he continued to read Greek, Latin, Italian and French.

To Jefferson education implied a vital view of the present; it combined facts and values; it meant public service and the search for public enlightenment. He believed that education should not be only for the élite but should be the basis for the cultural advancement of all.

In an age of extreme specialization, Jefferson reminds us of the value of general education. He was as much interested in agriculture as in history. He treasured practical inventions and intellectual exercises, and could converse with equal ease with Rush on medicine and with Paine on political theory. He believed that the human mind is capable of infinite improvement.

Jefferson believed that education was not to be tested by the books which a student read or the grades which he obtained, but by his understanding of himself and of society. If education alienated man from constructive relationships with others then it had failed, and a sterile culture would result. On the other hand, if education gave man an incentive to serve others and to improve humanity, then it lived up to its highest obligations.

Jefferson saw no opposition between the sciences and the humanities. The sciences he treasured because they added to man's control over nature and because they produced inventions which made life more exciting and which spread the impact of civilization. But to Jefferson science was not the goal of life; it was a method of understanding the external world. He valued the humanities because they enriched the mind; they represented the aristocracy of the spirit.

In a time when the past is often idolized, when some scholars want to return to the certainty of the 13th century, Jefferson reminds us that the past cannot be recovered and that traditionalism blocks the progress of education. Worship of the past leads to enslavement of the mind. The uniqueness of the present has to be explored if society is to advance and if democracy is to be safeguarded.

Jefferson was an excellent student of history, and he had a special interest in Greek culture. But students were to be taught that the great ages lay ahead, not that their own period was only a footnote to antique glories.

The Puritan educators had looked upon man as sinful, and preached about an arbitrary God who is enraged by the waywardness of man. Today many theologians are similarly enraptured by man's failings as they picture the awesome majesty of God. Jefferson, on the other hand, believed that religion is a simple matter, with a close relationship to education. Both are concerned with man's motivations; both are protests against pride and arrogance. Both are inward concerns which cannot be controlled by the state, and have as their aim a closer union between ideal and reality.

Like Socrates, Jefferson was a moralist in his educational views. Morality implied, to Jefferson, a sense of obligation and a sense of humility. Jefferson asked penetrating questions as a way of clarifying complex issues and so that he could live a more examined existence. Morality for private individuals implied tolerance and understanding, sound habits, and the willingness to listen to various viewpoints.

For the nation, according to Jefferson, morality implied the avoidance of Machiavellianism. The end did not justify the means. Freedom could not be curtailed in times of crisis. Power was to be checked by progressive laws. Rulers were to be responsive to the desires of the people. Lies were never to be tolerated in public life. Expenses of the government were to be kept to a minimum. Propaganda was to be avoided and instead a careful deliberation of issues was to be stressed. More money was to be spent for institutions of education than for institutions of warfare. The rights of the opposition were to be safeguarded. The privileges of the individual were to be protected. Tyranny was to be combated whether found in politics, religion or education.

The evils which Jefferson fought, such as organized ignorance, arbitrary government, authoritarianism, centralization of power, are even more significant in our own time than in his period. Today these evils threaten the survival of man and they could create a wasteland out of which no escape may be possible. Lincoln once remarked that Jefferson's ideas "represented the definitions and axioms of a free society."

The enemies of man, according to Jefferson, are not external; they are not represented by specific nations or civilizations, or by one religion or one philosophy; rather the enemies of man reside in his own heart and permit his seduction by superstition and ignorance.

Education starts by liberating man from the tabus of the past; it removes him from the prejudice of his environment; it teaches him the value of freedom; it imbues him with a vast sense of responsibility; it gives him an incentive to work for humanity; it stirs the resources of his intellect and his emotions; it appeals to his sense of purpose; it gives him a fervent sense of beauty; it gives him a genuine sense of morality which removes all social barriers.

Education in a Jeffersonian sense overcomes all forms of passivity and calls for strenuous participation in the drama of life. Education shows that democracy is not an unattainable ideal but an imperative reality. It points to the common rights of all individuals who are united in their quest for reason.

The task of the schools, according to Jefferson, is to inspire the young and the old, the rich and the poor with the possibilities of an open society. Democracy thus is to become a constant activity; it is to be the center of man's life; it is to dominate all his yearnings and ideals. It is to develop a genuine respect for individuality and for human integrity. It is to produce a new society which can look with confidence to the ideals of the future.

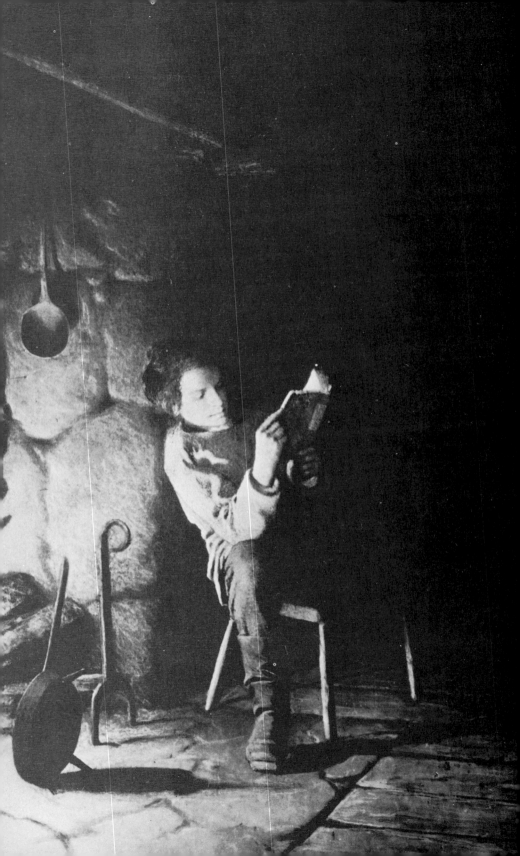

PART THREE

Pioneers of Progress and Education

CHAPTER ELEVEN

Impact of European Educators

ROUSSEAU

It is impossible to understand the development of 19th and 20th century American philosophy and education without a grasp of the impact of Rousseau, Pestalozzi, Herbart, Froebel and Spencer. Rousseau and Pestalozzi stimulated the development of progressive education, while Herbart aided the development of educational psychology and Froebel stimulated the growth of the kindergarten. Spencer's ideas contributed to an increased emphasis upon science in American education.

Jean Jacques Rousseau (1712–1778) accomplished almost a Copernican revolution in education. Before him, it was generally assumed that reason is man's highest good and that civilization leads to man's constant improvement. But Rousseau emphasized the primacy of emotion. Descartes had maintained that *"Cogito, ergo sum"* ("I think, therefore I am"). Rousseau found reality instead in man's feelings. He said, *"Je sens, donc je suis"* ("I feel, therefore I am").

Rousseau insisted that education should transcend specialization. Thus he wrote in *Émile:*

> Education by Nature will restore unsophisticated man, whose sole function is to be a man. In the natural order of things, all men being equal, their common vocation is manhood; and whoever is well trained for that, cannot fail to perform any vocation connected with it. Whether my pupil be destined for the army, the church, or the bar, is of small consequence. Regardless of the calling of his family, Nature calls him to human life. To live is the craft I desire to teach him.[1]

Rousseau stressed the importance of universal education. All were to be educated, the rich and the poor; since all were equal, no class differences were to be tolerated. This was indeed a revolutionary idea in his time.

He was opposed to the moral training of his time. A child should not be indoctrinated; moral precepts by adults were to be avoided. Rousseau recommended that the child follow his own instincts and his own ideals.

An opponent of intellectual education, he believed that book knowledge would only corrupt children. Books, according to Rousseau, "merely teach us to talk of what we do not know." Premature exposure to ideas would fill children with useless concepts and inhibit their creative drives. They should study the book of nature and thus sharpen their senses.

The education of Émile was divided into four states; (1) Infancy, (2) Childhood, (3) Boyhood, (4) Adolescence. In the first period, up to the age of five, the boy is like an animal; he is completely swayed by his feelings. In the second state, up to the age of twelve, he is in a state of savagery. His needs are still primitive, but now he is more interested in the exploration of nature. In the third state, up to the age of 15, he is like Robinson Crusoe; now he is developing the power of judgment. The last period, from 15 to 20, sees the emergence of his sexual drives, and he begins to reason more adequately.

Rousseau's recommendations for the education of women were extremely inadequate. He wanted women to be servants of men; their intellectual powers were not to be explored. Their physical development was to be stressed so that they could produce healthy children. They were to be taught singing, dancing, and embroidery so that they could entertain men. The principles of morality and

---

[1] *Émile, ou Traité de l'Éducation,* 1762.

religion were to make them virtuous, but women should not be educated to think for themselves; it would only serve to corrupt their minds and morals.

The educational influence of Rousseau was immense. Johann Pestalozzi in Switzerland believed, like the author of *Émile,* that the aim of education was a return to nature, and that through it humanity could be reformed. Froebel in Germany adopted Rousseau's belief in the goodness of man and he stressed the creative possibilities of children. In the United States, Horace Mann read *Émile* with vigorous interest and, like Rousseau, stressed the importance of love and compassion in education. Thoreau, like Rousseau, felt that nature could be man's most reliable guide.

There are reflections of Rousseau in Dewey and Kilpatrick. Both believed in the principle of interest, both stressed a child-centered system of education, both were suspicious of too much intellectualism, both were advocates of democracy in the classroom, both believed that no formal rules should be established. Furthermore, both Dewey and Kilpatrick rejected traditional education because it made too much of book knowledge. But the great difference between Rousseau and Dewey and Kilpatrick was in their divergent views toward science. To Rousseau, science was, at best, a second-rate study; he was certain that children would learn more from nature than from experiments in the laboratory. On the other hand, the great pragmatists believed that science is the model for education and that its method should be used in all areas of inquiry.

The real weakness of Rousseau was in his concept of reason. To be sure, reason is often perverted and can lead to a static view of life. But without reason man cannot control his emotions. We have never really explored the resources of our rational powers; most of the time we are subject to rationalizations which are part of our cultural heritage. Hutchins may exaggerate when he tells us that the main purpose of education is intellectual; but without intellectual training, education becomes only an exercise, and the teacher becomes an intellectual Babbitt.

This does not imply that we can neglect our feelings and our esthetic sensitivity. Ideas must be illuminated by desire and by intensity. We need a passion for ideas — otherwise our culture will be second-rate.

When Rousseau maintained that children are to be kept away from ideas and book knowledge he was profoundly wrong. Today, through television and other agencies of communication, the child has become part of the adult world. He grows up at a much faster pace than ever before, but his development is uneven: his body outgrows his mind, a fact often underestimated by timid parents and educators.

It should be our aim to expose children to books as early as possible. This develops not only excellent reading habits, but it creates wide interests and broad horizons for youngsters. A civilization can be defined by its love of books.

Rousseau underestimated the importance of discipline. To be sure, too much discipline has undesirable results and creates human robots who cannot think for themselves. Thus, some German scholars easily became subjects of totalitarianism because they were used to authoritarian ways in the classroom.

Discipline, however, can have positive features when based on sound habits. How much more successful we are if we develop as early as possible the habit of work and study! Good habits are never lost and, as James showed, they are the bases of intellectual advancement. But in a deeper sense, we need to develop our capacity for concentration. We allow intolerable inattention, even indifference, on almost all levels of education.

Habit, discipline, and concentration are not ends in themselves. They are only preludes to the development of genuine individuality. What matters ultimately is our inward development. The spark within us has to be nourished and expanded. *Beyond discipline is creativity, beyond concentration is self-expression.* We must be aware of the fact that significant achievement is not spontaneous, that it demands increasing effort and, to some extent, discipline.

Real education is always a protest against a fragmentary view of life. Rousseau was intoxicated by the realm of feelings; he overlooked the significance of reason. We can clarify our educational dilemmas only if we achieve a balance between the demands of our emotions and the discipline which our intellect imposes.

PESTALOZZI

Pestalozzi (1746–1827) reflected the influence of Rousseau and romanticism. Like Rousseau, Pestalozzi stressed the natural development of the child and, like Rousseau, Pestalozzi had great distrust for authoritarianism in education.

In Pestalozzi's time the education of the poor was especially neglected. He established several schools for underprivileged children of which the most famous was at Yverdun.

Pestalozzi believed that education, above all, is an individual process; he felt that collectivism was an illusory solution. Education should aim at the development of the *head* (our intellectual capacities), the *hands* (our physical activities), and the *heart* (our moral capacities).

In his view of methodology, he affirmed the *active* nature of the mind. We learn best, according to him, by starting with simple subjects in order to arrive at abstractions. Hence, practice comes before theory. Pestalozzi emphasized the happiness of the individual in education.

When men rush into the labyrinth of words, formulas, and opinions, without having gained a progressive knowledge of the realities of life, their minds must develop on this one basis, and can have no other source of strength.

A man's domestic relations are the first and most important of his nature.

A man works at his calling, and bears his share of the public burdens, that he may have undisturbed enjoyment of his home.

Thus the education which fits a man for his profession and position in the state must be made subordinate to that which is necessary for his domestic happiness.

It is the home that gives the best moral training, and restores to men the sense that God is their Father, and Jesus is indeed the Savior of the world. His teaching is justice itself, a simple philosophy of practical value for all, the revelation of God the Father to his erring children.[2]

In a letter on his work at Stanz he said:

The will can not be stimulated by mere words; its action must depend upon those feelings and powers which are the result of general culture. Words alone can not give us a knowledge of things; they are only useful for giving expression to what we have in our mind.

The first thing to be done was to win the confidence and affection of the children. I was sure that if I succeeded in doing that, all the rest would follow of itself. Think for a moment of the prejudices of the people, and even of the children, and you will understand the difficulties with which I had to contend.

And yet, however painful this want of help and support was to me, it was favorable to the success of my undertaking, for it compelled me to be always everything for my children. I was alone with them from morning till night. It was my hand that supplied all their wants, both of body and soul. All needful help, consolation, and instruction

---

[2] *The Evening Hour of a Hermit,* 1780.

they received direct from me. Their hands were in mine, my eyes were fixed on theirs.

We wept and smiled together. They forgot the world and Stanz; they only knew that they were with me and I with them. We shared our food and drink. I had neither family, friends, nor servants; nothing but them. I was with them in sickness and health, and when they slept. I was the last to go to bed, and the first to get up. In the bedroom I prayed with them, and, at their own request, taught them till they fell asleep.[3]

Pestalozzi upheld the power of love.

This is how it was that those children gradually became so attached to me, some indeed so deeply that they contradicted their parents and friends when they heard evil things said about me. They felt that I was being treated unfairly, and loved me, I think, the more for it . . .[4]

Pestalozzi's most famous educational work was probably *How Gertrude Teaches her Children,* which was widely read in the United States. Horace Mann was influenced by him, and around 1860, Oswego, New York, adopted the methods of Pestalozzi's system of education. Both John Dewey and W. H. Kilpatrick owed a great debt to Pestalozzi, who developed a truly child-centered philosophy of education.

HERBART

Johann Herbart (1776–1841) was mainly interested in the psychological foundations of education. From 1809 to 1833 he was a professor at the University of Königsberg and occupied the chair of philosophy formerly held by Kant.

Herbart felt that the main goal of education should be the development of morality. Like Socrates, he believed that virtue and knowledge were correlated.

Man, according to Herbart, recapitulates the development of culture through its various stages. First, like the primitive, he is exposed to sensation. Later he develops memory and imagination, but the most important stage is that of judgment, when man is able to discriminate between value and fact.

---

[3] *Letter on His Work at Stanz,* 1799.
[4] *Ibid.*

Herbart formulated five stages of learning:

(1) Preparation
(2) Presentation
(3) Association
(4) Generalization
(5) Application

Charles De Garmo, Charles McMurray and Frank McMurray, and Alexis Lange championed his views. In 1892 the national Herbartian Society was established; ten years later its name was changed to the National Society for the Scientific Study of Education. By 1902 American educators were following pragmatism rather than Herbartian psychology.

FROEBEL

Friedrich Froebel (1782–1852) was the most idealistic of the great European educators. Influenced by post-Kantian thought and Rousseau, he stressed a pantheistic view of the universe. He felt that man is part of God and that God is part of nature. History implies the unfolding of the divine essence. Man is good and has infinite possibilities.

Froebel felt that education should be concerned with character development. Education should start with the individual, for it is essentially an inward process.

In all things there lives and reigns an eternal law. This all-controlling law is necessarily based on an all-pervading, energetic, living, self-conscious, and hence eternal unity. This Unity is God. . . . All things are only through the divine effluence that lives in each thing, is the essence of each thing.[5]

Primarily and in truth man works only that his spiritual, divine essence may assume outward form, and that thus he may be enabled to recognize his own spiritual, divine nature and the innermost being of God. Whatever food, clothing, and shelter he obtains thereby comes to him as an insignificant surplus.

Play is the highest phase of child-development — of human develop-ment at this period; for it is self-active representation of the inner-most representation and represents freedom from necessity and impulse. Play is the purest, most *spiritual activity* of man at this stage.[6]

---

[5] *The Education of Man.*
[6] *Ibid.*

Activity should train both physical and moral powers.

What formerly the child did only for the sake of the activity, the boy now does for the sake of the result or product of his activity; the child's instinct of activity has in the boy become a *formative instinct,* and this occupies the whole outward life, the outward manifestations of boy-life at this period. How cheerfully and eagerly the boy and the girl at this age begin to share the work of father and mother![7]

Creativity thus is central in Froebel's system of education; he held that the function of the school is to stimulate our natural drive towards originality.

The home, as well as the school, contributes to educational progress. He thought that the family is the *basic* social institution.

Froebel gave special attention to early childhood education, and in 1837 he established the first kindergarten. He influenced many American educators, particularly Caroline Frankenburg, Elizabeth P. Peabody, W. T. Harris, and Kilpatrick.

SPENCER

Herbert Spencer (1820–1903), unlike Froebel, gave a mechanistic account of evolution. His life was devoted to writing and scholarship, although he received little formal schooling, which may have been fortunate, for the English public schools and universities in his period were still devoted to the classical tradition and neglected the study of the sciences. His father was secular in his outlook and had a distaste for the established Church. Herbert Spencer had little sympathy for any type of supernaturalism.

It may be asked how Spencer acquired his immense and encyclopedic knowledge, how could he synthesize so many aspects of science? The answer is that Spencer had extraordinary powers of concentration and observation. Through conversations with the scientists of his period he learned the essentials of their researches.

In his social philosophy, Spencer championed individualism and would tolerate no interference from government. Property rights he regarded as absolute. He admitted that at first all things were held in common, but he thought civilization could progress only under the spirit of individualism.

---

[7] *Ibid.*

The educational theories of Spencer are contained in his *Education: Intellectual, Moral and Physical* (1860).

We are none of us content with quietly unfolding our own individualities to the full in all directions, but have a restless craving to impress our individualities upon others, and in some way subordinate them. And this it is which determines the character of our education. Not knowledge is sought but what will bring most applause, honor, respect — what will most conduce to social position and influence — what will be the most imposing.

Education, Spencer stated, inevitably raises the problem of values.

Remembering how narrowly this time is limited, not only by the shortness of life, we ought to be especially solicitous to employ what time we have to the greatest advantage. Before devoting years to some subject which fashion or fancy suggests, it is surely wise to weigh with great care the worth of various alternative results which the same years might bring if otherwise applied.

In education, then, this is the question of questions, which it is high time we discussed in some methodic way. The first in importance, though the last to be considered, is the problem how to decide among the conflicting claims of various subjects on our attention. Before there can be a rational *curriculum*, we must settle which things it most concerns us to know; or, to use a word of Bacon's now unfortunately obsolete, we must determine the relative values of knowledge.

To this end a measure of value is the first requisite. And happily, respecting the true measure of value, as expressed in general terms, there can be no dispute. Everyone in contending for the worth of any particular order of information, does so by showing its bearing upon some part of life.

The conduct of life, according to Spencer, is central in education.

How to live? — that is the essential question for us. Not how to live in the mere material sense only, but in the widest sense. . . . Equally at present and in the remotest future must it be of incalculable importance for the regulation of their conduct that men should understand the science of life, physical, mental, and social, and that they should understand all other science as a key to the science of life.

Both American and English education have been greatly influenced by Spencer. The schools in both nations today emphasize the centrality of science. The spirit of Spencer is reflected in the pragmatism of James, Dewey, and Kilpatrick as well as in the technical ideas of Alfred North Whitehead, whose *The Aims of Education* reminds us of Spencer.

The study of these thinkers ought to convince us that education is a *continuous* process and that education demands constant change and experimentation. Usually the bold, new ideas of one century become the accepted customs of the next, and they may be outmoded by the breathtaking advances of science and technology. Progressive education, as championed by Parker and Dewey, is not of recent origin; it has existed throughout modern times as a protest against traditionalism and authoritarianism in education.

CULTURE DIFFUSION

We should not forget that many of the most important advances in American education in the 19th century were made possible by European institutions. Mann and Barnard believed that Prussian schools were superior in organization to our own and that Prussian teachers were extremely well trained and that they handled their classes in a proficient manner. This, however, did not imply a worship of Prussian totalitarianism or of authoritarian government.

The American university owed much to European precedents, especially to the German ideal of scholarship which stressed research and objective knowledge. The graduate school, as it developed at Johns Hopkins University, embodied the German concept of higher education. Nicholas Murray Butler, who made Columbia University into a first-rate institution, used the University of Berlin as his model.

In the 20th century, American ideas in education have had a powerful impact on Europe. The ideas of Dewey and Kilpatrick have invaded England and the Continent. The Ford Foundation has given vast grants to European educational institutions such as Oxford and Cambridge, and it helped establish the Free University in Berlin. Fulbright fellowships have contributed to a vigorous exchange program, and today many American professors are teaching at such scholastic centers as the University of Bonn, the University of London and the Sorbonne. American students in increasing numbers are studying in Europe, especially in France. Their background occasionally tends to be less extensive than that of their European colleagues, but they make up for it in their eagerness and interest in other cultures.

American educational leaders have lectured to a vast audience in Europe and Asia. James Bryant Conant spoke to large groups in Germany on the differences between European and American patterns of knowledge. Robert Hutchins' lectures have influenced the development of education in Israel. Brameld made a speaking tour of Korea and Japan where he was received with wide acclaim.

The American government has sponsored a vital cultural exchange program in the arts and sciences. This has been especially effective in Soviet Russia where American artists, such as Roy Harris and Leonard Bernstein, were greeted enthusiastically. The Franklin Institute has sponsored the translation of books into foreign tongues, including obscure Asian dialects. American textbooks in translation can be purchased in such distant lands as Pakistan and Afghanistan.

Many universities, like Stanford and Redlands, have established campuses abroad. At first, American universities were mainly interested in Europe; now their attention is shifting to the Orient. One of the most vital centers for the knowledge of Oriental civilization has been created at the University of Hawaii — a veritable beacon of culture diffusion. Under-developed countries have been helped not only by the Peace Corps, but also by the activities of large universities, especially by Michigan State University, which has helped pioneer new ideas in technology for Asia.

While the United States can learn from European models, it must not imitate or abandon its own individuality. When some educators urge an imitation of the vigor of the Russian system, they indicate a narrow spirit. Imitation leads to mediocrity. Imitation produces conformity to past standards. Imitation inhibits the originality without which education becomes an empty ritual.

In this sense, the United States can learn from Emersonian idealism. No educator in modern times has urged more strongly the cultivation of American ideas than did Emerson, who wanted to produce real cultural greatness in the United States.

CHAPTER TWELVE

Emerson and the Educational Renaissance

THE NEW AGE

Education in New England in the nineteenth century expressed a reaction against the harsh doctrines of Puritanism. Where Jonathan Edwards, John Cotton, and Cotton Mather had stressed the depravity of man, the followers of Unitarianism believed in man's perfection. The God of the Puritans was full of terrors, an awesome judge sparing no one who violated His commandments. The God of the Unitarians, on the other hand, was like a kind, cosmopolitan New England gentleman quite satisfied with His creation and not unreasonable in His demands for righteous living.

The religion of New England, as developed in the nineteenth century, shortened the distance between man and God. God became less arbitrary, while man became more divine. Creation, according to the Unitarians and the followers of Emerson, was characterized by an underlying unity.

It was an optimistic age. How far had the intellectuals of New England gone since the dark days of the witchcraft craze! How strong were the institutions of enlightenment! This was a real American renaissance. Its weakness was its overestimation of its own achievements. The same weakness was shown by the thinkers of the Italian enlightenment. Emerson and Thoreau, like Erasmus and More, were struggling against the medieval forces of life. They were humanists, appreciative of the power of man, suspicious of traditions, and hopeful that the rule of superstition lay far behind.

The educators of nineteenth century New England opened the door for American freedom. They destroyed old superstitions, weakened the hold of obsolete institutions, and re-examined the American heritage. The result was that the thinkers who followed them could live more comfortably in the present and could think independently instead of being bound by the sterile teachings of the past.

The mind of New England in its religious interpretation was best represented by William Ellery Channing (1780–1842).[1] As a boy he had heard Samuel Hopkins, a staunch defender of Calvinism, speak incessantly about damnation. He had attended Harvard University, which in his youth was still quite conservative. Then, in Virginia, he had accepted a position as a tutor to a rich feudal family. He had read William Godwin and Mary Wollstonecraft. From them Channing absorbed a fervent faith in liberal principles, yet he never went to extremes. His words were measured and analytical; he had not the torrential eloquence of William Garrison or the passionate conviction of Wendell Phillips.

In his political thinking, he followed Jefferson, distrusting those who exercised too much political power; he was an insistent believer in freedom. The Puritans believed that it was their task to censor the thoughts and behavior of their followers. Channing, on the other hand, believed in no absolute doctrine and allowed a wide variety of opinion in the Unitarian fold. In fact there was such a wide divergence of views in this religious group that no real intellectual unity could be achieved.[2]

INDUSTRIALISM AND ROMANTICISM

The development which conditioned political thinking most powerfully was industrialism. It changed the landscape of New

[1] For varying interpretations of Channing see Schneider, "The Intellectual Background of William Ellery Channing," *Church History* VII (1938-39), pp. 3-23.

[2] Important also was the influence of universalism. See Richard Eddy, *Universalism in America;* Abel C. Thomas, *A Century of Universalism in Philadelphia and New York.*

England as well as the rest of the United States. Almost everywhere in New England large factories were built, and their products were exported to all parts of the world. The factory system created two extremes, a wealthy class which practised conspicuous consumption in a state of relative idleness, and the oppressed wage earners who were most interested in overcoming economic insecurity and in enjoying the basic pleasures of life.

It is true that New England liberals were concerned with improving the lot of the common man. But they had no real contact with the people. Theirs was an idealized version of the man on the street; a version which they absorbed from their books in their study rooms.

Almost unanimously they opposed the spread of industrialism. Wistfully, Emerson and Thoreau spoke of an agrarian economy. They did not answer the most pressing question of the modern age: "How can man adjust himself to mechanized culture?" They evaded that problem and instead turned to the needs of the individual, who by his own spiritual and emotional resources might transcend the limitations of the machine.

The most illustrious defender of New England industrialism was Daniel Webster (1782–1852), best known in American history as a defender of the federal union in his debate with Hayne. He was a man of unusual oratorical talents. "Liberty and union, now and forever" — these words re-echoed throughout the nation. In reality he was a staunch supporter of the powerful financial interests; following his wealthy constituents, he usually voted for a high tariff. He upheld the power of the Bank of the United States and his efforts in the Dartmouth case made the law of the contract a sacred part of American legal thinking.[3]

In economics he supported the main doctrines of Adam Smith, stressing competition and the importance of individual initiative. But his economic gospel was well adjusted to the needs of his own contemporary society; thus his conscience was not bothered when he advocated strong protection for American industries. His stand on tariffs is imitated by many conservatives in our time.

While the intellectuals in New England were enraged at the injustices of slavery, Webster, in his thinking, took a very sane view, at least so he believed. He had no patience for agitators either in the South or the North. He supported the Fugitive Slave Bill, an action which enraged the liberals. In his famous speech on March 7, 1850, he spoke of the advantages of the United States, its great

---

[3] Regarding the general economic thought of this period consult Dorfman, *The Economic Mind in American Civilization*, I, 362 ff; Gabriel, *The Course of American Democratic Thought*, pp. 78-87.

popular constitutional government, its absence of a monarchy and militarism, its love for freedom and equality, its lack of imperialism; but his sentiments did not impress the liberals like Whittier, who spoke of him as a dead man:

> So fallen! so lost! the light withdrawn
> Which once he wore!
> The glory from his gray hairs gone
> Forevermore!

The philosophy of the New England thinkers was characterized by Transcendentalism. It stood for an idealistic metaphysics, a faith in intuition, in the spiritual potentialities of man, and consequently opposed all empiricism.[4]

The motivating influence upon the mind of the New England thinker was the gospel of romanticism. It represented not the philosophy of Rousseau but that of Wordsworth, Coleridge, and Carlyle. The romanticism of New England was restrained and bookish, occasionally almost sterile in its academic tone.

Great was the influence of the German thinkers, especially of Goethe. He had inspired the minds of New England with the concept of a universal man. The American liberals tried to be not merely poets or professors or critics, but attempted to perfect all aspects of their cultural development.

Germany, to these minds, was the fatherland of real civilization; they admired German culture just as much as their descendants in the twentieth century would show contempt for it. To Emerson, Parker and Alcott, Germany was the most educated nation in Europe. German philosophy, German science, and German literature were far superior to the products of other European nations. After 1830 the education of most American writers was not considered complete until they had visited Germany.[5]

It is true that the French influence was likewise very strong, especially in Margaret Fuller, but to the New England thinker the French mind was essentially alien; it lacked the discipline, organization and profound philosophy found in Goethe, Fichte and Schelling.

---

[4] Regarding the Spirit of Transcendentalism consult O. B. Frothingham, *Transcendentalism in New England;* Van Wyck Brooks, *The Flowering of New England;* F. O. Matthiessen, *American Renaissance; Art and Expression in the Age of Emerson and Whitman.*

[5] Besides romanticism, the influence of Plato, the Neo-Platonists, the *Upanishads* and the moral earnestness of Calvinism can be detected in the New England thinkers.

EMERSON AND THE AMERICAN SCHOLAR

Emerson (1803–1882) was probably the most eloquent apostle of Transcendentalism. He was an individualist throughout his entire life. He resigned from his pastorate in the second Unitarian Church in Boston when he lost faith in the symbols of religion and when he could not tolerate any definite ritual. No party or religious sect could claim him.

In his age individualism was much stronger than in the present century when life has become more stereotyped. Comparing the attitude of the community of 1850 with that of the 1960's, one finds that intellectual tolerance has lessened. What would happen to Emerson today if he expressed his radical thoughts concerning the state? What would be the fate of Thoreau if he refused to pay his taxes?

Emerson's most famous contribution to American thinking was made in his Phi Beta Kappa address. Oliver Wendell Holmes said that it marked America's declaration of intellectual independence. This is an exaggeration — it was simply a prelude, the opening shot in the struggle for the liberation of the American mind.

The scholar, according to Emerson, derives his knowledge from three sources: first, from nature; secondly, from action; thirdly, from books. Most important of these is nature. It is the first and the formative influence which governs life. Nature is not mere disjointed and atomic force. It is not a realm in which merciless competition occurs, nor can it be explained solely by physical laws. Nature is the expression of a moral purpose; behind it is a spiritual fact, the Over-Soul, the principle of reality. In it is an undeniable identity, for all things are part of it. Thus, Emerson said, the ancient precept, "Know thyself" and the modern maxim, "Study nature" are, at last, united.

How different is this ideal from the modern schools of thought. Reading the books of Steinbeck, one finds a constant struggle between man and nature. The tragedy of existence, according to Sartre, is that there can be no common meeting-ground between nature and man. Hence there is a feeling of despair and skepticism which has not only pervaded European Literature, but has made a powerful impression upon the American mind.

To Emerson the scientific method is utterly inadequate. Like the Neo-Platonists, he relied upon intuition. Truth, in Emerson's system, is to be discovered and envisioned; it cannot be gained through painstaking analysis.[6] Undoubtedly there is a strain of mysticism in his philosophy, but this element in his mental make-up was restrained and did not prevent him from having a sharp and penetrating social insight.

The task of the thinker, according to Emerson, is to be part of the rhythm of nature. To the twentieth century world, this would lead to a gospel of skepticism; to Emerson it was an affirmation because all of nature revealed an identical purpose and represented the perfection of the universe.

When Emerson turned to books, he showed how they could both stimulate and hinder the intellectual development of man. He reminded his listeners that the greatest works of the past, like those of Cicero, Locke, and Bacon, were written in the youth of these authors who, thus, could not be infallible guides to the problems of life. The professors in the audience, worshiping books for their own sake, must have disapproved most vigorously. Dr. John Pierce later compared Emerson's speech with the "misty, dreamy and unintelligible style of Swedenborg, Coleridge, and Carlyle."

It is unfortunate that the American intellectual has not listened to Emerson, for it is quite apparent that the academic life of the United States is still guided by the medieval academic traditions. To read a list of the dissertation topics for Ph.D. theses is a most disillusioning experience. Trivial subjects seem to rank high in this type of scholarship. The learned journals of American culture are almost scholastic in their endless debates concerning technical points.[7]

Emerson said that one must be creative to read well. There is too much respect in the United States for the printed word, too much intellectual conformity, too much tolerance for second and third-rate political and economic ideas. And in achieving oral expression, the lack of sophistication of American audiences is even more apparent.

Most important of all, Emerson urges the thinker to be a man of action. To be a recluse intellectually was distasteful to his mind. Living in the past as so many American intellectuals are wont to do is a betrayal, for their insight is needed by the man on the street.

[6] Cf. Stewart G. Brown, "Emerson's Platonism," *New England Quarterly,* XVIII (1945), 325-345.

[7] Regarding the separation of theory and practice and the medieval conception of learning see John Dewey, *The School and Society,* pp. 41-44, 72-73.

Scholarship that is confined to books is hopelessly incomplete, for it lacks the earthy touch of experience.

To Emerson, character has a higher role than intellect. It does not matter so much what a man thinks: it is more important what he is. The Puritans were quite different in this respect. They were more concerned with the thoughts of the man than with his character development. Most Americans today would agree with Emerson; indeed, they distrust those who have too much intellect.

Here a definite danger arises. Critics like Brogan have seen the activistic aspects of American culture, and show how the modern American worships movement and change and dislikes to think about the goal of his endeavor. In such an atmosphere thinking is not welcome, for it may challenge the basic postulates of action.

Strangely enough Emerson in his Phi Beta Kappa speech mentioned Swedenborg as a pattern for the future man.[8] Emerson had a great respect for this thinker because Swedenborg saw the symbolic spirit of nature and showed how close the bonds were between the material and the spiritual worlds. Swedenborg's greatness was based upon a combination of theology and mathematics. Emerson, perhaps, went too far in his enthusiasm. Certainly Swedenborg in his influence upon civilization has been a more regressive than a liberating influence.

What are the duties of the scholar? Emerson replies:

They are such as become Man Thinking. They may all be comprised in self-trust. The office of the scholar is to cheer, to raise, and to guide men by showing them facts amidst appearances. He plies the slow, unhonored, and unpaid task of observation. Flamsteed and Herschel, in their glazed observatories, may catalogue the stars with the praise of all men, and the results being splendid and useful, honor is sure. But he, in his private observatory, cataloguing obscure and nebulous stars of the human mind, which as yet no man has thought of as such— watching days and months sometimes for a few facts; correcting still his old records;—must relinquish display and immediate fame. In the long period of his preparation he must betray often an ignorance and shiftlessness in popular arts, incurring the disdain of the able who shoulder him aside. Long he must stammer in his speech; often forgo the living for the. dead. Worse yet, he must accept — how often! — poverty and solitude. For the ease and pleasure of treading the old

---

[8] Besides Swedenborg, Emerson's technical philosophy owes much to Plato, Berkeley, Coleridge, Cousin, and Goethe. Cf. Kenneth W. Cameron, *Emerson the Essayist: An Outline of His Philosophic Development Through 1836*, vol. 1. The Oriental influence on Emerson is fully discussed in F. I. Carpenter, *Emerson and Asia*, and A. Christy, *The Orient in American Transcendentalism*.

road, accepting the fashions, the education, the religion of society, he takes the cross of making his own, and, of course, the self-accusation, the faint heart, the frequent uncertainty and loss of time, which are the nettles and tangling vines in the way of the self-relying and self-directed; and the state of virtual hostility in which he seems to stand to society, and especially to educated society. For all this loss and scorn, what offset? He is to find consolation in exercising the highest function of human nature. He is one who raises himself from private considerations and breathes and lives on public and illustrious thoughts. He is the world's eye. He is the world's heart. He is to resist the vulgar prosperity that retrogrades ever to barbarism, by preserving and communicating heroic sentiments, noble biographies, melodious verse, and the conclusions of history.[9]

The scholar is to resist the popular cry:

These being his functions, it becomes him to feel all confidence in himself, and to defer never to the popular cry. He and he only knows the world. The world of any moment is the merest appearance. Some great decorum, some fetish of a government, some ephemeral trade, or war, or man, is cried up by half mankind and cried down by the other half, as if all depended on this particular up or down. The odds are that the whole question is not worth the poorest thought which the scholar has lost in listening to the controversy. Let him not quit his belief that a popgun is a popgun, though the ancient and honorable of the earth affirm it to be the crack of doom. In silence, in steadiness, in severe abstraction, let him hold by himself; add observation to observation, patient of neglect, patient of reproach, and bide his own time — happy enough if he can satisfy himself alone that this day he has seen something truly. Success treads on every right step. For the instinct is sure, that prompts him to tell his brother what he thinks. He then learns that in going down into the secrets of his own mind he has descended into the secrets of all minds. He learns that he who has mastered any law in his private thoughts, is master to that extent of all men whose language he speaks, and of all into whose language his own can be translated. The poet, in utter solitude remembering his spontaneous thoughts and recording them, is found to have recorded that which men in crowded cities find true for them also. The orator distrusts at first the fitness of his frank confessions, his want of knowledge of the persons he addresses, until he finds that he is the complement of his hearers — that they drink his words because he fulfills for them their own nature; the deeper he dives into his privatest, secretest presentiment, to his wonder he finds this is the most acceptable, most public, and universally true. The people delight in it; the better part of every man feels, This is my music; this is myself.

---

[9] *American Scholar.*

In self-trust all the virtues are comprehended. Free should the scholar be — free and brave. Free even to the definition of freedom, "without any hindrance that does not arise out of his own constitution." Brave; for fear is a thing which a scholar by his very function puts behind him.[10]

The scholar is to promote the affirmative trends of his time:

I have dwelt perhaps tediously upon this abstraction of the Scholar. I ought not to delay longer to add what I have to say of nearer reference to the time and to this country.

Historically, there is thought to be a difference in the ideas which predominate over successive epochs, and there are data for marking the genius of the Classic, of the Romantic, and now of the Reflective or Philosophical age. With the views I have intimated of the oneness or the identity of the mind through all individuals, I do not much dwell on these differences. In fact, I believe each individual passes through all three. The boy is a Greek; the youth, romantic; the adult reflective. I deny not, however, that a revolution in the leading idea may be distinctly enough traced.

Our age is bewailed as the age of Introversion. Must that needs be evil? We, it seems, are critical; we are embarrassed with second thoughts; we cannot enjoy any thing for hankering to know whereof the pleasure consists; we are lined with eyes; we see with our feet; the time is infected with Hamlet's unhappiness —

"Sicklied o'er with the pale cast of thought."

It is so bad then? Sight is the last thing to be pitied. Would we be blind? Do we fear lest we should outsee nature and God, and drink truth dry? I look upon the discontent of the literary class as a mere announcement of the fact that they find themselves not in the state of mind of their fathers, and regret the coming state as untried; as a boy dreads the water before he has learned that he can swim. If there is any period one would desire to be born in, is it not the age of the Revolution; when the old and the new stand side by side and admit of being compared; when the energies of all men are searched by fear and by hope; when the historic glories of the old can be compensated by the rich possibilities of the new era? This time, like all times, is a very good one, if we but know what to do with it.[11]

Emerson calls for self-affirmation.

Another sign of our times, also marked by an analogous political movement, is the new importance given to the single person. Every thing that tends to insulate the individual — to surround him with

---

[10] *Ibid.*
[11] *Ibid.*

barriers of natural respect, so that each man shall feel the world is his, and man shall treat with man as a sovereign state — tends to true union as well as greatness. "I learned," said the melancholy Pestalozzi, "that no man in God's wide earth is either willing or able to help any other man." Help must come from the bosom alone. The scholar is that man who must take up into himself all the ability of the time, all the contributions of the past, all the hopes of the future. He must be an university of knowledges. If there be one lesson more than another which should pierce his ear, it is, The world is nothing, the man is all; in yourself is the law of all nature, and you know not yet how a globule of sap ascends; in yourself slumbers the whole of Reason; it is for you to know all; it is for you to dare all. Mr. President and Gentlemen, this confidence in the unsearched might of man belongs by all motives, by all prophecy, by all preparation, to the American Scholar. We have listened too long to the courtly muses of Europe. The spirit of the American freeman is already suspected to be timid, imitative, tame. Public and private avarice make the air we breathe thick and fat. The scholar is decent, indolent, complaisant. See already the tragic consequence. The mind of this country, taught to aim at low objects, eats upon itself. There is no work for any but the decorous and the complaisant.[12]

What is the solution? Emerson gave an optimistic answer:

They did not yet see, and thousands of young men as hopeful now crowding to the barriers for the career do not yet see, that if the single man plant himself indomitably on his instincts, and there abide, the huge world will come round to him. Patience — patience; with the shades of all the good and great for company; and for solace and perspective of your own infinite life; and for work the study and the communication of principles, the making those instincts prevalent, the conversion of the world. Is it not the chief disgrace in the world, not to be a unit; — not to be reckoned one character; — not to yield that peculiar fruit which each man was created to bear, but to be reckoned in the gross, in the hundred, or the thousand, of the party, the section, to which we belong; and our opinion predicted geographically as the north, or the south? Not so, brothers and friends — please God, ours shall not be so. We will walk on our own feet; we will work with our own hands; we will speak our own minds. The study of letters shall be no longer a name for pity, for doubt, and for sensual indulgence. The dread of man and the love of man shall be a wall of defense and a wreath of joy around all. A nation of men will for the first time exist, because each believes himself inspired by the Divine Soul which also inspires all men.[13]

---

[12] *Ibid.*
[13] *Ibid.*

Emerson, in a prophetic vein, warned against technology as a tool of salvation.

This thousand-handed art has introduced a new element into the state. The science of power is forced to remember the power of science. Civilization mounts and climbs.

Yes we have a pretty artillery of tools now in our social arrangement; we ride four times as fast as our fathers did; travel, grind, weave, forge, plant, till and excavate better. We have new shoes, gloves, glasses and gimlets; we have the calculus; we have the newspaper, which does its best to make every square acre of land and sea give an account of itself at your breakfast table; we have money, and paper money; we have language — the finest tool of all, and nearest to the mind. Much will have more. Man flatters himself that his command over Nature must increase. Things begin to obey him. We are to have the balloon yet, and the next war will be fought in the air. We may yet find a rose water that will wash the Negro white. He sees the skull of the English race changing from its Saxon type under the exigencies of American life.

Tantalus, who in old times was seen vainly trying to quench his thirst with a flowing stream which ebbed whenever he approached it, has been seen again lately. He is in Paris, in New York, in Boston. He is now in great spirits; thinks he shall reach it yet; thinks he shall bottle the ware. It is however getting a little doubtful. Things have an ugly look still. No matter how many centuries of culture have preceded, the new man always finds himself standing on the brink of chaos, always in a crisis. Can anybody remember when the times were not hard, and money not scarce? Can anybody remember when sensible men, and the right sort of men, and the right sort of women were plentiful? Tantalus begins to think steam a delusion, and galvanism no better than it should be.

Many facts concur to show that we must look deeper for our salvation than to steam, photographs, balloons or astronomy. These tools have some questionable properties. They are re-agents. Machinery is aggressive. The weaver becomes a web, the machinist a machine . . .[14]

Emerson sees his period as a sign of culture lag.

The machine unmakes the man. Now that the machine is so perfect, the engineer is nobody. Every new step in improving the engine restricts one more act of the engineer — unteaches him. Once it took Archimedes; now it only needs a fireman, and a boy to know the coppers, to pull up the handles or mind the water tank. But when the engine breaks they can do nothing.

---

[14] *Works and Days.*

What sickening details in the daily journals! I believe they have ceased to publish the *Newgate Calendar* and the *Pirate's Own Book* since the family newspapers, namely the *New York Tribune* and the *London Times*, have quite superseded them in the freshness as well as the horror of their records of crime. Politics were never more corrupt and brutal; and Trade, that pride and darling of our ocean, that educator of nations, that benefactor in spite of itself, ends in shameful defaulting, bubble and bankruptcy, all over the world.

What have these arts done for the character, for the worth of mankind? Are men better? 'T is sometimes questioned whether morals have not declined as the arts have ascended. Here are great arts and little men. Here is greatness begotten of paltriness. We cannot trace the triumphs of civilization to such benefactors as we wish. The greatest meliorator of the world is selfish, huckstering Trade. Every victory over matter ought to recommend to man the worth of his nature. But now one wonders who did all this good. Look up the inventors. Each has his own knack; his genius is in his veins and spots. But the great, equal, symmetrical brains, fed from a great heart, you shall not find. Everyone has more to hide than he has to show, or is lamed by his excellence. 'T is too plain that with the material power the moral progress has not kept pace. It appears that we have not made a judicious investment. Works and days were offered us, and we took works.[15]

He felt that we must learn to live in the present.

The world is always equal to itself, and every man in moments of deeper thought is apprised that he is repeating the experiences of the people in the streets of Thebes or Byzantium. An everlasting Now reigns in Nature, which hangs the same roses on our bushes which charmed the Roman and the Chaldean in their hanging gardens. "To what end, then," he asks, "should I study languages, and traverse counties, to learn so simple truths?"

History of ancient art, excavated cities, recovery of books and inscriptions — yes, the works were beautiful, and the history worth knowing; and academies convene to settle the claims of the old schools. What journeys and measurements — Niebuhr and Müller and Layard — to identify the plain of Troy and Nimroud town! And your homage to Dante costs you so much sailing; and to ascertain the discoverers of America needs as much voyaging as the discovery cost. Poor child! that flexible clay of which these old brothers molded their admirable symbols was not Persian, nor Memphian, nor Teutonic, nor local at all, but was common lime and silvex and water and sunlight, the heat of the blood and the heaving of the lungs; it was that clay which thou heldest but now in thy foolish hands, and threwest away to

---

[15] *Ibid.*

go and seek in vain in sepulchers, mummy pits and old bookshops of Asia Minor, Egypt and England. It was the deep today which all men scorn, the rich poverty which men hate; the populous, all-loving solitude which men quit for the tattle of towns. He lurks, *he* hides—*he* who is success, reality, joy and power. One of the illusions is that the present hour is not the critical, decisive hour. Write it on your heart that every day is the best day in the year.[16]

Emerson advocated spontaneity.

But life is good only when it is magical and musical, a perfect timing and consent, and when we do not anatomize it. You must treat the days respectfully, you must be a day yourself, and not interrogate it like a college professor. The world is enigmatical— everything said, and everything known or done — and must not be taken literally, but genially. We must be at the top of our condition to understand anything rightly. You must hear the bird's song without attempting to render it into nouns and verbs. Cannot we be a little abstemious and obedient? Cannot we let the morning be?

Everything in the universe goes by indirection. There are no straight lines. I remember well the foreign scholar who made a week of my youth happy by his visit. "The savages in the islands," he said, "delight to play with the surf, coming in on the top of the rollers, then swimming out again, and repeat the delicious maneuver for hours. Well, human life is made up of such transits. There can be no greatness without abandonment. But here your very astronomy is an espionage. I dare not go out of doors and see the moon and stars, but they seem to measure my tasks, to ask how many lines or pages are finished since I saw them last. Not so, as I told you, was it in Belleisle. The days at Belleisle were all different, and only joined by a perfect love of the same object. Just to fill the hour — that is happiness. Fill my hour, ye gods, so that I shall not say, whilst I have done this, 'Behold, also, an hour of my life is gone' — but rather, 'I have lived an hour.' "

We do not want factitious men, who can do any literary or professional feat, as, to write poems, or advocate a cause, or carry a measure for money; or turn their ability indifferently in any particular direction by the strong effort of will. No, what has been best done in the world — the works of genius — cost nothing. There is no painful effort, but it is the spontaneous flowing of the thought.[17]

As the great prophet of individualism, Emerson asserted that self-reliance was a sacred duty for man. While the social reformers were appealing for institutional change, Emerson thought that man's destiny demanded his own fulfillment rather than the perfection of

---

[16] *Ibid.*
[17] *Ibid.*

institutions.[18] His faith in the great man was unbounded. Here he anticipated Nietzsche; like him he worshiped the full development of man's physical, emotional and intellectual powers. Like Nietzsche, Emerson was not afraid of egotism; he regarded it as the mainspring of life.

FREEDOM AND EDUCATION

In his stress upon freedom Emerson became the spokesman of the American way of life. Could not a man rise in the United States regardless of social origin? In the twentieth century, however, realistic critics do not hold with this belief. While in the nineteenth century the social makeup of the United States had been fluid and had found a constant outlet through the frontier, definite class lines have appeared today, and the opportunities have decreased with the closing of the frontier.

An institution, according to Emerson, is "the lengthened shadow of a great man." In his essay, *Self-Reliance,* he showed how the Reformation was a result of Luther, how Quakerism developed because of Fox, Methodism because of Wesley, and gave numerous other examples. History itself is a very simple matter to Emerson, for it represents the biography of greatness. However, with the development of sociology, economics, and a more scientific viewpoint of history, we could maintain the opposite, that man is only a shortened shadow of an institution. The latter view is much more sober and disillusioning, for if man is a product of immutable forces in his environment, his life is determined from the very beginning, and his struggle frequently merely becomes an expression of futility.

While Emerson believed in the theoretical greatness of democracy, he never shut his eyes to the actual shortcomings of the American system. For Jacksonian democracy he had little sympathy; he regarded it as a rule of the demagogue and of the untutored, although he approved of its principles. The Whigs, who represented the business interests, he reproached for their subservience to the financiers and for their disregard for human rights, although he admired their cultured leadership.

Certainly Emerson was not a detached thinker when it came to the political issues of his time. He blasted the Fugitive Slave Bill and attacked Harvard College for being subservient to financial interests. Boston he dismissed as depressing to an emancipated mind.

---

[18] Cf. Schneider, *A History of American Philosophy,* p. 282.

How different were the actual political conditions from his Utopian dreams; he believed in a society in which the best and wisest would govern. He thought that the end of all governmental functions should be the welfare of the people, not the perpetuation of power. Instead of Machiavellian principles in legislation, he looked forward to an age in which good will would triumph.[19]

Emerson reminds us that the state is an artificial institution.

In dealing with the State we ought to remember that its institutions are not aboriginal, though they existed before we were born; that they are not superior to the citizen; that every one of them was once the act of a single man; every law and usage was a man's expedient to meet a particular case; that they all are imitable, all alterable; we may make as good, we may make better. Society is an illusion to the young citizen. It lies before him in rigid repose, with certain names, men and institutions rooted like oak-trees to the centre, round which all arrange themselves the best they can. But the old statesman knows that society is fluid; there are such roots and centres, but any particle may suddenly become the centre of the movement and compel the system to gyrate around it.[20]

"The law is only a memorandum," he asserted in a famous phrase. He expected little from either the conservative or the radical party.

The philosopher, the poet, or the religious man, will of course wish to cast his vote with the democrat, for free-trade, for wide suffrage, for the abolition of legal cruelties in the penal code, and for facilitating in every manner the access of the young and the poor to the sources of wealth and power. But he can rarely accept the persons whom the so-called popular party propose to him as representatives of these liberalities. They have not at heart the ends which give to the name of democracy what hope and virtue are in it. The spirit of our American radicalism is destructive and aimless; it is not loving; it has no ulterior and divine ends, but is destructive only out of hatred and selfishness. On the other side, the conservative party, composed of the most moderate, able and cultivated part of the population, is timid, and merely defensive of property. It vindicates no right, it aspires to no real good, it brands no crime, it proposes no generous policy; it does not build, nor write, nor cherish the arts, nor foster religion, nor establish schools, nor encourage science, nor emancipate the slave, nor befriend the poor, or the Indian, or the immigrant.

---

[19] For an interesting interpretation of Emerson see George Santayana, *Interpretations of Poetry and Religion*, pp. 217-233.

[20] *Politics.*

From neither party, when in power, has the world any benefit to expect in science, art, or humanity, at all commensurate with the resources of the nation.[21]

NATURE AND MORAL EDUCATION

From the standpoint of technical education his *Essay on Nature* is especially revealing. He maintained that without a theory of nature, philosophy and science remain superficial. Nature, to Emerson, consisted of the Not-me, including the universe and other people; also it referred to essences which are independent of the individual such as time, space, causality, etc. Thus we have two substances, the soul, or subject, and nature, the object.

Unfortunately only a few can see Nature.

Most persons do not see the sun. At least they have a very superficial seeing. The sun illuminates only the eye of the man, but shines into the eye and the heart of the child. The lover of nature is he whose inward and outward senses are still truly adjusted to each other; who has retained the spirit of infancy even into the era of manhood. His intercourse with heaven and earth becomes part of his daily food. In the presence of nature a wild delight runs through the man in spite of real sorrows. Nature says — he is my creature and maugre all his impertinent griefs, he shall be glad with me. Not the sun or the summer alone, but every hour and season yields its tribute of delight; for every hour and change corresponds to and authorizes a different state of the mind, from breathless noon to grimmest midnight. Nature is a setting that fits equally well a comic or a mourning piece. In good health, the air is a cordial of incredible virtue. Crossing a bare common, in snow puddles, at twilight, under a clouded sky, without having in my thoughts any occurrence of special good fortune, I have enjoyed a perfect exhilaration. I am glad to the brink of fear. In the woods, too, a man casts off his years, as the snake his slough, and at what period so-ever of life, is always a child. In the woods is perpetual youth.[22]

There is a definite relationship between man and nature.

The greatest delight which the fields and woods minister is the suggestion of an occult relation between man and the vegetable. I am not alone and unacknowledged. They nod to me, and I to them.

---

[21] *Ibid.*
[22] *Nature.*

The waving of the boughs in the storm is new to me and old. It takes me by surprise, and yet is not unknown. Its effect is like that of a higher thought or a better emotion coming over me, when I deemed I was thinking justly or doing right.

Yet it is certain that the power to produce this delight does not reside in nature, but in man, or in a harmony of both. It is necessary to use these pleasures with great temperance. For nature is not always tricked in holiday attire, but the same scene which yesterday breathed perfume and glittered as for the frolic of the nymphs, is overspread with melancholy today. Nature always wears the colors of the spirit. To a man laboring under calamity, the heat of his own fire hath sadness in it. Then there is a kind of contempt of the landscape felt by him who has just lost by death a dear friend. The sky is less grand as it shuts down over less worth in the population.[23]

Nature is allegorical and symbolic; behind it we find a spiritual fact. There is a close relationship between the laws of matter and the laws of thought; thus Emerson's system is *monistic*.

Nature also serves as an educational discipline. First, it instructs us in intellectual truth.

Our dealing with sensible objects is a constant exercise in the necessary lessons of difference, of likeness, of order, of being and seeming, of progressive arrangement; of ascent from particular to general; of combination to one end of manifold forces. Proportioned to the importance of the organ to be formed, is the extreme care with which its tuition is provided, — a care pretermitted in no single case. What tedious training, day after day, year after year, never ending, to form the common sense; what continual reproduction of annoyances, inconveniences, dilemmas; what rejoicing over us of little men; what disputing of prices, what reckoning of interest, — and all to form the Hand of the mind; — to instruct us that 'good thoughts are no better than good dreams, unless they be executed!'

Secondly, nature reflects the moral conscience.

All things are moral; and in their boundless changes have an unceasing reference to spiritual nature. Therefore is nature glorious with form, color, and motion; that every globe in the remotest heaven, every chemical change from the rudest crystal up to the laws of life, every change of vegetation from the first principle of growth in the eye of a leaf, to the tropical forest and antediluvian coal-mine, every animal function from the sponge up to Hercules, shall hint or thunder to man the laws of right and wrong, and echo the Ten Commandments.

[23] *Ibid.*

Therefore is Nature ever the ally of Religion; lends all her pomp and riches to the religious sentiment. Prophet and priest, David, Isaiah, Jesus, have drawn deeply from this source.[24]

Natural processes are not independent, but reveal moral laws.

The moral law lies at the centre of nature and radiates to the circumference. It is the pith and marrow of every substance, every relation, and every process. All things with which we deal, preach to us. What is a farm but a mute gospel? The chaff and the wheat, weeds and plants, blight, rain, insects, sun, — it is a sacred emblem from the first furrow of spring to the last stack which the snow of winter overtakes in the fields. But the sailor, the shepherd, the miner, the merchant, in their several resorts, have each an experience precisely parallel, and leading to the same conclusion: because all organizations are radically alike. Nor can it be doubted that this moral sentiment which thus scents the air, grows in the grain, and impregnates the waters of the world, is caught by man and sinks into his soul. The moral influence of nature upon every individual is that amount of truth which it illustrates to him.[25]

Idealism questions the reality of nature.

Our first institution in the Ideal philosophy is a hint from Nature herself.

Nature is made to conspire with spirit to emancipate us. Certain mechanical changes, a small alteration in our local position, apprises us of a dualism. We are strangely affected by seeing the shore from a moving ship, from a balloon, or through the tints of an unusual sky. The least change in our point of view gives the whole world a pictorial air. A man who seldom rides, needs only to get into a coach and traverse his own town, to turn the street into a puppet-show. The men, the women, — talking, running, bartering, fighting, — the earnest mechanic, the lounger, the beggar, the boys, the dogs, are unrealized at once, or, at least wholly detached from all relation to the observer, and seen as apparent, not substantial beings.[26]

The poet likewise gives a symbolic interpretation of the universe.

By a few strokes he delineates, as on air, the sun, the mountain, the camp, the city, the hero, the maiden, not different from what we know them but only lifted from the ground and afloat before the eye. He unfixes the land and the sea, makes them revolve around the axis of his primary thought, and disposes them anew. Possessed himself

---

[24] *Ibid.*
[25] *Ibid.*
[26] *Ibid.*

by a heroic passion, he uses matter as symbols of it. The sensual man conforms thoughts to things; the poet conforms things to his thoughts. The one esteems nature as rooted and fast; the other, as fluid, and impresses his being thereon. To him, the refractory world is ductile and flexible; he invests dust and stones with humanity, and makes them the words of the Reason.[27]

The philosopher also emphasizes the ideal realm.

But the philosopher, not less than the poet, postpones the apparent order and relations of things to the empire of thought. "The problem of philosophy," according to Plato, "is, for all that exists conditionally, to find a ground unconditioned and absolute." It proceeds on the faith that a law determines all phenomena, which being known, the phenomena can be predicted. That law, when in the mind, is an idea. Its beauty is infinite. The true philosopher and the true poet are one, and a beauty, which is truth, and a truth, which is beauty, is the aim of both. Is not the charm of one of Plato's or Aristotle's definitions strictly like that of the *Antigone* of Sophocles? It is, in both cases, that a spiritual life has been imparted to nature; that the solid seeming block of matter has been pervaded and dissolved by a thought; that this feeble human being has penetrated the vast masses of nature with an informing soul, and recognized itself in their harmony, that is, seized their law.[28]

Emerson admonished us to look at nature with a fresh outlook.

Know then that the world exists for you. For you is the phenomenon perfect. What we are, that only can we see. All that Adam had, all that Caesar could, you have and can do. Adam called his house, heaven and earth; Caesar called his house, Rome; you perhaps call yours, a cobbler's trade; a hundred acres of ploughed land; or a scholar's garret. Yet line for line and point for point your dominion is as great as theirs, though without fine names. Build therefore your own world. As fast as you conform your life to the pure idea in your mind, that will unfold its great proportions. A correspondent revolution in things will attend the influx of the spirit. So fast will disagreeable appearances, swine, spiders, snakes, pests, mad-houses, prisons, enemies, vanish; they are temporary and shall be no more seen. The sordor and filths of nature, the sun shall dry up and the wind exhale. As when the summer comes from the south, the snow-banks melt and the face of the earth becomes green before it, so shall the advancing spirit create its ornaments along its path, and carry with it the beauty it visits and the song which enchants it; it shall draw beautiful faces, warm hearts, wise discourse, and heroic acts, around its way, until evil is no

---

[27] *Ibid.*
[28] *Ibid.*

more seen. The kingdom of man over nature, which cometh not with observation, — a dominion such as now is beyond his dream of God, — he shall enter without more wonder than the blind man feels who is gradually restored to perfect sight.[29]

THE OVER-SOUL

The synthesis of nature and the soul is accomplished by the Over-Soul, the principle of reality and oneness.

The Supreme Critic on the errors of the past and the present and the only prophet of that which must be, is that great nature in which we rest as the earth lies in the soft arms of the atmosphere; that Unity, that Over-Soul, within which every man's particular being is contained and made one with all other; that common heart of which all sincere conversation is the worship, to which all right action is submission; that over-powering reality which confutes our tricks and talents, and constrains every one to pass for what he is, and to speak from his character and not from his tongue, and which evermore tends to pass into our thought and hand and become wisdom and virtue and power and beauty. We live in succession, in division, in parts, in particles. Meantime within man is the soul of the whole; the wise silence; the universal beauty, to which every part and particle is equally related . . .
We are wiser than we know. If we will not interfere with our thought, but will act entirely, or see how the thing stands in God, we know the particular thing, and every man. For the Maker of all things and all persons stands behind us and casts his dread omniscience through us over things.[30]

Thus Emerson expressed in this essay almost a neo-Platonic concept of life. The universe is the emanation of the divine force; separateness is an illusion. The soul, not matter, is real. We realize that there is a union between man and God, and this indicates that evil has no real status. Like Plotinus, Emerson reacted against rationalism; he asserted that we can only have a *vision* of reality; we are unable to define it.

RELIGIOUS EDUCATION

Emerson was attacked sharply for his views which he expressed in his speech before the Senior Class in Divinity College of Harvard

---

[29] *Ibid.*
[30] *Over-Soul.*

in 1838. He started by asserting the reality of moral laws which are beyond spatial and temporal determinations.

> The sentiment of virtue is a reverence and delight in the presence of certain divine laws. It perceives that this homely game of life we play, covers, under what seem foolish details, principles that astonish. The child amidst his baubles is learning the action of light, motion, gravity, muscular force; and in the game of human life, love, fear, justice, appetite, man, and God, interact. These laws refuse to be adequately stated. They will not be written out on paper, or spoken by the tongue. They elude our persevering thought; yet we read them hourly in each other's faces, in each other's actions, in our own remorse. The moral traits which are all globed into every virtuous act and thought, — in speech we must sever, and describe or suggest by painful enumeration of many particulars. Yet, as this sentiment is the essence of all religion, let me guide your eye to the precise objects of the sentiment, by an enumeration of some of those classes of facts in which this element is conspicuous.
>
> The intuition of the moral sentiment is an insight of the perfection of the laws of the soul. These laws execute themselves. They are out of time, out of space, and not subject to circumstance. Thus in the soul of man there is a justice whose retributions are instant and entire. He who does a good deed is instantly ennobled. He who does a mean deed is by the action itself contracted. He who puts off impurity, thereby puts on purity. If a man is at heart just, then in so far is he God; the safety of God, the immortality of God, the majesty of God do enter into that man with justice. If a man dissemble, deceive, he deceives himself, and goes out of acquaintance with his own being. A man in the view of absolute goodness, adores, with total humility. Every step so downward, is a step upward. The man who renounces himself, comes to himself.[31]

Religion must be based on intuition, not on revelation.

> Meantime, whilst the doors of the temple stand open, night and day, before every man, and the oracles of this truth cease never, it is guarded by one stern condition; this, namely; it is an intuition. It cannot be received at second hand. Truly speaking, it is not instruction, but provocation, that I can receive from another soul. What he announces, I must find true in me, or reject; and on his word, or as his second, be he who he may, I can accept nothing. On the contrary, the absence of this primary faith is the presence of degradation. As is the flood, so is the ebb. Let this faith depart, and the very words it spake and the things it made become false and hurtful. Then falls the church, the state, art, letter, life. The doctrine of the divine nature being forgotten, a sickness infects and dwarfs the constitution. Once

---

[31] *The Divinity School Address.*

man was all; now he is an appendage, a nuisance. And because the indwelling Supreme Spirit cannot wholly be got rid of, the doctrine of it suffers this perversion, that the divine nature is attributed to one or two persons, and denied to all the rest, and denied with fury. The doctrine of inspiration is lost; the base doctrine of the majority of voices usurps the place of the doctrine of the soul.[32]

The error of historical Christianity is its emphasis on ritual and theology.

Historical Christianity has fallen into the error that corrupts all attempts to communicate religion. As it appears to us, and as it has appeared for ages, it is not the doctrine of the soul, but an exaggeration of the personal, the positive, the ritual. It has dwelt, it dwells, with noxious exaggeration about the *person* of Jesus. The soul knows no persons. It invites every man to expand to the full circle of the universe, and will have no preferences but those of spontaneous love. But by this eastern monarchy of a Christianity, which indolence and fear have built, the friend of man is made the injurer of man. The manner in which his name is surrounded with expressions which were once sallies of admiration and love, but are now petrified into official titles, kills all generous sympathy and liking. All who hear me, feel the language that describes Christ to Europe and America is not the style of friendship and enthusiasm to a good and noble heart, but is appropriated and formal, — paints a demigod, as the Orientals or the Greeks would describe Osiris or Apollo. Accept the injurious impositions of our early catechetical instruction, and even honesty and self-denial were but splendid sins, if they did not wear the Christian name.[33]

Moreover, Christianity stresses too much the sterile traditions of the past.

The Church seems to totter to its fall, almost all life extinct. On this occasion, any complaisance would be criminal which told you, whose hope and commission it is to preach the faith of Christ, that the faith of Christ is preached.

It is time that this ill-suppressed murmur of all thoughtful men against the famine of our church; — this moaning of the heart because it is bereaved of the consolation, the hope, the grandeur that come alone out of the culture of the moral nature, — should be heard through the sleep of indolence, and over the din of routine. This great and perpetual office of the preacher is not discharged. Preaching is the expression of the moral sentiment in application to the duties of life. In how many churches, by how many prophets, tell me, is man made sensible that he is an infinite Soul; that the earth and heavens are

---

[32] *Ibid.*
[33] *Ibid.*

passing into his mind; that he is drinking forever the soul of God? Where now sounds the persuasion, that by its very melody imparadises my heart, and so affirms its own origin in heaven? Where shall I hear words such as in elder ages drew men to leave all and follow, — father and mother, house and land, wife and child? Where shall I hear these august laws of moral being so pronounced as to fill my ear, and I feel ennobled by the offer of my uttermost action and passion?[34]

What are the remedies? Salvation must be found in the soul, in a living, dynamic faith.

The remedy is already declared in the ground of our complaint of the Church. We have contrasted the Church with the Soul. In the soul then let the redemption be sought. Wherever a man comes, there comes revolution. The old is for slaves. When a man comes, all books are legible, all things transparent, all religions are forms. He is religious. Man is the wonder-worker. He is seen amid miracles. All men bless and curse. He saith yea and nay, only. The stationariness of religion; the assumption that the age of inspiration is past, that the Bible is closed; the fear of degrading the character of Jesus by representing him as a man; — indicate with sufficient clearness the falsehood of our theology. It is the office of a true teacher to show us that God is, not was; that He speaketh, not spake. The true Christianity, — a faith like Christ's in the infinitude of man, — is lost.[35]

We must not be conformists.

Yourself a newborn bard of the Holy Ghost, cast behind you all conformity, and acquaint men at first hand with Deity. Look to it first and only, that fashion, custom, authority, pleasure, and money, are nothing to you, — are not bandages over your eyes, that you cannot see, — but live with the privilege of the immeasurable mind. Not too anxious to visit periodically all families and each family in your parish connection, — when you meet one of these men or women, be to them a divine man; be to them thought and virtue; let their timid aspirations find in you a friend; let their trampled instincts be genially tempted out in your atmosphere; let their doubts know that you have doubted, and their wonder feel that you have wondered. By trusting your own heart, you shall gain more confidence in other men.[36]

In concluding this essay, Emerson looked to a new teacher.

I look for the hour when that supreme Beauty which ravished the souls of those Eastern men, and chiefly of those Hebrews, and through

---

[34] *Ibid.*
[35] *Ibid.*
[36] *Ibid.*

their lips spoke oracles to all time, shall speak in the West also. The Hebrew and Greek Scriptures contain immortal sentences, that have been bread of life to millions. But they have no epical integrity; are fragmentary; are not shown in their order to the intellect. I look for the new Teacher that shall follow so far those shining laws that he shall see them come full circle; shall see their rounding complete grace; shall see the world to be the mirror of the soul; shall see the identity of the law of gravitation with the purity of heart; and shall show that the Ought, that Duty, is one thing with Science, with Beauty, and with Joy.[37]

EDUCATIONAL AND PHILOSOPHICAL CONTRIBUTIONS OF EMERSON

While Emerson's system lacked systematic organization, its main outlines can be clearly described.

(1)   In his approach to knowledge and philosophy, he urged an independent and creative attitude. We are not to be guided by the past, but by the present. We learn not merely from books, but also from nature and people. Ideas must be applied functionally to reveal the moral purpose of the universe. Most famous is his call for a declaration of independence on the part of the American scholar.

(2)   In his epistemology he dwelt on intuition. Both reason and sensation are inferior compared with intuition. Reality cannot be defined; it can only be visualized and felt. Self-knowledge and knowledge of nature are not opposed to each other; rather, both belong together and supplement each other.

(3)   In his metaphysical system he starts with a dualistic assumption: Nature and the Soul, the One and the Many, Unity and Variety. However, this dualism is not metaphysically real; both nature and the soul and all other phenomenal manifestations are part of the *Over-Soul*, the principle of reality.

As for the categories of science such as space, time, and causality, they do not characterize reality, which is beyond spatial and temporal determinations.

(4)   In religion Emerson was a mystic, but unlike the Eastern mystics he emphasized the pragmatic and concrete effects of contemplation. He rejected any type of religion based on tradition and revelation. To him the religious experience was dynamic and progressive and not confined to one sect, one nation, or one man. For its vitality it depended on the power of intuition, which precluded ritual.

[37] *Ibid.*

(5) In his ethical and political doctrines Emerson upheld the gospel of individualism. Thus he preached self-reliance and indicated that governments exist for the sake of man; that in fact wise men need no governments at all. He taught that evil has no metaphysical reality; that the universe is based on invariable moral laws, which establish a definite system of cosmic justice.

(6) His general philosophical viewpoint can best be described as idealism. This, however, did not lead Emerson to the subjectivism of Berkeley or to Hegel's absolute Idealism. Rather it implied to him that mind is more significant than matter and that nature reveals moral purposes and is symbolic of spiritual perfection.

This meant that Emerson did not welcome the gospel of naturalism. While there are evolutionary features in his system, they are on a qualitative plane. Emerson asserted that it is the task of man to realize the purity of the soul; in short to find the Over-Soul, in which all his doubts will be abolished and all his conflicts resolved.

The idealism of Emerson demanded a new type of education: not a system dedicated to the past, but one which explored the day after tomorrow: not one which stressed analytical knowledge but one which explored the wisdom of the heart.

CHAPTER THIRTEEN

Horace Mann

INFLUENCES

Among the pioneers of American education Horace Mann (1796–1859) deserves an honored place. His own career illustrates the importance of the educative process. Born in Franklin, Massachusetts, he received only the most rudimentary training until he was fifteen. A travelling schoolmaster gave him a few lessons during the year, but most of his learning he acquired himself. He studied day and night and was able to enter Brown University, where he made a brilliant record. At this time law was his major interest. In 1827 he was elected to the Massachusetts House of Representatives. A noted political career seemed to open up for him. But he became more interested in education than in law. Indeed, he was responsible for the establishment of the state board of education and became its first secretary. When asked why he exchanged law for education he replied that "the interests of a client are small compared with the interests of the next generation."

With single-minded dedication he labored for the cause of education. One of his aims was to abolish the cruel punishments which were current at his time. In most schools of his time there were at least ten to twenty floggings a day. Schoolmasters, influenced by the Calvinist gospel, believed that it was their duty to drive the devil out of the students. Was the child not a creature of sin? Was not hell-fire a fitting punishment for the child who disobeyed his teachers and parents? Was not flogging an aid to learning?

Horace Mann was brought up as a Calvinist, but became a Unitarian. He believed that human nature is basically good, that all human beings have the potential for creativity and growth. Excessive punishment only meant a stifling of individualism. It encouraged sadism and disregarded the rights and integrity of the students. In a report on Prussian education he noted that physical punishments were rarely used, and yet Prussia had excellent discipline.

The schoolmasters of his time were not convinced by his arguments. They felt that abolishing physical punishments would open the door to chaos. Such a step could diminish their authority and might be a prelude to open rebellion. Still, the ideals of Horace Mann prevailed and education has been elevated because of him.

The school buildings in his time were often like hovels. They symbolized the community's disrespect for education. Lighting was inadequate; many of the school buildings were unsafe and unsanitary. Mann saw to it that numerous new buildings were created and that they embodied better standards of planning and beauty and also were more conducive to learning. Through his reports, through many letters, through speeches and lectures, and lobbying in the state legislature and Congress he publicized the need for better public education. Often the response was hostile. Once when he and the governor of Massachusetts were to address an audience they arrived to find the hall dark and the floor unswept. Mann promptly took off his coat and swept the hall.

Education must be more than intellectual training, more than an exercise of one's abilities or a mere study of the past. Mann saw education as a tool of liberation, whereby the poor could rise on the social ladder; a tool whereby the Negro could become emancipated and the handicapped child learn to adjust to his environment and find a meaningful life.

To Horace Mann, the school was the foundation of democracy. Here rich and poor could learn together; here the young and the old were united in a common search; here were no frontiers to learning; here intellect and character merged and the past became the prelude to a more meaningful future.

Like Pestalozzi, who had a great impact on his thinking, Mann believed in training by vocational experience. He felt that the child should learn to use his senses, that he should take nature as the point of departure. He enriched the curriculum with such subjects as hygiene, drawing, and music. Rather than a classical basis, learning should have a utilitarian purpose so that man and society could be improved.

All this demanded a new conception of instruction. He was responsible for lengthening the school term and raising teachers' salaries. To make learning as enjoyable as possible he helped to introduce new textbooks designed to show a relationship between intellectual knowledge and the problems of society.

When he was a boy, he read almost all the 116 volumes in the library in Franklin, Massachusetts. Most schools of his time had inadequate library facilities. Mann organized many school libraries so that books could become part of the student's daily life. He believed less in formal assignments than in individual learning. What the student discovers for himself, when his own interests govern his reading, has more value than stereotyped assignments.

The basis of education, Mann argued, was reading. This meant an exercise of intellectual curiosity. It implied a knowledge of the great authors of the past. Books, to him as to Thoreau, are the real wealth of mankind. Their function was to liberate mankind from the narrow limitations of his environment.

Mann was responsible for the establishment of the first normal school, which opened its doors in 1839 in Lexington, Massachusetts. Only three students attended, but the idea soon spread to many parts of the nation and was widely imitated. Mann believed that teachers' training should be intellectual, moral and esthetic. Intellectually, they ought to have specific competence and a wide knowledge of the humanities. Morally, they should be models in their enthusiasm for education; indeed, to Mann education was the supreme embodiment of morality. Esthetically, they were to develop a sense of beauty in their students, who could eventually transform their own communities, so that ugliness would be supplanted by real esthetic appreciation.

His greatest controversy was with orthodox members of the clergy. Mann regarded Jesus as a supreme teacher whose ideals of love ought to be imitated, but he had no use for religion in the classroom. Did not ecclesiasticism lead to regression and was not dogmatism incompatible with the open mind which ought to prevail

in education? Were not the basic religious concepts, such as original sin and eternal punishment, replicas of an obsolete age? Should
not education be safeguarded from any outside interference?

The result was that Horace Mann was attacked in many sermons
in Boston. The Reverend Smith regarded him as a representative of
evil and viewed his ideas as being subversive both to religion and to
morality. To the Reverend Smith, Horace Mann was a radical reformer whose concepts would lead to the decline of society and whose
ideals of democracy might open the door to revolution.

Thus the Reverend Mr. Smith wrote to Mann:

1. I regard you as the representative of a system, or its head,
which seeks to change, slowly, perhaps, but surely, the whole system
of education in common schools—the result of which will be to elevate
the intellectual over the moral, and man above God. In detail and in
element I conceive your notions, in this matter, to be crude, their fruits
destructive; and the more I have seen your system explained, the
worse, to my mind, it appears.

2. Are you in favor of the use of the rod as the principal means of
enforcing obedience? That you tolerate it in deference to public sentiment, I do not dispute. But I am misinformed if you are not against its
use, and do not, as you have opportunity, discountenance its use.[1]

In a sermon Smith charged that "even now, in our best city
schools, insubordination and licentiousness abound." All this he attributed to the heretical opinions of Horace Mann.

IDEALS

In his Report in 1848 Mann stressed the importance of the schoolroom.

I proceed, then, in endeavoring to show how the true business of
the schoolroom connects itself, and becomes identical, with the great
interests of society. The former is the infant, immature state of those
interests; the latter their developed, adult state. As "the child is father
to the man," so may the training of the schoolroom expand into the
institutions and fortunes of the State.[2]

Next he turns to intellectual education as an aid to equality.

According to the European theory, men are divided into classes, —
some to toil and earn, others to seize and enjoy. . . .

[1] Smith, *The Ark of God on a New Cart*, pp. 23 ff.
[2] *Report of the Secretary of the Board of Education of Massachusetts for 1848.*

Our ambition as a State should trace itself to a different origin, and propose to itself a different object. Its flame should be lighted as the skies. Its radiance and its warmth should reach the darkest and coldest abodes of men. It should seek the solution of such problems as these: To what extent can competence displace pauperism? How nearly can we free ourselves from the low-minded and the vicious, not by their expatriation, but by their elevation? To what extent can the resources and powers of Nature be converted into human welfare, the peaceful arts of life be advanced, and the vast treasures of human talent and genius be developed? How much of suffering, in all its forms, can be relieved? or, what is better than relief, how much can be prevented? Cannot the classes of crimes be lessened, and the number of criminals in each class be diminished? Our exemplars, both for public and private imitation, should be the parables of the lost sheep and of the lost piece of silver. When we have spread competence through all the abodes of poverty, when we have substituted knowledge for ignorance in the minds of the whole people, when we have reformed the vicious and reclaimed the criminal, then may we invite all neighboring nations to behold the spectacle, and say to them, in the conscious elation of virtue, "Rejoice with me, for I have found that which was lost."

Now, surely nothing but universal education can counterwork this tendency to the domination of capital and the servility of labor. If one class possesses all the wealth and the education, while the residue of society is ignorant and poor, it matters not by what name the relation between them may be called; the latter, in fact and in truth, will be the servile dependents, and subjects of the former. But if education be equally diffused, it will draw property after it by the strongest of all attractions; for such a thing never did happen, and never can happen, as that an intelligent and practical body of men should be permanently poor. . . .[3]

Intelligence, he stated, is the condition of wealth.

For the creation of wealth, then, for the existence of a wealthy people and a wealthy nation, intelligence is the grand condition. The number of improvers will increase as the intellectual constituency, if I may so call it, increases. In former times, and in most parts of the world even at the present day, not one man in a million has ever had such a development of mind as made it possible for him to become a contributor to art or science. Let this development precede, and contributions, numberless, and of inestimable value, will be sure to follow. That political economy, therefore, which busies itself about capital and labor, supply and demand, interest and rents, favorable and unfavorable balances of trade, but leaves out of account the element of a widespread mental development, is nought but stupendous folly. The greatest of all arts in political economy is to change a con-

---

[3] *Ibid.*

sumer into a producer; and the next greatest is to increase the producer's producing power, — an end to be directly attained by increasing his intelligence.[4]

Then he turns to political education.

The necessity of general intelligence, — that is, of education (for I use the terms as substantially synonymous, because general intelligence can never exist without general education, and general education will be sure to produce general intelligence), — the necessity of general intelligence under a republican form of government, like most other very important truths, has become a very trite one. It is so trite, indeed, as to have lost much of its force by its familiarity. Almost all the champions of education seize on this argument first of all, because it is so simple as to be understood by the ignorant, and so strong as to convince the skeptical.[5]

Education, Mann believed, involves controversy.

Shall all teaching relative to the nature of our government be banished from our schools? and shall our children be permitted to grow up in entire ignorance of the political history of their country? In the schools of a republic, shall the children be left without any distinct knowledge of the nature of a republican government, or only with such knowledge as they may pick up from angry political discussions, or from party newspapers, from caucus speeches, or Fourth-of-July orations, — the Apocrypha of Apocrypha?

Surely, between these extremes, there must be a medium not difficult to be found. And is not this middle course, which all sensible and judicious men, all patriots, and all genuine republicans, must approve? — namely, that those articles in the creed of republicanism which are accepted by all, believed in by all, and which form the common basis of our political faith shall be taught to all. But when the teacher, in the course of his lessons or lectures on the fundamental law, arrives at a controverted text, he is either to read it without comment or remark; or, at most, he is only to say that the passage is the subject of disputation, and that the schoolroom is neither the tribunal to adjudicate, nor the forum to discuss it.

Such being the rule established by common consent, and such the practice observed with fidelity under it, it will come to be universally understood that political proselytism is no function of the school, but that indoctrination into matters of controversy between hostile political parties is to be elsewhere sought for, and elsewhere imparted. Thus may all the children of the Commonwealth receive instruction in all

[4] *Ibid.*
[5] *Ibid.*

the great essentials of political knowledge, — in those elementary ideas without which they will never be able to investigate more recondite and debatable questions; thus will the only practicable method be adopted for discovering new truths, and for discarding, instead of perpetuating, old errors; and thus, too, will the pernicious race of intolerant zealots, whose whole faith may be summed up in two articles — that they themselves are always infallibly right, and that all dissenters are certainly wrong, — be extinguished.[6]

He advocated moral education.

Moral education is a primal necessity of social existence. The unrestrained passions of men are not only homicidal, but suicidal; and a community without a conscience would soon extinguish itself. . .

Education has never been brought to bear with one-hundredth part of its potential force upon the natures of children, and, through them, upon the character of men and of the race. In all the attempts to reform mankind which have hitherto been made, whether by changing the frame of government, by aggravating or softening the severity of the penal code, or by substituting government-created for a God-created religion — in all these attempts, the infantile and youthful mind, its amenability to influences, and the enduring and self-operating character of the influence it receives, have been almost wholly unrecognized. Here, then, is a new agency, whose powers are but just beginning to be understood, and whose mighty energies hitherto have been but feebly invoked; and yet from our experience, limited and imperfect as it is, we do know, that, far beyond any other earthly instrumentality, it is comprehensive and decisive. . . .[7]

Religious education, he felt, adds to public education.

But it will be said that this grand result in practical morals is a consummation of blessedness that can never be attained without religion, and that no community will ever be religious without religious education. Both these propositions I regard as eternal and immutable truths. . . .[8]

He describes his own religious feelings.

. . . I was originally a member, and from which I have always sought counsel and guidance; and in justice to thousands of the most wise, upright, and religious-minded men in Massachusetts, who have been my fellow-laborers in advancing the great cause of popular education, under the auspices of this system, — I have felt bound to

---

[6] *Ibid.*
[7] *Ibid.*
[8] *Ibid.*

vindicate it from the aspersions cast upon it, and to show its con-
sonance with the eternal principles of equity and justice. I have felt
bound to show, that so far from its being an irreligious, an anti-
Christian, or an un-Christian system, it is a system which recognizes
religious obligations in their fullest extent; that it is a system which
invokes a religious spirit, and can never be fitly administered without
such a spirit; that it inculcates the great commands upon which hang
all the law and the prophets; that it welcomes the Bible, and therefore
welcomes all the doctrines which the Bible really contains; and that
it listens to these doctrines so reverently, that, for the time being, it
will not suffer any rash mortal to thrust in his interpolations of their
meaning, or overlay the text with any of the 'many inventions' which
the heart of man has sought out. It is a system, however, which leaves
open all other means of instruction – the pulpits, the Sunday schools,
the Bible classes, the catechisms, of all denominations ,– to be employed according to the preferences of individual parents. It is a
system which restrains itself from teaching that what it does teach is
all that needs to be taught, or that should be taught; but leaves this to
be decided by each man for himself, according to the light of his
reason and conscience, and on his responsibility to that Great Being,
who, in holding him to account for the things done in the body, will
hold him to the strictest account for the manner in which he has
'trained up' his children. . . .[9]

He praises the pilgrim fathers who felt

if they could give knowledge and virtue to their children, they gave
them all things. . . . *We have our futurity as they had theirs,* – a
futurity rapidly hastening upon us, – a futurity now fluid, – ready,
as clay in the hands of the potter, to be moulded into every form of
beauty and excellence; but so soon as it reaches our hands, so soon
as it receives the impress of our plastic touch, whether this touch be
for good or evil, it is to be struck into the adamant of the unchanging
and unchangeable past. Into whose form and likeness shall we fashion
this flowing futurity, – of Mammon, of Moloch, or of Jesus? Clear,
and more clear, out of the dimness of coming time, emerge to the
vision of faith the myriad hosts of the generations that shall succeed
us. Those generations are to stand in our places, to be called by our
names, and to accept the heritage of joy or of woe which we shall
bequeath them. Shall they look back upon us with veneration for our
wisdom and beneficent forecast, or with shame at our selfishness and
degeneracy? Our ancestors were noble examples to us; shall we be
ignoble examples to our posterity?[10]

---

[9] *Ibid.*
[10] *Ibid.*

FIGHTER FOR FREEDOM

Horace Mann did not remain neutral regarding the great issues of his time. When he was elected to Congress in 1848 he denounced slavery in bitter terms. He attacked the ravages of the industrial system. He urged that workers be better paid, that child labor be curbed, that factories become more sanitary and that slums be eliminated. No educator, he said, could remain neutral about social injustice. His ideals and aspirations were to be applied to society; otherwise, education would be mere theory.

How was the new society to be established? Mann rejected the doctrine of revolution. This would only create counter-violence; it would not abolish fundamental evils. A better way was through education which would open new doors to the underprivileged. Science and technology would aid the emancipation of the poor, who would use the machines to achieve higher economic standards and more leisure. While Thoreau viewed the machine as an aid to enslavement, Mann felt that it would enlarge human powers. The machine, Mann felt, would control nature and would increase human power so that human beings could become the kings of creation.

When Horace Mann became president of Antioch College in 1852, he again exhibited his independent genius. Antioch College was to be a unique institution: there were to be no class-barriers; women were to be admitted—a radical step for his time; there were to be no color bars. Students, he felt, ought to have intellectual and work experiences, the college was to be a truly democratic institution; indeed the students were to share in the administration.

In the classroom at Antioch the professor was not to be an oracle of Truth, rather a friendly guide to knowledge. Discussion and the seminar method were to be encouraged. Mann believed that a rigid curriculum was incompatible with intellectual democracy; hence he urged a stress upon electives. This meant that students could pursue their own interests and that their differences could be explored.

While most educators of his time stressed an exclusive mental training, Mann urged the cultivation of physical training. Would not the mind suffer when the body was neglected? Was not physical education a preparation for an active life? Did not physical exercises increase the enjoyment of human existence?

He had little regard for the lessons of the past. To him, history was a story of errors and follies. Like Jefferson, he felt that every generation had to make its own history.

He remarked that many of his students at Antioch had more brilliance than their professors. The task of the college, he felt, was to keep their interests alive, to intensify their curiosity and not to stifle their identity. To him, administration meant gentle encouragement and unwavering humanitarianism. In a commencement speech in 1859 he summarized his philosophy by saying: *"Be ashamed to die until you have won some victory for humanity."*

Engraved by H.W. Smith

Henry Barnard

CHAPTER FOURTEEN

Henry Barnard

CRUSADE FOR BETTER SCHOOLS

Henry Barnard (1811-1900) was secretary of the Board of Education in Connecticut, principal of an important normal school, in 1845 became State Superintendent of Education in Rhode Island, and in 1867 was elected as the first U. S. Commissioner of Education. He also served as Chancellor of the University of Wisconsin and President of St. Johns College in Maryland. He contributed widely to education by his editorship of the *American Journal of Education* which became a noted tool of dissemination of new ideas in Europe and in the United States.

Henry Barnard represents statesmanship in education. Elisha R. Potter, who was his successor in Rhode Island, declared that Barnard could attract the support of divergent parties and that he could work even with those who opposed him politically. Barnard saw himself as an apostle of knowledge. What mattered to him was not his own advancement and his own glory, but the cause of the teacher, who, to him, was the light of civilization.

Concerned with the improvement of pedagogy, he helped to initiate in 1859 the teachers' institute. The aim of the program was to acquaint teachers with new ideas and practices, to provide an opportunity for mutual stimulation and to remind educators that a teacher's education is never complete.

Barnard was interested in higher standards for the teaching profession. Was not the teacher as important as the physician? Was he not even more significant than the lawyer? Did he not decide the fate of the future? Superficial standards for teachers would impoverish the community, and lead to crime and delinquency; it would threaten the foundations of democracy. On the other hand, well-trained teachers would create better citizens, they would stimulate the intellectual life of the nation, and they would be symbols of the life of the spirit.

A member of the Episcopal church, he took his religion seriously. Jesus was the master teacher whose love was to inspire all instructors. Education, Barnard held, failed unless it developed a sense of moral and spiritual commitment. Education meant a correspondence of theory and action. The f·nction of the teacher was the same as that of the minister. Both should endeavor to convert humanity so that selfishness would be overcome and vice abolished.

Barnard believed that God was the center of the curriculum. Indeed, not to honor Him would be impious and would create a school system with a shallow foundation. Less concerned than Mann with the separation of state and church, he believed that the Bible should have an honored place in the classroom; its lessons should be taught to every student.

To Barnard, the teacher was a missionary of the intellect whose task was the formation of character. He should inculcate in his students a sense of civic virtue and responsibility. Sunday school teaching, Barnard held, was an excellent preparation for school life, for it indicated that truth had no dimensions and that the intellect and the spirit of man had to be joined in a common enterprise. Barnard was not a rationalist. An overdose of reason, he held, led to skepticism; it made man too cautious and did not create enthusiastic human beings with a sense of responsibility toward God and society. Both education and religion are emotional matters involving man's feelings toward himself and toward humanity.

Barnard was concerned with the improvement of instruction. His Annual Reports in Connecticut included the following:

1. Individual instruction, or the practice of calling up scholar after scholar for recitation, while it enables the teacher to adapt his questions

and explanations, to the peculiar mental habits, and attainments of each scholar, is devoid of interest, and in schools constituted like our common schools, is an immense waste of the labor of the teacher. Nevertheless it is the method most in use in the schools which I have visited, and even when they were properly classified, the recitations were still of this character, passing from scholar to scholar in regular succession.

2.   Simultaneous instruction, or the practice of addressing questions and explanations to an entire class is now generally introduced into the best regulated schools, to avoid the inconvenience of individual instruction. The answer is sometimes given by all together, and sometimes by an individual, called upon for this purpose, while the whole class is prepared mentally to reply. This method keeps every mind attentive, and enlists the great principle of sympathy in aid of the teacher. It is not resorted to, to so great extent in the district schools, as it might be, with electric effect. It answers admirably well in examinations, for many a diffident scholar is reassured and spurred up to his best, when sustained by the voices and sympathy of his fellows. It is very well adapted to lessons in spelling, to exercises in mental arithmetic, in geography, history, and to all questions in review.

3.   Interrogative or explanatory instruction, or the practice of questioning the pupil in regard to what he is reading or reciting, and of adding such explanations, and incidental instruction as may be called for and be appropriate, is one of the most useful improvements which has been introduced into school education. . . .

4.   Oral instruction, is closely connected, and indeed forms a part of the above method. It has however, its distinct province, and in the hands of a teacher properly trained and qualified, gives not only variety and interest to the ordinary exercises of the school, but arouses the mind to general activity, and enriches it with much useful knowledge, which cannot under ordinary circumstances be communicated in regular classes. The school should in all cases be questioned on what was said, and the older scholars required to write out what they remember. There is but little of this kind of instruction given in the schools I have visited.

5.   Exercises on the slate, both as a means of instruction and of amusing and useful employment for the younger children, and written answers both on the slate and black board in all of the studies, from the older scholars, although common in good public schools elsewhere, and in the best private schools with us, are not of very general use in the district school.

6.   Mutual instruction, or the practice of employing elder pupils, properly trained to teach the younger, and assist the teacher in other ways, has been tried in various parts of the State, and is still pursued to some extent. There has been a wide difference in the estimate placed in different counties, and by different educators in the same country, of the value of this method, and the extent to which it

should be introduced. In Germany, it has never attained to any public favor, but has been regarded with decided aversion.

Some of the best schools in England and Scotland, where the experiment was tried, are conducted on this plan. In this country, the system has met with different degrees of popularity, at different times and in different cities, where alone it has been tried.

This whole subject of methods of instruction, is but imperfectly understood. Teachers have no opportunity of learning, much less of practising any other than the old routine, mechanical process of the district school which they attended. We need model schools. . . .[1]

Henry Barnard decried the heavy turnover of teachers.

In the first place, nearly one month of the school is practically lost to the time consumed by the teacher in getting acquainted with the temper, wants, dispositions, and previous progress of his various pupils, with a view to their proper classification, and to the adaptation of his own peculiar modes of government and instruction. By the time the school is in good progress, the scholars begin to drop away, the school money is exhausted, and the school dismissed. After a vacation of unnecessary length, as far as the recreation and relief of the children are concerned, the summer school commences with reduced numbers, under a less vigilant supervision, with a poorly compensated teacher, to go through the same course as before; and so on from year to year. The loss of time consequent on the change of teachers, and the long intermission between the two seasons of schooling, not only retards the progress of the school, but leads to the breaking up of regular habits of study, which will be felt in the whole future life.

In the second place, it leads to the perpetual and expensive change of school books, so much complained of, and so justly complained of, by parents. Every teacher has his favorite text books, and is naturally desirous of introducing them wherever he goes. And as there is no system adopted in relation to this subject in any society, he usually succeeds in introducing more or less of them into every school. The money now expended in the purchase of new books, caused by the change of teachers, would go far to continue the same teacher another month in the same school. Thus the district might practically gain, without any additional expense, two months schooling each year by employing the same teacher year after year.[2]

He advocated a better treatment of women teachers.

It is time for every friend of improvement in our common schools to protest against the inadequate and disproportionate compensation

---

[1] *Second Annual Report*, 1840, pp. 29-33.
[2] *First Annual Report*, 1839, pp. 37-38.

paid to female teachers. I have no hesitation in saying, that in the schools which I have visited, the female teachers were as well qualified, as devoted to their duties, and really advanced their pupils as far as the same number of male teachers. Let but a more generous appreciation of the value of their services as teachers, especially in the primary departments, prevail — let the system be so far modified as to admit of their being employed more extensively than now, not only in the summer, but the winter schools, and, as far as possible for the year round, and a new and happy impulse would not only be felt, in the more thorough intellectual training of youth, but in the improved manners and morals of society. As it is now, that class of females best qualified, by having enjoyed the advantages of superior and expensive schools, cannot be induced to enter the common schools as teachers, on account of the inadequate compensation, and the unnecessary difficulties and inconveniences connected with the employment. If the State would but furnish an opportunity for a numerous and most deserving class of young females, who are forced by their necessities into the corrupted atmosphere and unhealthy employments of our workshops and factories, to prepare themselves for teaching, and then remove the obstacles in the way of their being employed to the best advantage, an untold amount of female talent and usefulness, now in part wasted, or if employed even at better compensation, at least to a far less useful purpose, would be enlisted in the so much needed work of molding the childhood and youth of this State and nation.[3]

While Barnard admired some of the European schools, he protested against European despotism.

Whatever may be thought of the practical value of the experience of European States in the organization and administration of Systems of Public Instruction, to those who are engaged in the work of establishing and improving Public Schools in this country, no one who had reflected at all on this subject can doubt the applicability, with some modifications, of many of the institutions and agencies which are employed there, especially in Germany, Holland, and Switzerland, to secure the thorough professional education and progressive improvement of teachers of elementary schools. Under the influence of these institutions and agencies, the public schools of certain districts of Europe have attained, within the last quarter of a century, a degree of excellence which has attracted the attention of statesmen, and commanded the admiration of intelligent educators in every part of Christendom. The course of instruction, even in the elementary schools of the people, is more thorough and comprehensive than is generally aimed at or reached in schools designed specially for the children of the wealthy, educated and privileged classes in other countries.

---

[3] *Ibid.*

It may, however, save some misapprehension of my own views, to remark, that with all these agencies for the education and improvement of teachers, the public schools of Europe, with their institutions of government and society, do not turn out such practical and efficient men as our own common schools, acting in concert with our religious, social, and political institutions. A boy educated in a district school in New England, taught for a few months in the winter, by a rough, half-educated, but live teacher, who is earning his way, by his winter's work in the school-room, out of the profession into something which will pay better, and in the summer by a young female, just out of the oldest class of the winter school, and with no other knowledge of teaching than what she may have gathered by observation of the diverse practices of some ten or twelve instructors, who must have taught the school under the intermittent and itinerating system which prevails universally in the country districts of New England — a boy thus taught through his school life, but subjected at home and abroad to the stirring influences of a free press, of town and school district meetings, of constant intercourse with those who are mingling with the world, and in the affairs of public life, and beyond all these influences, subjected early to the wholesome discipline, both moral and intellectual, of taking care of himself, and the affairs of the house and the farm, will have more capacity for business, and exhibit more intellectual activity and versatility than the best scholar who ever graduated from a Prussian school, but whose school life, and especially the years which immediately follow, are subjected to the depressing and repressing influences of a despotic government, and to a state of society in which everything is fixed both by law and the iron rule of custom.[4]

SOCIAL DOCTRINES

Barnard had little tolerance for radicals and dissenters. In Rhode Island, he recommended that no teacher be employed who showed a disrespect for the Bible. As a college president he did not provide for student participation in administration. A conservative, he was more interested in the rights of capital than in the achievements of labor.

This does not imply that he was uninterested in social issues. On the contrary, he denounced the factory system and pictured in somber terms the deprivations of the worker. He feared that if the economic abuses of the nation were not corrected, revolution and chaos might result. He attacked the long working hours which endangered the educational welfare of the nation.

[4] *Eighth Annual Report*, 1853, pp. 180-182.

Barnard tried to appeal to the conscience of the rich man. The task of the rich was to improve the lot of women and children, to care for the factory workers as would a father for his children, and to provide for the poor so that a decent society would emerge.

Barnard was convinced that society cannot be changed through socialist action but only through education. A friend, E. P. Grant, urged him to support the ideals of Fourier; Barnard almost gave money to the Ohio Phalanx which was started by Grant in 1844. But in the long run Barnard rejected socialism. He feared a decline of initiative, too much state interference, too much reliance on welfare agencies; in short, it was too utopian. Instead, he urged a vigorous cultivation of capitalism; free enterprise and the profit system were to be taught in the schools. As for economic equality, this was an impossible ideal. As the teacher was more important than the student, the entrepreneur was more important than the worker. The former deserved more recognition and better pay.

EDUCATIONAL GROWTH

Barnard held that economic ideals are closely tied to educational growth. Education could provide reservoirs of talent. No poor student should be denied an education. The common school would be an aid in preventing revolution by giving opportunity to all. He appealed to the rich merchants of his time to support education so that radicalism would not dominate the United States.

Barnard believed that the private school has only a negative influence, acting as a divisive agency creating snobs and social parasites. It militates against a sense of social responsibility and produces a permanent wall between the various strata of society. It creates a feeling of superiority on the part of its students and generates envy and hostility on the part of those who must attend the public schools.

He feared the development of a political aristocracy that would destroy the vitality of democratic institutions and create a culture-stifling caste system.

Like Horace Mann, he urged greater financial support for public education. The rich were to pay taxes as well as take care of the education of their own children, while the children of the poor were to be educated at the expense of the state or the community. Many contemporaries opposed Barnard in his stand. His opponents felt that the poor ought not to be educated — only the middle and upper classes should enjoy the pleasures of an intellectual life. They argued that educating the poor would give them false expectations — it would create too much democracy; it might be worthwhile theoretically but it would not be sound practise.

In urging that the schools "should be good enough for the best and cheap enough for the poorest," Barnard advanced the cause of real democracy. He was a strange mixture; while conservative in his religious philosophy and in some of his economic ideas, he was a strong liberal in his desire to universalize education and prevent the development of a strong class system.

He believed with Horace Mann that knowledge should have a utilitarian content, with more attention to such subjects as book-keeping, navigation, surveying and agriculture. Schools and business should cooperate in programs so that the prosperity of the nation would expand. All students, Barnard taught, were to have practical experiences so that they would learn to use their hands and so that they would appreciate the importance of work.

Barnard saw the importance of science in the curriculum. By giving systematic basis to knowledge, science would encourage new ideas and inventions. In fact, at St. John's he advocated that the sciences and the humanities be taught together, the humanities to give the students an appreciation of the past and the sciences to open the frontiers of the future.

As preparation for citizenship, all students were to be taught about the unique achievements of the United States. The ideals of the Bill of Rights and the Constitution were to be emphasized in the classroom.

This meant concentration upon patriotism. The schools could not be neutral regarding the great issues of the day; both students and teachers should be willing to die for their nation.

Barnard was interested in the teaching of history. Too often, he claimed, this was the dullest subject in the curriculum. It emphasized institutions and impersonal events instead of dwelling upon individual genius. It neglected the moral lessons without which the study of history becomes a merely theoretical concern. Like Emerson, he regarded institutions as manifestations of individual genius. He wanted students to be inspired by the past, to find models of inspiration so that their own creativity would be stimulated. To Barnard, the American experiment was a crusade against lethargy. America should demonstrate that man can overcome the limitations of his environment and achieve a veritable utopia through education.

He wanted to train captains of industry who would promote trade and advance the cause of science and who would regard education as a sacred cause.

Barnard was a scholar of education. In the *American Journal of Education* he exhibited an almost encyclopedic knowledge of the history of education. He regarded himself as a servant of a cause which transcended all classes and all nations.

The cause was better schools, more highly trained teachers, a more elaborate curriculum, more financial support on the local and state level, better school architecture, continuous education for instructors, education for the young and adults, and highly motivated administrators who would have something like a religious fervor for their mission. Schools were to become efficient tools for democratic living; they were to be laboratories for political leadership. Schools thus would be the link between ideal and actuality; they would give substance to the democratic dream that education is man's cardinal achievement and highest aspiration.

CHAPTER FIFTEEN

Thoreau and Educational Ideals

THOREAU'S SIGNIFICANCE IN AMERICAN CULTURE

Henry David Thoreau (1817–1862) was less appreciated during his lifetime than Barnard or Emerson. For many years afterwards, his works were not read widely, but in the twentieth century he has found an increasing following, and his voice is heard as far away as Gandhi's India. His anarchistic ideals appeal to many moderns more strongly than the humanistic culture of Emerson. The life of nature Thoreau advocated appears to be an excellent way out from the confusion and oppression of a mechanistic culture.

Like Emerson, Thoreau was a Harvard graduate, but he had no definite profession. When he graduated, he tried to be a teacher; he did this just to make a living, as he confessed later on. Being idealistic, he believed that his task in life was not just to make a living but to improve his fellowman, and so he gave up teaching. He later turned to manufacturing pencils, but this occupation did not satisfy him.

Most of his life was spent living close to nature. His experiences at Walden have become as famous as Tolstoy's life amidst the poor Russian serfs. Occasionally, Thoreau would do odd jobs helping his neighbors and assisting Emerson's editing of the *Dial*. Otherwise, his life was not at all noteworthy except for his refusal to pay the poll tax, which landed him in jail.

If his life was uneventful by conventional standards, it was picturesque as an intellectual pilgrimage. The problem of Thoreau was how to attain a meaning in life. His neighbors were intent upon amassing wealth, and they thought that the greatest goal lay in comfortable living. To them happiness was to be gained from material things; their aim was to get as far away as they could from the country and live a luxurious city existence.

Thoreau would have nothing to do with such a spirit. He deserted society. He never married, never was a slave to convention, never supported a church, never took any interest in political life, and was an anarchist when it came to the state. In every way his life was a protest.

While Americans of Thoreau's period, as well as of more recent times, were incessantly traveling to other nations, he stayed near Concord. Here he found everything: a magnificent countryside, abundant wild life, stimulating friends — what more could a man ask?

The Puritan heritage was strong in Thoreau. He used neither tobacco nor alcohol. As for women, his conduct was retiring, and he never seemed to partake of the pleasures of the flesh. He was remarkable for his self-sufficiency.

To some extent he underestimated the European tradition. He had contempt for England. He said he would rather go to Oregon than to London. He was proud of the fact that in Massachusetts the civilization had not been built upon the ashes of a previous culture.

PHILOSOPHY OF LIFE AND KNOWLEDGE

Thoreau was an individualist concerned about his own salvation and his own way of life rather than the reform of society. That is why he undertook his Walden experiment.

I went to the woods because I wished to live deliberately, to front only the essential facts of life, and see if I could not learn what it had to teach, and not, when I came to die, discover that I had not lived. I did not wish to live what was not life, living is so dear; nor did I wish to practice resignation, unless it was quite necessary. I wanted to live

deep and suck out all the marrow of life, to live so sturdily and
Spartan-like as to put to rout all that was not life, to cut a broad swath
and shave close, to drive life into a corner, and reduce it to its lowest
terms, and, if it proved to be mean, why then to get the whole and
genuine meanness of it, and publish its meanness to the world; or if it
were sublime, to know it by experience, and be able to give a true
account of it in my next excursion. For most men, it appears to me,
are in strange uncertainty about it, whether it is of the devil or of
God, and have somewhat hastily concluded that it is the chief end of
man here to "glorify God and enjoy Him forever."[1]

He felt melancholy when he looked at the manner in which most
people spend their lives.

This world is a place of business. What an infinite bustle! I am
awaked almost every night by the panting of the locomotive. It
interrupts my dreams. There is no sabbath. It would be glorious to see
mankind at leisure for once. It is nothing but work, work, work. I
cannot easily buy a blank-book to write thoughts in; they are commonly ruled for dollars and cents. An Irishman, seeing me making a
minute in the fields, took it for granted that I was calculating my
wages. If a man was tossed out of a window when an infant, and so
made a cripple for life, or scared out of his wits by the Indians, it is
regretted chiefly because he was thus incapacitated for — business! I
think that there is nothing, not even crime, more opposed to poetry,
to philosophy, ay, to life itself, than this incessant business.
  There is a coarse and boisterous money-making fellow in the outskirts of our town, who is going to build a bank-wall under the hill
along the edge of his meadow. The powers have put this into his
head to keep him out of mischief, and he wishes me to spend three
weeks digging there with him. The result will be that he will perhaps
get some more money to hoard, and leave for his heirs to spend fool-
ishly. If I do this, most will commend me as an industrious and
hard-working man; but if I choose to devote myself to certain labors
which yield more real profit, though but little money, they may be
inclined to look on me as an idler.[2]

We labor without any real goals.

If a man walk in the woods for love of them half of each day, he
is in danger of being regarded as a loafer; but if he spends his whole
day as a speculator, shearing off those woods and making earth bald
before her time, he is esteemed an industrious and enterprising citizen.
As if a town had no interest in its forests but to cut them down!

---

[1] *Walden, or Life in the Woods.*
[2] *Miscellanies, Life Without Principle.*

Most men would feel insulted if it were proposed to employ them in throwing stones over a wall, and then in throwing them back, merely that they might earn their wages. But many are no more worthily employed now. For instance: just after sunrise, one summer morning, I noticed one of my neighbors walking beside his team, which was slowly drawing a heavy hewn stone swung under the axle, surrounded by an atmosphere of industry, — his day's work begun, — his brow commenced to sweat, — a reproach to all sluggards and idlers, — pausing abreast the shoulders of his oxen, and half turning round with a flourish of his merciful whip, while they gained their length on him. And I thought, Such is the labor which the American Congress exists to protect, — honest, manly toil, — honest as the day is long, — that makes his bread taste sweet, and keeps society sweet, — which all men respect and have consecrated; one of the sacred band, doing the needful but irksome drudgery. Indeed, I felt a slight reproach, because I observed this from a window, and was not abroad and stirring about a similar business.[3]

The wise man, according to Thoreau, will treasure his own independence.

The community has no bribe that will tempt a wise man. You may raise money enough to tunnel a mountain, but you cannot raise money enough to hire a man who is minding *his own* business. An efficient and valuable man does what he can, whether the community pay him for it or not. The inefficient offer their insufficiency to the highest bidder, and are forever expecting to be put into office. One would suppose that they were rarely disappointed.

Perhaps I am more than usually jealous with respect to my freedom. I feel that my connections with an obligation to society are still very slight and transient. Those slight labors which afford me a livelihood, and by which it is allowed that I am to some extent serviceable to my contemporaries, are as yet commonly a pleasure to me, and I am not often reminded that they are a necessity. So far I am successful. But I foresee that if my wants should be much increased, the labor required to supply them would become a drudgery. If I should sell both my forenoons and afternoons to society, as most appear to do, I am sure that for me there would be nothing left worth living for. I trust that I shall never thus sell my birthright for a mess of pottage.[4]

Like Socrates, he was critical of organized education.

I hardly know *an intellectual* man, even, who is so broad and truly liberal that you can think aloud in his society. Most with whom you

[3] *Ibid.*
[4] *Ibid.*

endeavor to talk soon come to a stand against some institution in which they appear to hold stock—that is, some particular, not universal, way of viewing things. They will continually thrust their own low roof, with its narrow skylight, between you and the sky, when it is the unobstructed heavens you would view. Get out of the way with your cobwebs; wash your windows, I say! In some lyceums they tell me that they have voted to exclude the subject of religion. But how do I know what their religion is, and when I am near to or far from it? I have walked into such an arena and done my best to make a clean breast of what religion I have experienced, and the audience never suspected what I was about. The lecture was as harmless as moonshine to them. Whereas, if I had read to them the biography of the greatest scamps in history, they might have thought that I had written the lives of the deacons of their church. Ordinarily, the inquiry is, Where did you come from? or, Where are you going? That was a more pertinent question which I overheard one of my auditors put to another once, — "What does he lecture for?" It made me quake in my shoes.

To speak impartially, the best men that I know are not serene, a world in themselves. For the most part, they dwell in forms, and flatter and study effect only more finely than the rest. We select granite for the underpinning of our houses and barns; we build fences of stone; but we do not ourselves rest on an underpinning of granitic truth, the lowest primitive rock. Our sills are rotten.[5]

Thoreau had reverence for books:

I kept Homer's Iliad on my table through the summer, though I looked at his page only now and then. Incessant labor with my hands, at first, for I had my house to finish and my beans to hoe at the same time, made more study impossible. Yet I sustained myself by the prospect of such reading in future, I read one or two shallow books of travel in the intervals of my work, till that employment made me ashamed of myself, and I asked where it was then that I lived.

The student may read Homer or Aeschylus in the Greek without danger of dissipation or luxuriousness, for it implies that he in some measure emulate their heroes, and consecrate morning hours to their pages. The heroic books, even if printed in the character of our mother tongue, will always be in a language dead to degenerate times; and we must laboriously seek the meaning of each word and line, conjecturing a larger sense than common use permits out of what wisdom and valor and generosity we have. The modern cheap and fertile press, with all its translations, has done little to bring us nearer to the heroic writers of antiquity. They seem as solitary, and the letter in which they are printed as rare and curious, as ever. It is worth the expense

---

[5] *Ibid.*

of youthful days and costly hours, if you learn only some words of an ancient language, which are raised out of the trivialness of the street, to be perpetual suggestions and provocations. It is not in vain that the farmer remembers and repeats the few Latin words which he has heard. Men sometimes speak as if the study of the classics would at length make way for more modern and practical studies; but the adventurous student will always study classics, in whatever language they may be written and however ancient they may be. For what are the classics but the noblest recorded thoughts of man? They are the only oracles which are not decayed, and there are such answers to the most modern inquiry in them as Delphi and Dodona never gave. We might as well omit to study Nature because she is old. To read well, that is to read true books in a true spirit, is a noble exercise, and one that will task the reader more than any exercise which the customs of the day esteem. It requires a training such as the athletes underwent, the steady intention almost of the whole life to this object. Books must be read as deliberately and reservedly as they were written.[6]

He placed the written word above oratory.

The one is commonly transitory, a sound, a tongue, a dialect merely, almost brutish, and we learn it unconsciously, like the brutes, of our mothers. The other is the maturity and experience of that; if that is our mother tongue, this is our father tongue, a reserved and select expression, too significant to be heard by the ear, which we must be born again in order to speak. The crowds of men who merely *spoke* the Greek and Latin tongues in the Middle Ages were not entitled by the accident of birth to *read* the works of genius written in those languages; for these were not written in that Greek or Latin which they knew, but in the select language of literature.

. . . No wonder that Alexander carried the Iliad with him on his expeditions in a precious casket. A written word is the choicest of relics. It is something at once more intimate with us and more universal than any other work of art. It is the work of art nearest to life itself. It may be translated into every language, and not only be read but actually breathed from all human lips; — not be represented on canvas or in marble only, but be carved out of the breath of life itself.[7]

He attacked the reading done by his contemporaries.

The best books are not read even by those who are called good readers. What does our Concord culture amount to? There is in this town, with a very few exceptions, no taste for the best or for very good books even in English literature, whose words all can read and

---

[6] *Walden.*
[7] *Ibid.*

spell. Even the college-bred and so-called liberally educated men here and elsewhere have really little or no acquaintance with the English classics; and as for the recorded wisdom of mankind, the ancient classics and Bibles, which are accessible to all who will know of them, there are the feeblest efforts anywhere made to become acquainted with them. I know a woodchopper, of middle age, who takes a French paper, not for news as he says, for he is above that, but to "keep himself in practice," he being a Canadian by birth; and when I ask him what he considers the best thing he can do in this world, he says, beside this, to keep up and add to his English. This is about as much as the college-bred generally do or aspire to do, and they take an English paper for the purpose. One who has just come from reading perhaps one of the best English books will find how many with whom he can converse about it? Or suppose he comes from reading a Greek or Latin classic in the original, whose praises are familiar even to the so-called illiterate; he will find nobody at all to speak to, but must keep silence about it. Indeed, there is hardly the professor in our colleges, who, if he has mastered the difficulties of the language, has proportionately mastered the difficulties of the wit and poetry of a Greek poet, and has any sympathy to impart to the alert and heroic reader; and as for the sacred Scriptures, or Bibles of mankind, who in this town can tell me even their titles? Most men do not know that any nation but the Hebrews have had a scripture. A man, any man, will go considerably out of his way to pick up a silver dollar; but here are golden words, which the wisest men of antiquity have uttered, and whose worth the wise of every succeeding age have assured us of; — and yet we learn to read only as far as Easy Reading, the primers and class-books, and when we leave school, the "Little Reading," and story-books, which are for boys and beginners; and our reading, our conversation and thinking, are all on a very low level, worthy only of pygmies and manikins.[8]

Like Emerson, Thoreau called for an educational renaissance.

Shall the world be confined to one Paris or one Oxford forever? Cannot students be boarded here and get a liberal education under the skies of Concord? Can we not hire some Abelard to lecture to us? Alas! what with foddering the cattle and tending the store, we are kept from school too long, and our education is sadly neglected. In this country, the village should in some respects take the place of the nobleman of Europe. It should be the patron of the fine arts. It is rich enough. It wants only the magnanimity and refinement. It can spend money enough on such things as farmers and traders value, but it is thought Utopian to propose spending money for things which more intelligent men know to be of far more worth. This town has

---

[8] *Ibid.*

spent seventeen thousand dollars on a town-house, thank fortune or
politics, but probably it will not spend so much on living wit, the true
meat to put into that shell, in a hundred years. The one hundred and
twenty-five dollars annually subscribed for a Lyceum in the winter
is better spent than any other equal sum raised in the town. If we
live in the nineteenth Century, why should we not enjoy the advantages which the Nineteenth Century offers? Why should our life be
in any respect provincial? If we will read newspapers, why not skip
the gossip of Boston and take the best newspapers in the world at
once? — not be sucking the pap of "neutral family" papers, or browsing
"Olive-Branches" here in New England. Let the reports of all the
learned societies come to us, and we will see if they know anything.
Why should we leave it to Harper & Brothers and Redding & Co., to
select our reading? As the nobleman of cultivated taste surrounds himself with whatever conduces to his culture, — genius — learning — wit —
books — paintings — statuary — music — philosophical instruments, and
the like; so let the village do, — not stop short at a pedagogue, a
parson, a sexton, a parish library, and three select-men, because our
Pilgrim forefathers got through a cold winter once on a bleak rock
with these. To act collectively is according to the spirit of our institutions; and I am confident that, as our circumstances are more flourishing, our means are greater than the nobleman's. New England can
hire all the wise men in the world to come and teach her, and board
them round the while, and not be provincial at all. That is the
uncommon school we want. Instead of noblemen, let us have noble
villages of men.[9]

Real education, Thoreau stated, transcends poverty:

The setting sun is reflected from the windows of the alms-house as
brightly as from the rich man's abode; the snow melts before its door
as early in the spring. I do not see but a quiet mind may live as
contentedly there, and have as cheering thoughts, as in a palace. The
town's poor seem to me often to live the most independent lives of
any. Maybe they are simply great enough to receive without mis-
giving. Most think that they are above being supported by the town;
but it oftener happens that they are not above supporting themselves
by dishonest means, which should be more disreputable. Cultivate
poverty like a garden herb, like sage. Do not trouble yourself much
to get new things, whether clothes or friends. Turn the old; return
to them. Things do not change; we change. Sell your clothes and keep
your thoughts. God will see that you do not want society. If I were
confined to a corner of a garret all my days, like a spider, the world
would be just as large to me while I had my thoughts about me. The
philosopher said: "From an army of three divisions one can take away

---

[9] *Ibid.*

its general, and put it in disorder; from the man the most abject and vulgar one cannot take away his thought." Do not seek so anxiously to be developed, to subject yourself to many influences to be played on; it is all dissipation. Humility like darkness reveals the heavenly lights. The shadow of poverty and meanness gather around us, "and lo! creation widens to our view." We are often reminded that if there were bestowed on us the wealth of Croesus, our aims must still be the same, and our means essentially the same. Moreover, if you are restricted in your range by poverty, if you cannot buy books and news-papers, for instance, you are but confined to the most significant and vital experiences; you are compelled to deal with the material which yields the most sugar and the most starch. It is life near the bone where it is sweetest. You are defended from being a trifler. No man loses ever on a lower level by magnanimity on a higher. Superfluous wealth can buy superfluities only. Money is not required to buy one necessary of the soul.[10]

With such a philosophy he could not accept the theological dogmas of orthodox Christianity which, to him, represented a religion of negation rather than of joy. He had much more understanding of the gods of Greece, for they were part of nature.

When he saw the New Englanders worshiping in their churches, he felt a sense of pity, for the God they adored was a magnified image of a ruthless industrial system. As for himself, he literally followed the precepts of Christ. Had Christ not said, "Seek ye first the kindom of heaven; lay not up for yourself treasures on earth"? Thoreau knew the meaning of Christ's insight that a man would gain nothing if he conquered the world and lost his own soul.

Thoreau believed in man expressing himself in a complete and thorough-going manner; those who prostrated themselves before an arbitrary God had no understanding of the real meaning of religion; Thoreau found his religious experience much more readily in nature than in the churches of New England.

The more one reads Thoreau, not merely his *Walden* but his *A Week on the Concord and Merrimack Rivers,* his *Excursions, The Main Woods, Cape Cod, The Yankee in Canada,* the more one gets the impression of a saint-like nature. Though he detested formal theology and had only scorn for the clergy of his time, he had a basically religious interpretation of life. He measured all philosophy, all thinking, according to their contribution to the actual improvement of man's existence.

What did philosophy mean to Thoreau? It was not merely a systematized view of the world, nor an insight into its metaphysical

---

[10] *Ibid.*

structure; not an adherence to definite dogmas, but a love of wisdom which made it possible to give a practical solution to life's problems. To Thoreau, thought was an auxiliary to action. In this view he echoed the practices of the Stoic philosophers.

POLITICAL DOCTRINES AND EDUCATION

Politically, his doctrines were out of tune with the faith of his time. While great fortunes were being made in New England, the United States expanded in the war with Mexico, and Webster was defending high tariffs and the federal union, Thoreau detested the power of the state and preached a gospel of non-resistance.

The use of force was completely abhorrent to him, for he recognized clearly that modern society is based upon coercion. From the exaction of the tax collectors to the waging of war, governments usually use tyrannical means. Thoreau thought that it was his duty to protest against this trend. He was not willing to be coerced by the majority; in his system everyone was equipped with inalienable rights given to him by nature.

His philosophy resembled that of Rousseau in his scorn for laws. He emphasized that the law "will never make men free; it is men who have got to make the law free." As for the defenders of the law, he was extremely suspicious of them.

"The government," he stated in *Civil Disobedience,*

can have no pure right over my person and property but what I concede to it. The progress from an absolute to a limited monarchy, from a limited monarchy to a democracy, is a progress toward a true respect for the individual. Even the Chinese philosopher was wise enough to regard the individual as the basis of the empire. Is a democracy, such as we know it, the last improvement possible in government? Is it not possible to take a step further towards recognizing and organizing the rights of man? There will never be a really free and enlightened State until the State comes to recognize the individual as a higher and independent power, from which all its own power and authority are derived and treats him accordingly. I please myself with imagining a State at last which can afford to be just to all men, and to treat the individual with respect as a neighbor; which even would not think it inconsistent with its own repose if a few were to live aloof from it, not meddling with it, nor embraced by it, who fulfilled all the duties of neighbors and fellowmen. A State which bore this kind of fruit, and suffered it to drop off as fast as it ripened, would prepare the way for a still more perfect and glorious State, which also I have imagined, but not yet anywhere seen.[11]

Like Carlyle and Ruskin, Thoreau vigorously attacked the abuses of the industrial system. How different life was at Walden from that of Boston! How different fate was for him than for the wage earner in the textile mills! To Thoreau it appeared an undeniable truth that the industrial system was based upon serfdom. The majority of the people had only a bare existence for which they slaved enormously; for a few it meant wealth at a terrible price.

No wonder that Thoreau objected furiously to the capitalistic values. He thought that eventually the condition of the American worker would be as pitiful as that of the English wage earner, and he foresaw a period in which the United States would be covered with slums.

What was the solution? Could it be found through cooperative experiments like Brook Farm and Fruitlands? The answer was no, for this would have made him a part of society and he wanted to live by himself. He was not dogmatic about his solutions. He knew that he had found a satisfying way of life; others would differ in their methods.

The story goes that while he was on his deathbed he was asked if he could see anything of the world beyond. "One world at a time," Thoreau replied, "one world at a time."

This statement characterizes his educational outlook, for he never gave sweeping and categorical answers; in fact, if judged by his solution of the problems of modern society, he appears to be hopelessly inadequate. It is impossible for man in the atomic age to give up his scientific undertakings, desert his family, and live the type of life that Thoreau enjoyed at Walden. Thoreau's ideals were influenced too much by the gospel of anarchy.

This is especially evident in his attitude regarding political events.

Those things which now most engage the attention of men, as politics and the daily routine, are, it is true, vital functions of human society, but should be unconsciously performed, like the corresponding functions of the physical body. They are *infra*human, a kind of vegetation. I sometimes awake to a half-consciousness of them going on about me, as a man may become conscious of some of the processes of digestion in a morbid state, and so have the dyspepsia, as it is called. It is as if a thinker submitted himself to be rasped by the great gizzard of creation. Politics is, as it were, the gizzard of society, full

---

[11] *Civil Disobedience.*

of grit and gravel, and the two political parties are its two opposite halves, — sometimes split into quarters, it may be, which grind on each other. Not only individuals, but states, have thus confirmed dyspepsia, which expresses itself, you can imagine by what sort of eloquence. Thus our life is not altogether a forgetting, but also, alas! to a great extent, a remembering, of that which we should never have been conscious of, certainly not in our waking hours.[12]

His lasting significance for the American thinker lies in his penetrating question about the meaning and function of human life. It is not enough, according to Thoreau, to be an adherent to worthwhile causes if one neglects the inner self. Real leadership can come about only if the individual has an immediate awareness of nature.

In this respect no thinker can neglect Thoreau. Too frequently the intellectual in the twentieth century is tempted by the importance of reforms to overlook his inner self. Consequently, his ideas are academic, his outlook upon the world is stereotyped, and his personality is maladjusted. Educators must learn that lasting reform can be brought about only if there is a correspondence between outward action and personal development.

UTOPIAS AND REALITY

This was an age of utopias. One of the most notable, Brook Farm, was founded by George Ripley, a Harvard classical scholar. It was situated in the most impressive surroundings of Massachusetts, amidst splendid meadows and a nearby brook; in the summer its members could go swimming in the Charles River. The main concern of Brook Farm was a preservation of cultural values. There were classes in philosophy, German, Greek, music, botany, and geography. Among the instructors were Charles A. Dana, who later became editor of the New York *Sun*, Mr. Ripley, who turned to Catholicism, and Margaret Fuller, who found solace and love in Italy.

The two social reforms which were championed by Brook Farm were equality of wages and the absence of any domestic labor. It was Ripley's ideal to do away with all forms of social oppression; complete equality was to prevail and work would be done, not because of compulsion, but because of a real inner urge. Other utopian communities might preserve social stratification as Owen's community did in New Harmony; it was different at Brook Farm, where real freedom prevailed.

---

[12] *Ibid.*

Opposition, however, developed among the intellectuals. Emerson, after a while, had nothing to do with the experiments. Bronson Alcott founded Fruitlands, which believed in unlimited liberty and bordered on anarchy. Fourierism was ably championed by Albert Brisbane in *The Social Destiny of Man*. Horace Greeley was so impressed with the ideas of Brisbane that he allowed a daily column for his views in the New York *Tribune*. John Humphrey Noyes was interested in founding a perfect society in which the individual would be free from all restraints. He preached a gospel of sexual freedom which scandalized the conservatives, although he stressed that this liberty did not extend to the masses, and was only to be applied within his own community. Noyes wanted to change the basis of marriage and give greater freedom to women.

Together with community projects, which usually lasted only for a few decades, education was furthered by the reformers. Horace Mann, who was secretary of the State Board of Education of Massachusetts from 1838 to 1848, aided in the development of the public school. Much was done for the education of women. The kindergarten became an accepted American institution and was vigorously endorsed by Horace Mann.

At the same time, Frances Wright, who had spent several years in the United States as an agitator for educational reform, and was editing *The Free Enquirer*, urged that the state should erect schools for small children, who were to be taken away from their homes at the age of two. She was far ahead of her time; her proposal caused great opposition, for the parents thought that this would destroy the family system.

Bronson Alcott shocked many of his contemporaries by touching upon sex in his instruction. He did it in a most genteel manner and only pointed out to his pupils that human birth is not a divine event, but causes suffering to mothers. A Harvard professor thought that this was a most unfit and disgusting statement for children. Two Boston newspapers carried on a systematic campaign against Alcott, with the result that conscientious parents withdrew their children from his school.

It did not matter that Emerson defended Alcott. The genteel would have nothing to do with sex education. Alcott's school failed completely when he admitted a Negro girl. The intellectuals of New England might have great sympathy for the abolition movement, but they did not want their children in personal contact with an "inferior race." Many of them worshiped equality in the abstract, but when it came to real support of tolerance, they resisted most strenuously.

In New England and elsewhere women insisted upon greater privileges; they demanded the right to vote and wanted to be regarded as equals by their husbands. They were active in the temperance movement and attempted to make their husbands as pure and virtuous as they had to be. In the twentieth century their reform efforts continued, but were more organized and more vocal, with thousands of women's clubs like the P.T.A., W.C.T.U., and the Peace League.

New England was the stronghold of a persistent agitation for world peace. A linguist of New Britain, Connecticut, Elihu Burritt, gave vigor to this movement. He was the editor of *Christian Citizen*, which reached a wide audience. There were constant peace conventions which were attended by thousands of adherents who urged that wars be outlawed.

THE WEAKNESSES OF THE NEW ENGLAND SPIRIT

The philosopher in New England suffered from great illusions, since he thought that his reforms had provided a lasting change in American civilization. Ultimately, he was defeated by the fanaticism which developed during the Civil War and by the materialistic culture which followed.

The philosopher was too much concerned with upholding the propertied classes. He could not understand the man on the street. This trait was especially strong in the later writers like Holmes, Longfellow, and Lowell, who were so concerned with their narrow code of respectability that they lacked sympathy for the aspirations of the common man. Lowell himself thought that democracy could not be combined with an eight-hour day and a full extension of the suffrage.

Their culture was frigid, although Emerson and Thoreau cannot be so classified. But even they lacked the splendid compassion and insight of Walt Whitman for all aspects of American life. The thinker of New England was too much concerned with good manners, believed too much in correct forms, was too condescending regarding the laboring classes, and had too much faith in the wisdom of the intellectual.

The most consistent critics of the New England spirit were Hawthorne and Melville. The former had been greatly influenced by Transcendentalism, but he rebelled against this movement and most of his life maintained an attitude of complete skepticism. The

Scarlet Letter is representative of his mood, for in it there is no exact distinction between goodness and evil. Hawthorne regarded intellectual movements as a doctor might view a corpse. He discussed them thoroughly, he probed for their weaknesses, and he was more satisfied with their negative aspects than with their positive affirmations.

Melville likewise exemplifies the spirit of skepticism. Is not *Moby Dick* a symbol of man's inability to tame the force of nature? Did not Melville himself try to find a utopia all his life and yet never succeed? Melville, unlike Emerson, did not believe in categorical answers. Life, man, and God are mysteries that cannot be completely explored by human intelligence.

Thus the splendid and vigorous faith which was responsible for the New England renaissance turned into a soul-searching skeptical attitude. Henry Adams climaxed it by his works, in which the note of soul-searching doubt is dominant.

To some extent Henry Adams was the most critical of all American thinkers. Seldom has philosophy been stated with such vigor and grace as in his two works, *The Education of Henry Adams* and *Mont-Saint-Michel and Chartres*. At first he tried to follow in his family's footsteps and took up politics, but this occupation could not satisfy him. Wherever he looked he found greed, materialism and mediocrity. His view of the future was pessimistic: modern man was becoming a robot. With intense longing he looked back to the education of the Middle Ages as a period of unity and spirituality as compared with the heterogeneity and materialism of his own age.

BOOKER·T·WASHINGTON
1856   1915

HE LIFTED THE VEIL OF IGNORANCE
FROM HIS PEOPLE AND POINTED
THE WAY TO PROGRESS THROUGH
EDUCATION AND INDUSTRY

CHAPTER SIXTEEN

New Vistas

EDUCATIONAL AWAKENING

The great struggle in the first part of the nineteenth century was for free public schools. New York was a pioneer in the movement and under the leadership of Governor Clinton provided as early as 1795 $100,000 for the support of its schools. In 1812 New York followed the example of Massachusetts and established a district system of schools. Tuition for the poor was free, but parents who were financially able had to pay a fixed rate to the state.

In Pennsylvania education was privately controlled until 1818 when the legislature opened schools for pauper children. In Virginia a public school system was authorized in 1797, but adequate financial support was lacking. The same was true of North Carolina, where A. D. Murphey was an eloquent apostle of a more enlightened system of education.

Schools were supported in a variety of ways. Bequests by wealthy members of the community were a source of revenue. Taxes on liquor were applied. Sometimes lotteries were staged for the support of schools. The property tax, which became so common in later times, was resisted by many who regarded it as a radical scheme.

The Sunday school added to the expansion of education and provided not merely for religious instruction but also for a degree of secular learning. Many wealthy members of various communities became Sunday school teachers and they could see how inadequate the education was for the less fortunate members of society.

The monitorial system, initiated in England by Joseph Lancaster and Andrew Bell, attracted greater interest in learning. The new method provided for student assistants to a teacher and thus more students could be taught in an efficient way. The method was introduced into the U. S. in 1806 and political and educational leaders were so enthusiastic that it spread to all parts of the country. Indeed, the governors of New York and Pennsylvania made special pleas to their legislatures to adopt the new scheme and thus aid the progress of education.

Enthusiasm for education was promoted by the Lyceum movement. It attracted famous Americans like David Webster, Edward Everett and Albert Gallatin. Societies like the American Institute of Instruction founded by G. B. Emerson and James G. Carter aided the cause of public education. In Pennsylvania the Pennsylvania Society for the Promotion of Public Schools made many converts for a democratic system of schools. There were numerous educational conventions, especially in Illinois and New Jersey. Ohio was stimulated by the Western Academic Institute, which was founded in 1829.

The pioneers of the movement included the Rev. Charles Brooks in Massachusetts, Caleb Mills in Indiana, Gallaudet and Barnard in Connecticut, the Reverend C. E. Stowe in Ohio, Thaddeus Stevens in Pennsylvania, and Carter and Mann in Massachusetts. In the South, Henry Ruffner, Calvin H. Wiley, the Reverend Robert J. Breckenridge and Governor A. G. Brown labored tirelessly for the cause of public education.

Most significant in the spread of education were several journals. Note should be taken of the *Academician,* founded in 1818 and the *American Journal of Education,* established in 1826; it changed its name in 1832 to *The American Annals of Education.*

American educators were fascinated by European educational trends. In 1818 John Griscom gave a favorable report of Prussian education. Translations were made of French philosopher Victor Cousin's epoch-making work, *Report on the State of Public Education in Prussia.* Calvin E. Stowe, Barnard, Mann and Woodbridge all had a vigorous interest in European education, especially German education, and they issued reports which called for a system of education which would adopt higher standards of proficiency.

The spirit of this movement is exemplified by De Witt Clinton, who made an eloquent plea in 1809:

> In casting a view over the civilized world, we find an universal accordance in opinion on the benefits of education but the practical exposition of this opinion exhibits a deplorable contrast. While magnificent colleges and universities are erected and endowed and dedicated to literature, we behold few liberal appropriations for diffusing the blessings of knowledge among all descriptions of people. The fundamental error of Europe has been, to confine the light of knowledge to the wealthy and the great, while the humble and the depressed have been as sedulously excluded from its participation, as the wretched criminal, immured in a dungeon, is from the light of heaven. This cardinal mistake is not only to be found in the institutions of the Old World, and in the condition of its inhabitants, but it is to be seen in most of the books which have been written on the subject of education. The celebrated Locke, whose treatises on government and the human understanding have crowned him with immortal glory, devoted the powers of his mighty intellect to the elucidation of education; but in the very threshold of his book we discover this radical error: his treatise is professedly intended for the children of gentlemen.[1]

He contrasted European and American education.

> . . . This view of human nature is indeed calculated to excite the most painful feelings, and it entirely originates from a consideration of the predominating error which I have expressed. To this source must the crimes and the calamities of the Old World be principally imputed. Ignorance is the cause as well as the effect of bad governments, and without the cultivation of our rational powers, we can entertain no just ideas of the obligations of morality or the excellences of religion. Although England is justly renowned for its cultivation of the arts and sciences, and although the poor-rates of that country exceed five million sterling per annum, yet (I adopt the words of an eminent British writer) "there is no Protestant country where the education of the poor has been so grossly and infamously neglected as in England." If one tenth part of that sum had been applied to the education of the poor, the blessings of order, knowledge, and innocence would have been diffused among them, the evil would have been attacked at the fountain-head, and a total revolution would have taken place in the habits and lives of the people, favorable to the cause of industry, good morals, good order, and rational religion.

---

[1] *Address to the Public School Society*, 1809.

More just and rational views have been entertained on this subject in the United States. Here, no privileged orders, no factitious distinctions in society, no hereditary nobility, no established religion, no royal prerogatives, exist to interpose barriers between the people, and to create distinct classifications in society. All men being considered as enjoying an equality of rights, the propriety and necessity of dispensing, without distinction, the blessings of education, followed of course. In New England, the greatest attention has been invariably given to this important object. In Connecticut, particularly, the schools are supported, at least three fourths of the year, by the interest of a very large fund created for that purpose, and a small tax on the people, the whole amounting to seventy-eight thousand dollars per annum. The result of this beneficial arrangement is obvious and striking. Our Eastern brethren are a well-informed and moral people. In those States it is as uncommon to find a poor man who cannot read and write, as it is rare to see one in Europe who can.[2]

He pleaded for a universal system of education.

In such an extensive and comprehensive establishment we are to expect, according to the course of human events, that children of extraordinary genius and merit will rise up, entitled to extraordinary patronage. To select such from the common mass — to watch over their future destiny — to advance them through all the stages of education and through all the grades of knowledge, and to settle them in useful and honorable professions, are duties of primary importance, and indispensable obligations. This, however, will require considerable funds; but of what estimation are pecuniary sacrifices, when put in the scale against the important benefits that may result? And if we could draw aside the veil of futurity, perhaps we might see in the offspring of this establishment, so patronized and so encouraged, characters that will do honor to human nature. . . .[3]

Textbooks aided the progress of education. Horace Greeley in his *Recollections* describes their influence on his life. He tells how much he learned from Webster's *Spelling Book*, how hard he studied Morse's *Geography* and Lindley Murray's *Grammar* and *Spelling-Book*. Most of all, he prized the *Columbian Orator* which was a collection of important speeches in England and the United States. It inspired him to seek a higher level of public service and higher personal standards of morality.

The McGuffey Readers became standard texts in the nineteenth century classrooms. The first and second were compiled by McGuffey

---

[2] *Ibid.*
[3] *Ibid.*

in 1836. A year later saw the publication of the third and fourth. In 1841 the fifth was written. The textbook had great appeal and was revised frequently, it was last copyrighted in 1901. The book was especially attractive to Americans who lived on the frontier, for it stressed the virtues of self-reliance and individualism.

SIGNIFICANCE OF THE FRONTIER

The frontier has exerted an abiding influence upon American political life. As Turner pointed out, it has been a bulwark of American democracy. It has supported those who could not find employment in the East, it has been a symbol of unlimited opportunity, and it has prevented the existence of a decadent aristocracy. Again and again, the frontier has made for greater equality in American life.

However, the frontier likewise has produced many disadvantages. There, the refinements of a civilized existence were lacking. There, schooling was of the most inadequate type. In the camp meetings, the frontier sentiment was crystallized. They were crude, superstitious, and they produced mass orgies of half-disguised sexuality. They fought a strenuous struggle against vice, especially against drinking. Wholesale conversions took place, but these conversions were seldom lasting and thus the frontier community alternated between vice and religious puritanism. In this way, the frontier psychology aided in the development of extremes and intensified the instability of the American character.

Likewise, the frontier encouraged the spirit of lawlessness. Many criminals who were expelled from the East would find a refuge in the western lands where few questions were asked. The same process was repeated in the 20th century when members of the Pendergast or the Capone gang would emigrate to Las Vegas. A profound disrespect for the law developed. When the citizens finally got tired of the reign of anarchy, they usually banded together as they did in California in 1850 in vigilante committees, and they administered justice in a most crude manner without regard for the formalities of the law.

The frontier influence upon American life has also been responsible for an excessive dislike of central authority. To the settlers in Utah and Oregon in 1840, Washington was almost as far as Shanghai is from New York today. There was little contact with the government in Washington, except for the tax collectors, the periodical elections, and the postal service. The settlers in the West were certain that it was the main desire of the government to interfere in their own affairs and that a strong central authority would lead to a form of dictatorship. That suspicion still plagues many of the liberals who champion the doctrine of States' rights.

JACKSON

The real leader of this frontier democracy was Andrew Jackson (1767–1845). The crowds who came to see his inauguration had a feeling that he was one of them; seldom has an American president been as popular as Jackson.[4]

He was much more plebeian than Jefferson. Jefferson was essentially a Virginia aristocrat, too well educated to speak the language of the man on the street. Jackson, on the other hand, was not burdened by excessive knowledge, and his speech was direct and sufficiently ungrammatical to appeal to the most uneducated.

Democracy was expanded in the period of Jackson, which witnessed an extension of the suffrage, a persistent struggle against the Bank of the United States, and an encouragement of labor organizations. At the same time, thorough reforms were made in debtor's laws, national nominating conventions were introduced, and a more democratic educational system was established.

Jackson made the spoils system an integral part of the American political program. It must be remembered that Van Buren, one of his chief leaders, was the boss of one of the most efficient political machines in New York. He and Jackson's Kitchen Cabinet saw to it that their friends received the best governmental jobs. It is true that most of the appointees Jackson made were quite honest and that the spoils system started almost with the inauguration of the federal government. Yet, it cannot be denied that the spoils system is largely responsible for the political weakness of the United States. In the 20th century it prevents a continuity of administration. With a change of parties, it drives out many efficient public servants, whose only crime is that they did not vote for the right ticket. It makes for intensive rivalry among the job holders and prevents a truly unified government.

Jackson's democracy was too much a one-man show. To the people, Jackson was a hero who symbolized the advantages of the

---

[4] For a masterful survey of Jacksonian democracy, see Arthur M. Schlesinger, Jr., *The Age of Jackson.*

American way of life. They did not worry about his excessive personal control of the political system, and they were willing to follow him in 1836 when he suggested that Van Buren be selected as his successor.

SECTIONAL CONFLICT

As Jackson's administration drew to a close, the conflict between the states became more critical. Slavery was an issue which agitated both the North and the South. Upon this question, the Methodist and Baptist churches split, and other denominations experienced serious controversies. The northern Church leaders regarded slavery as an attack against the freedom of men and as a violation of basic Christian principles. Harriet Beecher Stowe, in *Uncle Tom's Cabin,* showed how the slave holder was an unprincipled villain, and she idealized the faith of the slave. It was pedestrian and sentimental literature, almost medieval in its allegorical spirit, but it caused a tremendous stir in the North.

In the South, the preachers pointed to the Old Testament, in which slavery had been a recognized institution. They could quote Paul, who did not favor emancipation, and they said that there was no reason to suppose that Christianity is a religion which favors complete equality.

Economic differences between North and South were even more significant. The South represented a feudal, agricultural society which could develop successfully only with low tariffs and cheap labor. No wonder that the South most vigorously protested the high tariffs of 1827 and 1832 and was ready to leave the Union in protest. The North was becoming more industrialized and needed protection for its infant industries. Northern legislators were successful in their agitation for higher tariff laws, although most of the intellectuals of the United States theoretically favored free trade.

The conflict between the states involved a profound difference in political interpretation. The South held the view that the states were supreme and championed a laissez-faire theory of government. The more the federal government left the states alone, the better the South liked it. At the present time, the most insistent demands for a decentralized government are coming from the South; thus not much has changed.

Most of the legislators in the North were opposed to an excessive reliance upon states' rights. They wanted a strong federal government which would not allow secession, and they believed that the government should undertake a vigorous program for internal improvements.

Fear was a motivating factor in the conflict. The Southerners were afraid of slave uprisings. Their leaders told them that the North was trying to establish a dictatorship. When humanitarians interfered, Southerners resented it as an invasion of their sacred political rights. Certain propagandists spread rumors that the slaves planned to murder their masters. To the South, the victory of Lincoln's policy was the last straw.[5] Lincoln, to them, was a representative of the northern agitators, of the "black" Republican party.

Lincoln's speech, delivered at Cooper Union, is an interesting document in this respect, for it contains many of the charges of the South against the Republican party. Lincoln shows how the Southerners regarded the Republicans as a sectional party, for it received no votes in the South, but he demonstrated that this is not true and that the South really represented the forces of sectional disunity.

Another charge was that the Republicans were revolutionists. How strange this accusation would sound in the atomic age! Lincoln, in his speech, tried to impress the South with the fact that the Republican party was only adhering to Constitutional principles and was supporting the philosophy of the Declaration of Independence.

The South blamed the Republicans for stirring up more controversy regarding slavery. Lincoln acknowledged that agitation had increased, but he blamed the South for giving up the old policy of compromise and for demanding an extension of slavery. As for the charge that the Republicans had aided in the insurrection of the slaves and that they were responsible for John Brown's raid, Lincoln denied this most emphatically.

He warned the South that it should not put too much faith in the Dred Scott decision, for the case was decided by only a small majority of the Court. If the South, said Lincoln, looked to the Constitution for a protection of slavery, it was certainly mistaken.

The position of Lincoln represents the dilemma of the liberal. His main purpose, throughout his career, was to save the Union. At the same time, he had a moral abhorrence of slavery. In his first inaugural address he stated that slavery in the slave states would be protected but that he would not tolerate extension of slavery. The tone of his speech generally was peaceful and compromising.

He showed that the unity of the nation was all-important and that secession could not be tolerated.

---

[5] L. K. Burgess, *The Civil War and the Constitution*, I, pp. 28-44. Channing *History of the United States*, VI, pp. 219-225. Chadwick, *Causes of the Civil War, 1859-1861*, 67-89.

I hold that, in contemplation of universal law and of the Constitution, the union of these states is perpetual. Perpetuity is implied, if not expressed, in the fundamental law of all national governments. It is safe to assert that no government proper ever had a provision in its organic law for its own termination. Continue to execute all the express provisions of our national Constitution, and the Union will endure forever — it being impossible to destroy it except by some action not provided for in the instrument itself.

Again, if the United States be not a government proper, but an association of states in the nature of contract merely, can it, as a contract, be peaceably unmade by less than all the parties who made it? One party to a contract may violate it — break it, so to speak; but does it not require all to lawfully rescind it?[6]

He expressed his faith in the people.

This country, with its institutions, belongs to the people who inhabit it. Whenever they shall grow weary of the existing government, they can exercise their constitutional right of amending it, or their revolutionary right to dismember or overthrow it. I cannot be ignorant of the fact that many worthy and patriotic citizens are desirous of having the national Constitution amended. While I make no recommendation of amendments, I fully recognize the rightful authority of the people over the whole subject, to be exercised in either of the modes described in the instrument itself; and I should, under existing circumstances, favor rather than oppose a fair opportunity being afforded the people to act upon it. . . . I understand a proposed amendment to the Constitution — which amendment, however, I have not seen — has passed Congress, to the effect that the federal government shall never interfere with the domestic institutions of the states, including that of persons held to service. To avoid misconstruction of what I have said, I depart from my purpose not to speak of particular amendments so far as to say that, holding such a provision to now be implied constitutional law, I have no objections to its being made express and irrevocable.

Why should there not be a patient confidence in the ultimate justice of the people? Is there any better or equal hope in the world? In our present differences is either party without faith of being in the right? If the Almighty Ruler of Nations, with His eternal truth and justice, be on your side of the North, or on yours of the South, that truth and that justice will surely prevail by the judgment of this great tribunal of the American people.[7]

He concluded with an appeal to reason.

In your hands, my dissatisfied fellow-countrymen, and not in mine, is the momentous issue of civil war. The government will not assail

---

[6] *First Inaugural Address.*
[7] *Ibid.*

you. You can have no conflict without being yourselves the aggressors. You have no oath registered in heaven to destroy the government, while I shall have the most solemn one to "preserve, protect, and, defend it."

I am loath to close. We are not enemies, but friends. We must not be enemies. Though passion may have strained, it must not break our bonds of affection. The mystic chords of memory, stretching from every battle-field and patriot grave to every living heart and hearthstone all over this broad land, will yet swell the chorus of Union when again touched, as surely they will be, by the better angels of our nature.[8]

Lincoln failed in his attempt to preserve peace. Fate forced upon him the role of a commander-in-chief who had to make decisions which cost the lives of thousands of soldiers and suspended fundamental liberties. He had to fight a bloody and bitter war while his heart yearned for peace.

In his second inaugural address we notice Lincoln's faith in a lasting peace.

Neither party expected for the war the magnitude or the duration which it has already attained. Neither anticipated that the cause of the conflict might cease with, or even before, the conflict itself should cease. Each looked for an easier triumph, and a result less fundamental and astounding. Both read the same Bible, and pray to the same God; and each invokes his aid against the other. It may seem strange that any men should dare to ask a just God's assistance in wringing their bread from the sweat of other men's faces; but let us judge not, that we be not judged. The prayers of both could not be answered — that of neither has been answered fully.

With malice toward none; with charity for all, with firmness in the right, as God gives us to see the right, let us strive on to finish the work we are in; to bind up the nation's wounds; to care for him who shall have borne the battle, and for his widow, and his orphan — to do all which may achieve and cherish a just and lasting peace among ourselves, and with all nations.[9]

For every liberal, an armed conflict is an agonizing experience, because he knows that violence creates more problems than it solves. The tragedy of Lincoln was that he died in the period when he was needed most. His cool and humanitarian views would have been a great benefit in the turbulent era of reconstruction; instead, the radical Republicans prevailed.

---

[8] *Ibid.*
[9] *Second Inaugural Address.*

The political ideas of Lincoln are best expressed by his faith in democracy by which he meant an equal chance for every member of American society. He was living in an era of expanding industrial technology. He did not shut his eyes to the realities of economic life, and he knew the importance of property. His concern was that every man would have an equal chance to get rich. Any power that curtailed this natural right, he could not tolerate.

The Republican party which Lincoln helped to create has long been divided over the problem of property rights. What is most important: the accumulation of wealth or the inalienable rights promised by the Declaration of Independence? Abraham Lincoln, Carl Schurz, and Wendell Willkie believed that man was more significant than property. The extreme conservative wing of the Republican party, on the other hand, has usually championed the opposite viewpoint and has so vigorously defended the rights of property that it has frequently denied the need for social reforms.

It must not be forgotten that Lincoln was a consummate political strategist. He faced opposition, not only from the South, but also from his own party, especially from the radical wing. He had to struggle against the lukewarm support of the Democrats; he had to combat a growing pacifist sentiment; he was forced to put down the draft riots and act vigorously against the growing number of deserters. Moreover, he had to get along with ambitious generals like McClellan, whose lust for power was unbounded.

All through his life, he had to face the contempt of sophisticated Easterners, who looked upon him as a crude product of the frontier society. That he was able to harmonize the various interests and to bring the Civil War to a victorious close, indicated how successful he was as a political strategist. In the 20th century, Dwight Eisenhower, in his effort to sustain the American system, would likewise meet with opposition from many diverse sources. Like Lincoln, Eisenhower had a supreme ability in preserving harmony among his various followers.

THE RECONSTRUCTION

American history seems to prove that while the nation achieves greatness during war periods, it usually fails when peace is to be made. The period that followed the Civil War verifies this contention, as do the policies pursued in the Philippines after the Spanish-American War, the Versailles Peace Treaty and the apparent failure of the American peace policy after World War II.

The policies pursued in the South after the Civil War bear a close similarity to American policies in Germany after World War II. There was a natural tendency, on the part of the radical Republicans to regard the South as an evil section and to condemn it wholesale just as many opponents of Germany associated all the Germans with the Nazi program. The radical Republicans in the South put into effect an arbitrary military government which was bound to fail. Instead of sending the best administrators to the South, corrupt northern officials took over, and they were aided by scalawags who exploited the political situation to the fullest.

The basic idea behind the reconstruction measures was to punish the South for the war of secession, but any peace that is based upon such a negative idea is bound to fail. Military force cannot be maintained for a long period, and it is usually succeeded by a reaction that goes to the other extreme and apologizes for the faults of the conquered. Thus today there are many well-meaning persons who stoutly maintain that Hitler's Germany should have been left alone, for it would never have constituted a real danger to peace.

It must not be forgotten that some positive results were achieved in the South. Many of the feudal estates were broken up, a more equitable system of taxation was established, public education was expanded, the Negro received greater legal protection, and property qualifications for voting were abolished.

The strange paradox was that now the South was opened up to full industrialization. It became a cheap reservoir of labor power. When wages were too high in the North, industries there could be closed down and the resources of the South could be exploited. For the northern entrepreneur, the South was like a green valley, and it afforded unlimited opportunities for expansion.

An outgrowth of the period of reconstruction was the formation of the Ku Klux Klan. At first, it was directed mainly at the Negroes, who were prevented from enjoying their political rights. It had fantastic ceremonies with secret initiation rites, white robes, secret passwords, and a system of leadership which resembled that of a medieval monastic order. It used flogging and lynching; at the same time, it supported "high" ideals of chivalry and maintained that its main function was to protect southern womanhood. After a while its program expanded, and it attacked Jews and Catholics and foreign-born persons, and started a crusade against "radical" ideas. In 1946, the philosophy of the Ku Klux Klan was brought up to date by the Columbians, who believed in open dictatorship, patterned after the German Nazi model.

The Ku Klux Klan reflects the frustration and tension that pervades part of the South. Its pressure is felt most strongly by the educated Negro, as Richard Wright shows in his autobiography, *Black Boy.*

BOOKER T. WASHINGTON

Born a slave, Booker T. Washington (1856–1915) taught himself how to read while he worked in a mine. At Hampton Institute he became a janitor and then a student. Only there did he learn the rudiments of civilized living such as how to use a knife and a fork and how to take care of his bodily needs. At Hampton he experienced a new world of scholarship and history and met individuals dedicated to humanitarian service.

In his autobiography he describes the spirit of the school.

I was among the youngest of the students who were in Hampton at that time. Most of the students were men and women — some as old as forty years of age. As I now recall the scene of my first year, I do not believe that one often has the opportunity of coming into contact with three or four hundred men and women who were so tremendously in earnest as these men and women were. Every hour was occupied in study or work. Nearly all had had enough actual contact with the world to teach them the need for education. Many of the older ones were, of course, too old to master the text-books very thoroughly, and it was often sad to watch their struggles; but they made up in earnestness much of what they lacked in books. Many of them were as poor as I was, and, besides having to wrestle with their books, they had to struggle with a poverty which prevented their having the necessities of life. Many of them had aged parents who were dependent upon them, and some of them were men who had wives whose support in some way they had to provide for.

The great and prevailing idea that seemed to take possession of every one was to prepare himself to lift up the people at his home. No one seemed to think of himself.[10]

In 1881 he was chosen to establish and head Tuskegee Institute in Alabama.

It was a formidable challenge. Tuskegee seemed an ideal place for the school. It was in the midst of the great bulk of the Negro population, and was rather secluded, being five miles from the main line of railroad, with which it was connected by a short line. During

---

[10] *Up from Slavery.*

the days of slavery, and since, the town has been a center for the education of the white people. This was an added advantage, for the reason that I found the white people possessing a degree of culture and education that is not surpassed by many localities. While the coloured people were ignorant, they had not, as a rule degraded and weakened their bodies by vices such as are common to the lower class of people in the large cities. In general, I found relations between the two races pleasant. For example, the largest, and I think at that time the only hardware store in the town was owned and operated jointly by a coloured man and a white man. This co-partnership continued until the death of the white partner.

I found that about a year previous to my going to Tuskegee some of the coloured people who had heard something of the work of education being done at Hampton had applied to the state Legislature, through their representatives, for a small appropriation to be used in starting a normal school in Tuskegee. This request the Legislature had complied with to the extent of granting an annual appropriation of two thousand dollars. I soon learned, however, that this money could be used only for the payment of the salaries of the instructors, and that there was no provision for securing land, building, or apparatus. The task before me did not seem a very encouraging one.[11]

There were other obstacles.

The first month I spent in finding accommodations for the school, and in traveling through Alabama, examining into the actual life of the people, especially in the country districts, and in getting the school advertised among the class of people that I wanted to have attend it. The most of my traveling was done over the country roads, with a mule and a cart or a mule and a buggy wagon for conveyance. I ate and slept with the people, in their little cabins. I saw their farms, their schools, their churches. Since, in the case of the most of these visits, there had been no notice given in advance that a stranger was expected, I had the advantage of seeing the real, everyday life of the people.

In the plantation districts I found that, as a rule the whole family slept in one room, and that in addition to the immediate family there sometimes were relatives, or others not related to the family, who slept in the same room. On more than one occasion I went outside the house to get ready for bed, or to wait until the family had gone to bed. They usually contrived some kind of a place for me to sleep, either on the floor or in a special part of another's bed. Rarely was there any place provided in the cabin where one could bathe even the face and hands, but usually some provision was made for this outside the house, in the yard.

---

[11] *Ibid.*

The common diet of the people was fat pork and corn bread. At times I have eaten in cabins where they had only corn bread and "black-eye peas" cooked in plain water.[12]

The schooling was most inadequate.

More than once, while on my journeys, I found that there was no provision made in the house used for school purposes for heating the building during the winter, and consequently a fire had to be built in the yard, and teacher and pupils passed in and out of the house as they got cold or warm. With few exceptions, I found the teachers in these country schools to be miserably poor in preparation for their work, and poor in moral character. The schools were in session from three to five months. There was practically no apparatus in the schoolhouses, except that occasionally there was a rough blackboard. I recall that one day I went into a schoolhouse — or rather into an abandoned log cabin that was being used as a schoolhouse — and found five pupils who were studying a lesson from one book. Two of these, on the front seat, were using the book between them; behind these were two others peeping over the shoulders of the first two, and behind the four was a fifth little fellow who was peeping over the shoulders of all four.[13]

The leadership of Washington was amazing. The school attracted students from many communities. It taught the Negroes how to improve their conditions. It emphasized moral values; thrift, industry, and inventiveness were to be encouraged.

Washington stressed the ideal of labor.

In addition to the agricultural training which we give to young men, and the training given to our girls in all the usual domestic employments, we now train a number of girls in agriculture each year. These girls are taught gardening, fruit-growing, dairying, bee-culture, and poultry-raising.

While the institution is in no sense denominational, we have a department known as the Phelps Hall Bible Training School, in which a number of students are prepared for the ministry and other forms of Christian work, especially work in the country districts. What is equally important, each one of these students works half of each day at some industry, in order to get skill and the love of work, so that when he goes out from the institution he is prepared to set the people with whom he goes to labour a proper example in the matter of industry.

---

[12] *Ibid.*
[13] *Ibid.*

The value of our property is now over $700,000. If we add to this our endowment fund, which at present is $1,000,000, the value of the total property is now $1,700,000. Aside from the need for more buildings and for money for current expenses, the endowment fund should be increased to at least $3,000,000. The annual current expenses are now about $150,000. The greater part of this I collect each year by going from door to door and from house to house. All of our property is free from mortgage, and is deeded to an undenominational board of trustees who have control of the trustees who have the control of the institution.

From thirty students the number has grown to fourteen hundred, coming from twenty-seven states and territories, from Africa, Cuba, Porto Rico, Jamaica, and other foreign countries.[14]

The schedule at the school was exacting.

5 A.M., rising bell; 5:50 A.M., warning breakfast bell; 6 A.M., breakfast bell; 6:20 A.M., breakfast over; 6:20 to 6:50 A.M., rooms are cleaned; 6:50, work bell; 7:30, morning study hour; 8:20, morning school bell; 8:25, inspection of young men's toilet in ranks; 8:40, devotional exercises in chapel; 8:55, "five minutes with the daily news"; 9 A.M., class work begins; 12, class work closes; 12:15 P.M., dinner; 1 P.M., work bell; 1:30 P.M., class work begins; 3:30 P.M., class work ends; 5:30 P.M., bell to "knock off" work; 6 P.M., supper; 7:10 P.M., evening prayers; 7:30 P.M., evening study hour; 8:45 P.M., evening study hour closes; 9:20 P.M., warning retiring bell; 9:30 P.M., retiring bell.[15]

Washington, who had a pragmatic philosophy of education, thought that culture was less important than concrete abilities which advanced the economic welfare of Negroes. He believed in the project method and encouraged the students to develop specialized skills. He attacked extravagance and laziness. Work, he stated, had the greatest educational value and was a prelude to social emancipation.

He was not discouraged in his outlook. When he traveled in Europe he found that the slums there were worse than what the Negroes faced in the United States. To Washington, education would provide the door for democratic participation.

He believed that the government should not interfere in business. In fact, he felt that the businessman with his drive and energy was the best prototype for America. He was a founder of the National

---

[14] *Ibid.*
[15] *Ibid.*

Negro Business League whose task was to encourage Negroes to rise in industrial life.

Washington did not pay enough attention to cultural subjects. He made little use of the arts in the Tuskegee curriculum. The reason for this neglect was that he faced more immediate challenges and that there was little time for a more liberal view of education.

Washington was admired as an educational leader in the United States and abroad. When President Eliot of Harvard conferred an honorary degree upon him he called Washington "a wise helper of his race, a good servant of God and country."

CHAPTER SEVENTEEN

Whitman and Education for Democracy

THE ACHIEVEMENT OF WHITMAN

Walt Whitman (1819–1892) forms a climax to the liberal movements of the nineteenth century. In his work, the beliefs of the frontier, the new city life, the struggles of the Union, the philosophical aspirations of America, all find their place. He represents a new type of American thinker as well as the highest expression of the American democracy. What Heine was to Germany, what Victor Hugo did for France, and what Tolstoy accomplished for Russia, Walt Whitman achieved for the United States. In his works the beliefs of the common man could be heard; not the common man of the scholar, but the common man of the poet, who had vast compassion and love for all.[1]

There was tragedy in Whitman's life. He lived through the period of the Civil War, and during this time he often doubted that America would emerge again a strong nation. His faith was tried

---

[1] Arvin, *Whitman;* Nathanson, *Forerunners of Freedom; the Re-Creation of the American Spirit,* ch. II.

247

even more strongly during the age which followed the war when America was following the gospel of unrestrained materialism. Still his faith, until the end, was firm. To him democracy was more than a political movement, more than a way of life, more than a guarantee of inalienable liberties. It was a veritable religion.

In his works, Lincoln became almost the God of democracy. In 1856 Whitman had expressed his grave disillusionment with the men who had occupied the presidential chair. Did not most of the presidents who preceded the Civil War regard their office as an incentive to private gain? In Lincoln, Whitman found the expression of the American genius. Seldom has a tribute to a political leader been so eloquent as his poems "Oh Captain, My Captain," and "When Lilacs Last in the Dooryard Bloom'd."

During the war Whitman had done heroic service in the hospitals. In his service he had made no distinction between southern and northern soldiers; he admired their quiet courage, but the struggle filled him with revulsion against violence.

Whitman was an earthy liberal. While Emerson and Thoreau retained a puritanical strain in their character, Whitman glorified the sensual life. *Leaves of Grass* outraged many of the respectable critics of the United States; nevertheless, Emerson immediately realized the lasting greatness of Whitman.

Probably his lasting achievement for the emancipation of the American spirit was his belief in nature. During the entire colonial period and most of the era of the Transcendentalists, America had witnessed a strange dualism between spirit and matter. The Puritans had despised the needs of the flesh, they had no understanding of the artistic value of nature and had negated the life-creating impulses. The Transcendentalists had rebelled against this attitude, but still were speaking only for the upper classes. Their appreciation of nature and of common things was aloof. Whitman, differing from the Transcendentalists, accepted life as he saw it and found an underlying greatness in it.[2]

Whitman was a poetic naturalist. The difficulty with the naturalistic tradition is that it has never been emancipated from the cold scientific cast which it absorbed in the eighteenth century. Essentially, it is the philosophy of mathematicians, not of poets. Walt Whitman contributed a new spirit to naturalism. He made it colorful and picturesque, and he believed that it could be the most illuminating philosophy for the American liberal.

---

[2] For an excellent interpretation of Whitman see Vernon Louis Parrington, *Main Currents in American Thought,* vol. 3, pp. 69-86.

Unfortunately, the intellectual has not chosen to follow Walt Whitman. Until the present day, most scholars have remained snobbish, separating life from their academic endeavors. Their study should have been the cab-driver, the carpenter, the revival preacher, the bartender, the policeman on the corner — all the characters Whitman described so well, instead of devoting their writing mostly to abstract, lifeless pursuits.

THE POETIC EDUCATOR

Walt Whitman gave the United States a new national poetry, fulfilling what Emerson had demanded in *The American Scholar*. His entire writings display a confidence in America's destiny. Was not America constantly expanding? Was not Jackson giving new forms to American democracy? Was not the struggle against slavery an expression of the everlasting struggle against injustice? In Walt Whitman, the experiences of the past depressions, of European slums, and European hatreds seemed distant. Instead, the voice of the vast, almost limitless Western frontier could be heard.

In many ways, Walt Whitman was too optimistic. His concept of government was essentially negative, like that of Jefferson. He thought that the best type of governmental organization would be one which governed least. This idea may have been sufficient for the nineteenth century, but it certainly will not solve the problems of our age, in which centralization prevails.

Walt Whitman remained a radical his entire life. More clearly than Emerson or Thoreau, he was able to appreciate the heritage of the United States. He knew how much America owed to the work of Paine, and remained unafraid of his individualistic attitude. Let the genteel call him immoral; let the conservatives attack his extremist attitude in politics; Whitman knew that without nonconformists, the United States could not progress. Thus he described himself:

> Walt Whitman, a Kosmos of Manhattan the son
> No more modest than immodest.
> Unscrew the locks from the doors!
> Unscrew the doors themselves from their jambs!
> Whoever degrades another degrades me,
> And whatever is done or said returns at last to me.
> Through me the afflatus surging and surging, through me
>   the current and index.
> I speak the pass word primeval, I give the sign of democracy,

> By God! I will accept nothing which all cannot have their
> counterpart of on the same terms.

The religion of Walt Whitman was derived from his Quaker background. It was not a matter of theology or of systematized beliefs, or
of adherence to conventional ideas; rather, an attitude regarding his
fellowman expressed by unceasing compassion. He understood what
the mystics of the fourteenth and fifteenth centuries had preached.
He knew the universe as part of a vast chain and that all men are
united by a common destiny:

> I celebrate myself, and sing myself,
> And what I assume you shall assume,
> For every atom belonging to me as good belongs to you.
> I loaf and invite my soul,
> I lean and loaf at my ease observing a spear of summer grass.
> My tongue, every atom of my blood, form'd from this soil,
>   this air,
> Born here of parents born here from parents the same, and
>   their parents the same,
> I, now thirty-seven years old in perfect health begin,
> Hoping to cease not till death.
> Creeds and schools in abeyance,
> Retiring back a while sufficed at what they are, but never
>   forgotten.
> I harbor for good or bad, I permit to speak at every hazard,
> Nature without check with original energy. . .[3]

All of life is interrelated, its essence is *earthy* not transcendent:

> I am the poet of the Body and I am the poet of the soul,
> The pleasures of heaven are with me and the pains of hell
>   are with me,
> The first I graft and increase upon myself, the latter I
>   translate into a new tongue.
> I am the poet of the woman the same as the man,
> And I say it is as great to be a woman as to be a man,
> And I say there is nothing greater than the mother of men.
> I chant the chant of dilation or pride,
> We have had ducking and deprecating about enough,
> I show that size is only development.
> Have you outstript the rest? are you the President?
> It is a trifle, they will more than arrive there every one,
>   and still pass on.

---

[3] *Song of Myself*, 1.

I am he that walks with the tender and growing night,
I call to the earth and the sea half-held by the night.
Press close bare-bosom'd night — press close magnetic
    nourishing-night!
Night of south winds — night of the large few stars!
Still nodding night-mad naked summer night.
Smile O voluptuous cool-breath'd earth!
Earth of the slumbering and liquid trees!
Earth of departed sunset — earth of the mountain misty-topt.
Earth of the vitreous pour of the full moon just tinged
    with blue![4]

Education is being close to nature; a part of man's essence.

Now I see the secret of the making of the best persons,
It is to grow in the open air and to sleep and eat with the
    earth.
Here a great personal deed has room,
(Such a deed seizes upon the hearts of the whole race of men.
Its effusion of strength and will overwhelms law and mocks
    all authority and all argument against it.)
Here is the test of wisdom,
Wisdom is not finally tested in schools,
Wisdom cannot be pass'd from one having it to another
    not having it,
Wisdom is of the soul, is not susceptible of proof, is its
    own proof,
Applies to all stages and objects and qualities and is content,
Is the certainty of the reality and immortality of things,
    and the excellence of things;
Something there is in the float of the sight of things that
    provokes it out of the soul.
Now I re-examine philosophies and religions,
They may prove well in lecture-rooms, yet not prove at all
    under the spacious clouds and among the landscapes
    and flowing currents.
Here is realization,
Here is a man tallied — he realizes here what he has in him,
The past, the future, majesty, love — if they are vacant of
    you, you are vacant of them.
Only the kernel of every object nourishes;
Where is he who tears off the husks for you and me?
Where is he that undoes stratagems and envelopes for you
    and me?

---

[4] *Song of Myself*, 21.

> Here is adhesiveness, it is not previously fashion'd, it is
>   apropos;
> Do you know what it is as you pass to be loved by strangers?
> Do you know the talk of those turning eye-balls?[5]

Truth is formed in all aspects of life. To achieve it we must use intuition, not logic or religious sermons. The entire universe has a certain significance.

> All truths wait in all things,
> They neither hasten their own delivery nor resist it,
> They do not need the obstetric forceps of the surgeon,
> The insignificant is as big to me as any,
> (What is less or more than a touch?)
> Logic and sermons never convince,
> The damp of the night drives deeper into my soul.
> (Only what proves itself to every man and woman is so,
> Only what nobody denies is so.)
> A minute and a drop of me settle my brain,
> I believe the soggy clods shall become lovers and lamps.
> And a compend of compends is the meat of a man or woman.
> And a summit and flower there is the feeling they have
>   for each other,
> And they are to branch boundlessly out of that lesson until
>   it becomes omnific,
> And until one and all shall delight us, and we them.
> I believe a leaf of grass is no less than the journey-work
>   of the stars,
> And the pismire is equally perfect, and a grain of sand, and
>   the egg of the wren,
> And the tree-toad is a chef-d'oeuvre for the highest,
> And the running blackberry would adorn the parlors of
>   heaven,
> And the narrowest hinge in my hand puts to scorn all
>   machinery,
> And the cow crunching with depress'd head surpasses any
>   statue,
> And a mouse is miracle enough to stagger sextillions of
>   infidels.[6]

He found God in man and in all parts of creation, although the essence of God cannot be comprehended.

> And I say to mankind, Be not curious about God,
> For I who am curious about each am not curious about God.

---

[5] Song of the Open Road, 6.
[6] Song of Myself, 30-31.

(No array of terms can say how much I am at peace about
   God and about death.)
I hear and behold God in every object, yet understand
   God not in the least.
Why should I wish to see God better than this day?
I see something of God each hour of the twenty-four, and
   each moment then,
In the faces of men and women I see God, and in my
   own face in the glass,
I find letters from God dropt in the street, and every one
   is sign'd by God's name,
And I leave them where they are, for I know that where-
   so'er I go,
Others will punctually come for ever and ever.[7]

Walt Whitman possessed a sense of piety which many of the
modern thinkers, who have only an attitude of negation, lack. They
know what they oppose, but when it comes to affirmations they are
lost. The reason for this nihilistic attitude of much of contemporary
thought is that it has lost its touch with reality; it has been uprooted
both physically and spiritually. Whitman, on the other hand, remained, until the end of his life, a champion of the people, giving
voice to the aspirations of the common man.

The foundation of democracy, according to Whitman, is faith
in the educability of man. The keynote of his age was the limitless
opportunity for the man on the street. With several depressions, and
industry occasionally unable to provide full employment, the West
was always ready to take up the slack. If a man could not make a
living in the East, he could always emigrate. Whitman looked to the
vast land of the frontier to provide a constant reservoir for American
prosperity. He admired the Westerner because he lived close to
nature and did not bow before authority. The ideal of Whitman was
that a new generation should grow up having no concept of class
oppression. He dreamt of a democracy which was to produce a new
perfect race whose mind, body, and emotions would be expressions
of the highest standards of civilization.

EDUCATION AND CULTURE

When Whitman wrote the *Democratic Vistas*, he had become
more pessimistic about the political development of the United States.

---
[7] *Ibid.*, 48.

For my part, I would alarm and caution even the political and business reader, and to the utmost extent, against the prevailing delusion that the establishment of free political institutions, and plentiful intellectual smartness, with general good order, physical plenty, industry &c. (desirable and precious advantages as they all are), do, of themselves, determine and yield to our experiment of democracy the fruitage of success. With such advantages at present fully, or almost fully, possess'd — the Union just issued, victorious, from the struggle with the only foes it need ever fear, (namely those within itself, the interior ones), and with unprecedented materialistic advancement — society, in these States, is canker'd, crude, superstitious, and rotten. Political, or law-made society is, and private, or voluntary society, is also. In any vigor, the element of the moral conscience, the most important, the vertebra to State or man, seems to me either entirely lacking, or seriously enfeebled or ungrown.

I say we had best look our times and lands searchingly in the face, like a physician diagnosing some deep disease. Never was there, perhaps, more hollowness at heart than at present, and here in the United States. Genuine belief seems to have left us. The underlying principles of the States are not honestly believed in, (for all this hectic glow, and these melo-dramatic screamings), nor is humanity itself believed in. What penetrating eye does not everywhere see through the mask? The spectacle is appalling. We live in an atmosphere of hypocrisy throughout.[8]

He described the shallowness dominating American institutions, how literature and religion were filled with second-rate ideas. As for the corruption of business, Whitman maintained that it was greater than commonly believed. Nor was that all. The federal government was corrupt, with this spirit extending to the state and city administrations. The speculator class seemed to be supreme in the United States. When he examined the manners of the United States, he found a lack of thorough culture and an abundance of small aims or no aims at all. City life, which he had admired so much before, now disgusted him. New York, he described as "flippant, infantile, unwholesome, and mean-mannered."

Whitman acknowledged that democracy in the United States had improved the material standards of society, and had popularized knowledge, but he questioned if the United States had improved in its educational life, or had absorbed the true spirit of religion.

Whitman lashed at the ideal of imperialistic expansion. What had it helped in the spiritual development of the United States that

---

[8] *Democratic Vistas.*

it had acquired Texas and Alaska and that it was reaching for Cuba? It had given this nation more power but had left it without a real soul.

In all this, Walt Whitman almost becomes prophetic in his insight. For when a nation becomes powerful and expands abroad, it tends to weaken its cultural structure. Thus the decline of the Greek civilization came after the expansion of Alexander the Great. When Rome created a world empire, it established a magnificent government, but the arts suffered. Walt Whitman made it clear that a nation could not expand physically and keep up its arts. Real power lay in knowledge, rather than in domination of other lands.

He asked:

> Are there, indeed, *men* here worthy the name? Are there athletes? Are there perfect women, to match the generous material luxuriance? Is there a pervading atmosphere of beautiful manners? Are there crops of fine youths, and majestic old persons? Are there arts worthy of freedom and a rich people? Is there a great moral and religious civilization — the only justification of a great material one? Confess that to severe eyes, using the moral microscope upon humanity, a sort of dry and flat Sahara appears, these cities, crowded with petty grotesques, malformations, phantoms, playing meaningless antics. Confess that everywhere, in shop, street, church, theatre, barroom, official chair, are prevailing flippancy and vulgarity, low cunning, infidelity — everywhere the youth puny, impudent, foppish, prematurely ripe — everywhere an abnormal libidinousness, unhealthy forms, male, female, painted, padded, dyed, chignon'd, muddy complexions, bad blood, the capacity for good motherhood deceasing or deceas'd, shallow notions of beauty with a range of manners, or rather lack of manners, (considering the advantages enjoyed), probably the meanest to be seen in the world.[9]

Certainly he did not give up his hope that democracy eventually would succeed. He did not despair, for his faith in democracy was based upon ideal educational principles, not upon an actual system of government.

He remained an individualist to the end; no party could claim him. He had hopes for the Socialists but never joined them. The Democratic party he had left a long time before when it espoused slavery. He was a lonely figure because he lived too much for the future—as Nietzsche might say, for the day after tomorrow.

---

[9] *Ibid.*

RAPHAEL SANTIVS PINX

IN AEDIBVS VATICANIS

CHAPTER EIGHTEEN

The Ideals of Harris

BROKMEYER AND ST. LOUIS

The genesis of speculative philosophy is connected with St. Louis and the labors of Henry Brokmeyer (1828–1906). It is strange that this city should have been the birthplace of one of the most fertile movements in American thought. Unlike Boston, it was a rather rough and unrefined place: here adventurers came who wanted to try their luck in the West; here merchants from all over the world congregated in search of profit and easy money.

The annals of St. Louis in the nineteenth century are full of crime and social conflict. The city was far less homogeneous than the Eastern centers of culture; all kinds of races came together and St. Louis, to a great extent, had the appearance of a frontier town.

Still, learning was appreciated there. This was mainly due to the large German population in the city. The revolution of 1848 had brought many German refugees to St. Louis; most of them were liberals who believed in the rights of man, and who looked upon education and philosophy as invaluable tools for the improvement of mankind.

We know very little about the life of Brokmeyer. He was born in Germany and came to this country when he was seventeen years old. Although he studied at Brown University for a short period, he was uninterested in formal education. At St. Louis he became involved in politics and was largely responsible for drawing up the Missouri constitution. He was elected Lieutenant Governor and became Acting Governor of the state. But in his last years he withdrew into solitude and spent most of his time as a trapper.

His ruling passion was his love for Hegel. He wanted to translate Hegel's *Larger Logic* into English, and he spent many years in the pursuit of this task, but he never succeeded. Somehow Hegel's terminology was so difficult and Hegel's language was so involved that the English translation became an impossible task for him.

We may wonder why Brokmeyer was so much attracted by Hegel. The reason appears to be that Hegel offered a complete explanation of intellectual and social phenomena, picturing life as an organic whole in which conflict is synthesized and in which constantly higher levels emerge. The writings of Hegel were regarded as almost sacred by Brokmeyer who, like the author of the *Phenomenology of Spirit,* felt that the real is rational and that the rational is real.

In his educational theories he preached self-control and self-reliance. He appreciated Hegel's concept of discipline, but, unlike Hegel, he relied upon democracy rather than monarchy in political affairs. Throughout his life Brokmeyer was an ardent advocate of liberty, which to him was the goal of all political institutions.

Like Socrates, he believed in rational ideals; merely to make a living was not adequate, rather it was the task of man to improve and reform education and to make a contribution to the future. He disliked a hedonistic concept of life, for he felt that we all have a social obligation and that it is our task to better our fellow-man.

HARRIS

W. T. Harris (1835–1909), who came from Connecticut, met Brokmeyer in 1858 and this event changed Harris' life. From then on he devoted himself to philosophy. Being from New England, he had a passing knowledge of Transcendentalism, but he certainly was not an expert in philosophy.

He became the outstanding member of the St. Louis Philosophical Society; he was also one of the eminent lights of the Concord School of Philosophy and later became United States Commissioner of Education. In establishing the *Journal of Speculative Philosophy*, he gave a vital impetus to technical thought in the United States. Among its contributors we find some of the most brilliant American thinkers such as Royce, Peirce, Howison, and James.

W. T. Harris regarded Brokmeyer as a great philosophical genius, and it was his desire to imitate his teacher. Harris also tried to translate Hegel, and the result of his labor was *Hegel's Logic*, which was published in 1890.

In his later years he dreamed of establishing a new center of culture at Concord. This was to become the Athens of the United States, and Hegel was to be its Socrates. However, the response of the audience at Concord was disappointing; Hegel was too difficult for them and too removed from the practical side of American life; literary topics were far more popular at Concord than Hegelian philosophy.

The Journal of Speculative Philosophy

The *Journal of Speculative Philosophy* was founded by Harris to counteract the empirical schools of philosophy which had become popular in the United States. W. T. Harris had no love for Spencer, J. S. Mill, and Comte. He looked upon their systems with considerable contempt, for he thought that they lacked speculative insight and intellectual vigor.

He made it clear in the *Journal* that he was interested above all in the great systems of thought which represented a cosmic insight and which had a metaphysical foundation. He wanted to popularize, most of all, the thoughts of Plato, Aristotle, Schelling, and Hegel.

Harris felt that Americans were too provincial and too nationalistic. Hence he wanted to impress his fellow countrymen with the fact that thought has no national boundaries, but is truly universal. He wanted to create a new group of thinkers who would transcend national ideals and who would speak for the deepest aspirations of humanity.

The new speculative philosophy, according to Harris, would negate all individualism. Thus it would strike a blow at those who were guided only by selfish interests and did not pay attention to the welfare of the group. Hegelian thinking represented to Harris a symbol of collective consciousness and collective needs. Hegel thus became the prophet of *unity*, based on reason and subordination to rational laws.

Like Hegel, Harris found in all movements three states: (1) thesis—positive assertion; (2) antithesis—standing for negation; and (3) synthesis—representing unification on a higher level. Like Hegel,

Harris was optimistic, for he thought that the future would witness a more rational culture and that the progress of mankind was assured.

Education and Philosophy

As a Hegelian, Harris was less interested in the individual than in institutions. Individual happiness and fulfillment were less important than the advancement of society.

Harris was deeply religious, stressing moral and spiritual factors in education. Christianity, he said, provides a synthesis between Oriental mysticism and Western skepticism. It provides both for a knowledge of man and a knowledge of God, a view of time and of eternity. It is a protection against barbarism and social anarchy, and against radicalism in politics and economics.

All this did not imply that the separation of state and church should be broken. Religion, according to Harris, had to appeal to dogmas, while education rested on reason and dialectical knowledge. The schoolroom, he stated, was not the place for ritual and religious ceremony.

The five basic subjects of Harris were grammar, literature and art, geography, mathematics and the sciences, and, most important, a knowledge of history. The study of the past which was not an impersonal inquiry, provided a platform for the present. The great ideas of the past, he held, were just as important in modern times as thousands of years ago.

Harris was opposed to a hedonistic view of education.

There is the same difficulty with the term 'interest' that there has been with the term *pleasure* or *happiness*, taken as a technical term for the highest end of man. Hedonism is a doctrine which has played a greater part in the history of ethics. It is not of any use to attack hedonism by asserting that the true end of man is not happiness or pleasure. Any end that you may name, other than happiness or pleasure, will be at once cunningly seized upon by the Epicurean. He will inquire with a smile whether your highest object and aim in life does not secure the greatest sum of pleasure and happiness in the long run? Your affirmative answer seems to him a fatal admission of the triumph of his principle. So, with regard to the doctrine of interest which affirms that the pupil should be developed through his teacher; that he must make it his first and foremost endeavor to interest his pupils in what they are studying. If you point out a higher object in studies — namely the acquaintance of the pupil with the rational order of the universe in which he lives: the attainment of wisdom and holiness — the advocate of interest will inquire with the same covert sarcasm whether this is not to be made interesting to the pupil — in fact whether it is not really the most interesting of all things, if rightly taught? The refutation of hedonism is not to be found in setting up an antithetic principle. It is not happiness, nor non-happiness, that should be regarded as the highest aim of man — "happiness is not," although Mr. Pope supposed it to be, "our being's end and aim."[1]

There is no self-contradiction in the refutation of hedonism.

If one approaches the subject by considering the undetermined character of the term 'happiness'; taking note of the fact that happiness includes all grades and kinds, namely a temporary happiness which is followed by a permanent injury to the soul as well as a highest happiness which leads through manifold trial and suffering to eternal blessedness. It is evident that happiness does not contain within it the determining principle: it demands a higher principle in order to correct its own indefiniteness and vagueness. . . . In order to define his chosen field of happiness, he must bring in a higher principle which relates to man's origin and destiny and to his realization of the Divine will in holiness and in the knowledge of truth. Then he will have introduced and justified his term "happiness," but at the same time will have subordinated it. Happiness is in this way proved to be a secondary principle by its own advocates.

Just so the principle of interest is a subordinate principle and it is shown to be such by its advocates, who attempt to point out what realm or sphere of interest is proper and to be encouraged. They make a study of the child's interest, and looking out upon the universe toward the careers which will arise from different species of interest, they select the kind of interest that leads in the surest manner toward human perfection in will and intellect. They also study the other kinds of interest and find out which of them will tend wholly toward the bad, and likewise which of them will lead by circuitous paths toward the good. In this way the Herbartians, and other advocates of interest as a principle of education, subordinate the principle of interest to a higher principle, namely the rational perfection of man, attainment of full self-expression; the realization of the reasonable in this universe and the attainment of full self-consciousness; the discovery of the Divine as the final end of human endeavor.[2]

---

[1] William T. Harris, "Professor Dewey's Doctrine of Interest as Related to Will," *Educational Review*, May 1896, pp. 490-491.

[2] *Ibid.*, p. 492.

Manual Training

Harris was not a proponent of stress upon manual training.

Neither apprenticeship nor the industrial school should be allowed to take possession of the youth until the completion of his twelfth year at least; the fifteenth year is still better, because physical maturity is necessary for the formation of the best muscular movements to produce skill. . . . Moreover, the serious occupations of life cannot be imposed on children without dwarfing their human nature, physically, intellectually, and morally, and producing arrested development. Not only the games of youth, but the youth's freedom from the cares of mature life, should be insured to him if the best preparation is to be made for manhood. It is sad to know that very many children are dwarfed by family necessity, which compels them to bear the weights and cares of mature years.[3]

He did not believe that the schools should be utilitarian institutions.

For when we inquire, we discover at once that the trade or vocation in life is but a small part of the total functions of anyone's life. It is what goes with the trade or vocation that makes even it a success or failure. What does one need to know besides his trade?

Under the head of behavior toward others, his success will depend on his treatment of his fellow-workmen and his employers; on his treatment of his neighbors, and of his family and children. Moreover his behavior as a citizen concerns vitally all who live with him under the same government; for he conditions to the extent of his single vote, and the proletariat class as a whole may form a majority and determine altogether what sort of government shall be placed over all, rich and poor, Christian or heathen, humane or selfish. The 'dude' citizen, who inherits large wealth and believes that the laboring classes should not be educated beyond the station they are to occupy in life, will find that the manual laborers are also voters, and that they decide whether there shall be rights of private property or protection of life and limb for him as well as for others.

The illiterate manual laborer, no matter how skillfully educated for his trade in wood and metal operations, cannot read and write. He cannot read the newspaper and take interest in the doings of town, State and nation or world at large, except as he hears of it in the turbid stream of personal gossip from fellow-workmen. He is essentially shut in, and his thoughts move around in a narrow circle like

---

[3] *The Educational Value of Manual Training*, p. 2.

the horse that turns the wheel of the mill. Nothing can prevent his being the victim of wild schemes of agitation that attack radically all the institutions of civilization. To the observer of the newer and newest phases of modern history, nothing is so clear as the fact that the first necessity of civilization is a system of universal education, not in industry, but in the ideas and thoughts that make up the conventional view of the world — such ideas and opinions as one learns in studying geography and history, and especially literature.[4]

Leadership

To Harris, a college education is one of the promises of American democracy. Higher education should not be restricted to a small minority, rather it should be available to a large portion of the population. Colleges should give more scholarships to graduates of the public schools who face financial difficulties.

The purpose of high school, according to Harris, is mainly cultural. A sound high school education would equip the student with an appreciation of the past so that he can understand the continuity of civilization. He would gain basic skills which would improve his facility of communication. But philosophical training and insight are the fruits of higher education which would give to the student and teacher a view of totality whereby all of history and all of human institutions could be surveyed. Higher education would make for a critical knowledge of the self, society, and education. Such knowledge would subordinate naturalism to spirituality and the sciences to the study of the humanities.

Harris believed that the college graduate would avoid all extremist philosophies. Would he not see that radicalism leads to the disintegration of society? Would he not oppose all magic formulas? Would he not be against all "isms" which tend to destroy the foundations of the state and the family? Would he not become a defender of established institutions?

The predictions of Harris were essentially correct. Most college graduates in our society tend to be more conservative in politics and economics than those who have not had a college education. A small minority of college graduates tends to be radical, while another small number will support reactionary ideas. The large majority, however, as Harris foretold, will support a middle of the road policy.

Harris felt that the educated man would champion a sober view of human institutions. He would not believe in sudden change or

---

[4] *Ibid.*, pp. 3-4.

in sweeping proposals for social legislation. He would realize that change is best achieved from within by a cultivation of sound habits and by more rational means of communication and administration. The educated man would not be overwhelmed by prejudice, for he would cultivate an attitude of critical analysis and he would look at life and social institutions with a spirit of objectivity.

The true intellectual, he believed, would stand above the social issues of his time; he would be essentially conservative, while the uneducated man in the street would be a partisan of fanatical courses. The true intellectual would cultivate the arts and the sciences; the uneducated would seek economic gain. The educated man would seek unity in education and philosophy, while the unlettered would be guided by fragmentary issues and ideas.

Harris had high hopes for adult education which would equalize educational opportunity. Adult education, Harris stated, would improve the leisure time activities of the average citizen and it would make culture part of his daily life. It would counteract the vulgarity of the yellow press which only portrayed the sensate drives of man. Harris, like Dewey, believed that education was a continuous process; hence the formal school would never stop and the intelligent individual would be as interested in improving his mind at the age of eighty as at eighteen.

Adult education ought to stress the responsibilities of citizenship and teach ethical values which make for a better society. Most important, adult education should stress the classics of the past so that the individual would understand the importance of cultural pursuits. Such education would strengthen the American way of life by preventing the rise of radicalism; it would provide a responsible audience for an enlightened leadership. Various groups in the community would find common goals in the pursuit of the humanities and philosophy.

The evils which Harris hoped to combat in education and society were determinism, socialism, and epicureanism. Determinism undermines man's needs to labor and develop his own goals. If the universe were determined from beginning to end, the individual effort would not count. Socialism leads to organized laziness whereby the individual relies on the state. In education, socialism curtails the freedom of the teacher and interferes with the authority of the administrator. Epicureanism he opposed because it makes pleasure the goal of life. Such a philosophy encourages mediocrity, for culture is based on man's sense of duty. Slavery to sensate desires invites moral disintegration. Instead, he urged vigorous labor so that both the individual and society might advance.

Harris felt that teachers would advance best by supporting the existing institutions. He did not favor a labor union for teachers, who are to look to their own professional advancement. He wanted teachers to set an example to society in ethical behavior, in the art of communication and in the depth of their background. He predicted a bright future for the American teacher who would become the leader of society if he had the insight and the skill to advance his cause and if he valued culture above utilitarian concerns.

The interests of Harris were prolific. He would speak to innumerable teachers and give lectures at universities. One of his favorite universities was Boston University where he delivered lectures on philosophy and education. His topics included religion, art, science, criminology, and the status of women. He felt that women ought to be completely emancipated and that their help was needed in fighting the tide of corruption and lawlessness.

Interested in improving the tone of newspapers, he urged editors to concentrate less upon scandal and to devote more space to education and cultural events. He urged young people to read the better newspapers through which they would realize that crime does not pay and that virtue is rewarded by society.

He was concerned about crime both on the juvenile and adult level. He believed that education should stress order and that waywardness among students should be punished so that they would realize that society does not tolerate an infraction of its rules. He urged that teachers aid the humanitarian causes in the various communities and that they support those who believe in honesty in government.

Harris stressed the importance of educational leadership. This meant, first, a larger physical investment in schools and higher salaries for teachers and administrators; second, it implied better trained teachers with a more prolific background; third, it meant a general appreciation of culture which was to improve the standards of public and private behavior; fourth, it meant the advancement of knowledge so that ignorance could be overcome and so that technology would be improved; fifth, it meant an appreciation of man's spiritual capacities, which could achieve new levels of excellence if he explored the resources of philosophy and education.

School and Society

Unlike Thoreau, Harris had a high regard for the machine. It would provide wider areas of enjoyment and prosperity. He thought it might produce the leisure which is the pre-requisite of a great culture. Furthermore, it would lift the level of intelligence of the masses who would need to learn new skills to operate the machines.

Unlike James, Harris welcomed the colonial expansion which took place in his time. The new colonies would be civilized, and the blessings of religion and education would make up for their loss of liberty. Mere political expansion was not enough; what was needed was a cultural diffusion so that real civilization would become universal.

Harris had little use for permissiveness in education. He wanted the child to accept the ideas of his teachers and be silent and punctual. He claimed that Rousseau's philosophy, that education should be largely negative and should avoid moralization, would only lead to barbarism.

Progressive educators of his time favored student participation in the government of the school, but Harris wanted the student to learn to take orders, and develop good habits. To give him too many privileges would only spoil his character.

He favored Greek and Latin as disciplinary subjects. Against Pestalozzi's emphasis on sensory knowledge, he dwelt upon the importance of reason which aimed at a view of totality.

Still, Harris had some advanced ideas. He felt that there ought to be special classes for the gifted and for slower students. The potentialities of each student were to be explored to the utmost. Discipline was not the end of learning, it was to lead to the rational emancipation of the individual who would make a real contribution to society.

The school should promote national progress. He felt that every civilization has its unique mission: for the Hebrews it was religion; for the Greeks philosophy; for the Romans law; for the United States it is a system of democracy which combines law and authority. The past and the present are to merge. History will show the triumph of reason over superstition, morality over anarchy. Patriotism, based on universal principles, is to be stressed in the public schools.

Education has more than an intellectual function: it must create an open society by providing opportunities for all classes; it must promote first-rate ideas and strengthen the United States in international competition; and it must give opportunities to minority groups so they can share the national prosperity.

PART FOUR

Dawn of Reform

CHAPTER NINETEEN

Man Against Nature

THE SIGNIFICANCE OF THE
EVOLUTIONARY THEORY

Evolution was the subject of the nineteenth century's most vigorous controversy. The startling theory that life evolves from lower to higher levels, the concepts of the prodigality of nature, natural selection, the animal ancestry of man — all upset the orthodox mind.

Before this period mathematics had replaced theology as the most important science; now biology succeeded mathematics. To see life from the viewpoint of biology is not the most inspiring and impressive experience; man does not like to think of himself as an integral part of nature, but makes special claims of uniqueness and importance and keeps on believing that his destiny is more glorious than that of the rest of nature.

Consoling voices could be heard which gave an optimistic note to the doctrine of evolution. They said, following Spencer, that Darwin's theory showed how far man had risen above the animal level;

others claimed that man had achieved a really enlightened stage; certainly there must be a divine purpose in the universe. In the twentieth century efforts were made to make God an indwelling principle in evolution. With Bergson the whole process is one which is guided by a vitalistic impulse, not by blind necessity. Thus the doctrine of evolution did not displace the purposive causes most philosophers cherish.

But there was another interpretation of evolution which was far more disturbing. Schopenhauer in *The World as Will and Idea* (1819) had already indicated than man is in everlasting bondage to his restless, dissatisfied will. All his activities are the result of its hunger; thus, love is merely a restless sexual drive, and compassion represents limited egotism. The life impulse itself is evil; the only hope is that man may transcend its bondage. Schopenhauer's philosophy ends with the Buddhist goal of ceasing to desire and negating the will. This pessimism appears later in a milder form in the death instinct of Freud, and it finds a climax in the modern movement of existentialism.

The new emphasis upon biology led to a pronounced interest in man's physiological heritage. Many studies were devoted to his sexual drives; love was now examined not as a romantic proclivity but as an animal passion. Reduced to its animal instincts, man's behavior was made more susceptible to exact scientific experiments. A new area was opened up through Freudian psychology — the study of man's unconscious drives. Religion now appeared to be the result of wish fulfillment rather than the product of rational thinking. Man's time perspective was radically changed as geological time together with the new astronomical concepts expanded his horizon immeasurably. His origins on earth thus were not a matter of a few thousand years but of millions of years.

Educators became more and more conscious of the importance of history; the factual method of the historian threw light upon the development of a Christianity now no longer considered as a supernatural institution. Comparative religion indicated the universal basis of various beliefs, and it showed that other religions had frequently been more tolerant than Christianity. The Bible was subjected to rigorous scholarship especially by the Tübingen School in Germany. The life of Christ was interpreted more critically by David Strauss and Joseph Renan, both of whom stressed his human experiences rather than his divine background. Renan's *Life of Christ* was, perhaps, too dramatic — its style was often bombastic — but it had an immense popular appeal. Many scholars followed Strauss in regarding the Bible as little more than a collection of poetic tales.

Thinkers now acknowledged the dynamic basis of history and thought. Fixed ideas became outmoded. The difficulty was that now modern man lacked intellectual stability; for there were no beliefs to which he could cling absolutely. Thus, the philosophy of evolution had positive as well as negative results. In its activistic emphasis it intensified the neurotic trends in western civilization. Restlessness became a way of life; scholars and common people alike would expect a constant change of values; society would be in a perpetual process of change.

Unfortunately, the doctrine of the survival of the fittest would give an intellectual justification to all kinds of oppression. It is self-evident that the new totalitarianism finds its rational basis in the Darwinian interpretation of life.

AMERICAN ECHOES

The most vigorous opponent of Darwinism in the United States was Louis Agassiz (1807–1873). Born in Switzerland, he had been influenced by Schelling and Cuvier, and he regarded the theory both as scientifically unsound and as a prelude to atheism.[1]

In his youth Agassiz had accepted an idealistic interpretation of reality; physical laws really are symbols of divine thoughts, and nature merely reflects the power of the Absolute. Throughout his career he held to the fixity of species, divine creation, and cosmic purpose.

To him the term "natural selection" reflected a serious omission. It omitted the creative power of God; without an understanding of teleology no valid view in science could be achieved. The possibility of classification indicated a harmonious adjustment in nature. Did this not indicate a higher harmony? Did it not demonstrate the omnipotence of God?

How can we explain existing life forms? How can we describe the diversity of phenomena? He examined various theories. First, life is explained according to the concept of spontaneous variation; but there is no scientific evidence for this principle. In fact, it does not explain anything. It is just another name for chance. Again, we might regard matter as the principle which causes all the changes in nature. However, matter is inert and passive. Furthermore, if we use

---

[1] For a critical survey of Agassiz consult James, "Louis Agassiz," *Memories and Studies*, pp. 3-16; Cooper, *Louis Agassiz as a Teacher*; Riley, *American Thought from Puritanism to Pragmatism and Beyond*, pp. 172-216.

matter we explain the highest principle, mind, by the lowest denominator, matter.

The third explanation, and the only rational and scientific one, is the providence and design of God. Without His intervention, nature would never have produced its most sublime product, man.

In his metaphysical theory, he held to a static, ontological system which almost reminds us of Plato. Nature rests upon types which are fixed and which are not subject to flux and change.

As for the specific parts of nature they are not real metaphysically. In fact, matter is only a cover for the spirit, which alone is eternal and real. The unity of nature indicated to Agassiz that this is the best of all possible worlds and that God's providence promotes the welfare of creation.

Among the works of Agassiz special notice should be taken of his *Essay on Classification*, which is found in part I of *Contributions to the Natural History of the United States of North America; Methods of Study in Natural History;* and "Evolution and Permanence of Type" which appeared in the *Atlantic Monthly* in 1874.

Although he was a noted scientist, his thinking was dogmatic and he was unwilling to acknowledge the validity of the viewpoints of his opponents. He felt that the theory of evolution was merely a passing fad which would surely become obsolete.

However, other scientists, especially Gray, Newcomb and Wright came to the defense of Darwin, and they turned against the ideals of Agassiz.[2] Asa Gray (1810–1888) was a botanist, and when he read the *Origin of Species* he realized that a new era had dawned for the scientific life of his time. He reviewed the *Origin of Species* in glowing terms and paid tribute to the genius of Darwin.

Religiously, Gray was a theist; thus Darwinism did not produce a naturalistic reaction in his life. He felt that the theory of evolution had strengthened rather than weakened religious ideals and that divine design was constant, creative, and not reserved to the past.

Simon Newcomb (1835–1909) was a noted astronomer who taught mathematics at the United States Naval Academy and Johns Hopkins University. He regarded the theory of evolution as a verification of the struggle for life which we observe in nature and which can be demonstrated scientifically. He held that science could progress only by a naturalistic concept of causality that disregards teleology. The trouble with the moralizing philosophers was their

---

[2] For a general survey of the scientific response to Darwinism see Loewenberg, "The Reaction of American Scientists to Darwin," *American Historical Review* XXXVIII (1932-1933), 657-760 and Wright, *Philosophical Discussions.*

proclivity to seek transcendent causes in nature, when in reality their function should have been to describe the processes of nature.

Chauncey Wright (1830–1875), a positivist in his educational philosophy, likewise defended Darwin and looked upon his theory as a great step forward in the emancipation of the human mind. Darwin had great respect for this American thinker, and they fought together against those who insisted upon a supernatural account of evolution. Wright did not jump to metaphysical conclusions regarding the theory of evolution as Spencer had; rather, he remained within the tentative, hypothetical framework of the scientific method.

PHILOSOPHICAL AND EDUCATIONAL IMPLICATIONS

The harshness of the Darwinian theory was lessened considerably by Alexander Winchell (1824–1891), who taught at Syracuse University and wrote *The Doctrine of Evolution, Theologico-Geology* and *Creation, the Work of One Intelligence.*

To Winchell, evolution indicated the prevalence of a spiritual force. Following Berkeley, he spoke of matter as inert; hence spirit was needed as the dynamic principle to produce the ascending ladder of creation.

He abhorred a mechanistic concept of man's mind; on the contrary, man's thoughts reflect the patterns of divine omniscience. We should realize that all things and all phenomena are guided by God, whose ideas have been the patterns of the universe and whose perfection is the model for all creatures.

Edward D. Cope (1840–1897) taught at the University of Pennsylvania and wrote, among other books, *The Origin of the Fittest* and *The Descent of Man in Evolution.* He felt that the proponents of evolution had overemphasized external factors and had ignored internal forces. He looked upon the universe as a dynamic creation in which energy is the ruling principle. In metaphysics he accepted the theory of panpsychism, which holds that all phenomena are alive and active.

His concept of the mind was more naturalistic than that held by Winchell. The mind has primarily an adaptive function and is guided by the environment. Through education we organize knowledge in order to increase our hold over our environment. His genetic view of the mind anticipated to some extent the systems of James, Baldwin, and Dewey.

Evolutionary theories were brought to the West by Joseph Le Conte, who taught at the University of California from 1874 till 1901. His main work is *Evolution: Its Nature, Its Evidences and Its Relation to Religious Thought.*

According to Le Conte, evolution indicates an upward trend in nature. Inorganic life is the prelude to organic life, and organic life is the prelude to man. Evil he regarded in the Stoic fashion: it has no reality. When we see the universe in perspective, we realize its perfection and we appreciate its teleological nature.

In his youth he had been a follower of Agassiz, but after studying the scientific evidence for evolution he became convinced that Agassiz had been mistaken, and that nature did not rest upon fixed species, but upon a dynamic derivation that manifests the divine will. He applied the law of evolution to all phenomena; he felt that it demonstrated a necessary truth which was even more important than the law of gravity.

More interested in a naturalistic interpretation of science than Le Conte was Paul Carus, who felt that man's emancipation could only be brought about by adherence to scientific truths. He was born in Germany, but his political views were so liberal that he had to leave that country and come to the United States, where he became editor of *The Open Court* and *The Monist.*

He regarded the new biological inventions almost with awe. He felt that progress could not be achieved without a surrender of human prejudices and partisanship and a willing acceptance of the scientific spirit. The great scientists were his apostles and their works were his bible. He urged an almost Spinozistic detachment through which truth can liberate man.

James Baldwin (1861–1934), who taught at Princeton and Johns Hopkins, intensified the naturalistic implication of the evolutionary theory. He emphasized the social side of evolution and stressed the fact that the individual is not autonomous but in his own development repeats the development of the race.

He described an organic theory of evolution which stressed adaptability and which makes possible the control of nature by intelligence. Idealism was socialized and made more practical and utilitarian. The same emphasis we find in John Dewey, whose philosophy of instrumentalism emphasized scientific control through the application of intelligence.

In the evolution of the mind, Baldwin referred to three levels: the first is pre-logical, the second is logical, the third is hyperlogical. The first stage is characterized by a naive and crude concept of the universe. Everything is regarded as chaotic and science as yet has not appeared. The second stage sees the development of scientific laws which establish causal relationships and experimental order in the universe. The third stage stands for the appreciation of esthetic factors, which are superior to causal laws and give an immediate insight regarding the nature of the universe.

Reality he conceived according to the theory of *Pancalism;* it stands for an esthetic description of experience which can be applied to the universe. Beauty thus has both a subjective and objective meaning. It stands for the orderly constitution of phenomena and for our own experience whereby we overcome all duality and find a serene and a contemplative perspective.

Among his works we find *Mental Development in the Child and the Race, Development and Education,* and *Genetic Theory of Reality.* He was the editor of the *Dictionary of Philosophy and Psychology* to which noted thinkers contributed, especially Peirce and Royce, and which was marked by a high level of scholarship.

THEOLOGICAL IMPLICATIONS

Orthodox theologians rejected the doctrine of evolution. They looked upon it with hostility, believing that it undermined revelation, destroyed the basis of morality, and denied man's immortality. The struggle against evolution is still going on today in Protestant fundamentalism, and in several Southern states evolutionary teachings are outlawed.

The anti-evolutionary forces were aided by the work of Andrew Peabody, of Harvard University, who felt that evolution could not be substantiated by science. To Peabody, Darwin's explanation was merely another chapter in the history of materialism, which attempted to undermine the certainty of the Christian faith.

An interesting version of evolution was contained in the theories of Henry James, Sr., who was influenced by Swedenborg and who regarded selfhood as the great obstacle in man's quest for salvation.

The keynote to his thinking was social and religious solidarity. Thus, in *Christianity, the Logic of Creation,* he pointed out that life reveals two processes; one leading to the creation of individuality; the other, the path of salvation, leading back to reunion with God. We shall see later how his son, William James, reversed the emphasis and placed his trust in the individual instead of the social group.

The Calvinistic view of evolution was expressed by James McCosh, who vigorously attacked the scientific version of evolution. He felt that the scientist is so much occupied with microscopic details and analysis that he cannot appreciate spiritual truths. Thus it becomes the task of the theologian to point out the divine principles unfolded in nature which demonstrate God's majesty. Evolution does not limit the activities of God, for He transcends all temporal and spatial categories and is the source of all natural laws.

George Frederick Wright, a professor at Oberlin College, was certain that Darwin had substantiated the truths of Calvinistic religion. Did not Darwin's concept of the survival of the fittest correspond to the doctrine of divine election? Did not Darwin destroy the ideals of the enlightment in picturing a merciless struggle in nature? Of course, Wright did not accept the mechanistic assumptions of evolutionism, for he held that God's plan was responsible for all natural changes.

This tough-minded interpretation of nature was not accepted by James Freeman Clarke, who founded the Church of the Disciples. In his view, evolution produced a higher type of humanity; he thus reflected the ideals of Transcendentalism.

He was certain that nature could be explained only according to both final and efficient causation. Thus he followed Leibnitz and Newton in trying to achieve a harmony between science and religion. Final causes, according to Clarke, do not imply that God intervenes in nature and that God is abitrary, but that design is *immanent* in nature. In this way, he used the evolutionary theory to preach the gospel of *pantheism*.

The dilemma of the theologian was fully demonstrated by James Woodrow (1828–1907), who taught at a Presbyterian seminary in South Carolina. He asserted that the theory of evolution is valid when interpreted as a mode of divine creativity.

He preached the doctrine of *mediate* creation, which he explained in the following way:

> In view of all the facts now presented—the way in which animals have succeeded each other, beginning as far back as we can go, and coming down to the present; the series of resemblances which connect them from the lowest to the highest, exhibiting such remarkable unity of plan; the existence of rudimentary organs; the geographical distribution of animals. . . . Are not the coincidences such as must almost compel belief of the doctrine, unless it can be proved to be contradictory of other known truth? For my part I cannot but so regard them; and the more fully I became acquainted with the facts of which I have given a faint outline, the more I am inclined to be-

lieve that it pleased God, the Almighty Creator, to create present and intermediate past organic forms not immediately but mediately, in accordance with the general plan involved in the hypothesis I have been illustrating.[3]

Evidently the Board of Directors of the seminary where he taught did not agree with him and so he was discharged from his position.

A more radical type of theology was taught by Theodore T. Munger (1830–1910), who wrote *The Freedom of Faith, Character Through Inspiration,* and other works.

He maintained that revelation was also a product of evolution and that there are no *a priori* scriptural truths. He criticized the Bible, not from a scholarly viewpoint, but from the standpoint of historical experience. Generally, he can be regarded as an excellent example of liberal Christianity.

Of greater philosophical importance than Munger was Francis Ellingwood Abbot (1836–1903), whose sincerity and passion for science caused his resignation from the Unitarian ministry, and who became one of the founders of *The Free Religious Association.*

He anticipated Peirce in his opposition to nominalism, and he was like Felix Adler in his stress on moral factors. He wanted to abolish all ecclesiasticism, all theology, and all dogmas. Education and religion were to be purified from their priestly origins.

He described his own faith in the following way:

Free Religion, the higher faith I hold, has no history, save the history of the human spirit, striving to work out its destiny in freedom. It is spiritual, not historical, — universal, not special, — inward, not outward. It has no list of doctrines to teach, no Church to extend, no rites to perform, no Bible to expound, no Christ to obey. With none of these things, it is the soul's deep resolve to love the truth, to learn the truth, and to live the truth, uncoerced and free. . . . It is the spirit of self-conscious freedom, aiming evermore at the best, and trusting itself as the architect of character. In fine, it is that sense of spiritual unity with boundless Being which fills the soul with reverence for human nature, and disables it from worshiping aught but the formless, indwelling, and omnipresent One.[4]

Among the writings of Abbot were *Religion and Science; Scientific Theism; The Way Out of Agnosticism, or the Philosophy of Free Religion.*

---

[3] Quoted in Blau, *American Philosophic Addresses.*
[4] *Ibid.*

Fiske

John Fiske (1842–1901) was more conventional than Abbot, and he was able to combine the evolutionary theories with religious faith. In his youth he had come under the spell of Spencer and so accepted the evolutionary theory.

At first his Harvard teachers did not like his radicalism. Spencer as yet had not become respectable. Strangely enough, in the twentieth century Spencer stands for arch-conservatism. After graduation he was invited to lecture at Harvard, where he was well-received. He was appointed an assistant librarian, but he did not continue in this position and devoted himself largely to writing and research. In his lifetime he won fame both as a philosopher and a historian.

Among his philosophical works we find *Outlines of Cosmic Philosophy;* Darwin reviewed it and said that he had never read "so lucid an expositor as Fiske." *The Destiny of Man* was applauded by liberal Christians, and *The Idea of God* indicated his theistic position. He also wrote *Darwinism and Other Essays; Myths and Myth-Makers; The Unseen World; Excursions of an Evolutionist;* and *Through Nature to God.*[5]

This last work gives an excellent summary of his system. In the first part, under the heading of the Mystery of Evil, he indicated the unity of nature.

The advance of modern science carries us irresistibly to what some German philosophers call monism, but I prefer to call it monotheism. In getting rid of the Devil and regarding the universe as the multiform manifestation of a single all-pervading Deity, we become for the first time pure and uncompromising monotheists, — believers in the ever-living, unchangeable, and all-wise Heavenly Father, in whom we may declare our trust without the faintest trace of mental reservation.

In a happy world there must be evil.

We are thus brought to a striking conclusion, the essential soundness of which cannot be gainsaid. In a happy world there must be sorrow and pain, and in a moral world the knowledge of evil is indispensable. The stern necessity for this has been proved to inhere in the innermost constitution of the human soul. It is part and parcel of the

---

[5] An evaluation of Fiske can be found in Clark, *The Life and Letters of John Fiske,* two vols., and Royce, "John Fiske as a Thinker," *Harvard Graduate's Magazine,* 10 (1901-2), pp. 23-33.

universe. To him who is disposed to cavil at the world which God has in such wise created, we may fairly put the question whether the prospect of escape from its ills would ever induce him to put off this human consciousness, and accept in exchange some form of existence unknown and inconceivable! The alternative is clear: on the one hand a world with sin and suffering, on the other hand an unthinkable world in which conscious life does not involve contrast.[6]

The second section of his book deals with Love and Self-Sacrifice. He made it clear that natural selection cannot explain the mind of man.

It must be borne in mind that while the natural selection of physical variations will go far toward explaining the characteristics of all the plants and all the beasts in the world, it remains powerless to account for the existence of man. Natural selection of physical variations might go on for a dozen eternities without any other visible result than new forms of plant and beast in endless and meaningless succession. The physical variations by which man is distinguished from apes are not great. His physical relationship with the ape is closer than that between cat and dog; which belong to different families of the same order; it is more like that between cat and leopard, or between dog and fox, different genera in the same family. But the moment we consider the minds of man and ape, the gap between the two is immeasurable.[7]

Man is distinguished from higher mammals (i.e. dogs, horses) in four ways: (1) man is more progressive, and his history indicates a wider advancement than that of mammals; (2) man is grouped in family relationships, whereas dogs come in packs and have no definite social organization; (3) man has the power of speech and thus is able to communicate his thoughts; (4) man has a longer infancy than mammals and thus needs a more extended period of care by his parents.

Fiske regarded the story of man as a thrilling episode in the development of the universe; it is a story with a definite educational background.

Surely if there is anywhere in the universe a story matchless for its romantic interest, it is the story of the genesis of Man, now that we are at length beginning to decipher it. We see that there is a good deal more in it than mere natural selection. At bottom, indeed, it is all a process of survival of the fittest, but the secondary agencies we have been considering have brought us to a point where our con-

---

[6] *Through Nature to God.*
[7] *Ibid.*

ception of the Struggle for Life must be enlarged. Out of the manifold compounding and recompounding of primordial clans have come the nations of mankind in various degrees of civilization, but already in the clan we find the ethical process at work. The clan has a code of morals well adapted to the conditions amid which it exists. There is an ethical sentiment in the clan; its members have duties toward it; it punishes sundry acts even with death, and rewards or extols sundry other acts. We are, in short, in an ethical atmosphere, crude and stifling, doubtless, as compared with that of a modern Christian homestead, but still unquestionably ethical.[8]

Nature preaches a moral sermon.

Though in many ways God's work is above our comprehension, yet those parts of the world's story that we can decipher well warrant the belief that while in Nature there may be divine irony, there can be no such thing as wanton mockery, for profoundly underlying the surface entanglement of her actions we may discern the omnipresent ethical trend. The moral sentiments, the moral law, devotion to unselfish ends, disinterested love, nobility of soul, — these are Nature's most highly wrought products, latest in coming to maturity; they are the consummation, toward which all earlier prophecy has pointed. We are right, then in greeting the rejuvenescent summer with devout faith and hope. Below the surface din and clashing of the struggle we hear the undertone of the deep ethical purpose, as it rolls in solemn music through the ages, its volume swelled by every history, great or small, of right over wrong, till the fulness of time, in God's own time, it shall burst forth in the triumphant chorus of Humanity purified and redeemed.[9]

The third part of his work is entitled *The Reality of Religion*. In it he especially attacks materialism. Already in the preface he had turned with scorn against Haeckel for his denial of a personal God and against De La Mettrie for his excessive reliance upon physical nature. Now Fiske expanded his arguments to justify his theistic conclusion.

Modern education, according to Fiske, supports the moral content of the unseen world.

All the analogies that modern knowledge can bring to bear upon the theory of a future life point to the opinion that the breach of physical continuity is not accompanied by any breach of ethical continuity. Such an opinion relating to matters beyond experience

[8] *Ibid.*
[9] *Ibid.*

cannot of course be called scientific, but whether it be justified or not, my point is that neither in the crude fancies of primitive men nor in the most refined modern philosophy can theology divorce itself from ethics. Take away the ethical significance from our conceptions of the Unseen World and the quasi-human God, and no element of significance remains. All that was vital in theism is gone.[10]

Nature teaches man the reality of religion.

So far as our knowledge of Nature goes the whole momentum of it carries us onward to the conclusion that the Unseen World, as the objective term in a relation of fundamental importance that has co-existed with the whole career of Mankind, has a real existence; and it is but following out the analogy to regard that Unseen World as the theatre where the ethical process is destined to reach its full consummation. The lesson of evolution is that through all these weary ages the Human Soul has not been cherishing in Religion a delusive phantom, but in spite of seemingly endless groping and stumbling it has been rising to the recognition of its essential kinship with the ever-living God. Of all the implications of the doctrine of evolution with regard to Man, I believe the very deepest and strongest to be that which asserts the Everlasting Reality of Religion.[11]

SIGNIFICANCE OF EVOLUTION IN AMERICAN THOUGHT

The controversy regarding evolution did not cease with the end of the nineteenth century. It led to the trial of John Scopes, who was defended by Clarence Darrow and prosecuted by William Jennings Bryan. Scopes was a biology teacher in Tennessee who had been dismissed for his evolutionary teachings in defiance of state law.

Probably no scientific theory caused as much change in critical thinking in the United States as the theory of evolution; not even Freudianism or Einstein's theory of relativity. Some of the changes were:

(1) Thinkers now relied more upon biology, which tended to replace theology. This trend is especially strong in James and Dewey. Man thus is considered as an evolving animal, not as a fallen angel. Philosophic truths had to be verified according to laboratory methods.

(2) Evolution caused a new emphasis on means and techniques. Gone were static goals and fixed values. Instead, the spirit of flux

---

[10] *Ibid.*
[11] *Ibid.*

characterizes most of the twentieth century philosophical systems. There was a pre-occupation with growth and movement: no *a priori* concepts were accepted.

(3) Evolution supported an agnostic philosophy. Before Darwin God had been the center of philosophical thinking. This had been especially true in the systems of Edwards and Johnson, but now nature replaced God, and the scientific method replaced the Bible.

(4) The historical approach to problems was favored because of the evolutionary theory. In the early nineteenth century the history of philosophy occupied a relatively minor place in the philosophical curriculum; now with the advance in scholarship and with greater interest in the history of ideas, the genesis of philosophical thoughts was studied assiduously. The naturalistic stress is especially strong in the standard texts of the history of philosophy, as can be seen in B. A. G. Fuller's *History of Philosophy.*

(5) Evolutionary theories changed the epistemological thinking of American scholars. More attention now was paid to hypothesis and correct verification. The mind was no longer regarded as an entity, but as a social function. Idealism to some extent was replaced by pragmatism, which gave a more dynamic approach to epistemological and metaphysical problems.

CHAPTER TWENTY

G. Stanley Hall

Evolutionary ideas found an educational application in the work of G. Stanley Hall (1846–1924). Hall studied in Leipzig under Wundt, the famous German psychologist, and he became a noted child psychologist. He attracted international attention as President of Clark University. His main books on education include *Aspects of Child Life and Education, Educational Problems,* and *Adolescence* in two volumes. He edited *Pedagogical Seminary,* an important educational magazine, which later became the *Journal of Genetic Psychology.*

Hall's interest in evolution made him champion the theory of acquired characteristics. Thus he extended the realm of heredity. The individual in his development repeats the development of his species. The growth of the individual is biological, mental and cultural.

Influenced by romanticism, he placed feeling above intellect and intuition above reason. He maintained that education fails if it does not appeal to the emotions of children.

Hall believed that sex is man's fundamental drive. This means that our unconscious urges will often triumph over our conscious desires. He popularized the ideas of Freud and Jung, but he was more influenced by the latter in his mysticism and his advocacy of a sound family life.

He stressed the biological differences between men and women. Women should not enter the professions; their main task is that of motherhood. The emancipated woman who escapes from her responsibilities is to be pitied. Motherhood is both a physical and spiritual responsibility; Hall described its glories in mystical terms.

PHILOSOPHY AND EDUCATION

To Hall, philosophy has more than a theoretical meaning. Its function is to serve humanity and to provide a foundation for action. In the past philosophy overemphasized theory and logic; it had established closed systems; it had often overlooked ethical problems. The philosophy of the future, on the other hand, will have an open perspective, be based on the insights of life and on concrete realities.

A valid philosophy must be in agreement with common sense. It cannot mistake appearance for reality; it cannot uphold a subjective reality and project it upon the universe. Philosophy should do more than explain the world; it has to become a platform for inspiration. Thus Hall opposed the pessimism typified by Schopenhauer. If we teach that this is the worst of all possible worlds, then we cannot inspire our youth and we end in moral paralysis. Philosophy grows out of feelings and temperamental preferences. Ideas are footnotes to experience. This means that abstraction is to be avoided and that psychological knowledge is more significant than metaphysical explanation.

Hall's philosophy implies that neither conventional idealism nor conventional materialism is a valid guide for action. Philosophical idealism overlooks the concrete setting of our drives, while philosophical materialism does not stress sufficiently the importance of motivation and noble aspiration.

Philosophy should make youth enthusiastic; it should lead to a love of knowledge; it should never develop a premature sophistication or cynicism. It should increase our interest in life and enhance our awareness of our own powers. It should not destroy the sense of mystery basic to the development of esthetic and scientific imagination. Truth has to pass a practical test; it must not lead away from action and involvement; it must not develop an ascetic attitude so that life becomes an endurance contest. Indeed, to Hall, "truth becomes a tool of evolution," it urges individuals to apply their insights to concrete matters.

Conventional philosophy, according to Hall, is too far removed from life. It is imbued with too much logic. It analyzes so much that it neglects the realm of feelings and it does not give the student an affirmative view of the self and of society. It upholds artificial first principles which inhibit inquiry. It has too much faith in tradition which blocks man's educational advancement.

A valid philosophy of education, Hall stated, can learn more from psychology than from conventional philosophy. For psychology studies the drives of man and examines his motives. Psychologists realize that man is a feeling animal intent upon significance and meaning. Psychology points to the need for constructive values which make life more abundant. Whether we are students or teachers, according to Hall, we need a wholesome perspective which combines interest in the self and humanitarianism.

To Hall, the universe is composed of space and motion. Space is the setting for energy. The world is guided by laws which can be understood by man. Evolution is the law of life which indicates that man can be perfected. Evolution implies growth, not merely in the physical realm but in morals. In fact, Hall believed that the weak and the ineffective are destroyed by nature, while the strong prevail and create a great culture.

Basic in his educational ideals is a persistent faith in a progress which governs all areas of life. Progress can be seen in physical life when new species appear; in science new laws are discovered, while in education our enlightenment is spreading to other nations.

Education, to Hall, is a tangible evidence of man's perfectibility. Education indicates that man's goodness outweighs his negative capacities. It is the task of the teacher to inspire youth with the thought that greatness belongs to the future, not to the past.

Man lives in two worlds. On the one hand, man is part of a physical setting and surrounded by objects. On the other hand, he lives in a world of imagination in which feeling and intellect meet. Imagination, which should be the center of education, is symbolized by the play activities of children and is climaxed by the artistic and scientific creativity of adulthood.

Hall points to specific needs in the development of the individual. First comes infancy — a stage between birth to the end of the second year. This phase sees the rapid physical development of the child whose senses are being stirred. The infant becomes aware of his own identity, and he becomes conscious of his environment. At the same time, he is dependent on parental love and understanding.

Next, comes the stage of childhood which lasts until the eighth year. Now imagination should dominate and it should be carefully cultivated. This implies no artificial restraints and discipline and no restrictive curriculum. Precise knowledge is to be avoided; fairy tales are the center of childhood, for they indicate that children yearn for an ideal realm.

Between eight to thirteen a different phase prevails for youth, for now education should stress drill and obedience. Good habits are to be cultivated. Exactness is to be stressed in school. Hall believed that youngsters of that age group need firm guidance. This period thus should be carefully supervised by teachers who are to stress the significance of hard work and are to be strict disciplinarians.

Between fourteen and twenty-two a flexible educational system is to prevail. Now the youngster is ready to enter the stage of civilization. He needs little drill, rather he requires inspiration. Now the arts and the humanities become especially important and interest is to prevail in the classroom. Now intuition rather than analysis is to be developed and the inward development of the student is to be attained.

Hall was opposed to examinations in this phase of the student's development. Instead, he urged a stress upon a complete view of life. The young student is to correlate the physical, spiritual and moral elements. He is to become conscious of the beauty of ideas. Ultimately, he is to become his own teacher and develop patterns of autonomy. What is needed thus is not accuracy of perception, but creativity which unites the ideal and the practical realm and which makes a unique contribution to civilization.

THE STUDY OF EDUCATION

Hall stressed the training of teachers.

More and more, everywhere, the value of a national system of instruction depends on the quality and quantity of the professional training of teachers, and, if confidence in the system is shaken, here is where we must first look. Unhappily, however, experience abundantly shows that no part of an educational system is so prone to deteriorate, and become not only sterile but injurious; so that normal schools need the most able supervision and inspection to protect them from the peculiar and insidious dangers inherent in the nature of their work.

The first need of teachers, even in lower grades, is a better knowledge of the subjects taught. Teaching is in no good sense professional until teachers not only are far beyond the need of keys and translations, far ahead of their best pupils, but can command the choicest resources of their subject. Even reading, school mathematics, history, geography, language, and writing are far more effectively taught by teachers who have been tempered for their work by the glow that comes from growing insight into some chosen mental field, and who know what devotion to truth for its own sake means; who have developed some interest in their subject and enthusiasm for it. Such teachers will be lovers, as Plato said, "not of truth alone, but of children and youth, whom they will burn to impregnate with it." They will really believe in education, and will bring out its power. To this end, the broad and uniform curriculum of our normal schools, which prevents them from taking a high rank, should be reconstructed, so that they may gradually specialize, both among themselves and within themselves. Some schools might lay slightly more stress upon letters, history, and literature, and others upon science; while each should permit and encourage special attention to favorite branches.[1]

Hall believed in experts.

With general training only, no one can do justice to himself in the intellectual world of today, which, in all its spheres, high or low, is now ruled by experts — by those who have attained more or less of the mastery that comes by concentration. This progressive specialization, while limiting the number of subjects for the individual teacher, save in the very lowest grades, would not only greatly increase his efficiency, but would enlarge his sphere. In all large towns the same teacher could teach his subject in different schools of the same grade, and, what is far more important, in different grades, gradually qualifying for higher classes, and thus working his way from the grammar school to the high school, and even to the university.

Such opening up of the way of promotion for the ablest teachers into professional chairs, is a common and approved method in Europe, and here would help to obliterate the dead lines and water-tight compartments that too often separate higher from lower grades. It would tend to vitalize colleges and elementary schools, and to bring the parts of our educational system into sympathy and unity. All important reforms in the highest educational grades would be felt in the lowest, and *vice versa*. A system in which each man is not kept doing his best work, is unbusinesslike and wasteful. Is there any reason why languages, sciences, geography, history, arithmetic, to say nothing of the mother tongue, writing, reading, and religion, sometimes down nearly to the beginning of primary grades, should not be thus taught here with as great gain in efficiency and economy as drawing, music, and gymnastics already are? While some schoolhouses would need changing, while some educators would oppose the system, while some additional appropriations to our normal schools would be required, it has

---

[1] Hall, "The Training of Teachers," *Forum*, 1890, p. 11.

been proved so economical and effective, and is in the current of so
many good and strong tendencies, that there is no doubt whatever
that it will gradually prevail. No intelligent man doubts that one
hour's teaching by an expert is worth more to a class than two hours'
instruction by a routine teacher.[2]

He asserted that methodology is less important than subject
matter.

The rage for analyses of processes that never should be analyzed,
kills the spontaneous in children at every point, and with its impertinent "hows" and "whys," pulls up every fresh thing in the juvenile
mind to see how it grows. Only those lacking in intuition and insight,
the slow or stupid, can explain and give reasons for their processes,
or the logical stages of them; just as it is only teachers not deeply
versed in their subjects that fall back upon these wretched substitutes
for learning. A child naturally loves to deal with wholes, and, if its
food is wholesome, its mental appetite is vast and its digestion mar-
velous. It was said that the habit of the Spartan nurses, of themselves
first chewing all the food of infants, was sometimes carried so far that
the growth of infant teeth was delayed, that children were underfed
because the virtue had already been chewed out, and that their stom-
achs were injured by adult, if not sometimes abnormal, saliva. But
apart from the effect of method to cram the pupils, it is most dangerous for the teachers, because it makes ignorance so easy to conceal
that few teachers can long remain proof against such a temptation.
The intolerant orthodoxy of one method, and the conceit and fraud of
teaching methods at all, in subjects where the instructor is not a
master, justify, or at least suggest, that insistence on methods and thor-
oughness in knowing the subject itself are usually in inverse ratio to
each other. There are always many equally good ways, and the best
probably has not yet been discovered; methods in teaching being at
best like copybook handwriting, always superseded if one writes
enough to get a hand of his own. It is the vice of tiros to begin a
subject by studying its methods; but to insist upon doing so, I have
long since, as a teacher, come to regard as a bad sign for a student's
further development. The old German lecture-room and textbook habit
of prefacing a topic by a prolix introduction on its methods, was long
ago dead in every topic save metaphysics and theology.[3]

He advocated the study of the development of education.

Next after proficiency in the subjects, I place the history of education, and the educational institutions, methods, and laws of today in

---

[2] *Ibid.*, p. 12.
[3] *Ibid.*, p. 13

our own and other countries. By history, I do not mean the grounds covered by such books as Gill's, Quick's, and Compayre's. These are good, but they give little idea of the scope and culture value of the history of education. It is natural that educational leaders who get their ideas of the history of education from such books, should think as unfavorably of it as Agassiz did of the development theory from perusing the works of such puerile representatives of it as Oken. If the history of education were as sad and full of error as that of chemistry, biology, or even theology, it would still have the peculiar value of a collection of admonitions of how not to do it; for how far from any city or university need we travel to find at least rudiments and survivals of most of the bad methods described in history?

Every European government keeps expensive agencies to learn promptly the latest changes and improvements in all political and military matters in other countries, and strives to be the first to adjust itself to every new condition, and to avail itself of it. Every enterprising manufacturer or business house studies new processes, supplies, fluctuations of taste or fashion, and markets in other lands. Every respectable man of science learns promptly of every important new discovery or treatise in his line throughout the world. But our professional schools for teachers, our city and State supervisors, and even our highest educational institutions, are conducted without utilizing or even studying, the experiences of other lands.[4]

He advocated the study of other educational systems.

Object lessons in industrial and technical education, of the most vital importance for our material interests, could be gathered in all the large countries of Europe. After a discussion continuing many years, and the collection of opinions from many sources, the university system of Russia underwent, in 1884, one of the most radical reconstructions known in the history of education. New departures of radical significance have been accomplished in France and, to a less degree, in Germany, profoundly modifying the status of science and learning of the higher grades. Many unique institutions have been started and many experiments made. In a word, there is a store of often long-accumulated experiences here, a wealth of suggestion and fact, shedding light upon all our educational problems, nearly all of which is accessible in French, German, or English. But where is the library in this country that contains these books? Where is the college or university man, the superintendent or normal-school teacher, in this country, who has studied the causes and effects, or can teach us the lessons, of these changes? Several American teachers, on a limited allowance of time, money, preliminary training, and knowledge of European languages, have brought us hints, and these, imperfect as they are, con-

---

[4] *Ibid.*, p. 14.

stitute, with a few translations, our most valuable educational literature of the last decade. The official heads of education in France, Germany, Italy, Switzerland, and other European lands, as I know in some cases from personal acquaintance and discussion with them, follow with eagerness all changes in other countries, almost as strategists in one country there follow the military movements of others. Here, leaders are too absorbed in serving the interests of single institutions, careless of others and of education in the country at large. To invite a discussion of great questions by a professor of education who is competent and independent, requires rare virtue in the head of a great institution of learning. Such a professor each chief university needs, if but to keep its authorities so posted that they may know their own interests in the widening environment in which they must act.[5]

He calls for comparative education.

Education is a mine of well-distilled experience, a laboratory of tried and recorded experiments. This rich material is found in the histories of individual universities, learned societies, academies, the relations of governments to science and learning expeditions, endowments, buildings, organization and administration, state examinations, the three learned professions, national educational policies, legislation both by academic senates and by political bodies. Indeed, the pedagogic standpoint is one of the very highest and most philosophical points of view for reading history in general.

Many read but the daily or weekly paper, which deals only with what is here and now, and though important, is ephemeral. Other readers of literature extend their interests to monthly and quarterly publications treating of State, national, and perhaps international questions. Third and higher comes interest in national literature reflecting races and history. Highest of all is the taste for the best, the great world classics, the great canons, the bibles of the race, which have interest for man as man in all places — Homer, Plato, Dante, Shakespeare. Thus, wherever a broader interest is substituted for a narrower one, there is enlargement, growth bibleward. The same scale holds of educational interests. Teachers begin with interest in their own room, grade, or city. A master, city superintendent, college president or professor of education must study in wider fields. As he who knows but one language or but one religion knows none well, so he who knows but one system of education knows none well. In every field it is the comparative method which does the best work.[6]

---

[5] *Ibid.*, p. 15.
[6] *Ibid.*, p. 16.

Europe can teach many lessons to the United States, according to Hall.

We have far more yet to learn from Europe, where teaching is much more of a profession, and is practiced by men who are less likely to change their vocation. In lands where no man can enter one of the learned professions, or hold any high political office or important position in government, railroad, or telegraph service, without a university course; where success in manufactures and in war depends directly upon the relative state of science; where hundreds of stipends, large and small, new and old, attached to churches, corporations, families, and professions, smooth the way for poor men; where universities elect their representatives to the highest educational bodies — in such countries courses of education are more deeply pondered, and become more unified, and almost as sacred as the canon of scripture itself. For the express study of these institutions, problems, and systems, as existing today, Clark University has appointed two instructors, and is selecting the best literature, so that young men may be qualified to represent education as superintendents, heads of normal schools, and professors in colleges, where the demand for such men now far exceeds the supply.

There was never before such fundamental unsettlement here as now. The parochial, technical, and professional problems, the shortening of the college course, the university movements at Washington — all these show that transformations as radical as those lately seen or now in progress in Italy, France, Sweden, and Russia may impend here. Thus, while we should not imitate "abroad" as Japan and South America do, broader studies have become inevitable for us.[7]

He was enthusiastic about the application of pedagogy to education.

Here psychology, which begins in tact and sympathy and ends in anthropology, has already laid the basis of pedagogy in a body of scientific facts and laws that no one questions. Even studies of crime and insanity are now utilized by the psychologist as nature's experiments for his benefit. Animal instinct, savage myth, custom, and belief yield valued contingents; while applied psychology considers the training of the blind, the deaf, and idiots, as well as of the criminal and the insane, and in each field finds matter of value to every teacher. The new psychology has as yet no presentation at all adequate in any textbooks; but a course of reading could now be wrought out, largely

---

[7] *Ibid.*, p. 17.

in English, that would yield a fair idea of it, beginning perhaps with Burnham's four articles on memory, aided by references to the most important articles he cites. It is physiological, and considers as one of its most important applications mental and school hygiene, physical training and gymnastics, the peculiar problem of female education, and student life and character, all of which have also their historical side.

Without going so far as Herbert Spencer, who says, "The subject that underlies all other subjects, and therefore the subject in which the education of every one should terminate, is the theory and practice of teaching," I am convinced of the need of two university chairs as above outlined, if they can be filled by men too judicious to do harm, and too able and learned to distill mediocrity or to dignify the commonplace. Educational history and psychology have each its own domain of fact, with a scientific soil so rich and deep that they would flourish with no parasitic life.

Besides commanding one of these two great fields, the university professor of education should, if possible, have felt the difficulties of the schoolroom, and have developed the tact to overcome them; should have learned that the most welcome expedients are likely to be petty, that ruts are apt to seem the king's highways, and that it is often of advantage to modulate from one method to another no better. He should be independent, and his undivided energies should be given to his department.[8]

CONTRIBUTIONS

Hall popularized the concepts of Jung and Freud and stimulated an interest in child psychology. He realized that the interests of children are different from those of adults; and that the integrity of childhood must be protected.

He believed that the group is more important than the individual, emphasizing common activities and the development of altruistic drives toward the service of humanity.

Intellect is less important than temperament. Hall's pragmatic philosophy looked to the consequences of ideas and made activity central in the educational experience. Like James, he opposed intellectualism as an obsolete view of life.

Education, to Hall, was the supreme study of man. It included the arts and the sciences, philosophy as well as religion. He felt that the history and philosophy of education should have a primary place in the college curriculum.

---

[8] *Ibid.*, p. 19.

His evolutionary theories tended to be optimistic. He felt that the individual in his development recapitulated the history of the race, and like Rousseau, he urged a curriculum which would be appropriate to the various phases in the development of man.

He stimulated interest in higher education by his emphasis on research and the creation of a genuine academic community. Knowledge was not to imitate the past, but to anticipate the frontiers of the future. Knowledge was to serve the interests of democracy and emancipate man from tribal taboos.

He called for a creative system of education which would explore all the powers of individuals. Teachers must be well-trained in subject matter and infectious in their enthusiasm.

Hall idolized the period of childhood, which should become the center of education. Through numerous questionnaires he tried to explore the attitudes and motivations of children.

Like Dewey, Hall favored more elastic instruction. The idea of uniformity in the curriculum he regarded as a roadblock. Let children advance according to their own needs and explore with fervor. Let them use all their gifts; the body as well as the mind should be stimulated. Science and art should be correlated. The entire curriculum ought to be based on the needs of children, not on adult authority.

Like Rousseau, Hall had an overly romantic vision of childhood. It is doubtful whether his questionnaires actually clarified the dilemmas and perplexities of children. But his influence was vast. It extended to scholars like Dewey, Kilpatrick, Starbuck, Terman, Cattell and Bode.

BLINDMAN'S-BUFF.

How long will this Game last?

CHAPTER TWENTY-ONE

The Progressives and Critics

THE PROGRAM OF REFORM

For the fifty years that followed the Civil War, the liberal thinker engaged in a bitter struggle for social progress. He stood at the side of the farmers who were fighting the railroads, he agitated for the women and children who were treated harshly by the industrial system. He worked for the general public so that prices would be low enough. The liberal exposed the abuses of monopoly and sought to have the rights of the people protected.

With equal vigor, the liberal leaders probed the inefficiency of government and exposed the abuses of political leaders. Through novels, the press, schools, lecture forums, and churches, the liberals tried to make the government more responsive to the demands of the common people.[1]

It was a struggle against the materialism which prevailed in American culture. The cultural atmosphere of the United States had

---

[1] Filler, *Crusaders for American Liberalism;* Regier, *The Era of the Muckrakers;* De Witt, *The Progressive Movement;* Moody, *Master of Capitalism.*

grown more sterile than before; the artist was regarded as a second rate person, while the captain of industry reigned like a king.

Materialistic evaluation dominated all aspects of American life. In politics it created the mediocre leader who was merely a spokesman for the interests of business. In journalism, it developed newspapers whose sole function seemed to be to popularize the ideals of business. It developed a style of living which was interested only in bigness, in conspicuous consumption and lacked even the most elementary idea of taste.

The progressive thinker was a strong supporter for the rights of labor. He thought that by establishing a strong and well-knit labor organization the influence of business could be counteracted. At the same time, he was still enough of a Jeffersonian to believe that the farm was the real backbone of America. Thus he tried to help the farmer to get his equitable share of the national income.

Most of the progressives were rebels against the institutions of the past. With a critical eye they examined the Constitution, the executive branch of the government, Congress, the Supreme Court, the state governments and the local mayors. They demanded that government should promote the general welfare of the people; they strenuously opposed the cynical idea that it was an end in itself.

Many progressives believed that the government should be a policeman, especially against big business. Thus the liberals were not afraid of entrusting the government with more power. The danger in the 20th century was that the government would become too strong and that in time it might become as oppressive as big business had been after the Civil War.

The progressives had faith in the rationality of the common man. They hoped that, if the abuses of government and of business were publicized sufficiently, the people would act to remedy the situation. They believed that only an informed electorate could preserve self-government.

To some extent they were too optimistic, because it appears that the man in the street is so occupied with the immediate problems of life that he has no time to think about the complicated issues of government. Moreover, since the period of the progressives, there have been so many currents of opinion that very often he is bewildered and does not know what is right and what is wrong.

The progressives' aim was to reform American society through legislation. Their accomplishments in this field are impressive, from the Sherman Anti-Trust Act to the development of the Federal Trade Commission. But laws can be interpreted in many different ways; corporation lawyers would find many ways of evading them. Moreover, reform depended upon the political outlook of the various administrations. If the party in power was conservative, it would find convenient methods to ignore the demands of the reformers.

The progressives favored a union of all liberal forces in the United States. They thought that the farmer and the shopkeeper and the worker had a common interest. Here again, they were too optimistic, for frequently since this period, there has been a sharp clash between the workers and the farmer, and sectionalism has triumphed over national interests.

The liberal cause attracted a wide variety of personalities. There was Carl Schurz, a German immigrant who tried to put into effect the ideals of the 1848 rebellion in Germany, who thought that it was possible to liberalize the Republican party. There was Henry George, who believed in the single tax; Eugene Debs, who was a socialist and was regarded as a danger to American society by the conservatives. There was William Jennings Bryan, the champion of the underdog, intensely religious — a strange mixture of idealistic demagogue, fundamentalist, and economic radical.

The Middle West produced John Peter Altgeld and Robert M. La Follette, with his insistent demand that the government should be more democratic. When he died, his sons would carry on in the progressive tradition. From the West came Lincoln Steffens, whose autobiography tells of the pilgrimage of a reformer who never gave up in his struggle to infuse democracy into city government. Upton Sinclair, whose novels were bitter denunciations of the abuses of industrial society, almost approached in vehemence Jack London, who infused a Marxist tone into American literature. American presidents caught this spirit, especially Theodore Roosevelt and Woodrow Wilson.

With such a varied following, the progressive cause found no unified leadership. The reformers could never agree on a common program; some believed in political action; other stressed humanitarian reform. Some extolled the Marxists' gospel; others represented merely local interests. They were usually more skillful in their opposition than in offering constructive programs for American society. Much time was wasted in a concentration upon minor issues; no wonder that they were unable to win lasting success.

THE LABOR MOVEMENT

In this period, the labor movement began to grow more rapidly. As the United States was becoming urbanized, as large scale industry developed, as the abuses of the financial system became more apparent, organization seemed the only answer to millions of Americans. Frequently, the conditions in the factory were incredibly bad. Elementary precautions for safety were omitted. In the coal mines, that state of affairs continued in the 20th century. When unemployment came, the worker was especially bitter, for usually he was unprepared for it.

The most significant early labor movement was that of the Knights of Labor, which was formed in 1869 in Philadelphia. Its program was extremely ambitious and included the demand for an eight-hour day, better public education, the abolition of child labor, workmen's compensation laws, arbitration of industrial disputes, and collective bargaining. The conservative forces were outraged by its demand for government ownership of public utilities and for the establishment of a system of cooperatives.

The Knights of Labor failed because they were too much concerned with political questions. Their strike strategy was inadequate, and their membership was not united. The ideal of its founders was that one large labor union was to be established, a task which proved to be impossible because of the internal difficulties of labor.

The American Federation of Labor, trying to remedy the weaknesses of the Knights of Labor, championed a conservative political program. Samuel Gompers, its leader, thought that unions should avoid supporting a specific political party and instead agitate only for specific measures of legislation which would aid their cause. To some extent, this strategy worked well, for labor thus would hold the power in the political scheme and both parties would bid for its support.

The weakness of this position was that it frequently split the vote of labor. Many times some unions would vote Republican, others for the Democratic ticket, and perhaps a third group for the Socialists. Moreover, the union leaders could never be certain that the politicians would carry out their promises once they were elected. Here Senator Joseph H. Ball is an excellent example. When he was first elected, he had the fervent support of the unions. Later, he became the most determined champion of restrictive anti-labor legislation.

A more radical organization called the Industrial Workers of the World grew up in this period. Its membership was drawn mostly from the lumber camps of the Northwest and from the textile mills of the East. This union urged a revolution, but American workers did not accept its gospel, and its decline was made certain by its pacifist beliefs during World War I.

The Committee for Industrial Organization, which was founded in 1936, tried to steer a middle course between the I.W.W. and the

A.F. of L. Its basis of organization was broad, for it included industrial as well as craft unions. It utilized the sit-down strike in a most effective manner, but, like the A. F. of L., it had difficulty in harmonizing the interests of its conservative and radical factions.

The success of American unionism depends, to a great extent, upon its strategy. When strikes, like those which took place in anthracite coal mines in 1919 and in the Southern textile mills in 1929, are accompanied by violence, the public usually reacts against unionism. The cause of the unions was not aided by the strike calls of John L. Lewis during World War II. Frequently a union leader is so much impressed by the needs of his own workers that he forgets the necessities of the nation and the public welfare.

REFORMERS

The cause of governmental reform was furthered immensely by the sensational articles which appeared in the opening years of the 20th century in *McClure's*, *Collier's*, and *Cosmopolitan*. Books were written which had vast popular appeal. Thousands read Ida Tarbell's *History of the Standard Oil Company*, Lincoln Steffens' *The Shame of the City*, and Thomas Lawson's *Frenzied Finance*. Among the reformers were even some conservatives — men like Charles Evans Hughes of New York and Hiram Johnson of California.

The progressive movement was responsible for the popular election of Senators, gave impetus to the drive for women's suffrage, championed the commission form of government for cities, and introduced the initiative, referendum, and recall. Moreover, the direct primary nomination was a result of progressive agitation.

Frequently, the progressives expected too much from these reforms; thus the direct primary nomination has not made for political liberalism because usually few of the voters bother to express their preference. Political machines have found it just as easy to control the primary as the party caucus. But even more important is the confusion which resulted from a long list of candidates, many of them unknown to the average voter.

The quality of the Senate improved because of progressive agitation. Still, in the South and elsewhere, the political machines had just as much power as before in selecting senatorial candidates. While the social outlook of many senators was liberalized, their international perspective did not broaden. No wonder that the Senate in the 1920's became a pillar of isolationism.

In city government, the reforms usually did not last very long. Bryce has pointed out that the city administration is usually the weakest point of American democracy. In spite of the efforts of the progressives the hold of the machine politicians was not broken. They might be ejected from office for a few years, but they were usually able to recuperate. In city as well as state administrations, the spoils system was not abolished. Psychologically, the progressive movement failed to imbue the public servant with the pride of office he has in England or Sweden. Usually he is underpaid, and envies the businessman, who receives a far better compensation for his efforts.

RELIGION AS EDUCATION

While the progressives were trying to reform politics, a reorientation took place in religion. Dynamic thinkers in Protestantism were carrying on a double crusade, first, against the traditionalists who still opposed the Darwinian interpretation of the universe, and secondly, against expediency and materialism in church affairs. Orthodox theologians received a rude blow when Andrew White (1832–1918) published his monumental *History of the Warfare of Science with Theology in Christendom*. Other writers stressed the idea that Darwinism could be harmonized with the conclusions of Christianity. Henry Ward Beecher explained to large audiences that evolution revealed God's purpose. Was not man's goal the final achievement of a spiritual perspective? Beecher's conclusions were extremely optimistic; to him science revealed a new form of theology; science was subordinated to the demands of Protestantism.

On the other hand, those who accepted Nietzsche's view of evolution had a more pessimistic view. Mencken and Dreiser accepted evolution as the basis of a naturalistic philosophy of life. In vain they looked for the high spiritual achievement of man which Fiske pictured; rather they saw man at the mercy of overwhelming natural forces.

Liberalism in religion and education was advanced by Walter Rauschenbusch (1861–1918). As a teacher at the Rochester Theological Seminary he was well acquainted with church history. He saw the evil effects of Christianity's compromise with the various institutions that dominate Western civilization. As a penetrating observer of his own time, he read widely in Henry George and other economic and sociological writers.

Rauschenbusch re-interpreted the Christian tradition. Before him it had been regarded mainly as a principle for salvation one had to believe in order to be saved. After Rauschenbusch the concept of the *social gospel* became dominant, and his followers used the idealism of Christ to measure the accomplishments of the contemporary economic system.

He was an insistent critic of the abuses of American society. Instead of love, the business philosophy dwelt upon competition; in many areas monopoly was triumphant. Under such conditions, how could the democratic ideal prosper? How could the Christian emphasis on equality be maintained? He showed that the middle man was a veritable parasite in the acquisitive society. As for the profit motive, it was as damnable, according to him, as the feudal oppression of the serfs.

How was a new society to be established? Rauschenbusch argued that the kingdom of God could be realized on earth. Let us not wait until a future life; let us make a new beginning in this world. Christ had preached a revolutionary gospel, but his meaning had been misinterpreted by the theologians, who were escapists. Even the Protestant reformers did not understand its implications in full.

The Kingdom of God could not compromise with the forces of unrighteousness. The outcome of the struggle was clear. The Kingdom of God would prevail and with it a real social democracy founded upon the sacredness of the individual.

THE STATE OF THE SOCIAL SCIENCES

The influence of Darwin forced a reorganization of the social sciences. Instead of stressing eternal laws which governed man's institutional behavior, their historical evolutionary nature was now emphasized. Karl Marx won many adherents in the United States, although his theories were modified. The dynamic nature of the American economic system did not fit the concept of class conflict as did the static economic system of Europe.

The new developments in the social sciences had also some destructive effects. William Graham Sumner (1840–1910), for example, followed Spencer quite literally in his belief in the survival of the fittest. He was a vigorous opponent of Upton Sinclair, who, he thought, was trying to interfere with the invariable laws of business competition. Sumner could give metaphysical explanations for the imperfections of American society. If competition produced

poverty and inequality, it might be regrettable from a moral standpoint, yet at the same time it would weed out the poor, incompetent,
and ignorant, and eventually a better race would emerge.

The progressive movement extended its ideals to institutional
education. Thus Jacob Riis regarded the battle over public schools
as the crucial struggle of his day. He felt that better vocational
training would be an aid in the battle against the slums and that
kindergartens would give a better chance for the underprivileged
members of society.

Governor La Follette declared in 1904 that the State University
was the most important institution of society. Did it not represent
the ideals of the common man? Did it not mean a union of theory
and practice? Was it not in the forefront of educational experimentation? The task of the State University, according to La Follette,
was to provide for the direct needs of the people. It was not to be
an ivory tower institution, but rather one which would directly contribute to reform.

National societies emerged, such as the National Society for the
Promotion of Industrial Education, which included labor leaders
and businessmen, teachers and lawyers, municipal crusaders against
corruption, people like Henry Bruere, Charles R. Richards and
Jane Addams.

A challenging economist was Thorstein Veblen (1857-1929), who
interpreted economics according to psychological motives. Throughout history he saw a conflict between two basic human drives: acquisition and social service. All the institutions associated with property
have as their foundation the desire for predatory exploitation, while
the institutions which aid the growth of civilization are based upon
technological cooperation. He showed how much of the profit system
is based merely upon conspicuous consumption. Thus he undermined
the concept of *laissez-faire*, both by wit and statistics. Indeed his
widely read *Theory of the Leisure Class* is as fascinating as a popular
study in psychology.

In sociology Lester Ward (1841–1913) likewise stressed the importance of psychology. His ideal was that democracy was to be
established, not upon the exploitation of industry, but upon the
foundation of science. Not for a moment did he doubt that man's
fate could be changed through intelligent planning and leadership.

A year before the World War broke out in Europe, Charles A.
Beard published his *Economic Interpretation of the Constitution*.
Many historians were rudely surprised by Beard's study, which claimed
that the founders of the Constitution were not acting in the interests

of high-minded idealism but only in the interests of their own class. Perhaps more than any other American historian Beard stressed the social factors that have guided American history. Consistently liberal in his outlook, he thought that it was the task of historians to provide an intelligent answer for the problems of education.

The new spirit made converts in the legal profession. Justice Brandeis showed how human rights are more important than the protection of property. Oliver Wendell Holmes brilliantly espoused the cause of the underdog. At Harvard University, Roscoe Pound and Felix Frankfurter argued for a humane interpretation of established laws.

CHAPTER TWENTY-TWO

The Ideals of Parker

BASIC FAITHS

The ideas of Francis Parker (1837–1902) are among the most progressive in the history of American education. What Whitman did for poetry and Emerson did for Transcendentalism, Parker did for education. He helped to emancipate education from its authoritarian and aristocratic biases.

Brought up in a rural atmosphere, he had a meager formal education, but he early acquired a love of books. He loved especially Bunyan's *Pilgrim's Progress*. He became a teacher at the age of sixteen, and took part in the Civil War. He hated the authority which he found in the Army and this feeling he extended to education, where he favored freedom and spontaneity. When an aunt died in 1872 he was left with a small inheritance which made it possible for him to study at the University of Berlin. Later he gained fame as superintendent of schools at Quincy, Massachusetts (1875–1880), and as principal of the Cook County Normal School in Chicago where he served between 1883 and 1899.

The great influences upon his life include Emerson, Mann, Pestalozzi and Froebel, and his friendship with John Dewey. Like Emerson,
Parker saw the unity of man and nature. Materialism was to him an
inadequate philosophy. Man is not merely part of nature; through
education man can transcend nature. Indeed, nature is guided by
design; its purpose is to produce a higher civilization.

He was a firm individualist. Society does not exist for itself; man
is never to be enslaved by the state. He was anti-Hegelian in his
insistence that all institutions, including the State, are only preludes to
man's moral emancipation.

Individuals, he stated in Emersonian terms, have a divine quality.
This includes the rich and the poor, the black and the white, the
young and the old. The task of the schools is to promote man's divinity, not to curb him by artificial means.

Horace Mann he admired for his faith in democracy. He felt
that he was a defender of humanity, and he opposed all forms of
sectarianism and authoritarianism.

Pestalozzi he respected for his emphasis that education involves
more than an intellectual ideal. Parker believed in the inspiration of
nature. He loved the serenity of the out-of-doors and used hikes as
educational devices. Like Pestalozzi he used the stimulation of the
senses, and believed that specific knowledge precedes general principles. In his nominalism he opposed the epistemological realism of
Harris who seemed to him the archetype of Hegelian absolutism.

Froebel's love of children deeply impressed Parker, who thought
that love should imbue all educational activities. This means that the
administrator should be a kind guide, the teacher should be a friend
of youth, and children should avoid all forms of antagonism.

There are basic similarities between Parker and Dewey. Both
were opposed to traditional education, were pragmatic in their outlook, had deep faith in democracy and were interested in social
reform. The difference was that Dewey had greater regard for
the scientific method than Parker, who still adhered to a type of
Transcendental philosophy.

Parker saw a conflict between two viewpoints and two ideologies
throughout history. One was that of aristocracy, which stresses hereditary privilege and divides people into classes. It employs force to
perpetuate injustice and uses patriotism as a means of subjugation.
It makes war necessary to defend private property.

Such a system is based upon a perverted view of religion. Did
it not believe in a God of fear? Did it not speak of supernaturalism?

Did it not neglect the problems of this world? Did it not develop a faith of exclusiveness? The only religion Parker believed in was one that taught the ideal of equality and emphasized compassion.

The educational system of an aristocratic nation would emphasize force and coercion. The student would not be allowed to think for himself and would not be encouraged to ask fundamental questions. He would become a serf of society. Education would become a tool of the most lasting oppression and would create a permanent slavery of the mind.

Opposed to the aristocratic view of education is that of democracy, which removes all artificial frontiers. In politics, it means the guarantee of liberty, a truly representative government and the perpetual right of revolution. In religion it means a common faith in man's divinity and the unity of man and God. In legislation it means a continuing concern for the underprivileged.

Parker helped in the work of Jane Addams and was an early proponent of better legislation for the working classes. In education, democracy means an expansion of opportunity and a new type of school which welcomes change and curriculum experimentation. The child must become a responsible adult; schooling should remove all forms of bias and prejudice and all class distinctions.

The revolution in teaching which he recommended would start with our view of history. The story of the past is to be re-examined. Instead of nationalism, internationalism would be encouraged. Instead of a stress upon competition, man's cooperative drives are to be encouraged. Instead of idolization of political leaders, man's spiritual and educational thinkers are to be studied. Instead of ancient history, modern history is to be emphasized. The view of history would be expanded through sociology, ethnology, and archeology. Culture must be seen as a total undertaking, not as a fragmentary study. In all these recommendations he anticipated James Harvey Robinson who in *Mind in the Making* uses historical lessons to remove rationalizations and prepare the way for a truly creative society. Parker, likewise, wanted to use the past to remove the biases and obsolescent beliefs of the present.

Parker was opposed to discipline and uniformity. Uniformity neglects individual and social differences. Education is to have a Heraclitean basis; change is to govern its philosophy and methodology.

Parker maintained that activity should govern the curriculum. Let the child move about freely and express his emotions. Let him rebel, if necessary, against his teachers. Let his interests govern the school, and let him take part in the school administration. If such a system could be developed, a new society would emerge which would have a real democratic basis.

Children need field trips; they must explore society; they should see the working conditions in factories. Their interest in reforming humanity is to be stimulated.

Grades and artificial incentives are to be avoided. If the school encourages competition it will create selfish adults who see only their own interests and neglect those of society. Cooperation and mutualism will produce altruistic citizens who will find happiness in humanitarianism.

THE MISSION OF THE TEACHER

To Parker, education is all-important.

There is but one question in this world: how to make man better; and but one answer: education. Education presents the conditions for man's complete development. To find the highest law of human growth, that law which determines the highest function of the human being, is the central problem in the *philosophy* of education; to train and develop that function in each and every human being, and as an essential sequence, to develop each and every power of the mind and soul is the central problem in the *art* of education. Man was made for man, and his one God-like function is to take knowledge from the eternity of human life. There is a perfect reconciliation between the application of unlimited altruism and the most complete education of the being who holds and fully applies it: for the knowledge of the needs of man, and the human acts which supply those needs, are in turn the essential means of the all-sided development of each human being. It is self-evident that the knowledge of the needs of man embraces all knowledge, and the application of that knowledge all proper human activities.

The explanation of human life, then, is that *it gives,* and just in proportion to the value of that which it gives *it grows.*

All we have to know are the needs of mankind; all we have to do is to supply those needs.[1]

He describes genuine education.

True education concentrates upon the development of the highest motive.

---

[1] Parker, *How to Study Geography.*

Upon this basis, the absolute and relative value of any branch of knowledge, the fundamental reasons for its teaching, the proportion of time and effort given to it, must be determined by the influence of such knowledge upon the human being in the outworking of its design into character.

The knowledge of life comprehends all knowledge, and therefore the study of life comprehends all studies. Inorganic or inanimate matter is the material basis of all animated organisms, and the purpose of the study of all the sciences that pertain to inorganic matter is to gain a knowledge of the preparation for life, its substantial basis, and the explanation of the laws and conditions of life. From the lowest germ of the plant up to the highest development of human consciousness life is in itself a unit of evolution.

The study of any item or detail of life, or of the preparation for life, becomes of vast importance when we appreciate its relations to the grand totality of life. There are no trifles in real teaching; the child studying the root, stem, leaves, flowers and fruit of a plant is gaining essential elements in all knowledge. What he learns is organically related to all truth; through the life of a simple plant he may one day see something of the complete unity of life. This beautiful truth adds great dignity to all real teaching and study.

All sciences, though isolated in name, are the organic factors of one great whole, — each is intrinsically related and bound to all; perfect knowledge of one means a perfect knowledge of all.[2]

Teaching, he stated, involves correct methodology.

Teaching has to do with the conscious activities. It may be defined as the presentation of those conditions which arouse, sustain, intensify and concentrate such conscious activities as directly induce growth and development.

The definition of teaching includes the definition of method. The method of teaching a subject or branch of knowledge consists:

1. In the arrangement of the details or particulars of the branch in the order and manner best adapted to the development of the mind. It follows, necessarily, that the order and arrangement best adapted to the mind's action and growth is also the best for the acquisition of knowledge. This arrangement of details is called a course of study.

2. In the presentation of the details in time, and stage of growth, so as to use the conscious activities in the most economical way; or, in other words, the adaptations of the subjects and objects of thought to conscious activities in such a manner as to concentrate all the powers of the being upon them.

The human being acquires knowledge and power by the action of immutable laws. No matter what external conditions may be presented

---

[2] *Ibid.*

to the teacher, the mind grows and acquires knowledge in its own unchangeable way. It follows undeviatingly its own divine laws.[3]

There is, however, no perfect method, according to Parker.

In teaching, any arbitrary adherence to an order of time, regardless of the order of growth, is fatal to development. Any teacher who pretends to have a perfect method of teaching any subject is a quack. Perfection in method is a pure ideal, far beyond the reach of present knowledge. The course of study here presented is divided into two distinct parts, namely, the elementary and the scientific. The purpose of the elementary part of the course is the collection of the psychic material indispensable to the inbuilding of an organic body of truth in the scientific course by observation, investigation, reading, hearing, language, and study. The elementary course is suggested for the first four grades. The process of thought in these grades is mainly inductive. The mental powers to be constantly exercised are those of synthesis and analysis—the latter used at all times to enhance the strength of the former. Color, form and number are the essential factors of synthetic power.

Observation, hearing, language and reading are the three mental processes conditioning the presence of objects and symbols.

Curiosity and fancy are the innate tendencies to be used by skillful teachers, in making fleeting impulses steady and constant.[4]

Teaching implies genuine integration.

Lastly, to intensify, enhance, there are the various modes of expression: making, modeling, painting, drawing, oral and written language. These agents of teaching are common to all teaching. The choice of subjects and objects of thought makes the method of teaching geography distinct from that of the teaching of all other branches. The main purpose of scientific geography is to build by the faculty of imagination the mental pictures of the continents and then to synthesize them into an image of the round world. The principal work, then, in the primary grades, is to collect sense-products needed for the work of the grammar grades. Field lessons, observations and investigations, that develop these ideas, should form the essential part of the course. The architect who designs one part of an edifice must know its relations to the whole; so the teachers in the lower grades should know the purpose and end of every subject and object of thought.

A science is one organic whole of truth; at each step each inference and generalization involve all preceding knowledge; each science, in turn, is only a part of one great science, the science of life and living.

---

[3] *Ibid.*
[4] *Ibid.*

Scientific geography illustrates this great truth in a beautiful way. The study of one continent requires all the most careful teaching the lower grades can furnish; one continent is the measure of another, and so on; the last generalization in the study of civilization demands for its thorough exposition every fact, inference and generalization that precedes it. The teacher who watches with great eagerness and insight the growth of her pupils in geography, never need to hesitate in regard to the new conditions that should be immediately presented.[5]

Theory demands correct application.

Failure in application of a theory does not always prove that the theory is false; there have been countless failures in the application of the Golden Rule, and of the principles of temperance, yet no one dares deny the truth of the theories. The question is, does the difficulty lie in a false theory, or is it found in the unskillful application of a true theory? The inclination is a very strong one to believe that the difficulty is in unscientific teaching and not in the mental powers of children. . . .

Teachers cannot teach that which they do not know, Jacotot to the contrary notwithstanding. If teachers know little else but mental pictures of maps and an isolated mass of conglomerated facts they cannot teach geography. The habit of thinking of the map and the map alone is an almost unsurmountable obstruction in the way of a teacher's ever learning to teach real geography. A teacher who has always taught figures and fancies them numbers, rarely learns what a number really is. The main difficulty in the way of the application of the science of teaching is the ignorance, on the part of teachers, of the subjects they pretend to teach. Habit and tradition stand in the way of their ever learning these subjects.[6]

He calls for intellectual courage.

The reasons why the number of excellent teachers is comparatively small are: 1. Teachers generally do not pay the price of genuine success, — *hard unremitting study of the subjects they teach.* 2. Many teachers study with commendable diligence, but the results of their study are meager, because in their study they do not comply with the immutable laws of human growth. Much hard study often leaves the student in the toils of petty details that weaken and often destroy the power to generalize, to reach universal truths.

Anyone who has struggled for years to overcome the bad methods and habits formed by previous study, knows full well the meaning of the divine saying, "Blessed is he that overcometh."

---

[5] *Ibid.*
[6] *Ibid.*

Courage and perseverance will always come to us when we feel deeply that all this hard work is for the salvation of the children and the consequent progress of the world.[7]

EXPERIMENTATION

"Variety is life," was Parker's slogan. Variety could be found both in science and art. Science would develop genuine individualism and it would encourage new explorations. There were to be no adult standards for the art of children. The adult should encourage all artistic efforts of children, otherwise creativity and individuality would be inhibited.

Parker reacted against the beliefs of Puritanism. To the Puritans, man was evil; to Parker, man is good. To the Puritans, learning was authoritarian; to Parker, education has to be democratic. To the Puritans, happiness had no value in education; to Parker, there could be no genuine education without happiness. To the Puritans, supernaturalism was all important; to Parker, nature was man's guide. Puritan truth was absolute; to Parker, truth is discovered in the relativity of experience. The Puritans thought children were evil; to Parker they are symbols of divinity.

The quality which Parker admired most in teachers was unbounded enthusiasm. Let the teacher experiment in a variety of ways, so that he becomes a perpetual learner. The formal education of the teacher, Parker thought, was less important than his feelings about himself, his students, his vocation, and his relationship to mankind.

The teacher thus becomes a reformer fighting a perpetual war against lethargy. He fought with vigor against cruelty. He championed democracy, equality, and the rights of children in this nation and throughout the world.

---

[7] *Ibid.*

CHAPTER TWENTY-THREE

Progress of Idealism

THE IDEALISTIC TRADITION

Between 1850 and 1900 idealism reigned supreme in the United States. The causes for this triumph were complex, and they illustrate the dependence of the American mind upon European developments. German philosophy, especially the systems of Kant and Hegel, was regarded as the model and as the starting point for the theoretical thinking. The idealistic movement owed much to the Puritan background, with its faith in cosmic values and its conception of the universe as a rational whole.

Philosophical education in this period was severely academic. The language used by thinkers like Royce, Creighton, and Howison was difficult for the student to understand and even more so for the layman. In reading their works, we notice an erudition and a technical proficiency which we frequently miss in the treatises of younger American philosophers.

In this period philosophy had a notable place in the college curriculum. As yet the sciences did not occupy the major attention of the student. The universe was explained according to teleological principles by the professor of philosophy, who frequently served as a clergyman in his spare time. Many American thinkers were intent not only upon describing the universe, but also in regarding it as a vehicle for God's providence and God's majesty.

THE LIFE OF JOSIAH ROYCE

Josiah Royce (1855–1916) was born in California, which, in this period, was largely undeveloped. Many of its communities were dominated by lawless elements. Gold had recently been discovered, and consequently those who were unable to prosper in the East migrated to the new state, where they expected a veritable Utopia. Education was neglected and lagged far behind Eastern standards.[1]

He studied philosophy at the University of California, but the courses there did not satisfy him. For his graduate training he went to Germany, where he was especially impressed by Lotze and Wundt. He returned to the United States and received his Ph.D. at Johns Hopkins University. Later he taught rhetoric and logic at the University of California. In 1882 he received a call to lecture at Harvard, where he taught for the remainder of his life.

THE WORKS OF ROYCE

The most popular introduction to Royce's philosophy is *The Spirit of Modern Philosophy*, in which he defends the idealistic thinkers, and in which he gives an excellent introduction to the great systems of philosophy. His ethical theories are best developed in *Philosophy of Loyalty*, while his religious concepts are contained in *The Problem of Christianity* and *The Religious Aspect of Philosophy*. His major work in philosophy was *The World and the Individual*. It is usually regarded as the most profound American work in metaphysics, and it can be compared with Bradley's *Appearance and Reality*.[2]

The beginner usually finds it difficult to read Royce. His style is repetitious and technical. Hence, it is necessary to read his works

---

[1] He wrote a book on California entitled, *California from the Conquest in 1846 to the Second Vigilance Committee in San Francisco, A Study of American Character*. (1886).

[2] For an evaluation of Royce consult Barrett, *Contemporary Idealism in America*, pp. 1-9; Cunningham, *The Idealistic Argument in Recent British and American Philosophy*, pp. 253-291; Albeggiani, *Il sistema filosofico di Josiah Royce;* Robinson, ed., *Royce's Logical Essays*.

several times, but after a while his philosophy becomes much easier to comprehend, and, if thoroughly understood, appears as one of the major contributions of American civilization.

THE PURPOSE OF ROYCE

It was the ideal of Royce to undermine the scientific agnosticism which had made such inroads in European culture. Like Kant, Royce believed that the scientific view applied only to phenomena. Time, space, and causality accordingly could not be applied to the thing-in-itself. As long as science described nature and remained within certain limits, Royce did not object to it. But when science tried to interpret metaphysics, Royce objected.

To appreciate the spirit of Royce, it is necessary to make a clear distinction between *description* and *appreciation*. The realm of causality depends upon scientific laws; yet they cannot explain the essence of the universe, which can be understood only through appreciation. To make this point clear, let us take a concrete example. A Frenchman visits the United States, and we try to describe our nation to him. We can describe our cities, cite statistics regarding industrial production, and mention universities, art museums, and scientific institutions. Still, our descriptions will be rather superficial, and they will omit some of the essential traits of the United States. These traits can be understood only through *appreciation* — when he understands the spirit of this nation by which it has a peculiar quality, and by which it is distinguished from other countries.

Yet it is this appreciation which, according to Royce, is the most certain method in education. Through it we realize that all fleeting phenomena are part of one whole, and that they are all part of the Absolute. We must beware, however, of attributing our own human mode of thinking to the Absolute. We make differentiations according to our temporal and spatial conditions; we think of the past, the present, and the future. To the Absolute, however, time and space lack meaning. Everything is apprehended all at once in a complete vision.

In *The World and the Individual,* Royce examined the various views of reality, such as realism, mysticism, and critical idealism, and he found all of them lacking. His standpoint in many ways was like that of Hegel. He justified the Absolute because of our own partial experience, which points to a larger whole.

Royce's Absolute almost reminds us of Calvin's concept of God. It includes all the aspects of man's experience. Everything that occurs in the universe, everything that has transpired in history, everything that we feel is part of the Absolute. The Absolute is conscious of evil and permits its existence; but evil is only a prelude to a larger good. Royce gave many examples to justify his standpoint and appealed to the Bible. For instance, he mentioned Christ's atonement. If this event had not happened, our religion would be superficial and inadequate.

This does not imply a moral fatalism. On the contrary, our view of reality, our belief in the victory of goodness, can give us faith and hope in our struggle against evil and wickedness. Generally, Royce was not pessimistic, for he believed in the supremacy of the good and pictured the triumph of the Absolute.

In his concept of knowledge he stressed *voluntaristic* factors, bringing a pragmatic element into his system. However, he was interested less in scientific than in philosophical verification. After all, the truth which we know is only partial and finite and requires an absolute truth which is the norm for all knowledge. If no absolute standard exists, how can we make any kind of valid judgment?

As he pointed out in his presidential address of 1903 before the American Philosophical Association, this standard of judgment is personal. It is eternal and infinite, yet it can be expressed in man's finite activities. The activities of reasoning which are practical and functional point to something eternal which embraces all human knowledge and which is our assurance that intellectual certainty is possible.

Thus in his theory of knowledge, he combined pragmatism and idealism; however, the idealistic element is the more significant in his system.

ETHICAL AND EDUCATIONAL IDEALS

Royce's moral philosophy can be found in *The Philosophy of Loyalty*, which is an attack against the new concepts of morality. With his background in absolute idealism, he had no love for Marx, Nietzsche or Henry George. He did not believe that moral standards are uncertain; on the contrary, he sought definite assurance and categorical beliefs.

Modern man is afflicted with a spiritual homesickness; he has lost balance and confidence. Royce wanted to guide humanity on the path to certainty, away from doubt and spiritual discontent.

We must seek a principle which commands our absolute obedience. *Be loyal to loyalty.* In this way we transcend narrow groups and narrow ideals. Our loyalty expands; first we are loyal to ourselves, then to our family, then to humanity. Our loyalty must be growing and dynamic; it must not be an obstinate attachment to an obsolete past.

The principle of loyalty requires us to respect other men's allegiances. Fair play is to govern our conduct even if we have to engage in war. Chivalry is not part of the past, it is just as vital for our own time. We may not agree with our opponents, but we must have regard for their sincerity.

In selecting a cause, we are to be decisive. Like William James, Royce had little use for hesitancy. Life is not a journey in limbo; in the great issues there is no neutrality. This may have been part of Royce's puritanical background; it was one reason why Santayana could not appreciate Royce, for Santayana enjoyed the role of the bystander, and he did not like decisive actions.

When Royce examined the American scene he found a distressing lack of loyalty among the immigrants and in our family system. He felt that the family system is not based on selfish desires, but on a spiritual fact, and that husband and wife must seek the welfare of the family unit, rather than individual gratification.

He was concerned with the condition of the labor unions. Too frequently, he found, they regard working-class welfare as more important than the national welfare.

> Further centralization of power in the national government without a constantly enriched and diversified provincial consciousness, can only increase the estrangement of our national spirit from its own life.[3]

Loyalty can be perfected in three ways. First, through the inspiration of outstanding leaders and teachers; they set a high standard for the average human being, and they demonstrate the possibilities of man. Second, loyalty can be bettered through an idealization of our cause. Third, loyalty is produced when we sacrifice and suffer for a cause. Thus we realize how important it is and how unimportant the individual is, compared to the welfare of the group.

His final definition of loyalty connects it with religion. *"Loyalty is the will to manifest, so far as possible, the Eternal, that is, the conscious and superhuman unity of life, in the form of the acts of an individual self."*[4]

Thus the ethical theory of Royce ended with a religious affirmation. Both knowledge and morality are rooted in metaphysical grounds. We cannot be satisfied with a partial and incomplete perspective but thirst for the Eternal Power in which and through which our education is fulfilled.

---

[3] *The Philosophy of Loyalty.*
[4] *Ibid.*

ROYCE AND AMERICAN PHILOSOPHY

Royce has been called the American Hegel. Yet Royce's influence on American culture has not been felt as much as that of Hegel on German culture. Royce was too much part of an alien tradition, and he did not stress concrete and living factors as did James in his theory of pragmatism, which appealed to the American mind.

Still, Royce widens our perspective and expands the range of our ideals. Unconcerned with the present and with immediate goals, he pointed to cosmic ends.

Some students of philosophy may regard the Absolute as a mere abstraction, as a faint ghost of Puritan philosophy. But this view is unwarranted. Royce held that all our goals and all our desires and all our thoughts point to a larger Self which, infinite and eternal in its essence, includes all temporal processes.

Moreover, his championship of loyalty has significant consequences. In this way he opposed the exaggerated individualism which dominated much of 19th century culture. Loyalty in his mind stood for a spirit of unity and cohesion and for a subordination of the individual to the group.

IDEALS OF BOWNE

The personalistic strains of idealism are best represented by Borden Parker Bowne (1847-1910), who was born in Leonardsville, New Jersey. He studied at New York University and afterwards went to Germany, where he studied at Halle and at Göttingen. Among his teachers Lotze was especially significant and probably supplied him with the fundamentals of his personalistic faith.

In 1876, after a brief excursion into journalism, he was appointed professor of philosophy at Boston University. In a short period he became one of the most influential teachers there and won a wide following among his students. However, the conservatives among the Methodist ministers disliked his liberal theology, and so he was accused of heresy. Nevertheless he retained his position until 1910, the year of his death.

His influence on American thought has been vast. After him, personalism became one of the most vigorous schools of thought;

and in the ministry, especially among the Methodists, he helped bring about a more progressive spirit.

As a teacher, Bowne had the capacity to make ideas an exciting subject. He directed his attention especially towards those who were mature and who were earnestly searching for truth. His knowledge of philosophy extended not merely to metaphysics and epistemology, but included psychology, esthetics, logic, and ethics. He enjoyed, above all, the graduate courses which he taught, especially his seminars dealing with Kant and Spencer.

Among his works we note *Philosophy of Theism; Principles of Ethics; Theory of Thought and Knowledge;* and *Kant and Spencer.* His best known work is probably *Personalism,* which gives a comprehensive summary of his system.[5]

He was influenced by a variety of thinkers. Among the Greek philosophers he found Plato, Socrates, and Aristotle especially congenial. The scholastics he disregarded to a large extent with the exception of St. Augustine, whose personalistic emphasis he appreciated. The modern thinkers who influenced his system include Leibnitz, Berkeley, Kant, Renouvier, Lotze and William James.

Naturally his membership in the Methodist church had an impact on his philosophical development. Some of his critics have regarded him primarily as a theologian, but a careful reading of his works does not support this view. True, he gave a philosophical explanation of religious truths, but to support his views he turned not to faith but to rational demonstrations. In many ways, he became the Socrates of the Methodist church.

Bowne's starting point is idealistic. Reality is not irrational, but governed by reason. Values are not merely temporary and subjective, but have an objective, metaphysical existence. He was also an idealist in the popular sense, believing that it is the function of philosophy to realize man's aspirations and to contribute to the moral improvement of humanity.

The gateway to reality is the self, which is not static, but is a dynamic manifestation of life. The self is not physiological as the materialists held, but is moral and spiritual.

Personalism primarily is not rationalistic; the self cannot be described merely by its rational activities. Personalism refuses to accept Descartes' "I think, therefore I am"; for Bowne, existence is prior to thought. The function of thought is to engender higher moral ideals.

---

[5] For a critical evaluation of Bowne see Jones, *Lotze und Bowne, eine Vergleichung ihrer philosophischen Arbeit;* Pyle, *The Philosophy of Borden P. Bowne;* McConnell, *Borden Parker Bowne.*

The world-ground depends on God; mechanism has no metaphysical reality; life must be conceived as a teleological process.

From the standpoint of epistemology we find that Bowne was a nominalist. Only individual things are real; universals are abstractions. Impersonalism had made the mistake of regarding universals as real, instead of realizing that they are artificial and depend on the perceiving subject.

The educational tone of Bowne's personalism owed much to the teachings of Kant; Bowne believed in good will as the foundation of morality.

Emphasizing dynamic factors in education, Bowne felt that it is the task of the individual to improve his behavior and universalize his ideals. We can never stand still and contemplate our perfection; the universe demands action and reformation.

All social systems can be measured by one essential standard: how do they contribute to the education of the individual and how do they actualize his moral and spiritual capacities? Bowne favored the democratic way of life, for he believed that it best recognizes the educational powers of man and his capacity to grow morally in an atmosphere of freedom and justice.

He was not blind to the weaknesses of the democratic society. He favored a rise in the standard of living of the masses. However, this is not to be done by a paternalistic government or by the revolutionary efforts of a political party. The extension of Christian ideals into politics and economics will provide for a new era in which poverty and war will cease.

With all his powers, he preached against an educational system which made pleasure or utility the highest good. Moral law is absolute; its violation leads to the disintegration of the individual and the destruction of society. He looked upon the family as a sacred institution, viewing the growing disunity in the American family with serious alarm.

Moral values are absolute and have a cosmic status. This necessitates personal immortality, for on earth our moral aspirations are often thwarted. We need a future life in which virtue can be fully triumphant. The freedom of the individual is an undeniable fact of our existence. We are not determined by the environment in which we live, but we can make creative choices which indicate our spirituality.

In education he championed the centrality of the teacher. The teacher inspires by his moral enthusiasm and thus creates the basis of progress.

IDEALISM AND EDUCATIONAL CONCEPTS

Idealism, as represented by Royce and Bowne, looks upon man as a spiritual creature. He is not defined by his biological heritage; he is qualitatively different from the animal world.

Idealism, following Plato, believes in two worlds: one is that of experience which is transitory, the other is that of ideals which have an eternal significance. Ideals in education become patterns of perfection for imitation. They indicate the possibilities of man who can find in them sources of perennial inspiration.

Idealism usually turns to the past rather than to the future. Its educational philosophy, as compared with pragmatism, tends to be more conservative. If the lessons of the past are overlooked, man develops a narrow perspective and exaggerates his own importance.

Idealists stress literature and the classics rather than scientific studies. In literature they find a representation of the soul of man, while science tends to be superficial. They emphasize the moral values of literature so that it becomes a pattern of ethical insight and ethical involvement.

The dignity of the teacher is important. He should not be too friendly with the students. He is not a mere resource person, rather he is a symbol of truth and authority and his ideas are to be respected.

Idealists stress the importance of rules in education. Without them, they believe, chaos will be the result. Rules represent the wisdom of the race; rebellion against them is discouraged.

Idealists tend to be more conservative in their political and economic views than pragmatists. They feel that social change is best promoted through personal insight and through higher moral values. They feel that political legislation often only creates a vast bureaucracy and gives too much power to the common man.

Loyalty in the teaching profession is central in idealism. This means not only loyalty to one's country, but loyalty to the profession and a sense of dedication. Students are to be taught that sacrifice for a noble cause should be a significant part of their career.

In every way, idealism rejects a naturalistic view of psychology. Man's learning is not governed by a stimulus-response relationship; man cannot be treated like a machine. Psychology, to idealists, is not an autonomous subject, but is the prelude to philosophy.

We must not forget that idealists also have more democratic tendencies. In the twentieth century, Felix Adler, the proponent of ethical culture, emphasized the integrity of the child and the need for a compassionate morality on the part of teachers and society. Some educational idealists, like Robert Ulich, have been the most vigorous foes of totalitarianism and thought control. Thus Ulich left Germany because he would not submit to the dictation of the Nazis. In the United States he fought with vigor and distinction for a more cosmopolitan view of learning and greater protection for the rights of the teacher.

CHAPTER TWENTY-FOUR

William James

THE CAREER OF JAMES

William James (1842–1910) was born into a wealthy family. His father traveled a great deal and was able to give an excellent education to his children, who spent several years in exclusive boarding schools in Europe. William James became very proficient in languages, and international in his outlook on life.

At first he aspired to be a painter and studied under William Hunt in Newport. But he changed his mind, and in 1861 he entered the Lawrence Scientific School. Two years later we find him at the Harvard Medical School. His study there was helpful, for it gave him a scientific foundation for philosophy. One of his teachers was Louis Agassiz, whom he assisted in various experiments and whom he accompanied on an expedition to the Amazon. In 1869 James received his M.D. from Harvard, to which he returned four years later as instructor in anatomy and physiology. Gradually his interests again shifted, this time to the field of psychology, and in 1876 he organized the first psychological laboratory in the United States. He became a professor of philosophy at Harvard in 1881.

James did not neglect his scientific labors during this entire period. He was still interested in physiology, but now his main love was philosophy. He approached it, not from the standpoint of idealism, but from a common-sense, down-to-earth viewpoint.

In his last years he suffered from ill health. He wanted to work on a systematic treatise to expound his viewpoint, but found neither the time nor the energy to fulfill this ambition.

THE WORKS OF JAMES

The most notable treatise of James in psychology can be found in his *Principles of Psychology* (1890), which constituted almost a major revolution in that field. In two volumes he discussed such subjects as "Functions of the Brain," "Association," "Perception of Space," "Perception of Reality," "Hypnotism," and "The Effects of Experience." Another significant work by James is *The Will to Believe,* in which he treated such topics as "Is Life Worth Living?" "The Dilemma of Determinism," "Great Men and Their Environment," "The Importance of Individuals," and "What Psychical Research Has Accomplished." In 1899 he published his *Talks to Teachers in Psychology.* In this book he stressed the laws of habit and the association of ideas.

In *The Varieties of Religious Experience* (1902), he dealt with such topics as "Religion and Neurology," "The Sick Soul," "Conversion," "Saintliness," and "Mysticism." In 1907 he published *Pragmatism.* Here he defined his philosophical method, showing how pragmatism is related to religion and life. Two years later appeared *The Meaning of Truth.* In this book he expanded some of the pragmatic concepts, and answered his critics.

The Hibbert Lectures appeared in 1909 under the title of *A Pluralistic Universe.* In this work he attacked Hegel, and showed how any type of monistic idealism is bound to fail. He also devoted much space to Bergson's criticism of intellectualism.

Memories and Studies, published posthumously, expounds his concept of the moral equivalent of war. Ralph Barton Perry edited James' Essays in *Radical Empiricism.* This volume is especially significant from a technical standpoint, for it contains among other subjects James' views on "Consciousness," "The Essence of Humanism," and "Absolutism and Empiricism."[1]

---

[1] For an evaluation of James consult Kallen, *William James and Henry Bergson;* Moore, *Philosophical Studies,* pp. 97-146; Perry, *In the Spirit of William James;* Flournoy, *The Philosophy of William James;* Baumgarten, *Der Pragmatismus.*

THE PURPOSE OF JAMES

James ushered in a new tradition in American education. Instead of definitions and abstractions, *experience* is made the criterion for truth. Concrete problems of life are emphasized. This makes the philosophy of James intelligible to the layman and accounts for its popularity.

James waged philosophical warfare against Hegelian idealism. The universe is not determined by ideas. It is not a dialectical process; rather, it can be understood through experience. Since it is not a deterministic whole, *freedom* has a place in it.

James describes his philosophy as radical empiricism. This means that it has no place for the thing-in-itself, for an Absolute Ego, or for a transcendental unity of apperception. Experience is continuous; it needs no substratum. Through it we perceive not merely objects but also *relations*.

Compare the view of James with that of Royce. To James experience is autonomous and needs no transcendent explanation. To Royce, experience refers to a higher principle of unity — the Absolute. Truth has meaning, according to Royce, only when it is part of a coherent whole. This view James rejected categorically.

PHILOSOPHY AND PSYCHOLOGY

Throughout his life, James was concerned with the relationship between philosophy and psychology. Philosophers are not concerned with eternal truths; their ideas arise out of concrete circumstances and are dependent upon their temperament. We start to think when we have a problem to solve. If our life were completely perfect, if we faced no obstacles, there probably would be no philosophical speculation at all.

James realized that no complete agreement is possible in philosophy, any more than in religion. The various philosophical and religious systems which we find in the world are expressive of emotional needs and emotional desires.

The pragmatic philosopher, in short, regards change as a necessary aspect of civilization, and will not try to coerce the opinions of those who come after him. It is merely pretentious to establish a completely systematic philosophical system, for ideas are subject to evolution. There can be no eternal truth in either philosophy or in any other area of inquiry.

In every way, the philosophy of James differs from that of rationalism, which upholds universals and stresses the validity of logic. James, on the other hand, regards the *specific* fact as ultimate; the universal is merely "an abstraction." In many ways his philosophy resembles that of Hume, and consequently he had no use for an absolute mind. But, unlike Hume, James stresses the fact that the relations that connect experiences must themselves be real. This faith in the validity of relations saves James from skepticism. In fact, in his own life doubt was never the ultimate standpoint. He rejected any philosophy which did not leave room for faith and for a spiritual explanation of life.

James made a famous distinction in his philosophy between two types of philosophers — the *tender-minded* and the *tough-minded*. The tender-minded are the idealists, who believe in free will, who are intellectual in their approach to the problems of life, and who favor optimism as against pessimism. They interpret the universe according to their own desires; in fact the world appears in their philosophies as an expanded classroom. Their most unpleasant trait is their dogmatism. Frequently, they pretend to know everything, and they explain the ways of the Absolute in exhaustive detail. Their style is pompous and dry, but their conclusions tend to be edifying to the religious-minded.

Quite different are the tough-minded philosophers, who tend to be pessimistic, and who regard science as the ultimate principle of explanation. They favor the materialistic viewpoint and have only contempt for the gospel of freedom as taught by the idealists.

To some extent James favors the tough-minded thinkers; he had a great respect for the conclusions of science. Nevertheless his basic purpose is to picture a universe consistent with his religious hopes and expectations.

By using a psychological approach to philosophy, James changed our perspective regarding technical thinkers. Instead of looking upon their systems as expressions of logic and pure reason, we now regard them according to their psychological presuppositions. We ask questions such as the following: What is the purpose of the thinker? How does he reflect the ideals of his period? Is he tough-minded or tender-minded? How do his educational views mirror his own experience?

With James, metaphysics and epistemology come down to earth, where they can be related to definite psychological motives. They become valuable if they have definite consequences; otherwise they are disregarded.

PRAGMATISM AND EDUCATION

In his second lecture on Pragmatism, James told of a camping trip during which everyone was very much occupied with a metaphysical dispute.

It dealt with a squirrel which was obscured from the sight of a man who tried to get near it. But no matter how rapidly he moved, the squirrel escaped in the opposite direction. The result was that no glimpse was caught of the squirrel. Now the problem is: *Does the man go around the squirrel or not?* He goes round the tree, sure enough, and the squirrel is on the tree; but does he go round the squirrel? In the unlimited leisure of the wilderness, discussion had been worn threadbare. Everyone had taken sides, and was obstinate; and the numbers on both sides were even. Each side, when I appeared, therefore appealed to me to make a majority. Mindful of the scholastic adage that whenever you meet a contradiction you must make a distinction, I immediately sought and found one, as follows: "Which party is right," I said, "depends on what you *practically* mean by 'going around' the squirrel. If you mean passing from the north of him to the east, then to the south, then to the west, and then to the north of him again, obviously the man does go around him, for he occupies these successive positions. But if on the contrary you mean first being in front of him, then on the right of him, then behind him, then on his left, and finally in front again, it is quite as obvious that the man fails to go around him, for by the compensating movements the squirrel makes, he keeps his belly turned towards the man all the time and his back turned away. Make the distinction and there is no further dispute. You are both right and both wrong, according as you conceive the verb 'to go around' in one practical fashion or the other."

Although one or two of the hotter disputants called my speech a shuffling evasion, saying they wanted no quibbling or scholastic hair-splitting, but meant just plain honest English "around," the majority seemed to think that the distinction had assuaged the dispute.[2]

The pragmatic method is primarily one which is able to settle metaphysical disputes. Such questions as: "Is the world one or many? Is it material or spiritual?" can lead to unending controversies. They can be settled only by tracing their *practical* consequences. If the differences between alternatives prove to be insignificant, then it is idle to dispute the problem.

---

[2] *Pragmatism*, Lecture II.

There is nothing new in this method, according to James. Did not Aristotle use it? Locke, Berkeley, and Hume resolved many philosophic controversies by the pragmatic frame of reference.

It may be asked then, what are the advantages of this method? James answered with conviction. Such a method abolishes all *a priori* philosophizing. It will not tolerate any closed system of thought, and it will have no patience for absolutes.

This means constant opposition on the part of academic philosophers, for they are bound by tradition, and many of them accept the Hegelian way of thinking. Still, James did not regard their hostility very seriously, for he maintained that their systems were obsolete. The pragmatic method, according to James, will bring about a close union between science and education, and will create a new renaissance in philosophical studies.

The pragmatic temper pays close attention to facts and despises abstraction. *Concreteness* is the keynote. Knowledge is not an end in itself, but a means to action and power. Dogmatism has no place. No finality can be accepted; instead, tentative conclusions are cherished. The pragmatic method neglects first principles and categories. Instead, it looks towards consequences and practical facts.

James pointed out that metaphysics has been dominated most of the time by a very primitive spirit.

> You know how men have always hankered after unlawful magic, and you know what a great part in magic *words* have always played. If you have his name, or the formula of incantation that binds him, you can control the spirit, genie, afrite, or whatever the power may be. Solomon knew the names of all the spirits, and, having their names, he held them subject to his will. So the universe has always appeared to the natural mind as a kind of enigma, of which the key must be sought in the shape of some illuminating or power-bringing word or name. That word means the universe's *principle,* and to possess it is after a fashion to possess the universe itself. "God," "Matter," "Reason," "the Absolute," "Energy," are so many solving names. You can rest when you have them. You are at the end of your metaphysical quest.
>
> But if you follow the pragmatic method, you cannot look on any such word as closing your quest. You must bring out of each word its practical cash-value, set it at work within the stream of your experience. It appears less as a solution, then, than as a program for more work, and more particularly as an indication of the ways in which existing realities may be *changed.*[3]

---

[3] *Ibid.*

Knowledge consequently is constantly changing; it is never static or final. Truth is not an expression of reality. It has to be tested in practice.

Pragmatism unstiffens all our theories, limbers them up and sets each one at work. Being nothing essentially new, it harmonizes with many ancient philosophic tendencies. It agrees with nominalism for instance, in always appealing to particulars; with utilitarianism in emphasizing practical aspects; with positivism in its disdain for verbal solutions, useless questions, and metaphysical abstractions.

All these, you see, are anti-intellectualist tendencies. Against rationalism as a pretension and a method pragmatism is fully armed and militant. But, at the outset, at least, it stands for no particular results. It has no dogmas, and no doctrines save its method. As the young Italian pragmatist Papini has well said, it lies in the midst of our theories, like a corridor in a hotel. Innumerable chambers open out of it. In one you may find a man writing an atheistic volume; in the next some one on his knees praying for faith and strength; in a third a chemist investigating a body's properties. In a fourth a system of idealistic metaphysics is being excogitated; in a fifth the impossibility of metaphysics is being shown. But they all own the corridor, and all must pass through it if they want a practicable way of getting into or out of their respective rooms.

No particular results then, so far, but only an attitude of orientation, is what the pragmatic school means.[4]

THE BASES OF EXPERIENCE

Unlike Spencer, James did not accept science as the ultimate explanation of reality. Like Schopenhauer, he believed that man is a metaphysical animal and that he is dominated not merely by reason but also by *faith*. Metaphysics then is inevitable, and we cannot escape from its domination.

In metaphysics, James stated, the primary controversy is between materialism and theism. Materialism traces all higher phenomena back to the lower constituents. Theism, on the other hand, is guided by the belief in spiritual powers and in a higher unity. Now this debate has definite consequences. Materialism, if followed to its logical conclusion, means that the world order is subject to mechanistic

---

[4] *Ibid.*

causation. It shows that man has no preferred position in the universe and that he is to be treated like any other part of creation.

In this connection, James quoted Balfour to bring out the full implication of materialism. The latter taught that ultimately the universe may be destroyed, that nothing may remain of man, and that death may triumph completely. Such a view James refused to accept. It would mean moral stagnation, for it would run counter to his fondest hopes.

On the other hand, the theistic order, with a personal God, gives us hope and consolation, expands our cosmic outlook, and gives vigor to our faith and to our religious beliefs. It makes God the ground of the universe. We feel less solitary, deserted, and impotent because we can look forward to a beyond in which we will experience eternal rewards.

All this may not be realized, and it may be merely an illusion. Still, such a faith creates less tragedy in the universe. If the world is destroyed, we can look forward to another existence. If wickedness flowers on this earth, we can be consoled by the thought of heaven. In short, morality is buttressed by such a metaphysical faith.

James reminded us that we cannot escape from metaphysical questions. A shallow thinker may say that ultimate answers are impossible and that we must be concerned merely with immediate problems. The true teacher realizes that man needs a transcendent explanation of phenomena, and that the universe must have a moral meaning.

James lays a Protestant stress on individualism, dislike of formal authority, hatred of scholastic reasoning, and emphasis on faith. As in the case of Protestantism, the opponents of pragmatism regarded it as a plebeian invention. Still, it had to be recognized; James himself predicted that the time would come when no one could remain ignorant of its contributions.

It may be asked now, what are the traits of the universe in the metaphysics of James? Above all, freedom of the will is recognized. James showed that the determinists picture the future according to the past and that their universe is austere and barren. Did not Spinoza speak of universal necessity? Did he not make it clear that our human wishes and desires do not affect the universe? The viewpoint of James is completely opposite to that of Spinoza. The future can be different from the past; real novelty is possible. It remains for us to change the world, to realize its potentialities and to make life more glorious than it has ever been.

The philosophy of James differs from absolute idealism, which pictures the universe as a perfect whole. Idealism, which is inconsistent with our own experiences, creates nothing but lethargy and complacency. If the world were a perfect oasis, a Shangri-La of delight, we would not strive so hard for perfection. The thinker of the future will reject both the materialistic and the idealistic concept of determinism. He will regard the universe, not as a static entity, but as a *dynamic* process in which we all cooperate and in which we all do our share.

James emphasizes *action*. Schopenhauer, he felt, was wrong in seeing only the unpleasant features of life. There is no reason to assume that the universe is guided by an irrational will and that everywhere evil triumphs over goodness. Likewise we cannot accept the viewpoint of Leibnitz that this is the best of all possible worlds, for Leibnitz's optimism merely indicates superficiality and shallowness.

His own viewpoint was that of *meliorism*. It is our task to improve the universe and to make life more perfect. Mere meditation regarding the nature of reality is not sufficient; such meditation must be followed by action, through which education can benefit and through which real progress can be made.

In metaphysics James attacks the monistic viewpoint on four grounds. First, monism does not account for finite consciousness. We are not merely modes of an absolute mind, for we possess a dignity and an autonomy of our own. Second, monism has no adequate solution for the problem of evil. Since it regards the Absolute as perfect, it cannot explain satisfactorily why imperfection should exist in the world. Yet we constantly wonder how it can exhibit so many limitations and so many disparities. Third, such an attitude cannot explain the process of change, since it regards the realm of the Absolute as eternal and unchanging. Here it contradicts experience, which is dominated by change and in which a constant flux reigns. Fourth, monism is fatalistic. Everything is determined; everything has its place and functions as part of an Absolute realm. In this way it neglects the realm of possibility which makes life meaningful and which creates real novelty.

RELIGIOUS EDUCATION

James, in *The Will To Believe*, writes that what mankind needs most is not unbounded faith, but rational criticism, but the scholarly world, swayed too much by the cult of skepticism, is unable to influence the life of common man. He attacks Huxley and Clifford, agnostics who denied the importance of religious experience. Religion cannot be determined and judged by pure reason, for it is primarily a manifestation of our emotional desires.

James points out that we can decide intellectually if we prefer Spinoza to Schopenhauer, and we can defend our viewpoint by various reasons. We might say that we like the detachment and moral courage of Spinoza while we dislike the irrationalism and egotism of Schopenhauer. But there are other decisions which must be made on emotional grounds, and here we take risks; we gamble. This is necessary in religion. Certain decisions may have *momentous* and *forced* consequences. If we believe in God, our life may be transformed and our perspective may be changed. Such faith is not a trivial matter, for it becomes the foundation of all philosophy.

The agnostics claimed that religious debate and religious fermentation characterize the prescientific mind. The positivistic stage, they thought, would eliminate all theological disputes. James disagreed with them; mankind will always need religion and will find deep meaning in it. Religious hypotheses can enrich our lives and can give us more drive and energy.

James' suggestions were not dogmatic but tentative and hypothetical. As an opponent of the established faiths, he called for a return to the mainsprings and sources of religious life. He analyzed the emotional experiences of the great saints and mystics of mankind. His religion was not genteel in any sense of the word. It was a rugged, masculine religion which contained traces of the old revival meetings.

James' concept of God is not clear. Occasionally he suggests that the polytheistic hypothesis may be more adequate than that of monotheism. He notes that there was more tolerance in ancient Greece, where many gods were worshipped, than in modern Europe, where God is pictured as an absolute monarch. Being a realist, James recognizes the importance of evil in the universe. If we say that God is all-powerful, we imply that he created evil, which would make a sadist out of him. Hence, it is better to speak of God as *limited*.

We must abandon, then, once and for all the medieval concept of deity, which viewed God as absolute and arbitrary. James rejects the transcendent concept of God; we can be certain that God is interested in our needs and that God helps us to realize our goals. We are engaged in a partnership with God in which all of us are struggling against evil, and are attempting to improve the universe.

Since the universe is characterized by freedom, and not absolutely determined, James believes that immortality may be possible. At any rate, there is no reason to suppose that scientific evidence is against immortality. Much interested in physical research, he thought it would prove that personal survival after death could be justified by empirical evidence. James postulated a definite personal continuation of life after death.

PHILOSOPHY OF EDUCATION

James opposed traditional instruction, which stressed memorization and relied on the classics. Instead, he favored functional training in laboratory work, which he thought would make for precision of thought and sharpness of observation.

In his period, moral philosophy frequently occupied the center of the curriculum, and it usually was taught by the college president, who was also a minister of the gospel. James opposed such instruction, which he thought cultivated mythologies and obscured the realities of our existence. Let the student explore life. Let him obtain a versatile view of science. Above all, let there be no fixed dogmas, traditional concepts, or obsolete superstitions.

James' educational philosophy rests upon psychology, not upon metaphysics. It is the task of the educator to study the laws of learning and become acquainted with the psychological facts which explain our nervous system. We must make habitual "as many useful actions as possible"; as in other realms of life, indecision is our great enemy. James despises the man who constantly frets over little things and who can never make up his mind. Education should see to it that such a type does not emerge; rather, it should develop bold leaders.

William James praised the structure of American education.

In the general activity and uprising of ideal interests which every one with an eye for fact can discern all about us in American life, there is perhaps no more promising feature than the fermentation which for a dozen years or more has been going on among the teachers. In whatever sphere of education their functions may lie, there is to be seen among them a really inspiring amount of searching of the heart about the highest concerns of their profession. The renovation of nations begins always at the top, among the reflective members of the State, and spreads slowly outward and downward. The teachers of this country, one may say, have its future in their hands. The earnestness which they at present show in striving to enlighten and strengthen themselves is an index of the nation's probabilities of advance in all ideal directions. The outward organization of education which we have in our United States is perhaps, on the whole, the best organization that exists in any country. The State school systems give a diversity and flexibility, an opportunity for experiment and keenness of competition, nowhere else to be found on such an important scale.[5]

To James education is . . .

. . . the organization of acquired habits of conduct and tendencies to behavior.

To illustrate. You and I are each and all of us educated, in our several ways; and we show our education at this present moment by different conduct. It would be quite impossible for me with my mind technically and professionally organized as it is, and with the optical stimulus which your presence affords, to remain sitting here entirely silent and inactive. Something tells me that I am expected to speak, and must speak; something forces me to keep on speaking. My organs of articulation are continuously innervated by outgoing currents, which the currents passing inward at my eyes and through my educated brain have set in motion; and the particular movements which they make have their form and order determined altogether by the training of all my past years of lecturing and reading. Your conduct, on the other hand, might seem at first sight purely receptive and inactive, — leaving out those among you who happen to be taking notes. But the very listening which you are carrying on is itself a determinate kind of conduct. All the muscular tensions of your body are distributed in a peculiar way as you listen. Your head, your eyes, are fixed characteristically. And, when the lecture is over, it will inevitably eventuate in some stroke of behavior, as I said on the previous occasion: you may be guided differently in some special emergency in the schoolroom by words which I now let fall. — So it is with the impressions you will make there on your pupil. You should get into the habit of regarding them all as leading to the acquisition by him of capacities for behavior, — emotional, social, bodily, vocal, technical, or what not. And, this being the case, you ought to feel willing, in a general way, and without hair-splitting or farther ado, to take up for the purposes of these lectures with the biological conception of the mind, as of something given us for practical use. That conception will certainly cover the greater part of your own educational work.[6]

James correlated reception and reaction.

No reception without reaction, no impression without correlative expression, — this is the great maxim which the teacher ought never to forget.

"An impression which simply flows in at the pupil's eyes or ears, and in no way modifies his active life, is an impression gone to waste.

---

[5] *Talks to Teachers*, pp. 3-4.
[6] *Ibid.*, pp. 29-30.

It is physiologically incomplete. It leaves no fruits behind it in the way of capacity acquired. Even as mere impression, it fails to produce its proper effect upon the memory; for, to remain fully among the acquisitions of this latter faculty, it must be wrought into the whole cycle of our operations. Its *motor consequences* are what clinch it. Some effect due to it in the way of an activity must return to the mind in the form of the *sensation of having acted* and connect itself with the impression. The most durable impressions are those on account of which we speak or act, or else are inwardly convulsed.[7]

James stressed the power of emulation.

Imitation shades imperceptibly into *Emulation*. Emulation is the impulse to imitate what you see another doing, in order not to appear inferior; and it is hard to draw a sharp line between the manifestations of the two impulses, so inextricably do they mix their effects. Emulation is the very nerve of human society. Why are you, my hearers, sitting here before me? If no one whom you ever heard of had attended a "summer school" or teachers' institute, would it have occurred to any one of you to break out independently and do a thing so unprescribed by fashion? Probably not. Nor would your pupils come to you unless the children of their parents' neighbors were all simultaneously being sent to school. We wish not to be lonely or eccentric, and we wish not to be cut off from our share in things which to our neighbors seem desirable privileges.

In the schoolroom, imitation and emulation play absolutely vital parts. Every teacher knows the advantage of having certain things performed by whole bands of children at a time. The teacher who meets with most success is the teacher whose own ways are the most imitable.[8]

Teaching depends on example.

Children admire a teacher who has skill. What he does seems easy, and they wish to emulate it. It is useless for a dull and devitalized teacher to exhort her pupils to wake up and take an interest. She must first take one herself; then her example is effective as no exhortation can possibly be.

Every school has its tone, moral and intellectual. And this tone is a mere tradition kept up by imitation, due in the first instance to the example set by teachers and by previous pupils of an aggressive and dominating type, copied by the others, and passed on from year to year, so that the new pupils take the cue almost immediately. Such a tone changes very slowly, if at all; and then always under the modi-

---

[7] *Ibid.*, pp. 33-34.
[8] *Ibid.*, pp. 49-50.

fying influence of new personalities aggressive enough in character to
set new patterns and not merely to copy the old. The classic example
of this sort of tone is the often quoted case of Rugby under Dr.
Arnold's administration. He impressed his own character as a model
on the imagination of the oldest boys, who in turn were expected
and required to impress theirs upon the younger set. The contagious-
ness of Arnold's genius was such that a Rugby man was said to be
recognizable all through life by a peculiar turn of character which he
acquired at school. It is obvious that psychology as such can give in
this field no precepts of detail. As in so many other fields of teaching,
success depends mainly on the native genius of the teacher, the sympathy, tact, and perception which enable him to seize the right moment
and to set the right example.[9]

James stressed both discipline and interest.

It is certain that most schoolroom work, till it has become habitual
and automatic, is repulsive, and cannot be done without voluntarily
jerking back the attention to it every now and then. This is inevitable,
let the teacher do what he will. It flows from the inherent nature of
the subjects and of the learning mind. The repulsive processes of
verbal memorizing, of discovering steps of mathematical identity,
and the like, must borrow their interest at first from purely external
sources, mainly from the personal interests with which success in
mastering them is associated, such as gaining of rank, avoiding punishment, not being beaten by a difficulty and the like. Without such
borrowed interest, the child could not attend them at all. But in
these processes what becomes interesting enough to be attended to is
not thereby attended to *without effort.* Effort always has to go on,
derived interest, for the most part, not awakening attention that is
easy, however spontaneous it may now have to be called. The interest
which the teacher, by his utmost skill, can lend to the subject, proves
over and over again to be only an interest sufficient to *let loose the
effort.* The teacher, therefore, need never concern himself about
inventing occasions where effort must be called into play. Let him
still awaken whatever sources of interest in the subject he can by
stirring up connections between it and the pupil's nature, whether in
the line of theoretic curiosity, of personal interest, or of pugnacious
impulse. The laws of mind will then bring enough pulses of effort into
play to keep the pupils exercised in the direction of the subject.[10]

James had little use for examinations.

The boy who tells us, "I know the answer, but I can't say what it is,"
we treat as practically identical with him who knows absolutely noth-

---

[9] *Ibid.,* pp. 50-51.
[10] *Ibid.,* pp. 109-111.

ing about the answer at all. But this is a great mistake. It is but a small part of our experience in life that we are ever able articulately to recall. And yet the whole of it has had its influence in shaping our character and defining our tendencies to judge and act. Although the ready memory is a great blessing to its possessor, the vaguer memory of a subject, of having once had to do with it, of its neighborhood, and of where we may go to recover it again, constitutes in most men and women the chief fruit of their education. This is true even in professional education. The doctor, the lawyer, are seldom able to decide upon a case off-hand. They differ from other men only through the fact that they know how to get at the materials for decision in five minutes or half an hour; whereas the layman is unable to get at the materials at all, not knowing in what books and indexes to look or not understanding the technical terms.

Be patient, then, and sympathetic with the type of mind that cuts a poor figure in examinations. It may, in the long examination which life sets us, come out in the end in better shape than the glib and ready reproducer, its passions being deeper, its purposes more worthy, its combining power less commonplace, and its total mental output consequently more important.[11]

James contrasts negative and positive motivation.

For instance, your pupils are wandering in mind, are listening to a sound outside the window, which presently grows interesting enough to claim all their attention. You can call the latter back again by bellowing at them not to listen to those sounds, but to keep their minds on their books or on what you are saying. And, by thus keeping them conscious that your eye is sternly on them, you may produce a good effect. But it will be a wasteful effect and an inferior effect; for the moment you relax your supervision the attractive disturbance, always there soliciting their curiosity, will overpower them, and they will be just as they were before: whereas, if, without saying anything about the street disturbances, you open a counterattraction by starting some very interesting talk or demonstration yourself, they will altogether forget the distracting incident, and without any effort follow you along. There are many interests that can never be inhibited by the way of negation. To a man in love, for example, it is literally impossible, by any effort of will, to annul his passion. But let "some new planet swim into his ken," and the former idol will immediately cease to engross his mind.

It is clear that in general we ought, whenever we can, to employ the method of inhibition by substitution. He whose life is based upon the word "no," who tells the truth because a lie is wicked, and who has constantly to grapple with his envious and cowardly and mean

---

[11] *Ibid.*, pp. 142-143.

propensities, is in an inferior situation in every respect to what he would be if the love of truth and magnanimity positively possessed him from the outset, and he felt no inferior temptations. Your born gentleman is certainly, for this world's purposes, a more valuable being than your "Crump, with his grunting resistance to his native devils," even though in God's sight the latter may, as the Catholic theologians say, be rolling up great stores of "merit."[12]

He turns to Spinoza who

. . . wrote in his *Ethics* that anything that a man can avoid under the notion that it is bad he may also avoid under the notion that something else is good. He who habitually acts *sub specie mali*, under the negative notion, the notion of the bad, is called a slave by Spinoza. To him who acts habitually under the notion of good he gives the name of freeman. . . . Make freemen of your pupils by habituating them to act, whenever possible, under the notion of a good. Get them habitually to tell the truth, not so much through showing them the wickedness of lying as by arousing their enthusiasm for honor and veracity. Wean them from their native cruelty by imparting to them some of your own positive sympathy with an animal's inner springs of joy. And, in the lessons which you may be legally obliged to conduct upon the bad effects of alcohol, lay less stress than the books do on the drunkard's stomach, kidneys, nerves and social miseries, and more on the blessings of having an organism kept in lifelong possession of its full youthful elasticity by a sweet, sound blood, to which stimulants and narcotics are unknown, and to which the morning sun and air and dew will daily come as sufficiently powerful intoxicants. . . .

If to some of you the things I have said seem obvious or trivial, it is possible that they may appear less so when, in the course of a year or two, you find yourselves noticing and apperceiving events in the schoolroom a little differently, in consequence of some of the conceptions I have tried to make more clear. I cannot but think that to apperceive your pupil as a little sensitive, impulsive, associative, and reactive organism, partly fated and partly free, will lead to a better intelligence of all his ways. Understand him, then, as such a subtle little piece of machinery. And if, in addition, you can also see him *sub specie boni,* and love him as well, you will be in the best possible position for becoming perfect teachers.[13]

James believed that progress could be achieved only through functional application. The education of the past was too much occupied with noble maxims. It had been too contemplative, and had neglected the everyday realm of action. The school room must be

---

[12] *Ibid.*, pp. 193-194.
[13] *Ibid.*, pp. 194-196.

equated with life and must become the center of action. Only in this way can education become constructive and dynamic in the experience of the individual.

There is a danger, James noted, that the teacher may moralize too much and that he may give too many sermons. Instead, he should appeal to the emotional drives of his students, and should make the process of knowledge as dramatic as possible. He should show that ideas can be as adventurous and as thrilling as other activities which at first appear more interesting to the students.

If learning is to be effective, James taught, it must be based upon daily exercise. We should not postpone our intellectual efforts. By devoting a few hours every day to poetry and philosophy we can increase our intellectual proficiency, and we can actualize our mental potentialities. Nothing worth-while is accomplished without constant effort. At first we regret it, for we believe we abandon some of our most cherished pleasures. But the more we indulge in intellectual effort, the more we improve ourselves and the more delightful life becomes.

At the same time, James realized the weaknesses of the American type of education. He was not an unqualified proponent of activism. For example, he mentioned the reaction of Hindu visitors who noticed the spiritual vacuity of American education. James agreed with them, for like them he felt that our life was becoming too tense and that anxiety was dominating our character. We must learn how to relax and how to control our desires. We must not be overcome by constant motion and by an unending expenditure of energy.

Many critics have been harsh with James because they have seen him merely as an apostle of utilitarianism. They have neglected the critical side of James' dynamic thought. He was interested, at the same time, in higher personal ideals, in a wider perspective, and he thought that education could develop a more adequate set of attitudes by which we can improve civilization. Action to him was not an end in itself. It was to be supplemented by self-discipline, and by meditation on the nature and destiny of man.

EDUCATION AGAINST WAR

The social philosophy of James was much concerned with the problem of war. He had no illusions about the pacifistic drives of man. Has not war been a constant aspect of civilization, glorified by the ministers of God? Is not man a beast of prey?

Since our culture is becoming more monotonous, we continually need excitement. Wars, consequently, especially for noncombatants, have been periods of relief from the tediousness of our existence. War fever, furthermore, is stimulated by the newspapers, which specialize in sensationalism and which dramatize the conflicts of nations.

To some extent, James believed that people actually want war. This may be disillusioning for the sentimentalist, but they do not understand human nature. War has a religious motive. It is part of our savage background, and it gives a certain intoxication to life.

James believed that universal disarmament is not the correct cure; we must put peaceful statesmen into power; we must educate the public, especially those who manufacture public opinion.

The best antidote is to find a substitute for war. Instead of military conscription, we should organize young men into battalions to build dams, to diminish the ravages of nature, and to expand our industrial system. Adventure would still remain with us. There would still be the thrill of new experiences, but our task would be constructive instead of destructive, and peace would reign supreme.

To bring about a better civilization, James looked to the outstanding individual. History is made not by the masses but by the outstanding leader. To establish peace, we must obtain a type of statesman who abhors all militaristic notions and dedicates himself to the welfare of humanity.

PART FIVE

Idealism and Pragmatism

CHAPTER TWENTY-FIVE

John Dewey

LIFE AND WORKS

Dewey (1859–1952), the outstanding student of William James, studied at the University of Vermont and at Johns Hopkins University; later he taught at Minnesota, Michigan, Chicago, and finally, from 1904, at Columbia. He travelled to China, Japan, Mexico, Russia, and Turkey. His philosophical theories exerted a wide influence abroad; he was instrumental in reorganizing the Turkish educational system.

Among his most important works are *Experience and Nature, The Quest for Certainty, Logic, Essays in Experimental Logic,* and *Reconstruction in Philosophy.* In esthetics he wrote *Art as Experience.* To religious philosophy he contributed *A Common Faith.* To ethics and social philosophy, he added *Human Nature and Conduct,* and *Freedom and Culture.* In political theory he gave voice to a pluralistic concept of the state in *The Public and Its Problems.*

Dewey continued the pragmatic tradition of William James, but his interest was mainly in education, while James' main interest was religion. Dewey had a powerful effect upon America's educational development. His *Democracy and Education* became a sort of Magna Charta of the American school system.[1]

Among the influences which conditioned Dewey's thinking, Hegelian philosophy occupies a prominent place. W. T. Harris thought that Dewey might become the foremost interpreter of Hegel in America. Dewey found in Hegel a sweeping explanation of history which appealed to his imagination; however, he noticed that Hegel's scientific views were defective and rested upon a superficial acquaintance with the experimental method.

More important than Hegel was the impact of Huxley, Spencer, and Darwin on Dewey's development. The theory of evolution became the cornerstone of Dewey's system. Like Darwin, Dewey believed in a *biological approach to knowledge*. Darwinism did not make a pessimist out of Dewey; he thought that science could control nature and that the struggle for existence could be modified by the judicious use of man's intelligence.

At the same time, Dewey had a pronounced interest in ancient philosophy. In his eighties he continued to be an avid reader of Plato. Like Plato, Dewey had a lifelong interest in social problems, and he was interested in the establishment of a new society. However, he did not appreciate Plato's authoritarian tendencies. Dewey believed in the common man and had no use for dictators, either in philosophy, politics or education.

The most significant single influence on Dewey was the work of William James, who had great respect for Dewey's philosophical insight. Dewey, in fact, became the St. Paul of pragmatism. There were heresies in pragmatic ranks. Peirce in his later views disliked the anti-intellectualism of James and adopted the term pragmaticism for his own philosophy. Schiller, who never liked an orthodox cause, styled his system humanism and devoted most of his time to an onslaught on the Aristotelian syllogism. Papini, the young Italian thinker, for whom James had great hopes, turned to Catholicism and devoted most of his labors to a defense of the Catholic saints, whose virtues and greatness he espoused. Dewey, however, remained faithful to pragmatism and defended its tenets against all opponents.

Like James, Dewey believed in an open universe, and he felt that traditional philosophy could not provide an adequate answer to the problems of education and human conduct. What matters then is not the goals of philosophy, but the *methods* utilized by the thinker.

---

[1] For a critical survey of Dewey see Hook, *John Dewey, an Intellectual Portrait; Leander, The Philosophy of John Dewey: A Critical Study;* Feldman, *The Philosophy of John Dewey: A Critical Analysis.*

But there are significant differences between the philosophies of Dewey and James. James was essentially religious. Dewey approached religion from the standpoint of the laboratory scientist, and had a strong bias for agnosticism. Dewey's system was more deterministic. Thus it reflected the growing stratification of American society. In James' time, individualism was the guiding voice of American culture; but in Dewey's era there was a strong trend in the direction of social action and social control.

Dewey dreamed of a welfare state which would provide economic security for its citizens and lift their standard of living.

Both men were liberals; both hated oppressive authority, but Dewey's liberalism was more sober and scientific. He expected no miracles; he had no faith in automatic solutions or in the laissez-faire spirit; instead, he urged the extension of democratic principles into the economic field.

Why did Dewey exert such an enormous influence on American life? First, he represented the down-to-earth tradition of pragmatism. He was not abstruse and theoretical like Royce and Edwards, rather he discussed *concrete and living issues.*

Second, he had immense faith in democracy. He did not look down on the masses; he had no sympathy for the upper classes, nor any respect for old-world culture. In Dewey the American way of life found an eloquent spokesman.

Third, he was an activist. He stressed constantly that mere contemplation is not sufficient, and that activity ennobles man. This spirit could easily be appreciated by the average American, who likewise had disdain for contemplation and whose energy was boundless. Americans are perhaps the most activist of all people; this spirit frequently produces anti-intellectualist currents in America.

Fourth, Dewey became the spokesman of the rebellion against authority. In education, students were demanding greater freedom and were trying to get away from the traditional curriculum; in religion, liberal Christianity was dissatisfied with the old supernaturalism and was attempting to establish a universal foundation for religion. In politics, the progressive movement was trying to reform federal and local government so that American democracy would be closer to Lincoln's ideal of a government of the people, by the people, and for the people. In art the same rebellion could be noticed. American artists tried their best to be up-to-date and with enthusiasm took up such European movements as cubism, surrealism, and dadaism, which they regarded as extremely progressive.

All these trends were reflected in Dewey's philosophy, which looked upon most of history as a dark and useless adventure. Instead, he urged his fellow-countrymen to look to a new scientific age which would not tolerate any type of dogmatism and which would witness the full triumph of the pragmatic method.

EDUCATIONAL IDEALS

Dewey's theory of education cannot be understood without a comprehension of his opposition to a merely cultural education, by which he understands the training of a parasitical leisure class. He opposed mere book knowledge in any area. He stressed actual practice, democratic cooperation, the fellowship of occupations, and the interests of the student which are to be measured by his growth.

In *My Pedagogic Creed,* Dewey turned to what the school is.

> The school is primarily a social institution. Education being a social process, the school is simply that form of community life in which all those agencies are concentrated that will be most effective in bringing the child to share in the inherited resources of the race, and to use his own powers for social ends.
>
> Education, therefore, is a process of living and not a preparation for future living.
>
> The school must represent life, as real and vital to the child as that which he carries on in the home, in the neighborhood, or on the playground.
>
> That education which does not occur through forms of life, forms that are worth living for their own sake, is always a poor substitute for the genuine reality, and tends to cramp and to deaden.
>
> The school, as an institution, should simplify existing social life; should reduce it, as it were, to an embryonic form. Existing life is so complex that the child cannot be brought into contact with it without either confusion or distraction; he is either overwhelmed by the multiplicity of activities which are going on, so that he loses his own power of orderly reaction, or he is so stimulated by these various activities that his powers are prematurely called into play and he becomes either unduly specialized or else disintegrated.
>
> As such simplified social life, the school should grow gradually out of the home life; it should take up and continue the activities with which the child is already familiar in the home.
>
> It should exhibit these activities to the child, and reproduce them in such ways that the child will gradually learn the meaning of them, and be capable of playing his own part in relation to them.
>
> This is a psychological necessity, because it is the only way of securing continuity in the child's growth, the only way of giving a background of past experience to the new ideas given in school.

It is also a social necessity because the home is the form of social life in which the child has been nurtured and in connection with which he has had his moral training. It is the business of the school to deepen and extend his sense of the values bound up in his home life.[2]

He attacks contemporary views.

Much of present education fails because it neglects this fundamental principle of the school as a form of community life. It conceives the school as a place where certain information is to be given, where certain lessons are to be learned, or where certain habits are to be formed. The value of these is conceived as lying largely in the remote future; the child must do these things for the sake of something else he is to do; they are mere preparations. As a result they do not become a part of the life experience of the child and so are not truly educative.

The moral education centers upon this conception of the school as a mode of social life, that the best and deepest moral training is precisely that which one gets through having to enter into proper relations with others in a unity of work and thought. The present educational systems, so far as they destroy or neglect this unity, render it difficult or impossible to get any genuine, regular moral training.

The child should be stimulated and controlled in his work through the life of the community.

Under existing conditions far too much of the stimulus and control proceeds from the teacher, because of neglect of the idea of the school as a form of social life.

The teacher's place and work in the school is to be interpreted from this same basis. The teacher is not in the school to impose certain ideas or to form certain habits in the child, but is there as a member of the community to select the influences which shall affect the child and to assist him in properly responding to these influences.

The discipline of the school should proceed from the life of the school as a whole and not directly from the teacher.

The teacher's business is simply to determine, on the basis of larger experience and riper wisdom, how the discipline of life shall come to the child.

All questions of the grading of the child and his promotion should be determined by reference to the same standard. Examinations are of use only so far as they test the child's fitness for social life and reveal the place in which he can be of the most service and where he can receive the most help.[3]

---

[2] *My Pedagogic Creed.* (Pamphlet issued in 1900.)
[3] *Ibid.*

Regarding the subject-matter of education he stated:

The social life of the child is the basis of concentration, or correlation, in all his training or growth. The social life gives the unconscious unity and the background of all his efforts and of all his attainments.

The subject matter of the school curriculum should mark a gradual differentiation out of the primitive unconscious unity of social life.

We violate the child's nature and render difficult the best ethical results by introducing the child too abruptly to a number of special studies, of reading, writing, geography, etc., out of relation to this social life.

The true center of correlation on the school subjects is not science, nor literature, nor history, nor geography, but the child's own social activities.

Education cannot be unified in the study of science, or so-called nature study, because apart from human activity, nature itself is not a unity; nature in itself is a number of diverse objects in space and time, and to attempt to make it the center of work by itself is to introduce a principle of radiation rather than one of concentration.

Literature is the reflex expression and interpretation of social experience; hence it must follow upon and not precede such experience. It, therefore, cannot be made the basis, although it may be made the summary of unification.

Once more that history is of educative value insofar as it presents phases of social life and growth. It must be controlled by reference to social life. When taken simply as history it is thrown into the distant past and becomes dead and inert. Taken as the record of man's social life and progress it becomes full of meaning. I believe, however, that it cannot be so taken excepting as the child is also introduced directly into social life.

The primary basis of education is in the child's powers at work along the same general constructive lines as those which have brought civilization into being.

The only way to make the child conscious of his social heritage is to enable him to perform those fundamental types of activity which make civilization what it is.

In the so-called expressive or constructive activities is the center of correlation.

This gives the standard for the place of cooking, sewing, manual training, etc., in the school.

They are not special studies which are to be introduced over and above a lot of others in the way of relaxation or relief, or as additional accomplishments. I believe rather that they represent, as types, fundamental forms of social activity; and that it is possible and desirable that the child's introduction into the more formal subjects of the curriculum be through the medium of these constructive activities.[4]

He emphasizes science and literature.

The study of science is educational insofar as it brings out the materials and processes which make social life what it is.

One of the greatest difficulties in the present teaching of science is that the material is presented in purely objective form, or is treated as a new peculiar kind of experience which the child can add to that which he has already had. In reality, science is of value because it gives the ability to interpret and control the experience already had. It should be introduced, not as so much new subject matter, but as showing the factors already involved in previous experience and as furnishing tools by which that experience can be more easily and effectively regulated.

At present we lose much of the value of literature and language studies because of our elimination of the social element. Language is almost always treated in the books of pedagogy simply as the expression of thought. It is true that language is a logical instrument, but it is fundamentally and primarily a social instrument. Language is the device for communication; it is the tool through which one individual comes to share the ideas and feelings of others. When treated simply as a way of getting individual information, or as a means of showing off what one has learned, it loses its social motive and end.

There is, therefore, no succession of studies in the ideal school curriculum. If education is life, all life has, from the outset, a scientific aspect, an aspect of art and culture, and an aspect of communication. It cannot, therefore, be true that the proper studies for one grade are mere reading and writing, and that at a later grade, reading, or literature, or science, may be introduced. The progress is not in the succession of studies, but in the development of new attitudes towards, and new interests in, experience.

Education must be conceived as a continuing reconstruction of experience; that the process and the goal of education are one and the same thing.

To set up any end outside of education, as furnishing its goal and standard, is to deprive the educational process of much of its meaning, and tends to make us rely upon false and external stimuli in dealing with the child.[5]

---

[4] *Ibid.*
[5] *Ibid.*

About the nature of method he stated:

The question of method is ultimately reducible to the question of
the order of development of the child's powers and interests. The
law for presenting and treating material is the law implicit within
the child's own nature. Because this is so I believe the following
statements are of supreme importance as determining the spirit in
which education is carried on.

The active side precedès the passive in the development of the
child-nature; that expression comes before conscious impression; that
the muscular development precedes the sensory; that movements come
before conscious sensations; I believe that consciousness is essentially
motor or impulsive; that conscious states tend to project themselves
in action.

The neglect of this principle is the cause of a large part of the
waste of time and strength in school work. The child is thrown into a
passive, receptive, or absorbing attitude. The conditions are such
that he is not permitted to follow the law of his nature; the result is
friction and waste.

Ideas [intellectual and rational processes] also result from action
and evolve for the sake of the better control of action. What we term
reason is primarily the law of order or effective action. To attempt
to develop the reasoning powers, the powers of judgment, without
reference to the selection and arrangement of means in action, is the
fundamental fallacy in our present methods of dealing with this matter.
As a result we present the child with arbitrary symbols. Symbols are
a necessity in mental development, but they have their place as tools
for economizing effort; presented by themselves they are a mass of
meaningless and arbitrary ideas imposed from without.

The image is the great instrument of instruction. What a child
gets out of any subject presented to him is simply the images which
he himself forms with regard to it.

If nine-tenths of the energy at present directed towards making
the child learn certain things were spent in seeing to it that the child
was forming proper images, the work of instruction would be indefinitely facilitated.

Much of the time and attention now given to the preparation and
presentation of lessons might be more wisely and profitably expended
in training the child's power of imagery and in seeing to it that he
was continually forming definite vivid and growing images of the
various subjects with which he comes in contact in his experiences.[6]

He dwells on emotions in learning.

Interests are the signs and symptoms of growing power. I believe
that they represent dawning capacities. Accordingly the constant and

---

[6] *Ibid.*

careful observation of interests is of the utmost importance for the educator.

These interests are to be observed as showing the state of development which the child has reached.

They prophesy the stage upon which he is about to enter.

Only through the continual and sympathetic observation of childhood's interests can the adult enter into the child's life and see what it is ready for, and upon what material it could work most readily and fruitfully.

These interests are neither to be humored nor repressed. To repress interest is to substitute the adult for the child, and so to weaken intellectual curiosity and alertness, to suppress initiative, and to deaden interest. To humor the interests is to substitute the transient for the permanent. The interest is always the sign of some power below; the important thing is to discover this power. To humor the interest is to fail to penetrate below the surface, and its sure result is to substitute caprice and whim for genuine interest.

The emotions are the reflex of actions.

To endeavor to stimulate or arouse the emotions apart from their corresponding activities is to introduce an unhealthy and morbid state of mind.

If we can only secure right habits of action and thought, with reference to the good, the true, and the beautiful, the emotions will for the most part take care of themselves.

Next to deadness and dullness, formalism and routine, our education is threatened with no greater evil than sentimentalism.

This sentimentalism is the necessary result of the attempt to divorce feeling from action.[7]

Regarding the school and social progress he remarked:

Education is the fundamental method of social progress and reform.

All reforms which rest simply upon the enactment of law, or the threatening of certain penalties, or upon changes in mechanical or outward arrangements, are transitory and futile.

Education is a regulation of the process of coming to share in the social consciousness; the adjustment of individual activity on the basis of this social consciousness is the only sure method of social reconstruction.

This conception has due regard for both the individualistic and socialistic ideals. It is duly individual because it recognizes the formation of a certain character as the only genuine basis of right living. It is socialistic because it recognizes that this right character is not to be formed by merely individual precept, example, or exhortation, but rather by the influence of a certain form of institutional or com-

---

[7] *Ibid.*

munity life upon the individual, and that the social organism through the school, as its organ, may determine ethical results.

In the ideal school we have the reconciliation of the individualistic and the institutional ideals.

The community's duty to education is, therefore, its paramount moral duty. By law and punishment, by social agitation and discussion, society can regulate and form itself in a more or less haphazard and chance way. But through education society can formulate its own purposes, can organize its own means and resources, and thus shape itself with definiteness and economy in the direction in which it wishes to move.

When society once recognizes the possibilities in this direction, and the obligations which these possibilities impose, it is impossible to conceive of the resources of time, attention, and money which will be put at the disposal of the educator.[8]

He values education for social progress.

It is the business of everyone interested in education to insist upon the school as the primary and most effective interest of social progress and reform in order that society may be awakened to realize what the school stands for, and aroused to the necessity of endowing the educator with sufficient equipment properly to perform his task.

Education thus conceived marks the most perfect and intimate union of science and art conceivable in human experience.

The art of thus giving shape to human powers and adapting them to social service is the supreme art; one calling into its service the best of artists; no insight, sympathy, tact, executive power, is too great for such service.

With the growth of psychological service, giving added insight into individual structure and laws of growth; and with the growth of social science, adding to our knowledge of the right organization of individuals, all scientific resources can be utilized for the purposes of education.

When science and art thus join hands the most commanding motive for human action will be reached, the most genuine springs of human conduct aroused, and the best service that human nature is capable of guaranteed.

The teacher is engaged, not simply in the training of individuals, but in the formation of the proper social life.

Every teacher should realize the dignity of his calling; that he is a social servant set apart for the maintenance of proper social order and the securing of the right social growth.

In this way the teacher always is the prophet of the true God and the usherer in of the true kingdom of God.[9]

---

[8] *Ibid.*
[9] *Ibid.*

His ideal is that the school should mirror the activities, interests, and aspirations of society. How foolish it is to divorce education from action, to make a monastery out of the school. Education is a *continuous* process. It does not start at any given time, and it certainly does not stop when we leave school. More than any other thinker, Dewey realizes how important education is for the development of a free society.

While the Greek thinkers, especially Plato and Aristotle, had too much respect for merely cultural subjects, and disdained manual labor, John Dewey and his followers emphasized perhaps too strongly the importance of manual work and industrial activity. The task of a genuinely progressive education should be to restore the balance between thinking and manual labor. America especially needs more concentrated courses in the fundamentals of modern civilization.

In fairness to John Dewey it should be pointed out that the weakness of progressive education is mostly due to *faulty application*. Many teachers who had no adequate educational training allowed their classes to do whatever they pleased. The lack of discipline they introduced bordered on anarchy; and his progressive ideal of education was constantly negated by the authoritarian tendencies both of the home and of social institutions.

SCIENTIFIC METHOD

In Dewey's philosophy, the scientific method plays an important role. He feels that philosophers can learn much from scientists; they should be open-minded and experimental in their approach to intellectual problems. Thus Dewey eliminates the consideration of metaphysical ideals from his system and instead views life from a secular standpoint.

Dewey demands a *reconstruction of philosophy*. Thinkers must abandon belief in eternal realities and avoid useless epistemological controversies; instead they should deal with the social and moral problems of their time.

> Any one of you who arrives at such a view of past philosophy will of necessity be left to entertain a quite definite conception of the scope and aim of future philosophizing. He will inevitably be committed to the notion that what philosophy has been unconsciously, without knowing or intending it, and so to speak, under cover, it must henceforth be openly and deliberately. When it is acknowledged

that under disguise of dealing with ultimate reality, philosophy has been occupied with the precious values embedded in social traditions, that it has sprung from a clash of social ends and from a conflict of inherited institutions with incompatible contemporary tendencies, it will be seen that the task of future philosophy is to clarify men's ideas as to the social and moral strifes of their own day. Its aim is to become so far as is humanly possible an organ for dealing with these conflicts.[10]

Applying this viewpoint to logic, Dewey points out that logic is not the key to reality and that it should follow an *experimental path*. Logic thus becomes a progressive discipline, occupied not with static syllogisms, but with the ever-changing data of experience.

Dewey's philosophy is characterized by *instrumentalism*, which is activistic and holds that growth is the main criterion for a meaningful life. There is no underlying substance; the mind is not an entity, but a *function*. There can be no division between object and subject, for both are interrelated.

In many ways, Dewey completed the work of Francis Bacon. Like Bacon, Dewey was concerned primarily with the *functional* aspects of knowledge, which could bring about a new renaissance of culture.

In modern culture Dewey finds four pronounced changes from medieval ideals.

First, there is the transfer of interest from the eternal and universal to what is changing and specific, concrete — a movement that showed itself practically in carrying over of attention and thought from another world to this, from the supernaturalism characteristic of the Middle Ages to delight in natural science, natural activity and natural intercourse. Secondly, there is the gradual decay of the authority of fixed institutions and class distinctions and relations, and a growing belief in the power of individual minds, guided by methods of observation, experiment and reflection, to attain the truths needed for the guidance of life. The operations and results of natural inquiry gained in prestige and power at the expense of principles dictated from high authority.

Consequently principles and alleged truths are judged more and more by criteria of their origin in experience and their consequences of weal and woe in experience, and less by criteria of sublime origin from beyond everyday experience and independent of fruits in experience. It is no longer enough for a principle to be elevated, noble, universal and hallowed by time. It must present its birth certificate, it must show under just what conditions of human experience it was

---

[10] *Reconstruction in Philosophy*, p. 26.

generated, and it must justify itself by its works, present and potential. Such is the inner meaning of the modern appeal to experience as an ultimate criterion of value and validity. In the third place, great store is set upon the idea of progress. The future rather than the past dominates the imagination. The Golden Age lies ahead of us, not behind us. Everywhere new possibilities beckon and arouse courage and effort. The great French thinkers of the later eighteenth century borrowed this idea from Bacon and developed it into the doctrine of the indefinite perfectibility of mankind on earth. Man is capable, if he will but exercise the required courage, intelligence and effort, of shaping his own fate. Physical conditions offer no insurmountable barriers. In the fourth place, the patient and experimental study of nature, bearing fruit in inventions which control nature and subdue her forces to social uses, is the method by which progress is made. Knowledge is power and knowledge is achieved by sending the mind to school to nature to learn her processes of change.[11]

Applying this viewpoint to science, Dewey believed that philosophers had not paid enough attention to scientific progress. They still believed in fixed ideas and they still adhered to *a priori* theories. However, science disclosed a universe which was neither fixed nor closed, but which revealed unlimited possibilities. Furthermore, science had a new respect for material facts. This implies that philosophers likewise had to adopt a new perspective which stressed experimentation and control, rather than a static contemplation of nature.

Such an experimental viewpoint was an expression of Dewey's democratic tendencies. He disliked static realities; instead, he favored change. In fact, his universe almost reminds us of Heraclitus in its dynamic pattern. Feudalism believed in fixed classes and in an absolute order; in philosophy it was represented by traditional idealistic theories which relied upon the fixity of species. Dewey's instrumentalism, however, stressed the reality of the individual and tolerated no absolute patterns. It believed in the future rather than in the past, and it had immense faith in the possibilities of man.

In this way, Dewey echoed the American spirit. Had not the pioneer negated the limitations of the old world? Was not progress the watchword of American culture? Was not growth a constant feature of American city life? The buoyant, energetic spirit of America is revealed in Dewey's technical philosophy.

Being a follower of the empirical tradition, Dewey stressed the importance of sensation. However, he did not follow Locke completely, for Dewey also emphasized the importance of intelligence.

---

[11] *Ibid.*, pp. 47-49.

It goes without saying that to him intelligence is not an abstract, hypothetical capacity; rather its function is to make possible for man a better adjustment to his environment. We cannot speak any more of pure reason, rather we must realize that man's reason is hypothetical.

This theory has important implications. It implies, first of all, that we must use our reason *concretely*. Education must come down to earth and contribute to the solution of man's social and political problems. Second, Dewey believes in tentative standards and hypothetical ideas. Reason has no exclusive key to reality. Our mind is not the gateway to the thing-in-itself; the standards of our generation should not necessarily guide the path of the future generation. In the third place our intelligence must be studied biologically since it evolved in the same way as all the other capacities of man. Dewey fought a perennial war against all those who tried to "deify" man's mind.

Like Machiavelli, Dewey was concerned with actuality, rather than with abstract ideals. The philosophers who had pictured only a Shangri-la and, like Royce, had appealed to the Absolute, had done serious harm to mankind, for they had divorced actuality from man's aspirations. To Dewey, ideals are not distant goals, but methods. They indicate our intellectual progress and must be applied to our daily life.

The philosopher of the future will not be concerned with a perfect realm. Nor will he seek to escape into a changeless reality; on the contrary, he will take part in the social strife of his time, and he will attempt to apply his ideals to the betterment of social institutions.

Our culture, especially poetry, art, and religion, cannot be sustained by relying upon the traditions of the past but only by anticipating the trends of the future.

Poetry, art, and religion are precious things. They cannot be maintained by lingering in the past and futilely wishing to restore what the movement of events in science, industry and politics has destroyed. They are an out-flowering of thought and desires that unconsciously converge into a disposition of imagination as a result of thousands and thousands of daily episodes and contact. They cannot be willed into existence or coerced into being. The wind of the spirit bloweth where it listeth and the kingdom of God in such things does not come with observation. But while it is impossible to retain and recover by deliberate volition old sources of religion and art that have been discredited, it is possible to expedite the development of the vital sources of a religion and art that are yet to be. Not indeed by action directly aimed at their production, but by substituting faith in the active tendencies of the day for dread and dislike of them, and by the courage of intelligence to follow whither social and scientific changes direct us. We are weak today in ideal matters because intelligence is divorced from aspiration. The bare force of circumstance compels us onward in the daily detail of our beliefs and acts, but our deeper thoughts and desires turn backwards. When philosophy shall have co-operated with the course of events and made clear and coherent the meaning of the daily detail, science and emotion will interpenetrate, practice and imagination will embrace. Poetry and religious feeling will be the unforced flowers of life. To further this articulation and revelation of the meanings of the current course of events is the task and problem of philosophy in days of transition.[12]

MORAL AND RELIGIOUS EDUCATION

Like James, Dewey was a *meliorist*. Neither the way of pessimism nor the way of optimism appealed to him. Pessimism makes us cynical and melancholy; it develops an attitude of resignation. Optimism creates a blindness whereby we assert that this is the best of all possible worlds, in spite of the evils which we see in life. Meliorism, as against pessimism and optimism, implies a plan of *action*. The meliorist believes that the condition of man can be improved and that philosophers should take a hand in social and intellectual reconstruction.

Like John Stuart Mill, Dewey believed in happiness. Thus he had no use for ascetic ideals. We cannot achieve salvation by starving our bodies. The goods of the world are to be enjoyed to the utmost. However, happiness is not a fixed state; it does not imply a utopia of comfort and luxury; rather, happiness is *dynamic* and demands constant effort and constant labor.

Moralists have been too abstract in their approach to philosophy. We want to know about the particular conditions in our culture, not about eternal values. Inquiry in morality should be guided by the concept of growth. The moral man is never self-righteous; he is never arrogant about his accomplishments; but is constantly trying to improve himself and to apply his knowledge to society.

Dewey felt that the scientific method would bring about an immense change in morality. By doing away with empty generalizations it would lead to the abandonment of dogmatism.

---

[12] *Ibid.*, pp. 212-213.

Notice how Dewey's moral philosophy differs from that of the Puritans. Dewey stressed growth, while the Puritans regarded morals as static. The Puritan saint felt self-righteous about his virtue; he thought that he was saved, while the rest of the world was damned. To Dewey, complacency is the great sin, and the intelligent person works hard so that all members of society can enjoy the fruits of civilization.

He insists that religion does not have doctrinal boundaries.

All religions, marked by elevated ideal quality, have dwelt upon the power of religion to introduce perspective into the piecemeal and shifting episodes of existence. Here too we need to reverse the ordinary statement and say that whatever introduces genuine perspective is religious, not that religion is something that introduces it. There can be no doubt (referring to the second element of the definition) of our dependence upon forces beyond our control. Primitive man was so impotent in the face of these forces that, especially in an unfavorable natural environment, fear became a dominant attitude, and, as the old saying goes, fear created the gods.

With increase of mechanisms of control, the element of fear has, relatively speaking, subsided. Some optimistic souls have even concluded that the forces about us are on the whole essentially benign. But every crisis, whether of the individual or of the community, reminds man of the precarious and partial nature of the control he exercises. When man, individually and collectively, has done his uttermost, conditions that at different times and places have given rise to the ideas of Fate and Fortune, of Chance and Providence remain. It is the part of manliness to insist upon the capacity of mankind to strive to direct natural and social forces to humane ends. But unqualified absolutistic statements about the omnipotence of such endeavors reflect egoism rather than intelligent courage.[13]

Knowledge cannot be divorced from our faith.

Understanding and knowledge also enter into a perspective that is religious in quality. Faith in the continued disclosing of truth through directed cooperative human endeavor is more religious in quality than is any faith in a completed revelation. It is of course now usual to hold that revelation is not completed in the sense of being ended. But religions hold that the essential framework is settled in its significant moral features at least, and that new elements that are offered must be judged by conformity to this framework. Some fixed doctrinal apparatus is necessary for *a* religion. But faith in the possibilities of continued and rigorous inquiry does not limit access to truth to any channel or scheme of things. It does not first say that

---

[13] *A Common Faith,* pp. 24-25.

truth is universal and then add there is but one road to it. It does not depend for assurance upon subjection to any dogma or item of doctrine. It trusts that the natural interactions between man and his environment will breed more intelligence and generate more knowledge, provided the scientific methods that define intelligence in operation are pushed further into the mysteries of the world, being themselves promoted and improved in the operation. There is such a thing as faith in intelligence becoming religious in quality — a fact that perhaps explains the efforts of some religionists to disparage the possibilities of intelligence as a force. They properly feel such faith to be a dangerous rival.[14]

To Dewey, God implies a unification of ideal values.

The idea that "God" represents a unification of ideal values that is essentially imaginative in origin when the imagination supervenes in conduct is attended with verbal difficulties owing to our frequent use of the word "imagination" to denote fantasy and doubtful reality. But the reality of ideal ends as ideals is vouched for by their undeniable power in action. An ideal is not an illusion because imagination is the organ through which it is apprehended. For *all* possibilities reach us through the imagination. In a definite sense the only meaning that can be assigned the term "imagination" is that things unrealized in fact come home to us and have power to stir us. The unification effected through imagination is not fanciful, for it is the reflex of the unification of practical and emotional attitudes. The unity signifies not a single Being, but the unity of loyalty and effort evoked by the fact that many ends are one in the power of their ideal, or imaginative, quality to stir and hold us.[15]

He criticized strongly the gospel of supernaturalism.

The objection to supernaturalism is that it stands in the way of an effective realization of the sweep and depth of the implications of natural human relations. It stands in the way of using the means that are in our power to make radical changes in these relations. It is certainly true that great material changes might be made with no corresponding improvement of a spiritual or ideal nature. But development in the latter direction cannot be introduced from without; it cannot be brought about by dressing up material and economic changes with decorations derived from the supernatural. It can come only from more intense realization of values that inhere in the actual connections of human beings with one another. The attempt to segregate the implicit public interest and social value of all institutions and social arrangements in a particular organization is a fatal diversion.

[14] *Ibid.*, p. 26.
[15] *Ibid.*, p. 43.

Were men and women actuated throughout the length and breadth of human relations with the faith and ardor that have at times marked historic religions the consequences would be incalculable. To achieve this faith and élan is no easy task. But religions have attempted something similar, directed moreover toward a less promising object — the supernatural. It does not become those who hold that faith may move mountains to deny in advance the possibility of its manifestation on the basis of verifiable realities. There already exists, though in a rudimentary form, the capacity to relate social conditions and events to their causes, and the ability will grow with exercise. There is the technical skill with which to initiate a campaign for social health and sanity analogous to that made in behalf of physical public health. Human beings have impulses toward affection, compassion and justice, equality and freedom. It remains to weld all these things together. It is of no use merely to assert that the intrenched foes of class interest and power in high places are hostile to the realization of such a union. As I have already said, if this enemy did not exist, there would be little sense in urging *any* policy of change. The point to be grasped is that, unless one gives up the whole struggle as hopeless, one has to choose between alternatives. One alternative is dependence upon the supernatural; the other, the use of natural agencies.[16]

Supernatural Christianity is basically aristocratic.

It is impossible to ignore the fact that historic Christianity has been committed to a separation of sheep and goats; the saved and the lost; the elect and the mass. Spiritual aristocracy as well as laissez faire with respect to natural and human intervention, is deeply embedded in its traditions. Lip service — often more than lip service — has been given to the idea of the common brotherhood of all men. But those outside the fold of the church and those who do not rely upon belief in the supernatural have been regarded as only potential brothers, still requiring adoption into the family. I cannot understand how any realization of the democratic ideal as a vital moral and spiritual ideal in human affairs is possible without surrender of the conception of the basic division to which supernatural Christianity is committed. Whether or no we are, save in some metaphorical sense, all brothers, we are at least all in the same boat traversing the same turbulent ocean. The potential religious significance of this fact is infinite.[17]

In the conclusion, Dewey sums up the elements of the common faith.

We who now live are parts of a humanity that extends into the remote past, a humanity that has interacted with nature. The things

---

[16] *Ibid.*, pp. 80-81.
[17] *Ibid.*, pp. 83-84.

in civilization we most prize are not of ourselves. They exist by grace of the doings and sufferings of the continuous human community in which we are a link. Ours is the responsibility of conserving, transmitting, rectifying and expanding the heritage of values we have received that those who come after us may receive it more solid and secure, and widely accessible and more generously shared than we have received it. Here are all the elements for a religious faith that shall not be confined to sect, class, or race. Such a faith has always been implicitly the common faith of mankind. It remains to make it explicit and militant.[18]

ARTISTIC IDEALS AND EDUCATION

The progressive spirit of Dewey is revealed in his esthetic theories. An excellent summary of them is contained in *Art as Experience* and chapter IX of *Experience and Nature*.

To Dewey, art has above all, a *social* significance. Thus Phidias represents the Greek ideal of life, and the Ionic style of architecture was best suited to the Greek taste. Roman art specialized in engineering and was especially concerned with public buildings. Here again the artist mirrored the mood of his society.

In the same manner Dewey gave a social interpretation of the medieval cathedral. The Gothic style of architecture gave a functional expression of medieval ideals. It was the product of a social experience which believed in supernaturalism. However, artistic goals are not static; they change just as much as political and economic ideals.

Dewey was not an enthusiastic supporter of medieval culture; we cannot go back to the age of Faith. Dewey had no use for Gothic architecture in modern America. It may have had its use in the Middle Ages; however, in a scientific civilization it is outmoded.

Art, according to Dewey, must be *dynamic*. Hence, he welcomed the new styles in painting and architecture. The artist who dwells in the past absorbs a one-sided perspective, for he becomes isolated and is unable to contribute to the progress of culture.

Art, Dewey asserted, has a utilitarian function. It cannot be divorced from life. Thus he felt that there should be a clear connection between industrial and fine arts. Esthetic principles are to be utilized not only in the museum, but in the home, school and factory.

In art education Dewey's influence was widespread. He showed that children often have a more adequate appreciation of art than adults. The teachers who tried to formalize the esthetic habits of

---

[18] *Ibid.*, p. 87.

children had been extremely shallow in their approach; for children, according to Dewey, are not to be trained in stereotyped esthetic patterns; rather their individuality is to be encouraged.

THE REFORMER

As a political philosopher Dewey expressed progressive ideals. In many ways he influenced the New Deal. He maintained that a laissez-faire concept of freedom is inadequate and that freedom and social security go together. The experimental method must be extended to politics if man's condition is to be improved. This again demands a real reconstruction of our institutional system. In politics, as in philosophy and in religion, he maintained an open mind and a flexible attitude.

Absolutism can best be prevented through voluntary organizations.

Associations of mathematicians, chemists, astronomers, business corporations, labor organizations, churches are trans-national because the interests they represent are worldwide. In such ways as these, internationalism is not an aspiration but a fact, not a sentimental ideal but a force. Yet these interests are cut across and thrown out of gear by the traditional doctrine of exclusive national sovereignty. It is the vogue of this doctrine or dogma, that presents the strongest barrier to the effective formation of an international mind which alone agrees with the moving forces of present day labor, commerce, science, art and religion.

Society, as was said, is many associations, not a single organization. Society means association; coming together in joint intercourse and action for the better realization of any form of experience which is augmented and confirmed by being shared. Hence there are as many associations as there are goods which are enhanced by being mutually communicated and participated in.[19]

CONTRIBUTIONS

Dewey's contributions to philosophy and education may be summarized briefly as follows:

(1) He gave a logical explanation of pragmatism and tried to divorce logic from metaphysics. To him logic was a *naturalistic* discipline.

---

[19] *Reconstruction in Philosophy,* p. 205.

(2) In his philosophy of instrumentalism he stressed the importance of change and opposed static ends and static ideals.

(3) In his methodology, he showed how the scientific method could be applied to all realms of inquiry. He stressed that the knowledge of the future must be functional, experimental, and subjected to the rigorous tests of the laboratory method.

(4) In his ethical system he was a meliorist. Rejecting both pessimism and optimism, he used the concept of growth as the standard of ethical evaluation.

(5) In religion he opposed all types of dogmatism and tried to develop a common faith which regards God as a unifying ideal and which uses scientific knowledge in religion.

(6) In education he emphasized the importance of the learner. A trenchant critic of traditional liberal education, he influenced the development of vocational education and the adoption of a student-centered curriculum.

(7) In esthetics he stressed that art is a progressive discipline and that it must be correlated with life. Thus he did not accept the Victorian ideal of art for art's sake.

(8) In his outlook on philosophy he was anti-metaphysical. He approached intellectual problems from the viewpoint of biology rather than of theology.

(9) In his social philosophy he was consistently liberal; he rejected all forms of authoritarianism.

(10) In his political views he was a pluralist. He did not favor concentration of governmental power, rather he favored voluntary cooperation of a variety of groups such as churches, labor unions, business corporations, and scientists who would work together for the common good.

In Dewey the voice of the pioneer, the stirring energies of the reformer, the patient method of the scientist, and the faith of the teacher are united in a search for a new education through which man can survive in a chaotic age.

CHAPTER TWENTY-SIX

The Culture of Normalcy

STATUS QUO

The period of the 1920's saw a frantic striving to get back to "the good old days." Americans regarded the World War as an abnormal adventure in international politics, as an unwarranted interference with their comfort and prosperity. They idealized the days before the war which, in the light of the 1920's, seemed to be extremely stable, sane and comfortable.

The middle class triumphed in this period. Middle class ideals, middle class conformity, middle class respectability, and middle class complacency prevailed. The ideal of this culture was to be safe and sound; it meant that divergent ideals in politics were to be avoided, that no new experiments in government were to be undertaken and that the world was to be ruled by business.[1]

This conservative atmosphere was strongly opposed to radicalism. The leaders in the 20's were determined to maintain the rule of busi-

---

[1] Cf. Charles Beard, ed., *Whither Mankind;* Schmalhausen, ed., *Behold America;* Malcolm Cowley, ed., *After the Genteel Tradition.*

ness. With pride, the political leaders pointed to the ever increasing prosperity. Was this not a sign that the American system was functioning well and that America could easily maintain the highest standards of living known in world history?

It was an age of conformity in politics. Wilson had always been distrusted by business leaders because he was a visionary, he did not speak the language of the service clubs, and his mind was academic. Harding was different. Everyone could understand his doctrine, "stabilize America first, prosper America first, think of America first, exalt America first." It is true that some members of his cabinet, like Forbes and Fall, thought of themselves first rather than of their country and that Harding inaugurated an era of political scandals. Still, most of the voters did not check too closely upon the state of morality of the federal government.

His successor, Coolidge, was pictured as a typical representative of the middle class; as a small town man who had worked his way up in life through industry, thrift, and ambition. He had an almost religious feeling about the importance of business, and that no innovation should be made in the government. Why should the administration tamper with the ownership of railroads or with the nationalization of public utilities when the old systems had worked so well? More strongly than any other President, perhaps, he opposed government regulation of business. In him, Adam Smith had won a complete victory.

It was a period of prosperity for the middle class. Everywhere evidences of the new wealth could be found. The new Country Club districts had all the latest conveniences and were equipped with the products of an ever-expanding technology. The American woman saw to it that her housework became lighter. Social status was symbolized by providing better education for the children; colleges now became not merely centers of intellectual training but refined matrimonial bureaus and gave social status through the fraternity and sorority system.

This cult of prosperity was motivated by the thought that each member of the middle class had to keep up with his neighbor. If the man next door bought a new car, this action had to be imitated. If his wife bought a new dress every month, it was certain that it would be noticed by other wives. America was striving frantically for material luxuries, while in Europe thousands were starving and the seeds were being sown for the rise of totalitarianism.

The 1920's strengthened the booster spirit in the United States. In countless service clubs, middle-aged men would gather to listen to enlightening speeches on the need of keeping taxes down. Like

Sinclair Lewis' Babbitt, they would be convinced that they lived in the best city and that theirs was the best civilization. The nationalistic spirit was expressed by the Republican policy of isolationism, and it found a stronghold in the Chambers of Commerce, which outdid each other in advertising the attractions of the various localities. It did not matter how small or how insignificant the community was, something always could be advertised.

The French visitors like André Maurois and André Siegfried noted that the manners of the United States were defective. This did not disturb the complacent American middle class, for they did not believe in being introverts. To reveal one's emotions, to be frank, was regarded as a mark of excellence. They could not understand the English proclivity for understatement and self-discipline. The extrovert triumphed as never before.

Nationalism made rapid headway in the United States. Except for a brief period of pacifism in the 30's, nationalism has continued to gain adherents. One reason is clear: the United States has always won the wars in which it has engaged. During the reign of Hitler, countless writers pointed out the difference between "barbarian" Germany and the democratic culture of America.

In the 1920's, nationalism developed an unquestioning faith in the superiority of American ways. Europe, to the citizens of Middletown, represented a continent of radicals. Its culture was completely outmoded, and its system of technology was far behind that of the United States.

The United States was regarded as an island of perfection. Isolationists were determined that they would never again interfere in quarrels abroad, and many citizens were outraged that American soldiers had been sacrificed for "European intrigues." Nationalism was represented by American intervention in South and Central America, by the constant rise of the tariff barriers, and by the tightening of immigration quotas.

MASS CULTURE

Advertising dominated American civilization. Politicians, militarists, opera singers, and movie stars all had their public relations experts. The technique of advertising was very simple. It used exaggeration, repetition, and sex. It pictured a new utopia in which middle-aged women could be as glamorous as Hollywood stars; balding businessmen could have the devastating charms of a Rudolph Valentino.

Advertising produced a new type of culture. The same products were sold from Maine to California; the same publicity slogans could be heard from New Orleans to New York. How different was this condition from the individualistic ideals of Thoreau and Emerson!

The automobile, in the 20's and 30's, became a necessity for the average American family, which kept up with its neighbor by purchasing a new model every year. It was not merely an instrument of transportation, but it served as a substitute for the bedroom. It almost became an indispensable sacrament to the American, who frequently was born in the automobile and died in it. The joy ride became an acceptable American institution; it signified the irresponsibility and unconcern of that generation.

Radio programs brought culture to the home of the middle class. The most popular programs were jazz and light music, the innumerable comedians, and the daytime serials, which broadened the perspective of the housewife. The radio came to all classes of society. Children with eager eyes listened to the gangster stories, housewives were thrilled by the romantic dramas, and businessmen relaxed through the jokes of the comedians.

The motion picture developed into a powerful institution. The formula used was quite simple. Producers realized that the man in the street did not want to be troubled by economic and social problems; he wanted to find an escape through a powerful illusion. No wonder that most movies featured upper-class homes, luxurious cars, and vast estates. Miracles often took place on the screen. A poor but beautiful stenographer might become the wife of a millionaire; the struggling salesman might become a captain of industry. Above all, the motion pictures featured the attraction of sex. Clara Bow became famous as a girl who represented the ideals of flaming youth. Rudolph Valentino almost became a second Byron in his appeal to the women of the United States.

ESCAPISM

Americans found escape in sports. The Red Sox became as popular as the President, perhaps even more so. The World Series attracted far more attention than the sessions of Congress. When Dempsey and Tunney had their famous match in 1927, it was a national event, and the gate amounted to over two and a half million dollars. Amusements were mechanized. Before this era, they had been patronized mostly by men; now women invaded them in large numbers. The scene was reminiscent of the last centuries of the Roman empire when the masses craved incessant amusement.

The newspapers adjusted themselves to the taste of the common man. The *New York Daily News* attracted millions of readers by its stress upon scandal, crime, and sex. It was soon imitated by Hearst's *New York Mirror*, and it was followed by magazines like *True Confessions* with the same type of approach. It must not be forgotten that liberal journalism still had its followers. William Allen White was struggling for freedom of the press with his *Emporia Gazette*. The *Indianapolis Times* was conducting a vigorous campaign against the Ku Klux Klan, and the *Christian Science Monitor* gave an excellent account of foreign developments, trying to imbue American citizens with a sense of their international responsibility. These papers were, however, in the minority. Most papers were so concerned with the Leopold-Loeb murder case, the Scopes trial, the activities of the Capone gang, and the St. Valentine's Day massacre that they had little time for the League of Nations or for the grave economic conditions in Europe.

Prohibition provided revealing sidelights in the American scene. This experiment was undertaken in the belief that it was possible to legislate the morality of the people. The advocates of prohibition could show by statistics that alcohol destroyed the unity of the family, produced divorces, undermined womanhood, lessened the efficiency of the workers, and produced insanity. Unfortunately the results of prohibition were quite different from what the proponents of the 18th Amendment had expected. To some extent, it increased crime in the United States, for millions of Americans would not be deprived of their liquor. It produced a new type of entertainment: the speak-easy, patronized by various social classes.

RADICALISM

Civil liberties had been seriously challenged during World War I. The national psychosis concentrated upon the German language. Anyone who admired Wagner, studied German literature, or used the German language, was regarded as unpatriotic. To criticize the conduct of the government was extremely dangerous. Eugene Debs was jailed because he was regarded as a fifth columnist who was trying to obstruct the war effort. Magazines like the *Milwaukee Leader* were suspended because they had socialistic tendencies. The Espionage and the Sedition Acts made punishable all subversive statements against the government. According to the Sedition Act, anyone who questioned the Constitution, the Army, or the American form of government could be prosecuted. Academic freedom was frequently violated, especially at Columbia University, where several professors were discharged because they would not support the war effort sufficiently.

The fear of radicalism in the 1920's can be seen in the reaction to the Communist danger. Russian influence was expanding in Europe; Communism had many followers in Austria; in Hungary a Soviet dictatorship was set up under Bela Kun; in Bavaria Kurt Eisner had established a radical government, and in Northern Germany the Spartakists were active. Many business leaders in the United States were alarmed. Editorial writers thought that if the Russian influence were not halted, the whole world would be conquered by it. So frightened were the conservatives in the United States and in England, that they were joyous when Mussolini established Fascism in Italy and when Ludendorff and Hitler preached a holy crusade against Bolshevism.

America undertook a program of European relief to stem the tide of radicalism. Hoover warned Congress that, if starvation were not halted, Europe would be an easy prey to Communism.

THE REBELS

Nevertheless, individualism reached a new climax in the 1920's. To some extent, this was a beneficial development, for an artist cannot create unless he is mainly concerned with his own development. Much great art is autobiographical; yet too much stress upon individualism leads to distintegration. The writers of the 1920's lacked the balance which had been achieved in Greek civilization, which had a more sane outlook regarding man and his environment.

The cult of individualism is almost a tradition in the United States. In this way the United States is quite different from Russia, which for many centuries had adhered to a collective way of life. The extreme leftists will say that this individualism is merely an illusion. They will point to the business control, to the stereotyped taste, to the standardized goods, to the universal advertising system, and they will be certain that individualism really does not exist in 20th-century America. But, if one looks deeper, one still finds an amazing mobility and individuality as Dos Passos shows in *The State of the Union*.

The rebels of the 1920's had no admiration for the saintly figures of American history. They were eager to debunk Lincoln and Washington. They treated the idols of the Victorian period even more contemptuously. Vernon Parrington subjected the American mind to a scholarly criticism which certainly could not lead to hero worship. V. F. Calverton, as a Marxist, was even less enthusiastic about the eminent figures of American literature, most of whom he treated with contempt.

The cynicism of this period was best represented by Ernest Hemingway in *The Sun Also Rises* and *A Farewell to Arms*. The latter novel was perhaps the most impressive reaction of American youth to the futility of war. Like Remarque's *All Quiet on the Western Front*, Hemingway's novel showed that the individual soldier was absolutely powerless, like an ant being squashed by a superior force.

Why was there such deep-seated antagonism to the war? To the writers of the 1920's, the World War had been a tragic delusion. Wilson had said that this was a struggle to make the world safe for democracy. They knew that there was less democracy in the 1920's than during the era of the New Freedom movement. Their parents had talked about honor and patriotism; all these phrases they debunked, for they knew no allegiance to the state. Their only effort was to live a full life and to express themselves completely. They resented the war because it was an outrage to their individuality, for they had to become a part of a vast mass, subject themselves to an inhuman machine, and follow decisions with which they could not agree. All this was against their individualistic gospel.

Many of these writers in the 1930's and during World War II changed their attitude. Thus Hemingway's *For Whom the Bell Tolls* is quite different from *A Farewell to Arms*. For Robert Jordan, his protagonist in the Spanish Civil War, was fighting for a holy cause in his struggle against the Spanish Fascists. When he died Jordan felt that he was not alone but part of the eternal human resistance to oppression.

Sex was especially important in the literature of the 1920's. If all of the other pleasures of life had been deflated, sex was still a welcome escape. The belief in sex marked a rebellion against conventional standards. American women issued a Declaration of Independence, which stated that they had just as much right as men to enjoy physical pleasures.

A new philosophy of life developed: extreme epicureanism. It said: live for the present; enjoy yourself to the fullest; do not worry about tomorrow. Be cynical and rebel against the code of respectability. Above all, do not accept any high-sounding ideals.

JAMES HARVEY ROBINSON

This period saw a constant expansion in the field of the social sciences. James Harvey Robinson, born in 1863, did much to bring about greater enlightenment in American culture. His *Mind in the Making* was directed not only against intellectual regression, but it pointed the way to a reconstruction of thought.

Robinson showed how the progress of civilization was hindered by blind prejudices, how modern man was still dominated by medieval ideals, and how the scientific method had not gained a full victory. In this book, he gave excellent examples which demonstrated that man's thinking is not guided by detachment but represents a response to emotional factors. Many of the facts which we accept are merely rationalizations. Many of the laws of social science are simply reflections of the dominant institutional forces. His book should have been required reading for all thinkers. If they had examined it carefully, they might have been more honest, less prejudiced, and less complacent.

Robinson's concept of history is humanistic. It is not the study of dates, kings, and political parties, nor merely a description of economic events. History represents the full drama of human development. It is the function of the historian to present a synthesis of civilization. Robinson's theory of educational reconstruction had a decided influence upon the curricula of American colleges in the years following World War II. Instead of specialized courses, frequently a core-curriculum was adopted. Educators realized that specialization was becoming so prevalent that no common cultural foundation existed. However, most of these courses were too superficial and were usually taught by immature instructors; hence, no real unity in intellectual matters was achieved.

The democratic ideal, as Jefferson showed, demands a common educational basis for citizenship. As long as millions in the United States do not even know the members of the President's Cabinet, and the significance of the legislation before Congress, democracy will be constantly endangered. As long as millions are utterly unacquainted with the meaning of the social relationships of science, no real control of the destructive weapons of the Atomic Age can be achieved. Thus the vision of James Harvey Robinson was only too correct. He saw that the scientific age made many ideas obsolete, that a re-examination has to be made of traditional ideals, and, above all, that the rationalizations of politics, economics, and religion will have to be eradicated if a new education for America is to be created.

CHAPTER TWENTY-SEVEN

Ideas of the New Deal

THE DEPRESSION

The Depression of 1930–39 marked a turning point in American history. The era of exaggerated optimism was finished. Gone were the days of easy spending and unbounded confidence in ever-rising levels of prosperity. As unemployment steadily increased, the people looked to the government for relief and new leadership.

The Depression came as a sobering experience to the American people. The average newspaper reader had heard about famines in Russia and India, had noticed headlines about nightmarish economic conditions in Germany, but these were remote and without personal meaning, for he was living in a nation of plenty. Now he was re-examining the position of the United States in the world. The American's social consciousness was becoming stronger, he asked more questions, and he became more skeptical regarding the old phrase, "Back to Normalcy."

Was the gospel of rugged individualism sufficient to meet the crisis? Could the traditional concept of non-interference in business affairs weather the storm, or was a new type of leadership and a new interpretation of democracy needed? President Herbert Hoover thought that business alone would be able to overcome the Depression. As unemployment increased, as the bread lines became longer, he maintained his optimism. The Depression, he thought, did not reveal any basic weakness in the economic system of America; rather, it was due to a lack of confidence. But his belief that normalcy was just around the corner proved unsound.

Never before had economic disaster affected so many Americans; never before had there been such a monumental collapse. The old philosophy of materialism, of vigorous faith in the future, could not be maintained. Business, which before had been regarded as a magic tool of prosperity, now was exposed to sharp criticism. During the depression public confidence in the captains of industry lessened considerably.

To the Democrats the depression furnished valuable campaign ammunition. They did not hesitate to blame the Republican administration for the business collapse. They pointed to Hoover as the man most responsible for bringing about the chaotic conditions.[1] Perhaps Franklin Roosevelt's most convincing argument for re-election, which he used over and over again, was that the Democrats had rescued the nation from disaster.

In the campaign preceding Roosevelt's first election, radical programs attracted many adherents. Socialist Norman Thomas, who had polled only 267,627 votes in 1928, received over 884,000 votes in 1932. William Z. Foster, the Communist candidate, received 102,991 votes, almost twice as many as in the previous presidential election. Thousands of Americans were impressed by the campaign oratory of Huey Long and Father Charles Coughlin. The latter advanced a platform of inflation reminiscent of Bryan's campaign in 1896. So desperate were the American people that some were willing to follow any leader who promised relief and rehabilitation.

PROGRAM OF THE NEW DEAL

President Roosevelt's New Deal tried to reform the capitalistic system from within.[2] The outstanding leaders of the New Deal had not lost their faith in the American system of government; they

[1] Hoover is ably defended by William S. Myers and Walter H. Newton, *The Hoover Administration: A Documentary Narrative,* and by Ray L. Wilbur and Arthur M. Hyde, *The Hoover Policies.* We must not forget Hoover's outstanding contribution to American politics in his chairmanship of the Hoover Commission, which did much for governmental reorganization.

[2] Cf. Charles and Mary Beard, *America in Midpassage;* Arthur M. Schlesinger, *The New Deal in Action.* For a vigorous criticism of the New Deal see Herbert Hoover, *Addresses Upon the American Road,* 1933-1938. Mr. Hoover exposes the New Deal to a penetrating analysis.

thought that through a program of reform the weaknesses of the economic system could be remedied and a new level of prosperity could be reached. The New Deal involved a new interpretation of the function of government; instead of having the central authority maintain a hands-off policy when it came to business, the New Dealers thought that it was the task of the government to become the chief agency for recovery.

Was the recovery of the New Deal permanent? No definite answer can be made. In 1937 economic conditions again became worse after a short period of improvement, and then the stimulus of war made for a new period of prosperity. The measures of the New Deal were shortlived; most of them were given up during World War II when concentration upon the armed forces became the primary consideration of America's policy.

During the Democratic administration millions of men were on relief. Traditionally, the American gospel was that anyone who really wanted to work would have no trouble in finding a job. Unemployment thus was regarded as a sign of laziness or as a punishment for anti-social habits. According to conservative writers, it was the task of charity, not of organized government, to take care of the poor and the underprivileged. The New Deal drew attention to the fact that one third of the nation really belonged to the lower strata of society.

It was the belief of the New Dealers that a measure of economic security should be guaranteed to all classes. The Social Security Act of 1935 represented a Magna Charta for the needy, the aged, the blind, dependent mothers, and crippled children. Still, it was incomplete, for many groups were excluded, and the traditional attitude of economic individualism had not yet been overcome.

Especially important was the Wagner Labor Relations Act, which climaxed the traditional struggle of the liberals to better the relationship between labor and employers. The Act was successful in protecting the rights of labor unions and restraining employers from interfering with collective bargaining, but it did not bring about industrial statesmanship nor did it solve the strike problem.

The New Deal fought vigorously against monopolies. Writers like Thurman Arnold had no doubt about the fact that international cartels were a basic cause for war. The Justice Department publicized the close interconnection between international monopolies which were trying to restrain trade and work against the distribution of goods.

The struggle of the New Deal against the Supreme Court likewise was unsuccessful. Roosevelt charged that the court was consistently nullifying the will of the majority, that it was engaged in a narrow type of judicial literalism, and that its members were too old to understand the new social developments. Proponents of his reorganization plan showed that the court had frequently reversed itself and that many decisions were made by a majority of only one member. But Roosevelt's attack against the court failed; the opposition to his reorganization scheme was well organized.

The New Deal used legislation as its primary tool. However, during Roosevelt's second term a powerful group of insurgent Democrats had organized against his program. Among them were Senator Walter George of Georgia, Senator Tydings of Maryland, and Senator "Cotton" Ed Smith of South Carolina. The latter was described by *Life* magazine as a conscientious objector against the twentieth century. Although Roosevelt made an eloquent appeal to the voters of the South to elect men who were sympathetic to the New Deal, he failed.

The 1936 primaries marked the beginning of the downfall of the New Deal. Not even Roosevelt was strong enough to counteract local politics. The opposition charged that he was violating basic liberties by interfering in sectional contests. Some called him a new Napoleon; others said that democracy was endangered because the President wanted only yes-men in Congress.

In his direct appeal to the voters, Roosevelt was extremely successful. His "fireside chats" were warm and intimate. He had the ability to simplify complex problems, to heighten their human interest, and to give the voters the feeling that he was speaking to them directly. As for his opponents, he frequently used a mixture of contempt and irony, and he used effective terms like "copperhead" and "economic royalist." He did not weary his audience by an overemphasis on statistics; there was always a light touch in his speeches.

More than ever before, the liberal program attracted the intellectual leaders of the nation. Conservatives spoke contemptuously of a brain trust, of an administration of college professors. Thousands of teachers and lawyers and social workers had gone to Washington to aid the country in meeting the economic crisis. Tugwell, Corcoran, Cohen, and Moley were especially influential; however, as the young men became mature and eminently successful, their liberalism sometimes waned and they often deserted the utopian ideals of their youth. Roosevelt believed in a better organization of administrative functions, but he was unsuccessful in creating an efficient civil service system and in reorganizing the various governmental bureaus.

FRANKLIN D. ROOSEVELT

Roosevelt powerfully represented the ideals of twentieth century liberalism. He came from one of the most distinguished American families; his education included lengthy studies abroad as well as intensive training at Harvard University and Columbia University law school. At the same time he received valuable practical experience when he fought the Tammany political machine and when he worked for Wilson's nomination. His war experience during World War I included service as Assistant Secretary of the Navy. To the man in the street his victory over infantile paralysis was a sign of his indomitable will.

Seldom has an American leader been as popular as Roosevelt. His personal charm was acknowledged even by his political enemies; his campaign technique was unexcelled; his way of handling the press showed political mastery.

Roosevelt believed that in foreign relations it was the task of the United States to mediate between the conflicting interests of England and Russia. He enjoyed the personal contacts which the Big Three meetings entailed. His grasp of foreign affairs was superior to that of most statesmen, for he had the opportunity to know intimately the outstanding leaders of other nations.

Even in the darkest days of 1941 and 1942 he did not show any signs of panic — calmness characterized his actions. Through deliberate planning and careful organization, he was able to master the most difficult problems both in foreign and domestic affairs.

It must be realized that throughout his career he had to harmonize conflicting interests in domestic politics, that he had to satisfy the professional machine politicians of the Democratic party as well as the enthusiastic liberals. In foreign policy he had to move carefully between a policy of non-interference as championed by the isolationists and the insistent demands for American participation in World War II.

To be objective, we must not overlook his weaknesses. As a strong man Roosevelt did not favor opposition to his policies; some members of his cabinet did not represent the highest type of statesmanship. It is true that it included efficient administrators like Harold Ickes, yet many lacked practical experience.

Roosevelt used too much the method of personal negotiation in foreign affairs. Wendell Willkie rightly charged that the people were uninformed about the activities of the State Department and that the policy of secrecy was exhausting the reservoir of good will. Thus, when Roosevelt died, the structure of peace was incomplete, for it rested mainly upon the personal agreement of the Big Three.

Frequently Roosevelt made concessions to political expediency. His most fateful step occurred at the Chicago convention. On the one hand, he endorsed Henry A. Wallace by writing a letter to the Democratic convention chairman, yet in private conversation he said that he was ready to accept Justice Douglas or Mr. Truman. All the time Wallace was certain that he had Roosevelt's complete endorsement. It is possible that Roosevelt foresaw the conservative trend in the nation and regarded Wallace as a liability, especially in the South.

WILLKIE

Wendell Willkie most of the time was opposed to the policies of Franklin D. Roosevelt but, fundamentally, perhaps his political philosophy was not very different. By temperament Willkie was likewise a champion of the underdog, and he never overcame the liberalism of his early college days. Like Roosevelt, Willkie had a powerful appeal to the voters who saw in him the fulfillment of the American success ideals.

Compared with Roosevelt, Willkie lacked political sophistication. His approach to economic and social problems was direct; he was less capable in manipulating political groups, and his speeches lacked the irony and sarcasm which Roosevelt often used. The Midwestern touch was very strong in Willkie, who always retained to some extent the homely philosophy of Indiana. Throughout his career Willkie spoke as a member of the middle class. Roosevelt, on the other hand, typified the social consciousness of the American aristocracy.

In every way Willkie's liberalism was unorthodox. He had supported La Follette; he had fought against the Ku Klux Klan, and had been a registered Democrat and a Roosevelt supporter in 1932. Then, as an executive of a large utilities company, he had become a violent foe of the TVA and had fought its measures most vigorously.

In his economic philosophy he favored full production; with considerable evidence he could point to the New Deal program, especially to the Agricultural Adjustment Act, as a policy of scarcity. Willkie thought that the business man should not be restrained in his endeavor to get ahead and that the farmer should not be made permanently dependent upon the government.

By free enterprise, Willkie did not imply business irresponsibility. Again and again he emphasized that American business leaders had a responsibility for the welfare of the people. Willkie, however, was more afraid of big government than of big business, and in his campaign speeches he stressed that the third term would be inimical to American liberty.

After he lost the election, his outlook broadened. In many ways Willkie's defeat was a victory. During the campaign he often lost sight of the broad international issues, so concerned was he with keeping America out of the war. He attacked the President for his provocative policy against Italy and Germany. After Pearl Harbor, Willkie adhered to a bi-partisan foreign policy and devoted all his efforts to building a sound and permanent peace.

His *One World*, written after a trip to the fighting fronts, which included personal conferences with Joseph Stalin, outlines the international vision of liberalism. Vigorously Mr. Willkie insisted upon a democratic foreign policy. It was his belief that the peace aims should be formulated before the war was over, for he realized how the idealistic hopes of humanity had been betrayed after World War I.

Unfortunately, the advice of Willkie was not heeded. Too much attention was paid to winning the armed struggle, while the peace problems were neglected. Moreover, the intellectuals of the democratic nations neglected specific issues while concentrating upon the promises of the Atlantic Charter.

Willkie realized that peace must be made on a world-wide basis. During his trip he not only talked to the official leaders of the various governments, to the diplomats and military commanders, but he listened to the ideas of ordinary citizens, to cab drivers, farmers, and the common soldiers. He understood that the people of the world wanted a new approach to world problems, and he believed that their voices should be heard.

Willkie was conscious of the future course of America's policy. In *One World* he showed how America must choose narrow nationalism, imperialism or genuine participation in the creation of a new world order.

Willkie's defeat in the Wisconsin primary in 1944 almost marked the end of the One-World idea. It showed that isolationism had not yet been conquered within the Republican party and that the conservative gospel of the stalwarts still triumphed. It showed that the Middle Western voters were so embittered about Roosevelt's policies that they wanted a more definite Republican stand than Willkie was prepared to take.

LITERARY AND EDUCATIONAL ECHOES

The ideals of the New Deal found ready adherence in literary circles. The Roosevelt administration made many attempts to aid the tenant farmer, especially through the Farm Security Administration, and every effort was made for soil conservation, but Steinbeck in 1939 publicized the fate of the tenant farmer in *The Grapes of Wrath.* Almost as influential as *Uncle Tom's Cabin,* it showed clearly the bitter fate of millions who are caught between the ruthlessness of a competitive system and the capriciousness of nature.

The same social consciousness appears in Richard Wright's *Native Son.* Bigger Thomas is the symbol of the warped and pathological mentality which a slum environment creates. Bigger was a Negro and that fact stamped his life. Only too clearly Wright shows that Bigger never really had a chance. Many New Dealers were, like Eleanor Roosevelt, fervent advocates of better race relations. Their reform efforts, however, were vigorously resented by the South.

The concepts of the New Deal were expressed in education by George Counts. He wrote a pamphlet in the midst of the Depression entitled *Dare the Schools Build a Social Order?* His answer was in the affirmative and in this way made a great impact on Brameld who stressed the social functions of American education.

Counts pointed to the failure of the earlier system of education. It had only appealed to an aristocratic audience and had inspired narrow loyalties. It had used the school to perpetuate a system of economic scarcity. It had appealed to the manufacturers and neglected the interests of labor.

To reconstruct the school system, Counts urged more popular representation on the school boards with a greater voice being given to labor. He favored vocational education and more extensive adult education. He maintained that schools should fight both social inequality and segregation. If the schools considered only intellectual issues they would fail. Their task was to be an agency of social and economic reform.

CHAPTER TWENTY-EIGHT

Santayana

CAREER AND WORKS

George Santayana (1863–1952), one of the most distinguished of American educators, sought exile and solace in Europe. Thus he represents a distinct tendency of twentieth-century American intellectuals to leave this country and to find a homeland somewhere else. Among notable expatriates we find Ezra Pound, Gertrude Stein, and T. S. Eliot — all of them found American culture to be incompatible with a thoroughly creative life.

Some of our expatriates became violent enemies of American democracy. This tendency we find especially in Ezra Pound, who was hired by Mussolini to give propaganda broadcasts on the disintegration of democracy and the shallowness and superficiality of American life.

Santayana never hated the United States; he only felt alien and out of place. He always retained his American friends, and he acknowledged his debt to them. He liked especially the Americans abroad who had been able to obtain a wide vision of culture.

Generally speaking, however, Santayana did not have a homeland. His was a universal profession. Wherever creativity was cherished, wherever the life of reason was valued, wherever real tradition reigned, he was at home. His life illustrates the maxim that for the philosopher the universe is his homeland.

He was born in Madrid and came to the United States when he was nine years old. Being the descendant of a well-to-do family, he was never plagued by financial worries.

He studied at Harvard, which as yet was not emancipated from the theological tradition. His description of his teachers is not flattering. Royce he regarded as a Protestant preacher dabbling in metaphysics; Royce's forced optimism, his explanation that this is the best of all possible worlds, displeased him. In Palmer he found an even more pronounced Sunday-school tendency, while in James he detected an expression of the American temper: impatient with tradition and intent upon novelty. Still, he appreciated James' sense of immediacy and his stress upon actual experience.

However, in James also, he found a lack of lyrical insight, and a moral compulsion which he could not accept. James' philosophy, like that of Royce, came from the subjective well and indicated the Protestant influence. Actually, James ought to have been a materialist, at least Santayana tells us that, but James was too religious to accept the consequences of his scientific postulates.

Santayana continued his studies abroad. In Berlin he attended the lectures of Friedrich Paulsen, who was lecturing on Greek ethics. Later, he studied the systems of Plato and Aristotle at Cambridge. Unfortunately, the philosophy department at Harvard had little knowledge of classical philosophy.

He began to teach philosophy at Harvard; his salary at first was $500 a semester. The invariable smallness of his classes caused distrust on the part of the administration at Harvard, which, like most American college authorities, measured wisdom by the number of students who were willing to listen to the teacher. The way Santayana lectured was memorable. He always searched for the right word; his sentences were formed like a classical symphony, and he regarded his instruction in a most leisurely manner. He was not interested in faculty politics; in fact, as he tells us in *The Middle Span*, he was bored by the long faculty meetings and by the petty spirit which prevailed among the Harvard faculty members.

He taught at Harvard until 1912, then he went to England and afterwards to Italy. In his later years he lived among a group of nuns in Rome in a perfectly platonic manner. He did not interrupt his philosophical labors during World War II and looked with detachment and also with a touch of melancholy upon the ideological struggle which he witnessed.

He was a most prolific writer. A few examples are: his autobiography *Persons and Places; The Middle Span;* and his novel, *The Last Puritan.* Then his description of the life of reason in *Introduction and Reason in Common Sense; Reason in Society; Reason in Religion; Reason in Art* and *Reason in Science.* His *Realms of Being* are significant, including *The Realm of Spirit, the Realm of Truth, The Realm of Essence,* and *The Realm of Matter.* In esthetics he distinguished himself with a notable work entitled *The Sense of Beauty.*

As a critic he wrote *Some Turns of Thought in Modern Philosophy, The Genteel Tradition at Bay, Platonism and the Spiritual Life, Dialogues in Limbo, Egotism in German Philosophy, Character and Opinion in the United States, Interpretations of Poetry and Religion, Winds of Doctrine, Obiter Scripta: Lectures, Essays and Reviews* and *Skepticism and Animal Faith.*

As a poet he contributed the *Hermit of Carmel and Other Poems* as well as several poetic collections. Finally, his most religious work, at least according to orthodox standards, is *The Idea of Christ in the Gospels.* For the student of education, all the works of Santayana are significant.

PHILOSOPHY OF LIFE

Santayana has no desire to coerce others to accept his system; they may choose their own if they find his to be inadequate.

Unlike the Marxists, he did not intend to appeal to the masses. His system is basically for the intellectual artistocracy, for those who really appreciate the life of reason. He was much more concerned in his philosophy with cultural problems than with an improvement of the living standard of the masses.

We do not perceive the material world directly, but through *essences.* Thus he was a critical realist. The words we use to describe the external world possess only an ideal reality.

Santayana called himself a materialist. To him, Berkeley's subjective idealism was an absurdity negated by our everyday experiences. All meaningful discourse involves a single system of events. However, material life serves as a preparation for the life of the spirit which is truly universal and which is based on natural facts.

The philosophy of Santayana is guided by the ideal of harmony. He tried to synthesize the various aspects of life: reason and faith, art and morality, science and poetry. In most of modern philosophy he found extremism — a spirit which displeased him; on the other hand, in Greece he found balance, sanity and harmony.

THE AMERICAN SCENE

What he found lacking in American culture was, above all, the sense of poetry. Probably we have produced more notable poets since he left the United States, but to him poetry is a way of life. The poetic way of life means an appreciation of symbolism and beauty, not for the sake of utility or ornamentation, but simply because it is the best expression of the life of reason.

As he remarked in *Character and Opinion in the United States,* this nation had not yet been emancipated from theology. Thus philosophy has to be comforting and teach a moral lesson. This strain can be observed in such divergent thinkers as Royce and James, who both were tender-minded when it came to religious verities.

Furthermore, he objected to the activistic spirit in America. There is not enough contemplation, not enough detachment, and not enough perspective. Santayana, however, believed in leisure and in a tranquil observation of life. By temperament he was aloof; he did not make friends easily. His students testify to the fact that he was reserved in his contacts with them; he never was one of the crowd.

His Catholic background made him suspect the Protestant tradition. New England religion he found to be drab and unimaginative. He was rather bored by the Unitarian discourses to which he was exposed. They illustrated the mixture in Protestantism of "waywardness and earnestness."

Physically, he looked quite different from other college professors. He dressed like a European nobleman; he was conscious of the tradition which was behind him. Inevitably he looked on his colleagues at Harvard as being rather plebeian and members of an inferior culture.

As he indicated in *The Last Puritan,* the puritanical heritage has done immense havoc to the American mind. It has given to the American people an awe-inspiring conscience, an all-important sense of ought. It has made for an avoidance of natural ideals and material concepts. It has alienated the American mind from the realm of matter; in short, it has made existence a metaphysical Sunday-school.

Nor was Santayana impressed by the growth of technology and material wealth in the United States. To his way of thinking, it constitutes only a plebeian dictatorship. The nervousness, haste, and activism of American life distressed him. No wonder that he found a welcome relief in his excursions into the realm of antique culture, where he found a true aristocracy of the spirit.

SOCIAL IDEALS

Santayana combined the naturalistic and the Platonic concept of love. While this emotion is rooted in physiological desire, it is not defined by this basis and thus reaches out to an ideal realm. Love connects actuality with ideals; it is a symbol of immortality.

Santayana measured political institutions according to their contribution to an ideal society. Democracy is found wanting. First of all, it encourages a stereotyped behavior; it standardizes human beings like automobiles. It leads frequently to the rule of the most mediocre and impotent. It prevents the emergence of genuine culture because it disregards tradition.

Still, in spite of these weaknesses, Santayana recognized some values in democracy; the individual is not sacrificed to the state, and he has freedom to express his own opinions and his own ideals.

He favored an aristocracy based on merit and achievement, not on heredity. He was not blind to the weaknesses of aristocracy, that it frequently led to lethargy and complacency and elevated incompetent persons to positions of responsibility.

He disliked most of all the revolutionary fervor of the Marxists. He believed that they only substituted one type of tyranny for another. The evils of the world, Santayana held, could not be abolished by an overthrow of governments. They could be overcome only through genuine education and through philosophic insight.

Philosophy's continuing function is to contemplate the eternal, timeless values, and to criticize the prejudices of the dominant systems of thought. Thus philosophy sharpens the tools of reason but remains aloof from the arena of social struggle.

Philosophers can best contribute to the enlightenment of our political leaders by preaching a gospel of cosmopolitanism. The philosopher should eschew chauvinism; he should not be bound by narrow loyalties; he must become a detached and timeless spectator of existence.

RELIGIOUS VIEWS

Santayana is at his best when he describes the "Christian Epic," in which life is conceived in dualistic terms. On the one hand, he finds the forces of good, which will experience the fruits of heaven; on the other hand, he sees the forces of evil, which will be damned to eternal destruction. This is the philosophy of St. Augustine, a Catholic like Santayana but more austere and somber.

The Catholicism of Santayana is tempered by his sense of poetry. In Catholic religion he found poetry, an esthetic ritual, and the Virgin Mary, who to him as to Henry Adams, appeared as the very symbol of a pious life. He did not look upon religion with a literalistic perspective; religion transcends theology.

Immortality can be viewed in three ways. First, in an Epicurean life of simplicity and detachment. Thus we appreciate the present, and we find serenity in intellectual speculation. Like Epicurus, we are not frightened then by the prospect of death, for we have risen beyond it.

Secondly, immortality may be obtained through contemplation of eternal objects. We know that science, art, and literature do not depend on us, but that they have a truly timeless existence. In contemplating intellectual objects, we feel that time has lost its meaning; we are lifted out of the present into a timeless stream of experience.

Here Santayana followed Plato and Spinoza. It is not physical immortality which he was seeking, but the immortality of truth. Let us remember that the essences which we apprehend are eternal and that they do not depend on corporeal manifestations.

Thirdly, immortality may be achieved through excellence of living. Our existence thus becomes our monument.

EDUCATIONAL VIEWS

Santayana attacked American education because it emphasizes society too much. The individual does not have enough privacy. He cannot think for himself; solitude is discouraged. In higher education the committee system prevails, leading to mediocre decisions and endless controversies which do not contribute to the life of reason. Santayana felt that the American teacher is too dependent on the reactions of his students. He wants to be liked and be part of their interests and outlook. Santayana cultivated instead an attitude of isolation and regarded himself as a stranger in modern society. He maintained that teaching becomes shallow when it is deliberately popular. He was satisfied when he could be understood by a few students and if he could have a permanent impact on their lives.

Santayana objected to the rule of methodology in education which implied a superficial procedure. The rules for good teaching, he claimed, could not be systematized. For some instructors the lecture method might be best; for others it might be the discussion or the seminar method. Even occasional silence had a place in education which tended to be too verbal. What really mattered was the insight of the instructor. What he advocated, what he developed within his own personality mattered—not the form of his communication.

Santayana felt that American education was still moralistic. There were still too many taboos about the behavior of teachers and students. There were still too many rules and restrictions which indicated a narrow view on the part of educational authorities. To Santayana, art was more important than morality. Art symbolized an ideal realm; morality constantly confused between essence and existence and attempted to force life into preconceived patterns.

Santayana missed an emphasis on poetry in American education. Like Confucius, he felt that no man could be truly educated who did not value the attractions of poetry and who had no real appreciation of literature. Santayana found that most of his colleagues at Harvard were concerned about the formal aspects of literature and they classified works without understanding the basic spirit of literature. They lacked style in writing and in their personal behavior.

Santayana objected to the quantitative evaluations in education. Once when he had only a few students in philosophy, he was called into the president's office. The president was concerned that Santayana was not reaching enough students and was not living up to his obligations. Santayana felt that he had no duty to communicate his ideas to a large number of students, that it was better to be an unforgettable event in the life of a few than a minor event in the existence of many.

He valued leisure as the condition of a life of reason. Education, he stated, should be spontaneous. Instead he found it to be full of compulsions. Thus teachers instructed too many classes, attended too many meetings, undertook too many community responsibilities, wrote too many articles and books which were bound to be insignificant. Thus teachers became technicians who regarded the intellectual life as a mechanical process.

Santayana did not believe in social responsibility. The scholar had to live for himself, develop his own insights and cultivate a sense of inwardness. If he neglected to do these things he would be a pilgrim in superficiality. Society, to Santayana, was not a substitute for existential development.

He did not believe that modern man had progressed. Was he not a slave to the machine? Was he not a prisoner of society? Was he not in a perpetual hurry to accomplish something which was bound ·to be unimportant? Was he not guided by false values? Was he not a victim of extremist philosophies? To make the present the point of departure in education was regarded as a major fallacy by Santayana who looked to the past for inspiration.

The type of education which he admired could not be found in the institutions of his time which were symbols of quantification and superficiality. Nor could real education, Santayana stated, be found in the medieval universities which prohibited heresy. To be sure, medieval universities were more profound than modern institutions of higher learning and they achieved a sense of unity and coherence which could not be found at Harvard or Yale. What Santayana admired was the intellectual life as represented by Athens in the time of Aristotle. Here was a teacher who understood the demands of the body and of the spirit, who saw physical existence and metaphysical ideals, who was urbane in his sense of moderation, and who was concerned about principles rather than specific facts.

Aristotle realized that education should stress the liberal arts.

Santayana was certain that a real liberal education could be achieved only by a minority. The masses should best be instructed in the three R's, and they should be taught the necessity of following the insights of a true intellectual aristocracy.

The idea that all are equal in education was rejected by Santayana. He felt that there is a natural aristocracy of talent and that history is guided by the few. The minority are bound to be misunderstood by the majority which wants magic formulas in ethics and education. The true teacher requires no absolute certainty; he needs no popular response. He achieves a degree of immortality by his preoccupation with the ideas he is developing.

Such greatness, Santayana declared, has no frontiers. It could be found a thousand years ago as well as in our own time. The past was our constant companion; its ideas and ideals, its attitudes and motivations continued to influence the present. To ignore the past was to cultivate an attitude of deliberate blindness.

The progress of culture and education, according to Santayana, was delayed by fanaticism. The fanatic tried to coerce facts. Whenever he triumphed, freedom was endangered and a mass culture emerged. The fanatic in religion, politics and education was conspiring against the independent spirit who treasured his own integrity.

Utilitarianism was just as dangerous, according to Santayana. It reduced ideals to a narrow matrix and ultimately appealed to majority decisions. In education this meant that the needs of the student were to be stressed. Santayana instead stressed the needs of culture which should not have utilitarian applications and which would often dwell on the "unessential" aspects of life.

Like Robert Hutchins, Santayana attacked the cult of specialization. The ideal teacher would be a philosopher who would relate the arts and the technical sciences and who would have a profound view of the past. He would see all of history as a quest for a rational life in which extremes could be avoided. He would be concerned about principles which can give guidance to modern man, who is so often defeated by fragmentary concerns and fragmentary endeavors.

CHAPTER TWENTY-NINE

William Heard Kilpatrick

THE PROGRESSIVE IDEAL

Progressive education is the product of both European and American ideas. Rousseau, Pestalozzi and Froebel contributed to its development. In America, James, Peirce, Parker, and Hall stimulated its growth. The progressive movement in politics had educational implications, for it held that free schools are the bastions of democratic living.

The Progressive Education Association was established in 1919. At first, under the impact of Kilpatrick, it emphasized individualistic ideals. After the Depression in 1930, through the ideas of John L. Childs, George Counts, V. T. Thayer and Boyd H. Bode, it turned more to the consideration of social issues. After World War II, the movement lost impetus. This was due to a shift of interest. Reconstructionism, as championed by Brameld, gained new adherents. It made social reform the primary concern of educators. The conservative reaction in politics had educational consequences and thinkers like Russell Kirk criticized the assumptions of progressivism and urged a return to tradition. Neo-scholastics pleaded for the type of unity represented by the medieval church. Hutchins and Adler advocated the Great Books as the center of the curriculum. Essentialists attacked the neglect of discipline in progressive education. Conant in his report on the American high school gave a subject-centered emphasis and urged the study of solid material rather than concentration on experimental projects.

Still, the progressive movement has attracted able proponents in our time. Among them mention should be made of Ernest Bayles, Lawrence G. Thomas, H. Gordon Hullfish, George Axtelle, Frederick C. Neff and Bruce Raup. Their concern is with the experimental foundations of knowledge and they regard the traditional view of education as obsolete.

Progressive educators believe that subjects should not be taught in isolation. They feel that planning should be cooperative on the part of teachers, administrators and children. Learning involves no preconceived goals, but implies a constant reconstruction of the ideas and ideals of students and teachers. Mere reflection is inadequate, for it leads to unending abstractions. There is an emphasis upon activity. Learning becomes a theory of inquiry; knowledge becomes active participation. Specific ideas rather than general concepts are stressed. This means a specific project, like the city in modern life, may become the subject of extended investigations in the school.

Freedom and cooperation govern the progressive school, which objects to traditional controls. Freedom implies that no dogmas are allowed and that indoctrination is shunned. Progressive educators thus have fought against loyalty oaths and against other types of thought control. Progressive education is interested in evidence, not in static beliefs. Cooperation implies that the students learn best when they share ideas and experiences. The progressive educator feels that competition leads to anxiety which vitiates a genuine educational experience.

The teacher in such a system has a unique role. His task is not that of a disciplinarian. He works with children so that mutual goals are achieved and creative capacities are actualized. The progressive administrator does not impose his ideas upon the school, rather he encourages his associates, who are regarded as equals in the educative process, to think for themselves.

Education in this way becomes an experience in relatedness. The school becomes a miniature democracy, where the interests of all are safeguarded. The effectiveness of the school is measured not by its capacity to transmit knowledge, but by its ability to develop constructive attitudes and motivations so that cooperation and freedom may prevail and all forms of discrimination may be abolished.

KILPATRICK

The most influential of the progressive educators was William Heard Kilpatrick (1871–   ). His influence was felt at every level of education and extended to adult and vocational education. The various state departments of education often gave voice to his ideas. In the 1960's, especially in California, a reaction took place. In fact, Max Rafferty in California viewed the ideas of Kilpatrick as being false and leading to a superficial education. Admiral Rickover charged him with being the champion of an overemphasis on methodology which, according to the admiral, is the real road-block to educational advancement.

Educated in Georgia schools, Kilpatrick attended Mercer University, eventually becoming its acting president. In 1909 he went to Teachers College at Columbia University, where he soon became its most famous teacher. After his retirement in 1938 he continued his lecturing and writing.

Among his books, special note should be made of his *Foundations of Method* and *Philosophy of Education*. The latter is the climax of his mature thinking and is an eloquent defense of the progressive educational philosophy.

Kilpatrick was especially influenced by Darwin. Life is an evolving process; man is an organism who survives by adjusting himself to new environments.

The scientific method, Kilpatrick held, can be extended to all areas of inquiry. It stands for an open mind and free inquiry; it is the foe of all forms of dogmatism and avoids absolutes.

Science means rigorous honesty. He challenged the conservatism which prevailed at Mercer University and he was promptly accused of heresy. Kilpatrick felt that the logic of evidence is stronger than the logic of faith and that, if necessary, the educator should be a martyr for his beliefs.

Kilpatrick had great admiration for both Peirce and James. Peirce he respected for his stress upon fallibilism and his opposition to determinism. William James he admired because James had seen the intimate connection between philosophy and psychology. Like James, Kilpatrick was certain that there could be no advance in philosophy without an adequate theory of learning. Philosophy is not an expression of eternal truths but rather a struggle for social welfare, an intellectual expression of man's search for the good life.

John Dewey became the main guide for Kilpatrick. Like Dewey, Kilpatrick regarded education as a democratic process and stressed that learning involves experience and the reconstruction of our environment; like Dewey, he believed in group action and favored a child-centered program. Kilpatrick especially championed the activity method, which appeals to the interests of children.

Kilpatrick attacked the evils of traditional education, which he called an "Alexandrian conception of learning." Ancient Alexandria represented a decline in culture because it imitated Greek learning and was book-centered.

Kilpatrick had little use for the great books. They may have been of some value in the time they were produced but now they are mostly obsolete. Book learning is authoritarian, and leads the student away from the real conflicts of life to a conservative view of society.

The prevailing emphasis on liberal education was rejected by Kilpatrick who felt that it creates only snobbery on the part of the ruling class. Liberal education was less important than vocational education which involved direct experience and democratic participation. Professors in the liberal arts promptly charged Kilpatrick with an over-emphasis on methodology and with a consequent proliferation of the curriculum.

Man's social nature is more important than his intellectual traits. The intellect cannot exist in isolation; it should not be trained through grammar and memorization, rather it should be used to solve the conflicts of our time. Religion, if it were to be taught anywhere, would have to be subjected to critical analysis and would have to submit to scientific evidence.

Kilpatrick was a strong supporter of reforms in government and better social legislation. Education cannot be separated from social action. As long as war and poverty threaten the survival of mankind, the educator cannot be passive. His aid is needed in protecting the public interest and in advancing humanitarian causes. Kilpatrick was interested in adult education and in improving the lot of the Negro, and in ending segregation both in the South and the North.

Like Dewey, Kilpatrick believed that life is a process of flux and that there can be no absolutes in ethics, politics or religion. Religion represents a positive attitude toward one's greatest value; it needs no supernatural exemplification. To Kilpatrick, a liberal religion has positive consequences, for it aids man in his concerns in this life, while a conservative religion obscures the real problems and the real conflicts of man.

To Kilpatrick, both American materialism and Russian materialism represent perverted religions and false values. American materialism reduces human values to property standards and emphasizes efficiency over human happiness. It creates a soulless and mechanized culture. Russian Marxism, on the other hand, subordinates man to a political party and stifles free inquiry. It creates an absolutism of conformity and denies the value of democracy. It overemphasizes the economic factors in history. It inhibits education, because in Marxism the teacher becomes the tool of the state.

To Kilpatrick, education fails if it does not provide real experience for children. Education is not the prelude to adult existence, rather the school is an autonomous center designed for democratic living. Mere study, mere discipline are secondary devices which enhance the prestige of the institution but often have no genuine educational value.

Kilpatrick believed that such ideals as cooperation and personal happiness cannot be postponed until adult life. The student has to learn how to share, how to work as a member of a group, and how to cooperate with others, but his integrity must be protected; no artificial discipline may be imposed upon him.

Kilpatrick was certain that democracy failed so often because of the distance between theory and action. We preach freedom, and yet we enact authoritarianism in the classroom. We stress the individual, and still we regard him as a statistic. We believe in the equality of all and at the same time we develop a scholastic hierarchy. Let the schools, he said, become centers of cooperative learning in which the project method prevails. Let learning be not merely an intellectual process but one which involves the totality of one's reactions. Let memorization be abandoned; let examinations be regarded as obsolete devices; let there be no static curriculum. Above all, let the teacher and the student plan the curriculum together. Let the teacher be a friend, a resource person rather than a stern taskmaster. Let the schools become laboratories for our society; then a new civilization will emerge.

Kilpatrick in this way emphasized the child rather than the teacher, concomitant learning rather than subjects, experience rather than study, action rather than intellectual training, and, most important perhaps, interest rather than effort. The project method is central in his philosophy. It involves common planning; children pursue their own interests and learn to cooperate with the group. Learning in this way is made vital and relevant.

Kilpatrick believed that specific subjects are far less important than general education. There is to be no specialization on the elementary level and not very much in high school. Even in college, core courses, which involve activity and participation, should be emphasized. General education, to Kilpatrick, means something else than to Hutchins. It is not the study of books, it is not an exploration of theory, it is not a study of the past, rather it involves projects which explore the dilemmas of the present and which bridge the gap between school and community.

Kilpatrick, as can be expected, was no supporter of traditional discipline. It develops submissive, hypocritical human beings. Integrity cannot be legislated, standards cannot be coerced by administrative pressures. The school can frame certain elastic rules of conduct, but they will not work if the students do not support them and make them part of their own philosophy of life.

"We learn what we live" is the keynote of Kilpatrick's philosophy. Participation rather than contemplation is to govern our school system.

Learning Theory

Kilpatrick makes a sharp distinction between two types of learning.

The common or conventional theory, hereinafter called "learning theory A" (or type A for short), has the following characteristics: (i) it is primarily a theory for learning from books; (ii) it thus consists typically of learning the words or statements of others; (iii) it expects the learning to come in a situation abstracted from life and so (typically) to center around a content of little or no present meaning to the learner; (iv) it expects the learning to be got mainly, if not solely, by repetition; and (v) it counts that the learning will be applied generally, if not always, in an experience different from that in which the learning takes place, usually appreciably later.[1]

He contrasts the other theory.

The other theory called herein "learning theory B" (type B), shows the following characteristics: it holds (i) that behaving is typically an essential part of the learning process; (ii) that the learning goes forward best, if not solely, in a situation of concrete personal living; (iii) that the learning comes from behaving, not from mere repetition of words, as with type A; (iv) that the first application of the learning comes, normally, within the experience in which the learning takes place, in fact that the learning comes typically in order to carry on this experience. As a corollary it is here maintained that the best learning under type A really came chiefly when it operated *not* as A — learning in an abstracted situation, to be applied later in life — but when it operated as B (iv), that is, when the content was in fact

---

[1] *Philosophy of Education*, pp. 237-238.

used to carry on some experience. Study of the biological evolution of man may help us to contrast and evaluate these two learning theories.

It is a recognized principle of evolution that "acquired characters," learned instances of behavior, are not transmitted by birth from parent to child. Evolution does not proceed that way. The theory of evolution does, however, hold that the more useful any organic functioning is for survival, the more surely will a variation in the direction of its better functioning win out in the struggle for existence and so more surely will it be transmitted. For example, ability to learn is highly important to survival; thus increased ability to learn means greater chance of survival and so greater chance of being transmitted.[2]

His conclusion was

. . . that type B certainly is true learning, and that its presence in experience is essential to the very existence of human experience as such.

Is type B learning so important biologically that evolution would seize upon it to fix it as an abiding feature in the life of the species? The answer is yes. The importance seen just above would suffice to bring about this effect. Even in subhuman organisms the unity of a life episode is fixed by and in the type B of learning, working, of course, at the same time alongside other kinds of learning from previous experiences. It seems probable that at least some of the deer's fear of the tiger is the result of such previous learning. What happens *now* in *this* activity to give unity to *this* episode or *this* experience is, however, largely the fact of its own B type learnings.

Is not type B the principal source of the learning used by the typical adult in life? It is clear that in each life experience this adult learns some things directly in and through this very experience as he works at it to make it go. This learning is of course type B. But the adult in this experience also uses many kinds of learning that have come to him in the past. It is this past learning that we wish to study further. How were these past items learned? Were they learned by the type A process as outlined in the original definition of type A? Or were most of them learned by the type B process? To answer this question consider our possible sources of the past learnings used in this experience: (i) those learned before the adult left school or college, but learned entirely outside of school or college; (ii) those learned in school or college; (iii) those learned since leaving school or college, but learned in and through life; (iv) those learned since leaving school or college, but learned by type A school learning procedures. It is clear that the learning under (i) and (iii) is type B learning and that the learning under (ii) and (iv) is type A learning. Which pair gives the greater aggregate? Is it not highly probable that the ordinary nonscholarly adult's learning of (iv) kind are very, very few in number,

---

[2] *Ibid.*, p. 238.

and also that a large portion of the original (ii) kind have been forgotten? And is it not probable that for any typical adult, (i) and (iii) are largest in number? Is not the answer that type B is the principal source of learning used by the typical adult?[3]

He turns to biology in its view of learning.

It is generally believed that man has not developed biologically in any significant manner or degree since he became *Homo sapiens;* culturally, yes—greatly so; biologically as regards mind, no, not so far as we can tell. If this be accepted, then man's present capacity to learn was developed during the long period which ended with the coming of *Homo sapiens.* As we contrast theory A with theory B, it becomes clear that B stands closer to man as a behaving organism, and that A came into existence only after *Homo sapiens* had invented writing. As between the two, then, theory B is the only one that certainly appears in the biological evolution of man. Man thus naturally behaves according to B; A belongs solely to cultural development.[4]

He asks a crucial question:

Specifically, what does it mean to say that if I wish my pupil to learn anything, such as a thought or a feeling or a movement, the pupil has to *live* that thought or that feeling or that movement? Suppose as principal of a high school in a fair-sized village, I set as one of my aims or goals that my pupils shall, if I can effect it, learn (acquire, build, develop, each in himself) a spirit of public service to the village. There are really two questions here: (i) What does it mean in such a case to *learn* a thought or a feeling or a movement? (ii) What does it mean to *live* that thought or feeling or movement?

Taking the first question, we can at once name some things which the verb *learn* does *not* mean in this case. It does not mean that any pupil who can get an A on a written examination on the subject has therein learned (achieved) the desired spirit of service. A written examination might disclose *knowledge* (so far as words prove knowledge) *about* such a spirit, but a pupil might have full knowledge *about* the spirit and not have (or feel) the spirit itself. Learning a spirit certainly means more than learning knowledge *about* it. Nor could ability and willingness to say a pledge of allegiance to such a spirit tell us that the pupil had got (learned) the spirit. No, a pupil has not *learned* this desired spirit until he has so got the spirit in him that he will of himself, as opportunity may open, really work for the public good of the community. Learning means, in this case, to build (acquire, develop) the habit, the attitude and the interest of so working; it means so to build this habit and attitude that others can rely on him,

[3] *Ibid.,* p. 241.
[4] *Ibid.,* pp. 241-242.

when occasion demands, to work this way both outwardly and inwardly. This is what learning means in such a case.[5]

Kilpatrick stressed cumulative and concomitant learning.

Some things we learn in full strength all at once. When I got a telegram telling me that my long-time friend had passed away, I did not need repeated messages on successive days to strengthen the learning; the first one sufficed. But my regard for my friend had not come to me thus all at once. It was growing the years I had known him. Each experience we lived through together contributed its added increment of insight into his character and to my regard for his worth. My feeling for him stands forth as a clear instance of cumulative learning. So likewise is it with our standards, our ideas, our principles of action, as we have previously seen. Each is an instance of cumulative learning.

Simultaneous or Concomitant Learning. In any significant experience the human organism acts as an organized whole; thought and feeling, internal glandular secretion, heart and nerve—all act together. Each experience is thus a complex of many interacting parts and aspects. Any similar experience will repeat in some measure certain of the same thoughts or feelings or movements. Suppose now a series of related experiences, such as my successive experiences with my friend just discussed; the related *thoughts* of the successive experiences I had with him, and so of him, were accumulated and organized into my insight into his character. Similarly the *related* feelings of the successive experiences were accumulated and organized into my *attitude* of regard for him.

In this way every school child, in addition to the arithmetic or history or geography which the old type of school sets him to learn, is thinking and feeling and concluding about the teacher, about school, about himself, about the subject. And these successive thoughts about the teacher are being collected to build the cumulative learning we call the child's conception of the teacher, what the child would expect of the teacher, under this, that, or the other condition.[6]

Impact

The impact of Kilpatrick was furthered by his unusual personality. He had unbounded faith in democracy and in the possibilities of education. Even after he retired he spoke at countless gatherings and held seminars at his home. He corresponded with educators throughout the world and in his eighties kept up a schedule which might have exhausted a younger man.

---

[5] *Ibid.*, p. 243.
[6] *Ibid.*, p. 246.

When he spoke, he sounded like an ancient prophet. With this author he addressed an education seminar at New York University in 1952. Kilpatrick had just recovered from a major illness. At first his voice was faint; then as he proceeded his intensity mounted. He told how the world had been governed by superstition, how the aristocracy had prevailed, how wars had conspired against human progress. He was certain that universal education would usher in a new period in which real democracy would prevail. Theological students questioned him about his religious beliefs. He answered with complete sincerity that he did not believe in a religion of dogmas but only in one which gave support to ideal values and which went beyond denominational barriers.

When he finished his discourse, there was a moment of silence, then there was prolonged applause. Even those who opposed his ideas were impressed by his sincerity and his missionary fervor for education.

As a teacher, Kilpatrick had the ability to lecture with eloquence and at the same time be a most stimulating discussion leader. He made education relevant to the issues of our time. His classes were so popular that many students had to stand. His audience included parents, political leaders, and businessmen. To Kilpatrick, progressive education was not a movement, it was a cause which had to prevail or democracy would be endangered.

In his classes, Kilpatrick emphasized the importance of questions. He did not try to give final answers, rather he stressed more penetrating inquiries. He was not trying to build a system of philosophy, for he wanted to develop the personal understanding of the student.

He was a most proficient counselor. When students experienced psychological problems, they found him to be extremely understanding. When they needed a letter of recommendation, he would oblige and take time out to advance their careers. His kindness was unfailing. His home was open to all: freshmen were received with as much attention as graduate students.

He was certain that freedom would fail if the schools adhered to authoritarian philosophies. He wanted to emancipate parents, children, teachers and administrators from the old education. Parents were to become better counselors; they were to safeguard the interests of the child. Youngsters were to develop without the rigid standards of the adult world. Teachers were to find a new dignity in their vocation. Administrators, who were to open the door to significant educational experimentation, were to welcome new ideas and aid genuine educational advancement.

Kilpatrick was certain that our theory of learning has vast consequences for education and society. If we regard learning as an abstract process, if we view it as a theory of books, we shall create a second rate civilization, one which imitates and is bound to be eclectic. Like Alexandria, it may produce magnificent buildings and libraries and laboratories but it will create no sound educational growth, which depends on shared experiences and active participation.

A theory of learning which involves participation and situations which are relevant today produces individuals who can work together, who have faith in their originality, and will face the future without having recourse to the obsolete views of the past.

CHAPTER THIRTY

Contemporary Trends in Philosophy and Education

RECENT TENDENCIES IN AMERICAN PHILOSOPHY

Since World War II there has been a renewed interest in philosophy. There is an emphasis on integrated education and liberal training in the arts, and thus the study of philosophy has been encouraged. This does not always have fortunate results; in some large universities hundreds of students assemble in an auditorium where the professor addresses them through a microphone. This is a far cry from the personal type of instruction which prevailed in the Boston of Emerson.

The "Great Books" movement, which had its center at the University of Chicago, has also contributed to the renaissance of philosophical thinking. People who would never have dreamed of reading Plato, Aristotle, Kant, Royce, or James are turning to them and are finding new horizons.

Durant's *Story of Philosophy* sold several hundred thousand copies and became a standard book in middle-class homes. Edman's *Philoso-*

417

pher's Holiday and *Philosopher's Quest* almost achieved the status of best seller and attracted favorable notices.

THE CONFLICT OF THE SCHOOLS

The school spirit is probably more pronounced in the 20th century than in earlier times. Pragmatism has continued to flourish, especially at the University of Chicago where George Herbert Mead taught from 1893 to 1931. Among his works we find *The Philosophy of the Present; Mind, Self, and Society; Movements of Thought in the Nineteenth Century;* and *The Philosophy of the Act.*[1]

Mead is especially significant for developing the social side of pragmatism. Thus he distinguished between the *I* and the *me.* The *I* is really a social *I* and is controlled by the *me,* which represents a sociological super-ego. Like Dewey he relied on the scientific method, which best describes the structure of the universe.

Dewey's influence has been enormous. He is probably the best known American thinker of the 20th century. His influence is particularly strong in the works of Sidney Hook, and it governs many education departments of leading universities.[2]

Realism, like pragmatism, has expanded its influence in the 20th century. Much of the pioneering work was done by R. B. Perry, who in 1910 wrote his noted treatise in *The Journal of Philosophy* on "The Ego-Centric Predicament," in which he showed that idealism leads to logical paradoxes and that realism is a more rational theory than idealism.[3]

The realist reaction resulted in the founding of neo-Realism, which believes that we have an immediate knowledge of the external world, and which tries to get away from the egocentric proclivity of idealism.

The thinkers who took part in this movement included Walter T. Marvin, who, in *The New Realism,* discussed "The Emancipation of Metaphysics from Epistemology"; Ralph B. Perry, who described "A Realistic Theory of Independence"; Edward G. Spaulding, who gave

---

[1] An evaluation of Mead's philosophy can be found in Grace Chin Lee, *George Herbert Mead, Philosopher of the Social Individual;* T. V. Smith, "The Social Philosophy of George Herbert Mead," *American Journal of Sociology,* XXXVII (1931–1932), 368–385.

[2] The pragmatic influence also can be seen in the work of Albion Small, James H. Tufts, W. S. Thomas, Thorstein Veblen, Arthur F. Bentley, Charles E. Merriam, H. D. Lasswell and T. V. Smith.

[3] Others regard Wm. James' article, "Does 'Consciousness' Exist?" *Journal of Philosophy,* 1904, as the milestone in the advancement of American realism.

"A Defense of Analysis"; William P. Montague, who outlined "A Realistic Theory of Truth and Error," Edwin B. Holt, who explained "The Place of Illusory Experience in a Realistic World," and Walter B. Pitkin, who discussed "Some Realistic Implications of Biology."

However, a civil war soon broke out among the realistic thinkers and a new group emerged; the critical realists. They felt that the neorealists had not been critical enough in their analysis and that we do not know the external world directly but through a medium which was called *essence* by Santayana.

The thinkers who favored this viewpoint issued a cooperative study entitled *Essays in Critical Realism*. In it Durant dealt with "The Approach to Critical Realism"; Arthur O. Lovejoy attacked pragmatism in "Pragmatism vs. the Pragmatist";[4] James B. Pratt discussed "Critical Realism and the Possibility of Knowledge"; Arthur K. Rogers dealt with "Three Proofs of Realism"; and C. A. Strong wrote "On the Nature of the Datum."

Naturalism, which is closely related to realism, has opposed all types of spiritual metaphysics. It has given a sober account of evil, and it has fought against intellectual dogmatism. It has been ably championed by thinkers such as Sellars, Otto, Cohen, Woodbridge, Lewis, and Santayana. Frederick Woodbridge is especially significant in this group for his study on *Nature and Mind*.

The American naturalists, as compared to their British colleagues, are not quite so pessimistic. The British philosopher Bertrand Russell speaks of a hostile universe, which has no regard for human values, in an eloquent essay, "Free Man's Worship." Woodbridge pictures a more benevolent universe in which intellectual values have validity.[5]

Logical empiricism, which has done much to negate metaphysics in science and to give a more truly mathematical foundation to logic, has been influenced by a variety of American scholars, from Peirce to Dewey. It has been ably championed by Reichenbach, Carnap, Bridgman, Feigl, Frank, Lewin, Ayer and a host of other scholars.[6] It has been applied to ethical problems by Dewey in *Theory of Valuation* and H. Gomperz on "Some Simple Thoughts on Freedom and Responsibility," which appeared in *Philosophy*, in 1937.[7]

[4] See also Lovejoy's discerning article on the weaknesses of neo-Realism in "Realism versus Epistemological Monism," *Journal of Philosophy*, X (1913), 561–572.

[5] Closely related to naturalism is the humanist movement. Cf. "A Humanist Manifesto," in the 1936 issue of *The New Humanist*.

[6] Logical empiricism owes much to the work of Wittgenstein, whose *Tractatus Logico-Philosophicus*, and *Der Wiener Kreis: Wissenschaftliche Weltauffassung* are important contributions to this movement.

[7] A valuable survey of the writing of the logical empiricists can be gained in Feigl and Sellars, *Readings in Philosophical Analysis*.

Idealism continues to be an active movement in American philosophy. Mary Calkins for many years was an expert in the interpretation of classical German philosophy, and her classes at Wellesley were inevitably popular. William E. Hocking is probably the best known of contemporary idealists; his main work is *The Meaning of God in Human Experience*, which combines mysticism with pragmatism, and which comes to a conclusion that can be likened to that of Malebranche, namely, that we first know God and then human beings. Hocking was influenced by Royce, but he reacted against the latter's absolute idealism and instead made more of the independence of the individual.

John E. Boodin also reflects the idealist influence, although he calls his system a combination of empirical realism and metaphysical energism. He believes in cosmic interaction and in the objective status of values. Among his works we find *Time and Reality; A Realistic Universe; Cosmic Evolution;* and *The Religion of the Future*.

The practical application of idealism can be found in Felix Adler, the founder of the Ethical Culture Movement. Adler stresses the ideal of universality and the educational integrity of the individual. He wanted to transform society on an ethical basis, including the family, the vocational groups, and the state. His interpretation of morality was dynamic and gave full recognition to the need for individual differences.

He conceived of religion in ethical terms. Instead of priests he wanted moral teachers. Religious faith should be emancipated from supernaturalism and dogmatism. All members, are to be guided by high moral values and by dedication to ideal ends.

His doctrines are summarized in *An Ethical Philosophy of Life; The Reconstruction of the Spiritual Ideal*, and *Creed and Deed*.[8]

The same moralistic emphasis, although in a more theistic form, can be found in personalism. Brightman in *The Problem of God* and *The Finding of God* represented this movement and reflected the influence of Bowne. Brightman, however, believed in a finite God who is limited by evil. Brightman bases his philosophy on scientific grounds and stresses the need for hypotheses in religious faiths.

R. T. Flewelling brought the personalistic view to the philosophy of history in *Survival of Western Culture*, in which he opposed Oswald Spengler's pessimism and pointed to the infinite spiritual

---

[8] Among other thinkers who contributed to 20th century idealism we find G. P. Adams, W. G. Everett, Edgar A. Singer, Radoslav A. Tsanoff and Wilbur M. Urban.

capacities of human personality. He viewed personalism as a mediating philosophy which could establish a synthesis between Eastern and Western culture.[9]

Catholic philosophy has become increasingly important in 20th century American culture. It has been championed in such journals as *The New Scholasticism, The Modern Schoolman, The Thomist,* and in the *Proceedings of the American Catholic Philosophical Association.*

It has been stimulated by visits to the United States by distinguished neo-scholastic European philosophers like Maritain and Gilson and by a renewed interest in medieval culture.

Neo-scholasticism has already had important reverberations in educational theory. Probably the American neo-scholastic thinkers are somewhat more orthodox than their European colleagues, who have been exposed to centuries of skepticism.

Neo-scholasticism upholds the validity of Aquinas and regards his philosophy as the most meaningful for our century. It does not neglect modern scientific developments, but they are subordinated to the phenomenal realm, and in the noumenal world only final causation is valid. The aim of this movement is to fight materialism, agnosticism, and skepticism and to lead modern man back to the certainty of the Roman Catholic Church.

The growth of religious mysticism can be observed in our own era. To some it appears as an escape from unpleasant reality, to others as a recovery of the essential self and a reaction against an overly activist civilization. Huxley, Heard, and Isherwood have lent support to this movement. Huxley, especially in *Perennial Philosophy,* makes an eloquent appeal for a mystical interpretation of life.

The Quakers have contributed to mysticism. Two representatives are Rufus Jones and Elton Trueblood. Both combined mystical tendencies with a faith in the goodness of man and in the vitality of nonviolence as the best way of life. A more conservative approach to religion appeared in Niebuhr's *Nature and Destiny of Man.* With a Kierkegaardian approach to religion, Niebuhr emphasized the transcendence of God and the reality of human evil.

Various European philosophical movements have left their traces in this country. Especially, phenomenology has had an effect upon the social sciences, mathematics, art, religion, psychology and a host of other fields. The outstanding representative of this movement is

---

[9] The personalistic emphasis is also strong in A. C. Knudson. Cf. Knudson, *The Philosophy of Personalism; The Doctrine of God;* and *The Validity of Religious Experience.*

Marvin Farber, who in 1943 published *The Foundation of Phenomenology,* and who edits *Philosophy and Phenomenological Research,* published at the University of Buffalo.

Existentialism has been the subject of much interpretation and criticism in American philosophical journals.[10] The lectures of Jean Paul Sartre, chief exponent, have been accompanied by widespread interest.

In the twentieth century the philosophy of history has become exceedingly important in American culture. This may be due to the vast influence of Spengler on the American mind, and it may also reflect our perplexity regarding our ultimate destiny. P. A. Sorokin wrote in 1941 *The Crisis of Our Age,* which is a summary of his *Dynamics of Culture.* Sorokin feels that history presents an incessant conflict between ideological and sensate factors, and he gives numerous examples to back up his viewpoint.

Lewis Mumford developed a personalistic perspective in such works as *Man and Technics,* in which he traced the effect of the machine on human thinking, and in *Faith for Living* and in *The Condition of Man,* in which he called for a new dynamic interpretation of the liberal tradition.

Northrop gained fame with his *Meeting of East and West,* in which he pointed out the distinguishing features of Eastern and Western culture and also presented a plan for synthesis and harmony of the two worlds.

TRENDS IN EDUCATIONAL PSYCHOLOGY

In educational psychology the conflicts between the schools is just as intense as in philosophy. Pioneers in educational psychology, like Edward Lee Thorndike, emphasized the quantitative nature of learning. Thus Thorndike in his masterpiece, *Educational Psychology* (3 volumes), deals with three parts of learning: Volume I is concerned with the bases of learning; volume II with the laws of learning; and volume III with individual differences. He held that subjects like mathematics and Latin have little transfer value. His basic idea was that educational research should be based upon experimentation and exact statistics.

In our time existential psychology, as represented by Rollo May, deals more with qualitative factors, especially with value analysis. The choices of the individual, May asserts, have to be clarified; this

---

[10] In education Kneller and van Cleve Morris champion existential ideas.

cannot be done through statistical analysis. Existential psychology pleads for a close union of psychology, ethics, and philosophy.

Behaviorism, as championed by Watson and Meyer, tries to eliminate the concept of mind and instead stresses the stimulus response matrix. It is opposed to all forms of introspection and attempts to make psychology a truly naturalistic discipline. Skinner, who was influenced by behavioristic concepts, used its principles in the creation of teaching machines. Purposivism, as represented by McDougall, is concerned, on the other hand, with man's ideals and goals and regards behaviorism as a gross simplification of the essential psychological problems.

Functionalism, as taught by Dewey, Judd, and Thorndike, stresses man's conscious adaptation to the environment, which involves a continuous process based on evolutionary presuppositions. Freudianism, on the other hand, which is making many converts in education, stresses the unconscious factors in man's life and points to the irrational as a basis of man's emotional life. It speaks of basic dualisms: the drive toward pleasure versus pain, the life impulse versus the death drive, the id — our passionate driving self — versus the restraints of the superego.

Some psychologists are concerned more with the measurement of specific abilities. This was accomplished by individuals like Seashore, who measured musical ability, Lasker, who measured racial attitudes, Bernreuter, who studied the degree of introversion, and Bogardus, who studied the problem of social distance. Gestalt psychologists, on the other hand, are more concerned with man's total response. A German exile, Bruno Klopfer, applied the techniques of the Rorschach test, a valuable projective device, to the total educational situation.

Psychologists are divided on the efficiency of tests. The I.Q. test determines the degree of intelligence. An I.Q. of 105 indicates average intelligence, while an I.Q. of 160 would indicate the capacities of a genius. In the 1960's the reliance upon I.Q. tests has been challenged by psychologists like Anderson, Torrance and McKinnon, who have demanded a more creative attitude in testing, which considers the subject's intangible traits and motivations which might lead to significant educational growth.

SOCIAL IDEALS

The social conception of man is gaining more followers in our period. It was championed by Dewey in his *Human Nature and*

Conduct and by George Herbert Mead who stressed the self which emerges as a reaction to group ideals. Neo-Freudians, like Karen Horney, point out that individual psychology cannot explain the total nature of man and that Freud was preoccupied with individual rather than social needs. The growing popularity of sociology and anthropology point to a re-examination of prevailing views of psychology. Margaret Mead, Ruth Benedict, and Ralph Linton all stress the effect of culture on the behavior of the individual. Thus, Ruth Benedict, in *Patterns of Culture,* shows that what is normal and abnormal is guided by group standards and that frequently the group in power may determine our values.

In education this emphasis has changed the outlook of teachers. More of them now are concerned with minority problems and they realize that the value system of the middle class cannot be imposed on a slum environment. More instructors are aware of the eroding effect of prejudice, which makes for social disorganization and precludes the good life for a large number of people.

To see the school in its social setting is to become aware of the tensions which prevail in the community and, ideally, to develop a conscience about social lags and a determination to make education the agency of enlightenment.

The development of group dynamics and the sociodrama include a merging of educational, psychological and sociological ideals. These techniques are based upon man's social needs and his dependence on group standards. The way the group looks upon the individual and the way he reacts to its standards may determine his effectiveness in life and his capacity to learn.

With the new psychological and sociological emphases, educators have become conscious of the way millions of children are brought up in rural and urban slums. Conant made a graphic study of the devastating effect of the slum on the social environment. The level of expectancy in such an environment would be low. Education would be thought of in vocational, not in academic terms. The dropout rate in such communities would be a fact which would predispose many to a life of idleness and delinquency.

Psychologists today are divided over the nature of therapy. Should it be client-centered, as Rogers urges? Should it utilize group situations as Moreno and Bach emphasize? Should it be concerned with values? Should the therapist remain objective or should he be involved in the personal life of the client? Should the therapy deal with past events or be goal-directed? Should the therapy dwell upon personal deficiencies or the social situation? Should it deal with pathological elements or should it emphasize affirmative possibilities? Should it be guided by the postulates of one school of thought or should it be eclectic? Should it emphasize or minimize man's religious drive? Should the therapist who deals with children and adolescents work in close conjunction with school authorities or should he be mainly concerned with the clinical aspects of his work? Most important perhaps is the question: Should the counseling function of the teacher be intensified or should counseling become a specialized function to be undertaken only by experts?

Educational philosophy without psychological applications becomes a journey in abstractions. *Psychology, in a sense, is the concrete verification of philosophical concepts.* It makes philosophy a more human and a more dramatic enterprise. Psychology without philosophy tends to develop too many uncritical assumptions. *In isolation both disciplines stagnate; in a common enterprise both subjects develop greater depth and more universality.*

The need for a close union between the two disciplines was expressed by William James who felt that no teacher should be ignorant of basic human motivation. Without such knowledge, education and philosophy are superficial disciplines and have no real impact on the lives of individuals and nations.

The psychology of education, according to James, combines analysis and intuition.

The science of psychology, and whatever science of general pedagogics may be based on it, are in fact much like the science of war. Nothing is simpler or more definite than the principles of either. In war, all you have to do is to work your enemy into a position from which the natural obstacles prevent him from escaping if he tries to; then to fall on him in numbers superior to his own, at a moment when you have led him to think you far away; and so, with a minimum of exposure of your own troops, to hack his force to pieces, and take the remainder prisoners. Just so, in teaching you must simply work your pupil into such a state of interest in what you are going to teach him that every other object of attention is banished from his mind; then reveal it to him so impressively that he will remember the occasion to his dying day; and finally fill him with devouring curiosity to know what the next steps in connection with the subject are. The principles being so plain, there would be nothing but victories for the masters of the science, either on the battlefield or in the schoolroom, if they did not both have to make their application to an incalculable quantity in the shape of the mind of their opponent. The mind of your own enemy, the pupil, is working away from you as keenly and eagerly as is the mind of the commander on the other side from the scientific general. Just what the respective enemies want and think, and what they know and do not know, are as hard things for the teacher as for the general to find out. Divination and perception, not psychological pedagogics or theoretic strategy, are the only helpers here.

But, if the use of psychological principles thus be negative rather than positive, it does not follow that it may not be a great use, all the same. It certainly narrows the path for experiments and trials. We know in advance, if we are psychologists, that certain methods will be wrong, so our psychology saves us from mistakes. It makes us, moreover, more clear as to what we are about. We gain confidence in respect to any method which we are using as soon as we believe that it has theory as well as practice at its back. Most of all, it fructifies our independence, and it reanimates our interest, to see our subjects at two different angles — to get a stereoscopic view, so to speak, of the youthful organism who is our enemy, and, while handling him with all our concrete tact and divination, to be able, at the same time, to represent to ourselves the curious inner elements of his mental machine. Such a complete knowledge as this of the pupil, at once intuitive and analytic, is surely the knowledge at which every teacher ought to aim.[11]

CURRENTS IN EDUCATIONAL THOUGHT

In turning to educational philosophy we find that the progress of idealism has been especially advanced by H. H. Horne (1874–1946), a student of Josiah Royce. Horne fought a vigorous war against the naturalism of Dewey and Kilpatrick. He taught at New York University and lectured at Dartmouth, North Carolina, and Harvard. Especially signficant are his *Philosophy of Education* and *The Democratic Philosophy of Education.*

In his technical system he calls his views idealistic theism. This implies that man is part of a larger reality—God—and that the universe has a spiritual meaning. Empirical knowledge is subordinated to speculative knowledge. Mechanical events are symbols of teleology. What matters are not facts but values which depend on an Absolute Standard.

Man, to Horne, represents the highest stage of evolution. His destiny is different from that of animals for he has the power of thought and can make moral decisions. To reduce man to his animal ancestry is to degrade man's mission.

---

[11] *Talks to Teachers,* pp. 9–11.

Education is to give to the student a view of the majesty of the Absolute. Education has three parts: theoretic, which deals with the sciences; esthetic, which develops awareness of our artistic heritage; and volitional, which deals with man's actions. Horne was not friendly to the elective system which, he felt, destroyed the unity of the curriculum. He urged seven main areas of concentration required for all students. They include biology, physics, mathematics, psychology, grammar, literature and history. The last subject he regards as being especially significant, for it can give to man a view of his potential greatness and inspire him to transcend his material limitations.

Horne was certain that education implied something more than social living. It meant the training of the mind which is man's highest achievement and his link with divinity. While Dewey and Kilpatrick stressed the importance of interest and spontaneity, Horne upheld the significance of effort and discipline.

In our time realism has had a new revival. Both Russell and Whitehead have stimulated this movement in education; Russell in his emphasis upon intelligence and objectivity, and Whitehead in his eloquent essay *The Aims of Education*, plead for a scientific and esthetic reconstruction of education in which knowledge is utilized for the adventure of ideas.

In educational circles, Breed and Broudy represent realist ideals. At the same time the impact of Thorndike cannot be neglected. Thorndike felt that whatever exists can be measured. He tried to give a scientific foundation to our learning theory based upon statistical knowledge and exact verifications.

The realist stresses the importance of fundamentals. This includes language training and acquaintance with logic and mathematics. The student is to learn that his biases do not determine the course of the universe which exists independent of man. Stress is placed upon factual competence, especially in the natural sciences. The realist believes that the world is not a place of chance but one in which a structure abides. To ignore this structure is to become a romanticist who may end like Don Quixote fighting philosophical windmills. To understand this structure is to become truly educated. It implies objectivity, a respect for facts, a knowledge that science proceeds by a view of particulars, analyzing problems and then arriving at a general conclusion. It implies that particulars exist beyond our own consciousness.

The educational system which the realist favors is one which emphasizes careful testing and objective data. To say that examinations are obsolete, as Kilpatrick does, leads to a lowering of standards, as realists like Breed point out.

For the realist, communication is a vital part of education. It implies a mastery of mathematics, skilled analysis and adequate study habits. In this way the mind achieves an almost effortless use and is able to apply the data which science supplies and which makes human progress possible.

Both idealists and realists contributed to the Essentialist platform represented by individuals like Bagley, Kandel and Brickman. Essentialists were vigorously opposed to progressive education. They urged greater concentration on subject matter, more development of fundamental skills, and they did not feel that the authority of the teacher ought to be slighted. More conservative in their social philosophy than the pragmatists, the essentialists were in favor of defending traditional values so that the school would mirror the dominant mood of the community.

Brameld, in such works as *Philosophies of Education in Cultural Perspective, Design for American Education for the Emerging Age,* and *Toward a Reconstructed Philosophy of Education,* takes a different view of education. He feels that education ought to have a utopian basis. It ought to help to overcome the crisis of our time. This implies an active reconstruction of our institutional system.

We face the choice today of merely adding to cultural lag by becoming pawns of our environment or using our intelligence for group action, for goal seeking, searching for the unity of events — he uses Whitehead's term, prehension — and in this sense contributing to the future. Brameld maintains that the same revolution that is taking place in the physical sciences is occurring in the behavioral sciences — a revolution which indicates that universal values exist and that they can be realized through intelligent group action and cross-cultural fertilization.

In practice this means an emphasis on adult education, especially the education of workers, a stress upon the organization of teachers for peace and economic abundance, and a realization that teaching requires political as well as intellectual courage.

The neo-scholastic philosophy in education has won favor from professional philosophers like Mortimer Adler. An eloquent representative of this viewpoint was W. I. Cunningham (1885–1961) who taught at Portland University and at Notre Dame. His *Pivotal Problems of Education* and *General Education and the Liberal College* represent the Catholic viewpoint.

Education, according to Cunningham, involves a four-fold development. There is man's growth in the home and in the community and his mental training, but most important is his religious development. Cunningham stresses man's supernatural destiny. Man's relationship with God is all-important and it is guided by the Church, which strengthens man's faith and which helps him to live with God.

The fundamental issue in education, according to Cunningham, is naturalism or supernaturalism. Naturalism emphasizes man's biological nature; it is fragmentary, it leads to anxiety and uncertainty. Supernaturalism, as interpreted by the Church, leads to eternal happiness; it combines reason and faith and represents a recognition of man's divine nature.

The believer takes Jesus as his example and is guided by the teachings of the Church. He views knowledge as a divine instrument and uses the arts and sciences for the advancement of the spiritual kingdom, realizing that the knowledge of God is the beginning and end of our education.

CHAPTER THIRTY-ONE

Robert Hutchins Revisited

THE REBEL

No one can deny the brilliance of Robert Hutchins, who became dean of Yale while still in his twenties and president of the University of Chicago at the age of thirty. Even more impressive are his achievements in his mature years. When he felt that civil liberties were threatened, he started the Center for the Study of Democratic Institutions in Santa Barbara — an organization which has made important contributions to the understanding of Western ideals. It is the ambition of Hutchins to create an institution which will rival Plato's *Academy*. Like Plato, Hutchins feels that education is a total process and that it fails unless it can change man's institutional relationships.

Hutchins speaks and writes in a provocative manner. If, as Whitehead indicates, style is the ultimate morality of man, Hutchins indeed must rank high. His sentences are crisp and clear. He is a master of irony and his sense of humor is penetrating.

Few have fought more vigorously for academic freedom. This means to him not merely protection of the rights of those who agree

431

with him, but tolerance even of those who disagree in a most violent manner. He has never succumbed to the expediency of the moment, but instead has concentrated upon the long-range objectives of education.

While Dewey and Whitehead stress the unitary aspects of knowledge, Hutchins upholds fundamental dualisms. In his system there is conflict between theory and action, education and training, wisdom and knowledge, philosophy and science, and permanence and change. The true scientist, Hutchins asserts, will be concerned with general principles. The lesson of science is not, as Dewey thought, flux and change; rather, it is the permanence of life.

Hutchins is engaged in a warfare against utilitarianism. College courses in typewriting and home economics are anathema to him. He scorns the cult of athletics. The purpose of education is intellectual; talk about educating the whole child is mere sentimentalism. Universities are not substitutes for the finishing school, the Salvation Army, the Boy Scouts, or the home environment. They should be independent centers of thinking. They should be concerned not with usefulness but with the cultivation of reason.

Hutchins has great faith in the powers of rationality. While Dewey looks upon reason as an activity, Hutchins regards reason as an end. The man who cultivates his reason, according to Hutchins, will be effective in any activity. Reason is disciplined by grammar and logic. Without fundamental skills our entire education will be an adventure in chaos.

To identify experience with nature is- inadmissible. The true naturalist, Hutchins says, is concerned with the nature of things, not with our valuation of them. Nature as such is blind; to understand nature we must go beyond it.

Dewey's naturalism has helped undermine the unity of the curriculum. Instead of time-honored subjects, trivial inquiries are conducted. Instead of being concerned with the problem of the good, students now try to learn about cosmetics or the intricacies of population statistics.

REFORMS

Hutchins describes three types of curriculum and finds them defective.

The life-activities centered curriculum is exemplified by the course of study of a women's college, which is based on a job analysis of the diaries of several hundred mature women. The categories of the activities of these women constitute the structure of the college curriculum, although women, perhaps, ought to do and may even be doing things that these mature women did not do. The student-interest centered curriculum, apparently on the theory that it is hopeless to try to understand education or to figure out what an education should be, simply takes the expression of interest on the part of the student as revealing what he should study, for who knows what he should study, anyway? The professor-interest centered curriculum is the more usual variety. Each professor and each department want the whole time of the student so that he can be thoroughly trained in the professor's or the department's specialty. Since it is obviously impossible for the student's whole time to be spent in this way, the curriculum is determined by a process of pulling, hauling, and log-rolling; and finally emerges as a sort of checkerboard across which the bewildered student moves, absorbing from each square, it is hoped, a little of something that each professor or each department has to offer him.[1]

These courses are not related to thinking.

The activities of mature women may have had little to do with thinking. Some students may not be interested in thought. And I have heard of professors and departments who believed that their function was to cram their students with information. It is hard to contemplate such courses of study without agreeing with Henry Adams, who said, "The chief wonder of education is that it does not ruin everybody concerned in it, teachers and taught."

If we insist that colleges and universities should be devoted to thinking, and if we insist that they should, if possible, think about important things, we may perhaps find the way in which higher education may make its unique contribution to morals and religion. Most of our educational institutions are and will probably remain secular, in the sense that they are not controlled by any church and are open to everybody regardless of his religious faith or lack of it. But there is another kind of secularism that besets the higher learning in America, and that is secularism in the sense in which we say that religion is insignificant, it is outmoded, it is equivalent to superstition. This kind of secularism higher education can and should repel. If a college or university is going to think and to think about important things, then it must think about religion. It is perhaps not necessary that all the faculty should be religious; it would be desirable that most of them, at least, should take religion seriously.[2]

Hutchins attacks moral relativism.

According to the dogmas of scientism, skepticism, and secularism there is no truth. If there is truth at all, it is truth discoverable in the

---

[1] Bedell Lecture, 1948.
[2] *Ibid.*

laboratory, by what is called the scientific method. I recently heard a minister of a Protestant church state at a public meeting that no man could tell whether a given act was right or wrong. I replied that he was a moral relativist, thinking that he would be so stung by this reproach that he might reconsider his position. Instead he proudly answered, "Of course I am a moral relativist," as if to say that anybody who is not a moral relativist is an unenlightened, unscientific, medieval reactionary.

We should all admit, I suppose, that a moral act is one performed in the right way under the right circumstances; but the notion that under some circumstances it could be right, for example, for one man to kill another with malice aforethought must mean that there is no difference between good and bad, between right and wrong, that there is no moral law and there are no moral principles that higher education can take seriously. It must mean that there are no morals; there are only the mores; and there is no religion; there is only superstition. If higher education is to take morality and religion seriously, it must repudiate these dogmas; for the truths of morality and religion never have been and never can be discovered by experiment or by any allegedly "scientific" means. Morality and religion cannot be taken seriously unless the possibility of attaining truth by philosophical inquiry and by revelation is admitted. It is necessary to believe that philosophy is something more than words and that it is possible to be rational and religious at the same time.

By the commitments to which I have referred, higher education may directly contribute to the formation of character. The indirect contributions it may make are, perhaps, almost as important. These are the moral by-products of its intellectual work. The life of learning requires the support of the moral virtues; and an arduous academic career must tend to develop these virtues. Without courage or fortitude no one can long stick at the painful task of thinking and studying.[3]

He pleads for a real educational community.

I should add that there is a certain moral failure on the part of an educational institution that does not try to make its work something other than the accumulation of miscellaneous credits; for it seems unjust to expect the student to work hard on trivial, irrelevant, incoherent, and meaningless material. The vice of the adding-machine method of education is that it has a way of making even important subject matter seem trivial, irrelevant, incoherent, and meaningless.

There is a certain moral failure, too, on the part of an educational institution that does not allow the student to make his own the treasure of the accumulated thoughts of the race. So the failure of the elective system was a moral failure. The official historian of Harvard said of President Eliot that he had defrauded the Harvard

---

[3] *Ibid.*

students of their cultural heritage. The failure of vocational education is of the same variety: in the name of a specious commercial or industrial dexterity it cheats the student out of his place in the stream of human history.

An educational institution should be a community. A community must have a common aim, and the common aim of the educational community is the truth. It is not necessary that the members of the educational community agree with one another, for the basis of community is communication. In order to communicate with one another, the members of the community must understand one another, and this means that they must have a common language and a common stock of ideas. Any system of education that is based on the training of individual differences is fraudulent in this sense. The primary object of education should be to bring out our common humanity. For though men are different, they are also the same, and their common humanity, rather than their individual differences, requires development today as at no earlier era in history.[4]

VISION OF THE FUTURE

The idea that nothing is true unless it works is received with scorn by Hutchins. Does this not lead to an emphasis upon utilitarianism? Does this not imply a worship of technology? Is this not materialism in a new disguise?

Hutchins makes a sharp distinction between knowledge and opinion. Opinion is relative, while knowledge is absolute. We can disagree regarding matters of opinion, but when it comes to knowledge we should be guided by the expert. Hutchins charges that the progressive educator reduces all knowledge to opinion and thus makes relativism supreme in education.

With irony, Hutchins speaks of the higher learning in America. He attacks especially three evils: (1) the emphasis upon professionalism, (2) the stress upon scientism, and (3) the prevalence of anti-intellectualism. Hutchins has little use for professional and vocational education. Universities should stress the great books and the liberal arts. Specialism, especially in science, leads to a narrow mind with vast knowledge and little education. The universities have become social and athletic centers. Hutchins wants them to become centers of independent thinking and inter-departmental inquiry.

Hutchins has outlined the university of Utopia. It would consist of three departments: natural sciences, social sciences, and metaphysics. Controversial subjects would be welcomed; complete freedom

---

[4] *Ibid.*

of inquiry would prevail; professors and students would be engaged in the discussion of timeless subjects.

All this does not imply that Hutchins is uninterested in social issues. He has been one of the leaders in the movement seeking to establish a world government, he has served on a commission studying the freedom of the press, he has fought consistently for racial equality, he has defended political diversity, and he has resisted the attempts of political organizations to dominate the affairs of educational institutions.

Hutchins has a vision of one world. This world, he believes, cannot be established by force or by military power, but only through the cultivation of reason. Ultimately, he hopes that the educational curriculum everywhere will stress the great books and the great ideas of mankind. Imbued with a sense of the past, Hutchins feels that the study of previous cultures and civilizations will give to modern man a broad perspective which he desperately needs if he wants to survive.

The philosophy of Hutchins is summarized by the famous statement: "Education implies teaching. Teaching implies knowledge. Knowledge is truth. The truth is everywhere the same. Hence education should be everywhere the same."

It is easy to criticize this statement on semantic grounds. Stuart Chase in *The Tyranny of Words* has attacked the semantic fallacies involved in the view that education should be everywhere the same. But in a deeper sense, this statement is based on a fundamental vision. To understand a thinker the verbal meaning is less important than the symbolic significance involved in his views. The word, after all, is only a reflection of experience; it stands for an underlying faith, a basic world view.

Hutchins believes that truth is eternal and that education should give us a concept of absolute truth. Education should train the intellect; all other goods are subordinated to the cultivation of reason, which exists as an end in itself. Once we accept this premise, the particular aspects of education appear to be insignificant compared with its universal mission: to train man in the life of reason.

Still, the weaknesses of Hutchins' philosophy cannot be overlooked. Hutchins has too much faith in reason. Our rational capacities cannot be separated from our emotional drives. Reason is not an entity, but a process. It is cultivated best not by the discipline of grammar or by the study of the Aristotelian syllogism, but by scientific experimentation, by esthetic experience, and by realizing the problematic nature of knowledge.

To Hutchins, the intellectual experience is the highest form of knowledge, yet the intellectual life suffers when it is aloof from society. To be more concrete, a work experience for a college student can be as significant as the study of the great books. Knowledge without action leads to intellectual isolation; action without knowledge leads to social sterility. Both extremes are undesirable in education.

This certainly does not eliminate the need for the reading of the classics. But they must be accepted in a more critical spirit, not as absolute guides to knowledge, but as points of reference showing both the similarities and contrasts between modern and ancient ideals of knowledge. The great book, as Descartes points out, is the book of the world. Its study should be our supreme task and vocation.

Yet, despite these reservations, we must acknowledge Robert Hutchins as one of the truly great educational thinkers of Western civilization. He has helped to clarify our problems; he has demolished some of our most cherished idols; he has strengthened the foundations of liberal education. In an age of conformity his is the voice of vigorous dissent and valiant individualism.

PART SIX

Levels of Education

CHAPTER THIRTY-TWO

The Bases for Elementary Education

BASES

In the history of education an authoritarian bias has often prevailed. It holds that the child is evil, that he must be thoroughly disciplined, that he cannot be trusted to develop his own abilities. This was the philosophy of the early settlers who regarded children as creatures of evil. They felt that sin starts in early childhood, and that rebellious children would be damned. Were not whippings the best means to discipline youngsters?

Rev. Thomas Brainerd gave a summary of the Puritan child.

He was taught that time was a talent always to be improved; that industry was a cardinal virtue, and laziness the worst form of original sin. Hence he must rise early and make himself useful before he went to school; must be diligent there in study, and be promptly home to do "*chores*" at evening. His whole time out of school must be filled up by some service, such as bringing in fuel for the day, cutting potatoes for the sheep, feeding the swine, watering the horses, picking the berries, gathering the vegetables, spooling the yarn. He was expected never to be reluctant, and not often tired.

He was taught that it was a sin to find fault with his meals, his apparel, his tasks, or his lot in life. Labor he was not allowed to regard as a burden, nor abstinence from any improper indulgence as a hardship.

His clothes, woolen and linen, for summer and winter, were mostly spun, woven, and made up by his mother and sisters at home; and as he saw the whole laborious process of their fabrication, he was jubilant and grateful for two suits, with bright buttons, a year. Rents were carefully closed and holes patched in the "every day" dress, and the Sabbath dress always kept new and fresh.

He was expected early to have the stops and marks, the abbreviations, the multiplication table, the Ten Commandments, and the Lord's Prayer, and the Shorter Catechism, at his tongue's end.

Courtesy was enjoined as a duty. He must be silent among his superiors. If addressed by older persons, he must respond with a bow. He was to bow as he entered and left the school, and bow to every man or woman, old or young, rich or poor, black or white, whom he met on the road. Special punishment was visited on him if he failed to show respect to the aged, the poor, the colored, or to any persons whatever whom God had visited infirmities. He was thus taught to stand in awe of the rights of humanity.[1]

In such a system the rules were strict, as can be seen from some of the prohibitions of the North Carolina schools:

Rules of School	Lashes
Boys and Girls Playing Together	4
Quareling	4
Fighting	5
Fighting at School	5
Quarreling at School	3
Gambling or Betting at School	4
Playing at Cards at School	10
Climbing for Every foot Over three feet up a tree	1
Telling Lyes	7
Telling Tales Out of School	8
Nick Naming Each Other	4
Giving Each Other Ill Names	3
Fighting Each Other in Time of Books	2
Swearing at School	8
Blackgarding Each Other	6
For Misbehaving to Girls	10
For Leaving School without Leave of the Teacher	4
Going Home with Each Other without Leave of the Teacher	4
For Drinking Spirituous Liquors at School	8
Making Swings & Swinging on Them	7

[1] Barnhard's *American Journal of Education*, XVI (1866), 335.

Rules of School	Lashes
For Misbehaving when a Stranger is in the House	6
For Wearing Long Finger Nails	2
For Not Making a Bow when a Stranger Comes in or goes out	3
Misbehaving to Persons on the Road	4
For not Making a Bow when you Meet a Person	4
For Going to Girls' Play Places	3
Girls Going to Boys' Play Places	2
Coming to School with Dirty Face and Hands	2
For Calling Each Other Liars	4
For Playing Bandy	10
For Bloting Your Copy Book	2
For Not Making a bow when you go home and when you come away	4
Wrestling at School	4
Scuffling at School	4
For not making a Bow when Going out to go Home	2
For Weting Each Other Washing at Play Time	2
For Delaying Time Going Home or Coming to School	4[2]

A more liberal viewpoint is represented by Comenius, Rousseau, Froebel, and Pestalozzi in Europe and by Kilpatrick, Dewey, Hall, Alice Temple, F. D. Baker, Elizabeth Harrison, and F. Parker in the United States. They believed that human nature is basically good and that all children have creative potentialities which can be stimulated by the cooperation of school and community. The second viewpoint accepts love as the fundamental basis of life. Love implies trust. It means a sharing of experience. It leads to a pattern of understanding so that the teacher is like a parent. He will never give up hope. He becomes the symbol of unending encouragement.

It may be asked whether the second viewpoint is practical. Do we not live in a competitive society? Are not love and hate equally balanced? Does not our society encourage a subtle antagonism? Do not our agencies of communication feature the cult of violence?

The answer to these questions is that in our schools we must create an environment in which compassion and understanding can flourish. This means greater emphasis on leadership. We can tell at once when a school treasures personality and avoids coldness and rigidity. For example, in a Santa Monica school in a low economic area for which the author was a consultant, the principal was well-intentioned, but she disliked the children from minority groups. A new principal, Richard Key, was enthusiastic about education and strengthened the morale of the children and teachers, and saw to it that the parents became involved in the school. The result was a

---

[2] C. L. Coon, *North Carolina Schools and Academies (1700–1840)*, pp. 163–166.

new school in which teachers seldom quit, in which the children do creative work, including poetry which has been published in book form. Most important of all, a training institution has become a genuine community center.

HISTORICAL TRENDS

Nursery education is especially important today. The first nursery school in the U.S. was established in 1919. Fourteen years later a federal program for nursery schools was undertaken. During World War II, with many mothers working, the federal government aided nursery school education through the Lanham Act.

Universities such as Columbia Teachers College, Ohio State and Iowa State have been especially active in this field. Nursery schools offer valuable laboratory experience for psychologists and psychiatrists. They often are cooperative ventures between teachers and parents. In this way learning is applied to life situations and parents gain a new understanding of their children. In the future, nursery school education will probably be as widespread as Kindergartens are today. Froebel was the pioneer in the Kindergarten movement. To Froebel, play activities had genuine educational functions. He felt that children want to learn at an early age and that their creative drives should be stimulated. The first German Kindergarten was founded by Mrs. Carl Schurz in 1855 at Watertown, Wisconsin. The first English Kindergarten was the work of Elizabeth Peabody in 1860. Thirteen years later, under the inspiration of W. T. Harris, Susan Blow opened the first public school Kindergarten in St. Louis.

The elementary school, like the Kindergarten, has its roots in Europe. Comenius was a pioneer who explored the natural capacities of children. He produced, in 1659, the first children's book, *The Visible World*, which was beautifully illustrated. Jean J. Rousseau stimulated the study of child psychology. In *Emile* he outlined a system of education which was based upon an absence of coercion.

Pestalozzi was especially interested in the education of the poor. His experimental school at Yverdun attracted attention in many parts of the world, and he had major followers in the U.S. His major disciple in the U.S. was Charles Sheldon of Oswego, New York, who believed in a more enlightened view of discipline. Sheldon favored the cultivation of the senses and the exploration of man's physical, moral, and intellectual capacities.

Herbart had a pronounced influence upon both primary and secondary instruction. He believed that learning should produce a many-sided individual. Herbart's influence was felt in the U.S. through the McMurrays and through the National Herbartian Society. Herbartian ideals triumphed in education until Dewey subjected them to a searching criticism.

In the 20th century the greatest European influence on American elementary education has been Maria Montessori. She believed in the natural capacities of children. She encouraged systematic stimulation of the senses in a prepared environment combining both discipline and creativity. The Montessori movement has grown rapidly in the second half of the 20th century. For example, a Montessori school was established in 1959 in Santa Monica by Tom Laughlin, a brilliant educator. He began with six students and four years later had a waiting list of 800.

American interest in European elementary education was stimulated in 1837 by a report of C. E. Stowe who showed that much could be learned, especially from German practices. Horace Mann in his *Reports* lauded the Prussian school system. He wanted elementary education to be better organized and more adequately financed. Henry Barnard looked upon Pestalozzi as the model educator for children. Barnard wanted to improve the quality of teachers for the elementary profession; hence he was especially interested in teachers' institutes. Francis Parker was a pioneer in progressive education. He introduced crafts and arts into the elementary school curriculum. Inspired by Froebel, he dwelled upon the play activities of children whose growth was not to be inhibited by coercion. He tried to change the classroom so that instead of being "old, stiff and unnatural," it would be a place of work and full expression.

The achievements of Dewey and Kilpatrick made the elementary school a place of life activities. Projects were encouraged. The interests of children became paramount. Community understanding was furthered in progressive education.

The ideals of Helen Parkhurst should not be omitted. She based her educational program, the Dalton plan, upon the principles of freedom, cooperation and careful budgeting of time. A student in the Dalton plan had a flexible program; he was like a junior scientist in a laboratory and he could move freely from class to class and proceed according to his own rate of achievement.

Free elementary education was unknown in the 18th century. Only in 1834 did Pennsylvania enact a law which made provision for free elementary schools. In 1890 Connecticut made elementary education compulsory. At the end of World War I this became a requirement for all the states of the Union.

SCHOOLS TODAY AND YESTERDAY

The curriculum of the early schools was extremely authoritarian, as the regulations of Rhode Island indicate. These were first issued in 1800.

The Instruction shall be uniform in the several schools, and shall consist of spelling, Reading, the use of Capital letters and Punctuation, Writing, English Grammar & Arithmetic.

The Pronunciation shall be uniform in the several schools & the standard shall be the *Critical Pronouncing Dictionary* of John Walker.

The following Books, and none others, shall be used in the several schools, viz: Alden's *Spelling Book*, first & second part, *New Testament, American Preceptor*, Murray's *Sequel to the English Reader*, Murray's *Abridgement of English Grammar* and Dabols' *Arithmetic*.

The scholars shall be put in separate classes according to their several improvements, each sex by itself. . .

The Scholars shall be excused from attending the schools on Saturdays, on Christmas day, on the 4th of July, on public feasts and Thanksgiving, on the last Monday in April, on the day of Regimental Training; on the day succeeding each quarterly visitation and during the whole of Commencement Week. But on no other days shall the Preceptors dismiss the Schools without permission obtained from the Town Council.

As Discipline and Good Government are absolutely necessary to improvement it is indispensible that the scholars should implicitly obey the Regulations of the Schools.[3]

In Boston Caleb Bingham describes elementary instruction.

The books used in the reading schools were, the *Holy Bible*, Webster's *Spelling Book*, Webster's *Third Part*, and the *Young Lady's Accidence*. The *Children's Friend* and Morse's *Geography* were allowed, not required; and "Newspapers were to be introduced, occasionally, at the discretion of the masters." . . .

Furthermore, it was ordered that, in the writing schools, the children "should begin to learn arithmetic at eleven years of age; that, at twelve, they should be taught to make pens." Until eleven years old, all the pupils did, in a whole forenoon or afternoon, was to write one page of a copy book, not exceeding ten lines. When they began to cipher, it

---

[3] *Centennial Report School Committee, 1899-1900,* pp. 42-43.

rarely happened that they performed more than two sums in the simplest rules. These were set in the pupil's manuscript, and the operation was there recorded by him. No printed book was used. Such writing and ciphering, however, were too much for one day, and the boys who ciphered, only did so every other day. If it be asked, how were the three hours of school time occupied? The answer is, in one of three ways, — in mischief; in play; or in idleness. . . .

In the reading schools, the course was for every child to read one verse of the *Bible*, or a short paragraph of the *Third Part*. The master heard the first and second, that is, the two highest classes, and the usher heard the two lowest. While one class was reading, the other studied the spelling lesson. The lesson was spelled by the scholars in turn, so that, the classes being large, each boy seldom spelled more than one or two words. In grammar, the custom was to recite six or more lines once a fortnight, and to go through the book three times before any application of it was made to what was called parsing.[4]

An elementary school of 1857 was described in the following terms by Superintendent Philbrick:

The accommodations were generally, judged by the present standard, poor in respect to light, air, play-grounds, out-buildings, ventilation, the size of rooms, heating, furniture, and, indeed, in almost every particular that could be named. The schoolrooms were excessively crowded, each teacher having an average of upwards of sixty pupils. The percentage of attendance was low, and truancy was rife. The principle of gradation had not been introduced, and each teacher had six classes. There were no desks for the use of slates, the pupils being seated in movable arm chairs, which, in their day, were considered a great improvement; no tablets of any value, and few blackboards. The school-books were objectionable, and there was no program, in the proper sense of the word. There was no systematic teaching of writing, drawing, music, object lessons, gymnastics, or phonic exercises. In numbers little or nothing was taught beyond the mechanical memorizing of the elementary tables. And, although the efforts of the teachers were concentrated principally upon reading and spelling, the pupils were very deficient in these branches, judged by the present standard.[5]

School architecture was inadequate, as a report of Mayhew in Michigan indicates.

Under this head it will be sufficient to enumerate the principal features of school-houses as they are.

---

[4] *American Journal of Education*, V, pp. 325–334.
[5] *Twenty-ninth Semi-Annual Report of the Superintendent of Public Schools of the City of Boston*, 1874, pp. 162-165.

They are, almost universally, badly located, exposed to the noise, dust, and danger of the highway, unattractive, if not positively repulsive in their external and internal appearance, and built at the least possible expense of material and labor.

They are too small. There is no separate entry for boys and girls appropriately fitted up; no sufficient space for the convenient seating and necessary movements of the scholars; no platform, desk, or recitation room for the teacher.

They are badly lighted. The windows are inserted on three or four sides of the room without blinds or curtains to prevent the inconvenience and danger from cross-lights, and the excess of light falling directly on the eyes or reflected from the book, and the distracting influence of passing objects and events out of doors.

They are not properly ventilated. The purity of the atmosphere is not preserved by providing for the escape of such portions of the air as have become offensive and poisonous by the process of breathing, and by the matter which is constantly escaping from the lungs in vapor, and from the surface of the body in insensible perspiration.

They are imperfectly warmed. The rush of cold air through cracks and defects in the doors, windows, floor and plastering is not guarded against. The air which is heated is already impure from having been breathed, and made more so by noxious gases arising from the burning of floating particles of vegetable and animal matter coming in contact with the hot iron. The heat is not equally diffused, so that one portion of a school-room is frequently overheated, while another portion, especially the floor, is too cold.

They are not furnished with seats and desks, properly made and adjusted to each other, and arranged in such a manner as to promote the comfort and convenience of the scholars, and the easy supervision on the part of the teacher. The seats are too high and too long, with no suitable support for the back, and especially for the younger children. The desks are too high for the seats, and are either attached to the wall on three sides of the room, so that the faces of the scholars are turned from the teacher, and a portion of them at least are tempted constantly to look out at the windows, — or the seats are attached to the wall on opposite sides, and the scholars sit facing each other. The aisles are not so arranged that each scholar can go to and from his seat, change his position, have access to his books, attend to his own business, be seen and approached by the teacher, without incommoding any other.

They are not provided with blackboards, maps, clock, thermometer, and other apparatus and fixtures which are indispensable to a well regulated and instructed school.[6]

---

[6] *American Journal of Education*, IX, pp. 491–492.

The physical setting of the modern elementary school is completely different from what it was a hundred years ago. Today the elementary school emphasizes adequate lighting, and it employs an international style of architecture influenced by such masters as Wright, Neutra, and Saarinen. The buildings are designed for multiple purposes; laboratories are included, and in many schools there is movable furniture. The modern school is informal and friendly. Frequently it employs a vivid color scheme. Sometimes children are encouraged to work on murals so that they can make their own contribution to the physical setting of the school.

The range of books has become extensive. Not only are there basic texts, but supplementary reading is stressed. School libraries and audio-visual material have been added to the elementary curriculum. In many school-rooms reference books and pamphlets add to the stimulation of children.

Before children are taught how to read today, they are exposed to stories, and their psychological readiness is tested. An attempt is made to correlate pictures and the written material. With the advent of television, children are more exposed to visual stimuli; hence they learn to read at an earlier age.

In the early part of the 20th century, reading was usually taught to one group. This procedure standardized learning. The student who was called upon by his teacher would rise and read aloud. If he was outstanding, he would not receive enough encouragement and individual attention. The child who had visual or psychological difficulties would not receive the individual counseling he needed. To overcome these difficulties, reading now is taught in small groups; special aid is available for the under achiever and enrichment is available for the gifted.

In considering the elementary curriculum we should be conscious of its advances. The elementary schools have been successful in developing a degree of original expression in writing. The process starts with children dictating a story to their teacher. Later, simple letters are written to parents or friends. There is still too much reliance on workbooks and on texts, and not enough emphasis on the appreciation of poetry and the writing of poems and short stories. Many teachers are so critical that they discourage the first efforts of children and thus inhibit their efforts toward self-expression.

On the elementary level, concerted attempts are made to develop better speech patterns. Some teachers stress mainly the formal, grammatical parts of speech; others regard them as tools for more creative communication through which the student expresses his total personality. It is especially important that personality factors be observed at the elementary level. Frequently, children are shy and do not want to express themselves. It is the task of the teacher to bring out their ability and to develop their powers of communication.

In the teaching of arithmetic, drill is not used as much as in former times. The emphasis now is to explain the meaning of arithmetic and apply it to life situations. Some of the new mathematical advances, which usually have been introduced at the secondary and college levels, are now being explored in elementary school.

Science activities are being intensified in every grade. Children are interested in the space age and often know more about some of its aspects than their teachers. Science fairs have made experimentation more exciting and have created community interest. Foreign languages are being introduced on the elementary level; in the Montessori schools a foreign language is taught on the nursery level. Language programs tend to be sequential. Thus in the Beverly Hills school system a child may have eight years of French or Spanish. In some schools even Russian is given on the elementary level.

The arts are not neglected on the elementary level. Music involves rhythmic activity as well as singing, listening and the playing of instruments. Folk dancing is especially valuable at the elementary level.

Both applied and fine arts are taught. Dramatics has become popular. Children work in various media; some do weaving, others block prints, still others do finger-painting. There are classes in art employing crayons, water colors, colored paper, wood and clay.

Social studies have a prominent place in the elementary curriculum. This frequently involves correlation of history and geography; in some schools the social studies and the sciences are fused. Children are taken on many field-trips. In culturally deprived communities, enrichment along academic and cultural lines is especially important.

To indicate the variety of subjects on the elementary level let us look at the California Education Code, which decrees that all elementary schools provide instruction in the following:

(1) reading
(2) writing
(3) spelling
(4) language study
(5) arithmetic
(6) geography

(7) history of the United States and of California
(8) civics, including a study of the Declaration of Independence and of the Constitution of the United States
(9) music
(10) art
(11) preparation for healthful living
(12) manners and morals
(13) nature of alcohol and narcotics
(14) fire prevention
(15) public safety and accident prevention
(16) thrift
(17) humane treatment of animals
(18) American history and
(19) physical education

In addition, the State Code, in section 11271, includes the study of science. The Code further declares that elective subjects may be added by the local Board of Education. The Los Angeles County Course of Study makes provision for industrial arts and homemaking.

Many children are handicapped because of social, economic, or racial origin. The majority of Mexican-American children do not graduate from high school; many have difficulty in speaking English. When they do not obtain special help and orientation, they tend to be unmotivated and fall behind in their studies. It is almost axiomatic that those who dislike school tend to develop anti-social tendencies. Thus delinquency is a special problem in children so handicapped.

Much can be done to curb delinquency at all levels of education. Prevention of delinquency should start, not in junior high school, but as early as nursery school. Parents and community leaders should be involved in the educative process. Special orientation teachers with warm personalities should be hired; social workers should discuss problems of child guidance with parents. The class size should be reduced so that the teacher can do more counseling. A more flexible curriculum should be devised to meet the needs of a variety of special groups, including the gifted as well as the underprivileged.

P.T.A. attendance for parents should be encouraged. For example, if many parents are Spanish speaking, some of the P.T.A. programs should be in Spanish. There should never be a condescending attitude toward another culture; indeed, the richness and vitality of the Spanish background should be emphasized. The principal should have a constant open house for students and parents; he should work closely with ministers, lawyers, doctors, business men and other responsible members of the community.

The need for this type of program is illustrated in many schools in Southern California. For example, in one school near Los Angeles the population moves in and out of the district. The economic standard is low. The school may start with 500 children and end with 800. In one class during the first month six new children were added; one was a boy of eight from Mexico City who could not speak English. The I.Q.'s in the class ranged from 85 to 150.

The school had employed an orientation teacher who held special classes for children with language handicaps. A budget cut forced the elimination of this program. The result was that the needs of the minority groups were not met.

THE TEACHER'S ROLE

In elementary education the teacher performs many functions. He is a counselor, friend, artist, scientist, psychologist, and he provides for flexibility of action. Gladys Andrews describes his various roles:

HELPING — David, to understand an abstraction, for instance, of *opening* the garage door.

— Tim, Sue and Jane develop a sketch to show what happens when they turn on the light switch.

— Steve, a sixth grader, take a series of photographs to show the stages of the moon as he observed them during the month of October.

ENCOURAGING — The sixth grade group to chart the flow of traffic past the school, every hour during the day. The facts collected were used in a series of editorials prepared by the class. They also made posters and developed a campaign for younger children in the school concerning safety practices in crossing the street and for getting in and out of automobiles. Information secured from their study ultimately helped to redirect traffic near the school, thus making the school less of a thoroughfare. Visits to the city council followed the editorials in the newspaper, and graphs and charts were prepared to support the proposals made. Two of the boys depicted the traffic problems through a chalked mural.

. . .

MAKING — Bulletin board space available for each group in the school. Extensive bulletin board space was arranged in the halls for individual groups to keep the displays current for describing a variety of products of their work. Some of these displays were made on an individual basis; at other times displays were the result of small group work; and often the bulletin boards showed a contribution of the entire class. Samples of bulletin boards included: two and three dimensional forms, stabiles, collages, murals, pictures, sketches, graphs, charts, songs, poems, stories, miniatures, constructions of playground equipment, descriptions of games, ideas in science, formulas, questions and answers, photographs, musical scores, information in foreign languages, and various paper and wood constructions. . . .

EXPLORING — The contents of the cracks of the sidewalk provided interest for the fifth grade group who developed and charted animal communities residing in these cracks. Some members of the group also wrote their own stories about an animal or community of animals they had seen. . . .

— With old automobile tires and different size balls to develop games by the fifth grade to be taught to the third grade.

— The different kinds of materials being used in constructing a nearby bridge. Small samples of the materials were collected and a miniature of the bridge constructed by some of the fourth graders.

. . .

ORGANIZING — Trails in the woods around the school. One trail led to places where children could see different rock formations; another trail was called the fungi trail, and the third trail had to do with the parade of the plant kingdom. In order to develop these trails children had to make extensive studies of available rocks, fungi, and plant life. They then arranged tours. Designs were made for trails with original symbols appropriate for the type of observation to be made.

— Plans for the sixth grade week at the conservation camp. Children made plans for transportation, clothing, menus, recreation, first aid, and safety. A bulletin was prepared by the committee to report its work. A daily newspaper for each day at camp was planned, printed, and distributed.

.   .   .

CHANGING

— The classroom around by arranging the seats so that each person represented a particular place in South America. Care was taken in terms of relationships of places to each other and distances approximated. The discussion centered around people, places, customs, work and products.

TAKING

— The second grade class down the street to find out about the new kinds of disturbing sounds being made in construction of the new apartment house. Upon returning to the classroom they recalled some of the sounds and tried to represent them first by verbal symbols and then by organizing them into *sound studies* and *chants*.

— The fifth grade to the State Capitol to see the legislature in session. Upon returning to school they set up a miniature legislative assembly to debate ways of solving the traffic problem created by the bicycles at school. This was extended to the entire school. Representatives from various classrooms in the school represented the counties of the state. The public interest was debated and actual policies were planned concerning the bicycle problem at Jolof School.

.   .   .

DISCOVERING — The challenges in stunt or trick activities with a group of first graders. The children were divided into pairs and asked to challenge each other to a new and different stunt which they *made up*. Each twosome had a space in which to work, and they were asked to avoid the kind of stunt which would need a mat. When their stunts were completed and had been given as a challenge to their partner, they then had to think of a name which would describe the stunt. In turn, the twosome challenged the whole class to their stunts.

LISTENING — For "found sounds" with the fourth grade, and recording the sounds. Effort was made to help several small groups within the group capture their sounds, reproduce them and put them into a total sound composition. As the group visited the seashore, one group captured the sounds of the breaking of the waves while another group identified the sounds that came from the smashing of the water against the rocks. The third group reproduced the sounds the wind made as it passed through the shrubs and trees. There were also peculiar insects making sounds at intervals; these were recorded and reproduced. The class as a whole organized their sounds and reproduced them in a composition.

— To Haydn's *Surprise Symphony*. Children described responses or a personal feeling they had to one of the symphonic movements. The descriptions of their feeling were expressed in form, color or words.

. . .

INVITING — Questions about things that come to the minds of youngsters. The teacher played the role of raising questions such as:
Wonder why?
What makes you think so?
What do you suppose it would be like?
How do you know?

Tell us more, could you?

Does it have a use? What's it used for?

How old is it?

Does it feel (look, move)?

Talk some more about that.

Do you see anything wrong with this?

What suggestions could you make for improving it?

What variations in colors do you see?

What do other people think about this?

What about its beauty?

What do you see in this?

What impressions do you have?

Wonder what makes it like this?

PROVIDING — Selections of meaningful materials from the day's newspaper. These selections took the form of incomplete situations or unfinished stories. The children were encouraged to complete each account showing alternate ways that the article or news item could turn out. This also took the form of unfinished stories with marked human interest items. After the children's work had been completed, some compared their ideas with the original item.

.   .   .

EVALUATING — The group's trip to the United Nations. The teacher asked the group to describe briefly observations made at the United Nations. A series of observations was listed. The teacher then asked the group to look at the composite list and satisfy themselves if their feelings and information about the United Nations were covered. Following the extension and refinement of the group's impressions, plans were made for a huge mural. The class was given time for planning, organizing, and portraying their ideas. When the mural was finished it not only served as an evaluation device for the group but was placed in the hall for others to enjoy. Other impressions of the United Nations were portrayed through mobiles, sculpture and a story of the "United Nations in the Future."

ASSESSING — The sixth grade's understanding of the meaning of the concept of Thanksgiving. The teacher opened the discussion with the group using the question, "What does Thanksgiving really mean to you?" Ideas were discussed. They were then classified, organized, and terminated into a class proclamation. The children were pleased with their efforts and wanted to print it in "Proclamation Style." They then sent representatives to a local printing company to find out about styles of printing. With their information and with some original ideas of their own they constructed a huge easel at the front door of the school on which they printed their original Thanksgiving proclamation. These are but a few of the many experiences which emerge daily in classrooms which teachers could capitalize upon to begin the process of releasing creativity in boys and girls.[7]

With the expansion of knowledge it appears that drastic changes will occur in the elementary school. Special laboratories will be needed to meet the needs of children who are extremely sophisticated in their scientific quest. Great artists and poets may become scholars in residence on the elementary level. Guidance facilities will have to become more organized and more readily available for elementary schools. A concentrated attempt will have to be made to attract male teachers so that a better ratio between men and women can exist on the elementary level. This does not mean that the work of dedicated women should be slighted; women like Peabody were the great pioneers in elementary education. There will be greater stress upon parental involvement, upon lifting the level of minority groups and thus aiding the democratic process.

It should be pointed out that status seeking is a constant danger in education. It is a mistake to value higher education and to underrate the early education of children. All levels are equally significant. Indeed, psychology teaches us that as we are guided, loved, and motivated in our earliest, most impressionable years, so our entire personality is affected.

A more concerted investment in elementary education will produce happier adults, a more stable society and a more creative spirit, not only in our schools, but in our entire institutional system.

[7] Gladys Andrews, "Releasing Creativity" in Fleming, *Curriculum for Today's Boys and Girls*, pp. 418–430.

CHAPTER THIRTY-THREE

The High School

HISTORICAL TRENDS

One of the main achievements of the American system of education is the comprehensive public high school. A symbol of cultural diffusion, it unites various groups in the community. It offers a variety of programs, for both those with academic goals and those with vocational goals. It contributes to equality of opportunity. It was the basis of the Americanization of millions in the past; today it is the foundation for the mastery of the complexities of the Atomic Age.

Yet, severe critics, like Admiral Rickover, have attacked the comprehensive high school. They want more selective education and hope to imitate certain parts of European education which are essentially aristocratic. They feel that the high school today retards the most gifted and appeals only to the mediocre students.

Their criticism is superficial. To be sure, more imaginative programs could be established for the gifted and more academic training could be given to the able students, but democracy would be injured if the public high school were not supported and if private education would take the place of our public schools. Indeed, English and German educators are so impressed with the structure of the American high school that they want to use it as a pattern for European education.

The early high school, as exemplified by the Boston Latin Grammar School, was not a democratic institution. Its appeal was for the few and it stressed mainly the classical languages. Discipline was harsh. Wealthy people supported it liberally; sometimes, as we have seen, lotteries added money to the school. There were few scholarships; most of the students belonged to the professional or to the capitalist class.

The curriculum of the Boston Latin Grammar School was based upon a grammatical knowledge of ancient languages; utilitarian subjects were slighted; drill and memorization were used by the instructors; homework was excessive. The thought behind the school was that if education was painful it was bound to be beneficial to the students and to society.

Between 1751 and 1800 the Academy made its appearance. The first was founded in 1751 by Franklin. It taught modern languages as well as the sciences. Practical subjects, such as bookkeeping, were not slighted. The Academy admitted both sexes; its clientele came not only from the upper and middle classes, but included members of the working class as well.

The Academy, which expanded educational opportunity, reacted against narrow denominationalism, although most academies provided for religious training. The philosophy of the Academy was close to Locke's. Its aim was to produce men and women of the world who had practical interests and a sense of public responsibility.

Thousands of academies flourished in the nineteenth century. The Academy did not provide free tuition. Its standards varied from state to state; its financial support often was inadequate.

The first public high school, founded in 1821 in Boston, was a school for boys. In 1826 a school for girls was established. The Boston high school had a three year course and emphasized the knowledge of English and utilitarian studies.

In 1827 James Carter became a leader in making the high school a common institution in Massachusetts. Chicago, in 1856, established the first co-educational high school and thus created a pattern which has influenced all of secondary education.

19TH CENTURY TRENDS

An excellent description of the 19th century teacher is given by Oliver Wendell Holmes.

The morning came: I reached the classic hall;
A clock-face eyed me, staring from the wall;
Beneath its hands a printed line I read:
YOUTH IS LIFE'S SEED-TIME: so the clock-face said:
Some took its counsel, as the sequel showed,
Sowed their wild oats, and reaped as they had sowed.

How all comes back! The upward slanting floor,
The master's throne that flanked the central door,
The long, outstretching alley that divides
The rows of desks that stand on either side,
The staring boys, a face to every desk,
Bright, dull, pale, blooming, common, picturesque.
Grave is the Master's look; his forehead wears
Thick rows of wrinkles, prints of worrying cares;
Uneasy lie the heads of all that rule,
His most of all whose kingdom is a school.
Supreme he sits; before the awful frown
That bends his brows the boldest eye goes down;
Not more submissive Israel heard and saw
At Sinai's foot the Giver of the Law.[1]

The 19th century high school was classical in outlook, as the following description of a Cincinnati high school indicates:

FIRST YEAR

First Session	*Second Session*
English Grammar, Brown or Pinneo, Completed	Weld's Latin Lessons, to Part II.
English History, Goodrich or Markham, Completed	Fitch's Physical Geography Andrews' and Stoddard's Latin Grammar
Ray's Algebra to Sec. 172	Ray's Algebra, to Sec. 305
	Physical Geography (3 lessons)
	Reading (2 lessons)

(Five lessons in each of the above weekly)

Once a Week During the Year
Lectures, by the Principal, on Morals and Manners
Aids to Composition, completed
Composition and Declamation, by sections, each
    one in three weeks
Reading and Vocal Music
Penmanship, if needed.

---

[1] Holmes, "The School Boy."

SECOND YEAR

First Session	Second Session
Weld's Latin Lessons, to History	Weld's Latin Lessons, completed
Andrews' and Stoddard's Latin Grammar	Andrews and Stoddard, completed
Geometry, Davies' Legendre, to Book V	Geometry, Davies' Legendre, to Book IX
Gray's Natural Philosophy, to Pneumatics	Gray's Natural Philosophy, completed

(Five lessons in each of the above weekly)

Once a Week During the Year

Reading, Elemental Sounds
Rhetoric and Vocal Music
Composition and Declamation, by sections

THIRD YEAR

First Session	Second Session
Silliman's Chemistry, to Sec. 282	Silliman's Chemistry, to Vegetable Chemistry
Algebra and Spherics, Ray's and Davies' Legendre completed	Davies' Trigonometry, completed
Andrews' Caesar or Sallust, 50 Sections (3rd)	Cooper's Virgil's Aeneid, 3 books (3rd)
German or French (3 days)	German or French (3 days)

Once a Week During the Year

Constitution of the United States
Hedge's Logic
Reading, Rhetoric, and Vocal Music
Composition and Declamation, by sections

FOURTH YEAR

First Session	Second Session
Cutter's Physiology & Hygiene	Davies' Navigation and Surveying
McIntire's Astronomy	Weber's General History
Gray and Adams' Geology	Wayland's Mental Philosophy
Folsom's Cicero, 3 Orations (3 days)	Evidences of Christianity (1 day)
Moral Philosophy (1 day)	German or French (3 days)
German or French (3 days)	

Once a Week During the Year
Critical Readings, Vocal Music
Compositions, by sections
Original Addresses, by sections

College Class
For those preparing to enter college, the following may be substituted
for the regular studies of the fourth year,
Virgil's Aeneid, six books
Caesar or Sallust, completed
Cicero's Orations, six
Crosby's Greek Grammar
Felton's Greek Reader.[2]

THE OUTSTANDING TEACHER

What makes for a good high school teacher? What qualities are
most important? What are his greatest contributions? The following
papers may supply a clue.

A student of education described his most important high
school teacher:

Beyond a doubt my most important teacher was one that I had in
my senior year in high school. He was young, well-dressed, filled
with humor and had a most understanding smile. He was dynamic
and exciting in his speech and he was sad when the occasion demanded. He was interesting and interested . . . he was warm and
at times, hard — but always was he real.

Strangely, up until that time I had detested any course in English —
but he made it different. Poetry came alive and the drama exciting. His
requirements were not stringent and yet I found, as did others, that
more of my spare time was involved in reading and even memorizing
works like Rudyard Kipling's "Gunga Din" and finding pleasure in
plays by Ibsen and others.

And never once did I feel that he was trying to manipulate or mold
me. Never did he ridicule and yet he could be angered. Each of his
students, I am sure, felt somehow needed, wanted, accepted and successful — he gave you a feeling of great self-respect (and how I needed
that).

[2] *Journal of American Education*, Vol. IV, 1858, pp. 520–525.

As I recall his classroom scene I don't see a sea of immobile faces and clasped hands which so often had prevailed. He was a lecturer, to be true, but never dull. I find that often have I tried to pattern myself in his fashion — not in his teaching exactly, but in him as a person. How he would have reacted, what he would have said, what he would have advised.

In short, he was contagious, refreshing, challenging, different. He did not allow you to think . . . he made you ponder about life.

Another great teacher is described in the following terms:

Bette Sherman stands out above all because she inspired me to pursue my present profession — teaching physical education. As a sophomore student in high school I was a pupil in her class. She was new to California and showed a definite enthusiastic attitude toward her work. A native of Minnesota, she had, what I would call, mid-western zip and stimulated her students into performing well. She demanded certain things — motivated a sense of responsibility on the student's part and most important I feel — she commanded respect. She was skilled in athletics, very well groomed, possessor of a pleasing personality, and interested in the student.

This teacher set an example of character of the highest type. She was firm, but fair and always positive in approach. I looked up to her and still do. I feel that any success I have had during my first semester of teaching is, in part, due to her influence upon me. I have gained both tangible and intangible things from her.

A choir director left a deep impact.

Mr. Tom Sanderson, my high school choir director, was the best teacher I have ever had. He loved what he taught and he loved whom he taught. He was wise and gracious. His pupils respected him and everything he did, for he never did anything he didn't whole-heartedly believe in.

When he explained music to the class, it was almost as if he worshipped the pages it was written on. He studied every meaning in every piece of music he gave us and conveyed those meanings to us so that we might be able to sing the words with the proper attitude and understanding. In doing this, he taught us the value of an open mind in the understanding of others and what they think. I never appreciated the finer things in life until I met Mr. Sanderson.

Although the trait of conveying the innermost meanings of things and the understanding to appreciate them is a highly admirable one, I think I valued him most because he was so happy in what he was doing. So often, it seems that people don't do what they're happy in and they have a certain air about them that shows it. This is not true with Mr.

Sanderson; he loved his work and just seemed to glow at the very mention of it.

He was the perfect example of my ideal teacher: poet, philosopher, teacher, counselor, and friend all rolled up into one.

A young woman became truly unforgettable to one of her students.

Young, attractive, and unmarried was my wonderful ninth grade teacher of social studies and English. But her physical beauty is not what drew the students to her — she was a friend and a very intelligent woman. So highly respected was she that she motivated an earnest desire to study and learn. What more can a teacher do?

One of her strong points was her absolute control over the class. Usually the chatter or whisper of a high school class is almost uncontrollable, especially if lunch hour is approaching! Here, however, silence prevailed. The students listened devotedly to her lucid explanations because she was able to make learning an enjoyable and dramatic process.

As an incentive for better work, she posted a chart on the bulletin board indicating the total number of points each person had received from assignments and tests. Of course, no one wanted to lose such an obvious race as that! Occasionally she made extra credit available to raise the points.

Class assignments were by no means easy. Weekly assignment sheets were distributed, accompanied by several questions, charts to make, and reports to give. We compiled a Civil War notebook of approximately eighty pages and, at the end of the year, a complete history of some phase of American life, which amounted to almost 100 pages of written material.

Tests were also of a high level for the age group. They were extremely comprehensive, including up to six pages of extensive essays, fill-ins, and the like. We were even given a final exam from Leif Erickson to Eisenhower! I can honestly say that, throughout high school, I never took a more difficult test. It was always a challenge, certainly, but because of our eagerness and her excellent guidance, we were able to accomplish a great deal and earn an 'A' besides.

Outside of class, as well as in, her outstanding qualities were made known to the students. Every day students occupied her classroom during the lunch hour, visiting her. Through casual conversation, she taught us much more of life than merely academic ideas.

Another student remembers his mathematics teacher.

Donald Cross is head of the mathematics department at John Marshall High School in Los Angeles. Being in his thirties, he has acquired knowledge and experience as a mathematics teacher without losing touch with the younger generation. His subtle humor often broke up my drowsy afternoon algebra class. He always claimed the ancient "cross" product as his own invention. Half way through a complex derivation he was liable to turn around and ask the class what the class was going to get him for Christmas. You could not dislike Mr. Cross even if he was failing you.

His tests were tough but comprehensive and fair. These were the two most important qualities of his tests. The element of luck was an insignificant feature of anybody's success in his class. It was simply a matter of studying enough. His points of emphasis were no secret. This learning climate with respect for the teacher and absence of tension in the classroom was conducive to the maximum absorption of the material by the students.

Mr. Cross had complete command of his subject. This was important because indecision in the presentation of an argument often negates its logic. This is especially significant for a math teacher because his effectiveness depends on the logical development of the topic. This fine instructor conveyed to me an enthusiasm for the order, logic, and organization of mathematics. Since my major will be either math or engineering, I will always be indebted to him for the fine foundation he gave me for future mathematics courses.

The most important qualities of the good high school teacher can be summarized as follows:

(1) He has the ability to learn from his students
(2) He is enthusiastic about his work
(3) He makes his subject vital and important
(4) He has developed a degree of self-reliance without an attitude of arrogance
(5) He is able to change his methods
(6) He is interested in his students and looks upon them as individuals
(7) He has the ability to motivate students to learn for themselves
(8) He has developed genuine friendliness and a sense of humor
(9) He projects a sense of physical and emotional vitality
(10) He is youthful in his attitude toward life and is never shocked by the behavior of youngsters
(11) He controls the class without using arbitrary discipline
(12) He relates class learning to community problems
(13) He is patient with the slow learner
(14) He respects all students and never talks down to them
(15) He is expanding his own knowledge

(16) He cooperates with his colleagues and is interested in inter-departmental work

(17) He is a trusted counselor whom students seek out when they have emotional or scholastic difficulties

(18) He makes learning more significant than grades

(19) He teaches not just ideas but an understanding of the complexity of life

(20) He regards the life of education as a vocation and a sacred privilege

OBJECTIVES OF SECONDARY EDUCATION

The aims of secondary education were best defined by the Commission on the Reorganization of Secondary Education of the National Education Association in 1918. The report called for a reformulation of secondary education to meet the needs of a dynamic society. It noted that secondary education, like many other American institutions, tends to be too conservative to reach its goal, which is the realization of democracy. This involves both the individual and his social needs. The individual is not to be exploited by society; at the same time the society's needs are not to be disregarded by the individual.

Seven areas are covered by the Report. The first deals with health.

Health needs can not be neglected during the period of secondary education without serious danger to the individual and the race. The secondary school should therefore provide health instruction, inculcate health habits, organize an effective program of physical activities, regard health needs in planning work and play, and co-operate with home and community in safe-guarding and promoting health interests.

To carry out such a program it is necessary to arouse the public to recognize that the health needs of young people are of vital importance to society, to secure teachers competent to ascertain and meet the needs of individual pupils and able to inculcate in the entire student body a love for clean sport, to furnish adequate equipment for physical activities, and to make the school building, its rooms and surroundings, conform to the best standards of hygiene and sanitation.[3]

Next the report discusses fundamentals.

Much of the energy of the elementary school is properly devoted to teaching certain fundamental processes, such as reading, writing,

---

[3] Commission on the Reorganization of Secondary Education, N.E.A., *Cardinal Principles of Secondary Education*, 1918.

arithmetical computations, and the elements of oral and written expression. The facility that a child of 12 or 14 may acquire in the
use of these tools is not sufficient for the needs of modern life. This
is particularly true of the mother tongue. Proficiency in many of these
processes may be increased more effectively by their application to
new material than by the formal reviews commonly employed in grades
seven and eight. Throughout the secondary school, instruction and
practice must go hand in hand, but as indicated in the report of the
committee on English, only so much theory should be taught at any
one time as will show results in practice.[4]

Next the report turns to the family.

Worthy home-membership as an objective calls for the development of those qualities that make the individual a worthy member
of a family, both contributing to and deriving benefit from that
membership.

This objective applies to both boys and girls. The social studies
should deal with the home as a fundamental social institution and clarify its relation to the wider interests outside. Literature should interpret and idealize the human elements that go to make the home.
Music and art should result in more beautiful homes and in greater
joy therein. The coeducational school with a faculty of men and
women should, in its organization and its activities, exemplify wholesome relations between boys and girls and men and women.

Home membership as an objective should not be thought of solely
with reference to future duties. These are the better guaranteed if
the school helps 'the pupils to take the right attitude toward present
home responsibilities and interprets to them the contribution of the
home to their development.[5]

The fourth area discussed is vocational education.

Vocational education should equip the individual to secure a livelihood for himself and those dependent on him, to serve society well
through his vocation, to maintain the right relationships toward his
fellow workers and society, and, as far as possible, to find in that
vocation his own best development.

This ideal demands that the pupil explore his own capacities and
aptitudes, and make a survey of the world's work, to the end that he
may select his vocation wisely. Hence, an effective program of vocational guidance in the secondary school is essential.

Vocational education should aim to develop an appreciation of
the significance of the vocation to the community, and a clear con-

---

[4] *Ibid.*
[5] *Ibid.*

ception of the right relations between the members of the chosen vocation, between different vocational groups, between employer and employee, and between producer and consumer. These aspects of vocational education, heretofore neglected, demand emphatic attention.

The extent to which the secondary school should offer training for a specific vocation depends upon the vocation, the facilities that the school can acquire, and the opportunity that the pupil may have to obtain such training later. To obtain satisfactory results those proficient in that vocation should be employed as instructors and the actual conditions of the vocation should be utilized either within the high school or in cooperation with the home, farm, shop, or office. Much of the pupil's time will be required to produce such efficiency.[6]

The fifth area is civic education which

. . . should develop in the individual those qualities whereby he will act well his part as a member of neighborhood, town, or city, State, and Nation, and give him a basis for understanding international problems.

For such citizenship the following are essential: A many-sided interest in the welfare of the communities to which one belongs; loyalty to ideals of civic righteousness, practical knowledge of social agencies and institutions; good judgment as to means and methods that will promote one social end without defeating others; and as putting all these into effect, habits of cordial cooperation in social undertakings.

The school should develop the concept that the civic duties of men and women, while in part identical, are also in part supplementary. Differentiation in civic activities is to be encouraged, but not to the extent of loss of interest in the common problems with which all should cope.

Among the means for developing attitudes and habits important in a democracy are the assignment of projects and problems to groups of pupils for cooperative solution and the socialized recitation whereby the class as a whole develops a sense of collective responsibility. Both of these devices give training in collective thinking. Moreover, the democratic organization and administration of the school itself, as well as the cooperative relations of pupils and teacher, pupil and pupil, and teacher and teacher, are indispensable.[7]

The sixth is concerned with worthy use of leisure.

Education should equip the individual to secure from his leisure the re-creation of body, mind, and spirit, and the enrichment and enlargement of his personality.

---

[6] *Ibid.*
[7] *Ibid.*

This objective calls for the ability to utilize the common means of enjoyment, such as music, art, literature, drama, and social intercourse, together with the fostering in each individual of one or more special avocational interests.

Heretofore the high school has given little conscious attention to this objective. It has so exclusively sought intellectual discipline that it has seldom treated literature, art, and music so as to evoke right emotional response and produce positive enjoyment. Its presentation of science should aim, in part, to arouse a genuine appreciation of nature.[8]

Seventh is ethical character.

In a democratic society ethical character becomes paramount among the objectives of the secondary school. Among the means for developing ethical character may be mentioned the wise selection of content and methods of instruction in all subjects of study, the social contacts of pupils with one another and with teachers, the opportunities afforded by the organization and administration of the school for the development on the part of pupils of the sense of personal responsibility and initiative, and above all, the spirit of service and the principles of true democracy which should permeate the entire school — principal, teachers, and pupils.[9]

LEADERS

In the development of the high school two Harvard presidents deserve special notice: Charles W. Eliot and James Bryant Conant. Eliot, as chairman of the National Committee of Ten, also gave impetus to the founding of the junior high school. The first junior high school opened in Berkeley in 1909. The junior high school became a place of transition where curricular experimentation could be carried on and special attention could be paid to the needs of adolescents.

Conant made a searching study in the 1950's of the high schools in the U.S. He criticized small school districts, inadequate facilities, and poor counseling. He felt that English, the sciences, and foreign languages were not taught with sufficient vigor. Still, he was a firm champion of the comprehensive high school which he regarded as a pillar of the American system.

His recommendations included an expansion of guidance facilities, more stress on English composition, smaller classes and the consolida-

[8] *Ibid.*
[9] *Ibid.*

tion of school districts. He advocated that the most gifted should receive college level courses in high school and that those going on to university work should have four years of mathematics and extensive work in foreign languages.

The weakness of the Conant study lies in its neglect of the arts. With an inflexible curriculum they tend to assume a minor place. Moreover, he did not emphasize sufficiently the study of social issues, which broaden the students' outlook on domestic and world affairs. His view was too traditional, reflecting 19th century standards. The need of the high school is to examine the problems of our time, to develop the type of student who regards the present as his major concern.

Conant recommended that the number of small high schools be reduced. Certainly, large high schools can often provide better instruction. With better facilities, they can provide excellent laboratory equipment. They are often located near university centers and thus give additional intellectual stimulation. However, large high schools often have an impersonal spirit; only if he is outstanding does the student win favorable notice from the teachers and administrators. Small high schools frequently develop greater warmth of atmosphere and more concern for the individual student.

The real issue is not large versus small schools but developing a valid approach to education. Does the high school seek community involvement? Is its program dynamic? Is it a genuine intellectual center? Is it a therapeutic community? Does it encourage creativity and the arts? Is its administration democratic in practice as well as in theory? Does it appeal not only to the average but to the gifted student? Most important, does it produce alumni who have a vital sense of mission, who are concerned about humanity, who want to contribute to this civilization and who regard education as a continuous and self-activating process? The answer to these questions will determine the ultimate success of the comprehensive high school, which is one of America's great contributions to world civilization.

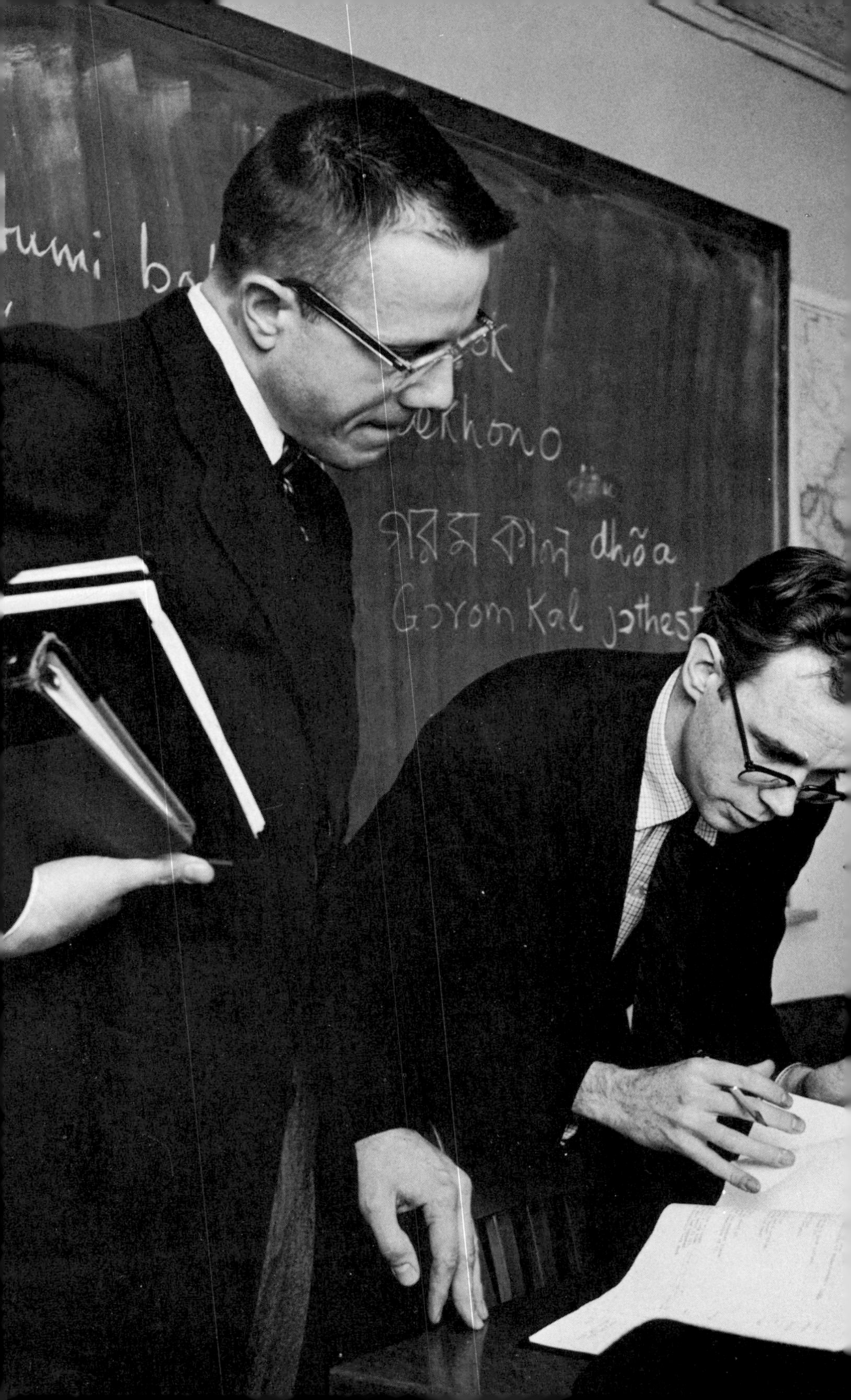
dhõa
Gɔrom Kal

CHAPTER THIRTY-FOUR

Leadership in Higher Education

SIGNIFICANCE OF LEADERSHIP

Leadership is the realization of genuine individuality. It is a *state of being*, not so much a state of doing. Where others see only vague possibilities, the genuine leader exemplifies the Aristotelian dictum that actuality precedes potentiality.

The quality of higher education depends on the quality of its leaders like Paul Smith at Whittier College and Norman Topping and Tracy Strevey at the University of Southern California. When college administrators are inspired and forward looking, their universities prosper. When they protect freedom in times of crisis, they set an example for the nation. When they develop a genuine philosophy of education, their ideals radiate to faculty members and students. On the other hand, when college leaders are guided merely by expediency and reflect only the wishes of their constituency, their institutions stagnate.

The United States has produced some notable college presidents. Some, like John Witherspoon, distinguished themselves both in politics and in higher education. Witherspoon, who came from Scotland, was an adherent to the common-sense school of philosophy, and he became enthusiastic about America's possibilities. A signer of the Declaration of Independence, he believed that freedom should prevail in politics and in higher education. Under his regime, Princeton became a more liberal place. A dedicated teacher, he instructed courses in moral philosophy, history, and theology. Before he came, the idealism of Berkeley had prevailed at Princeton; through his efforts the ideas of common sense realism took over. He was not a profound thinker, but a man of action who was constantly engaged in fund-raising campaigns. Although he was blind the last ten years of his life, he never lost enthusiasm for his position, and he was a vigorous proponent of higher education and a friend to his students until the last days of his college presidency.

At Union College, Eliphael Nott was president for sixty-two years, a unique achievement in American educational history. As a strong believer in progress he felt that the future would be glorious for the United States and would witness the end of wars and poverty. A foe of liquor, he would give long speeches in chapel on the evils of alcoholism and the need for temperance. When a student was found guilty of an offense, he would see President Nott personally who dealt with him in a paternal way. In fact, Nott regarded the college as an expanded family and tolerated no opposition from the faculty.

Nott's lasting impact came mainly through his course in moral philosophy. Like Witherspoon, he was not a profound or original thinker; his aim was to produce men who would read the book of the world. Thus, he reminded his students that academic concerns were not as significant as constructive citizenship. He wanted them to study modern languages as well as Greek and Latin. Books, he maintained, were to be studied thoroughly, but they were not substitutes for actual experience, which could be obtained only by understanding and analyzing various types of people. Like Mark Hopkins, he influenced his students not so much by his formal ideas as by his sincerity and his moral fervor.

One of his students was Francis Wayland, President of Brown, who tried to introduce democratic ideals into higher education. He advocated an elective system which meant that a student could proceed at his own speed under faculty guidance. An opponent of the overemphasis on the classics, Wayland urged more cultivation of science, history, modern languages, and even agriculture. He urged that higher education should appeal to all classes, the rich and the poor, the merchant and the minister, the lawyer and the farmer. To accomplish this goal, he felt that the present should be stressed rather than the glories of antiquity.

Opposition to his views was strong. Many intellectuals deplored his modern ideas. High-brow magazines denounced him as a cheap innovator. The Brown B.A. was attacked as being inferior, just as the B.A. at Chicago was attacked when Hutchins accelerated the program. The opposition was so vigorous that when Wayland resigned, Brown went back to its old curriculum and abandoned the new ideas. In our time, Chicago gave up the reforms of Hutchins when the latter resigned as chancellor and joined the Ford Foundation.

College presidents who left their imprint upon American education include Henry P. Tappan at Michigan, who was mainly interested in graduate work and who wanted his university to be as scholarly as Göttingen. He was denounced by his contemporaries as being an intellectual aristocrat. At Williams, Mark Hopkins became famous for his lofty idealism. He knew every student, and his aim was to make real thinkers out of them. Out of his college came a President of the United States, members of the Supreme Court, and many senators. At Cornell, White fought a constant warfare against external control and he showed how freedom could prosper only when the state and church were separated.

ELIOT

Outstanding among 19th-century college presidents was Charles W. Eliot who became president of Harvard in 1869. He had been a noted teacher at M.I.T. and Harvard, and he was determined to change Harvard's entire curriculum. When he took over as president, the graduate professional schools were in a decline and the financial basis of the university was precarious.

Eliot believed that no real conflict exists between literature and the sciences; all subjects should be taught in an open-minded manner. The classics must not dominate the curriculum.

Eliot was interested in increasing the quality of teaching and expanding research. He wanted his teachers to avoid all forms of authoritarianism and to encourage open-mindedness.

Eliot has been attacked because he instituted the elective system. Hutchins and Adler were especially vigorous in their denunciations of Eliot who, to them, was an apostle of expediency and shallow pragmatism.

Viewed from the perspective of the present-time, Eliot appears as one of the foremost leaders and innovators in higher education. In his time, the elective system was most progressive, and it invigorated the curriculum at Harvard. To be sure, it was abused at many universities because trivial elective courses were offered and counseling facilities were inadequate. But the other extreme, which prevails today at St. John's College is far worse, for a prescribed, rigid curriculum stifles the individuality and originality of the student.

TOWARD GENERAL EDUCATION

While general education is today a most important movement in our universities, we must not be deluded by its claims. A course in the history of civilization which lasts a year certainly can touch only the surface. Courses in art appreciation, introductory biology, physics or geology provide only bare essentials, and the student may emerge with a distaste for general culture. The fault is in trying to cover too much in too superficial a way. General education has more lasting significance in the senior year and at the graduate level when the student has enough of a factual background to synthesize the ideas which he is studying.

It is as easy to be mediocre in an elective system as in one which stresses specific requirements. General education depends more on point of view than on specific course content. It has no limitation; it certainly should not end, as it often does, by the end of the sophomore year. Scripps College has pioneered with notable results in teaching humanities for four years. There is no reason why a B.A. and even a Ph.D. degree should not be given in general education.

A specific major is important for those who go into the professions, especially for future scientists. But for thousands of co-eds who will be housewives, for future philosophers, artists, and ministers, the best type of education is one which stresses broad relationships and which evokes lasting interests. The traditionalist will reply at once that this does not develop depth. But does a major in sociology, economics or philosophy on the undergraduate level develop significant depth? It is vitally important to produce students and instructors who go beyond specialization and who are able to communicate with each other.

The implication is that the need exists in our time, as in Eliot's, to liberalize our curriculum, which too often has become rigid. Eliot was wise when he realized that the curriculum itself is not the major matter in higher education, that far more important is the spirit of the institution and the quality of its instruction. Eliot's ambition was to attract the greatest teachers to Harvard. His ideal university would simply include the most inspired teachers and the most enthusiastic students. This view of education is as significant in our time as it was in Eliot's.

INNOVATIONS

In the 19th century, higher education was expanded, especially at Johns Hopkins, which was founded in 1876. Freedom from external control was emphasized there by Daniel C. Gilman who was enraptured by the German ideal of scholarship. Gilman held that research should be central; graduate work was the basis of Johns Hopkins. A believer in complete academic freedom, Gilman was unconcerned about the political and religious opinions of his instructors whose main function, he maintained, was to be excellent teachers and independent researchers.

David Starr Jordan, who made Stanford into a first-class institution, favored original research as the main purpose of higher education. General culture to him was secondary compared to specific knowledge. As for the study of Greek and Latin, these are inadequate tools for modern man who needs above all an understanding of science. From his time to the present, Stanford has emphasized the importance of graduate work.

Woodrow Wilson transformed Princeton into a dynamic institution of learning. When he took over as president, he found it to be in a state of decline. Certain that the main purpose of a university is intellectual, he hired fifty young scholars to invigorate scholarship and upset traditionalism. Some alumni attacked him in violent terms, for they wanted Princeton to be a center of aristocratic leisure. With such a view Wilson had no patience. He constantly tried to improve Princeton's academic standards.

From the standpoint of educational history, William R. Harper at Chicago deserves special notice. He was most unusual; he received his Bachelor of Arts from Yale at 14 and his doctorate at eighteen, and became President of the University of Chicago at 35. A veritable dynamo, he was unique as a teacher and as an administrator. Unlike Eliot, he believed that the first two years of the curriculum should consist of prescribed introductory courses, to open new horizons to the student. He advocated that the junior college should become part of American education; his advice was followed especially in California. When complaints were made to him that his instructors were too radical he protected their right to voice unorthodox opinions. Like Hutchins, Harper felt that a college experience should not be made dependent on formal credits; hence, he allowed students to graduate according to their level of achievement, not according to residence requirements.

Harper attracted internationally famous scholars to Chicago by paying more money than they could have received anywhere else. Again he was very wise, although his opponents called him a materialist. Today we can almost rank universities according to their salary schedules. Presidents who feel that teaching ought to be a sacrificial profession have been shown to be unrealistic. In our civilization, underpaying a professor is a mark of disrespect, indicating that we do not value his attainments.

Professors were attracted to Chicago in the period of Harper and Hutchins not only because of financial considerations, but also because of its intellectual climate. Nobel prize winners graced its faculty. Pragmatists would engage in controversies with scholars like Adler. A real sense of intellectual excitement prevailed at Chicago, especially under Hutchins. When he left, the university became a more conventional institution and soon lost some of its outstanding professors.

HUTCHINS AND THE HIGHER LEARNING

Hutchins was certain that a university depended on the communication of principles, not on relative concepts. He felt that naturalism produced a fragmented view of man and of ideas.

> The result is that there is no such thing as the intellectual life of man. The mind is regarded as a biochemical mechanism developed to solve practical problems. There is no such thing as the truth. All the ideas that men have had were conventions of their time and place and may be disregarded, since we live in a different time and usually in a different place. The thing to do is to get together and pull for the benefit of the community. But what is the benefit of the community? Science cannot tell us. It may secure us the control of nature; but it cannot tell us what to do with it after we have got it. The wisdom of our forefathers cannot tell us. By definition they lived in a different time. The naturalists say that philosophy cannot tell us because it is mere words; it isn't about "scientific facts"; science is always correcting it and limiting its scope just as it is always restricting religion and other superstitions. It is, therefore in those fields in

which the aim of the activity as well as the laws of it is important that the doctrine of naturalism has caused the most confusion. In courses in law, ethics, politics, economics, and history, we have descriptions of what is and has been because we can have nothing else. The critic must have some standard for criticism. What works is an unworkable standard. What is in accordance with man's nature, and hence best for man, is inadmissible because our naturalists will have nothing to do with man's nature. There is nothing left but description which makes no distinction between what is natural and what is conventional. It is impossible to reconcile insistence on convention with the possibility of principles in human action. Yet a contemporary economist tells us that "we must remember that there are certain economic principles which have validity irrespective of the historical framework in which they operate." If this is so, it must be because of the consistency of human nature and of the world in which we live. If there are such principles, it would appear that there must be principles of equal validity in law, history, sociology, ethics, and politics, for these disciplines also deal with man. If human nature is constant in economics, it must be constant in these other disciplines, too. In these other disciplines, too, our principal aim should be to communicate these principles.[1]

To unify ideas and to encourage an understanding of principles, Hutchins furthered interdisciplinary work which combined science and humanities, literature and philosophy, and all branches of social science. Professors from various disciplines met frequently to exchange ideas. The school of theology was reorganized so that major Protestant denominations worked together in a common program. Hutchins envisioned a true community of scholars, but the faculty resisted his moves and favored more rigid departmentalism.

It does not matter so much whether Hutchins was an efficient university administrator. He had vision and he realized that convention is the deadly enemy of creativity. He maintained that higher education is dominated by the cult of conformity; he favored constant controversy. He shocked the traditionalists when he granted the B.A. according to proficiency tests; he outraged some alumni when he abolished the football team. He made philosophers indignant by his advocacy of absolute truths. Some conservative trustees were opposed to him because he was never afraid of radicalism. Sensational newspapers reported that the University of Chicago was a hotbed for "subversive" opinions; actually, most of its students were too immersed in their studies to pay much attention to political events. The opinions

---

[1] Hutchins, "The Philosophy of Education" in R. N. Montgomery, (ed.), *The William Rainey Harper Memorial Conference.*

of Hutchins both in politics and education were denounced in violent terms by the extreme right and the extreme left.

As an administrator, Hutchins showed contradictory tendencies. He said that a college president ought to be well educated, consequently he took up the study of the classics and the great books. His autobiography contains a chapter on the lags in his own college education. He felt that most administrators were so busy with public relations and raising funds that they did not have time to think about the purposes of education. Still, he was an excellent fund raiser who expanded the endowment of the University of Chicago by millions of dollars. In his relationship with the faculty he could be both aloof and warm. To his friends he was extremely kind; to his enemies he could be sarcastic. He spent so much time away from Chicago that occasionally he felt like a visitor. Students who came into contact with him found him to be an incisive teacher who could be critical and yet encouraging at the same time.

CONANT

Conant's background was different from that of Hutchins. Conant was a distinguished chemist when he became president of Harvard in 1933. Twenty years later he became ambassador to Germany. Devoted to public education, Conant later worked for the Carnegie Foundation trying to improve the quality of American high schools.

He was not an ivory tower administrator, as he showed in his work with the government during World War II and in the post-war period. He wrote specialized papers in chemistry as well as popular books on such subjects as *Understanding Science*. Few students will forget his course in "The Growth of Experimental Science." A dramatic lecturer, he would make concrete demonstrations to illustrate the development of the scientific method.

Conant felt that the curriculum was only a partial basis for the education of the student. He believed that self-education was more important than formal instruction. Both the arts and the sciences had an equal place, and he favored great teaching as well as research. Great teaching creates enthusiastic students, while research expands the bases of knowledge and makes for constant progress.

While Hutchins regarded the University of Paris as the model for modern colleges, Conant felt that the university cannot imitate past standards but must rely upon the experimental spirit. The purpose of the university is fourfold: (1) there should be stress upon learning for its own sake; (2) specialization should be encouraged; (3) general education should give a common foundation to intellectual endeavors; (4) students should develop their esthetic as well as their civic talents.

While President Butler at Columbia often succumbed to expediency when he dealt with dissenting opinions, Conant believed that controversy is important in education. As a student of history, Conant realized that dissent was the basis of the industrial revolution and of modern democracy. A like-minded faculty would create a stifling atmosphere. Let the scholar desert the ivory tower and take part in the conflicts of society; only let him not become a fanatic, for real knowledge is a subtle process, not mere categorical affirmation.

Under Conant's guidance, a committee worked for two years studying *The Objectives of a General Education in a Free Society*. It resulted in broad introductory courses through which the student received basic knowledge in the sciences, humanities, history and philosophy. The report influenced not only the Harvard curriculum but also many other universities, which formed committees to develop new patterns for general education.

Conant saw the dilemmas of the modern university. As knowledge becomes more complex, as new discoveries are multiplied, specialization becomes more and more imperative. A chemist can know well only a small part of his field; a physicist only one aspect of his science; frequently professors in the same field are unable to communicate with each other. The professor of ethics might have difficulty understanding the theories of his colleagues whose major interest was symbolic logic. Still, Conant wanted to develop a university in which a common foundation prevailed. This could be accomplished, he felt, through a vigorous system of general education, through interdisciplinary seminars and through an open attitude toward the co-operative nature of knowledge.

CHAPTER THIRTY-FIVE

Arts of Communication

THE GIFTED

One of the most promising aspects of the current educational scene is the encouragement of the gifted. In earlier times there were few programs for those who had special capabilities. Today special programs for the gifted can be found on all levels of education.

A word of caution: Such programs must not create a new status consciousness. A student who feels he deserves special privileges just because he has unusual intellectual capacities will not be very successful in life. In fact, at a social meeting in Southern California one group of parents would not associate with the others. One of the mothers, when asked about her isolationist attitude, said that she would have nothing to do with parents of average children because she was the mother of a gifted child.

Enrichment programs should not stress merely intellectual experience. They should include a knowledge of community trends, a work-study program and travel on a wide scale. For those going into education, summer camp work is especially worth-while. Social awareness should be stirred through experiences in Quaker work-camps, helping out in slum areas or working for social agencies.

The teacher for the gifted should not be authoritarian. He should not try to answer too many questions, but instead should encourage original projects. Gifted students can develop seminars of their own which may rival American colonial discussion groups in vitality and significance.

We need to know the structure and outlook of the gifted person. He tends to be individualistic and persistent in his inquiries, and to dislike pedestrian work.

The progress of programs for the gifted depends on the atmosphere of the school. Does the school encourage new ideas and avoid authoritarianism? Does it give real freedom to its teachers?

Certain attitudes should be encouraged in the gifted student. First, he has to develop self-trust, becoming confident of his capacities without being arrogant. Second, he should have a sense of social obligation to bridge the gap between theory and reality. Society becomes the laboratory for his insights and achievements. Third, he should develop sound moral judgment. This implies an awareness of his own feelings as well as the capacities of others. Ideas have to be humanized; they have to bridge the gap which so often exists in our society. The gifted can become the leaders of society if they have the boldness and the humanity and the affirmative view of man and if they realize that their achievements are only preludes to a larger insight and to more concrete application.

Often we feel that we know the answer to a pressing problem when our insights are fragmentary. Did not Socrates say that, knowing he did not know, he knew more than those who thought they knew but did not know? Premature certainty is the enemy of progress. It is also the greatest road-block in the development of the gifted into cultural leaders.

An excellent example of an effective program for the gifted can be found at Beverly Hills High School under the leadership of Kenneth Peters and Willard Robinson. The first program is in English.

Four years of English is required of all students at Beverly Hills High School. In addition to the regular English courses, the department offers two years of journalism, two of drama, two of forensics, and one of speech. Honors sections are provided only in the English courses.

The work in the honors sections consists of a great deal more reading and a great deal more writing than is required in the regular sections. In composition, stress is laid more on style and structure than on mechanics, which the honors students are presumed to have mastered. In literature, analysis of the materials read is carried to much greater depths and is much more detailed than in the other sections.

A class of special interest is one of the twelfth grade honors sections, which compresses the work of both semesters into one, giving a full year's credit for the course. This section is for the special benefit of those seniors who are attending classes at UCLA.[1]

The second program is in Social Studies.

Course offerings in the social sciences include ancient and medieval history, United States history, modern history, world geography, and problems of democracy. Each of these courses, with the exception of ancient and medieval history and world geography, offers an honors section. Department feeling is that ninth grade pupils do not have adequate background to do honors work in history, and since ancient and medieval history is a ninth grade course it is used partly to inculcate the principles of studying history. In this way those students capable of honors work in this field can be identified and are prepared to undertake serious high-level work in subsequent courses.

The honors sections in social science use the same text as do the regular sections, but little time is spent on it. Instead the students are obliged to use a variety of sources in their work, which often takes the form of special assignments. As an example, the course in U.S. history makes use of such sources as Commager, de Tocqueville, Parrington, Churchill, and Schlesinger. Topics assigned are such thought-provoking ones as making a comparison of the first and second New Deals, or discussing the Puritan mind and thought and its influence on America.[2]

The third program is in foreign languages.

In view of the paucity of foreign language offerings in American high schools noted by the Conant study, it is refreshing to find that Beverly Hills High School offers not only four languages — French, Spanish, Latin, and German — but four full years of each language. The foreign language program also has available for all classes a language laboratory to supplement the work of the teachers.

The work of honors sections in foreign language is distinguished chiefly by a much larger amount of reading and conversation in the language being studied, as well as by a much greater degree of mastery of the mechanics of the language.[3]

The fourth is in science.

The course offerings in science at Beverly Hills High are ample to provide a thorough grounding even for future scientists. A year of

---

[1] "Education for the Academically Able and Talented," *Beverly Hills Report*, p. 27.

[2] *Ibid.*, pp. 27–28.

[3] *Ibid.*, pp. 28–29.

general science is given in the ninth grade, followed by biology, two years of chemistry, physiology, and physics. Naturally not all the courses are elected by all students.

Honor sections are provided in chemistry, physics, and general science. The department is contemplating the addition of an honors section in botany as well. The second year of chemistry is offered only in summer session and is restricted to students who have shown outstanding achievement in chemistry during their first year. A similar course in experimental physics is being considered as an addition to the department's offerings.

The laboratory facilities for science courses at Beverly Hills High School are exceptional in that the science classrooms are separate from the laboratories, so that students can use the laboratories to do extra work or advanced projects even while other courses are in session in the adjacent room. Naturally, this provision is of special value to gifted students, who are most likely to be making use of the laboratories outside of regular class hours.[4]

The fifth program is in mathematics.

The course offerings in mathematics at Beverly Hills High School include not only the usual elementary algebra and geometry, and the fairly common advanced algebra and trigonometry, but a course in mathematical analysis which introduces the students to analytical geometry and calculus, topics ordinarily reserved for college-level courses. . . .

A very interesting feature of the mathematics program for the gifted, and one which is made possible by the relatively small size of the community, is an arrangement through which high school teachers go to the elementary schools to teach algebra to selected eighth grade pupils for one hour each day. In general, the top twenty-five per cent of the student population in achievement and aptitude are selected to participate in this program.

Honors sections are provided in geometry and trigonometry as well as in both years of algebra. The class in mathematical analysis is essentially an honors course, being restricted to students with special interest in and capability for mathematics.[5]

Most important is the seminar program.

During the current school year there are four seminars; each seminar extending across four grade levels.

Participants are chosen according to the criteria as outlined on the seminar chart. The seminar meets once a week during the first period

---

⁴ *Ibid.,* pp. 29–30.
⁵ *Ibid.,* pp. 30–31.

of the day. Credit is given for this work and the student's participation is recorded on the cumulative record.

In its current method of operation, the seminar consists of 18 to 20 students who meet with a leader to discuss the current topic. The theme for the current year, and probably for an indeterminate number of future years, is "The Great Ideas that Have Contributed to Man's Culture." Reading is assigned for each meeting two weeks or so in advance, and each reading assignment is discussed three times. The first time the leader and students discuss the writer and the times in which he lived. For the second discussion, a line-by-line analysis is made of the reading selection; the leaders feel that such detailed analysis is desirable because it is seldom done in regular classes, provides valuable insights, and is difficult for most American students because of its unfamiliarity. The third discussion of each selection takes up the students' reactions to the work and the ways in which they can relate it to their own lives and times.

The Great Ideas theme is implemented by making a sampling, chosen appropriately for each group, of the work of outstanding thinkers from Plato to contemporary thinkers. New selections from the same group of writers are chosen in each succeeding year.

The work of the seminars also includes occasional field trips or visits to places of cultural or intellectual interest, and once each month a session is devoted to techniques of efficient reading and study of material such as that covered by the seminar.[6]

Beverly Hills High School cooperates with UCLA and has an

. . . arrangement . . . through which selected high school seniors are enabled to take courses at the university for regular college credit. The proximity of the university makes the physical problem a fairly simple one . . .

Those who are selected attend several orientation meetings at which they are informed of various aspects of the program and are assisted in making their selections of university courses. These meetings are conducted by two members of the counselling staff at UCLA, one of whom administers the tests while the other is assigned by the university as counselor for this program. The students enroll in the university in the regular manner and attend the same courses as other university students, although an effort is made to place them in sections where they will encounter well-qualified and sympathetic fellow students. The participants in this program ordinarily attend their university classes in the morning and attend their high school classes during the last four periods of the day. Their high school work consists usually of two or three solid subjects during this period, although their graduation requirements are not reduced in any respect. They

---

[6] *Ibid.*, pp. 31–32.

have usually arranged to complete their requirements by additional or summer work before the senior year, except for those which they can handle at the same time as their university classes.[7]

Most stimulating is the summer session in Europe.

In cooperation with the Institute of European Studies, University of Vienna, two summer schools for Beverly Hills High School students have been organized: one in Madrid, Spain for students of Spanish; and one in Gmunden, Austria for students of German. The purpose of the project is to combine intensive language instruction with a certain degree of immersion into the European scene through combined study and travel. This will help the students gain a better understanding of the artistic, literary, and political aspects of our common Western heritage and provide an additional incentive for their academic work at home.[8]

FUTURE WRITERS

The educational possibilities of students are especially revealed in creative writing. Perhaps never before have so many youngsters been interested in this field. Classes in creative writing are extremely popular in high school and college, and editors are swamped by an abundance of manuscripts. The passion to write extends not only to the young, but also to the old who are attending adult education classes trying to polish up their style, and perhaps write the great American novel.

What specific steps can be taken to improve our writing ability? Let us take the field of novel writing. Imagine a young student in college who intends to become a second Hemingway or Thomas Wolfe.

First of all, a student should cultivate an extensive interest in literature. He should read the great novels of the United States, Europe, and South America. Above all, he should select one author and he should read him carefully and think about his writing technique.

Let us say he selects Flaubert's *Madame Bovary*. There is an important scene in this book when Madame Bovary receives a letter from her lover informing her that he cannot elope with her. Her reaction is pictured in a penetrating way. We almost see the letter dropping to the ground, and we feel the emotions of her heart. At the same time everything outside is calm and tranquil. Let the young

---

[7] *Ibid.*, pp. 32–33.
[8] *Ibid.*, pp. 34–35.

writer visualize the scene and let him describe it in his own words and then he should compare his own description of the scene with that of Flaubert.

But the admiration of one author is not enough, for the young writer must develop his own style, his own perspective, and his own philosophy of life. For that purpose he should travel, meet all types of people and become a part of them. He should keep a journal, like André Gide, and record the conversations which he hears; he should describe his own thoughts in a diary, for this process aids in self-analysis and sharpens his senses.

When he starts to write the novel he should not choose a subject about which he knows little or which is alien to his way of life. Rather, the subject should be of vital concern to him; he should have a passionate interest in it. It is best if he describes himself as much as possible. In most of the great modern novels, like those of Kafka, Joyce, and Gide, the autobiographical element is dominant.

When he finishes the manuscript he should lay it aside for a while and then submit it to friends who have a penetrating critical ability. He may rewrite it several times; every time he does so he will feel a new insight and a new freshness. At first there will, undoubtedly, be rejection slips, but still the young author should not give up hope. Eventually, if his work has merit, he will find recognition.

The rules for a work of non-fiction are different from those governing a novel. A book on religion or philosophy or literature should, above all, avoid one quality — dullness. The essayist can learn especially from Emerson who was able to say so much with an economy of words. Furthermore, the essayist should cultivate an intense sense of satire. In our own time perhaps no author is quite as thought-provoking and as stimulating as Bertrand Russell. He has never written a book which is dull. He may be wrong, but it is a delight to read him because he is witty, irreverent, and delightfully sarcastic.

ON WRITING EXAMINATIONS

A sense of originality should also be cultivated by the student who writes an essay examination. There is perhaps nothing more enlightening in college teaching than to be exposed to the tests of the average student. Basically there is not much difference between the "C" student and the "A" student when they answer certain essay questions. The "A" student usually has studied more, and probably listened more thoroughly than the "C" student. But this does not mean that the "A" student is creative, for in some cases he only repeats what his teacher has said and he is suitably rewarded for his imitation.

Especially important in writing a test is organization. The student need not make a formal outline, but at least he should have a plan in his head of what he is going to say. He should define his terms and he should actually think while he is writing, not try to fill up paper with as many unrelated facts as possible. He should cultivate a critical attitude, and, if necessary, should differ from his professor and his text. Unfortunately, some instructors believe in quantity and they are inclined to give the student a better grade when he fills up as much space as possible.

Hayakawa has often remarked that the English themes in high school and college are the worst obstacles to creativity. They usually deal with such pedestrian topics as descriptions of a building, a visit to the country, a visit to the county museum, and other innocuous subjects. Most of the time they are graded by the teacher in a superficial manner. It would be much better if the themes were criticized by the class, for the students very often have a sharper opinion than their teachers. Furthermore, content should be stressed rather than proficiency in grammar. It appears that some English teachers are in love with commas and semicolons and they see only the mechanics of expression instead of understanding the creative spirit of writing.

THE ART OF ORATORY

Proficiency in speaking is just as significant as development of writing ability. Our ability in public speaking is increased when we listen to the great orators, analyze their methods, and find out why they had such a powerful influence on civilization. Take such orators as Wendell Willkie and Franklin D. Roosevelt. When you listen to recordings of their speeches your imagination is stirred. You notice that they use words in a unique way. Their language is colorful and plastic; it is never dull. Humor and satire constantly appear. At the same time they are able to stir our emotions and to guide our actions.

If we want to cultivate our speaking ability we must become conscious of words. Most of the time we repeat the same words over and over again. Our language is drab, unimaginative, and repetitious. We should constantly learn new words, and use them in our daily conversations. We should study semantics, which deals with the meaning of words, so that we may not be ruled by word magic and so that we do not regard words as objects or entities.

At the same time we should become conscious of our voice quality; we should listen for example to great actors like Olivier and notice how his voice is able to portray all types of emotion and various shades of feeling, and practice daily so that our language is more melodious and more expressive of our emotions.

When you have to give a speech investigate carefully the subject which you have to discuss. Let us imagine the subject is Hitler's Germany. Study men like Hitler and Goebbels; read authors like Rauschnigg, Thomas Mann and Shirer. Do not just accept one opinion or one standpoint but try to analyze the conflict of viewpoints. After you finish your reading prepare a rough outline, and perhaps practice the speech before a mirror. Be very relaxed the hour before you give the speech, for tension makes the speaker uncertain and often ineffective. Never be afraid of the audience; direct your remarks especially to one individual. In this way you feel a sense of intimacy and also you can understand the effect of your speech.

To be successful, the public speaker should study the nature of his audience. Aristotle in his *Rhetoric* gives us some excellent advice on this matter. Thus he said when a public speaker addresses young men he should realize that they are changeable in their behavior, hot tempered and eager for victory. Aristotle believed that young men live in the expectation of the future. Hence, a public speaker should stimulate their sense of adventure and their love for excitement.

On the other hand, when a public speaker addresses old men, according to Aristotle, he should keep in mind that they are cynical and smallminded. Old men are cowardly; they do not like to take risks, they are afraid of death, and thus they are fervently attached to life. They love security because they have learned that life is bitter without material advantages. Therefore, the orator must appeal to their sober realism and to their conservative instincts.

Aristotle also had some challenging advice to orators when they address rich men. The rich, according to Aristotle, love ostentation; they believe that material standards are all important, and that money can buy everything. Aristotle told the orator that he should flatter the vanity of the wealthy; in this way he will be successful.

What method should we follow when we give a controversial speech? Should we be completely objective? Ideally, yes, according to Aristotle, but usually the orator should follow the path of persuasion.

He should try to excite the emotions of his audience and repeat his points so that they can be easily remembered. He should justify his own case and tear down the arguments of his opponent.

However, in creative speaking we should never appeal to prejudice; we should not deny our ideals in action. We gain more by being fair and objective than by using the methods of the demagogue. This does not mean that we should lack conviction; rather, we should recognize that others may have an equally valid insight and that we can learn as much from our opponents as from our friends.

HOW TO READ CREATIVELY

One of the great needs of modern education is the development of better reading habits. Many students are unable to analyze a paragraph of a difficult author, others do not want to read because they find manual activities so much more attractive.

As Bacon already pointed out, not all books should be read with equal care. Some books should be read casually, others should be studied diligently. We should read not for ornamentation, but for insight and self-improvement.

When we read a vital book we should know something about the author. This humanizes our reading and gives us a more meaningful association. Before we start to read the book we should preview it so that we catch a glimpse of the purpose of the author and the points he tries to cover. Our attitude, while we read, should be one of sympathy; above all, we should try to understand what the author wants to say; at the same time, we should not curb our critical capacities.

It is an excellent practice to underline certain passages. Naturally this method cannot be followed when the book belongs to the public library. Therefore, it is important that, as soon as possible, we acquire our own library. Occasionally, when the book belongs to us, we might even make notes on the margin. This method was used by almost all the great German philosophers. For example, when Schopenhauer read Leibnitz's *Monadology* he made notes on almost every page of the book, and these notes are almost as enlightening and meaningful as the original manuscript.

When you read a serious book in philosophy or science or religion do not try to read it all at once. Close the book after every third or fourth chapter, then ask yourself questions, test yourself, and try to remember the main points of the author. This method has several advantages. It sharpens our memory, it makes the material which we read more meaningful, and it serves as a valuable intellectual discipline.

Most important in reading is our *ability to concentrate*. If possible we should avoid all noise and all outside disturbances. Even when we are tempted by our friends to go to a movie or to pursue other distractions we should not succumb, for discipline is perhaps the most important element in creativeness.

Naturally it is easier to concentrate upon a novel than upon a serious work like Spinoza's *Ethics*. A novel deals with concrete situations, excites our passion for life, and stimulates our imagination, while Spinoza's great book is written in a very technical manner and his language is abstract and difficult to comprehend. This does not mean, however, that we should disregard Spinoza, for difficult books have a reward of their own. We feel a sense of accomplishment when we have mastered them; they remain with us long after we have forgotten the plot of the latest best-seller.

HOW TO LISTEN CREATIVELY

An Indian visitor who came to the United States was asked what feature he found to be most unpleasant in the United States. He replied, "Your eternal noise; you do not know how to listen." This indeed has become a verbal civilization. From the time we get up until we go to sleep we are exposed to a niagara of words from commentators, friends, business associates, and a variety of other sources.

We must cultivate, above all, our listening ability. Silence is a prelude to genuine learning. We should meditate more and talk less.

In teaching I have found how difficult it is for students to concentrate upon a lecture unless it is enlivened by humor or by human interest. This restlessness begins very early, for our students have a super-abundance of energy and they lack the power of concentration.

To be sure, some lecturers are exceedingly dull. They have monotonous voices and deal with insignificant details; hence our temptation is to fall asleep. Yet, often our first impression is erroneous. I know one teacher, for example, who is extremely boring to the freshman class, although he is fascinating to graduate students.

The listener must use his imagination. He must constantly ask questions, such as, what is the purpose of the lecture? What is the basic motivation of the speaker? Do I agree with him or do I disagree and why?

Our sensitivity is sharpened especially when we listen to music, for music is a direct key to reality. It mirrors moods and emotions more exactly than any verbal expressions. In listening to music we are transported to a new realm in which our own passions and desires appear to be insignificant and trivial. Sometimes, when we listen to the great masters like Bach, Beethoven, or Bartok, we forget about our own ego and tend to lose consciousness of the self. We feel almost that our physical nature is an illusion and we become part of the eternal medium of music.

Schopenhauer describes the importance of music.

According to all this, we may regard the phenomenal world, or nature, and music as two different expressions of the same thing, which is therefore itself the only medium of their analogy, so that a knowledge of it is demanded in order to understand that analogy. Music, therefore, if regarded as an expression of the world, is in the highest degree a universal language, which is related indeed to the universality of concepts, much as they are related to the particular things. Its universality, however, is by no means that empty universality of abstraction, but quite of a different kind, and is united with thorough and distinct definiteness. In this respect it resembles geometrical figures and numbers, which are the universal forms of all possible objects of experience and applicable to them all *a priori*, and yet are not abstract but perceptible and thoroughly determined. All possible efforts, excitements, and manifestations of will, all that goes on in the heart of man and that reason includes in the wide, negative concept of feeling, may be expressed by the infinite number of possible melodies, but always in the universal, in the mere form, without the material, always according to the thing-in-itself, not the phenomenon, the inmost soul, as it were, of the phenomenon, without the body. This deep relation which music has to the true nature of all things also explains the fact that suitable music played to any scene, action, event, or surrounding seems to disclose to us its most secret meaning, and appears as the most accurate and distinct commentary upon it. This is so truly the case, that whoever gives himself up entirely to the impression of a symphony, seems to see all the possible events of life and the world take place in himself, yet if he reflects, he can find no likeness between the music and the things that passed before his mind.[9]

---

[9] *World as Will and Idea,* Bk. 4, 52.

THE SOCIAL MATRIX

Not only esthetic events, but social crises as well, condition the life of creative communication. When Franco bombed the defenseless city of Guernica many idealists in the Western world were outraged, but no one gave a more graphic account of the horror of this air raid than did Picasso in his painting of Guernica. It is a vivid impression of death, despair, and destruction.

In literature personal misfortune has frequently inspired creative work: Bunyan wrote *Pilgrim's Progress* while he was in jail; Boethius composed *The Consolation of Philosophy* while he was waiting for execution; Dante wrote *The Divine Comedy* under the impact of his exile from Florence. Grillparzer, a famous German dramatist, tells us how he wrote one of his plays, *The Argonauts*. He was in Italy where he became ill, and suddenly heard that his mother had died and so he hurried home. His shock was so great that he had forgotten almost everything; he could not create and his mind was in a state of absolute chaos. For relaxation he played the piano, and occasionally he would play the piano with a girl in the neighborhood. Then suddenly, while listening to music, his ideas about the new play were clarified; he felt a new freshness and vitality, and he finished his work.

In some artists creativity is an all absorbing process, and may even lead to self-destruction. This is especially true in the paintings of Van Gogh. His self-portraits reveal a tortured mind. To Van Gogh the distinction between man and nature was almost obliterated; nature was brilliantly alive and burned with intensity. He was not only a superb artist but also a social reformer and he felt most at home when he was with the lower classes of society. But still, he was uncertain of his genius and he was tortured by a perpetual feeling of melancholy; hence, his final step was suicide.

It may be asked how art can become a way of life? How can art invigorate our institutions and change our sense of values? Above all, we should patronize our own artists instead of looking back to ancient traditions. For example, we should give special scholarships to American composers whose work should be performed by the outstanding symphony orchestras of this nation. At the same time we should contribute to an international exchange of writers, musicians, and painters, for culture develops most vigorously amidst a diversity of patterns and ideals. All this means that we should put more stress upon *originality* in art than upon technique.

Also, we should train great teachers of art. Too many teachers of art are dominated by tradition and are conscientious objectors to our own civilization. Unorthodox teachers of art can present us with a new vision of beauty which may create a real American renaissance.

The importance of art is revealed in the following incident: A city in Germany was almost completely destroyed during World War II. The theatre, the local school, the city hall — all were in ruins. The problem after the war was what building should be erected first. Some suggested that certainly the school was most vital, others felt that political institutions were most significant and hence the city hall should be rebuilt at once, but the majority decided that the theatre should come first.

Some might say that this reveals a very impractical spirit. But we must remember that man does not live by utility alone and that he yearns for a creative way of life.

CREATIVE COMMUNICATION

The primary aim of education should be the stimulation of creativity. In summary, how can this be accomplished?

(1)   An attitude of awareness should be developed; the student should become conscious of his abilities.

(2)   The student should be taught how to concentrate upon a given subject. Creativity requires immense *self-discipline*.

(3)   The great works of art, literature and music should be brought into the classroom. Classical music should be used even in nursery school.

(4)   Activities in art, literature and music should emphasize the individuality of the student, not the imitation of adult standards.

(5)   Outstanding artists and writers of the community should be invited to take part in classroom activities. A special fund should be set up to attract great artists to the campus.

(6)   Art and literary clubs should be found on every campus. The school should publish a magazine containing the outstanding literary works of the students.

(7)   Field trips to museums and other institutions of art and learning should be made as frequently as possible.

(8)   The appreciation of the arts and literature should be a central concern of the teacher, who should stress, above all, the art of the present. A literature course should start with Hemingway instead of *Beowulf*.

(9) Criticism of students' work should be positive rather than negative. Areas for improvement should be indicated. The teacher should remember that his own standards of criticism are fallible.

(10) Enriched experiences should be given to gifted students. Tutors should be assigned to them to take advantage of their creative ability.

CHAPTER THIRTY-SIX

Delinquency and Education

SIGNIFICANCE

Delinquency is one of America's foremost educational problems. It touches the rich and the poor, and rural as well as urban communities. Vandalism is a form of delinquency. Los Angeles schools report many cases of wilfull destruction of school property; New York loses over 300,000 panes of glass every year; Baltimore estimates that vandalism costs $100,000 a year. Most disconcerting is the fact that the majority of drop-outs, of which there will be over 7,000,000 in the 1960's, may end as delinquents.

Delinquency points to the confusion of values and the inadequacy of many adults. The majority of American youngsters have constructive attitudes, but *a small minority make the headlines.* Society appears to be more willing in some cases to enlarge the jails than to develop a truly constructive educational system. It is not enough to be concerned about delinquency; what matters is to create schools that are genuine community centers and can be effective agents in the struggle against juvenile and adult waywardness.

CASES

Not so long ago a newspaper headline announced: KILLER, 15, GIVEN DEATH SENTENCE. The article explained how Isaiah Greene, aged fifteen, whom the judge had called a young savage, was the youngest killer in Pennsylvania history and how together with two companions, Edwin Walker, fourteen, and James ("Smiley") Crowson, he had held up a drugstore and killed the owner. When the judge pronounced the sentence Greene collapsed, but his two companions, who were given life imprisonment, showed little emotion.

Recently I visited the home of a juvenile killer. He had confessed firing the shotgun during a gang fight. He lived in a slum section. He was an only child whose parents were divorced. Since the father had deserted the family, the mother had to work to support the boy. I asked her whether she had any idea that he was a delinquent. She said that she had not had enough time for the boy and that two years ago he had started hanging around a neighborhood gang. She blamed one boy especially who was apparently the leader and who had instigated the gang fight. I asked her how the boy acted in school, and she replied that he hated his teachers and often went to the movies when he should have been in school.

In their personal relationship he was completely uncommunicative and there was no closeness between them. She felt bewildered. She had worked so hard and sacrificed so much and now this tragedy had occurred to her.

When I talked to the boy, a different picture of the mother emerged. Apparently, she was seldom at home and she kept company with all kinds of men. There was no supervision and he was left free to roam the streets. I asked him whether he felt repentant and he remarked that he was sorry he got caught; he wouldn't kill again. His only thought was how he could get out of the state training school; at the same time he wanted to "get the squealer."

His attitude is ambivalent. On the one hand, he wants to live along civilized lines; on the other hand, he thirsts for revenge. It is doubtful whether he can be rehabilitated in the reform school; statistics indicate that half our adult criminals obtained early lessons in crime in state training schools and detention homes.

A basic lack in this boy's background was the absence of a father figure. There was no voice of authority, no one who could discipline him, and no one to respect. In school he had mainly grades of D and F, and when he tried athletics he did not make the team. When the coach found him smoking and drinking his athletic chances were gone. As for policemen, he hated them vigorously.

When asked what kind of people he admired he replied that he liked boxers. He respected men like Sonny Liston, Cassius Clay, Sugar Ray Robinson and Jack Dempsey. His reason was that they could beat up anybody and they made a lot of money. He had frequented a boxing gym and he admired physical strength above all. Furthermore, he thought that fighters could have any girl they wanted and drove flashy cars.

The boy he had killed was Mexican, aged sixteen. I also visited the victim's family. They lived in a broken-down shack without indoor plumbing. There were eight children in the family. The home was kept spotless and there were even flowers on the table. The parents had been in this country for ten years but they still had not adjusted to our ways. In Mexico the father exercised absolute authority; here he was disrespected. There were no juvenile gangs in the village from which they came. They had warned the boy to stay away from the gang, but in vain; and now he was gone. The mother cried as she showed me some of his belongings and a picture taken of him when he was in junior high school.

TYPES

It is a mistake to believe that delinquents are qualitatively different from normal youngsters. A Buddhist priest has said that the same key that opens the doors to heaven will open the doors to hell. This statement can be applied to the delinquency problem. Like normal youngsters, wayward youths love adventure and excitement; but they are more impulsive and less hindered by convention and social restrictions. Normal children are more responsive to the values of the community; they have a guilty conscience when they commit a wrong act and when they disobey their parents. Delinquents, on the other hand, feel they are misunderstood. When they get into trouble they blame their companions or their parents or teachers or the police. They lack the power to criticize their own actions. In their emotional make-up they tend to go to extremes, from elation to depression and from submission to stubborn defiance.

In their sexual development, they start very early to experiment with the opposite sex. The case of Jean comes to my mind. Her foster father had made physical advances to her. After that came a long succession of both young and old men. At the age of sixteen she was extremely cynical and remarked, "Men are only interested in one thing."

Delinquents as a group, as Sheldon and Eleanor Glueck point out, tend to be exhibitionists. The boys tend to be loud, extroverted and uninhibited, and the girls tend to be hostile toward adult authority. This does not mean that they live without rules, but their standards are at variance with those of society. When they belong to groups they will often do anything to conform to the standards of the gang and its taboos, and even subject themselves to extremely arduous initiation rites.

In some cases the delinquent may be a quiet boy who apparently has not given his parents any trouble or a shy girl who has always avoided group activities. Not so long ago a boy in Los Angeles killed his father when the father tried to discipline him. The boy explained that he just got mad. Another boy recently killed his father when the latter beat up his mother.

We can distinguish between two types of delinquency; in one case it is like a slow disease. The delinquent may start by staying away from school, then by stealing and participating in gang fights. He may advance in his delinquency through armed robbery and, eventually, even killing. As we survey his total development we usually find an unhappy childhood and frustrated emotions. The second type of delinquency with a less obvious background is guided by the impulse of the moment. An apparently well-behaved girl who comes from an adequate home may go to a department store and see a sweater which she wants. She may not be able to restrain herself and so will become a thief. Or a boy may become involved in a fight and seriously injure someone else. Ordinary youngsters will not go to extremes; for example, when they fight they will stop at a certain point, but delinquents will not have such compunctions and they may fight with any kind of weapon.

AMBIVALENT STANDARDS

There is no fundamental difference between juvenile and adult delinquents. In many neighborhoods the junior gangs may help the local syndicate, and the local bookie may employ boys as his helpers. Drug peddlers use adolescents to an alarming degree.

A young delinquent told me that in his neighborhood the local "hoods" had the biggest and most expensive cars, they wore the best clothes, and they had the flashiest women. Their parties were the most exciting. He told about his own father who was a mailman trying to support his family. His father drove an old-model car and he never had any luxuries. He was honest, but apparently honesty did not pay.

I tried to tell the boy about the consequences of crime and what would happen if he got caught. He said that only the dumb ones got caught. He mentioned a major city where ten gang slayings had taken place within five years and not one had been solved. He maintained that if one wanted to eliminate an enemy a telephone call could be made to Detroit or Chicago and a hired "torpedo" would come and do the job. There would be no overt motive and no traces would be left. How would it be possible to apprehend the criminal?

Then he told me about a case in which a member of the gang had been apprehended by the police. He had not "squealed" and had been supplied with the best lawyer. While he was in prison his family was taken care of, and when he was released he became a local hero. A party was given in his honor and, according to the boy, it resembled a Roman festival.

More and more in our society white-collar crimes are being committed. Every day we read about check forgeries and trusted employees who abscond with their employers' funds. The possibilities for crimes are greater than their detection, and law-enforcement agencies often do not use the latest scientific techniques in their battle against criminals.

It is true, of course, that only a small minority among delinquents are deliberately antisocial. They often suffer from impulses which they cannot control. One young psychopath in our community was found to be suffering from a brain tumor; another one had diabetes. Still, some deliberately and with forethought enjoy the life of crime. They like its adventure and its romance. They look forward to easy money and fast cars. They do not want to work hard and they will do anything to avoid strenuous efforts. They enjoy terrorizing others and they feel self-important because they are feared.

In some ways they are like the Nazi SS troops who guarded Hitler's concentration camps and killed thousands of helpless human beings. Most of them felt no guilty conscience; they even enjoyed their role and their leaders left exact diaries in which they daily recorded the executions. Of course, in the case of the SS this was a policy sponsored by the government, whereas all our conventions and laws are against such behavior.

All this indicates, however, that moral standards are relative and that the human conscience is elastic. We are determined more by our immediate environment than by abstract moral goals. Occasionally, our actions are only guided by consequences and legalistic considerations; we have no concern for the dignity of the persons and the security of property.

We are living in an age of violence. Read the books by Mickey Spillane which have sold millions of copies, especially to adolescents, and one finds brutal killers and an equally brutal detective who enjoys the sadistic punishment of the guilty. The detective loves physical violence for its own sake and delights in breaking bones. His prowess is rewarded by beautiful girls whom he loves passionately.

This is the eternal struggle between good and evil. It goes back to the Persian dualism in the *Zend-Avesta,* which sees a constant conflict between light and darkness. But the American version as expressed by Mickey Spillane in such books as *One Lonely Night* and *I, the Jury* makes the "good" man, the detective, fully as sadistic and bloodthirsty as the killer.

One of the most penetrating authors of our time is James M. Cain, whose books, *Double Indemnity, The Moth, The Postman Always Rings Twice,* picture a world of unbridled selfishness, unnatural passion, and quick violence. Thus in *The Postman Always Rings Twice* a young man is befriended by a café owner who takes care of him as if he were his own son and yet the young man will stop at nothing, including murder, to make love to the café-owner's wife. He has one aim and one desire and whatever stands in his way has to be eliminated. The girl he loves is equally brutal and has no feeling of gratitude for her husband who has treated her generously and rescued her from being a waitress in a cheap café. She wants the young man, and she collaborates in his design to get rid of her husband.

If we watch many of our most successful movies like *Asphalt Jungle* and *The Killers* we find a world of unrestrained violence and torture. The same applies to television. Innumerable Westerns and mysteries which are watched religiously by our youngsters night after night offer a sordid succession of assault, robbery, and murder.

We should not make the mistake of singling out TV or the movies for the wave of delinquency. Still, there is a pressing need for more educational programs and for a limitation upon the crime serials and Westerns. We must not forget that youngsters develop morals and attitudes through the popular agencies of communication and that antisocial acts may leave a lasting impression upon them.

In our time we have an unprecedented increase in scandal magazines and pornographic literature. Horror and crime comics often appear to be the favorite literature of some of our young people. How can they develop constructive attitudes when they read about the misdeeds of their favorite movie star or the unnatural lusts of their sports idol? How can they develop a calm view of sex when its attractions are constantly being publicized?

This is not a call for Puritanism, but for sanity. In some communities, local censors have even banned the works of Steinbeck, Faulkner, and Hemingway as being detrimental to the young mind. If they were consistent, as has often been pointed out, they would also have to ban certain parts of the Bible.

There is widespread confusion regarding moral standards. In a survey made by Farleigh Dickinson College in New Jersey of 1,000 college students and 2,500 high-school students it was found that over 70 per cent did not consider lying and cheating as being part of delinquency; 17 per cent believed that sexual offenses did not imply delinquency and 15 per cent could see nothing wrong with vandalism regarding property. In a more recent poll of Purdue University a large number of teen-agers showed a shocking disregard for civil liberties, maintaining that the police should curb politically undesirable opinions. Their ideas were in direct opposition to the Declaration of Independence. Another poll by *Scholastic Magazine's* Institute of Student Opinion involving 5,855 teen-age high-school students showed that a large number preferred big business over small business and that they wanted government employment rather than jobs in private industry. Their main concern appeared to be security and to be taken care of by a paternalistic government.

In surveys made by various colleges it was found that a surprising number of students cheat. Occasionally, as many as 50 per cent would cheat on examinations. In some colleges the honor system was instituted, but it had to be withdrawn because of student opposition. Cheating was discovered a few years ago at West Point and the offenders had to be expelled.

Naturally, this is not always the fault of students. Some professors encourage cheating by giving impossible examinations and by being too harsh. Frequently, students both in high school and in college regard cheating as being perfectly normal, as an "innocent" sport.

SLUMS

In certain cities Negroes live in a virtual ghetto. For example, in Los Angeles thousands of colored people arrive every year and they can live only in a restricted district. Their children frequently rebel and find status through gang associations. When their housing is improved and when they live in a decent environment, the delinquency rate usually drops.

It has been estimated that in a slum area in Pittsburgh, 87 per cent more policemen are needed and that there are 250 per cent more deaths from T.B. and almost 267 per cent more cases of juvenile offenses. Adult crime in this area is 200 per cent more prevalent than in a normal residential district. Such is the financial and human cost of our blighted areas.

ORGANIZATION

Ours is an age of large-scale organization. David Riesman in *The Lonely Crowd* describes the increase of the other-directed personality, the individual who is concerned mainly with social approval and who feels a terrible social emptiness. Thus we have a host of organizations in the adult world which attempt to cultivate our gregarious drives and overcome our sense of loneliness.

Yet it is an apparent fact that loneliness is one of our most pressing problems. We may feel it in a big city as well as in a small town. Certain existentialist thinkers, like Jaspers and Sartre, see it as the primary condition of modern life. Most individuals hate to meditate and to be by themselves. They want to be on the go and to share in social activities.

When we observe delinquent youngsters we often find this feeling of loneliness; this demands insight and understanding on our part. Thus a girl who bore an illegitimate child said to me that no one ever understood her. Her parents only yelled at her and her teachers only looked upon her as a wayward child. She felt that she was an orphan and that she did not belong anywhere. Only when she made love did the sense of loneliness disappear.

Another delinquent who was a truant from school, a boy of thirteen, described how he would wander through the streets of the city. He would go to movies and pool halls and sit in the park. His main ambition was to get away from home.

Today we have thousands of gangs in practically every city. This is not a new phenomenon, but the juvenile gangs of today are far tougher than ever before. They fight with zip guns and even with Molotov cocktails. Members of these gangs feel they have acquired status and they look down on law-abiding youngsters. They are at war with their parents whom they despise, with the police whom they hate, and with teachers whom they view with contempt.

The gang creates a split attitude in its members. Toward the outside world, defiance is cultivated. A gang member gains respect by antisocial attitudes. The worst crime for him is to be disloyal to his comrades or to be cowardly when battling rival gangs.

Fights may start in the most trivial way. A rival group may trespass on gang territory or one of its members may have been insulted. Then war is inevitable and it is fought in the most ferocious way.

The world of the gangs is a strange one. Some members are dope addicts and they feel very adult in cultivating this habit. They love the sound of rock-and-roll music; their parties are scenes of incredible debauchery. To be sure, we must not generalize for there are a large number of peaceful gangs with relatively civilized standards, but the number of young criminal gangs is constantly increasing.

Youngsters love excitement and adventure, thus the more daring their existence is, the more satisfaction they find. Excitement has many dimensions; there can be a sense of adventure in the intellectual life or in artistic endeavor or in science, but some youngsters, especially in gangs, find excitement in vandalism and in destruction.

Delinquency arises out of a search for security, a false security, in which the delinquent subordinates his own uniqueness to group standards and group ideals.

To understand the values of the delinquent, we should take a close look at the values of the adult world. On the one hand, he rebels against them; on the other hand, he tries to find substitutes which will gratify his own ego.

The essential desires and attitudes of the typical delinquent are:

(1)   He admires physical strength
(2)   He yearns for material satisfactions
(3)   He hates to be alone
(4)   He despises the squealer
(5)   He loves freedom and yet, as Fromm would say, he escapes from it
(6)   He despises authority
(7)   He looks upon sex in purely sensate terms
(8)   He regards work as an activity fit for squares
(9)   Most of the time he daydreams about impossible schemes
(10)   He needs new thrills and new adventures all the time
(11)   He feels that the world is conspiring against him; "no one understands him"
(12)   He enjoys annoying adults
(13)   He looks upon life as a jungle
(14)   He is governed by impulse

REFORMS

To fight delinquency we must stress the counseling available in the school. It is obvious that not every teacher can be a skilled counselor; guidance has to become an important profession with the highest standards. Today we often assign a teacher who has an inadequate load to be a counselor. This means he will only be interested in the academic standards and performance of the student. What is important, however, is the psychological development of the youngster.

When I started to teach, my main concern was with academic excellence. I had rigorous standards and divided my classes into two categories: the brilliant and the stupid. I was uninterested in the inferior ones and appealed mainly to the élite.

Today, I am more interested in the personal development of a student, and I ask such questions as:

What is he really like?

What are his goals?

What is his home environment?

What are his strengths and weaknesses?

What type of people does he admire?

What are his intellectual, esthetic and religious interests?

How does he conceive of himself?

How does he conceive of society?

What is his adjustment to the opposite sex?

How does he meet failure?

What traits does he like and dislike in others?

Is he basically compassionate or egocentric?

What values does he treasure most?

How does he react toward materialism?

Is he an exciting individual?

Is he happy? If not, why not?

These questions may be helpful to parents, teachers, and workers in the fields of delinquency. Once they are answered—though they never can be completely answered—they throw new light upon the individual.

Teachers need to be psychologically oriented; they need an understanding of mental hygiene. The concept of the teacher's role is changing; in the future it will involve more of the therapeutic function. Undoubtedly, we need more male teachers to guide the early experi-

ences of the child. A more elastic curriculum should be developed
so that we can avoid the many drop-outs who become delinquents.
*A more concentrated investment in education is the best insurance
against delinquency.*

An excellent illustration of creative community planning in child
guidance is the Children's Bureau of Passaic, New Jersey—a community of 68,000. The bureau was established in 1937. Referrals at
first came mainly from the police department; today they usually
come from the schools. The bureau employs a director, a psychologist,
a social worker, a reading specialist, three attendance officers, several
policemen, and one policewoman, as well as a well-qualified secre-
tarial staff. The bureau is concerned with the normal as well as the
delinquent child; it also has pioneered in the study of gifted children.
The director is the chief guidance officer of the community, and he
directs the counseling activities of the local schools.

When a child is referred to the bureau, a total effort is made by
the staff to find the causes of his difficulty. He is given a thorough
medical examination, then a battery of psychological tests; the social
worker investigates his home environment and talks to his family
and neighbors; she also interviews his teachers and even his friends
and playmates. Then the child is given a reading test; failure in reading accomplishment often leads to delinquency. The entire staff meets
and the problem is reviewed from the legal, medical, social, psychological, family, and educational viewpoints, and a decision is made
involving the cooperation of several community agencies.

The bureau has been so successful that there has been a steady
decline in delinquency in the community, and its activities are regarded as a model to be imitated by other cities. The family, the
school, the church, the police, all must work together for the welfare
of our youngsters. The ideal of cooperation is best manifested by
the Youth Studies Center at the University of Southern California
under the magnificent guidance of Dr. Kim Nelson, who tries to
bring about a total awareness of the community.

In the field of inter-racial education to prevent delinquency the
attainments of Dr. Fred Weaver, Dr. Evis Coda, Opal Jones, and
Sam Hamerman deserve special notice. They all are pioneers in
human relations and democratic idealism. Most important of all is
continued slum clearance and better housing for the underprivileged.
As long as the slums infest major American cities we shall have to
fight an uphill battle against delinquency. This demands action and
support on both the national and the community level. Certainly
there is a need for better recreational facilities and the elimination

of "gin mills" and other undesirable places for our youngsters. We need more psychiatric clinics and better trained police officers who can deal with delinquents. Correctional institutions should be carefully checked so that they can be centers of education rather than breeding grounds for adult criminals.

All this will be costly. But in the end we will save millions of dollars. In a state institution a boy costs the taxpayers thousands of dollars a year, while in school he only costs a few hundred. We must discard nineteenth-century penal systems; harshness and cruelty only create viciousness.

CHAPTER THIRTY-SEVEN

New Horizons

Ever since 1787 the federal government has been active in the support of education. 1787 was the date of the Northwest Ordinance which tried to promote organized knowledge. Ohio, specifically, was to use the 16th section of each township for the support of its schools. States that were newly admitted to the Union were later given direct grants by Congress for educational purposes.

For the defense of the U. S. the Military Academy was established at West Point in 1802. Twenty-three years later the Naval Academy was founded at Annapolis. The Coast Guard owes its inception to Alexander Hamilton who, in 1790, established a Revenue-Marine Service to enforce the Custom Laws. In 1876 a Coast Guard Academy was established in New London, Connecticut. In the 20th century the Merchant Marine has its educational headquarters at Kings Point, New York. In 1956 this institution became a permanent service academy. In 1954 an Air Force Academy was established near Colorado Springs, Colorado. Its campus is one of the most impressive in the U.S. and its instructors and students have a high degree of motivation.

Important for the progress of education was the First Morrill Act in 1862 which provided for the establishment of land-grant colleges. Institutions established under the Act were to be related to "agriculture and the mechanical arts." In the 20th century the agricultural and mechanical schools became strong centers of liberal education also. In 1887 the Hatch Act aided the advancement of agricultural stations. In 1914 the Smith-Lever Act gave financial aid to land grant colleges and made possible the promotion of scientific agriculture. In 1917 the Smith-Hughes Act furthered the cause of vocational education and established a Federal Board of Vocational Education. In 1936 the George-Allen Act expanded vocational education.

Franklin D. Roosevelt, during his presidential administration, provided emergency grants to the states and established the National Youth Administration and the Civilian Conservation Corps.

Vocational rehabilitation was furthered by the Smith-Sears Act in 1918 and by the Smith-Bankhead Act two years later. In 1943 a Vocational Rehabilitation Act was passed by Congress which provided veterans with hospitalization, various types of therapy and other benefits. Veterans of the Korean War received aid through Public Law 16.

Most important from an educational standpoint was the "G.I. Bill of Rights," which provided aid to veterans of World War II to continue education in high school, junior college, university, graduate school, and other specialized institutions. The act provided tuition which was paid directly to the educational institution; also, some of the veterans' living expenses were taken care of by the government. Almost eight million veterans benefited by this Bill. The cost amounted to over $14,500,000. Veterans of the Korean War also received educational benefits. The difference was that they received a lump sum which had to provide for both their educational and living expenses.

In 1958, during the Eisenhower Administration, a Defense Education Act was passed. This was largely the result of concern over lags in education and a feeling that Russian competition was especially severe in the sciences. A year before, a Russian artificial satellite had convinced many legislators that Russian progress in technology posed a dangerous threat. The act provided for special aid in languages, science, mathematics, and counseling. Through financial incentives more capable students were to be encouraged to go into college teaching.

The establishment of the Peace Corps and extension of the scope of the National Defense Education Act were the major successes of the Kennedy Administration in education. Under the Kennedy Administration federal aid to education became an issue of vigorous controversy; it remains so under the Johnson Administration. Federal aid is opposed by political conservatives. In addition, some religious groups feel that federal funds should aid all schools at all levels.

U.S. OFFICE OF EDUCATION

Henry Barnard was one of the pioneers who urged a central government agency for education. In 1867 a "Department of Education" was set up; a year later it became the "Office of Education" as part of the Interior Department. In 1870 it changed its name again and became a "Bureau of Education." In 1929 it again became the "Office of Education." It was transferred to the Federal Security Agency in 1939; in 1953 it became part of the Department of Health, Education and Welfare.

The history of the Department indicates that it has never been regarded with the respect which education deserves. Actually, the Commissioner of Education ought to have full cabinet status.

Among the U.S. Commissioners we note the following:

Commissioner	President Making Appointment	Years in Office
Henry Barnard	A. Johnson	1867-1870
John Eaton	Grant	1870-1886
N. H. R. Dawson	Cleveland	1886-1889
William T. Harris	Harrison	1889-1906
Elmer E. Brown	T. Roosevelt	1906-1911
Philander P. Claxton	Taft	1911-1921
John J. Tigert	Harding	1921-1928
William J. Cooper	Hoover	1929-1933
George F. Zook	F. Roosevelt	1933-1934
John W. Studebaker	F. Roosevelt	1934-1949
Earl J. McGrath	Truman	1949-1953
Lee Thurston	Truman	1953 (2 mos.)
Samuel Brownell	Eisenhower	1953-1956
Lawrence G. Derthick	Eisenhower	1956-1961
Sterling McMurrin	Kennedy	1961-1962
F. Keppel	Kennedy	1963-

Commissioners H. Barnard, W. T. Harris, E. J. McGrath, L. Derthick, and F. Keppel deserve special notice for their attempts to universalize educational opportunities. The report which Derthick issued on Russian education gave great impetus to more effective support of American schools on all levels.

The office issues voluminous reports. Its journal, *School Life,* and its *Annual Report* and *Biennial Surveys* have a wide circulation. It cooperates with universities and state departments of education in significant educational projects, aids land grant colleges, and provides for library facilities in rural areas.

Its activities are constantly expanding, especially through the National Defense Act. Its library resources are formidable. It assists in the Fulbright Fellowship program and aids in a large-scale exchange of students. It sponsors programs for all agencies of communication and initiates conferences during which new educational ideas are discussed. The Commissioner of Education advises the President in his legislative program and usually defends it before Congressional Committees.

ORGANIZATIONS

Professional organizations have aided the development of the teaching profession. Especially significant is the National Education Association, which was started in 1857 and was first called the National Teachers' Association. Its purpose was to expand education and "elevate the character of the teaching profession."

The philosophy of the N.E.A. is based upon a desire to unite all members of the teaching profession into one strong organization, neither pro-capital nor pro-labor, but concerned with the welfare of the teacher. Its aim is to improve the public conception of the teacher, so that his position becomes more important in society. The N.E.A. has supported federal legislation for support of the schools. It has protected the profession against wild attacks from regressives who charge the schools with being subversive and atheistic.

N.E.A. leaders in our time like W. Carr and L. G. Derthick have continued in the spirit of Horace Mann and have vigorously promoted the cause of education.

Its auxiliary organizations include the state teachers' groups of which the California Teachers' Association is especially significant. Charles Ruby, Jessie Moses, J. Wilson McKenney, Daniel Dawson, Arthur Corey and Lionel de Silva have given vigorous leadership for the schools in California. The C.T.A. has been successful in raising salaries and professional standards in California. It has stimulated the California legislature to give billions of dollars for better schools. It has a Commission on Higher Education which promotes new ideas and new concepts on the junior college and university level. In 1963 the C.T.A. celebrated its 100th anniversary. Noted speakers, including foreign ambassadors, paid tribute to its work.

The National Education Association, as well as its member associations, has been especially concerned about the ethics of the teaching profession. In 1952 a code of ethics was formalized. It contains five major principles.

The first holds that

The primary obligation of the teaching profession is to guide children, youth, and adults in the pursuit of knowledge and skills, to prepare them in the ways of democracy, and to help them to become happy, useful, self-supporting citizens. The ultimate strength of the nation lies in the social responsibility, economic competence, and moral strength of the individual American.

In fulfilling the obligations of this principle the teacher will—

(1) Deal justly and impartially with students regardless of their physical, mental, emotional, political, economic, social, racial, or religious characteristics.

(2) Recognize the differences among students and seek to meet their individual needs.

(3) Encourage students to formulate and work for high individual goals in the development of their physical, intellectual, creative, and spiritual endowments.

(4) Aid students to develop an understanding and appreciation not only of the opportunities and benefits of American democracy but also of their obligations to it.

(5) Respect the right of every student to have confidential information about himself withheld except when its release is to authorized agencies or is required by law.

(6) Accept no remuneration for tutoring except in accordance with approved policies of the governing board.[1]

The second principle states:

The members of the teaching profession share with parents the task of shaping each student's purposes and acts toward socially acceptable ends. The effectiveness of many methods of teaching is dependent upon cooperative relationships with the home.

In fulfilling the obligations of this second principle the teacher will—

(1) Respect the basic responsibilities of parents for their children.

(2) Seek to establish friendly and cooperative relationships with the home.

(3) Help to increase the student's confidence in his own home and avoid disparaging remarks which might undermine that confidence.

---

[1] *N.E.A. Code of Ethics*, 1952.

(4) Provide parents with information that will serve the best interests of their children, and be discreet with information received from parents.

(5) Keep parents informed about the progress of their children as interpreted in terms of the purposes of the school.[2]

The third principle maintains that

The teaching profession occupies a position of public trust involving not only the individual teacher's personal conduct, but also the interaction of the school and the community. Education is most effective when these many relationships operate in a friendly, cooperative, and constructive manner.

In fulfilling the obligations of this third principle the teacher will —

(1) Adhere to any reasonable pattern of behavior accepted by the community for professional persons.

(2) Perform the duties of citizenship, and participate in community activities with due consideration for his obligations to his students, his family, and himself.

(3) Discuss controversial issues from an objective point of view, thereby keeping his class free from partisan opinions.

(4) Recognize that public schools belong to the people of the community, encourage lay participation in shaping the purposes of the school, and strive to keep the public informed of the educational program which is being provided.

(5) Respect the community in which he is employed and be loyal to the school system, community, state, and nation.

(6) Work to improve education in the community and to strengthen the community's moral, spiritual, and intellectual life.[3]

The fourth principle asserts that

The members of the teaching profession have inescapable obligations with respect to employment. These obligations are nearly always shared employer-employee responsibilities based upon mutual respect and good faith.

In fulfilling the obligations of this fourth principle the teacher will —

(1) Conduct professional business thru the proper channels.

(2) Refrain from discussing confidential and official information with unauthorized persons.

(3) Apply for employment on the basis of competence only, and avoid asking for a specific position known to be filled by another teacher.

(4) Seek employment in a professional manner, avoiding such practices as the indiscriminate distribution of applications.

---

[2] *Ibid.*
[3] *Ibid.*

(5) Refuse to accept a position when the vacancy has been created thru unprofessional activity or pending controversy over professional policy or the application of unjust personnel practices and procedures.

(6) Adhere to the conditions of a contract until service thereunder has been performed, the contract has been terminated by mutual consent, or the contract has otherwise been legally terminated.

(7) Give and expect due notice before a change of position is to be made.

(8) Be fair in all recommendations that are given concerning the work of other teachers.

(9) Accept no compensation from the producers of instructional supplies when one's recommendations affect the local purchase or use of such teaching aids.

(10) Engage in no gainful employment, outside of his contract, where the employment affects adversely his professional status or impairs his standing with students, associates, and the community.

(11) Cooperate in the development of school policies and assume one's professional obligations thereby incurred.

(12) Accept one's obligation to the employing board for maintaining a professional level of service.[4]

The fifth principle declares:

The teaching profession is distinguished from many other occupations by the uniqueness and quality of the professional relationships among all teachers. Community support and respect are influenced by the standards of teachers and their attitudes toward teaching and other teachers.

In fulfilling the obligations of this fifth principle the teacher will —

(1) Deal with other members of the profession in the same manner as he himself wishes to be treated.

(2) Stand by other teachers who have acted on his behalf and at his request.

(3) Speak constructively of other teachers, but report honestly to responsible persons in matters involving the welfare of students, the school system, and the profession.

(4) Maintain active membership in professional organizations and, thru participation, strive to attain the objectives that justify such organized groups.

(5) Seek to make professional growth continuous by such procedures as study, research, travel, conferences, and attendance at professional meetings.

(6) Make the teaching profession so attractive in ideals and practices that sincere and able young people will want to enter it.[5]

---

[4] *Ibid.*
[5] *Ibid.*

Opposed to the principles of the N.E.A. is the American Federation of Teachers—an organization which is affiliated with the AFL and which was started in 1916. The AFT is less concerned with pedagogical problems and more interested in the bargaining power of the teacher. It advocates the use of strikes to accomplish better working conditions for the teacher. It holds that the teaching profession must eliminate all forms of segregation, must advance industrial education, promote the ideals of academic freedom and, most important, has to be part of the labor movement rather than leaning toward the propertied class. Its philosophical spokesman has been Myron Lieberman who in such books as *Teaching as a Profession* and *The Future of Public Education* has argued for one strong organization for teachers which would stress social involvement and which would develop higher standards of proficiency on every level.

Also important in the development of American education has been the Parent-Teachers Association. Established in Washington in 1894, it was first called the National Congress of Mothers. Its aim was to improve the effectiveness of the child, parents, schools, and society. In 1900 it held a convention and a charter was issued together with a new name: The National Congress of Parents and Teachers. Today it has millions of members, both fathers and mothers. It has been a vigorous agency in promoting better schooling and advancing the welfare of children and has supported a more adequate financial investment in education, has helped underprivileged children, and has given hundreds of scholarships to deserving youngsters. It has made education a true community concern.

Critics, like Admiral Rickover, charge the PTA with too much interference in educational affairs and too much emphasis on social activities. Indeed, in 1963 Rickover even proposed that the PTA be abolished. Nothing could be more irresponsible. The PTA is one of the most dynamic educational agencies in this nation. Foreign visitors are impressed by the diversity of its membership and its enthusiasm for progress in education. Many schools can virtually be measured by the quantity and quality of their PTA involvement. In underprivileged communities it has made valiant efforts to interest parents in child guidance and to make the school a symbol of community unity. In linking the child, the home and the community, the PTA represents American idealism in action.

TRENDS

In our time there has been a greater popular interest in education than ever before. The election for state superintendency in California, which featured Max Rafferty against Ralph Richardson, was followed with eagerness by a vast audience. Television, magazines and newspapers devote more space to education than ever before. Even the image of the teacher, who used to be pictured as a rather anemic creature, is changing. Now the more prevalent conception is of a dynamic personality who is enthusiastic and personable and who is dedicated to youth. Still, much has to be done to make the teacher the real leader of American society.

Educational journals have improved in quality and appeal. This is especially true of the *Phi Delta Kappan,* the *N.E.A. Journal,* the *Teachers College Record, School and Society* and the *Harvard Educational Review.* Educators are now concerned about the implication of inquiries in other areas and in cooperative endeavors with various departments of the academic community. This has been a period of soul-searching—always a healthy symptom of educational growth.

New instructional techniques include team teaching, the use of educational television, more comprehensive textbooks, the widespread use of teaching machines, paperback books, language instruction in the first grade or kindergarten, and the introduction of new scientific concepts on the elementary level. Science fairs have promoted student interest in individual projects. The non-graded high school has attracted nation-wide attention. Much has been done for the gifted. For example, in California outstanding high school seniors are able to take college courses for credit. In Santa Monica the seminar method is used even on the elementary level.

A determined attempt has been made to deal with delinquency and the drop-out problem. Encouraging is the activity of the Youth Opportunity Board in Los Angeles, which has united all school agencies in an onslaught against delinquency. Still, the obstacles are immense when we remember that more than half of the Mexican-American children do not finish high school.

In a provocative speech Daniel Schreiber describes the Higher Horizons Program in New York.

Its main premise was that, regardless of what past records and I.Q. scores might indicate, many human talents—human lives, in fact—were going to waste. As of today, sixty-five schools with a population of 45,000 participate in the program, and the accuracy of its premises has been substantiated many times.

The program begins with third-grade students and extends to cover the population of thirteen junior high schools. At the beginning of the year these students are given intelligence tests, plus reading and arithmetic ability tests. They are then exposed to a program of instruction which employs every productive technique available, emphasizing remedial teaching in arithmetic and reading. But these classroom activities are supplemented and balanced by others which are considered of equal, if not greater, importance.

First of all, the guidance staff of each of the schools participating in the program has been enlarged so that each school has at least one full-time guidance counselor. I cannot possibly overstate the importance of guidance being provided to *every* child, to assure him in a continuing way of the school's positive commitment to him and his potential; and not just to the child who is in need, or when he is overtly in need. Secondly, an extensive program in cultural enrichment was initiated to expose these often incredibly impoverished children and young people to many aspects of this world to which they belong — through trips to theatres, concerts, museums, libraries — experiences taken for granted in the instance of the average middle-class child — which they might otherwise never come to know. Finally, in recognizing that the child's aspirational uplift must be sustained and encouraged by his total environment, great attention is being given to involving the parents of the Higher Horizons students in the schools' endeavors through guidance, newsletters, and workshops.

Let me record some of the accomplishments of the original demonstration guidance project of students. In various studies, they showed an average individual gain of thirteen I.Q. points in three years. The average gain for the boys was seventeen points; for the girls eleven points. The boys, incidentally, had lower scores than the girls on the first test. Let me quote from a study of eighty-one pupils who had taken both tests: "Sixty-six showed an increase; twelve showed a drop; and three remained the same. . . ." This ratio of increase to decrease of five to one remained constant in all of the studies made. Twenty-one students, or more than one-fourth of the group, showed gains of more than twenty-one points; thirteen between twenty-one and thirty points; six between thirty-one and fifty; and two between fifty-one and sixty points. In 1957, 26 per cent of the students had scored in the I.Q. category of 110 and above. In 1960, 58 per cent scored 110 and above. What is particularly interesting is the increase in the I.Q. in view of previous findings that boys and girls from this background usually show a decrease in I.Q. as they grow older.

In general, approximately 40 per cent more pupils are finishing high school than did before. Two and one-half times as many are completing academic courses, and three and one-half times as many are going on to some type of post-secondary education. In fact, of those who completed the academic course in June 1961, 91 per cent went on to further education. Sixty-six per cent of the group graduated from senior high school, compared to an average of 40 per cent for previous groups.[6]

---
[6] Daniel Schreiber, "Promising Practices Gleaned from a Year of Study," *Phi Delta Kappan*, February, 1963, p. 220.

The non-graded high school represents one of the challenges of our time. Frank Brown gained fame as principal of such a school in Melbourne, Florida. He describes his experiment in eloquent terms.

The first step in recovering from decades of intellectual disaster wrought by the grade must be to reclassify youngsters for learning on the basis of their achievement rather than the grade to which they have been chronologically promoted. They must be fanned out in a new design. This is accomplished by clustering students intellectually on the basis of their performance on nationally standardized achievement tests. The intelligent quotient, which has been a primary measure in the past, is of little or no value in the non-graded school. . . . The plan for continuous learning at Melbourne accommodates youngsters by placing them in temporary learning situations from which they can move at any time. These *ad hoc* learning arrangements are called phases. A phase is a stage of development with a varying time element. One student may remain in a low phase indefinitely; another may progress rapidly into higher phases.

When students enter Melbourne High School they are sorted on the basis of nationally standardized achievement tests. They are then clustered into a new spectrum in line with their various aptitudes and abilities.

Phase 1: — Subjects are centered around remedial work.

Phase 2: — Subjects are concerned with basic skills.

Phase 3: — Subjects are designed for students seeking an average education.

Phase 4: — Subjects are available for students desiring education in considerable depth.

Phase 5: — Subjects are open to students who are willing to assume responsibility for their own learning and plan to go far beyond the boundaries of a single course.

Phase Q: — Students whose creative talents are well developed in special areas should give consideration to this "Quest" phase of the curriculum. This is an important dimension of the phased organization designed to give thrust in the direction of individual fulfillment. In this phase a student may research in an area in which he is deeply and broadly curious, either to develop creative powers or in quest of knowledge. A student may spend from one to three hours a day in Quest.

Phase X: — Non-academic subjects which do not accommodate student mobility; e.g., typing, physical education. These subjects are ungraded but unphased.

This realignment of students brings about a major difference in course content between the non-graded and conventionally graded school. The motion of the non-graded curriculum compels the school to resort to a much wider range of materials. No standard textbooks are used in any phase. A multiplicity of material has replaced them. A gradeless curriculum designed for student mobility must be saturated with variegated materials.

The effect of non-grading is to change the educational process so that students are accelerated through subject matter on a continuing rather than a yearly basis. Learning is both more appropriate and more viable when children of comparable academic accomplishment and pace are grouped together.

There are no study halls in the Melbourne plan for a non-graded school. The study hall, like the grade, belongs to the remote past. In a non-graded curriculum students are expected to take responsibility for their own learning and the monitored type of study hall becomes a useless appendage.

Changes wrought by the gradeless plan

What are some of the changes that have taken place at Melbourne High School after three years of gradeless learning?

First, it is evident that a non-graded school is different from a graded school in more ways than just a re-ranking of students. Some classes must be smaller; others must be larger.

Another reform which is spurred by non-graded education is a change in the function of the teacher. Students who are unbridled intellectually are no longer content with a passive "telling" kind of education. Teachers must throw out the old kit bag.

Gradeless schools are moving from memorized learning and simplified explanations to the process of inquiry for each individual. What is inquiry? In its simplest form, inquiry is curiosity linked to action. It means newer and deeper perceptions for the individual. In its ultimate form, it leads to the development of traits of imagination and creativity and eventually to new discoveries for science and the humanities.

In the non-graded school, the intellectual pace of various students is more separate and unequal than in graded education. As the curriculum is expanded and becomes variegated, achievement becomes a hallmark of the school. The illusory aim of evenness in achievement which is characteristic of graded schools is not evident here.

Rebellion against the grade lockstep is one of the missed revolutions of our time. Still poised and full of ferment, it may never occur, although the grade curtain which was rung down around learning has been pierced by a new system of learning where the flashpoints are phases instead of annual promotion.

As Philip Coombs said when he was executive secretary of the Fund for the Advancement of Education, "What the schools need is not simply more money from the outside but sweeping changes on the inside." Sweeping changes do take place in a non-graded school, and without an increase in the budget.[7]

Colleges have been caught by the wave of experimentation. There are an increasing number of honors programs, better inter-collegiate cooperation, more independent study and tutorial work, more research on the undergraduate level, more programs abroad, and more involvement with the public school system. But the American university is still too much bound by tradition. As yet, it does not educate enough students. There is not sufficient involvement with pressing social issues. A truly creative spirit is lacking in most colleges.

Most encouraging in our time has been the work of the Peace Corps. It has demonstrated the idealism of American youth both at home and abroad; it has changed some foreign conceptions of the United States; it has fought valiantly against poverty and ignorance, not by superimposing artificial standards but by cooperative work and cooperative planning. The Peace Corps is a triumph for American democracy and for the American ideal of education.

ADULT EDUCATION

As early as 1661 an adult evening school was established in New York. In New England the churches often combined education and spiritual training. In 1808 Yale University offered extension classes. 1831 marks the beginning of the American Lyceum, which provided valuable support of public education and expanded the horizons of countless adults.

The Chautauqua movement had its inception in 1874. Its early objective was religious—to provide better Sunday school teachers. But its purpose broadened and many small communities were enriched in their scientific, esthetic and social activities. Noted lecturers reached a wide audience, bringing ideas in the arts and sciences.

Adult education was promoted especially through the public library. The YMCA and YWCA not only provided social services to youth but also served as educational agencies. Women's clubs gave platforms to countless lecturers. Universities did not lag behind—they established evening and correspondence courses. Today in community colleges the adult evening program often attracts more students than

[7] Brown, "The Non-Graded High School," *Phi Delta Kappan*, Feb., 1963, pp. 207–209.

the day program. In 1891 the International Correspondence School opened at Scranton, Pa. The University of California and other state universities have programs for adults which include a great variety of courses.

In 1926 the American Association of Adult Education was established. It merged in 1951 with the Department of Adult Education of the N.E.A. and formed a new organization, the Adult Education Association. Its magazine, *Adult Leadership,* serves as a clearing house for new ideas.

Under President Roosevelt the Works Progress Administration provided employment for unemployed artists. Writers and teachers were enlisted in a vast adult program. Newton Minow, FCC chairman, appointed in the Kennedy administration, made strong efforts to improve the quality of both commercial and educational television so that they could become genuine adult media.

The Carnegie Foundation has sponsored organized adult education programs. This was especially due to the leadership of F. P. Keppel who was influenced by English and German interests in adult education. The Ford Foundation has a thriving adult division which includes international relations, human relations, radio and television programs, the humanities and the promotion of the American ideal of freedom. The Ford Foundation has made considerable grants to the Great Books Foundation and to the American Library Association.

It is encouraging to note that both labor and management are promoting adult education. Many unions have special classes for their officers and members, and they sponsor extension work and offer scholarships. Enlightened industrial leaders send their executives back to college for specialized studies and for work in the humanities.

The Great Books Movement has attracted a wide audience. It has popularized works which otherwise would have been neglected, and has served as a meeting place for executives and housewives, artists and scientists, educators and laymen who have joined in a common intellectual enterprise. It has trained teachers to use the discussion method more effectively and has expanded the intellectual horizons of countless communities.

The greatest educational expansion in our time will take place in adult education. The need is not merely for more programs but more imaginative planning which can enrich our communities, make them more beautiful esthetically and erase the social barriers which tend to create ghettoes. Adult education is not merely a supplement to the education of the young; it is an autonomous enterprise, and demonstrates that education need never stop, that it implies more than mere cultural ornamentation. Adult education is a part of American democratic idealism. It provides new outlooks and new ideas, and thus becomes the foundation of an open society.

Part of the greatness of ancient Athens was its adult education. It was not institutionalized but spontaneous; much of it was centered in the market place and in the banquet hall. Athenian leaders realized that the life of reason had to be cultivated by all; the young and the old, the rich and the poor. Such a life involved an active support of the arts. Indeed, Athenian citizens were paid to support the drama festivals. When a great thinker like Protagoras spoke it was like a public holiday.

Adult education should lead to an active interest in music, poetry and the other arts, and should improve both the social and intellectual life of our communities. It should elevate our taste and our appreciation so that we gain a knowledge of what is truly first-rate in civilization.

CHAPTER THIRTY-EIGHT

The Education of Women

BACKGROUND

The education of women is a complex matter. Their attraction lies in their ability to see the centrality of life and their capacity to feel profoundly and to project with warmth and imagination. Too much emphasis upon facts and analysis may limit this capacity by stifling spontaneity. DeMaistre wisely observed that the great fault of many women is their desire to feel like men.

In colonial times women received only the rudiments of education. They were taught reading, writing and arithmetic, but they were not admitted to the colonial colleges. It was thought that women were designed by God to become homemakers and that too much education would corrupt them. A girl eager for knowledge was regarded as being eccentric, but was expected to change after she got married.

One of the most progressive men in colonial times was Benjamin Rush, who remarked on the subject of education for women:

To qualify our women, they should not only be instructed in the usual branches of female education, but they should be taught the principles of liberty and government; and the obligations of patriotism should be inculcated upon them. The opinions and conduct of men are often regulated by women in the most arduous enterprises of life; and their approbation is frequently the principal reward of the hero's danger and the patriot's toils. Besides, the first impressions upon the minds of children are generally derived from the women. Of how much consequence, therefore, it is in a republic that they should think justly upon the great subject of liberty and government.[1]

Thomas Jefferson in a letter to Nathaniel Burwell noted that the minds of women are corrupted by too much novel reading. He recommended instead authors like Molière, Racine, Corneille, Dryden and Shakespeare. The French language should be taught to both men and women, and he recommended dancing, drawing and music as valuable forms of amusement for young ladies. Most important, however, is household economy, which is the foundation of our society.

One of the pioneers in the education of women was Mrs. Emma Willard. At 17 she began her career as a teacher. She taught in a variety of schools before and after her marriage. Her father, after a few years, faced financial ruin and Emma had to support the family.

In 1814 she established a boarding school for girls at Middlebury, Massachusetts. Its inadequate facilities made her acutely conscious of the neglect of the education of women; neighboring Middlebury College for men had a fine plant, an excellent library, and well-trained teachers.

In 1821 she opened a new school in Troy, New York, which had the support of the governor. To it came the daughters of the most influential families from New York and other states. It soon achieved an international reputation and educators came from other nations to study its system.

The Troy Female Academy was different because it taught "masculine" subjects like geography, history, and mathematics, as well as the painting and embroidery which were usually stressed at girls' schools. Even physiology had a place in its curriculum. Some parents were shocked to hear that their daughters were becoming acquainted with human anatomy. They felt that this might rob them of their "delicacy" and even lead to immorality. Several parents protested vigorously to Mrs. Willard to eliminate physiology from the curriculum, but she would not budge.

The examinations at the Troy Female Academy were held in February and July. The examinations in July, which represented the climax of the academic semester, usually lasted eight days. She in-

---

[1] Rush, *On the Mode of Education Proper in a Republic.*

vited eminent teachers from other parts of the country to conduct the tests and thus see how well prepared her girls were.

In her school no class distinctions were tolerated. Rich and poor received the same treatment. When a girl was found to be wayward, Emma would talk to her as a friend and counselor. She was admired by her students whom she taught to develop their minds and their bodies. She counseled them never to neglect their appearance, for scholarship alone would not assure their success in life.

Hundreds of teachers were trained by her. She demanded the highest standards of proficiency from prospective instructors, and became a close friend of Horace Mann and Henry Barnard and helped them in their efforts to improve the standards of the teaching profession. With Woodbridge, she wrote a geography text which became a standard book in many schools in the 19th century.

In 1839 she gave up the active management of the Troy school. Two years later she became superintendent of schools at Keningston, Connecticut, a unique honor at the time. In 1845 she was an honored guest at the World Education Convention in London.

Emma Willard was a tireless traveler. She toured New England, the West, and the South and spoke to all kinds of groups, always advocating better education for women. She would lecture for a few dollars; many times she was not paid at all. Many attacked her views which were unorthodox and too advanced for her time. Some newspaper editors called her visionary and radical. Still, when she died in 1870 at the age of 83, she was generally regarded as one of the important pioneers in American education.

PIONEERS

Coeducation was making rapid headway in the 19th century. Oberlin College admitted both boys and girls if they had adequate academic qualifications. Antioch College likewise was liberal in its admissions policy and encouraged coeducation. Iowa State was open to both sexes from its establishment in 1856. The Ohio State University and the University of Wisconsin also admitted coeds. The University of Michigan even admitted women into its graduate school.

Another pioneer of female education was Catherine Beecher, who organized the Western Female Institute in Cincinnati and also established the Hartford Female Seminary. She was a prolific writer and organized the Woman's Education Association. Like Emma

Willard, she lectured all over the country on behalf of better education for women.

Elizabeth Peabody, who was influenced by Froebel, opened the first English-speaking kindergarten in America; she edited the *Kindergarten Messenger* which stimulated the development of early childhood education. Always advocating the cause of popular education, she traveled widely and, as one of her disciples wrote, "kindled a blaze which was seen and answered from a hundred heights across the land."

Mary Lyon, a pioneer in the development of higher education for women, founded Mount Holyoke College and served as its first president. She set high standards of academic proficiency and at the same time took a personal interest in her girls. Entrance examinations at the college were unusually severe. Emily Dickinson, who was a student there, wrote home saying: "You cannot imagine how trying they are." The curriculum included the sciences, mathematics and languages as well as philosophy. The arts also found a prominent place at Mount Holyoke. Students and teachers were required to share in doing the housework. This meant that often girls had to rise at 5 o'clock in the morning to prepare meals. It made for simplicity in their way of living, and also made possible low tuition costs, in line with the democratic ideals of its founder.

Religion had a prominent place at Mount Holyoke. Courses in moral philosophy taught belief in God's providence. Piety was encouraged. Many graduates became wives of missionaries and helped spread the Christian Gospel. The students were encouraged to search their consciences every day and to confess their waywardness to the school executives.

Vassar, founded in 1865, placed even more emphasis upon intellectual stimulation than did Mount Holyoke. In 1875 Wellesley College was established; it reflected the ideals of Henry Durant who supervised both the curriculum and the management of the college. The same year saw the founding of Smith College, which provided a broad education for women and gave a secondary place to specialization. Bryn Mawr, founded in 1885, embodied the spirit of Martha Carey Thomas who was its first president. At Bryn Mawr, internationally famous scholars formed the nucleus of the faculty. Miss Thomas was a notable scholar in philology and had taken graduate work at Johns Hopkins and at the University of Zürich where she received her Doctorate. The college pioneered in giving autonomy to students and encouraging them to learn self-government. Traditional educators were shocked by this procedure and predicted the ruin of the college; instead it prospered and other colleges adopted its student government scheme.

Alice Freeman Palmer distinguished herself as head of the history department at Wellesley and later as its president. In 1892 she became dean of women at the University of Chicago. Each summer she taught underprivileged children in the slums of Boston.

Ella Flagg Young was superintendent of the Chicago schools and in 1910 became president of the National Education Association. She made important contributions to vocational education and to the professional study of education in universities. She believed in applied democracy and encouraged divergent opinions among her subordinates.

TRENDS TODAY

Today co-education is an accepted fact, and colleges for women, such as Smith, Wellesley, and Radcliffe, compete with the best colleges for men and have excellent academic standards.

Among contemporary women's colleges Sarah Lawrence and Bennington deserve special notice. Since 1925 when Sarah Lawrence was founded, it has been a liberalizing influence on American education. There the influence of John Dewey was especially strong; while many of its students came from wealthy homes, they were encouraged to develop a genuine social perspective. Entrance requirements were extremely liberal; classes were conducted on a seminar basis. Grades played a secondary role in admission; what mattered most was the personality of the girl, her motivation and interest in higher education. The college progressed especially under the leadership of Harold Taylor, who was a philosopher of the pragmatic school and who felt that the social sciences should have a prominent place in the Sarah Lawrence curriculum.

Bennington College, established in 1932, soon earned a national reputation. Its counseling services were especially proficient and the student was encouraged to develop originality and creative thinking. Since the arts had a prominent place at Bennington, eminent poets were invited to share their ideas with the students. Progressive concepts of education were treasured as much at Bennington as at Sarah Lawrence; participation and active experience in the arts and sciences became the foundations of the Bennington curriculum.

Colleges for women were the first to uphold the importance of poetry, painting, the dance and drama—subjects frequently slighted at the men's colleges and regarded by them as unnecessary frills. Today these so-called unessential subjects have a notable status in all universities and may have a deep impact in developing cultural sensitivity among students.

PARADOXES

The triumph of co-education has created unfortunate dilemmas. The co-ed is encouraged to develop her mind and to be proficient in her studies. Often she surpasses the boy in originality and intellectual curiosity. At the same time, she lives in a civilization which prizes physical beauty. This frequently means that she curbs her intellectul interests and subordinates herself to group standards.

The dilemma is exemplified by Carol Kennicott in Sinclair Lewis' *Main Street*. Carol, the graduate of a women's college, was inspired by the beauties of literature and her dream was that she would marry a poet. Instead, she became a librarian occupied with utilitarian tasks and answering routine questions. She married a doctor who was also a real estate operator in a small community. She thought that Gopher Prairie could become a center of culture. Instead, she found that it was dominated by a rigid class system and that it was a veritable intellectual desert. Instead of intellectual excitement, she experienced measureless boredom; instead of contact with like-minded individuals, she was exposed to innumerable parties which were exercises in futility.

Gopher Prairie is still with us today. It may have more conveniences; it may have a few cultural opportunities; but in countless communities the intellectual level is on a mediocre plane, and many women feel that their college experience has filled them with too many expectations and hopes so that disenchantment becomes inevitable.

We must not forget that most women students are governed by the drive for security. As one of my students wrote so perceptively:

> We are about fourteen or fifteen of us that do practically everything together. We live on the same floor in the best freshman women's dormitory at that dear old university; we eat meals together, we spend the weekends (when we aren't on dates) doing asinine things together. We laugh, talk, and when there is nothing better to do, we study as a group. We figure that college is the best and practically the only time to just have fun. We don't seem to have many financial worries, we have sufficient independence to make it interesting, and we are secure

enough in the group that opinion of others matters little to us. This is why we have fun. The others look on us with envy, sometimes with scorn. We don't care because we are having what is commonly known as a "blast."

Take last week-end for example. Fifteen couples, well-chaperoned, went on an overnight beach party at Laguna. We ate at the beach, sang old songs, and danced until two-thirty in the morning. The next day we spent at the beach, improving our tans while our dates surfed and went skin-diving. We didn't get any studying done that week-end, but as I said before, we sure had fun.

Oh, there are a few of us who have our more serious moments. We discuss religion or psychology or more often, sex. We feel that we have a fairly intelligent outlook on sex — well, we should have, we've talked about it enough. We don't know if we are typical examples of the younger generation, and we don't particularly care one way or the other.

We like our group. It gives us enough security so that we can act as we please, but it doesn't stifle our individuality. We enjoy ourselves, and like I said, right now that is one of our main goals. How successful it makes us feel to attain a goal so early in life.

IMPLICATIONS

A pressing need exists for a better relationship and understanding between men and women. This means not only more courses and better counseling for marriage in our colleges and high schools but a more realistic analysis of the role of the two sexes in contemporary life. Women must learn to moderate their economic desires and demand less from their husbands, who otherwise develop tension and anxiety. The cult of romantic love must be modified so that a more mature philosophy of life emerges. One of the aims of education at all levels is to establish a genuine appreciation of the sexes. This means more closeness in family life, more sharing of activities, and less dependence on popular stereotypes. Too many homes are as transitory as locker rooms. Too many men are so absorbed in their occupations that their home life recedes and they become strangers to their children. Too many wives, who are college graduates, are so occupied with trivial clubs and social activities that they live in unexamined, noisy futility.

This does not imply that women should be only homemakers. On the contrary, the aesthetic and intellectual interests of women are important, such things should make them more feminine, not more masculine. One of the best examples of the creative use of higher education is Mary Tinglof, who distinguished herself as a member of the Los Angeles Board of Education. She had strong convictions about the need for a liberal philosophy of education so that academic freedom would be protected. She read constantly; her intellectual interests kept her young. In great demand as a speaker, she addressed college meetings all over the country.

Agnes Meyer, like the early feminine pioneers, was utterly courageous in the support of education. Through books and articles, television appearances, and speeches before congressional committees, she championed freedom of inquiry. She became a spokesman for minority groups. She reminded legislators of the need for more and better schools and for an increasing investment in higher education. Her example indicates that the age of pioneering for women has not passed and that their leadership is needed in developing creative patterns for our schools.

The suggestion was made by a college instructor not so long ago that the enrollment of women should be restricted in our colleges because, in a time of limited facilities, it was more important to educate men. This view is completely inadequate. To be sure, we do not need more coeds whose main ambition is to be socialites and who regard college as a prelude to the country club. We need more women who will become scientists and artists and who will contribute to the advancement of our civilization. *We need women who are intellectually alive and exciting with innerdirected motivations.* We need women who are concerned about community life as well as international relations. *We need women with an enlightened conscience who are genuine individualists.* We hope that out of our colleges will come women who will improve the tone of family life; who will combine a thirst for knowledge with warmth and understanding and who will cherish "the wisdom of the heart."

CHAPTER THIRTY-NINE

Education and Parents

PARENTS AS TEACHERS

Education has no frontiers, but is a limitless process with limitless possibilities. It is the awareness with which we explore life and through which we try to make human existence meaningful. Man is defined by his hopes, and education is the ultimate expression of man's yearning for a better life.

In the seventeenth and eighteenth centuries, parents often acted as teachers, but now public education has taken over, and often parents take their responsibilities very lightly and believe that the schools have an automatic solution for the problems of their offspring. I remember a letter which I received when I started to teach; it was from the mother of a boy who was a *conscientious objector to any form of knowledge.* She asked in the letter, "Why don't you lern my boy how to spell?" The letter is symbolic of the smugness of many parents who believe that the schools are to be blamed when their children make little intellectual progress.

The letter reminds me of a nineteenth century poem:

I Have Brought My Daughter to You to Be Taught Everything

Dear Madam, I've called for the purpose,
Of placing my daughter at school;
She's only thirteen, I assure you,
And remarkably easy to rule.

I'd have her learning painting and music,
Gymnastics and dancing, pray do,
Philosophy, grammar, and logic,
You'll teach her to read, of course, too.

On the harp she must be proficient,
And play the guitar pretty soon.
And sing the last opera music
Even though she can't turn a right tune.

You must see that her manners are finished,
That she moves with a Hebe-like grace;
For though she is lame and one-sided,
That's nothing to do with her case.

Now to you I resign this young jewel,
And my words I would have you obey;
In six months return her, dear madam,
Shining bright as an unclouded day.

She's no aptness, I grant you, for learning
And her memory oft seems to halt,
But remember, if she's not accomplished
It will certainly be your fault.[1]

HOME ENVIRONMENT

The first moral and intellectual attitudes are learned at home; children are extremely perceptive, and they tend to imitate the behavior of adults. They often see through hypocrisy and therefore are disturbed when there is a basic dualism in the attitude of their parents — when the parents negate by their actions what they profess to believe. The atmosphere of the home is all-important; the material standards are generally secondary. What matters most is that intellectual concepts are treasured and that there is a genuine interest

---

[1] *Godey's Lady's Book*, XLVI.

in knowledge. Interest in knowledge can be stimulated in many ways; an excellent library, good records, reproductions of famous paintings— all are conducive to an atmosphere which encourages the child to seek genuine enlightenment.

The importance of early education is illustrated by the following anecdote:

Alfred Francis Wayland Parker, the great Chicago teacher, had lectured to a fashionable audience. A woman came up to him and asked:

"How early can I begin the education of my child?"

"When will your child be born?"

"Born? Why, he's already five years old."

"My goodness, woman," he exclaimed. "Don't stand there talking to me — hurry home; already *you have lost the best five years!*"

In the nineteenth century, the father was regarded as the absolute head of the family. He usually was extremely staid and respectable, especially in middle-class circles. He was somewhat arbitrary, easily angered and disturbed by the sins of children. He had a rigorous sense of justice and meted out physical punishment to the unruly. His word was law; to oppose it meant excommunication from the family circle. He often looked upon his offspring as naturally depraved and given to sinful ways. Authority had to be used to drive the devil out of the children and develop in their hearts a sense of justice and propriety.

Under these circumstances there could be little comradeship between parents and children. Respect for parents was the ideal virtue and parents were supposed to be looked upon as models of perfection. Yet, there were grave deficiencies in this attitude. One needs only to read representative nineteenth century novels, like Flaubert's *Madame Bovary*, Tolstoy's *Anna Karenina*, or Hawthorne's *Scarlet Letter*, to realize that the unity of the family was rather artificial and that it was mainly based upon coercion. The wife was often regarded as a machine for reproduction; her sphere was supposed to be the kitchen and the raising of children. As for her intellectual capacities, they were entirely secondary. Her task was to obey her husband, who was her lord and master.

CHANGES

In the twentieth century a basic change has taken place in the family system. Co-education, technology, the political and economic emancipation of women, the new leisure — all these trends have led to greater equality in the family system. Today the father usually is not a tyrant, but is more like a friend to his children. Often he acts like his offspring, and he is usually casual in his ways. Now the wife plays a dominant part in the family, while the father is busy as a provider, trying to get ahead in the strenuous economic struggle.

How should parents educate their children? No exact outline can be given; there are no absolute formulas in education. Still, parents must learn to avoid certain harmful attitudes.

Just as a great teacher is a constant learner, so the best parents are those who learn from their children. Thus one of my students describes how she learned from her daughter:

My most unforgettable teacher is not someone whom I have known in the past or under whom I have studied during my schooling. She is a young lady entering first grade this year and is only six years old.

Brenda was born following a period of international war. A personal war in my own life had not stopped, because of bitter experiences during previous months. Entering her physical life in this rather unstable environment did not trouble her one bit. It almost seemed as if she had one jump on life before she had to face its problems.

Through her own inquisitiveness and wonderment we have explored, in a small way, the world of nature and creation. The tenderness with which she picks a flower and examines its petals and later places it in a special place of honor in our home has given me a new reverence for all life. The collection of sea shells on our fireplace opened up a new world to her small mind. It challenged me to do extra reading so I would be able to talk with her about the God who created the sea from which we were picking the shells. To her each shell had a special assignment. She gave to each a family of mother, father, sisters, and brothers. In her simple love for the sea shells, she taught me that God not only created man, but created a world of beauty to explore. The experience that instantly sets the pace for her wildest imagination is the very quiet game of "listening to the ocean waves" through a large sea shell.

A world without love and trust does not exist, to her knowledge. She has faith in every contact she makes. This is not to say she is not an individual in her own right. She has strong ideas about human behavior, but through my daily association with her I have become more tolerant and warmer in my own relationship with others. She is not old enough to tell you how love is defined. The love in her eyes is the same when she finds a baby bird who has fallen from the nest or when she tries in her excitement to tell of her school activities.

The expression she so often uses early in the morning, "Let's open the door and see what the world is made out of," has taught me to think of human creativity.

IMPACT OF PARENTS

Parents can have a lasting educational impact on their children by stressing the importance of culture. Robert Browning tells about the debt which he owed to his father, who taught him Greek when he was six and who gave him a lasting appreciation of Greek literature. Mozart received his early education in music from his father, who set very high standards. John Stuart Mill owed a vast debt to his father, who saw to it that the boy received rigorous intellectual exercise.

One of my best students once remarked to me that he owed his real education to his mother, who was widowed when he was seven. She had to work for a living, but when she came home she would discuss art and philosophy and talk about the history of civilization. To her a good book meant more than material possessions and she encouraged her son to read widely. She took night school courses so that she would not regress and so that she would be intellectually stimulating. She was poor, according to her son, but he never felt the poverty; rather, he felt privileged that he had been brought up in such a stimulating environment.

Nelson Rockefeller tells how much he owes to his upbringing. Although his parents were immensely wealthy, he was never spoiled. His allowance as a boy was 25 cents a week and he had a shoe shine concession in his home to make extra money. He chose one of the less fashionable colleges of the Ivy League, Dartmouth, and there he received only a limited allowance every month. To make ends meet, he worked in the cafeteria. No wonder that he became a dedicated public servant and that he developed a simple and unaffected way of life.

Parents should not be perfectionists. Often they inhibit the growth of their children by not allowing for the full development of their individuality; on other occasions, parents encourage too much the precocious tendencies of their offspring.

When I was in college I usually spent my summers as a counselor in a Y.M.C.A. camp. One of my problem cases was Bobbie, a boy of eight, who had been brought up by his mother. She assured me that Bobbie was a genius, and Bobbie agreed.

The second week of camp I took Bobbie aside and asked him how he liked it up in the mountains. I expected him to give a simple answer. Instead he said: "I have not been quite adjusted yet."

Parents should not encourage a too permissive attitude in the home. Not all the impulses of the child are to be tolerated. Children can be just as tyrannical as adults. At the same time, parents should not establish excessively rigid standards of behavior. Too much rigidity only gives an incentive to rebellion on the part of children.

Parents should avoid allowing community and business activities to interfere with a full, well-planned home life. The education of children is the primary obligation of the father and mother. Family unity is cemented when parents participate in the activities of their children and when they show a profound interest in their esthetic and educational development.

Intellectual curiosity on the part of children must not be stifled. Too many fathers and mothers inhibit their youngsters by being impatient and by taking the questions of their offspring too lightly. The child is naturally curious and this is the best foundation for his educational growth. It goes without saying that parents should not stand still in their own intellectual and emotional development. When they become lethargic in their own outlook upon life they are unable to influence their children creatively. Most of the time children look down on parents who have ceased to grow and do not keep up with the changing patterns of the time.

Should parents use physical punishment? No definite answer can be given. In certain cases spanking may be helpful, but in many cases physical punishment indicates that the parents are failing in their educational philosophy. When physical punishment is applied, it should be with a humanitarian spirit.

Discipline in the home depends on an inward attitude on the part of parents. Firmness is best achieved through mutual understanding and when the parents act in such a manner that their children can admire them.

The home can and should act as a supplementary agency to the school. Parents should see to it that the arts become vital influences in the lives of their children and that real culture is part of the family environment. This process cannot start too early. The child should be stimulated so that he will share his ideas with his parents; in this way the cooperative spirit triumphs, and real democracy is achieved in the relationship between parents and their offspring.

A mother recently came to me very much perplexed, for her husband was dying and she had not said anything about this to her son, who was five years old. She told him that his father had gone on a vacation, for she did not want her boy to be exposed to the somber atmosphere of the hospital. Her husband agreed with her, although he missed his son very much.

I advised her to take her son to the hospital. Undoubtedly this experience would come as a shock to him, but it was time for him to be enlightened about life and death. I told her to approach her boy in a positive way, to explain to him that no one lives forever, that now he must show how big he is, and that he can carry on in the spirit of his father.

To children death is not such an awe-inspiring event as to adults. They may grieve more when their pet dog dies than when an immediate member of the family passes away. Only when death is surrounded by mystery does it become terrifying to them.

As Antoine de Saint-Exupéry remarked:

Already at the age of fifteen I might have learnt this lesson. I had a younger brother who lay dying. One morning towards four o'clock his nurse woke me and said that he was asking for me.

"Is he in pain?" I asked.

The nurse said nothing, and I dressed as fast as I could.

When I came into his room he said to me in a matter-of-fact voice, "I wanted to see you before I died. I am going to die." And with that he stiffened and winced and could not go on. Lying in pain, he waved his hand as if saying, "No!" I did not understand. I thought it was death he was rejecting. The pain passed, and he spoke again. "Don't worry," he said, "I'm all right. I can't help it. It's my body." His body was already foreign territory, something not himself.

He was very serious, this younger brother who was to die in twenty minutes. He had called me in because he felt a pressing need to hand on part of himself to me. "I want to make my will," he said; and he blushed with pride and embarrassment to be talking like a grown man. Had he been a builder of towers he would have bequeathed to me the finishing of his tower. Had he been a father, I should have inherited the education of his children. A reconnaissance pilot, he would have passed on to me the intelligence he had gleaned. But he was a child, and what he confided to my care was a toy steam engine, a bicycle, and a rifle.

Man does not die. Man imagines that it is death he fears; but what he fears is the unforeseen, the explosion. What man fears is himself, not death. There is no death when you meet death. When the body sinks into death, the essence of man is revealed. Man is a knot, a web, a mesh into which relationships are tied. Only those relationships matter. . . .[2]

---

[2] *Flight to Arras,* pp. 182–184.

PART SEVEN

Conclusion

CHAPTER FORTY

Art and Creativity

IMPORTANCE OF ART

Art gives a central meaning to education and links the realm of the intellect and that of the senses. Art is the bond between the past and the future, between the world of our dreams and the realm which we actually experience.

The artist is a subtle moralist. He teaches a lesson by direct experience and vivid awareness. His sermons need no translation; they can be understood by all. He does not superimpose ideas upon life but he allows the rhythm of existence to develop freely. By liberating himself, the artist contributes to the emancipation of humanity.

Progress in civilization means more than technological improvement. The machine can enslave us or it can be a bringer of freedom. Nor does progress imply more comforts for the individual; our luxuries may simply alienate us from nature. Nor is mere knowledge an unqualified blessing; knowledge may paralyze us for action and create unending dilemmas. Progress can be measured best by the expansion of sensitivity — moral and aesthetic — so that beauty invades our soul and dominates all our relationships. In *Endymion,* John Keats celebrates the importance of beauty:

> A thing of beauty is a joy forever:
> Its loveliness increases; it will never
> Pass into nothingness; but still will keep
> A bower quiet for us, and a sleep
> Full of sweet dreams, and health, and quiet breathing.
> Therefore, on every morrow, are we wreathing
> A flowery band to bind us to the earth,
> Spite of despondence, of the inhuman dearth
> Of noble natures, of the gloomy days,
> Of all the unhealthy and o'er-darkened ways
> Made for our searching: yes, in spite of all,
> Some shape of beauty moves away the pall
> From our dark spirits.

Art represents genuine universality. Whether we are young or old, poor or rich, whether we have much formal education or are self-educated, we need the stimulation of art. This does not imply that we should all paint or compose or become designers or poets, rather that we should learn to become aware of the stimulation of art, its infinite variety and its impact on human development.

Art has been defined in various ways. James Huneker speaks of it as "an instant in eternity." Jean Cocteau remarked that "art is science in the flesh." Robert Browning believed that "art is the one way possible of speaking truth"; Seneca asserted that "all art is but imitation of nature"; Salvador de Madariaga felt that "art is the conveyance of spirit by means of matter"; and Emerson said that "art is the path of the creator to his work."

There is a nexus between science and art. Both fields depend on imagination and intuition; they substitute a new universe for the one which the ordinary man experiences; they construct patterns from the multitude of phenomena; both contribute to man's need for self-expression; they necessitate a discipline which heightens our senses; both are forms of profound awareness. The difference is that science is interested in prediction and control, while art represents both order and chaos, both integration and deliberate disequilibrium.

The tragedy of many individuals is that they feel separated from life. Many students merely endure education, which they view as a mechanical process. They listen to lectures, but the words of the instructor become monotonous phrases. They cram for tests and a week later they have forgotten most of the material covered in the book. They give answers in class which they feel will please their instructor and improve their grade. They study not to become educated, but only to obtain a better job after graduation.

Many instructors likewise are not at all interested in reaching the individual student; rather they are concerned about their own economic and professional advancement. In college this means the publication of books and articles and unending research. They strive for respectability rather than for understanding. They are not emotionally involved with the process of learning. In fact, they studiously cultivate an attitude of neutrality toward the great issues of our time.

Art demands emotional involvement. Through art our emotions are stirred, we become conscious of parts of our personality which were ignored amidst everyday experience. The greyness of existence is replaced by new contrasts and climaxes.

Art is a protest against inhumanity. When we look at the paintings of Goya and Orozco we become aware of the inhumanity of man and his ability to compartmentalize his conscience. When we view the productions of Kirchner and Munch we feel the threat of mass society which tends to enslave the individual. But art is more than an expression of social reform. It points to a new universe, to new possibilities, to ideal vistas. It transforms experience so that uniqueness and genuine individuality are achieved.

When Sinclair Lewis wrote *Babbitt* and *Main Street* he did not want to expose merely the drabness of middle class life and the ugliness of the small town; he wanted to point to new realms of experience in which generosity was treasured and beauty valued, in which art had an autonomous function. When Sherwood Anderson wrote *Winesburg, Ohio* he exposed the inner life of the pillars of small town society, showing how far their actual lives differed from their social masks. Yet all the time Anderson stressed man's need for authentic communication which overcomes loneliness. Art, according to Anderson, presents us with a paradox. On the one hand, it reminds us of the mortality of all occasions, that we will become a part of the stream of time, that our hopes and ideals and desires do not have a cosmic status. On the other hand, art gives us an awareness which transcends the moment. It is our link with infinity.

THE STRUGGLE AGAINST FRAGMENTATION

The modern artist shows the fragmentation of society and its profound sense of alienation. The sharp division between the humanities and the sciences reflects a vast difference between the realms of value and fact. Modern life encourages physical and spiritual ghettoes. Education illustrates the paradox of modern man who seeks peace and yet creates the conditions for war.

Art faces life in its nakedness and creates an order which has a transcendental value. Art makes education vital and emotional. The individual, through artistic experience, is reminded that it is not enough to know and to verbalize, he must learn to express himself and become a participant in the drama of life.

Art demands allegiance to a cause which illuminates and intensifies all feelings and all occasions. The artist becomes so absorbed in his work that its expression becomes more real than his own existence. Carl Jung maintained that in a sense Goethe did not create Faust, rather Faust created Goethe.

The child who truly values art achieves a uniqueness which adults often lose. His curiosity is not stifled; he does not become a slave to convention. He retains the capacity to feel deeply and to appreciate with fervor. To him, life is a process of relatedness in which the larger self is discovered. His values are less dependent on materialism and social approval; rather they center on warmth and creativity. He does not live an other-directed life, for he finds society within himself and he discovers new vistas and new areas of the self. Solitude is not a burden, but an invitation to renewal and to more deliberate inwardness.

As Emerson stated:

How cheap even the liberty then seems; how mean to study, when an emotion communicates to the intellect the power to sap and upheave nature; how great the perspective! Nations, times, systems, enter and disappear like threads in tapestry of large figure and many colors; dream delivers us to dream, and while the drunkenness lasts we will sell our bed, our philosophy, our religion, in our opulence.

There is good reason why we should prize this liberation. The fate of the poor shepherd, who, blinded and lost in the snowstorm, perishes in a drift within a few feet of his cottage door, is an emblem of the state of man. On the brink of the waters of life and truth, we are miserably dying. The inaccessibleness of every thought but that we are in, is wonderful. What if you come near to it; you are as remote when you are nearest as when you are farthest. Every thought is also a prison; every heaven is also a hell. Therefore we love the poet, the inventor, who in any form, whether in an ode or in an action or in looks and behavior, has yielded us a new thought. He unlocks our chains and admits us to a new scene.

This emancipation is dear to all men, and the power to impart it, as it must come from greater depth and scope of thought, is a measure of intellect. Therefore all books of the imagination endure, all which ascend to that truth that the writer sees nature beneath him, and uses it as his exponent. Every verse or sentence possessing this virtue will take care of its own immortality. The religions of the world are the ejaculations of a few imaginative men.[1]

To live in the realm of imagination is to transcend mortality. This is the feeling of the artist, whether he is young or old in whatever civilization he may live. External barriers do not matter. We can admire the art of the paleolithic age as well as of today. We can be partisans of the realism of the Renaissance as well as non-objective art. We can appreciate Picasso in advanced age as well as the tentative attempts toward self-expression of a school boy. Art thus develops genuine generosity and charity. It indicates that complexity is to be welcomed, that an idea should be judged more by its fertility and impact than by its accuracy.

Art reminds us that man is not a statistic. He cannot be subordinated to a method in education, politics or religion. *Art is defiant individuality in action.* In education art indicates that standards and evaluations are secondary; in politics it shows that man cannot fulfill himself by abdicating his individuality and by conformity to mass standards; in religion art points to the inner experience rather than to the outer ritual.

If education gives only a minor place to the arts, it will aid the forces of disintegration; in every way it will become more specialized and more diffuse. It will become more anemic and ever less emotional. In this way the distance between ideal and actuality will be widened. On the other hand, if the arts become central in education, a vital culture will emerge which will rejoice in its individuality and which will not become a victim of neurotic utilitarianism. It will leave its stamp upon history because it will encourage authentic self-expression.

Art is a protest against waste. In *Our Town,* Thornton Wilder shows that the real tragedy of man is not death; it is deliberate unawareness; it is our inability to see the preciousness of the moment; it is our proclivity toward triviality and our failure to explore the full dimensions of life. There are infinite reservoirs of beauty, and yet we tolerate incredible ugliness. The life of the spirit creates unending adventure, and yet we neglect it for the pedestrian pursuits of materialism. Novelty is a constant element in life and yet we succumb to the patterns of sameness. We are reminded by Thoreau that "life is sweetest at its core," and yet we are pilgrims on the surface.

---

[1] *The Poet.*

To see beyond the surface, to become involved in life, to heighten its significance, to express our individuality without fear and without anxiety, to make beauty part of everyday existence, to overcome drabness in all dimensions — this is the challenge of art in contemporary education.

CHAPTER FORTY-ONE

The Philosophy of Creative Teaching

THE BATTLE OF IDEAS

A great teacher is a dramatist of ideas. He builds the bridge between the world of reality and the world of our dreams. He makes the past as vivid as the present. The biases and prejudices from which so many suffer are beneath him. He has learned to view life with detachment.

The importance of the teacher is described in Matthew Arnold's *Rugby Chapel*.

> And through thee I believe
> In the noble and great who are gone;
> Pure souls honour'd and blest
> By former ages, who else —
> Such, so soulless, so poor,
> In the race of men whom I see —
> Seem'd but a dream of the heart,
> Seem'd but a cry of desire.
> Yes! I believe that there lived
> Others like thee in the past,
> Not like the men of the crowd
> Who all round me to-day

> Bluster or cringe, and make life
> Hideous, and arid, and vile;
> But souls temper'd with fire,
> Fervent, heroic, and good,
> Helpers and friends of mankind . . .

This is an ideal portrait. Many teachers are fragmentary human beings. They suffer frequently from the limitations of their time. Thus a noted professor of physics refused to accept the new quantum theory; it just was not physics. Wilamowitz, a famous philologist, refused to believe in the genius of Nietzsche, who, he thought, was unscholarly. In the United States, William James, one of our most brilliant teachers, was regarded with suspicion by academic thinkers who thought that his ideas were too popular and that he was not profound enough in his philosophical system.

Teachers frequently have compromised with the social system of their time. Hegel proved the superiority of the German states. Gentile was a loyal follower of Mussolini. Heidegger, as rector of Freiburg, supported the doctrines of Hitlerism. Even in democratic nations, thinkers, in times of crisis, have become victims of hysteria.

Teaching thus is basically an existential process. It reflects the personality, outlook, ideals, and background of the instructor who, though he may claim to be objective, in reality represents the spirit of his time, what the Germans call the *Zeitgeist*.

A great teacher not only knows his subject, he radiates it. To a brilliant French teacher, the study of language is something more than the study of grammar. It becomes the study of the soul of a nation. To a scientist who is dedicated to his work, science becomes an avenue to truth and the foundation of progress. To an artist like Richard Neutra or Frank Lloyd Wright, architecture is not just an ornamental expression of man; rather it becomes an introduction to his innermost physiological and spiritual needs. To a poet like Robert Frost, poetry is not merely a lyrical expression, but man's encounter with a timeless reality.

Any student who is so fortunate as to have great teachers will feel that knowledge ennobles and elevates, and that it substitutes unity for separateness and dualism; knowledge gives not only power, but a justification for existence.

A great teacher is never a mere technician. For example, when we listen to the ideas of Neutra we learn not only about architecture but about society, physics, politics, ethics, and biology. When Robert Oppenheimer lectures, he may touch upon philosophy and Zen Buddhism, as well as upon relativity and nuclear physics. Ernest

Rutherford, the great English physicist, was an expert in contemporary literature. Alfred North Whitehead was at home both in higher mathematics and in the latest theory of poetic criticism. A great teacher is in an unending state of self-discovery; he can never stand still; thus he communicates a sense of excitement to the student.

VALUES OF INSPIRATION

A profound historian like James Harvey Robinson will see history as a cultural story in which man's mind evolved and was released from the bondage of superstition and rationalization. When Beard lectured about American civilization, it became like a dramatic play. When Felix Frankfurter discussed constitutional history at Harvard he influenced a generation of lawyers with his concepts of social justice.

At the University of Southern California, few will forget B. A. G. Fuller, the noted historian of philosophy, who could make Greek thought as vivid as modern times. A skeptic and a naturalist, Fuller poked fun at convention, especially at puritanism.

At Boston University, Brightman had a different view from Fuller's, for Brightman was a personalist who felt that the universe had a spiritual purpose. Utterly dedicated to his students, he would spend hours with them discussing their problems and their philosophy of life.

At Harvard University, Robert Ulich, in philosophy of education, attracted international attention. He fled from the tyranny of National Socialism and came here certain that culture could flourish only in a democratic society. An idealist like Kant and Emerson, Ulich pointed to the responsibilities of the teacher, "the guardian of society." His students received something beyond severe academic training and the inspiration of profound scholarship. They obtained a vision of living greatness, and were in contact with a man who never stood still in his intellectual development.

F. C. S. Northrop at Yale became one of the noted attractions of his university. In his *Meeting of East and West*, he demonstrated his encyclopedic knowledge and he showed that philosophy has a universal meaning. Interested in both the physical and social sciences, an expert in logic, and a student of Asiatic thought, Northrop projected intellectual excitement in his seminars.

Herbert Schneider at Columbia made formidable contributions to the study of American thought. He was interested especially in young instructors and encouraged them to follow their researches.

At international conferences he was always a champion of moderation and enlightenment. At the same university, Irwin Edman became an unforgettable event in the life of thousands of students who were grateful to him for the beauty of his style and his attempt to make philosophical problems relevant to our own time.

Philip Wheelwright at University of California at Riverside impressed many students with his eloquence. Broad in his interests and well acquainted with Oriental culture, he tried to show the relationship between philosophy and other cultural enterprises. In his style of speaking, he almost approached the greatness of Santayana and like the latter he regarded much of man's intellectual quest as a poetic enterprise.

At Scripps College, T. M. Greene, a prolific author, taught with vigor after years at Princeton and Yale. Greene preferred the calmness and relatively slow pace of a small college. He impressed the students at Scripps with his erudition and his ability to dramatize philosophical problems. He demanded high standards of expression in both oral and written work. At the same time he was interested in the personal development of his students, who found in him a warm and understanding friend. He maintained that a professor should be like a psychiatrist and look upon a student's problem with an open mind, instead of regarding him as a wayward sinner.

These are only a few examples of proficient teachers in philosophy. They represent various views of man and the universe. They usually differed in their concepts of education. Their backgrounds were diverse. But they had one belief in common: the study of philosophy and education should serve as a means to a wider perspective in daily life.

Every university has a few professors whose lectures are so stimulating, challenging, and exceptional that a student feels that his education is not complete unless he takes their classes. Professors of this type like Phelps at Yale, Wilder at Chicago, Melnitz at UCLA, and Melbo at Southern California, have become truly unforgettable.

To watch a great teacher is like seeing an unforgettable play. Millions of viewers have seen Frank Baxter on television. He describes himself as the last of the romantics, and when he talks about Shakespeare, his favorite subject, the students feel as if they were back in Elizabethan times. He never stands still and occasionally he will act out, with great skill, certain parts of Shakespeare's plays. He reads the dramas of Shakespeare with fervor and deep emotion.

William James at Harvard became famous for his informal style of lecturing. He would never prepare and constantly improvised.

To him every question was precious. Impatient with abstraction, he would demand clarity of expression. He had sympathy for all causes—from psychic investigations to revivalism. Was not man defined by emotion rather than by reason? Was not the universe receptive to our wishes? Was not our heart the source of wisdom?

Woodrow Wilson impressed a generation of students at Princeton with his command of political economy. To him it was the most vital subject. He was in absolute control of the classroom. His ideal was to make real gentlemen and scholars out of his students. When he became President of the United States, he often yearned for the academic days at Princeton.

Judge Medina has written a moving tribute to Christian Gauss, the great Dean at Princeton, who influenced so many students. Gauss, a specialist in Dante, could recite the *Inferno* by heart. More important, he was a discerning critic who always looked for ways to improve the students' work. A famous author wrote, "Gauss gave us hell and made us love it."

There are no absolute rules for teaching. A teacher like Dewey may have been dry and lifeless to many students, yet those who appreciated his ideas were enthralled. Thus, Irwin Edman tells us that to listen to Dewey was to see philosophy in action, with new ideas being discovered and new relationships being established. Dewey's disciple, Kilpatrick, who taught thousands of students at Teachers College, was as eloquent as a prophet, and when he talked about the new education, his sincerity was apparent even to those who opposed him.

Creative teaching necessitates deep conviction about the importance of ideas. It means that the teacher is interested in something more than facts. He is concerned with the realm of significance and thus builds a bridge between the realm of actuality and that of ideas. Creative teaching involves a profound change both on the part of the instructor and the student. Ultimately, they realize that they are involved in a timeless process which demands a reconstruction of the heart as well as of the intellect. Creative teaching is like a conversion experience except that it has more lasting effects. It produces initial torment and profound doubts, yet it demands total loyalty. Creative teaching produces dissatisfaction with all forms of partiality and fragmentariness; it liberates the individual from the cave of egocentricity and leads him to the broader vistas of enlightenment.

CHAPTER FORTY-TWO

Existentialist Ideals and Education

SIGNIFICANCE OF EXISTENTIALISM

Existentialism stresses the centrality of man, his aloneness and his commitment, his freedom and his limitations, his affirmations and negations. It emphasizes sincerity, intuition, inwardness, and indeterminism. Existentialists include Paul Tillich, who has a solid faith in God, and Jean Paul Sartre, who is a determined atheist. Some existentialists, like Karl Jaspers, are professional philosophers, while Rollo May is a psychologist, and Albert Camus was a celebrated author. The common link in existentialism is not a conclusion, but a preoccupation with man's mood and a concern for the awesome choices which human existence demands. Existentialism sees the flux of life. The universe is not closed, it is emerging, and man's values have a central part in it. Like Thoreau, the existentialist wants to reduce life to its lowest denominator so that it can be experienced with deep involvement.

Existentialism has no common viewpoint; it is not a philosophy which believes in slogans or in party lines; it is deliberately subjective. Just as we all have to make our own decisions, so the educator has to develop his own framework of ideas. When I speak of an existential philosophy of education, I express *my* ideas and ideals which I cannot impose on others. These ideas are the product of personal awareness and a long search for meaning as an educator and a human being facing the uncertainties of the 20th century. To accept these ideals without reflection would be a disservice to them; to reject them uncritically would be equally invalid. Philosophy is like a work of art; it aims to stir and unsettle; it demands a response which is individualized and which is the product of self-examination and self-discovery.

In every way the existential viewpoint is divergent from conventional education and philosophy. To existentialism, philosophy is not a theoretical matter, it is not a prelude to objectivity. On the contrary, philosophy is an aspect of subjectivity. Our choice of values, then, has lasting consequences on both the theoretical and the practical level.

In contemporary educational philosophy many attempts are made to classify ideas. Thus one may say that Hutchins is a perennialist for he believes that truth is absolute, and that it can best be understood through the Great Books. Actually, the more we know about such great thinkers as Hutchins, the less any classification is accurate. For example, in Hutchins' *Education for Freedom* we find both existential and perennialist tendencies. Likewise, William James is the fountainhead for both pragmatism and existentialism. Thus classification is a superficial procedure, because educational philosophy involves choice and commitment and intangible factors which defy categorization.

If philosophy reflects the openness of life, there can be no absolute system, no complete truth, and no educational system valid for all nations. The unifying factor lies in a complex exploration of life, in the striving for authenticity, in the attempt "to internalize the external" and to make education a living, subjective reality.

Existentialism is concerned with attitudes and motivation. It feels that more significant than professional competence is the life-view of the teacher and his actual dedication to educational goals. In essence, he teaches through being. What he represents through action is more eloquent than the theories which he propounds.

Such a philosophy points to the basic responsibilities of the teacher. He can retard civilization by conforming and by soul-less actions or he can be an agent of moral advancement by fearless questioning and bold nonconformity. His obligation goes beyond the classroom and extends to the family and society. At the same time the student has deep obligations to himself and to humanity. It is not enough for him to acquire knowledge and to be an expert, rather he must have an emotional involvement with knowledge so that his life is transformed and so that culture becomes a living actuality. He can never achieve certainty, for he must realize that education has no beginning and no end and that his own insights are bound to be incomplete.

In such a fallibilistic setting there can be no prescribed curriculum. The teacher can never cover a complete field of knowledge nor can he be neutral regarding the great issues of the day. His digressions and value judgments may be more significant than the subject matter which he conveys. When he speaks with the wisdom of the soul he becomes a real influence upon his students, otherwise he becomes a mere footnote to a textbook.

Existentialism, unlike pragmatism, subordinates society to the demands of the individual. This does not imply social lethargy. But existentialism points out that individual tensions would remain even in a social utopia; the issues of life go beyond social reform. In fighting for a better society existentialism aims at the emancipation of the individual who is striving for "the freedom of all." The struggle, as Boris Pasternak observed, is not for an objective truth as determined by a party, but rather for a subjective ideal which is being universalized in a tentative manner. Existentialism upholds the concrete individual against the masses which forever threaten to inhibit his creativity.

In education this implies a stress upon the individual student. The existential teacher will not demand adjustment, rather he will fight against adjustment. In avoiding indoctrination like a deadly sin, he will encourage rebellion and opposition as bases of progress. He will not be concerned with externals and instead will dwell upon the need for inwardness both in his own life and in the existence of his students.

For existentialist thinkers there can be no objective knowledge of history. Historical facts are subordinated to value judgments which illuminate and clarify the dilemmas of the present. Existentialists refuse to acknowledge an inevitable pattern in history; rather they see it as an open possibility. In Emersonian terms they view the institution as the replica of man whose ideals and values are the center of study. Since no inevitability is recognized, history implies change which can be directed toward individual betterment. To existential historians, history shows the conflict between the authentic individual and the mass-man. Education's function is to fight against the idols of the masses so that genuine freedom can be achieved.

Art has a central place in existential education. Mere appreciation of art is inadequate. Mere historical knowledge about it is regarded as secondary. What is demanded is an active participation in art "which can never be an objective enterprise."

To clarify the esthetic issue, we must draw a distinction between the creator of art and the critic. The creator speaks from within; he is eternally restless; he becomes what he does; he is in a state of constant receptivity; his vision is always unfulfilled. The critic (who tends to dominate education) speaks from without—he lacks inwardness and cannot understand the subjective agonies of the creator. The task of education is to create participants in the enterprise of art who will view the creator with deep sympathy and see art as the center of human existence.

In such a philosophy the humanities are even more valuable than the academic study of the sciences. The humanities give us an immediate view of life, they introduce us to the flux of experience; they transform our inner being, while the sciences demand detachment and present an impersonal view of the universe. However, it should be pointed out that science can be a part of the humanities if its philosophical and esthetic aspects are stressed, if it sharpens our powers of perception and illuminates the existential choices which we face in this age of uncertainty.

Liberal education, in existential terms, means education that molds our inner being. Liberal education can be measured by its capacity to emancipate us from the idols of the tribe so that we develop a strong sense of identity based upon an awareness of inner freedom.

The center of existential education is the dialogue between the teacher and a student and, even more important, the inward dialogue which is part of the educational process of all individuals. Thus Socrates and Kierkegaard agree and become our guides, for they teach that truth is not an external process but an inward achievement which depends on our own receptivity. In existentialist circles the lecture method is regarded as a secondary device, for it often creates a mechanical relationship between teacher and student. As for teaching machines, they may be acceptable aids, but only as preliminary steps in an education which depends on existential inter-stimulation.

Moral ideas can never be excluded from an existential scheme of education. This does not mean teaching about morality or censoring books, or presenting abstract schemes of ethics, but rather a development of perspective. The teacher thus becomes a moralist without absolutes who develops within the student a feeling about the alternatives which he faces.

While most existentialists are opposed to conventional religion —indeed, Sartre and Camus are atheists—reason is subordinated to faith, and the need for a cosmic perspective is recognized. Victor Frankl, an existentialist psychiatrist, feels that man's real sickness is religious; man chooses false values and idolizes them. Existentialism opposes all forms of religious dogmatism which make man an appendage to an institution.

PSYCHOLOGY AND EDUCATION

Against a mechanistic view of psychology, existentialists point to man's uniqueness and his qualitative difference from other parts of nature. The existential therapist tries to avoid preconceptions and he himself changes in the therapeutic process.

Carl Rogers expresses the innermost spirit of existentialist therapy:

> I launch myself into the therapeutic relationship having a hypothesis or a faith, that my liking, my confidence, and my understanding of the other person's inner world, will lead to a significant process of becoming. I enter the relationship not as a scientist, not as a physician who can accurately diagnose and cure, but as a person entering into a personal relationship. I risk myself, because if, as the relationship deepens, what develops is a failure, a regression, a repudiation of me and the relationship of the client, then I sense that I will lose myself or a part of myself . . . I let myself go into the immediacy of the relationship where it is my total organism which takes over and is sensitive to the relationship, not simply my consciousness.[1]

While Freudian therapists stress the past in its deterministic aspects, the existential counselor is more concerned with the present and the future. His question is: Where are you going and why?

---

[1] Carl Rogers, "Persons or Silence? A Philosophical Question." *American Psychologist*, 10:267–278, 1955.

He deals with three worlds: the world outside *(Umwelt)*, the world of relationships *(Mitwelt)*, and the world within *(Eigenwelt)*. All are equally significant and a dynamic relationship has to be established so that the ego can function without being inhibited by self-limitation.

Sincerity is the keynote to existential education. "Be frank with yourself and with your children," the advice given by Tolstoy to teachers, has deep meaning for existentialists. All the questions of children are to be answered with frankness; they are never to be evaded. The problems of pupils are to be viewed with real concern and compassion, not with academic detachment. The aim of the teacher is to become, not an absolute guide, but a source of emancipation so that the pupil becomes an autonomous center of creativity.

The task of existential education is not preparation for life. We are not merely lawyers or doctors or artists or teachers but human beings exploring the preciousness of the moment, strenuously striving for significance. Specialization, then, is never adequate, for all significant problems have a subjective meaning. What man is counts for more than his external achievements.

Specifically, this means in education that general knowledge is not the preparation for specific competence; on the contrary, specific competence is the prelude to general understanding. Our colleges usually reverse that process. They have introductory general courses while their advanced work is excessively specialized without real integration and genuine interdisciplinary understanding. The result is enormous fragmentation and the absence of a coherent philosophy of education. Thus a reform is needed which would look upon specialization as a mere platform upon which general understanding could be built.

This type of education looks to the concrete individual and is concerned with his actual preoccupations. Its conception of life is problematic, its aim is not a static balance but a dynamic equilibrium, which recognizes the dilemmas and perplexities of human existence. Such a philosophy begins and ends with questions. The difference is that the first questions touch the surface of our being and arise out of external needs, while the final queries are symbols of inwardness and commitment and go to the heart of the matter.

The soul searching questions, which are the bases of the educative process, indicate that no generation can be taught in a formal way, that the basic attitudes and motivations must be reshaped and redefined by every generation. We may be able to instruct others in quantification, we may be able to give them practical competence, but values can only be suggested; they have no real meaning unless the individual finds them in the maze of his own experience.

Such a view of education and man accepts the fragmentary aspect of all experience. Totality is an abstraction; my insight is but a pebble in the stream of eternity. Yet I must not subordinate it to the commands of authority and fail to express it because it cannot approach a view of totality. The existentialist view is deliberately ego-centered for he believes that unless the individual has explored himself thoroughly and subjectively, life is merely a cyclical exercise. It says to the individual: You are qualitatively different from all parts of nature, if you will become aware of your awareness, and if you seek an authentic existence through which real communication can be achieved. You have the choice of freedom through self-exploration or slavery through unthinking dependence. The issue of existence goes beyond life and death; it is the issue of drifting impersonally or living creatively with a Faustian thirst for subjective depth and unending enlightenment.

Real education becomes a constant protest against externality. It appears that man forever externalizes his problems and his situations. *A subject, he wants to become an object; a creator, he wants to become a disciple.* Having an infinite capacity for self-deception, man mistakes the symbol for reality, the myth for God, the tribe for humanity.

The existentialist perspective calls for a rendezvous of man with himself so that life becomes a dawn rather than a twilight experience. The basic questions that educators should ask are: Has the individual awakened from dogmatic slumber? Has he been emancipated from the tabus of society? Has he overcome the seductions of technology? Has he striven with sincerity and with a degree of agony? Has he become an active participant in the search for knowledge? Has he cultivated a sense of inwardness? Has he developed a sense of relatedness with others so that they are not merely objects for his own desires? Has he involved himself in a cause without abdicating his own identity? In short, has he become genuinely creative?

No individual can give an affirmative answer to all these questions. This is part of the existentialist challenge which shows that education moves from the partial to the larger self.

In its central doctrines there are basic similarities between existentialism and Zen Buddhism. In common they stress a basic simplicity and regard the unessential as being essential; both cherish spontaneity and limit the powers of reason; both appeal to imagination and insight. The great difference is that existentialism demands an agonizing self-examination, which involves a sense of being forlorn in the universe.

In a society concerned with the externals of education, governed by technology and the multiplication of desires, and other-directed in its status consciousness, existentialism fills a desperate need. It calls for strenuous self-examination so that life may not be wasted in triviality and superficiality and so that the authentic individual can emerge with a sense of limitation and a sense of unfulfilled possibilities.

CHAPTER FORTY-THREE

The Coming American Renaissance

A TIME OF DECISION

"We must all choose and choose in time." This statement by Kierkegaard symbolizes the extent of our responsibilities. We face decisions as individuals and as a society. Stagnation or creativity, meaninglessness or striving for significance, conformity or audacious individualism, egocentricity or service to humanity — these issues may determine our destiny.

Education thus depends upon our views of life. We have the choice of adhering to the mores of society, of merely cultivating our social self, and of living the life of Babbittry. If we choose this path then frustration and disenchantment will result. Eventually we will feel the waste in our existence. On the other hand, we can choose a life of exploration, of restless longing, of a search for inwardness, of affirmation of humanity whereby we see, as William James pointed out, the larger Self. This choice promises no magic rewards, no material success; it makes life, however, a journey in depth; it immortalizes our experience; it gives poignancy to the moment.

Man is governed by his ideals. He dreams even amidst a sordid actuality. *He is a poet realizing the biological limitations of his existence.* Ideals are not patterns of perfection; they are not static outlines; they represent the motives for action, the foundations of the human enterprise. What is needed is for man to dream boldly and then to apply those dreams to the realities of our institutional system.

Education implies awakening. Thoreau said:

> To him whose elastic and vigorous thought keeps pace with the sun, the day is a perpetual morning. It matters not what the clocks say or the attitudes and labors of men. Morning is when I am awake and there is a dawn in me. Moral reform is the effort to throw off sleep. Why is it that men give so poor an account of their day if they have not been slumbering? They are not such poor calculators. If they had not been overcome with drowsiness, they would have performed something. The millions are awake enough for physical labor; but only one in a million is awake enough for effective intellectual exertion, only one in a hundred million to a poetic or divine life. To be awake is to be alive. I have never yet met a man who was quite awake. How could I have looked him in the face?

> We must learn to reawaken and keep ourselves awake, not by mechanical aids, but by an infinite expectation of the dawn, which does not forsake us in our soundest sleep. I know of no more encouraging fact than the unquestionable ability of man to elevate his life by a conscious endeavor. It is something to be able to paint a particular picture, or to carve a statue, and so to make a few objects beautiful; but it is far more glorious to carve and paint the very atmosphere and medium through which we look, which morally we can do. To affect the quality of the day, that is the highest of arts. Every man is tasked to make his life, even its details, worthy of the contemplation of his most elevated and critical hour.[1]

A nation can deliberately achieve cultural greatness. The choice which America faces today is whether it should follow the patterns of Hellenic civilization as represented by Athens or be like Hellenistic civilization. For a short time under Pericles, the Athenians cultivated the life of reason. Philosophy was the central enterprise and curiosity was treasured; almost no question was tabu. Refinement and art governed the life of the citizen; the drama united the young and the old, kings and common citizens. Democracy extended not merely to politics but to other areas of social life.

Compare, on the other hand, Hellenistic civilization with Athenian ideals. In Alexandria, schooling was institutionalized and knowledge

---

[1] *Walden.*

was compartmentalized; applied science was stressed; the arts lacked great themes; there was a deep division between the wealthy and the poor; philosophers taught man how to adjust himself to a sordid reality or how to escape to a transcendental realm. Imitation and professionalization governed Hellenistic culture. Instead of refinement, extravagance was cultivated.

Is the U.S. today following the Athenian or the Hellenistic pattern? The answer is that despite the fact that American democracy is more extensive than that of Athens, its cultural emphasis is more like that of Alexandria. But this emphasis can be reversed through a new education which stresses the centrality of the teacher and the need for unending questions, which regards the arts as the core of experience, which emphasizes originality, and which views the present as the point of departure. The Athenians had to depend on themselves. There were no Babylonian or Egyptian cultural patterns to serve as points of reference. We must develop the same independence and take the problems and dilemmas of our time as the foundations of education.

PERIODS

So far American educational thought has passed through four discernible periods. The first was governed by the Puritan spirit. It was authoritarian and stressed the limitations of man; it viewed man as a sinner who would end in hell-fire. It regarded the teacher as a disciplinarian aiding the ministry in the process of salvation.

Such a view had both positive and negative consequences. It produced individuals with a deep sense of duty who labored hard to conquer the wilderness. But the negative result was a conformist spirit and a vast intolerance. Quakers, Jews and Catholics had an inferior position in colonial education. Dissenters were persecuted.

The second great period saw the enlightenment and the emancipation of the American spirit. It was the time of the framing of the Constitution and the Bill of Rights. The possibilities and the freedom of man were stressed by thinkers like Franklin and Jefferson. It was the period of the Academies which emphasized useful knowledge. Reason was enshrined; its analysis was to be applied to all areas of life and was expected to bring about a new utopia.

The American enlightenment produced "philosopher kings" like Jefferson who gave an immortal view of democracy. It made the subsequent advances possible. We are all indebted to the founders of the American system, especially in education.

But their optimism was unfounded. Man is not only a rational but a believing creature. Progress is never automatic; it depends on moral and intelligent leadership and a dedicated citizenry interested in first-rate ideas.

The third phase was the time of Emerson. It was a romantic reaction against science, empiricism, and an over-reliance on reason. Emerson favored the teacher who spoke from within and saw the unity of all life.

This transcendental view was inspiring. It made for bold institutions and a type of cosmopolitanism, but it slighted detailed analysis and overlooked the importance of science. It contributed to what Santayana called the genteel spirit in American philosophy.

Quite different was the fourth period — the era of pragmatism. Its eloquent protagonists were James, Dewey and Kilpatrick. Education was to become progressive and was to center on the interests of the child. Democracy was to become a reality. Group standards were to dominate. Subject areas were to be supplanted by the problem-centered inquiry. Interest was to be more significant than effort and discipline.

Such a system of education made for a more colorful school system. It expanded educational opportunity and made learning more dramatic. It focused upon childhood development.

At the same time it created vast problems. Some of the disciples of Dewey looked upon him with awe and regarded his views as the final statements of education. They forgot that education has pluralistic goals and that no final educational philosophy is possible.

The first-rate mind is interested in queries. The follower seeks answers. *Genius is unafraid of the complexities of life. The follower seeks compulsive simplification.* The first-rate thinker is guided by fundamental intuitions, while the second-rate philosopher becomes a pedestrian critic who always uses the past as the point of reference.

Pragmatic education slighted subject matter; it underrated the importance of discipline; it overlooked the significance of attention; it did not explore sufficiently the capacities of children, adults, teachers and administrators.

DYNAMIC EDUCATION

The education which can meet the needs of our time is based upon the need for individual and social enlightenment. Society becomes the verification of our theories, the laboratory of our ideas.

Social problems such as war, economic privation, intolerance, and delinquency, become of concern to all educators. If these problems are not solved, if the schools are only theoretical centers, if imagination and social concern are not applied to these issues, then humanity may not survive. It is self-evident that the vision of education has to be expanded. Just as civilization has moved from a fluvial to a thalassic to an oceanic and now to a cosmic basis, so education has to move from a local to a cosmopolitan view, from fragmentary concerns to a philosophy of inter-relatedness.

The foundation of the new education is perceptual awareness. All the senses are to be mobilized at a far younger age than they are in conventional schooling. Good habits and concentration are to be stressed. Attention is to be emphasized so that the moment achieves significance and so that the individual becomes aware of his awareness.

Books are central in such a system. They develop new areas of exploration. They are links with the past and preludes to the future. But they demand active thinking; mere worship of books is a denial of their significance. Books develop the authentic individual, determined to leave his mark on society. Books indicate that greatness is not of the past but that it is possible in our time, that greatness has no limitations and no frontiers.

THE IDEALS OF CULTURE

This philosophy tells the individual: You have creative capacities. You must not lose them in self negation and traditionalism. You must work strenuously in a Socratic spirit. You must be conscious of your genius. You must strive for universality in thought and in action.

Are we too specialized for such a viewpoint? Is our culture too fragmented? Are we like the monads of Leibnitz—unable to communicate with each other? Have the sciences hopelessly outstripped the humanities?

These are sobering questions. But no trend in history is inevitable. Education indicates that man can create a new society and that a renaissance is a perpetual possibility. Thoreau expressed this optimistic view in *Walden*.

The life in us is like the water in the river. It may rise this year higher than man has ever known it, and flood the parched uplands; even this may be the eventful year, which will drown out all our muskrats. It was not always dry land where we dwell. I see far inland the banks which the stream anciently washed, before science began to record its freshets. Everyone has heard the story which has gone the rounds of New England, of a strong and beautiful bug which came out of the dry leaf of an old table of apple-tree wood, which had stood in a farmer's kitchen for sixty years, first in Connecticut, and afterward in Massachusetts, — from an egg deposited in the living tree many years earlier still, as appeared by counting the annual layers beyond it; which was heard gnawing out for several weeks, hatched perchance by the heat of an urn. Who does not feel his faith in a resurrection and immortality strengthened by hearing of this? Who knows what beautiful and winged life, whose egg has been buried for ages under many concentric layers of woodenness in the dead dry life of society, deposited at first in the alburnum of the green and living tree, which has been gradually converted into the semblance of its well-seasoned tomb, — heard perchance gnawing out now for years by the astonished family of man, as they sat round the festive board, — may unexpectedly come forth from amidst society's most trivial and handselled furniture, to enjoy its perfect summer life at last!

I do not say that John or Jonathan will realize all this; but such is the character of that morrow which mere lapse of time can never make to dawn. The light which puts out our eyes is darkness to us. Only that day dawns to which we are awake. There is more day to dawn. The sun is but a morning star.[2]

GOALS

The type of education which will bring about true greatness may be outlined as follows:

(1) It must be centered on man — his ideals and possibilities — rather than on material considerations. The keynote to the new type of education is flexibility and total involvement. Such an education will start earlier; nursery school will be as universal as the kindergarten is today, and a great expansion will take place in adult education.

(2) This education will accelerate learning in a creative way. We have underestimated the capacities of children, teachers, and adults. Much of junior high school will come down to the elementary level; part of college will be taught in high schools. Graduate school methods will be applied to the undergraduate colleges. The aim of such a system is to produce self-reliant individuals intent upon making their best contribution to civilization.

---

[2] *Ibid.*

(3) Intercultural understanding will be a primary goal. Comenius realized that without peace, education has no future. To promote mutuality among nations, an international exchange of students, teachers, artists and scientists will be intensified. International houses will be found even on the high school campus. The comparative approach will be brought to the study of politics, economics, history, religion and philosophy. The history of other cultures will be taught in a sympathetic way; at the same time a genuine appreciation of our own heritage will be fostered.

(4) The seminar and the discussion method will be central in the new education. This implies an appreciation of diversity and a pluralistic concept of life. Knowledge thus ceases to be an ornamental process and becomes instead a Socratic achievement in which the question, not the static answer, rules.

(5) Education will be regarded as both an intellectual and a therapeutic process. This means close collaboration with all the agencies — formal and informal — which educate. To strive against loneliness and anxiety, such a system will deepen and strengthen genuine human contacts, especially on the adult level.

(6) The arts will be regarded as the foundations of life. This does not imply a neglect of the sciences or a distrust of the scientific method. Both fields will be cultivated with intensity. The centrality of art lies in its development of style and appreciation; it forms a link between school and society, and it lends significance to all human actions. As a symbol of man's cultural immortality, it adds dignity to the educational enterprise.

(7) Since decisions in modern times must be made by the few for the many, a pressing need arises to train future leaders in intellectual and moral responsibility. Such training would counteract the amorality and Machiavellianism which threaten to destroy modern man. The new training for leadership will have a Jeffersonian basis, emphasizing the responsibilities of the leader for public service and public improvement.

(8) Liberal education will be the core of learning. This does not imply fixed requirements or the abandonment of professional schools. Liberal education builds an active appreciation of our total cultural heritage, and emancipates us from the perspective of immediacy. It leads to a bold, imaginative way of life. Liberal education is concerned with the spirit of man and points to the vistas of the future.

(9) Since education has no frontiers and no limitations, the isolation of the various levels of education must be overcome. This means an active interchange of instructors and ideas and much more inter-institutional cooperation than prevails today. It means also less departmentalization and more general education. Education involves a common loyalty and a common dedication transcending scattered and diffuse concerns.

(10) Education will be a means of liberation from all forms of authoritarianism. This means less stress upon rules, less reliance upon bureaucracy, and the development of genuine democracy. The teacher and the administrator should welcome the expansion of education which will take place in our time. Until all are enlisted in the educative process, until enlightenment replaces superstition, until the crusade against ignorance succeeds, mankind will have at best a precarious future.

Such a system is based on unwavering humanitarianism. The genuine teacher will affirm man's dignity and show that democracy is not a vain ideal, but a way of life that can be extended to all aspects of our institutional system. By his actions and his philosophy the genuine teacher will exemplify the possibilities of man, and he will show that permanent enlightenment and a new renaissance can be achieved.

The teacher must become the prophet of our time. His task is to guide and advance civilization. He teaches by soul-searching example and by facing without fear the dilemmas of our time.

The new 'teacher may start at 18, and he may not finish at 85. We have never fully explored the creative possibilities of youth or the potentialities of maturity. Wilson changed Princeton for decades by hiring a group of young instructors. Hastings College of Law achieved a national reputation by hiring the retired deans and professors of Eastern colleges. There is no reason why occasionally the Ph.D. could not be given at 18 or why many teachers should not be active in advanced age.

The exploration of human ideals is the real challenge of our time. What matters is not quantitative knowledge but the determination of the individual to be educated and to radiate his insights to others and thus help create a great culture.

A lasting culture demands more than academic ornamentation. It demands more than the orthodox scholastic ritual. It certainly requires more than efficiency. *A great culture demands boldness of insight, a dedicated leadership, and, above all, a cordial hospitality for new ideas.*

The kind of revolution that Jefferson accomplished in his time can be achieved in ours. It is a revolution demanding a deep sense of responsibility and an intense dedication to the arts and sciences — not as playthings for the élite, but as imperatives for all. A great culture demands constant re-examination. It calls for a meeting of theory and application. It demands that education become the center of American life. We have the resources; we need only courage and vision to achieve a new world.

Glossary

Absolutism—The belief that an unconditioned standard of truth and values exists.

Aesthetics—The study of the principles of beauty.

Agnosticism—First used by Herbert Spencer and popularized by T. H. Huxley indicating that no definite knowledge can be obtained of certain subjects. Applied to theology, it means that we can have no certain assurance of either the existence or non-existence of God.

Altruism—The belief in the transcendence of the self and in the possibility of compassionate moral actions.

Anthropomorphism—Viewing God and reality according to human parallels.

Antithesis—Negation of a proposition.

A Posteriori—Stands for knowledge based upon experience. It is the opposite of *a priori* reasoning which is reasoning prior to experience. In logic, *a priori* reasoning is deductive, whereas *a posteriori* reasoning is inductive.

Atheism—A concept in philosophy which stands for the negation of the belief in a supreme being.

Atman—A term frequently used in the *Upanishads* which stands for man's essential self which transcends the categories of space and time. While the empirical self is constantly changing and shifting and is dependent on individual manifestations, Atman is truly universal.

Augustinianism—Applies to the philosophy of Augustine (354–430) who stressed the majesty of God, the reality of original sin and who developed a Christian philosophy of history.

Authoritarianism—A term in philosophy which states that the source of knowledge can be found in an absolute standard; this standard can be represented by an ecclesiastical organization, a sacred book, the personal will of a god, history, or the laws of society.

Axiology—The organized and systematic consideration of values; especially important in this subject is the relationship between values and reality.

Brahma—An important god of Hinduism; also used to describe the personal form of the World Soul.

Brahman—The impersonal essence of the universe; also used to describe the members of the priestly class.

Calvinism—The religious movement initiated by John Calvin, who stressed the perfection of God, predestination, puritanism, and the wickedness of man. Calvinism stressed authority in education.

Categorical Imperative—The basis of Kant's moral philosophy which stands for the absolute, unconditioned moral law.

Cosmological argument—An argument which attempts to prove the existence of God by postulating the necessity of a first cause. All causes are based upon prior causes which depend upon something which is absolute and uncaused, namely God.

Cosmology—The study of the origin and nature of the universe.

Cosmopolitanism—A world-minded view of man which transcends local biases.

Cyrenaicism—A school of philosophy founded by Aristippus who stressed the importance of physical pleasures.

Deduction—The process of reasoning whereby conclusions are made on the basis of assumed premises. Aristotelian logic is generally deductive, while Baconian logic is inductive. Medieval religious philosophy, which followed Aristotle, is generally deductive. Modern religious philosophy, especially in Protestantism, is inductive.

Deism—A term which stands for the religious philosophy of the 18th century and interprets religion according to the principles of reason. Deism is opposed to fervent emotionalism and revelation and regards God as a supreme scientist who does not intervene directly in the affairs of the universe. Deism believes in an enlightened view of education.

Determinism—The doctrine that all events in the universe can be understood according to their causal relationship. It is opposed to *indeterminism,* which believes in the freedom of the will. Determinism upholds the view that human behavior is governed by laws — physical or psychic.

Dialectic—Stands for a thorough examination of the categories and presuppositions of knowledge. Dialectic reasoning has been used in various ways by Kant, Hegel, and Marx. It is especially important in modern Communism which believes that knowledge reflects social conditions and applies Hegelian principles to institutional problems.

Dualism—Belief that reality is composed of two divergent elements.

Élan Vital—A concept used by Bergson to describe the vital impulse in evolution; this impulse is the source of creative activity.

Empiricism—The type of philosophy which claims that knowledge is based on experience and denies the knowledge of innate truth. The classic exponent of this school of philosophy is John Locke, who considered man's mind a blank tablet with no capacity to understand concepts transcending experience.

Epicureanism—The school of philosophy which maintains that the highest pleasures are those of the mind. Opposed to supernaturalism, Epicureanism believes in a scientific interpretation of the universe and tries to get away from the fear of God and the dread of death. The founder of this school was Epicurus (342–270 B.C.) whose theories were popularized by Lucretius in a poem *On the Nature of Things.*

Epistemology—The subject in philosophy which deals with the analysis of the grounds, content, and limitations of human knowledge.

Essentialism—The view that education ought to emphasize tradition and sound habits and transmit the ideas of the past.

Eternal Recurrence—The view of Nietzsche that reality is part of a cosmic cycle.

Existentialism—Stresses freedom, intuition and the primacy of the self. In education existentialism emphasizes personal development and inwardness.

Experimentalism—Emphasis on experience and science as the criteria of knowledge.

Formalism—The belief in a categorical principle of ethics; a view often identified with the philosophy of Kant.

Hedonism—The doctrine that all human behavior is motivated by pleasure. There are two types of hedonism: (a) ethical hedonism which regards pleasure as the absolute value; and (b) psychological hedonism which holds that all conduct is guided by the quest for pleasure and the avoidance of pain.

Heracliteanism—View that nature is in a state of change.

Heterodox—A view opposed to conventional standards.

Humanism—A term which has various meanings in philosophy. It generally stands for an opposition to supernaturalism and regards man as the main factor in the universe.

Idealism—Used popularly to describe the spiritual content of life and to denote a faith in ultimate values. Technically, it holds the view that existence is dependent on thought. It has various forms such as in Hegel (experience is reduced to an Absolute Mind) and in Berkeley (experience depends upon perception, a pluralistic concept of reality). In education, as in Horne, idealism stresses inspiration, standards of excellence, and the primacy of the teacher.

Immanence—Sometimes used as though synonymous with pantheism. It holds that God is an indwelling principle in the universe. It is opposed to the viewpoint of transcendence which claims that God is beyond the universe.

Instrumentalism—A school of philosophy associated with John Dewey, who regards ideas as instruments and tools whose main function is to clarify social issues. Instrumentalism is based on the pragmatism of William James and looks with disdain on metaphysical reasoning. Instrumentalism favors an experimental view of education.

Intuitionism—The view that reality can only be comprehended through supra-rational vision or insight.

Machiavellianism—Applies to the theories of Machiavelli, who taught that might makes right and who stressed that the end justifies the means.

Materialism—A school of thought which holds that all events in life can be reduced to their material origin. According to Hobbes, there are only two realities: matter and motion. Materialism denies the independent existence of spiritual values; it views ideals according to their physiological origin. A distinction should be made between ancient materialism as in Democritus, which is concerned mainly with a consideration of cosmology, and modern materialism as championed by Marx, which is dialectic and tries to change the universe rather than interpreting it.

Maya—A term in Indian philosophy which stands for illusion. The veil of Maya is everything which obscures reality.

Meliorism—A concept which tries to mediate between optimism and pessimism. It holds that life can be improved through concentrated human effort and education.

Metaphysics—A study of reality, of "what comes after physics." The term is used in various contexts. To Descartes it stood for knowledge of immaterial entities, to Kant it dealt with things-in-themselves and objects of faith, to Aquinas it was the subject which dealt with supernatural ideals.

Modernism—The view in theology which tries to combine science and religious ideals.

Monism—The belief that only one principle of reality exists.

Mysticism—The view that reason is inadequate when it comes to the search for the ultimate principle of reality. Mysticism appeals to intuition and holds that the highest state of knowledge is beyond all intellectual categories.

Neo-Platonism—A school of philosophy established by Plotinus, who believed in the transcendence of the One, mysticism and the nonreality of evil.

Nirvana—A term in Indian philosophy which has various meanings. On the psychological side it stands for the extinction of lust, hatred, covetousness, and craving. Metaphysically, it stands for the extinction of finitude or of all becoming.

Noumenon—A term representing Kant's view that a thing-in-itself exists. This term is used in opposition to the concept of phenomenon, which stands for the appearance of things.

Ontological argument—Was first used by Anselm (ca. 1100), who held that the idea of God as greatest being presupposes His existence. It was subjected to a strong criticism by Kant in the *Critique of Pure Reason.*

Perennialism—Emphasizes intellectual virtues and tradition in education.

Personalism—A school of philosophy with a theistic orientation and which stresses the reality of the self. In education it stresses the moral role of the teacher.

Positivism—A doctrine developed by Comte who holds that knowledge does not extend to ultimate principles but only to phenomena. Positivism rests on the scientific method and is opposed to metaphysical reasoning.

Pragmatism—A school of philosophy associated with James, Dewey, Mead, and F. C. S. Schiller. It believes that knowledge should deal with man's adaptation to his environment and that it is to be tested by practical consequences. It is concerned with the effects rather than the motives of men. In education it stresses a child-centered view.

Progressivism—An educational philosophy which is experience-centered and which urges constant experimentation in our schools.

Puritanism—The moral and religious philosophy which believes in rigorous ethical standards and which is opposed to all types of hedonism. Puritanism dwells upon disciplinary values in education.

Rationalism—A school of thought which holds that reason is the standard of truth and that knowledge is to be verified by intellectual rather than empirical factors. It was popular on the Continent with such thinkers as Leibnitz, Descartes, and Spinoza; in England, however, empiricism was more important than rationalism.

Reconstructionism—An educational philosophy championed by Brameld which urges the use of the schools as vigorous centers of social reform.

Relativism—The view that no absolute truth exists in ethics; it implies an emphasis on the flux and change of moral standards.

Self-Realization—The ethical view that perfection lies in the cultivation of the potentialities of the self.

Stoicism—One of the important ethical schools of philosophy which emphasizes self-discipline, the rational nature of the universe, resignation, and control of emotions. This school holds that it is man's task to follow the laws of the universe. Metaphysically, Stoicism owed much to the philosophy of Heraclitus.

Summum Bonum—Applies to the Supreme Good. Various values are regarded as the highest good, such as pleasure, reason, self-sufficiency, and classless society, etc.

Supernaturalism—In opposition to naturalism, this view maintains that the universe represents the creation of a supreme being. It regards man's life as an interlude in the cosmic process and affirms the reality of heaven and hell.

Synthesis—Combination of various viewpoints. In Hegel thesis and antithesis form a synthesis.

Taoism—A Chinese philosophy developed by Lao-tse, who looked upon Tao (Nature) as the criterion of all values. Opposed to city life, Taoism glorified simple virtues and upheld an ethical system of non-assertion and compassion.

Teleological argument—Tries to prove the existence of God based on the concept of design. It holds that the universe reveals a purposeful structure which must be ascribed to a supreme being.

Theism—The doctrine that the universe is guided by a personal God who is eternal and all-powerful and that there is a personal relationship between man and his Creator.

Theology—The investigation of God and His relationship to the universe.

Thomism—The authoritative views of the Church as given by Aquinas who tried to combine Aristotelianism and ecclesiastical ideals and who developed an educational system based on supernatural virtues.

Transvaluation of Values—The view of Nietzsche who desired a new code of ethics based on the will to power.

Utilitarianism—The theory that all movements should be judged according to the principle of the greatest good for the greatest number. The chief exponents of this belief were Jeremy Bentham and John Stuart Mill, who were more concerned with social legislation and education than with metaphysical reasoning.

Value—Applied to anything which possesses significance. Persistent controversies are carried on regarding such subjects as the objectivity and relativity of values.

Vedas—The Hindu holy books. The Vedas are divided into the following parts: Rigveda, Yajurveda, Samaveda, and Arthaveda.

Vitalism—A biological concept which holds that the events of life are not to be explained by materialistic assumptions but only by postulating an independent substance which is essentially unknowable and immaterial. Various names for this substance are Élan Vital, Vital Principle, etc.

Voluntarism—The position in philosophy which emphasizes the will as the fundamental part of life and reality.

Zen—A view of philosophy and education which stresses spontaneity, simplicity and self-discovery. In Zen Buddhism the teacher is not an authority but simply a creative person who reminds the student of his own powers to find enlightenment. In its flexible views, Zen has some similarities with the ideals of progressive education. Zen attempts to overcome a rationalistic view of the universe and it accepts the serenity and unity of nature as an example for philosophical and educational thinking.

Questions for Discussion
and Investigation

CHAPTER 1

1. Who are the pioneers who contributed to the development of American education?
2. What is the significance of Horace Mann?
3. How does Helen Keller represent the greatness of the human spirit?
4. Who, in your opinion, are the pioneers of 20th century education? Justify your selection.
5. What is Emerson's view of scholarship?
6. Do you agree with Hutchins that education is mainly an intellectual process?
7. What, in your opinion, are America's main contributions to civilization?
8. What is the significance of *Escape from Freedom* by Erich Fromm?
9. What are the causes for the rise of fanaticism in our time?
10. What are the advantages and disadvantages of technology?

11. What is the relationship between education and morality? Evaluate your own moral views.
12. Make a list of what you regard to be the main aims of education and justify your selection.
13. What is the relationship between education and happiness?

CHAPTER 2

1. What is the significance of creativity?
2. What are the phases of creative thinking?
3. What are the traits of the creative individual?
4. Why is *Survival through Design* by Neutra a major work for our time?
5. How can creativity be stimulated in the classroom?
6. What are the main obstacles to creativity?
7. How can administrators further educational creativity?
8. What can parents do to evoke creative traits on the part of their children?
9. How can students become more creative in their intellectual life?
10. Who have been your most creative teachers? Justify your selections.
11. How creative is American society? Is genuine creativity increasing or decreasing?
12. Do you feel that America is more or less creative than Athens was in the time of Pericles? Explain your position.

CHAPTER 3

1. Why has philosophy been a stepchild in American culture?
2. Analyze the weaknesses of the academic method of philosophy.
3. How was idealism manifested in American thought?
4. What has been the influence of science on American philosophy?
5. In what ways is American civilization like that of Rome?
6. What is the relationship between philosophy and education?
7. What are the main problems of education in our time?
8. Should the humanities or the sciences be the center of education?
9. How important are academic standards in education?
10. Should American education be controlled by the states or by the federal government? Justify your answer.

CHAPTER 4

1. What is the relationship between education and religion?
2. What are the advantages and disadvantages of the separation of state and church?
3. What are the main doctrines of Catholicism? How do they relate to education?
4. Should federal aid be given to parochial schools? Justify your answer.
5. What are the principal educational ideals of Protestantism?
6. What are the educational views of Calvin?
7. Why did intolerance arise in Calvinism?
8. What are the principles of Jesuit education?
9. Should American education be more or less secular?
10. What are the educational ideas of the Quakers? How do they compare with those of Catholicism?
11. In what ways has religion influenced the American mind?
12. Discuss the strengths and weaknesses of the major American religious groups.

CHAPTER 5

1. Evaluate the ideals of Puritanism.
2. Who were the main Puritan scholars?
3. Discuss the weaknesses of colonial education.
4. What was the status of the teacher in colonial life?
5. Describe the main events in the life of Samuel Johnson.
6. What are the principal works of Johnson? Why is he so important as a thinker?
7. Why did Johnson object to the Calvinistic view of determinism? What is your own concept regarding predestination?
8. Describe Johnson's moral philosophy.
9. What are the educational views of Johnson?
10. Describe the development of Harvard in the 17th century.
11. What causes are basic in the founding of American colleges?
12. Compare and contrast the colonial and the modern American student.

CHAPTER 6

1. How did Jonathan Edwards represent the Calvinist tradition?
2. Analyze the status of God in the philosophy of Jonathan Edwards.
3. Why did Jonathan Edwards believe in the depravity of man?
4. Enumerate the outstanding works of Jonathan Edwards.
5. Was Jonathan Edwards completely orthodox in his Calvinism?
6. What are the educational views of Edwards?
7. What, in your opinion, are the strengths and weaknesses of the educational system of Edwards?
8. What is the significance of John Woolman?
9. Why did Woolman believe in simplicity?
10. Compare and contrast the educational views of Edwards and Woolman.
11. Can Woolman's ideas be applied to our time? Justify your answer.

CHAPTER 7

1. What is the relationship between humanism and education?
2. Discuss the educational ideals of Spinoza.
3. What is the significance of Deism? What did Deism teach in regard to religion?
4. How did Paine express the Deistic principles? In what ways was Paine unorthodox?
5. Describe Franklin's educational views.
6. Why did the Deists believe in progress and science?
7. Describe the philosophical views of Ethan Allen.
8. What is the significance of Palmer?
9. Why did the Deists stress the power of education?
10. Compare and contrast Deism and Puritanism.

CHAPTER 8

1. Why did materialism become popular in American thought?
2. Describe the philosophical views of Colden. Why did he object to Berkeley's idealism?
3. How did Priestley influence American materialism?

4. Evaluate Rush's contribution to American philosophy and education.
5. Compare the philosophy of Buchanan with that of Jonathan Edwards. Which do you find more valid? Explain your answer.
6. What are the main differences between idealism and materialism?
7. In what way is science based on a materialistic view of life?
8. What is the relationship between education and materialism?
9. Make a list of the great materialists in history and explain their contributions.
10. What are the weaknesses of materialism?

CHAPTER 9

1. What are the basic causes for the American Revolution?
2. What is the significance of Thomas Paine's *Common Sense?*
3. How did the American Revolution influence American culture?
4. What is the philosophy of the Declaration of Independence?
5. Compare and contrast the American Revolution with the Soviet Revolution in 1917.
6. How did Washington influence education?
7. How did the Revolution encourage American education?
8. In what ways was the American Revolution unsuccessful?
9. Why is the problem of leadership so important in America?
10. How did the states provide for education?
11. In what ways were the Articles of Confederation defective?
12. What are the basic principles behind the American Constitution?

CHAPTER 10

1. What are the principal accomplishments of Jefferson?
2. What was Jefferson's concept of philosophy?
3. Why did Jefferson object to Platonism in Christianity?
4. What was Jefferson's attitude regarding centralization in government?
5. Analyze Jefferson's moral philosophy. In what ways was it Epicurean?
6. What was Jefferson's view of Epicurus?
7. How did Jefferson criticize the educational ideas of his time?
8. Why did Jefferson object to European education?

9. What was Jefferson's concept of higher education?
10. What are the advantages and disadvantages of Jefferson's educational views?
11. Can Jefferson's educational ideals be applied to our time? Justify your answer.

CHAPTER 11

1. What is the significance of Rousseau in education?
2. What is Rousseau's view of specialization?
3. What are the four phases of Émile?
4. What is the importance of Pestalozzi?
5. How did Pestalozzi influence American education?
6. What is Pestalozzi's view of love?
7. What are the stages of learning, according to Herbart?
8. Compare the ideas of Herbart with those of Rousseau.
9. How did Froebel influence childhood education?
10. What educational contributions did Spencer make?
11. How has the U.S. influenced European education in the 20th century?
12. What, in your opinion, are the advantages and disadvantages of European education, especially in England, France and Germany?
13. How can education develop the bases of a peaceful world?

CHAPTER 12

1. Describe the background of Transcendentalism.
2. How did Emerson contribute to the emancipation of the American mind?
3. What was the substance of Emerson's *Divinity School Address?*
4. Why did Emerson believe in individualism?
5. What was Emerson's concept of nature?
6. Describe the metaphysical views of Emerson.
7. What was Emerson's view of society? What is your own view of society?
8. How did Emerson regard the cult of tradition?
9. What is the function of the teacher, according to Emerson?
10. Compare and contrast the educational and philosophical ideals of Emerson and Jefferson.
11. What is Emerson's view of Christianity?
12. How can Emerson's educational ideals be applied to the dilemmas of our time?

CHAPTER 13

1. Describe the life of Horace Mann.
2. Discuss the educational practices in the period of Horace Mann.
3. What were Mann's main goals?
4. Why was Mann attacked by some orthodox ministers?
5. How can education aid equality, according to Mann? What is your own view?
6. What is the relationship between education and controversy, according to Mann?
7. How did Mann further moral education?
8. What were Mann's religious views?
9. How did Mann regard revolution?
10. Analyze Mann's statement "Be ashamed to die until you have won some victory for humanity."

CHAPTER 14

1. Describe the career of Barnard.
2. How did the example of Jesus influence Barnard?
3. What is the function of the teacher, according to Barnard?
4. How did Barnard view the instruction of his time?
5. What was Barnard's attitude toward women teachers?
6. How did Barnard regard European education?
7. What was Barnard's view of radicalism?
8. How did Barnard further the tenets of capitalism?
9. What was Barnard's view of private schools?
10. Compare the ideas of Barnard with those of Mann.

CHAPTER 15

1. Why did Thoreau rebel against American society?
2. Why did Thoreau prefer the life of nature?
3. Evaluate Thoreau's concept of religion.
4. In what ways was Thoreau an anarchist?
5. What was Thoreau's concept of wisdom?
6. How did Thoreau react to organized education?
7. What was Thoreau's view of books?
8. How did Thoreau view the reading which was done by his contemporaries?

9. How practical are the educational ideas of Thoreau?
10. Do you agree or disagree with the main educational concepts of Thoreau? Justify your answer.

CHAPTER 16

1. How did the frontier influence American education?
2. What is the significance of Jacksonian democracy?
3. What was Lincoln's political philosophy?
4. How did Lincoln try to preserve the Federal Union?
5. What were the main results of the Civil War?
6. Discuss the educational awakening in the 19th century.
7. What were the advantages and disadvantages of the monitorial system?
8. How was education supported in the early 19th century?
9. What is the significance of the Lyceum movement?
10. What contributions did B. T. Washington make to education?

CHAPTER 17

1. Why was there tragedy in Whitman's life?
2. Describe Whitman's theory of knowledge.
3. Evaluate Whitman's concept of God.
4. What was Whitman's criticism of democracy? Do you agree with him?
5. In what ways was Whitman's philosophy opposed to that of Puritanism?
6. What is the relationship between education and nature, according to Whitman?
7. What was Whitman's concept of truth? What is your own concept of truth?
8. What was the role of intuition in education, according to Whitman?
9. What should be the goals of education, according to Whitman?
10. Do you agree or disagree with the ideas of Whitman? Justify your answer.

CHAPTER 18

1. What did Brokmeyer contribute to American educational philosophy? Why was he interested in Hegel?
2. Who founded the *Journal of Speculative Philosophy?* What was its purpose?

3. What was Harris's view of religion?
4. What were the basic subjects, according to Harris?
5. Why was Harris opposed to hedonism? What is your own view of hedonism?
6. How did Harris view manual training?
7. Why did Harris support adult education?
8. How did Harris regard capitalism?
9. What should be the role of teachers, according to Harris?
10. Compare the views of Harris with those of Whitman.

CHAPTER 19

1. Why did the theory of evolution cause a storm in philosophical circles?
2. How did Agassiz react to evolution?
3. What was Newcomb's concept of evolution?
4. How did evolution affect theological viewpoints?
5. How did Fiske interpret the theory of evolution? How did he defend the reality of religion?
6. What was Fiske's view of evil? Do you agree or disagree with him? Explain your position.
7. How did Fiske view the power of love?
8. How is man distinguished from other animals, according to Fiske?
9. Fiske believed that nature preaches a moral sermon. Do you agree or disagree? Why?
10. How did the new evolutionary ideas affect the course of American education?
11. How did evolution lead to religious agnosticism?

CHAPTER 20

1. What are the main works of Hall?
2. How did Hall view the theory of evolution? What is your own concept of evolution?
3. What is the function of philosophy, according to Hall? What is your own view?
4. Why did Hall criticize conventional philosophy?
5. How did Hall feel about progress? Do you agree or disagree? Why?
6. What is the relationship between education and psychology, according to Hall?
7. What are the main stages in the life of the individual, according to Hall?

8. What measures did Hall recommend for the training of teachers?
9. How did Hall view experts?
10. What was Hall's view of methodology?
11. What are the strengths and weaknesses in Hall's educational philosophy?

CHAPTER 21

1. What are the major aims of the progressive movement?
2. Why did the progressive movement fail?
3. Who were the leaders of the progressive movement?
4. What was the significance of Andrew White?
5. How did Labor advance in this period?
6. What is the importance of the "social gospel"?
7. What was Rauschenbusch's view of American society?
8. Discuss the contributions of Sumner.
9. What was the relationship between progressivism and education?
10. Why was Veblen important in American culture?

CHAPTER 22

1. Discuss the career of Parker.
2. What thinkers were the main influences upon Parker?
3. What are the similarities between Parker and Dewey?
4. How did Parker view an aristocratic system of education?
5. How did Parker try to teach history?
6. What was Parker's view of democracy?
7. How did Parker view discipline in education? What is your own viewpoint?
8. What was Parker's concept of grades? What is your own philosophy regarding grades?
9. What is the function of the teacher, according to Parker?
10. Compare the views of Parker with those of Harris. Who, in your opinion, is more valid in his concept of education?

CHAPTER 23

1. Why did Royce accept the philosophy of idealism?
2. What did Royce imply by the principle of loyalty?
3. What is the status of the Absolute in Royce's philosophy?
4. Why did the idealistic movement become so important in American thought and education?

5. Enumerate Bowne's main works.
6. Why did Bowne accept the philosophy of personalism?
7. What was Bowne's view of materialism?
8. Describe Bowne's moral philosophy. In what ways did Bowne reflect Kant's moral teachings?
9. What is the significance of Bowne in American philosophy?
10. What were Bowne's educational views?

CHAPTER 24

1. In what ways was James different from Royce?
2. What is the significance of pragmatism?
3. Why did James rebel against traditional philosophical views?
4. What did James mean by tough-minded and tender-minded philosophers? What type do you prefer? Explain your position.
5. What did James contribute to religious theories?
6. How did James view traditional instruction?
7. How did James regard moral philosophy?
8. Why did James stress the importance of good habits?
9. What does James mean by emulation?
10. Why does teaching depend on example, according to James?
11. Evaluate the educational philosophy of James.
12. Why did pragmatism become such an influential philosophy?

CHAPTER 25

1. What are Dewey's principal philosophical works?
2. Analyze Dewey's philosophy of religion.
3. What does Dewey mean by instrumentalism?
4. How did Dewey influence American culture?
5. Analyze Dewey's political views. How would they be judged by Fascists and Marxists?
6. How did Dewey view the scientific method?
7. What criticisms did Dewey make of traditional education?
8. How did Dewey contribute to progressive education?
9. Why has Dewey been attacked so vigorously in our time?
10. Evaluate the advantages and weaknesses of Dewey's concepts of education.
11. Compare the views of Dewey with those of Thoreau. Who do you find more suggestive? Why?
12. What are the implications of Dewey's views for the teacher, parent, and administrator?

CHAPTER 26

1. Describe the philosophy of normalcy.
2. How did the 1920's react to radicalism?
3. Describe the cult of individualism in the 1920's?
4. Why was Hemingway admired so much in the 1920's?
5. What was the literary reaction to the culture of the 1920's?
6. Why did nationalism increase in the 1920's?
7. How did economics influence the American way of life in the 1920's?
8. What was the role of advertising in this period?
9. What were the marks of escapism in the 1920's?
10. Compare the culture of the 1920's with that of the 1950's.
11. Why did many educators rebel against the culture of the 1920's?

CHAPTER 27

1. Analyze the philosophy of the New Deal.
2. Describe Roosevelt's political philosophy. What is your own evaluation of his work?
3. In what ways did Willkie aid the cause of internationalism?
4. Why was Willkie opposed to a planned economy?
5. How did the New Deal influence education?
6. What is the significance of *Native Son?*
7. Describe the contributions of Steinbeck to American culture.
8. Why was Counts important?
9. How did Counts criticize an aristocratic system of education?
10. What is the relationship between the "New Deal" and Kennedy's "New Frontier"?
11. In your own opinion what should be the role of the central government in education?

CHAPTER 28

1. How did Santayana evaluate American culture?
2. Why did Santayana prefer the life of detachment?
3. Compare Santayana's philosophy with that of William James.
4. What was Santayana's concept of society?
5. Why did Santayana oppose American education?
6. What was Santayana's concept of progress?

7. Why did Santayana favor the rule of tradition?
8. How did Santayana view specialization?
9. Do you prefer the educational ideals of Dewey or those of Santayana? Justify your position.

CHAPTER 29

1. Who were the main leaders in progressive education?
2. What is the significance of reconstructionism?
3. Why does progressive education favor freedom in the classroom?
4. What are the main works of Kilpatrick?
5. How does Kilpatrick view the scientific method?
6. What is Kilpatrick's attitude toward the Great Books?
7. What is Kilpatrick's view of Dewey?
8. Why does Kilpatrick attack traditional liberal education?
9. What learning theory does Kilpatrick uphold?
10. Why did Kilpatrick become so influential in American education?

CHAPTER 30

1. How has American philosophy been popularized?
2. Describe the contributions of realism to American philosophy. What is the difference between Neo-realism and critical realism?
3. Why is personalism important in 20th century philosophy?
4. Analyze the educational views of Horne. In what ways do they differ from John Dewey?
5. What advances have been made in educational psychology?
6. Do you agree or disagree with the tenets of behaviorism? Explain your answer.
7. What is the significance of neo-scholasticism?
8. Why has existentialism become popular?
9. What is the importance of essentialism?
10. Discuss the ideals of realism in education.
11. What contributions has Brameld made to 20th century education?

CHAPTER 31

1. Discuss the career of Hutchins. What do you regard as his most important achievement?
2. What are the main differences between Dewey and Hutchins?
3. Why does Hutchins favor the Great Books? What is your own view of the Great Books?

4. How does Hutchins view academic freedom? Would you extend academic freedom to those who follow a totalitarian ideology? Explain your position.
5. Why does Hutchins believe in a world government?
6. What criticism did Hutchins make of higher education?
7. What is Hutchins' view of religion?
8. What is Hutchins' concept of the curriculum?
9. What is the goal of education, according to Hutchins?
10. How does Hutchins view vocational education?
11. Why has Hutchins been attacked so vigorously?
12. Compare the ideals of Hutchins with those of Plato.

CHAPTER 32

1. How did Brainerd describe puritan education?
2. Who were the main pioneers in elementary education?
3. Discuss the work of Montessori.
4. How did European ideas influence American elementary education?
5. What was the significance of Parkhurst?
6. What contributions did Dewey and Kilpatrick make to elementary education?
7. Describe the curriculum of the early modern elementary school.
8. What are the goals of elementary education today?
9. How can elementary education aid the cause of democracy?
10. What is the teacher's role in elementary education?

CHAPTER 33

1. What is the significance of the comprehensive high school?
2. How has Rickover attacked secondary education?
3. Discuss the development of the Academy movement.
4. Why did the Academies decline in the U.S.A.?
5. Compare the high school in the 19th century and today.
6. What, in your opinion, are the main problems in high school teaching?
7. What are the traits of the outstanding high school teacher?
8. What are the objectives of secondary education?
9. Describe the high school of the year 2000 A.D. What changes will occur in its structure and curriculum?

CHAPTER 34

1. Who have been the notable college presidents in the U.S.?
2. Discuss the achievements of Nott.
3. Why was Wayland significant?
4. What innovations did Eliot make at Harvard?
5. Do you agree or disagree regarding the elective system? Justify your answer.
6. What are the main problems in general education?
7. What were the accomplishments of W. R. Harper?
8. How did Hutchins view the philosophy of naturalism?
9. What contributions did Conant make?
10. What are the main weaknesses of higher education today?
11. What measures would you suggest to improve higher education?
12. Give a detailed description of what you would consider "the university of utopia"?

CHAPTER 35

1. Why has there been intense interest in the gifted students in our time?
2. How should gifted students be educated?
3. What is the relationship between I.Q. and creativity?
4. Describe the Beverly Hills program for gifted students.
5. How can our reading tastes be improved?
6. What are the principles of successful oratory?
7. What can be done to improve English instruction on every level?
8. How can creative listening be developed?
9. What was Schopenhauer's view of music?
10. How can creative communication be developed in our school system? What can be done in this field by teachers, administrators, parents and community leaders?

CHAPTER 36

1. What are the main causes of delinquency?
2. What are the traits of the delinquent?
3. Discuss the relationship between slums and delinquency.

4. What is the role of the gangs in delinquency?
5. How does society indirectly encourage delinquency?
6. What is the relationship between juvenile and adult delinquency?
7. Discuss the cheating problem in our colleges.
8. Evaluate the moral standards of the American middle class.
9. Why is violence increasing in our time?
10. How can education curb delinquency?

CHAPTER 37

1. What is the significance of the First Morrill Act?
2. Discuss the development of military education in the U.S.
3. What are the functions of the U.S. Commissioner of Education?
4. How has the federal government promoted education?
5. What is the significance of the N.E.A.?
6. What are the main educational journals today?
7. What is the role of the P.T.A.?
8. Should teachers be allowed to strike? Justify your own viewpoint.
9. Discuss the N.E.A. code of ethics.
10. What is the significance of the non-graded high school?
11. What are the main problems of adult education in the U.S.?
12. Why is adult education the intellectual foundation of democracy?

CHAPTER 38

1. How did Rush view the education of women?
2. What is the significance of Emma Willard?
3. What did Jefferson recommend for the education of women?
4. Discuss co-education in the 19th century.
5. Why did many teachers object to co-education? What are the values and disadvantages of co-education?
6. Discuss the development of Vassar College in the 20th century.
7. What contributions did Sarah Lawrence and Bennington make to higher education?
8. Discuss the dilemmas of Carol Kennicott in *Main Street*.
9. Should girls have the same education as boys? Defend your answer.
10. What contributions did Agnes Meyer make to contemporary education?

CHAPTER 39

1. What are the obligations of parents in developing moral and spiritual values in the home?
2. How does "momism" affect the security of the child?
3. Compare the 19th century father and his role today.
4. How can family unity be developed?
5. How permissive should parents be?
6. Should parents use physical punishments?
7. What should be the relationship between teachers and parents?
8. How can the home encourage intellectual curiosity?
9. Do you feel that more homework should be given to our children? Justify your answer.
10. What steps can be taken to curb divorce?
11. What can parents do to prevent delinquency?

CHAPTER 40

1. What is the relationship between art and morality?
2. What is the role of the machine in civilization?
3. What are the various definitions of art?
4. What is the relationship between science and art?
5. Why is art a protest against inhumanity?
6. How does art strive for integration?
7. What is the significance of *Winesburg, Ohio?*
8. What is Emerson's view of art?
9. What is the role of art in education?
10. How can art improve the quality of man's relations?
11. Should a course in art appreciation be required for all students in college? Explain your answer.
12. How can students best develop a genuine understanding of modern art?

CHAPTER 41

1. What is the function of the great teacher?
2. How can teaching be made dramatic?

3. Why is there much pedestrian teaching in our colleges?
4. What is your view of educational television?
5. What were the contributions of Woodrow Wilson to higher education?
6. Discuss the educational philosophy of Ulich.
7. How did William James approach teaching?
8. What are your own prescriptions for creative teaching?
9. How can we bridge the gulf between school and society?
10. What method of teaching do you prefer: the lecture or the discussion group? Explain your answer.

CHAPTER 42

1. What are the central ideas of existentialism?
2. What is the difference between existentialism and conventiona philosophy?
3. Why does existentialism point to the importance of attitudes
4. What is the existentialist view of the teacher?
5. How does existentialism regard society?
6. What is the existential view of history?
7. What is the existential role of art?
8. How does existentialism view liberal education?
9. Discuss the non-directive views of Carl Rogers.
10. What are the goals of existential education?

CHAPTER 43

1. How do ideals affect education?
2. What are the significant choices for American society?
3. Discuss the relationship between education and awakening.
4. Compare Hellenistic with Athenian education. What are the similarities between the U.S. and Hellenistic civilization?
5. What have been the main periods in American education? Which one has been most important?
6. What are the dangers of the disciple spirit?
7. What are the advantages and disadvantages of pragmatic education?
8. How can education lead to a new renaissance?
9. What is the role of books in education?
10. Evaluate the author's program for the improvement of American education. What are your own viewpoints regarding this subject
11. What are your central beliefs regarding education and democracy

Selected Bibliography

Adler, Mortimer J. *Art and Prudence.* New York, Longmans, Green & Company; 1937.

Adorno, T. W., and others. *The Authoritarian Personality.* New York, Harper and Brothers; 1950.

Aikin, W. M. *The Story of the Eight-Year Study.* New York, Harper and Brothers; 1942.

Allport, Gordon. *Becoming.* New Haven, Yale University Press; 1955.

American Council on Education, Committee on Religion and Education. *The Function of the Public Schools in Dealing with Religion.* Washington, D. C., The Council; 1953.

Ames, Edward S. *Religion.* New York, Henry Holt & Co., Inc.; 1930.

Anshen, Ruth Nanda, ed. *Freedom: Its Meaning.* New York, Harcourt, Brace and Company; 1940.

——, ed. *Moral Principles of Action.* New York, Harper and Brothers; 1952.

Ashley-Montagu, Montague Francis. *Darwin, Competition and Co-operation.* New York, H. Schuman; 1952.

——. *The Direction of Human Development.* New York, Harper and Brothers; 1955.

Bagley, William C. *Education and Emergent Man.* New York, Thomas Nelson and Sons; 1934.

Ballou, Richard B. *The Individual and the State: The Modern Challenge to Education.* Boston, Beacon Press, Inc.; 1953.

Bantock, G. H. *Freedom and Authority in Education.* Chicago, Henry Regnery Company; 1953.

Barker, Roger G., Kounin, Jacob S., and Wright, Herbert F., eds. *Child Behavior and Development.* New York, McGraw-Hill Book Company; 1943.

Barnard, Chester I. *The Functions of the Executive.* Cambridge, Mass., Harvard University Press; 1947.

Barth, Karl. *Against the Stream.* New York, Philosophical Library; 1954.

Barzun, Jacques. *Of Human Freedom.* Boston, Little, Brown and Company; 1939.

Beard, Charles A. *The Myth of Rugged American Individualism.* New York, The John Day Company; 1932.

Becker, Carl L. *Freedom and Responsibility in the American Way of Life.* New York, Alfred A. Knopf, Inc.; 1945.

Bendix, Reinhard, and Lipset, Seymour. *Class, Status, and Power.* Glencoe, Ill., The Free Press; 1953.

Benedict, Ruth. *Patterns of Culture.* Boston, Houghton Mifflin Company; 1934.

Benjamin, Harold. *Emergent Conceptions of the School Administrator's Task.* Stanford, Stanford University Press; 1942.

Benne, Kenneth D. *A Conception of Authority.* New York, Teachers College, Columbia University; 1943.

Berdyaev, Nicolai. *Freedom and the Spirit.* London, Centenary Press; 1935.

Berger, Morroe, and others, eds. *Freedom and Control in Modern Society.* New York, D. Van Nostrand Company, Inc.; 1954.

Berkson, Isaac B. *Education Faces the Future.* New York, Harper and Brothers; 1943.

————. *Preface to an Educational Philosophy.* New York, Columbia University Press; 1940.

Bertocci, Peter Anthony. *Introduction to the Philosophy of Religion.* Englewood Cliffs, N. J., Prentice-Hall, Inc.; 1951.

Bestor, Arthur. *The Restoration of Learning.* New York, Alfred A. Knopf, Inc.; 1955.

Bettelheim, B. *Love Is Not Enough.* Glencoe, Ill., The Free Press; 1950.

Blanshard, Brand, and Others. *Philosophy in American Education.* New York, Harper & Brothers; 1945.

Bloch, Ernst. *Freiheit und Ordnung: abriss der Sozial-Utopien.* New York, Aurora Verlag; 1946.

Bode, Boyd H. *Democracy as a Way of Life.* New York, The Macmillan Company; 1937.

———. *How We Learn.* Boston, D. C. Heath and Company; 1940.

———. *Modern Educational Theories.* New York, The Macmillan Company; 1927.

Borsodi, Ralph. *This Ugly Civilization.* New York, Harper and Brothers; 1933.

Bossard, James H. S. *Parent and Child; Studies in Family Behavior.* Philadelphia, University of Pennsylvania Press; 1953.

———. *The Sociology of Child Development.* New York, Harper and Brothers; 1948.

Bower, William C. *Church and State in Education.* Chicago, University of Chicago Press: 1944.

———. *Moral and Spiritual Values in Education.* Lexington, University of Kentucky Press; 1952.

Bowers, Claude G., *Jefferson and Hamilton.* Boston, Houghton-Mifflin Co.; 1925.

Brameld, Theodore. *Cultural Foundations of Education.* New York, Harper and Brothers; 1957.

———. *Ends and Means in Education.* New York, Harper and Brothers; 1950.

———. *Philosophies of Education in Cultural Perspective.* New York, The Dryden Press, Inc.; 1955.

———. *Toward a Reconstructed Philosophy of Education.* New York, The Dryden Press, Inc.; 1955.

Breed, Frederick S. *Education and the New Realism.* New York, The Macmillan Company, 1939.

Briggs, Thomas H. *The Great Investment.* Cambridge, Mass., Harvard University Press; 1930.

Broudy, Harry S. *Building a Philosophy of Education.* Englewood Cliffs, N. J., Prentice-Hall, Inc.; 1954.

Brown, Junius Flagg. *Psychology and the Social Order.* New York, McGraw-Hill Book Company; 1936.

Brubacher, John S. *A History of the Problems of Education.* New York, McGraw-Hill Book Company; 1947.

———, ed. *The Public Schools and Spiritual Values.* New York, Harper and Brothers; 1944.

Bryson, Lyman, and others, eds. *Aspects of Human Equality*. New York, Conference on Science, Philosophy, and Religion in Their Relation to the Democratic Way of Life; 1953.

Buber, Martin. *Between Man and Man*. Ronald Gregor Smith, trans. Boston, Beacon Press, Inc.; 1955.

Burton, William H. *The Guidance of Learning Activities*, 2nd ed. New York, Appleton-Century-Crofts, Inc.; 1952.

Burtt, Edwin A. *Types of Religious Philosophy*, 2nd ed. New York, Harper and Brothers; 1951.

Bury, J. B. *The Idea of Progress*. New York, The Macmillan Company; 1932.

Butler, J. Donald. *Four Philosophies and Their Practice in Education and Religion*, 2nd ed. New York, Harper and Brothers; 1957.

Butler, Nicholas Murray. *True and False Democracy*. New York, The Macmillan Company; 1907.

Butts, R. Freeman. *The American Tradition in Religion and Education*. Boston, Beacon Press, Inc.; 1950.

――――. *A Cultural History of Western Education*, 2nd ed. New York, McGraw-Hill Book Company; 1955.

Calkins, Mary W. *The Good Life and the Good*. New York, The Macmillan Company; 1918.

Callahan, Raymond E. *An Introduction to Education in American Society*. New York, Alfred A. Knopf, Inc.; 1956.

Cannon, Walter Bradford. *The Wisdom of the Body*. New York, W. W. Norton and Company, Inc.; 1932.

Cantor, Nathaniel. *The Teaching-Learning Process*. New York, The Dryden Press, Inc.: 1953.

Carmichael, Leonard, ed. *Manual of Child Psychology*, 2nd ed. New York, John Wiley and Sons, Inc.; 1954.

Cassirer, Ernst. *An Essay on Man*. New Haven, Yale University Press; 1948.

Childs, John L. *American Pragmatism and Education*. New York, Henry Holt and Co., Inc.; 1956.

Coghill, George Ellet. *Anatomy and the Problem of Behavior*. Cambridge, England, University Press; 1929.

Cohen, Morris R. *The Faith of a Liberal*. New York, Henry Holt and Co., Inc.; 1946.

――――. *Reason and Nature*. New York, Harcourt, Brace and Company; 1931.

Colardarci, Arthur, and Getzels, Jacob W. *The Use of Theory in Educational Administration*. Stanford, Stanford University Press; 1955.

Cole, Lawrence E., and Bruce, William F. *Educational Psychology*. Yonkers, New York, World Book Company; 1950.

Commager, Henry S., *The American Mind*. New Haven, Yale University Press; 1950.

Conant, James Bryant. *Education and Liberty*. Cambridge, Mass., Harvard University Press; 1953.

Counts, George S. *Dare the School Build a New Social Order?* New York, The John Day Company; 1932.

————. *Decision Making and American Values in School Administration*. New York, Teachers College, Columbia University; 1953.

————. *The Prospects of American Democracy*. New York, The John Day Company; 1938.

————. *Social Foundations of Education*. New York, Charles Scribner's Sons; 1934.

Cunningham, William F. *Pivotal Problems of Education*. New York, The Macmillan Company; 1940.

Curti, Merle. *The Growth of American Thought*. New York, Harper and Brothers; 1943.

————. *The Social Ideas of American Educators*. New York, Charles Scribner's Sons; 1935.

Davis, Allison. *Intelligence and Cultural Differences*. Chicago, University of Chicago Press; 1951.

————. *Social-Class Influences Upon Learning*. Cambridge, Mass., Harvard University Press; 1948.

DeGrazia, Sebastian. *The Political Community*. Chicago, University of Chicago Press; 1948.

Demiashkevich, Michael. *An Introduction to the Philosophy of Education*. New York, American Book Company, 1935.

Dewey, John. *Art as Experience*. New York, Minton, Balch and Company; 1935.

————. "Authority and Social Change," in Harvard Tercentenary Publications, *Authority and the Individual*. Cambridge, Mass., Harvard University Press; 1937, pp. 170-190.

————. *Characters and Events*, 2 vols. New York, Henry Holt and Co., Inc.; 1929.

————. *The Child and the Curriculum*. Chicago, University of Chicago Press; 1902.

————. *A Common Faith*. New Haven, Yale University Press; 1934.

————. *Democracy and Education*. New York, The Macmillan Company, 1916.

————. *Education Today*. New York, G. P. Putnam's Sons; 1940.

————. *Experience and Education*. New York, The Macmillan Company; 1938.

————. *Experience and Nature*. New York, W. W. Norton and Company, Inc.; 1929.

――――. *How We Think,* 2nd ed. Boston, D. C. Heath and Company; 1933.

――――. *Human Nature and Conduct.* New York, Henry Holt and Co., Inc.; 1922.

――――. *Individualism Old and New.* New York, Minton, Balch and Company; 1930.

――――. *Intelligence in the Modern World,* Joseph Ratner, ed. New York, Random House; 1939.

――――. *Liberalism and Social Action.* New York, G. P. Putnam's Sons; 1935.

――――. *Moral Principles in Education.* Boston, Houghton Mifflin Company; 1909.

――――. *The Public and Its Problems.* New York, Henry Holt and Co., Inc.; 1927.

――――. *The Quest for Certainty.* New York, G. P. Putnam's Sons; 1929.

――――. *Reconstruction in Philosophy.* New York, Holt and Co., Inc.; 1920.

――――. *The School and Society,* 2nd ed. Chicago, University of Chicago Press; 1943.

――――. "Theory of Valuation," *International Encyclopedia of Unified Science,* Vol. II, No. 4. Chicago, University of Chicago Press; 1939.

――――, and Bentley, Arthur. *Knowing and the Known.* Boston, Beacon Press, Inc.; 1949.

――――, and Tufts, James H. *Ethics,* 2nd ed. New York, Henry Holt and Co., Inc.; 1932.

Dewey, Richard S., and Humber, W. J. *The Development of Human Behavior.* New York, The Macmillan Company; 1951.

Drake, Durant. *Invitation to Philosophy.* Boston, Houghton Mifflin Company; 1933.

Eby, Frederick, and Arrowood, C. F. *The Development of Modern Education.* Englewood Cliffs, N. J., Prentice-Hall, Inc.; 1940.

Edman, Irwin. *Arts and the Man.* New York, New American Library of World Literature, Inc.; 1949.

――――, ed. *Fountainheads of Freedom.* New York, Harcourt, Brace and Company; 1941.

Educational Policies Commission, National Education Association. *Learning the Ways of Democracy.* Washington, D. C., National Education Association; 1940.

Ehlers, Henry. *Crucial Issues in Education.* New York, Henry Holt and Co., Inc.; 1955.

Emerson, Ralph W. *Essays — First and Second Series.* Boston, Houghton Mifflin Company, 1883.

Ferguson, Charles W. *A Little Democracy Is a Dangerous Thing.* New York, Association Press; 1948.

Fleming, Robert S. *Curriculum for Today's Boys and Girls.* Columbus, Charles E. Merrill Books, 1963.

Fromm, Erich. *Escape From Freedom.* New York, Farrar and Rinehart, Inc.; 1941.

Garrison, Noble L. *The Improvement of Teaching, A Two-Fold Approach.* New York, The Dryden Press, Inc.; 1955.

Gold, Milton. *Working to Learn.* New York, Teachers College, Columbia University; 1951.

Gotshalk, Dilman W. *Art and the Social Order.* Chicago, University of Chicago Press; 1947.

Gouldner, Alvin W., ed. *Studies in Leadership.* New York, Harper and Brothers; 1950.

Graff, Orin B., and Street, Calvin M. *Improving Competence in Educational Administration.* New York, Harper and Brothers; 1956.

The Great Books Foundation. *Great Issues in Education*, 3 vols. Chicago, The Great Books Foundation; 1956.

Griffin, Alan F. *Freedom: American Style.* New York, Henry Holt and Co., Inc.; 1940.

Hadley, Arthur H. *The Conflict Between Liberty and Equality.* Boston, Houghton Mifflin Company; 1925.

Hanna, Paul Robert. *Youth Serves the Community.* New York, D. Appleton-Century Company; 1936.

Havighurst, Robert J. *Human Development and Education.* New York, Longmans, Green and Company; 1927.

———, and Neugarten, Bernice L. *Society and Education.* New York, Allyn and Bacon, Inc.; 1957.

Hayek, Friederich A. *Individualism and Economic Order.* Chicago, University of Chicago Press; 1947.

Henderson, Stella V. *Introduction to Philosophy of Education.* Chicago, University of Chicago Press; 1947.

Highet, Gilbert. *The Art of Teaching.* New York, Alfred A. Knopf, Inc.; 1950.

Hill, Thomas E. *Contemporary Ethical Theories.* New York, The Macmillan Company; 1950.

Hocking, William E. *What Man Can Make of Man.* New York, Harper and Brothers; 1942.

Hofstadter, Richard, and Metzger, Walter P. *The Development of Academic Freedom in the United States.* New York, Columbia University Press; 1955.

Hollingshead, August R. *Elmtown's Youth.* New York, John Wiley and Sons, Inc.; 1949.

Hook, Sidney. *Education for Modern Man.* New York, The Dial Press, Inc.; 1946.

———. *John Dewey: An Intellectual Portrait.* New York, The John Day Company; 1939.

Hoover, Herbert. *American Individualism.* New York, Doubleday and Company, Inc.; 1922.

Horne, Herman H. *The Democratic Philosophy of Education.* New York, The Macmillan Company; 1935.

———. *The Teacher as an Artist: An Essay in Education as an Aesthetic Process.* Boston, Houghton Mifflin Company; 1917.

Horney, Karen. *The Neurotic Personality of Our Time.* New York, W. W. Norton and Company, Inc.; 1937.

Hullfish, H. Gordon. *Educational Freedom in an Age of Anxiety.* New York, Harper and Brothers; 1953.

Hutchins, Robert M. *The Conflict in Education.* New York, Harper and Brothers; 1953.

———. *The Higher Learning in America.* New Haven, Yale University Press; 1936.

Hutchinson, John A. *Faith, Reason, and Existence.* New York, Oxford University Press; 1956.

James, William. *The Varieties of Religious Experience.* New York, Longmans, Green and Company, Inc.; 1902.

———. *Pragmatism.* New York, Longmans, Green and Company; 1907.

———. *Talks to Teachers on Psychology.* New York, Henry Holt and Company; 1900.

Jefferson, Thomas. *Letters.* (Edited by Saul Padover). New York, The John Day Company; 1956.

Jennings, H. S. *The Biological Basis of Human Nature.* New York, W. W. Norton and Company, Inc.; 1930.

Johnson, F. Ernest, ed. *American Education and Religion.* New York, Harper and Brothers; 1952.

Kallen, Horace M. *Art and Freedom,* 2 vols. New York, Duell, Sloan and Pearce, Inc.; 1942.

———. *The Education of Free Men.* New York, Farrar, Straus and Cudahy, Inc.; 1949.

———, ed. *Freedom in the Modern World.* New York, Coward-McCann, Inc.; 1928.

———. *Individualism — An American Way of Life.* New York, H. Liveright, Inc.; 1933.

Kallenbach, W. Warren, and Hodges, Jr., Harold M., eds. *Education and Society.* Columbus, Charles E. Merrill Books, Inc.; 1963.

Kandel, Isaac L. *Conflicting Theories of Education.* New York, The Macmillan Company; 1938.

Kelley, Earl C., and Rasey, Marie I. *Education and the Nature of Man.* New York, Harper and Brothers; 1952.

Kelso, Louis O., and Adler, Mortimer J. *The Capitalist Manifesto.* New York, Random House; 1958.

Kilpatrick, William H. *Education and the Social Crisis.* New York, Liveright Publishing Corporation; 1932.

———. *Education for a Changing Civilization.* New York, The Macmillan Company; 1926.

———, ed. *The Educational Frontier.* New York, The Century Co.; 1933.

———. *Group Education for a Democracy.* New York, Association Press; 1940.

———. *Philosophy of Education.* New York, The Macmillan Company; 1951.

———. *Selfhood and Civilization.* New York, The Macmillan Company; 1941.

———. *Source Book in the Philosophy of Education.* New York, The Macmillan Company; 1934.

Klubertanz, George P. *The Philosophy of Human Nature.* New York, Appleton-Century-Crofts, Inc.; 1953.

Kluckhohn, Clyde. *Modern Education and Human Values.* Pittsburgh, University of Pittsburgh Press; 1952.

———, and Murray, Henry A. *Personality in Nature, Society, and Culture.* New York, Alfred A. Knopf; 1949.

Koopman, G. R., Miel, Alice, and Misner, Paul J. *Democracy in School Administration.* New York, Appleton-Century-Crofts, Inc.; 1943.

Kroeber, Alfred L. *The Nature of Culture.* Chicago, University of Chicago Press; 1952.

La Barre, Weston. *The Human Animal.* Chicago, University of Chicago Press; 1955.

Langer, Suzanne. *Philosophy in a New Key.* Cambridge, Mass., Harvard University Press; 1942.

Lashley, K. S. *Brain Mechanisms and Intelligence.* Chicago, University of Chicago Press; 1929.

Leary, Lewis. *The Unity of Knowledge.* Garden City, New York, Doubleday and Company, Inc.; 1955.

Lerner, Max. *America as a Civilization.* New York, Simon and Schuster, Inc.; 1957.

———. *Ideas Are Weapons.* New York, The Viking Press, Inc.; 1939.

Lewin, Kurt. *Resolving Social Conflicts.* New York, Harper and Brothers; 1948.

Lieberman, Myron. *Education as a Profession.* Englewood Cliffs, N. J., Prentice-Hall, Inc.; 1956.

Lilienthal, David E. *Big Business: A New Era.* New York, Harper and Brothers; 1953.

———. *TVA: Democracy on the March.* New York, Harper and Brothers; 1944.

Lindberg, Lucille. *The Democratic Classroom.* New York, Teachers College, Columbia University; 1954.

Lippmann, Walter. *The Method of Freedom.* New York, The Macmillan Company; 1934.

———. *Preface to Morals.* New York, The Macmillan Company; 1929.

Lodge, Rupert C. *Philosophy of Education,* 2nd ed. New York, Harper and Brothers; 1947.

Lowenfeld, Viktor. *Creative and Mental Growth.* New York, The Macmillan Company; 1949.

Lynd, Robert S. *Knowledge for What?* Princeton, Princeton University Press; 1939.

———, and Lynd, Helen M. *Middletown.* New York, Harcourt, Brace and Company; 1929.

———. *Middletown in Transition.* New York, Harcourt, Brace and Company; 1937.

MacDonald, John. *Mind, School and Civilization.* Chicago, University of Chicago Press; 1952.

MacIver, Robert M. *Academic Freedom in Our Time.* New York, Columbia University Press; 1955.

———. *The Web of Government.* New York, The Macmillan Company; 1948.

McKeon, Richard, Merton, Robert K., and Gellhorn, Walter. *The Freedom to Read: Perspective and Program.* New York, R. R. Bower for the National Book Committee; 1957.

McNerney, T. *The Curriculum.* New York, McGraw-Hill Book Company; 1953.

Madden, Ward. *Religious Values in Education.* New York, Harper and Brothers; 1951.

Malinowski, Bronislaw. *Freedom and Civilization.* New York, Roy Publishers; 1944.

Mann, Horace. *The Republic and the School,* Lawrence A. Cremin, ed. New York. Teachers College, Columbia University; 1957.

Mannheim, Karl. *Diagnosis of Our Time.* London, Kegan Paul, Trench, Trubner & Co.; 1947.

———. *Ideology and Utopia.* New York, Harcourt, Brace and Company; 1936.

———. *Man and Society in an Age of Reconstruction.* New York, Harcourt, Brace and Company; 1940.

Maritain, Jacques. *Art and Poetry.* New York, Philosophical Library; 1943.

———. *Education at the Crossroads.* New Haven, Yale University Press; 1943.

———. *An Introduction to Philosophy.* New York, Longmans, Green and Company; 1930.

Martin, William O. *The Order and Integration of Knowledge.* Ann Arbor, Michigan, University of Michigan Press; 1957.

Mason, Robert E. *Moral Values and Secular Education.* New York, Columbia University Press; 1950.

Mathewson, Robert H. *A Strategy for American Education.* New York, Harper and Brothers; 1957.

May, Rollo. *Man's Search for Himself.* New York, W. W. Norton and Company, Inc.; 1953.

Mayer, Frederick. *A History of Ancient and Medieval Philosophy.* New York, American Book Company; 1950.

———. *A History of Modern Philosophy.* New York, American Book Company; 1951.

———. *Education and the Good Life.* Washington, D. C., Public Affairs Press; 1957.

———. *Philosophy of Education for Our Time.* New York, Odyssey Press; 1958.

———. *A History of Educational Thought.* Columbus, Charles E. Merrill Books, Inc.; 1960.

Mead, George H. *Mind, Self and Society.* Chicago, University of Chicago Press; 1934.

———. *The Philosophy of the Act.* Chicago, University of Chicago Press; 1938.

Mead, Margaret. *Male and Female.* New York, William Morrow and Company; 1949.

Meadows, Paul. *The Culture of Industrial Man.* Lincoln, Nebraska, University of Nebraska Press; 1950.

Meiklejohn, Alexander. *Education Between Two Worlds.* New York, Harper & Brothers; 1942.

———. *What Does America Mean?* New York, W. W. Norton and Company, Inc.; 1953.

Melby, Ernest O. *Administering Community Education.* Englewood Cliffs, N. J., Prentice-Hall, Inc.; 1955.

———, ed. *Mobilizing Educational Resources.* New York, Harper and Brothers, 1943.

Menninger, Karl. *Man Against Himself.* New York, Harcourt, Brace and Company, Inc.; 1938.

Mercer, Blaine E., and Carr, Edwin R. *Education and the Social Order.* New York, Rinehart and Company; 1957.

Merriam, Charles E. *Public and Private Government.* New Haven, Yale University Press; 1944.

Meyer, Adolph. *The Development of Education in the Twentieth Century.* Englewood Cliffs, N. J., Prentice-Hall, Inc.; 1949.

Miller, Perry. *The New England Mind.* New York, The Macmillan Company; 1939.

Montague, William P. *Great Visions of Philosophy.* Chicago, Open Court Publishing Company; 1950.

Morris, Charles. *Six Theories of Mind.* Chicago, University of Chicago Press; 1932.

Morris, Van Cleve. *Philosophy and the American School.* Boston, Houghton Mifflin; 1961.

Mowrer, Orval. *Learning Theory and Personality Dynamics.* New York, The Ronald Press Company; 1950.

Mumford, Lewis. *The Condition of Man.* New York, Harcourt, Brace & Co., Inc.; 1941.

———. *The Culture of Cities.* New York, Harcourt, Brace & Co., Inc.; 1938.

———. *The Story of Utopia.* New York, Liveright Publishing Corporation; 1933.

———. *Technics and Civilization.* New York, Harcourt, Brace & Co., Inc.; 1934.

———. *Values for Survival.* New York, Harcourt, Brace & Co., Inc.; 1934.

Murphy, Gardner. *Personality: A Biosocial Approach to Origins and Structure.* New York, Harper and Brothers; 1947.

Myrdal, Gunnar. *An American Dilemma.* New York, Harper and Brothers; 1944.

National Society for the Study of Education, Thirty-ninth Yearbook, Parts I and II. *Intelligence: Its Nature and Nurture.* George D. Stoddard, ed. Chicago, University of Chicago Press; 1940.

———. Forty-first Yearbook, Part II. *The Psychology of Learning.* Chicago, University of Chicago Press; 1942.

———. Fifty-fourth Yearbook, Part I. *Modern Philosophies and Education.* Chicago, University of Chicago Press; 1955.

Nef, John U. *The United States and Civilization*. Chicago, University of Chicago Press; 1942.

Newlon, Jesse H. *Educational Administration as Social Policy*. New York, Charles Scribner's Sons; 1934.

Niebuhr, Reinhold. *The Nature and Destiny of Man*, 2 vols. New York, Charles Scribner's Sons; 1941-1943.

Nisbet, Robert A. *The Quest for Community: A Study in the Ethics of Order and Freedom*. New York, Oxford University Press; 1953.

Nock, Albert J. *Our Enemy the State*. New York, W. Morrow and Company; 1935.

————. *The Theory of Education in the United States*. New York, Harcourt, Brace and Company; 1932.

Northrop, F. S. C. *The Logic of the Sciences and the Humanities*. New York, The Macmillan Company; 1947.

O'Connor, D. J. *An Introduction to the Philosophy of Education*. New York, Philosophical Library, Inc.; 1957.

O'Neill, James M. *Religion and Education Under the Constitution*. New York, Harper and Brothers; 1949.

Otto, Max C. *The Human Enterprise*. New York, Appleton-Century-Crofts, Inc.; 1940.

————. *Science and the Moral Life*. New York, New American Library; 1949.

Park, Joe, ed. *Selected Readings in the Philosophy of Education*. New York, The Macmillan Company; 1958.

Parrington, Vernon L. *Main Currents in American Thought*. New York, Harcourt, Brace and Company; 1930.

Parsons, Talcott, and Shils, Edward A. eds. *Toward a General Theory of Action*. Cambridge, Mass., Harvard University Press; 1951.

Peirce, Charles Sanders. *Philosophical Writings of Peirce*. Justus Buchler, ed. New York, Dover Publications, Inc.; 1955.

Perry, Ralph Barton. *General Theory of Value*. New York, Longmans, Green and Company; 1926.

————. *Realms of Value*. Cambridge, Mass., Harvard University Press; 1954.

Peters *et al*. *Counseling: Selected Readings*. Columbus, Charles E. Merrill Books, Inc.; 1962.

Pfeffer, Leo. *Church, State, and Freedom*. Boston, Beacon Press, Inc.; 1953.

Phenix, Philip H. *Intelligible Religion*. New York, Harper and Brothers; 1954.

————. *Philosophy of Education*. New York, Henry Holt and Co., Inc.; 1958.

President's Research Committee on Social Trends. *Recent Social Trends.* New York, McGraw-Hill Book Company; 1933.

Raup, R. Bruce. *Complacency, the Foundation of Human Behavior.* New York, The Macmillan Company; 1930.

———. *Education and Organized Interests in America.* New York, G. P. Putnam's Sons; 1936.

———, Axtelle, George E., Benne, Kenneth D., and Smith, B. Othanel. *The Improvement of Practical Intelligence.* New York, Harper and Brothers; 1950.

Reavis, William C., and Judd, Charles H. *The Teacher and Educational Administration.* Boston, Houghton Mifflin Company; 1942.

Redden, J. D., and Ryan, F. A. *A Catholic Philosophy of Education.* Milwaukee, Bruce Publishing Company; 1942.

Reichenbach, Hans. *Experience and Prediction.* Chicago, University of Chicago Press; 1952.

Riccio, Anthony C., and Cyphert, Frederick R. *Teaching in America.* Columbus, Charles E. Merrill Books, Inc.; 1962.

Riesman, David. *Individualism Reconsidered.* Glencoe, Ill., The Free Press; 1955.

———, Glazer, Nathan, and Denney, Reuel. *The Lonely Crowd.* New Haven, Yale University Press; 1950.

Rogers, Carl. *Client Centered Psychotherapy.* Boston, Houghton Mifflin Company; 1951.

Royce, Josiah. *The Spirit of Modern Philosophy.* Boston, Ginn and Company; 1892.

Santayana, George. *Character and Opinion in the United States.* New York, Charles Scribner's Sons; 1920.

Schlesinger, Arthur M. *The Age of Jackson.* Boston. Little, Brown; 1945.

Schneider, Herbert W. *A History of American Philosophy.* New York, Columbia University Press; 1946.

Selznick, Philip. *Leadership in Administration: A Sociological Interpretation.* Evanston, Illinois, Row, Peterson and Company; 1957.

Sinclair, William. *The Conditions of Knowing.* New York, Harcourt, Brace and Company; 1951.

Skinner, B. F. *Science and Human Behavior.* New York, The Macmillan Company; 1953.

Smith, Philip G. *Philosophic-Mindedness in Educational Administration.* Columbus, Ohio, College of Education, The Ohio State University; 1956.

Smith, T. V. *The American Philosophy of Equality.* Chicago, University of Chicago Press; 1927.

————. *The Democratic Way of Life*. Chicago, University of Chicago Press; 1929.

Snyder, Richard C., and Wilson, H. Hubert, eds. *Roots of Political Behavior*. New York, American Book Company; 1949.

Sorokin, Pitirim A. *Social Philosophies of an Age of Crisis*. Boston, Beacon Press, Inc.; 1951.

Soule, George. *The Future of Liberty*. New York, The Macmillan Company; 1936.

Spindler, George D., ed. *Education and Anthropology*. Stanford, Stanford University Press; 1955.

Stace, Walter T. *Religion and the Modern Mind*. Philadelphia, J. B. Lippincott Company; 1925.

Stanley, William O. *Education and Social Integration*. New York, Teachers College, Columbia University; 1953.

————. Smith, B. Othanel, Benne, Kenneth D., and Anderson, Archibald W. *Social Foundations of Education*. New York, The Dryden Press, Inc.; 1956.

Stoddard, George D. *The Meaning of Intelligence*. New York, The Macmillan Company; 1943.

Tead, Ordway. *College Teaching and College Learning*. New Haven, Yale University Press; 1949.

Tillich, Paul. *The Courage To Be*. New Haven, Yale University Press; 1952.

Toynbee, Arnold. *A Study of History*. New York, Oxford University Press; 1939.

Ulich, Robert. *Conditions of Civilized Living*. New York, E. P. Dutton & Co.; 1946.

————. *Fundamentals of Democratic Education*. New York, American Book Company; 1940.

————. *History of Educational Thought*. New York, American Book Company; 1945.

————. *Human Career*. New York, Harper and Brothers; 1957.

UNESCO. *Freedom and Culture*. New York, Columbia University Press; 1951.

Van Doren, Mark. *Liberal Education*. New York, Henry Holt and Co., Inc.; 1943.

Wahl, Jean. *A Short History of Existentialism*. New York, Philosophical Library; 1949.

Wahlquist, John T. *The Philosophy of American Education*. New York, The Ronald Press Company; 1942.

Ward, Virgil S. *Educating the Gifted*. Columbus, Charles E. Merrill Books, 1961.

Washburne, Carleton. *A Living Philosophy of Education.* New York, The John Day Company, 1940.

Watson, John B. *Behaviorism.* New York, W. W. Norton and Company, Inc.; 1930.

Whitehead, Thomas N. *Leadership in a Free Society.* Cambridge, Mass., Harvard University Press, 1936.

Whyte, William H., Jr. *The Organization Man.* New York, Simon and Schuster, Inc.; 1956.

Wieman, Henry N. *The Directive in History.* Boston, Beacon Press, Inc.; 1949.

Index

DATE DUE